SEXUAL OFFENCES REFERENCER

A Practitioner's Guide to Indictments and Sentencing

THIRD EDITION

HHJ PATRICIA LEES
ELEANOR LAWS QC

Great Clarendon Street, Oxford, OX2 6DP,
United Kingdom

Oxford University Press is a department of the University of Oxford.
It furthers the University's objective of excellence in research, scholarship,
and education by publishing worldwide. Oxford is a registered trade mark of
Oxford University Press in the UK and in certain other countries

© Patricia Lees and Eleanor Laws 2022

The moral rights of the authors have been asserted

First Edition published in 2007
Second Edition published in 2014
Third Edition published in 2022

Impression: 1

All rights reserved. No part of this publication may be reproduced, stored in
a retrieval system, or transmitted, in any form or by any means, without the
prior permission in writing of Oxford University Press, or as expressly permitted
by law, by licence or under terms agreed with the appropriate reprographics
rights organization. Enquiries concerning reproduction outside the scope of the
above should be sent to the Rights Department, Oxford University Press, at the
address above

You must not circulate this work in any other form
and you must impose this same condition on any acquirer

Public sector information reproduced under Open Government Licence v3.0
(http://www.nationalarchives.gov.uk/doc/open-government-licence/open-government-licence.htm)

Published in the United States of America by Oxford University Press
198 Madison Avenue, New York, NY 10016, United States of America

British Library Cataloguing in Publication Data
Data available

Library of Congress Control Number: 2021952245

ISBN 978–0–19–284443–9

DOI: 10.1093/law/9780192844439.001.0001

Printed and bound by
CPI Group (UK) Ltd, Croydon, CR0 4YY

Links to third party websites are provided by Oxford in good faith and
for information only. Oxford disclaims any responsibility for the materials
contained in any third party website referenced in this work.

SEXUAL OFFENCES REFERENCER

THIRD EDITION

This third edition is dedicated to you, the practitioners who use this work and whom we thank for your patience and voracity.

HHJ Patricia Lees
Eleanor Laws QC
May 2022

ACKNOWLEDGEMENTS

We owe huge thanks to Lucy Luttman for her assistance with updating the book and her meticulous hard work in ensuring this third edition continues to work as an easy to use referencer.

Our thanks also go to Jocelyn Ledward, Treasury Counsel, for updating the cases which may be the subject of an Attorney-General's Reference.

CONTENTS

Table of Cases   xi
Table of Statutes and Statutory Instruments   xix
List of Abbreviations   xli
Index to Indictments/Charges   xlv

1. Indictments   1
2. Rape   21
3. Sexual Assaults   37
4. Offences Involving Children   57
5. Buggery and Offences of Indecency   131
6. Familial Offences   159
7. Offences Involving the Mentally Disordered   185
8. Prostitution and Trafficking   243
9. Indecent Images/Obscene Publications   299
10. Offences Against Public Decency   327
11. Preparatory Offences   343
12. Sentencing   359
13. Special Measures Including Section 28 Pre-trial Recorded Cross-examination   431
14. Notification Requirements   451
15. Publicity   467
16. Sexual Harm Prevention Orders   477
17. Sexual Offences Committed Outside the Jurisdiction   509

Appendix A: Specified Sexual Offences   513
Appendix B: Sentencing Guidelines Council—Sexual Offences Act 2003 Definitive Guidelines   517
Appendix C: PD-5 CPD I to PD-8 CPD I General matters 3: Vulnerable People, Ground Rules, Intermediaries, Vulnerable Defendants   647
Index   653

TABLE OF CASES

Abbott v Smith [1965] 2 QB 662, [1964] 3 All ER 762 .... 8.130
A-G's Reference (No 1 of 1975) 8.80
A-G's Reference (No 5 of 1980) 72 Cr App R 71 CA 9.59
A-G's Reference (No 1 of 1989) [1989] 3 WLR 1117 .... 6.29
A-G's Reference (No 2 of 1995) [1996] 1 Cr App R(S) 274 .... 3.22
A-G's Reference (No 145 of 2006) 12.97
A-G's Reference (No 21 of 2007) (R v Oakes) [2007] All ER (D) 281 May 9 .... 12.171
A-G's Reference (Nos 74 and 83 of 2007) [2007] EWCA 2550 .... 4.89
A-G's Reference (No 107 of 2007) [2008] EWCA Crim 198 .... 12.193
A-G's Reference (No 55 of 2008) [2008] EWCA Crim 2790 .... 12.118
A-G's References (Nos 11 and 12 of 2012) (Channer and Monteiro),
    [2012] EWCA Crim 1119 .... 4.89, 12.191
A-G's Reference (No 27 of 2013) [2014] EWCA Crim 334 (R v Burinskas) 12.121, 12.128
A-G's Reference (No 53 of 2013) (R v Wilson) [2013] EWCA Crim 2544 .... 12.192
A-G's Reference (R. v O); R. v O [2018] EWCA Crim 2286, [2019] CrimLR 353, CA 2.24, 12.156
A-G's Reference (No 1 of 2020) [2020] EWCA Crim 1665 .... 3.49
A-G's Reference (Darren Rose) [2021] EWCA Crim 155 .... 12.94, 12.159
A-G's Reference (Olawale Hassan) [2021] EWCA Crim 412 .... 12.97
Allen [2019] EWCA Crim 1772 .... 12.98
Atkins v DPP; Goodland v DPP [2000] EWHC Admin 302 .... 9.06

B (A Minor) v DPP [2000] 2 AC 428 HL 4.13
Beal v Kelley (1951) 35 Cr App R 128 .... 3.05, 5.33, 5.34
Behrendt v Burridge (1976) 63 Cr App R 202 DC 8.118
Bevan [2011] EWCA Crim 654 .... 4.261

C v Sevenoaks Youth Court [2009] EWHC 3088 (Admin) 13.32
Clarke and Others [2018] EWCA Crim 18 .... 12.146

Dinc [2017] EWCA Crim 1206 .... 13.61, 13.63
DJ [2015] EWCA Crim 563 .... 12.24, 12.79
Dooley [2005] EWCA Crim 3093 .... 9.06
DPP v Armstrong [2000] Crim LR 379 .... 9.18
DPP v Burgess [1971] QB 432 .... 4.13
DPP v Morgan [1976] AC 182, 61 Cr App R 136 .... 2.26

E (Edwards) [2011] EWCA Crim 3028; [2012] Crim LR 563 .... 13.61
Evans v Ewells [1972] 2 All ER 22, [1972] 1WLR 671 .... 10.09, 10.17

Fairclough v Whipp (1951) 35 Cr App R 138 CA 3.05, 5.34
Fethney [2011] EWCA Crim 3096 .... 4.261
Francis & Lawrence [2014] EWCA Crim 631 .... 12.24, 12.79
Fruen [2016] EWCA Crim 561 .... 12.113

G v UK [2012] CLR 46 .... 4.04

Hall (1987) 86 Cr App R 159 .... 7.13
Harrison [2007] EWCA Crim 2976 .... 9.06
Hemsley [2010] EWCA Crim 225 .... 16.25

Hogg [2007] EWCA Crim 1357 .... 12.134
Hulme v DPP [2006] EWHC 1347 (Admin) 7.25
Hunt v DPP [1990] Crim LR 812 .... 10.17

Ibbotson v UK [1999] Crim LR 153 .... 14.04
IM v LM (Capacity to consent to sexual relations) [2014] EWCA Civ 37 .... 2.49
Invicta Plastics Ltd v Clare [1976] RTR 251 .... 8.38, 8.44

Jonas [2015] EWCA Crim 562 .... 13.63
Julian Assange v Swedish Prosecution Authority [2011] EWHC 2849 (Admin) 2.47

Longworth [2006] UKHL 1 .... 12.231
Lord Goddard CJ Beal v Kelley (1951) 35 Cr App R 128 .... 3.03
Lubemba and Pooley [2014] EWCA Crim 2064 .... 13.61, 13.63

Mark Le Brocq v Liverpool CC [2019] EWCA Crim 1398 .... 13.63
Marshall (2.12.2009) Unreported, Woolwich CC 1.29
Massey [2007] EWCA Crim 2664 .... 7.187
McLoughlin & Newell [2014] EWCA Crim 188 .... 12.132

Pinnell and Joyce [2010] EWCA Crim 2848 .... 12.24, 12.78–12.79, 12.82, 12.86
PMH (Hampson) [2018] EWCA Crim 2452 .... 13.63
Prince [2013] EWCA Crim 1768 .... 12.191
Privett [2020] EWCA Crim 557 .... 1.51, 12.175–12.179, 12.183–12.184

R (D) v Camberwell Green Youth Court [2005] UKHL 4 .... 13.07
R (F and T) v Secretary of State for Justice [2010] UKSC 17 .... 12.234
R (F) v DPP [2013] EWHC 945 (Admin) [2013] Cr App R 21 .... 2.47
R (on the application of AS) v Great Yarmouth Youth Court [2011] EWHC
    2059 (Admin); [2012] Crim LR 478 .... App C 3F.3
R (on the application of C) v Sevenoaks Youth Court [2009] EWHC 3088 (Admin);
    [2010] 1 All ER 735 .... App C 3F.3
R (on the Application of Christopher Prothero) v Secretary of State for the
    Home Department [2013] EWCA 2830 .... 14.11
R (on the application of D) v Camberwell Green Youth Court [2005] UKHL 4,
    [2005] 1 WLR 393; [2005] 2 Cr App R 1 .... App C 3F.3
R (on the application of F (by his litigation friend F) and Thompson (FC)
    (Respondents)) v Secretary of State for the Home Department (Appellant)
    [2010] UKSC 17 E 14.05
R (on the application of Monica) v DPP [2018] EWHC 945 (Admin) 2.47
R (on the application of TP) v West London Youth Court [2005] EWHC 2583 (Admin);
    [2006] 1 WLR 1219, [2006] 1 Cr App R 25 .... App C 3F.3
R v A [2014] EWCA Crim 299 .... 2.49
R v A [2015] EWCA Crim 177 .... 1.18, 1.20
R v Abdullahi (Osmund Mohammed) [2006] EWCA Crim 2060 .... 4.202, 4.205, 4.206, 10.31
R v AD [2016] EWCA Crim 454 .... 1.39–1.40
R v Aldridge and R v Eaton [2012] ECWA Crim 1456 .... 16.44
R v Ali (Yasir) [2015] EWCA Crim 1279 .... 2.47, 8.184
R v Alison [2021] EWCA Crim 324 .... 16.34
R v Almilhim [2019] EWCA Crim 220 .... 12.17
R v AM [2018] EWCA Crim 279 .... 12.154
R v Arifin [2018] EWCA Crim 145 .... 12.131
R v Ashton (John) [2006] EWCA Crim 794, [2007] 1 WLR 181 .... 1.55–1.56
R v B (A Minor) v DPP [2000] 2 Cr App R 65 .... 8.22
R v B (M) [2012] EWCA Crim 770 .... 10.31
R v B (MA) [2013] EWCA Crim 3 .... 2.47, 3.59

R v B [1999] Crim LR 594 CA 4.13
R v B [2006] EWCA Crim 2945, [2007] 1 WLR 1567 ....2.47
R v B [2018] EWCA Crim 1439 ....4.195
R v B [M] [2012] EWCA Crim 770 ....10.31
R v Baillie-Smith (Raymond) (1977) 64 Cr App R 76 CA 6.25
R v Balderstone (1955) 39 Cr App R 97 CCA 7.62
R v Banks [1916] 2 KB 621, 12 Cr App R 74 ....4.60, 4.80
R v Bassett (Kevin) [2008] EWCA Crim 1174 ....10.31
R v Bateman (Paul Michael) [2020] EWCA Crim 1333 ....9.23, 9.35, 12.195
R v Beale [2019] EWCA Crim 665 ....15.01
R v Beale 10 Cox 157 ....4.51
R v Beaney [2004] 2 Cr App R (S) 441 ....16.18
R v Bingham [2013] EWCA Crim 823 ....2.50
R v Boateng [2016] 1.39
R v Bostock (1893) 17 Cox 700 ....3.20, 3.30, 4.63, 5.37
R v Bourke [2017] EWCA Crim 2150 ....12.75
R v Bourne (1952) 36 Cr App R 125 ....5.11
R v Bowden [2002] 2 Cr App R 438 CA 9.06
R v Bowker [2008] 1 Cr App R (S) 72 ....12.156
R v Boyea [1992] Crim LR 574 CA 3.05
R v Brant (David Charles) [2018] EWCA Crim 2800 ....12.188
R v Bree [2007] EWCA Crim 804 ....2.47, 3.39
R v Broadfoot (1977) 64 Cr App R 71 CA 5.125, 8.22, 8.80
R v Brown (1993) UK HL 19, (1994) 1 AC 212 ....3.05
R v Brown [1984] 3 All ER 1013 ....8.80, 8.81
R v Burinskas [2014] EWCA Crim 334 ....12.159
R v Burrows 35 Cr App R 180 ....5.45
R v C (Barry) [2004] EWCA Crim 292 ....2.37
R v C [2005] EWCA Crim 3533 ....12.45
R v C [2009] UKHL 42 ....2.47
R v C [2012] EWCA Crim 2034 ....2.47
R v Cairns [1998] Crim LR 141 ....1.30, 1.32
R v Canavan; R v Kidd; R v Shaw [1998] 1 WLR 604, [1998] 1 Cr App R 79,
    [1998] 1 Cr App R (S) 243 ....1.15, 1.19
R v Cardwell [2012] EWCA Crim 3030 ....12.119
R v Carmona [2006] EWCA Crim 508 ....12.244
R v Cawthron [1913] 3 KB 168 ....4.54
R v Chall and Others [2019] EWCA Crim 865 ....12.149, 12.185, 12.197
R v Chaney [2009] EWCA Crim 52 ....1.29, 12.47
R v Chapman 42 Cr App R 257 CCA 8.23
R v Cheyne (Marco) [2019] EWCA Crim 182 ....16.22, 16.43
R v Choung [2020] 1 Cr App R (S) 13 ....16.18
R v Ciccarelli [2011] EWCA Crim 2665 ....2.50
R v Clarke [2015] EWCA Crim 350 ....1.39
R v Clarke [2017] EWCA Crim 393 ....12.114
R v Clarke 63 Cr App R 16 CA 8.98
R v Clarke and R v Cooper [2017] EWCA Crim 393 ....12.157
R v Claydon [2005] EWCA Crim 2827 ....4.263
R v Clayton and Halsey [1963] 1 QB 163, 46 Cr App R 450 ....10.08
R v Clifford (1988) 8 CL 86 ....10.09
R v Clifford [2014] EWCA Crim 2245 ....12.142
R v Coates [2008] 1 Cr App R 52 ....2.47
R v Cogan (John Rodney) [1976] QB 217 ....2.50
R v Collard [2005] 1 Cr App R (S) 34 ....16.18
R v Collier (Edward John) [2004] EWCA Crim 1411 ....9.27
R v Connor [2019] EWCA Crim 234 ....16.11

R v Court [1989] AC 28 HL..3.12, 3.26
R v Courtie [1984] AC 463...4.256, 5.16, 5.19
R v Cox [2012] EWCA Crim 549; [2012] 2 Cr App R 6 ....App C 3D.4, App C 3F.6
R v D [1993] Crim LR 542...5.15
R v D (Sexual offences prevention order) [2005] EWCA Crim 3360..................16.06, 16.94
R v D [2005] EWCA Crim 2951, [2006] CLR 364............................6.67, 6.73, 6.81
R v Davies [1998] 1 Cr App R(S) 380 CA..5.63
R v Dawes (Robert Houghton) [2019] EWCA Crim 848..12.30
R v DCA [2013] EWCA Crim 1017 ....12.142
R v De Munck 13 Cr App R 113 CCA, [1918–19] All ER Rep 499 ....8.08, 8.15
R v Debnath (Anita) [2005] EWCA Crim 3472 ....12.226
R v Delroy Grant (March 2011)— The 'Night Stalker' trial..................................15.03
R v Dicken 14 Cox 8 ....4.51
R v DJ [2015] EWCA Crim 563..12.85
R v DO [2014] EWCA Crim 2202..12.188
R v Dogra [2019] EWCA Crim 145, [2019] 2 Cr App R (S)9..................................12.97
R v Donovan [1934] 2 KB 498..3.05
R v Dooley [2006] 1 Cr App R 21 ....9.06
R v Dougal [2005] Swansea Crown Court...3.39
R v Drury (1975) 60 Cr App R 195 CA...8.15
R v Dunn [2015] EWCA Crim 724..3.16, 4.11
R v Durrant (Andrew) [2018] EWCA Crim 2400..4.253
R v ET 163 JP 349, CA 9.06
R v Evans (Chedwyn) [2012] Crim 2559..3.39
R v E [2011] EWCA Crim 3028; [2012] Crim LR 563 ....App C 3D.4
R v F [2009] CLR 462..12.233
R v F [2011] EWCA Crim 1844...1.60
R v F 74 JP 384..7.06
R v Falder [2019]1 Cr App R (S) 46...12.86
R v Farrugia and Others (1979) 69 Cr App R 108 CA..8.102
R v Faulkner v Talbot (1982) 74 Cr App R 1 ....3.28
R v Fellows and Arnold [1997] Cr App R 244 CA......................................9.06, 9.59
R v Fernandez [2002] The Times 26 June..5.94
R v Fitzmaurice [1983] QB 1083..8.38, 8.44
R v Flitter (Julian) [2000] 12 WLUK 345 ....2.40
R v Forbes and Others [2016] EWCA Crim 1388; [2016] 2 Cr App R (S) 44............1.05, 1.15, 1.18,
                                    1.39–1.40, 12.23, 12.200, 12.136, 12.146, 12.148,
                                    12.155, 12.157, 12.180, 12.186, 12.190
R v Fowler [2002] EWCA Crim 620, [2002] Crim LR 521......................................2.40
R v Francis (1989) 88 Cr App R 127 CA...4.13
R v Francis [2014] EWCA Crim 631...12.85
R v Franklin [2018] EWCA Crim 1080 ....16.36
R v Fruen and DS [2006] EWCA 561..12.110
R v G [2003] UKHL 50..11.52
R v G [2006] EWCA Crim 821 ....4.92, 4.96
R v G [2008] UKHL 37..4.04
R v Gavrina [2010] EWCA Crim 1693..4.226
R v GD [2021] EWCA Crim 465..16.29
R v Gibson and Sylveire [1990] 2 QB 619, 91 Cr App R 341 CA........................9.60, 10.04
R v Gillespie [1998] Crim LR 139..3.22
R v Goddard (1990) 92 Cr App R 185 CA 8.119
R v Goldfinch [2019] EWCA Crim 878 ....12.148, 12.155–12.156
R v Goodyear [2005] 3 All ER 117 ....12.16
R v Goodyear [2005] EWCA Crim 888 ....12.17
R v Gordon (1927) 19 Cr App R 20 CA 1.53, 6.06
R v Goss and Goss (1990) 90 Cr App R 400 CA 4.11, 4.13

R v Graham and Others [1997] 1 Cr App R(S) 302. . . . . .1.37
R v Graham-Kerr [1988] 1 WLR 1098. . . . . .9.06
R v Grant Murray [2017] EWCA Crim 1228. . . . . .13.63
R v Grewal [2010] EWCA Crim 2448. . . . . .2.50
R v Grout [2011] EWCA Crim 299. . . . . 1.48, 3.55, 4.26, 4.37
R v Gwilym [2018] EWCA 377 . . . . .12.89
R v H [2003] EWCA Crim 1208; *The Times* 15 April 2003. . . . . .App C 3F.3
R v H [2005] EWCA Crim 732, [2005] Crim LR 735 . . . . 3.35, 3.39
R v H [2005] 2 All ER 859 CA 6.49, 6.57
R v H [2005] EWCA Crim 732 . . . . .3.49
R v H [2007] EWCA Crim 2056 . . . . .3.41
R v H (J) and Others [2011] EWCA Crim 2753; [2012] 1WLR; [2012] 2 All ER 340;
    [2012] 2 Cr App R (S)21. . . . . App B p 642
R v H [2011]. 12.137, 12.187
R v Hall [1964] 1 QB 273, 47 Cr App R 253 . . . . .5.42
R v Hamer [2017] EWCA Crim 192. . . . . .16.69
R v Hamilton [2007] EWCA Crim 2062 . . . . .10.08
R v Hardy (James) [2013] EWCA Crim 2125 . . . . .10.12
R v Hardy (James) [2013] EWCA Crim 2125 . . . . .10.12
R v Hardy [2019]. 10.12
R v Hare [1934] 1 KB 354, 24 Cr App R 108. . . . . 3.05, 3.28, 5.35
R v Harling (1938) 26 Cr App R 127 CA 2.04
R v Hartley [2011] EWCA Crim 1299 . . . . 1.15, 1.20
R v Heard [2007] EWCA Crim 125 . . . . .2.50, 3.39, 4.26, 4.40, 4.92, 4.100, 4.110,
                                                                     4.122, 4.132, 4.195, 4.206, 4.227
R v Henderson (Trevor) [2007] EWCA Crim 3264 . . . . .10.53
R v Hewitt [2018] EWCA Crim 2309. . . . . .16.32
R v Hewitt [2020] 1.60
R v Hibbert [2015] EWCA Crim 507 . . . . .12.89
R v Hill 10 Cr App R 56 CCA. 8.98
R v Hoath; R v Standage [2011] EWCA Crim 274 . . . . .16.42
R v Hobson [2013] EWCA Crim 819. . . . . .1.09
R v Hodgson [1973] QB 565 CA, (1973) 57 Cr App R 502. . . . . 3.14, 4.72
R v Howarth [2021] 16.23
R v Hunt 34 Cr App R 135 CCA 5.43
R v Hussain (Tayyab) [2019] EWCA Crim 1542. . . . . .12.30
R v Hysa [2007] EWCA Crim 2056 . . . . .2.50
R v IP [2005] 1 Cr. App. R. 102 . . . . .10.34
R v IS [2016] EWCA Crim 1443 . . . . .12.88
R v Isles [1998] Crim LR 140. . . . . .3.22
R v J [2004] UKHL 42. . . . . .2.20, 2.31, 3.15, 3.22, 4.60, 4.80
R v J.F. [2002] Crim 2936. . . . . .2.49
R v JH [2015] EWCA Crim 54; [2015] 1 Cr App R (S) 59 . . . . 12.200
R v J.M. [2015] EWCA Crim 1638; [2016] 1 Cr App R (S) 21 . . . . 12.185
R v Jacobs (1817) Russ & Ry 331 . . . . .5.11
R v Jellyman 8 C&P 604 . . . . .5.13
R v Jennings 4 C&P 249 . . . . 4.50, 4.58
R v Johnson and Others [2006] EWCA Crim 2486 [2007] 1 Cr App R (S) 112. . . . . 12.247
R v Jones (Ian) [2007] EWCA Crim 1118 . . . . .4.37
R v Jones [2009] EWCA Crim 237 . . . . 12.216
R v Jones [2014] EWCA Crim 1859; [2015] 1 Cr App R (S) 9 . . . . .12.41
R v Joseph (Verna Sermanfure) [2017] EWCA Crim 36 . . . . 4.195, 4.206, 4.239, 4.248, 5.04, 5.78,
                                                                     5.118, 7.179, 7.187, 8.89, 8.140, 9.07, 9.28, 9.48, 9.60, 9.70, 10.09, 10.43
R v JTB [2009] UKHL 20. . . . . .4.261
R v K (Robert) [2008] EWCA Crim 1923 . . . . 2.40, 2.50
R v K (Robert) [2009] 1 Cr App R 24 CA. 2.51

R v K [2001] 3 All ER 897 .... 8.22
R v K [2002] 1 AC 462 HL 5.94
R v Kaitamaki (1985) AC 147 (PC) 2.05, 2.50
R v Kamki [2013] EWCA Crim 2335 .... 2.47, 3.39
R v KC [2019] EWCA Crim 2311 .... 12.97–12.98
R v Kehoe [2009] 1 Cr App R(S) 12.119
R v Khellaf [2016] EWCA Crim 1297 .... 12.227
R v KPR [2018] EWCA Crim 2537 .... 12.104
R v Kulah [2008] 1 All ER 16 .... 12.16
R v Kumar [2005] Crim LR CLR 470, [2004] EWCA Crim 3207 .... 5.05
R v L [1999] 1 Cr App R 117 CA 3.22
R v L [2017] 1 Cr App R (S) 51 .... 12.156
R v L [2017] EWCA Crim 43 .... 12.154
R v L.F. [2016] EWCA Crim 561 .... 1.41–1.42
R v Land [1999] I Cr App R 301; QB 65 .... 9.06
R v Lang [2005] EWCA Crim 2864 .... 12.88, 12.97, 12.99
R v Lawrance [2020] EWCA Crim 971 .... 2.47
R v LDG [2018] EWCA Crim 2264 .... 12.154
R v LM [2010] EWCA Crim 232 .... 7.187
R v LM [2010] EWCA Crim 2327 .... 8.140
R v Longworth [2006] UKHL 1 .... 14.20
R v M [2011] EWCA Crim 252 .... 9.06
R v M'Rue (1838) 8 C & P 641 .... 2.17
R v Mackenzie and Higginson (1910) 6 Cr App R 64 CCA 8.23
R v Malone (1998) 2 Cr App R 447 CA 2.04, 2.50
R v Marsden [1891] 2 QB 149 .... 2.04, 7.05, 7.56, 7.110, 7.158
R v Maughan (1934) 24 Cr App R 130 .... 3.05
R v Mayling [1963] 2 QB 717, 47 Cr App R 102 .... 10.08
R v MC [2012] EWCA Crim 213 .... 1.37
R v McCann [2007] 1 Cr App R (S) 4 .... 10.34
R v McCann, Sinaga & Shah [2020] EWCA Crim 1676 .... 12.133
R v McLellan [2018] 1 Cr App R (S) 18 .... 16.08
R v McLellan and Bingley [2017] EWCA Crim 1464 .... 16.23, 16.29
R v McNally (Justine) [2013] EWCA Crim 1051 .... 2.47
R v Mearns (1990) 91 Cr App R 312 .... 3.20, 3.30, 5.37
R v Michael Harries and Others [2007] EWCA Crim 1622 .... 1.26
R v Miskell 37 Cr App R 214 .... 5.45
R v MJ [2019] 1 Cr App R (S) 10 .... 1.58
R v Morris [1951] 1 KB 394, 34 Cr App R 210 .... 10.11
R v Morris-Lowe [1985] 1 All ER 40 .... 8.81
R v Morris-Lowe [1985] 1 All ER 400 .... 8.08
R v Nazari [1980] 71 Cr App R (S) 87A 12.244
R v NC [2016] EWCA Crim 1448 .... 16.09, 16.25–16.26, 16.28
R v Nelson (Keith) [2020] EWCA Crim 1615 .... 12.202
R v Newbon [2005] Crim LR 738 .... 12.45
R v Newland (1988) 87 C. App R 1.02
R v O [2018] EWCA Crim 2286, [2019] CrimLR 353, CA 2.24
R v Okoro [2018] EWCA Crim 1929 .... 9.27, 9.38
R v Oliver [2011] EWCA Crim 3114 .... 12.196
R v Olugboja (1981) 73 Cr App R 344 CA 2.04
R (OP) v Secretary of State for Justice [2014] EWHC 1944 (Admin) 13.32
R v Orritt [2018] EWCA Crim 2286 .... 12.147
R v Owen [1988] 1 WLR 134 .... 9.06
R v P [2013] EWCA Crim 1143 .... 12.122
R v Pacurar [2016[EWCA Crim 569 .... 11.53
R v Parsons; R v Morgan [2017] EWCA Crim 2163 .... 16.09, 16.26, 16.31, 16.34, 16.50, 16.93–16.97

R v Pelletier [2012] EWCA Crim 1060. . . . . .16.11
R v Penguin Books Ltd [1961] Crim LR 176 ('Lady Chatterley's Lover case'). 9.60
R v Perkins [2013] EWCA Crim 323 . . . . 12.150
R v Perrin [2002] 4 Archbold News 2 CA 9.59
R v PH [2006] EWCA Crim 2394. . . . . .12.98
R v Phillips [2018] EWCA Crim 2008 . . . . .12.84
R v Phillips 8 C&P 736 . . . . .4.51
R v Pickford [1995] 1 Cr App R 420 CA. 6.34
R v Pinkerton [2017] EWCA Crim 38 . . . . 12.195
R v PK; R v TK [2008] EWCA Crim 434 . . . . .2.47
R v PMH [2018] EWCA Crim 2452. . . . . .13.61
R v Poole [1961] AC 223 . . . . .1.58
R v Porter [2006] 2 Cr App R 25 . . . . .9.27
R v Porter [2006] EWCA Crim 560 . . . . .9.06
R v Preece and Howells (1977) QB 370, 63 Cr App R 28 CA 5.42
R v Prince [1875] LR 2 CCR 154. . . . . 4.51, 4.70
R v PS [2013] EWCA Crim 1592. . . . . .1.60
R v PS, CF, Abdi Hadir [2019] EWCA Crim 2286 . . . . 12.203
R v R (Paul Brian) [1993] Crim LR 541 . . . . 1.10, 1.33, 3.18, 12.44
R v R [1992] 1 AC 599. . . . . 2.01, 2.37
R v R [1993] Crim LR 541 . . . . .3.18
R v Rackham [1997] 2 Cr App R 222 . . . . 4.102, 4.113, 4.124
R v Radcliffe [1990] Crim LR 524 CA. 4.13
R v Ram (1893) 17 Cox CC 609. . . . . 2.05, 2.50
R v Rawlinson [2018] EWCA Crim 2825. . . . . 12.231, 14.04
R v RD [2013] EWCA Crim 1592. . . . . .1.60
R v Reakes [1974] Crim LR 615 CA 5.16, 5.19
R v Reynolds [2021] EWCA Crim 10. . . . . .12.133, 12.202
R v Richards (Tony) 2020 [EWCA] Crim 95 . . . . .10.31
R v RK (Knight) [2018] EWCA Crim 603 . . . . .13.61
R v Robinson [2011] EWCA Crim 916 . . . . .2.47
R v Rogers (1914) 10 Cr App R 276. . . . . .4.268
R v Rolfe (1952) 36 Cr App R 4 . . . . .3.49
R v Rosser [2014] EWCA Crim 22015 . . . . 12.133
R v Rowley [1991] Crim LR 785 . . . . .10.08
R v RT & MAM [2020] EWCA Crim 1343 . . . . .9.06
R v Russen 1 East PC 4.50, 4.58
R v S and Others [2005] EWCA Crim 3616. . . . . .12.99
R v Saunders and Others [2013] EWCA Crim 1027. . . . . 12.118, 12.120–12.121
R v SG and DG [2009] EWCA Crim 2241 . . . . .1.10
R v Shott 3 C&K 206. . . . . .4.58
R v Silverwood and Chapman [2015] EWCA Crim 2401 . . . . .1.39
R v Slocombe [2005] EWCA Crim 2297 . . . . .14.08
R v Smethurst [2002] 1 Cr App R 6 CA 9.06
R v Smith (Gavin) [2012] EWCA Crim 398 . . . . .9.59
R v Smith and Jones (1976) 63 Cr App R 47 CA 11.28, 11.52
R v Smith and Others [2011] EWCA Crim 1772 . . . . 16.04, 16.08, 16.25,
         16.28–16.30, 16.33, 16.35, 16.50, 16.63, 16.93
R v Smith and Tovey [2005] EWCA Crim 530 . . . . .1.13
R v Smith; R v Jayson [2003] 1 Cr App R 13. . . . . .9.06
R v Sokolowski [2017] EWCA Crim 1903 . . . . 16.08, 16.23, 16.27, 16.34
R v Speck (1977) 65 Cr App R 161 CA 4.13
R v Stephenson [1912] 3 KB 341 . . . . .3.05
R v Stocker [2013] EWCA Crim 1993 . . . . 1.36–1.37, 1.40
R v Tambedou (Seedy) [2014] EWCA Crim 954 . . . . .2.50
R v Terrell [2008] 2 Cr App R (S) 49 . . . . .16.18

R v Thompson and others [2018] EWCA Crim 639 . . . . 12.80, 12.104
R v Thwaites [2006] EWCA Crim 3235 . . . . 1.55–1.56
R v Touhey (1961) 45 Cr App R 23 . . . . 2.20, 2.31
R v Tovey and Smith [2005] EWCA Crim 530 . . . . 1.03
R v Turner [1886] CCC Sess Papers 7.06
R v Turner (Mark) [2006] 2 Cr. App. R. (S). 51 . . . . .10.53
R v Ulhaqdad [2017] EWCA Crim 1216 . . . . .12.88
R v Utton [2019] Crim 1341 . . . . .12.17
R v W [2018] EWCA Crim 265; [2018] 1 Cr App R (S) 55. . . . . 12.188
R v Walker; R v Coatman [2018] 1 Cr App R 19 . . . . .1.37
R v Watts (James Michael) [2010] EWCA Crim 1824, [2011] CLR 68. . . . . .7.79
R v Webb [1964] 1 QB 357, [1963] 3 All ER 177 CCA 8.15
R v West [1898] 1 QB 174. . . . . .4.80
R v White [2014] EWCA Crim 714 . . . . .1.39
R v Whitta [2006] EWCA Crim 2626. . . . . .2.50
R v Wiles [2004] Cr App R (S) 88 . . . . .14.29
R v Wilkinson [2010] 1 Cr App R(S) 100 . . . . 12.119
R v Williams [1893] 1 QB 320 . . . . 2.05, 4.51, 4.61, 4.70
R v Williams EWCA Crim 281 . . . . .1.56
R v Willis (1974) 60 Cr App R 146, [1975] 1WLR 292 CA. 5.09
R v Wills [2011] EWCA Crim 1938, [2012] 1 Cr App R 2 . . . . App C 3D.4, App C 3D.5
R v Wiseman (1718) Fortes KB 91 . . . . .5.11
R v Wollaston 12 Cox CCR 5.35
R v Woods [2012] EWCA Crim 2753. . . . . 12.142
R v Wright [2020] EWCA Crim 1696
R v Younas [2017] EWCA Crim 1. . . . . .1.04
Rackham [1997] 2 Cr App R 222. . . . . .1.07
Reed & Others [2021] EWCA Crim 572 . . . . 1.51, 2.31, 2.52, 3.07, 3.20, 3.30, 3.43, 3.51, 3.62, 4.17,
    4.31, 4.34, 4.43, 4.47, 4.53, 4.63, 4.72, 4.83, 4.94, 4.96, 4.103, 4.105,
    4.114, 4.116, 4.125, 4.127, 4.136, 4.149, 4.160, 4.169, 4.178, 4.187,
    4.198, 4.200, 4.109, 4.209, 4.211, 4.217, 4.220, 4.222, 4.232, 4.234,
    4.241, 4.243, 4.250, 5.37, 5.52, 5.56, 5.80, 5.97, 5.109, 5.120, 6.11,
    6.19, 6.27, 6.36, 6.52, 6.60, 6.70, 6.79, 7.08, 7.15, 7.27, 7.35, 7.43,
    7.51, 7.58, 7.65, 7.73, 7.81, 7.89, 7.97, 7.105, 7.118, 7.126, 7.134,
    7.142, 7.149, 7.181, 8.11, 8.18, 8.25, 8.35, 8.41, 8.47, 8.49, 8.55, 8.60,
    8.62, 8.68, 8.74, 8.76, 8.83, 8.91, 8.114, 8.121, 8.128, 8.135, 8.142,
    8.154, 8.161, 8.168, 8.186, 9.18, 9.34, 9.42, 9.63, 9.72, 10.53, 11.08,
    11.15, 11.23, 11.31, 11.39, 11.47, 11.55, 12.175–12.179, 12.183
RK (Knight) [2018] EWCA Crim 603 . . . . 13.61, 13.63
RL [2015] EWCA Crim 1215 . . . . .13.63
Ross Hillman Ltd v Bond [1974] QB 435 DC 9.06
RT & Stuchfield [2020] EWCA Crim 155 . . . . 13.61, 13.63

Shaw v DPP [1961] 2 All ER 446 HL. 8.97
Shaw v DPP [1962] AC 220 HL. 8.98
Stevens v Christy 85 Cr App R 249 DC, [1987] Crim LR 503 . . . . .8.132
Stewart v DPP (1986) 83 Cr App R 327 CA 8.98

Thompson v Lodwick [1983] RTR 76. . . . . .9.06
Tolhurst v DPP [2008] EWHC 2976 (Admin). 4.94

Walker [1996] Cr App R 111 CA. 10.08
Wills 2011 EWCA Crim [1938] 13.63

YGM [2018] EWCA Crim 2458 . . . . .13.63

TABLE OF STATUTES AND STATUTORY INSTRUMENTS

STATUTES

Adoption Act 1976 (AA 1976)
   s 47(1).......................6.25, 6.34
Age of Marriage Act 1929 (AMA 1929)
   s 1..............................3.18
   s 1(1).......................4.60, 4.80
   s 2..............................3.18
Assaults on Emergency Workers
   (Offences) Act 2018
   s 2..............................3.53
Attempted Rape Act 1948
   s 1..............................2.11
Aviation and Maritime Security Act 1990
   s 1.............................16.87
   ss 9–13........................16.87
Aviation Security Act 1982
   ss 1–4.........................16.83
British Nationality Act 1981
   Pt 4............................8.175
   s 50(1).........................8.152
Child Abduction Act 1984
   ss 1–2.................16.84, 12.221
Children Act 1989 (CA1989)..........16.95
   s 53,............................7.78
   s 60(3).........................7.78
   s 108(4)........................8.15
   Sch 12, para 14.................8.15
Children and Young Persons Act 1933
   (CYPA 1933)..................4.265
   s 1....................12.248, 16.79
   s 3............................8.114
   s 39...........................15.19
   s 44..........................12.204
   s 46(1).........................4.269
   s 49...........................15.25
   s 50.......................2.36, 5.05
   s 99(1).........................4.264
   s 99(2).........................9.06
Civil Partnership Act 2004..............9.27
   s 261(1).........................6.76
   Sch 27, para 174............6.67, 6.76
Communications Act 2003
   s 127(1)........................16.89
Coroners and Justice Act 2009
   (CAJA 2009).......9.06, 9.27, 12.249, 13.32
   s 17...........................13.01
   s 62..............1.61, 9.37, 12.221

s 62(1)..................9.41, 14.29, 16.75
s 62(2)(a).........................9.38
s 62(2)(b).........................9.38
s 62(2)(c).........................9.38
s 62(3)......................9.38–9.39
s 62(4)...........................9.39
s 62(5)...........................9.39
s 62(6)(a)...................9.38, 9.41
s 62(9)(a)........................9.40
s 63(3)(b)..................9.38–9.39
s 63(7)......................9.38–9.39
s 64(1)...........................9.40
s 65(2)(a).........................9.39
s 65(2)(b).........................9.39
s 65(3)...........................9.39
s 65(5)...........................9.39
s 65(6)...........................9.39
s 65(7)...........................9.39
s 65(8)...........................9.39
s 66..............................9.43
s 104............................13.32
s 125(1).................12.171, 12.206
Crime and Disorder Act 1988 (CDA 1988)
   s 51.............................1.55
   Sch 3...........................1.55
Crime and Disorder Act 1998..........12.249
   ss 7–13.........................1.55
   s 8(1)(b).......................16.67
   s 37(1)........................12.204
   s 51.............................1.55
   s 51B..........................12.248
   s 29...........................16.89
   s 31(a)........................16.89
   s 31(b)........................16.89
   s 34...........................4.261
   s 37(1)........................12.204
   Sch 3, para 2..................12.248
   Sch 9, para 1...................4.261
Crime (Sentences) Act 1997 (C(S)A 1997)
   s 30..........................12.132
   s 52...........................5.112
Criminal Appeal Act 1968
   s 3.............................1.37
Criminal Attempts Act 1981
   (CAA 1981).........1.61, 2.52, 3.07, 3.30,
      3.43, 3.51, 3.62, 4.17, 4.43, 5.56, 5.120
   s 1........................3.20, 5.46

s 1(1)........1.51, 2.31, 2.34, 4.17,4.31, 4.72, 4.83, 4.94, 4.103, 4.114, 4.125, 4.136, 4.149, 4.160, 4.169, 4.178, 4.187, 4.198, 4.209, 4.220, 4.232, 4.241, 4.250, 5.57, 5.80, 5.97, 5.109, 5.120, 6.27, 6.36, 6.52, 6.60, 6.70, 6.79, 7.15, 7.27, 7.35, 7.43, 7.51, 7.73, 7.81, 7.89, 7.97, 7.105, 7.118, 7.126, 7.134, 7.142, 7.149, 7.181, 7.189, 8.18, 8.25, 8.41, 8.47, 8.55, 8.60, 8.68, 8.74, 8.83, 8.91, 8.114, 8.121, 8.128, 8.135, 8.142, 8.154, 8.161, 8.168, 8.186, 9.18, 9.34, 9.42, 9.63, 9.72, 10.53, 11.08, 11.15, 11.23, 11.31, 11.39, 11.47, 11.55	
s 4 ....5.46	
s 4(5).............................5.21	
s 11(1).............................5.56	
Criminal Attempts Act 1985 (CAA 1985)................. 1.50, 3.20	
Criminal Damage Act 1971	
s 1 .... 16.82	
s 1(2)............................. 16.82	
Criminal Justice Act 1948 (CJA 1948)	
s 1 ....2.11	
s 1(1)...........................6.12, 6.20	
Criminal Justice Act 1972	
s 48 ....4.13	
Criminal Justice Act 1987	
s 4 .... 12.248	
s 6(1)............................. 12.248	
Criminal Justice Act 1988 (CJA 1988)	
s 134............................. 16.86	
s 160........ 1.61, 9.01, 9.06, 9.25, 9.38, 9.72, 12.166, 12.221, 12.248, 14.29, 16.72, 17.10, 17.17, App A p 514	
s 160(1)...............9.25, 9.27, 9.29, 9.30	
s 160(2A) 9.28	
s 160(3)............................9.28	
s 160(4).........................9.27–9.28	
s 160A(1) 9.27	
s 160A(3) 9.27	
s 160A(4) 9.27	
Sch 3............................. 12.250	
Criminal Justice Act 2003 (CJA 2003) 12.05, 12.11, 12.117, 12.128, 12.131	
ss 1–7 .... 12.161	
s 7(3)........................4.126, 4.138	
s 9(3)............................. 4.127	
s 100 ....13.61, 13.63	
s 142(2)........................... 12.131	
s 143(1)........................... 12.131	
s 144 .... 12.211	
s 154 .... 12.240	
s 154(1)..................... 9.52, 9.64, 9.73	
s 156(3)........................... 12.97	
s 156(4)........................... 12.97	
s 224A............................ 12.124
s 224A............................ 12.124
s 225 .... 14.29
s 224A................. 12.120, 12.123, 12.127, 12.129, 12.131
s 224A(1)(b) 12.123
s 224A(12)........................ 12.123
s 225 .... 12.118, 12.120, 12.127, 12.129–12.130
s 225(1)........................... 12.119
s 225(2)........................... 12.119
s 225(2)(b)........................ 12.131
s 226A............................ 12.113
s 229(3)........................... 12.247
s 236A................... 1.41, 12.106, 12.153
s 243A............................ 12.161
s 244 .... 12.13, 12.92, 12.165, 12.160
s 246A............................ 12.131
s 246A............................ 12.131
s 247A............................ 12.161
s 249(1)........................... 12.160
s 254 .... 12.161
s 256AA 12.162
s 264 .... 12.13, 12.92, 12.165
s 265 .... 12.161
s 266 .... 12.161
s 278 .... 12.161
s 279 .... 12.161
s 282 .... 8.143
s 282(2)....... 4.126, 4.137–4.138, 7.28, 7.36, 7.44, 7.52, 7.82, 7.98, 7.106, 7.127, 7.135, 7.143, 7.150, 7.182, 7.190
s 282(3)............................7.90
s 282(4)...... 3.31, 3.52, 3.63, 4.18, 4.33, 4.46, 4.84, 4.150, 4.161, 4.170, 4.179, 4.188, 4.221, 4.233, 4.242, 4.251, 6.53, 6.61, 6.71, 8.34, 8.48, 8.61, 8.75, 8.92, 8.136, 8.155, 8.162, 8.169, 8.187, 9.19, 10.26, 10.37, 10.45, 11.40, 11.48, 11.56
s 320 ....10.01, 10.09
Sch 15........................... 12.166
Sch 15B 12.119, 12.124, 12.126
Sch 18A 1.41
Criminal Justice and Court Services Act 2000 (CJCSA 2000)............ 16.59
ss 26–34 .... 12.217
s 39 ....4.10
s 41(1)...............................9.19
s 41(3).........................9.25, 9.28
Criminal Justice and Courts Act 2015............... 9.45, 9.48, 12.11, 12.91, 12.164, 12.165
c 2, Pt 3 s 78(2)...................... 15.19
Pt 1 s 5(1) 12.123
s 33 ....9.67
s 33(1)..............................9.71

Criminal Justice and Immigration
Act 2008 (CJIA 2008) 9.06, 9.50, 12.05,
17.02, 17.11, 17.15
s 63 . . . . 1.61, 9.45, 12.221, 14.29, 16.75
s 63(1). 9.46
s 63(3). 9.46
s 63(4). 9.46
s 63(5). 9.46
s 63(5A)(a). 9.46
s 63(5A)(b) 9.46
s 63(7). 9.46
s 63(7)(a) 9.46
s 63(7)(b) 9.46
s 63(7)(c) 9.46
s 63(7)(d). 9.46
s 63(7B) 9.46
s 63(8). 9.47
s 63(9). 9.47
s 64(3)(b) 9.47
s 64(7). 9.47
s 65(2). 9.48
s 66 . . . . .9.48
s 66(3). 9.49
s 67(4)(a) 9.52
s 69 . . . . .9.06
s 83 . . . . 12.196
Sch 15, para 1. . . . . 4.225
Sch 15, para 5(4) 6.49, 6.57
Criminal Justice and Public Order
Act 1994 (CJPOA 1994). 5.62,
5.90, 9.01, 9.05–9.06
s 84(1). 9.06, 9.26
s 84(2). 9.06, 9.26
s 84(1)(3) 9.06
s 84(4). 9.25
s 142 . . . . 2.01, 2.37, 5.63, 5.12, 11.297
s 143 . . . . 5.127
s 143(1). 5.43
s 144 . . . . .5.46
s 145 . . . . 5.04, 5.08, 14.22
s 146(2). 5.13
s 168(1). 11.05, 11.12
s 168(3). 2.38, 11.05, 11.12
Sch 9. . . . . 11.12
Sch 11 . . . . 11.05, 11.12, 11.20
Criminal Law Act 1967 (CLA 1967)
s 6 . . . . 5.16, 5.19
s 7(2). 5.21
s 10 . . . . .2.21
Criminal Law Act 1977 (CLA 1977)
s 1 . . . . .9.18
s 54 . . . . 1.27, 1.61, 6.40, 6.44, 6.47, 12.49,
12.166, 12.221, 12.248, 14.29,
15.04, 16.72, App A p 514
s 54(1). 6.02, 6.41
s 54(2). 6.42–6.43

s 54(4). 6.43
s 54(4)(a) 6.45
s 54(4)(b). 6.45
Criminal Law Amendment Act 1885
(CLAA 1885). 1.61, 2.07, 4.67,
4.77, 7.10, 11.02
s 2 . . . . 8.01, 8.06, 12.221
s 2(1). 8.10
s 3 . . . . .2.07, 12.221
s 4 . . . . 2.07, 3.05, 4.48–4.49, 4.53–4.54,
4.56, 4.52, 6.12, 12.223
s 5 . . . . 2.07, 3.05, 4.664.56–4.57,
4.63, 12.221
s 5(1). 4.62, 4.80, 12.248
s 5(2). 7.03, 7.05, 7.07
s 6 . . . . 12.221
s 7 . . . . 12.221
s 8 . . . . 12.221
s 9 . . . . 2.05, 4.53, 4.63, 4.72
s 11 . . . . 5.01, 5.40, 5.44, 5.101, 12.221
Criminal Law Amendment Act 1922
(CLAA 1922)
s 1 . . . . 3.05, 5.35
s 2 . . . . .4.60
Criminal Law Amendment Act 1928
s 1 . . . . 4.59, 4.80
Criminal Procedure Act 1851
(CPA 1851)
s 9 . . . . .4.53
Criminal Procedure and Investigations
Act 1996 (CPIA 1996) 13.59
Customs and Excise Management
Act 1979. . . . . 12.249
s 170 . . . . 12.166, 12.221, 14.29,
16.72, App A p 514
Customs Consolidation Act 1876
s 42 . . . . 12.166, 14.29, 16.72, App A p 514
Domestic Violence, Crime and Victims
Act 2004 (DVCVA 2004) 1.21
s 5 . . . . 12.221, 16.89
s 12 . . . . 12.229
ss 17–21 . . . . .1.21
s 17(2). 1.25
Explosive Substances Act 1883
s 2 . . . . 16.79
s 3 . . . . 16.79
Firearms Act 1968
s 16 . . . . 16.80
s 16A. 16.80
s 17(1). 16.80
s 17(2). 16.80
s 18 . . . . 16.80
Immigration Act 1971 . . . . 12.246
s 3(6). 12.242, 12.244
s 6 . . . . 12.242
s 6(2). 12.245

Indecency with Children Act 1960
  (IwCA 1960) 1.61, 3.16, 3.21, 5.104
  s 1 .... 1.27, 3.16, 4.07–4.08, 4.12, 4.20,
      5.34, 12.49, 12.166, 12.221, 12.248,
      14.29, 15.04, 16.72, App A p 514
  s 1(1)............ 3.05, 4.14, 4.15, 4.18, 5.112
  s 2(1).................................3.14
Indictments Act 1915................1.01, 3.05
  s 1 .... 16.79
Infanticide Act 1938
  s 1 ....12.221, 16.79
International Criminal Court Act 2001
  s 51 .... 16.89
  s 52 .... 16.89
Justice Act (Northern Ireland) 2016........9.48
Legal Aid, Sentencing and Punishment
  of Offenders Act 2012
  (LASPO 2012).......12.11, 12.117, 12.119,
      12.128–12.131, 15.08, 15.24, 15.31
  s 122 ....12.118, 12.123
  s 123 .... 12.119
Magistrates Court Act 1980 (MCA 1980)
  s 17 ....5.43
  s 17(1)......................5.127, 8.106
  s 17A-17C 1.55
  s 24 .... 4.260
  s 32(1)............................. 10.11
  s 34(3)............................. 10.19
  s 150(4)........................... 4.267
  Sch 1 ....5.43, 8.106
Maritime Security Act 1990
  s 1 .... 16.87
  ss 9–13 .... 16.87
Marriage Act 1949 (MA 1949)
  s 2 ....4.60, 4.80
Mental Deficiency Act 1913
  (MDA 1913) 1.61, 7.61, 7.64
  s 1 ....7.56
  s 56 .... 7.54, 7.60, 7.108, 7.113, 7.161
  s 56(1)............................. 7.152
  s 56(1)(c) 7.152
  s 56(1)(d)....................7.152, 7.156
  s 56(1)(e) 7.56, 7.59, 7.110, 7.112,
      7.154, 7.156, 7.158, 7.160
  s 56(4)..............7.57, 7.111, 7.155, 7.159
  s 56(5)................... 7.57, 7.111, 7.155
Mental Health Act 1959 (MHA 1959) 7.20
  s 127 ....7.20
  s 127(1)(b) 7.20
  s 128 .... 1.27, 1.61, 7.01, 7.70,
      7.76, 12.49, 12.166, 12.220,
      12.221, 15.04, App A p 514
  s 128(a)............................7.72
  s 128(1)............................7.68
  s 128(3)............................7.74
  s 128(4)........................7.13, 7.71

Mental Health Act 1983................ 13.41
  s 1 ....7.24
  s 127 .... 16.84
Mental Health (Amendment) Act 1982
  Sch 3...............................7.20
Misuse of Drugs Act 1971 .... 12.249
  s 4(3)........................... 12.221
Modern Slavery Act 2015 (MSA 2015) 1.61,
      8.188, 12.236–12.239, 12.248, 13.24, 16.91
  s 1 ....8.181, 12.239, 12.248,
      13.15, 13.27, 13.42
  s 2 ..... 1.61, 4.247, 4.248, 8.176, 8.181, 8.184,
      8.188, 12.166, 12.221, 12.239, 12.241,
      12.248, 13.15, 13.27, 13.42, 15.04, 16.91
  s 2(1)......................... 8.182, 8.185
  s 2(2)............................. 8.184
  s 2(3)............................. 8.183
  s 2(4)............................. 8.183
  s 2(5)............................. 8.183
  s 2(6)............................. 8.184
  s 3 .... 8.183
  s 3(3)........................4.247, 8.183
  s 4 ....12.239, 12.248
  s 5(1)(a) 8.187
  s 5(1)(b) 8.187
  s 8 ....8.189, 12.239
  s 11 ....8.189, 12.235
  s 14 ....8.189, 12.236
  s 17(4)......................12.238, 13.43
  s 18 .... 12.237
  s 18(5)........................... 12.237
  s 19 .... 12.237
  s 23 .... 12.236
  s 45 .... 2.50, 3.39, 3.49, 3.59, 4.26, 4.40,
      4.92, 4.100, 4.110, 4.122, 4.132, 4.135,
      4.157, 4.166, 4.175, 4.184, 4.195, 4.198,
      4.206, 4.209, 4.217, 4.227, 4.239, 4.248,
      4.258, 5.04, 5.78, 5.118, 6.50, 6.58, 6.67,
      6.76, 7.25, 7.33, 7.41, 7.49, 7.79, 7.87,
      7.95, 7.103, 7.124, 7.132, 7.140, 7.147,
      7.179, 7.187, 8.31, 8.39, 8.45, 8.53, 8.58,
      8.66, 8.72, 8.89, 8.140, 8.184, 9.07, 9.28,
      9.48, 9.60, 9.70, 10.09, 10.24, 10.35,
      10.43, 10.51, 11.37, 11.44, 11.53
  Sch 4......... 4.195, 4.206, 4.239, 5.04, 5.78,
      5.118, 7.179, 7.187, 8.89, 8.140, 9.07,
      9.28, 9.48, 9.60, 9.70, 10.09, 10.43
  Sch 4, para 33.......2.50, 3.39, 3.49, 3.59, 4.26,
      4.40, 4.92, 4.100, 4.110, 4.122, 4.132,
      4.135, 4.157, 4.166, 4.175, 4.184, 4.198,
      4.209, 4.217, 4.227, 4.258, 6.50, 6.58,
      6.67, 6.76, 7.25, 7.33, 7.41, 7.49, 7.79,
      7.87, 7.95, 7.103, 7.124, 7.132, 7.140,
      7.147, 8.31, 8.45, 8.53, 8.58, 8.66, 8.72,
      10.24, 10.35, 10.51, 11.37, 11.44, 11.53
  Sch 4, para 36...................... 8.184

National Assistance Act 1948
  Pt III 7.69
Nationality, Immigration and Asylum
  Act 2002
  s 145 .... 1.27, 12.49, 12.221
Obscene Publications Act 1959
  (OPA 1959) 9.03, 9.55
  s 1(1) 9.59
  s 1(2) 9.59
  s 1(3)(a) 9.59
  s 1(3)(b) 9.59
  s 1(4) 9.59
  s 1(6) 9.59
  s 2 .... 1.61, 9.04, 9.56–9.57, 9.60
  s 2(1) 9.61, 9.62
  s 2(1)(a) 9.64
  s 2(1)(b) 9.64
  s 2(3) 9.03, 9.55, 9.60
  s 2(3A) 9.60
  s 2(4) 9.60
  s 2(4A) 9.60
  s 2(5) 9.60
  s 3 .... 9.66
  s 4(1) 9.60
  s 4(1A) 9.60
Obscene Publications Act 1964
  (OPA 1964) 9.03, 9.55, 9.57
  s 1 .... 9.04
  s 1(1) 9.58
  s 1(2) 9.59
  s 1(3) 9.60
  s 1(4) 9.66
  s 2 .... 9.59
Offences Against the Person Act
  1861 (OAPA 1861) 16.78
  s 4 .... 16.78
  s 16 .... 12.248, 16.78
  s 18 .... 16.78
  ss 20–23 .... 16.78
  s 21 .... 12.221
  ss 27–32 .... 16.78
  s 35 .... 16.78
  s 37 .... 16.78
  s 38 .... 5.90, 16.78
  s 47 .... 16.78
  s 52 .... 1.61, 2.08, 3.02, 3.06, 3.08,
              3.11, 4.63, 4.117, 12.221, 12.248
  s 53 .... 12.221
  s 54 .... 12.221
  s 55 .... 12.221
  s 61 .... 1.27, 1.61, 5.01, 5.07, 5.09,
                    5.14, 5.48, 5.78, 12.221
  s 62 .... 1.27, 1.61, 4.53, 5.20, 5.22, 5.24,
            5.28, 5.31, 5.36–5.39, 5.86, 5.92, 12.221
  s 63 .... 2.04, 6.08, 6.16, 6.33,
                      7.05, 7.56, 7.110, 7.158

Offender Rehabilitation Act 2014
  (ORA 2014) 12.161–12.163
  ss 1–7 .... 12.161
  s 2 .... 12.162
  s 4 .... 12.163
  s 6 .... 12.163
Policing and Crime Act 2017
  s 164 .... 5.01
  s 176 .... 8.42, 8.56, 8.69
Postal Services Act 2000
  s 85(3) 16.89
  s 85(4) 16.89
Powers of Criminal Courts (Sentencing)
  Act 2000 (PCC(S)A 2000) 12.05, 12.163
  s 91 .... 4.260
  s 91(1)(b)–(e) 4.260
Proceeds of Crime Act 2002
  (POCA 2002) 7.184, 12.05
  s 75(2)(c) 1.19
  s 75(3)(a) 1.19
  Sch 2 ...... 7.184, 7.192, 8.50, 8.63, 8.77, 8.93,
                    8.145, 8.156, 8.163, 8.170, 8.180
  Sch 2, para 8(2)(a) 4.223
Prohibition of Female Circumcision
  Act 1985
  s 1 .... 16.84
Protection from Harassment
  Act 1997 .... 12.249, 16.88
  s 2 .... 16.88
  s 2A 16.88
  s 4 .... 16.88
  s 4A 16.88
  s 5A 12.224, 12.229
Protection of Children Act 1978
  (PCA 1978) 9.01, 9.25
  s 1 .... 1.27, 1.61, 4.247, 9.04, 9.33, 9.38,
              9.72, 12.49, 12.166, 12.221, 12.248,
              14.29, 16.72, 17.10, 17.17, App A p 514
  s 1(1) 9.05
  s 1(1)(a) 8.151, 8.175, 8.183,
                              9.06, 9.08, 9.09
  s 1(1)(b) 9.06, 9.10–9.11
  s 1(1)(c) 9.06, 9.12–9.13
  s 1(1)(d) 9.14–9.15
  s 1(2) 9.06
  s 1(3) 9.07
  s 1(4) 9.06
  s 1(4)(a) 9.06
  s 1(4)(b) 9.06
  s 1A 9.06
  s 1A(1) 9.06
  s 1A(3) 9.06
  s 1A(4) 9.06
  s 1A(5) 9.06
  s 1A(6) 9.06
  s 1B 9.06

s 1B(1)(a) 9.06
s 1B(1)(b) 9.06
s 1B(1)(c) 9.06
s 2 . . . . .9.06
s 2(3) 9.06
s 3 . . . . .9.07
s 6(1) 9.07
s 7(2) 9.06
s 7(3) 9.06
s 7(4) 9.06
s 7(5) 9.06
s 7(6) 9.01
s 7(7) 9.06
s 7(8) 9.06
s 7(9) 9.06
Protection of Freedoms Act 2012
  (PFA 2012) 8.149, 16.53, 16.56
  Pt 5, Ch 4 . . . . 12.221
  Pt 5, Ch 5 . . . . 3.32, 5.47, 5.54, 5.59, 5.67, 5.111
  s 67 . . . . 16.35
  s 87(1) 12.217
  s 92 . . . . .5.01
  s 109(1) 8.172
  s 109(2) 8.172
Public Order Act 1986 (POA 1986)
  ss 1–3 . . . . 16.85
  s 4 . . . . .10.14, 16.89
  s 4A 16.89
  s 5 . . . . 10.14
Punishment of Incest Act 1908
  (PIA 1908) 1.61, 2.09, 6.01, 6.06
  s 1 . . . . 6.06–6.09, 12.221
  s 1(1) 6.09–6.10, 6.12
  s 1(2) 6.08, 6.18
  s 1(3) 6.12
  s 1(4) 6.13
  s 2 . . . . 6.15–6.17, 6.20, 12.221
  s 3 . . . . 6.08, 6.16–6.17
  s 4(2) 6.09, 6.17
  s 4(3) 2.09
  s 6 . . . . .6.09, 6.17
Regulation and Inspection of Social
  Care (Wales) Act 2016
  Pt 1 . . . . .7.78
Regulation of Investigatory Powers
  Act 2000
  s 53 . . . . 16.89
  s 54 . . . . 16.89
Road Traffic Act 1988
  s 1 . . . . 16.86
  s 3A 16.86
Safeguarding Vulnerable Groups Act
  2006 (SVGA 2006) 16.51, 16.52, 16.62
  s 2 . . . . 16.52
  s 18A 16.56
  Sch 3 . . . . 16.52

Sentencing Act 2020 (SA 2020)
  ('Sentencing Code') 1.41, 12.02–12.15,
              12.25, 12.117, 12.204, 12.252,
              16.03, 16.05, 16.21, 16.25
  Pt 1 . . . . 12.04
  Pts 2–13 . . . . 12.04
  Pt 11, Ch 2 . . . . 16.03, 16.07
  s 1 . . . . 12.04
  s 1(1) 12.25
  s 2 . . . . 12.04
  s 30 . . . . 12.59, 12.62, 12.65,
                  12.66, 12.69, 12.70
  s 30(1) 12.96
  s 30(1)(c) 12.59, 12.62, 12.65, 12.66, 12.70
  s 30(1)(d) 12.69
  s 54(4)(a) 16.66
  s 54(4)(b) 16.66
  s 54(5) 16.66
  s 57 . . . . 12.10
  s 58 . . . . 12.204
  s 59 . . . . 12.171
  s 59(1) 12.206
  s 63 . . . . 12.10
  s 79 . . . . 14.21
  s 80 . . . . 14.21
  s 82(2) 14.21
  s 173(1) 12.36
  s 174 . . . . 12.36
  s 177(1) 12.35
  s 177(2) 12.35
  s 177(3) 12.35
  s 180(1)(a) 12.35
  s 180(1)(b) 12.35
  s 181 . . . . 12.35
  s 181(a) 12.35
  s 181(b) 12.35
  s 181(4) 12.35
  s 181(6) 12.35
  s 184 . . . . 12.36
  s 186(10) 12.36
  s 186(11) 12.36
  s 187(2) 12.36
  s 187(3) 12.36
  s 200 . . . . 12.39
  s 201 . . . . 12.39
  s 202(2)(a) 12.37
  s 202(2)(c) 12.37
  s 203 . . . . 12.37
  s 206 . . . . 12.39
  s 208(10) 12.39
  s 208(11) 12.39
  s 208(12) 12.39
  s 208(13) 12.39
  s 209(2) 12.38
  s 216 . . . . 12.40
  s 249(1) 12.62

s 250 . . . . 12.57, 12.59, 12.62, 12.64, 12.68	
s 254 . . . . 12.61, 12.161	
s 254(1). 16.65	
s 255 . . . . 12.61, 12.62	
s 256 . . . . 12.62	
s 258 . . . . 12.57, 12.59	
s 258(2). 12.62	
s 263(2). 12.27	
s 264(2). 12.27	
s 264(3). 12.27	
s 265 . . . . 4.97, 4.106, 12.12,
12.101, 12.153, 12.161
s 266 . . . . 12.66, 12.124, 12.161
s 267 . . . . 2.55, 3.46, 3.65, 4.35, 4.48, 4.97,
4.106, 4.117, 4.128, 4.201, 4.212,
4.223, 4.235, 6.73, 6.81, 7.30, 7.38,
7.129, 7.137, 8.36, 8.50, 8.63,
8.77, 8.189, 9.24, 11.50, 12.66
s 268 . . . . 12.66
s 272 . . . . 12.65
s 273 . . . . 2.55, 3.46, 3.65, 4.35, 4.48,
4.97, 4.106, 4.117, 4.128, 4.201, 4.212,
4.223, 4.235, 6.73, 6.81, 7.30, 7.38, 7.129,
7.137, 8.36, 8.50, 8.63, 8.77, 8.189, 9.24,
11.50, 12.66, 12.118, 12.123–12.131
s 273(3). 12.118, 12.124
s 273(14) 12.123
s 274 . . . . 12.64–12.66, 12.118, 12.123–12.131
s 275 . . . . 12.118
s 277(2). 12.27
s 277(3). 12.27
s 278 . . . . 4.97, 4.106, 12.12,
12.101, 12.153, 12.161
s 279 . . . . 12.70, 12.161
s 280 . . . . 2.55, 3.46, 3.65, 4.35, 4.48, 4.97,
4.106, 4.117, 4.128, 4.201, 4.212,
4.223, 4.235, 6.73, 6.81, 7.30, 7.38,
7.129, 7.137, 8.36, 8.50, 8.63,
8.77, 8.189, 9.24, 11.50, 12.70
s 281 . . . . 12.70
s 283 . . . . 2.55, 3.46, 3.65, 4.35, 4.48,
4.97, 4.106, 4.117, 4.128, 4.201, 4.212,
4.223, 4.235, 6.73, 6.81, 7.30, 7.38, 7.129,
7.137, 8.36, 8.50, 8.63, 8.77, 8.189, 9.24,
11.50, 12.70, 12.118, 12.123–12.131
s 283(3). 12.118, 12.124
s 283(14) 12.123
s 285 . . . . 12.68, 12.69–12.70,
12.118, 12.123–12.131
s 286(1). 12.26
s 286(2). 12.28
s 288(2). 12.27
s 288(4). 12.27
s 289 . . . . 14.29
s 290 . . . . 12.28
s 291 . . . . 12.28

s 292(3). 12.28
s 292(4). 12.28
s 306 . . . . 2.25, 2.55, 3.23, 3.32, 3.46, 3.54,
3.65, 4.19, 4.35, 4.48, 4.75, 4.86, 4.97,
4.117, 4.163, 4.172, 4.181, 4.190, 4.212,
4.201, 4.223, 4.235, 4.244, 5.47, 5.89, 5.99,
6.30, 6.38, 6.46, 6.55, 6.63, 6.73, 7.17, 7.30,
7.38, 7.46, 7.54, 7.137, 7.144, 7.151, 7.169,
7.175, 7.184, 7.192, 8.20, 8.27, 8.36, 8.50,
8.63, 8.77, 8.86, 8.93, 8.116, 8.123, 8.130,
8.137, 8.145, 8.156, 8.163, 8.170, 8.180,
8.189, 9.24, 9.37, 10.28, 10.39, 10.56, 11.10,
11.17, 11.25, 11.33, 11.42, 11.50, 11.58
s 306(1). 12.59, 12.62, 12.65, 12.66, 12.69
s 307 . . . . 12.65, 2.55, 3.46, 3.65, 4.48, 4.97,
4.106, 7.30, 7.38, 7.129, 7.137, 8.36, 8.189
s 308 . . . . 12.59, 12.62, 12.65,
12.66, 12.69, 12.70
s 328 . . . . 12.158
s 344 . . . . 16.09
s 344(1). 16.18
s 345 . . . . 2.13, 2.25, 2.55, 3.09, 3.23, 3.32,
3.46, 3.54, 3.65, 4.19, 4.35, 4.48, 4.55, 4.65,
4.75, 4.86, 4.97, 4.106, 4.117, 4.151, 4.163,
4.172, 4.181, 4.190, 4.201, 4.212, 4.223,
4.235, 4.244, 4.254, 5.24, 5.40, 5.47, 5.54,
5.59, 5.67, 5.83, 5.89, 5.99, 5.111, 5.123,
5.130, 6.13, 6.21, 6.30, 6.38, 6.46, 6.55,
6.63, 6.73, 6.81, 7.17, 7.30, 7.38, 7.46,
7.54, 7.67, 7.75, 7.84, 7.120, 7.129, 7.137,
7.144, 7.151, 7.169, 7.175, 7.184, 7.192,
8.20, 8.27, 8.36, 8.50, 8.63, 8.77, 8.85,
8.93, 8.103, 8.109, 8.116, 8.123, 8.130,
8.137, 8.145, 8.156, 8.163, 8.170, 8.180,
8.189, 8.197, 9.24, 9.37, 9.45, 9.54,
9.66, 9.75, 10.13, 10.20, 10.28, 10.39,
10.47, 10.56, 11.10, 11.17, 11.25,
11.33, 11.42, 11.50, 11.58, 16.97
s 345(1). 16.07
s 345(2). 16.07
s 347(1)(a) 16.21
s 347(1)(b) 16.21
s 347(2)(a) 16.21
s 347(2)(b) 16.21
s 347(3). 16.21
s 350 . . . . 16.22
s 350(1). 16.37
s 350(2)(a) 16.37
s 350(2)(b) 16.37
s 350(2)(c) 16.37
s 350(5). 16.38
s 350(6). 16.38
s 350(8). 16.41
s 350(9)(b) 16.40
s 350(9(c) 16.40
s 352(1). 16.48

s 352(2)	16.49	Sch 15, para 9(l)	4.223
s 353	16.45	Sch 15, para 9(m)	4.235
s 353(a)	16.45	Sch 15, para 9(n)	.6.73
s 353(b)	16.45	Sch 15, para 9(o)	.6.81
s 355	16.67	Sch 15, para 9(p)	.7.30
s 358	16.09–16.10, 16.33	Sch 15, para 9(q)	.7.38
s 359	12.224	Sch 15, para 9(r)	7.129
s 360(2)	12.224	Sch 15, para 9(s)	7.137
s 379(1)	12.236	Sch 15, para 9(t)	.8.36
s 379(2)	14.02	Sch 15, para 9(u)	.8.50
s 385	16.10	Sch 15, para 9(v)	.8.63
s 386	12.243	Sch 15, para 9(w)	.8.77
s 399	12.37	Sch 15, para 9(x)	11.50
s 405	4.264	Sch 15, para 12(b)	8.189
Sch 6, Pt 4	12.36	Sch 15B	12.124
Sch 6 pt 4, para 12(1)	12.36	Sch 18	12.16
Sch 9, Pt 3	12.33, 12.39	Sch 18, Pt 2	12.166
Sch 13	1.41, 12.101	Sch 18, para 7	.9.37
Sch 13, para 6(a)	4.97, 4.106	Sch 18, para (af)	.7.92
Sch 14	12.70	Sch 18, para 27	7.137
Sch 14, para 9(6)	.9.24	Sch 18, para 29(a)	.2.25
Sch 14, para 9(a)	2.55, 3.46, 3.65	Sch 18, para 29(b)	11.10
Sch 14, para 9(d)	.4.97	Sch 18, para 29(c)	11.17
Sch 14, para 9(e)	4.106	Sch 18, para 29(d)	11.25
Sch 14, para 9(f)	4.128	Sch 18, para 29(e)	.4.75
Sch 14, para 9(g)	.4.48	Sch 18, para 29(f)	.4.86
Sch 14, para 9(h)	4.117	Sch 18, para 29(g)	.7.17
Sch 14, para 9(i)	.4.35	Sch 18, para 29(h)	7.120
Sch 14, para 9(j)	4.201	Sch 18, para 29(i)	6.30, 6.38
Sch 14, para 9(k)	4.212	Sch 18, para 29(j)	.3.23
Sch 14, para 9(l)	4.223	Sch 18, para 29(k)	3.32, 5.47, 5.99
Sch 14, para 9(m)	4.235	Sch 18, para 29(l)	.5.89
Sch 14, para 9(n)	.6.73	Sch18, para 29(q)	.8.86
Sch 14, para 9(o)	.6.81	Sch 18, para 29(r)	.8.27
Sch 14, para 9(p)	.7.30	Sch 18, para 29(s)	8.116
Sch 14, para 9(q)	.7.38	Sch 18, para 29(v)	7.175
Sch 14, para 9(r)	7.129	Sch 18, para 29(w)	.8.20
Sch 14, para 9(s)	7.137	Sch 18, para 29(x)	7.169
Sch 14, para 9(t)	.8.36	Sch 18, para 29(y)	8.123
Sch 14, para 9(u)	.8.50	Sch 18, para 29(z)	8.137
Sch 14, para 9(v)	.8.63	Sch 18, para 31	.4.19
Sch 14, para 9(w)	.8.77	Sch 18, para 32(b)	8.130
Sch 14, para 9(x)	11.50	Sch 18, para 33	11.33
Sch 14, para 12(b)	8.189	Sch 18, para 34	.6.46
Sch 15	12.09, 12.118, 12.123–12.126	Sch 18, para 35	.9.24
Sch 15, para 9(6)	.9.24	Sch 18, para 38(a)	.2.55
Sch 15, para 9(a)	2.55, 3.46, 3.65	Sch 18, para 38(aa)	7.129
Sch 15, para 9(d)	.4.97	Sch 18, para 38(ab)	7.137
Sch 15, para 9(e)	4.106	Sch 18, para 38(ac)	7.144
Sch 15, para 9(f)	4.128	Sch 18, para 38(ad)	7.151
Sch 15, para 9(g)	.4.48	Sch 18, para 38(ag)	7.100
Sch 15, para 9(h)	4.117	Sch 18, para 38(ah)	7.108
Sch 15, para 9(i)	.4.35	Sch 18, para 38(ai)	.8.36
Sch 15, para 9(j)	4.201	Sch 18, para 38(aj)	.8.50
Sch 15, para 9(k)	4.212	Sch 18, para 38(ak)	.8.63

Sch 18, para 38(al) 8.77	Sch 19, para 20(l) 11.50
Sch 18, para 38(am) 7.184, 8.93	Sch 19, para 22(b). 8.189
Sch 18, para 38(an). 7.192, 8.145	Sch 27. . . . . 12.08
Sch 18, para 38(ao) 8.156	Sentencing (Pre-consolidation
Sch 18, para 38(ap) 8.163	Amendment) Act 2020 . . . . 12.09
Sch 18, para 38(aq) 8.170	Serious Crime Act 2007 (SCA)
Sch 18, para 38(ar) 8.180	Serious Crime Act 2015 . . . . 12.249
Sch 18, para 38(as) 11.42	Pt 5 . . . . 8.42, 8.55, 8.69
Sch 18, para 38(at) 11.50	s 68(3)(a) 8.42, 8.55, 8.69
Sch 18, para 38(au) 11.58	s 69 . . . . 16.75
Sch 18, para 38(av) 6.55	Sex Offenders Act 1997
Sch 18, para 38(aw). 6.63	Pt 1 . . . . 14.01
Sch 18, para 38(ax) 10.28	s 5A. 16.01
Sch 18, para 38(ay) 10.39	s 7 . . . . .17.01–17.02
Sch 18, para 38(az) 5.83	Sch 3 . . . . 14.01
Sch 18, para 38(b). 3.46	Sexual Offences Act 1956 (SOA 1956) 1.35,
Sch 18, para 38(ba) 10.56	1.37–1.38, 1.61, 3.02, 3.10, 3.25, 3.28,
Sch 18, para 38(c) .3.54	4.88, 4.118, 7.03, 8.01, 8.81, 8.146,
Sch 18, para 38(d). 3.65	11.02–11.03, 12.43, 12.45, 12.126
Sch 18, para 38(e) .4.97	c 69 . . . . 1.27, 12.49
Sch 18, para 38(f) 4.106, 4.128	s 1 . . . . 2.01, 2.05, 2.14, 2.38, 11.29, 12.220,
Sch 18, para 38(h). 4.48	12.221, 14.29, 16.71, App A p 513
Sch 18, para 38(i) 4.117	s 1(1). 1.36, 2.15–2.16, 2.19,
Sch 18, para 38(j) .4.35	2.22, 2.30, 2.32, 2.34
Sch 18, para 38(k). 4.201	s 1(2). 2.15–2.16
Sch 18, para 38(l) 4.212	ss 1–7 . . . . 12.166
Sch 18, para 38(m) 4.35,	s 2 . . . . 2.20, 2.31, 8.147, 11.18,
4.117, 4.201, 4.212	12.221, 15.04, App A p 513
Sch 18, para 38(n). 4.223	s 2(1). 11.03, 11.07
Sch 18, para 38(o) 4.235	s 3 . . . . 2.20, 2.31, 8.147, 11.18,
Sch 18, para 38(p) 4.244	12.221, 15.04, App A p 513
Sch 18, para 38(q) 4.163	s 3(1). 11.10–11.14
Sch 18, para 38(r) 4.172	s 3(4). 5.106
Sch 18, para 38(s) 4.181	s 4 . . . . .2.20, 2.31, 5.72, 11.26, 12.221,
Sch 18, para 38(t) 4.190	15.04, App A p 513
Sch 18, para 38(u). 6.73	s 4(1). 11.18–11.22
Sch 18, para 38(v) .6.81	s 5 . . . . 1.42, 2.21, 4.56, 4.66–4.71, 12.220,
Sch 18, para 38(w) 7.30	14.29, 15.04, 16.71, App A p 513
Sch 18, para 38(x) .7.38	s 6 . . . . .2.21, 4.66, 4.76, 4.81, 4.87,
Sch 18, para 38(y) .7.46	6.27, 12.221, 12.223, 12.248,
Sch 18, para 38(z) .7.54	14.29, 15.04, 16.71, App A p 513
Sch 18, para 39 . . . . 8.189	s 6(1). 4.78
Sch 19. . . . . .12.16, 12.57, 12.59,	s 6(2). 4.80
12.64–12.65, 12.68–12.69, 12.119	s 6(3). 4.80
Sch 19, para 20(a) .2.55	s 7 . . . . 2.21, 7.10, 7.11, 7.13, 7.
Sch 19, para 20(b) .3.46	14, 7.22, 12.221, 15.04, App A p 513
Sch 19, para 20(c) .3.65	s 7(2). 7.13
Sch 19, para 20(d) .4.97	s 8 . . . . 2.21, 7.61, 7.62, 7.64, 7.68
Sch 19, para 20(e) 4.106	s 8(1)(2) 7.63
Sch 19, para 20(f) .4.48	s 9 . . . . .7.113, 12.221, 15.04, App A p 513
Sch 19, para 20(g) .7.30	s 9(1). 7.121, 7.117
Sch 19, para 20(h) .7.38	s 9(2). 7.115
Sch 19, para 20(i) 7.129	ss 9–11 . . . . 12.166
Sch 19, para 20(j) 7.137	s 10 . . . . .2.21, 6.14, 6.22, 6.31, 12.221,
Sch 19, para 20(k). 8.36	14.29, 15.04, 16.71, App A p 513

s 10(1)............................6.02, 6.26	s 28(3).................................8.15
s 10(2)............................6.24, 6.25	s 28(5).................................8.15
s 11 ....6.22, 6.31, 6.39, 12.221,	s 29 ....7.162, 7.163, 7.167, 7.176,
15.04, App A p 513	8.78, 12.221, App A p 514
s 11(1)............................6.02, 6.35	s 29(2)................................7.165
s 11(2)............................6.33, 6.34	s 30 ....8.13, 8.140, 8.147, 12.221
s 12 ....1.42, 5.01, 5.04, 5.48, 5.72,	s 30(1).............................8.95, 8.99
5.73–5.74, 5.78, 12.221,	s 30(2)................................8.126
14.29, 15.04, 16.71	s 31 ....8.13, 8.103–8.107, 8.147, 12.221
s 12(1)............................5.57, 5.64	s 32 ....8.03, 8.116–8.120,
s 12(1A) 5.62	12.166, App A p 514
s 12(1C) 5.62	s 33 ....8.94, 8.133, App A p 514
s 13 ....1.39, 5.01, 5.101, 5.105, 5.107,	ss 33–36 ....8.13, 8.94
5.113, 12.221, 14.29, 16.71	s 33A............8.94, 8.130, 12.166, 12.241
s 14 ....1.42, 2.20, 2.31, 3.11, 3.16, 3.17,	s 33A(1) 8.134
3.19, 3.34, 4.12, 4.83, 12.221, 12.248,	s 33A(2) 8.133
14.29, 15.04, 16.71, App A p 513	s 37 ....2.18, 2.20, 2.23, 2.31, 3.15, 3.21,
s 14(1)..................................1.37	3.31, 4.59, 4.72, 4.73, 4.80, 4.83, 5.46,
s 14(2).................................3.18	5.98, 7.13, 7.16, 7.63, 7.66, 7.115,
s 14(3).................................3.18	7.119, 7.166, 7.168, 7.172
s 14(4).................................3.18	s 37(2)................6.25, 6.34, 8.81, 8.84
ss14–17 ....12.166	s 37(3)...............3.31, 4.73, 4.84, 6.28,
s 15 ....1.42, 3.24, 3.34, 5.45, 12.221,	6.37, 8.101, 8.115, 8.122
12.248, 14.29, 15.04, 16.71, App A p 513	s 37(5)................................6.27
s 15(1)......................3.29, 5.92, 5.96	s 44 ....4.69, 4.79, 6.24, 7.12, 7.70, 7.115
s 15(2).................................3.28	s 45 ....7.20, 7.115
s 15(3)............................3.28, 7.01	s 45(1)................................7.62
s 15(4).................................3.28	s 46 ....3.10, 3.25, 4.68, 4.78,
s 16 ....3.33, 5.86, 11.03, 12.221,	8.97, 8.105, 8.107, 8.112
14.29, 15.04, 16.71, App A p 513	s 47 ....7.13, 7.63, 7.115, 7.171
s 16(1)....................5.31, 5.83, 5.87	s 47(2)................................7.70
s 17 ....12.221, 15.04, App A p 513	s 51 ....5.48
s 19 ....12.221, App A p 513	Sch 1 ....2.14
ss 19–29 ....12.166	Sch 2 ....2.20, 6.27, 6.34
s 20 ....12.221, App A p 513	Sch 2(1) 7.13
s 21 ....12.221	Sch 2(1)(a)............................2.23
s 22 ....8.13, 8.147, 11.02,	Sch 2(1)(a)(ix).........................3.15
12.221, App A p 513	Sch 2(1)(b)............................2.23
s 22(1)...........................8.78–8.82	Sch 2(2) 7.13
s 22(1)(a) 8.80	Sch 2(2)(a)......................3.15, 4.73
s 23 ....8.13, 8.20, 8.28, 11.02,	Sch 2(2)(b)............................4.73
12.221, App A p 514	Sch 2(8) 11.09
s 23(1)................................8.24	Sch 2(9) 11.24
s 24 ....8.13, 8.109–8.113, 8.147,	Sch 2(10)(a)..............4.59, 4.80, 4.84
12.221, App A p 514	Sch 2(10)(b)..............4.59, 4.80, 4.84
s 24(1)...............................8.113	Sch 2(11)(a)...........................7.13
s 24(3)...............................8.112	Sch 2(11)(b)...........................7.16
s 25 ....12.221, App A p 514	Sch 2(12) 7.63
s 26 ....12.221, App A p 514	Sch 2(12)(a)...........................7.66
s 27 ....7.163, 7.169, 7.173, 7.176,	Sch 2(12)(b)...........................7.66
12.221, App A p 514	Sch 2(13) 7.116
s 27(2)................................7.171	Sch 3(13)(a)..........................7.119
s 28 ....8.13, 8.28, 8.147, 12.221,	Sch 3(13)(b)..........................7.119
14.29, 16.71, App A p 514	Sch 2(14) 7.13
s 28(1)....................8.13, 8.16, 8.17	Sch 2(14)(a)...........................6.28

Sch 2(14)(b)	6.28
Sch 2(15)(a)	6.37
Sch 2(15)(b)	6.37
Sch 2(17)	3.21, 4.83
Sch 2(18)	3.31
Sch 2(18)(i)	5.98
Sch 2(19)(i)	5.98
Sch 2(23)	8.81, 8.84
Sch 2(25)	8.115
Sch 2(27)	7.172, 7.174
Sch 2(30)(i)	8.101
Sch 2(30)(ii)	8.101
Sch 2(32)(i)	8.122
Sch 2(32)(ii)	8.122
Sch 2(39)	7.166
Sch 4	5.48
Sch 37	4.72
Sch 214(a)	6.25
Sch 214(b)	6.25
Sch, para 29	7.168

Sexual Offences Act 1967
(SOA 1967) 1.45, 5.02, 5.13, 5.43

s 1	5.04, 5.43, 5.126
s 1(1)	5.13
s 1(2)	5.13
s 1(4)	7.70
s 2	5.13
s 3	5.08
s 3(1)(a)	5.55
s 3(2)	5.108
s 3(4)(b)	5.21
s 3A	5.13
s 4	1.27, 1.61, 5.113, 11.02, 12.49, 12.166, 12.221, App A p 514
s 4(1)	5.123, 5.126, 5.128
s 4(3)	5.43
s 5	1.27, 1.61, 8.03, 8.123, 8.127, 12.49, 12.166, 12.221, App A p 514
s 5(1)(a)	8.129
s 5(1)(b)	8.129
s 7	5.04, 5.08, 5.43
s 8	5.04, 5.43
s 10	5.08, 5.13
s 10(1)	7.70
s 11(3)	3.10, 3.25
s 13	5.04

Sexual Offences Act 1985 (SOA 1985)

s 1	8.95
s 2	8.95
s 3	2.31
s 3(2)	2.09, 2.11, 2.23
s 3(3)	3.14, 3.21, 4.72, 4.83

Sexual Offences Act 1993 (SOA 1993)

s 1	2.36, 4.61, 4.70, 4.262, 5.05, 6.25
s 2	5.05
s 2(2)	2.36, 6.25
s 3	6.25

Sexual Offences Act 1994
s 1	5.08

Sexual Offences Act 2000
(SOA 2000) 5.01, 5.70
s 1(1)	5.70
s 3(2)(a)	4.147

Sexual Offences Act 2003 (SOA 2003) 1.27, 1.29, 1.35–1.38, 1.44, 1.45, 1.47, 1.53–1.54, 1.61, 2.01, 2.46–2.51, 3.02, 3.15, 3.24, 3.28, 3.34–3.35, 3.55, 3.66, 4.32, 4.44, 4.92, 4.136, 4.226, 4.260, 5.01, 5.05–5.06, 5.71, 5.91, 5.127, 6.03, 6.40, 6.50, 7.01–7.02, 8.03, 8.28, 8.148, 9.01–9.02, 9.21, 9.27, 10.01, 10.05, 10.12, 10.14, 10.18, 10.21, 10.37, 11.02, 11.17, 12.14, 12.43–12.48, 12.50, 12.116–12.117, 12.139, 12.147, 12.182, 12.190, 12.224, 12.237, 12.248, 14.19–14.20, 15.05, 16.01, 16.03, 16.21, 16.25, 16.40, 16.49, 16.90, 17.09, 17.16

Pt 1	8.183, 13.27
Pt 2	16.97
s 1	2.48–2.50, 4.26, 5.73, 12.220, 12.221, 14.29, 16.73, App A p 514
s 1(1)	1.36, 2.51
s 1(4)	2.52
ss 1–19	12.166
ss 1–71	4.247
ss 1–4	3.40, 4.26, 4.40, 4.100, 4.110, 4.122, 4.132, 4.195, 4.206, 4.227, 17.09, 17.16
ss 1–56	11.44, 11.52
ss 1–79	4.226, 8.151
s 2	3.37–3.41, 12.220, 12.221, 14.29, 16.73, App A p 514
s 2(1)	3.42
s 2(2)	4.206
s 2(3)	9.06
s 3	2.52, 3.35, 3.46–3.50, 4.260, 12.221, 12.248, 14.29, 16.73, App A p 514
s 3(1)	3.50
s 4	2.53, 3.55–3.59, 5.113, 12.221, 12.248, 14.29, 16.73, 16.78, App A p 514
s 4(1)	3.60, 3.61
s 4(1A)	12.221
s 4(2)	3.59
s 4(3)	3.59
s 4(4)	3.61
s 5	1.41, 4.76, 4.88–4.92, 5.73, 8.33, 12.105–12.106, 12.220, 12.223, 14.29, 16.73, App A p 514
s 5(1)	4.93
s 5(2)	4.95
s 5(2)(b)	7.182

TABLE OF STATUTES AND STATUTORY INSTRUMENTS

ss 5–8	4.03, 4.214
ss 5–15	3.40, 4.26, 4.40, 4.100, 4.110, 4.122, 4.132, 4.195, 4.206, 4.227, 17.09
s 6	1.41, 4.76, 4.88, 4.97–4.100, 8.33, 12.105–12.106, 12.220, 12.223, 14.29, 16.73, App A p 514
s 6(1)	4.101
s 6(2)	4.104
s 7	4.119–4.122, 4.256, 8.33, 12.220, 12.223, 12.248, 14.29, 16.73, App A p 514
s 7(1)	4.123
s 7(2)	4.126
s 8	1.48, 4.35–4.41, 5.113, 12.220, 12.223, 12.248, 14.29, 16.73, App A p 515
s 8(1)	1.51, 4.41–4.42
s 8(2)	4.42, 4.46
s 8(3)	3.63, 4.46
s 9	1.37–1.38, 3.66, 4.218, 4.257, 8.33, 12.221, 12.248, 14.29, 16.73, App A p 515
s 9(1)	4.106–4.112, 4.129–4.134
s 9(2)	4.87, 4.106–4.112, 4.115, 4.137
s 9(3)	4.137, 4.138
s 9(3)(b)	4.137
ss 9–12	4.153, 4.218, 4.256, 12.215
ss 9–13	4.03
s 10	4.20–4.26, 4.218, 4.257, 5.113, 12.221, 12.248, 14.29, 16.73, App A p 515
s 10(1)	1.51, 4.27–4.30
s 10(2)	4.28, 4.30
s 11	4.192–4.195, 4.218, 4.257, 12.221, 12.248, 14.29, 16.73, App A p 515
s 11(1)	4.196–4.197
s 11(2)	4.199
s 12	4.201–4.206, 4.218, 4.257, 10.31, 12.221, 12.248, 14.29, 16.73, App A p 515
s 12(1)	4.207, 4.208
s 12(a)	4.210
s 12(b)	4.210
s 13	1.54, 4.23, 4.112, 4.197, 4.203, 4.208, 4.218, 4.256, 4.257, 4.259–4.260, 12.215, 14.28, 14.29, 16.73, App A p 515
s 13(1)	4.29–4.30
s 13(2)	4.115, 4.138
s 13(a)	4.210
s 13(b)	4.210
s 14	4.202, 4.212–4.217, 12.182, 12.221, 12.241, 12.248, 14.29, 16.73, App A p 515
s 14(1)	4.218
s 14(4)(a)	4.221
s 14(4)(b)	4.221
s 15	4.224–4.227, 12.221, 12.248, 14.29, 16.73, App A p 515
s 15A	4.191, 4.236–4.239, 12.166, 12.175–12.179, 14.29, 16.73
s 15A(1)	4.240
s 15(1)	4.226, 4.228–4.230
s 15(1)(a)	4.226
s 15(1)(i)	4.226
s 15(1)(ii)	4.226
s 15(1)(iii)	4.226
s 15(1)(b)	4.226
s 15(1)(c)	4.226
s 15(1)(d)	4.226
s 15(2)(b)	4.226
s 15(4)	4.227, 4.233
s 15A	4.05, 4.191
s 15A(3)	4.239, 4.242
s 16	3.66, 4.152, 4.154–4.157, 12.221, 12.248, 14.29, 16.73, 16.78, App A p 515
s 16(1)	4.158
s 16(3)	4.157
s 16(4)	4.157
s 16(5)(a)	4.161
s 16(5)(b)	4.161
ss 16–19	16.33
ss 16–41	17.09
s 17	4.163–4.171, 12.221, 12.248, 14.29, 16.73, App A p 515
s 17(1)	4.167
s 17(3)	4.166
s 17(4)	4.166
s 17(5)(a)	4.170
s 17(5)(b)	4.170
s 18	4.172–4.175, 12.221, 12.248, 14.29, 16.73, 16.78, App A p 515
s 18(1)	4.176
s 18(3)	4.175
s 18(4)	4.175
s 18(5)(a)	4.179
s 18(5)(b)	4.179
s 19	4.181–4.185, 12.221, 12.248, 14.29, 16.73, App A p 515
s 19(1)	4.185
s 19(3)	4.184
s 19(4)	4.184
s 19(5)(a)	4.188
s 19(5)(b)	4.188
s 20	4.143, 16.78
s 21	4.142, 4.154, 16.33, 16.78
s 21(4)(a)	4.167
s 21(4)(d)	4.176
s 21(5)	4.158–4.159, 4.185
s 22	4.154, 16.78
s 22A	4.144

s 23	4.144, 4.154, 16.78
s 24	4.144, 4.154
s 25	3.66, 4.260, 6.03, 6.05, 6.31, 6.63–6.67, 12.166, 12.221, 12.248, 16.33, 14.29, 16.73, App A p 515
s 25(1)	6.68–6.69
s 25(2)(a)	6.65
s 25(3)	6.65
s 25(4)(a)	6.71
s 25(4)(b)(i)	6.71
s 25(4)(b)(ii)	6.71
s 25(5)(a)	6.71
s 25(5)(b)	6.71
s 25(6)	6.65, 6.68
s 26	4.260, 6.03, 6.05, 6.47, 6.73–6.76, 12.166, 12.221, 12.248, 14.29, 16.33, 16.73, App A p 515
s 26(1)	6.77–6.78
s 26(2)	6.75
s 26(3)	6.75
s 26(4)(a)	6.80
s 26(4)(b)(ii)	6.80
s 26(5)	6.80
s 26(6)	6.77
s 27	6.03, 6.65, 16.78
s 27(1)(b)	6.67, 6.76
s 27(2)	6.03
s 27(2)(a)	6.66
s 27(2)(b)	6.66
s 27(3)(a)–(d)	6.66
s 27(4)	6.67
s 27(4)(a)	6.66
s 27(4)(b)	6.66
s 27(4)	6.03
s 27(5)	6.67
s 27(6)	6.67
s 28	16.78
s 28(1)(a)	6.67, 6.76
s 28(1)(b)	6.67, 6.76
s 29	6.67, 16.78
s 30	7.22–7.25, 12.220, 12.221, 12.222, 12.223, 12.248, 14.29, 16.73, 16.78, App A p 515
ss 30–41	12.166, 17.16
s 30(1)	7.26
s 30(2)	7.24
s 30(3)	7.28
s 30(3)(c)	7.25
s 30(4)	7.25
s 30(4)(a)	7.28
s 30(4)(b)	7.28
s 31	7.22, 7.30–7.33, 12.220, 12.221, 12.222, 12.223, 12.248, 14.29, 16.73, 16.78, App A p 515
s 31(1)	7.34
s 31(2)	7.24
s 31(3)	7.33, 7.36
s 31(4)	7.33, 7.36
s 32	7.22, 7.38–7.46, 12.220, 12.221, 12.222, 12.223, 12.248, 14.29, 16.73, 16.78, App A p 515
s 32(2)	7.24
s 32(3)	7.41
s 32(3)(a)	7.44
s 32(3)(b)	7.44
s 33	7.22, 7.46–7.50, 12.220, 12.221, 12.222, 12.223, 12.248, 14.29, 16.73, App A p 515
s 33(2)	7.24
s 33(3)	7.49
s 33(3)(a)	7.52
s 33(3)(b)	7.52
s 34	7.121–7.124, 12.220, 12.221, 12.222, 12.223, 14.29, 16.73, App A p 515
s 34(1)	7.125
s 34(2)	7.124–7.125, 7.127
s 34(2)(c)	7.124
s 34(3)	7.124
s 34(3)(a)	7.127
s 34(3)(b)	7.127
s 35	7.121, 7.129–7.132, 12.220, 12.221, 12.222, 12.223, 14.29, 16.73, 16.78, App A p 515
s 35(1)	7.133
s 35(2)	7.132–7.133, 7.135
s 35(3)	7.132
s 35(3)(a)	7.135
s 35(3)(b)	7.135
s 36	7.121, 7.137–7.140, 12.220, 12.221, 12.222, 12.223, 14.29, 16.73, App A p 515
s 36(1)	7.141
s 36(2)	7.140
s 36(2)(a)	7.143
s 36(2)(b)	7.143
s 37	7.121, 7.144–7.147, 12.220, 12.221, 12.222, 12.223, 14.29, 16.73, 16.78, App A p 515
s 37(1)	7.148
s 37(2)	7.147
s 37(2)(a)	7.150
s 37(2)(b)	7.150
s 37(3)	8.108
s 38	7.76–7.79, 12.216, 12.220, 12.221, 12.222, 12.223, 14.29, 16.73, 16.78, App A p 515
s 38(1)	7.80
s 38(3)	7.79–7.80, 7.82

s 38(3)(c)	7.79
s 38(4)(a)	7.82
s 38(4)(b)	7.82
ss 38–41	7.78
s 39	7.76, 7.85–7.87, 12.220, 12.221, 12.222, 12.223, 14.29, 16.73, App A p 515
s 39(1)	7.88
s 39(3)	7.87–7.88, 7.90
s 39(4)	7.87
s 39(4)(a)	7.90
s 39(4)(b)	7.90
s 40	7.76, 7.92–7.96, 12.220, 12.221, 12.222, 12.223, 14.29, 16.73, App A p 515
s 40(3)	7.95
s 40(3)(a)	7.98
s 40(3)(b)	7.98
s 41	7.76, 7.100–7.103, 12.220, 12.221, 12.222, 12.223, 14.29, 16.73, App A p 515
s 41(1)	7.104
s 41(3)	7.103
s 41(3)(a)	7.106
s 41(3)(b)	7.106
s 42	7.78, 7.80, 7.88, 7.96, 7.104
s 43	7.79, 7.87, 7.95, 7.103, 8.31
s 44	7.79, 7.87, 7.95, 7.103
s 45(1)(3)	9.06
s 45(2)	9.06, 9.25
s 46(1)	9.06
s 47	8.28, 12.221, 14.29, 16.74, 16.73, 16.78, 16.90, App A p 515
s 47(1)	1.51, 8.28–8.32
s 47(2)	8.31
s 47(3)	8.31, 8.34
s 47(4)	8.31
s 47(4)(a)	8.34
s 47(4)(b)	8.34
s 47(5)	8.31
s 47(5)(b)	8.34
s 47(6)	8.31
ss 47–50	12.166, 12.248, 17.09
s 48	8.28, 9.02, 12.221, 12.241, 14.29, 16.73, App A p 515
s 48(1)	8.36–8.40, 8.46
s 48(2)(a)	8.48, 8.61
s 48(2)(b)	8.48
s 49	8.28, 9.02, 12.221, 12.241, 14.29, 16.73, App A p 515
s 49(1)	8.50–8.54, 8.59
s 49(2)	8.39, 8.45
s 49(2)(b)	8.61
s 50	8.152, 9.02, 12.221, 12.241, 14.29, 16.73, App A p 516
s 50(1)	8.63–8.67, 8.73
s 50(2)(a)	8.75
s 50(2)(b)	8.75
s 51(1)	8.38, 8.44, 8.57, 8.71
s 51(2)	7.178, 7.186, 8.38, 8.44, 8.133
s 51(3)	8.38, 8.44, 8.57, 8.71
ss 51–53	16.74
s 52	7.176–7.184, 8.04, 8.86, 12.166, 12.221, 12.241, 12.248, 16.90, App A p 516
s 52(1)	7.180, 8.86–8.90
s 52(2)	7.179, 8.89
s 52(2)(a)	7.182, 8.92
s 52(2)(b)	8.92
s 53	8.04, 12.166, 12.221, 12.241, 16.90, App A p 516
s 53A	8.190, 8.194
s 53A(1)	8.190
s 53A(2)(a)	8.193
s 53A(2)(b)	8.193
s 53A(3)	8.193
s 53A(3)(a)	8.193
s 53A(3)(b)	8.193
s 53A(4)	8.195
s 53(1)	7.184–7.188, 8.137–8.141
s 53(2)(a)	7.190, 8.143
s 53(2)(b)	7.190, 8.143
s 54(1)	7.178, 7.186, 8.88, 8.139
s 54(1)(a)	8.193
s 54(1)(b)	8.193
s 54(2)	7.178, 7.186, 8.193
s 55	8.94, 8.133
s 56	8.04
s 57	8.149–8.152, 12.166, 12.221, 16.90, App A p 516
s 57(1)(a)	8.153
ss 57–59	8.171
ss 57–59A	12.241, 12.248, 16.74
s 57(2)(b)	8.155
s 58	8.149, 8.156–8.159, 12.166, 12.221, 16.90, App A p 516
s 58(1)(a)	8.160
s 58(2)(b)	8.162
s 59	8.149, 12.221, 16.90, App A p 516
s 59(1)	8.164–8.167
s 59(1)(a)	8.167
s 59(2)(b)	8.169
s 59A	8.171–8.176, 12.166, 12.221, 16.90, App A p 516
s 59A(1)(a)	8.177
s 60A	8.156, 8.163, 8.170, 8.180, 12.235
s 61	11.26, 12.221, 12.248, 14.29, 16.73, 17.09, 17.16, App A p 516
s 61(1)	11.35–11.38
s 61(2)	11.37
s 61(2)(b)	11.40

ss 61–70	12.166
ss 61–71	11.44, 11.52
s 62	11.34, 12.221, 14.29, 16.73, 17.09, 17.16, App A p 516
s 62(1)	11.43–11.46
s 62(3)	11.45, 11.48
s 62(4)	11.45
s 62(4)(b)	11.48
s 63	11.34, 12.221, 14.29, 16.73, 17.09, 17.16, App A p 516
s 63(1)	11.50–11.54
s 63(3)	11.53
s 63(3)(a)	11.56
s 63(3)(b)	11.56
s 64	6.04, 6.31, 6.48–6.50, 15.06, 14.29, 16.73, App A p 516
s 64(1)	6.51
s 64(1)(e)	6.49, 6.57
s 64(3)	6.49
s 64(3A)	6.49
s 64(4)	6.49
s 64(5)(a)	6.53
s 64(5)(b)	6.53
s 65	6.04, 6.39, 6.55–6.58, 14.29, 16.73, App A p 516
s 65(1)	6.59
s 65(3)	6.57
s 65(3A)	6.57
s 65(4)	6.57
s 65(5)	6.61
s 66	10.05, 10.12, 10.14, 10.15, 12.221, 14.29, 16.73, App A p 516
s 66(1)	10.21–10.25
s 66(2)	10.24, 10.26
s 67	10.05, 10.14, 10.29–10.35, 12.221, 14.29, 16.73, App A p 516
s 67(1)	10.29, 10.36
s 67(1)(a)	10.31, 10.36
s 67(1)(b)	10.31, 10.36
s 67(1)(c)	10.36
s 67(1)(d)	10.36
s 67(2)	10.29
s 67(2)(a)	10.32–10.33
s 67(2)(b)	10.32
s 67(3)	10.29
s 67(4)	10.29
s 67A	10.05, 10.40–10.43, 14.29, 16.73
s 67A(1)	10.44
s 67A(2)	10.44
s 67A(4)	10.43
s 67A(4)(b)	10.45
s 67(3)(b)	10.33
s 67(3)(c)	10.33
s 67(4)	10.34
s 67(4)(a)	10.45
s 67(5)	10.35
s 68(1)	10.31, 10.32–10.33
s 68(1A)	10.32, 10.42
s 68(2)	10.34
s 69	4.191, 5.74–5.78, 10.02, 14.29, 15.06, 16.73, App A p 516
s 69(1)	5.79
s 69(3)	5.78, 5.81
s 70	10.02, 10.48–10.51, 14.29, 16.73, App A p 516
s 70(1)	10.52
s 70(2)	10.54
s 71	5.114–5.123, 10.02, 15.06
s 71(3)	5.121
s 71A	5.01
s 72	2.50, 3.39, 3.49, 3.59, 4.26, 4.40, 4.92, 4.100, 4.110, 4.122, 4.132, 4.157, 4.166, 4.175, 4.184, 4.195, 4.206, 4.217, 4.227, 4.258, 6.67, 6.76, 7.25, 7.33, 7.41, 7.49, 7.79, 7.87, 7.95, 7.103, 7.124, 7.132, 7.140, 7.147, 8.39, 8.45, 8.53, 8.58, 8.66, 8.72, 11.37, 11.44, 11.53, 12.221, 17.01–17.02, 17.08, 17.11
s 72(1)	17.11
s 72(1)(a)	17.03
s 72(1)(b)	17.03
s 72(1)(b)	17.04
s 72(1)(d)(i)	9.07
s 72(1)(d)(ii)	9.28
s 72(2)	17.03, 17.11
s 72(3)	17.11
s 72(4)	17.05
s 72(4)(a)	17.06
s 72(4)(b)	17.06
s 72(4)(c)	17.06
s 72(5)	17.06, 17.14
s 72(3)	17.07
s 72(6)	17.07, 17.12
s 72(6)(a)	17.13
s 72(6)(b)	17.13
s 72(6)(c)	17.13
s 72(7)	17.08, 17.13
s 72(8)	17.14
s 72(9)	17.11
s 73	4.257
s 73(1)	6.67
s 73(2)(d)	6.67
s 74	2.47, 3.39, 10.42, 11.37
s 75	2.47, 3.59
s 76	2.47, 3.59
s 78	3.39, 3.49, 4.26, 6.49, 6.57, 7.24, 7.25, 8.31
s 78(b)	3.39
s 79	6.49, 6.57, 6.75
s 79(1)	7.25

s 79(2)	2.49, 5.78, 6.50, 6.58, 6.65, 6.75, 7.25, 10.51
s 79(3)	2.49, 3.39, 3.59, 5.78, 6.50, 6.58, 6.65, 6.75
s 79(4)	4.206, 7.49, 7.103, 7.147, 10.42
s 79(5)	4.195, 7.49, 7.103, 7.147
s 79(6)	7.24
s 79(7)	7.41, 7.95, 7.140
s 79(8)	3.35, 3.49, 6.65, 6.75, 7.24
s 79(9)	2.49, 3.39, 3.59, 5.78, 6.50, 6.58, 6.65, 6.75, 7.25
s 79(10)	5.78
s 79A	10.03
s 80	10.13
s 80(1)	2.13, 2.25, 2.55, 3.09, 3.23, 3.32, 3.46, 3.54, 3.65, 4.19, 4.35, 4.48, 4.55, 4.65, 4.75, 4.86, 4.97, 4.106, 4.117, 4.128, 4.151, 4.163, 4.172, 4.181, 4.190, 4.212, 4.254, 5.24, 5.30, 5.40, 5.54, 5.59, 5.67, 5.83, 5.89, 5.99, 5.111, 5.130, 6.13, 6.21, 6.30, 6.38, 6.46, 6.55, 6.63, 6.73, 6.81, 7.16, 7.30, 7.38, 7.46, 7.54, 7.67, 7.75, 7.120, 7.129, 7.137, 7.144, 7.151, 7.169, 7.184, 7.192, 8.27, 8.36, 8.50, 8.63, 8.77, 8.85, 8.93, 8.103, 8.109, 8.116, 8.123, 8.130, 8.137, 8.145, 8.156, 8.163, 8.170, 8.180, 8.197, 9.24, 9.37, 9.45, 9.54, 9.66, 9.75, 10.20, 10.39, 10.47, 11.10, 11.17, 11.25, 11.33, 11.42, 11.50, 11.58
s 80(1)(a)	14.02
s 80(1)(b)	14.02
s 80(1)(c)	14.02
s 80(1)(d)	14.02
s 81	14.01
s 82	14.29
s 82(1)	14.09
s 82(2)	14.09
s 82(3)	14.14, 14.29
s 82(4)	14.29
s 83(2)	14.10
s 83(5)	14.10
s 83(5A)	14.11
s 83(5)(h)	14.10–14.11
s 84	14.12
s 85(5)(a)	14.13
s 85(5)(b)	14.13
s 86(2)(a)	14.14
s 86(2)(b)	14.14
s 87(1)	14.16
s 87(2)	14.16
s 89	14.07
s 91	14.17
s 91A	14.05, 14.23
s 91A(2b)	14.23
s 91B(2)	14.24
s 91B(3)	14.26
s 91B(4)	14.26
s 91B(5)	14.26
s 91C(1)	14.25
s 91D	14.25
s 91E(2)	14.25
s 92(2)(a)	14.04
s 92(2)(b)	14.04
s 97	14.03
s 103A	16.18
s 103A(2)	16.02
s 103A(2)(a)	16.12
s 103A(2)(b)	16.12
s 103A(3)(b)	16.17
s 103A(4)	16.13, 16.16
s 103A(4)(a)	16.14
s 103A(5)	16.16
s 103A(7)	16.16
s 103B(1)	16.17, 16.33
s 103B(2)(a)	16.15
s 103B(2)(b)	16.15
s 103B(2)(c)	16.15
s 103B(2)(d)	16.15
s 103B(3)(a)	16.15
s 103B(3)(b)	16.15
s 103B(3)(c)	16.15
s 103B(3)(d)	16.15
s 103B(9)	16.02
s 103C(1)	16.24
s 103C(2)(a)	16.21
s 103C(2)(b)	16.21
s 103C(3)(a)	16.21
s 103C(3)(b)	16.21
s 103C(4)	16.24
s 103C(6)	16.13
s 103C(6)(6)	16.39
s 103D(1)	16.22
s 103D(2)	16.22
s 103D(3)	16.22
s 103D(4)	16.22
s 103E(1)	16.37
s 103E(2)(a)	16.37
s 103E(2)(b)	16.37
s 103E(2)(d)	16.37
s 103E(4)	16.38
s 103E(7)	16.41
s 103E(8)	16.41
s 103E(9)(a)	16.40
s 103E(9)(b)	16.40
s 103E(9)(c)	16.40
s 103E(9)(d)	16.40
s 103F(1)	16.19
s 103F(3)	16.19
s 103F(4)(a)	16.19
s 103F(4)(b)	16.19
s 103G(1)	16.48
s 103G(2)	16.49

s 103G(4)	16.48
s 103G(7)	16.20
s 103H(1)	16.45
s 103H(1)(b)	16.45
s 103H(1)(c)	16.46
s 103H(2)	16.47
s 103H(3)(a)	16.45
s 103H(3)(b)	16.45
s 103I(1)(a)	16.65
s 103I(1)(b)	16.65
s 103I(1)(c)	16.65
s 103I(1)(d)	16.65
s 103I(1)(e)	16.65
s 103I(3)(a)	16.66
s 103I(3)(b)	16.66
s 103I(4)	16.66
s 114	16.01
s 131(1)(a)	14.08
s 134(1)(a)	14.21
s 141	1.27, 12.45
s 224A	12.119
s 225(1)	12.119
s 225(2)	12.119
s 225(3)	12.119
s 244(3)	12.165
s 256B	12.163
s 348(4)	16.22
s 348(7)	16.22
Sch 1	8.04
Sch 2	17.11, 17.15
Sch 2, para 1	17.08
Sch 2, para 1(d)(i)	17.10, 17.17
Sch 2, para 1(d)(ii)	17.10, 17.17
Sch 2, para 3	17.10, 17.17
Sch 2, para 8	11.16
Sch 2, para 31(i)	8.108
Sch 2, para 31(ii)	8.108
Sch 3	2.13, 3.09, 4.55, 4.65, 5.24, 5.30, 5.40, 5.123, 5.130, 6.13, 6.21, 6.38, 7.17, 7.67, 7.75, 7.120, 7.169, 7.175, 7.184, 7.192, 8.27, 8.85, 8.93, 8.103, 8.109, 8.116, 8.123, 8.130, 8.137, 8.145, 8.156, 8.163, 8.170, 8.180, 8.197, 9.66, 9.75, 10.20, 11.10, 11.17, 11.25, 11.33, 11.42, 12.225, 14.02, 14.28–14.29, 16.02, 16.07, 16.09, 16.15, 16.70–16.75
Sch 3, para 1	2.25
Sch 3, para 2	4.75, 4.86
Sch 3, para 3	4.86
Sch 3, para 4	6.30
Sch 3, para 5	5.54, 5.59, 5.67, 5.54, 5.59, 5.67
Sch 3, para 6	5.111
Sch 3, para 7	3.23
Sch 3, para 8	3.32, 5.99, 5.47, 5.99
Sch 3, para 9	5.89, 5.89
Sch 3, para 10	8.20
Sch 3, para 11	4.19
Sch 3, para 12	6.46
Sch 3, para 13	9.24
Sch 3, para 15	9.37
Sch 3, para 16	4.151
Sch 3, para 17	2.55, 3.46
Sch 3, para 18	3.54
Sch 3, para 19	3.65, 4.97, 4.106, 4.117
Sch 3, para 20	4.128
Sch 3, para 21	4.35, 4.48, 4.117, 4.201, 4.212
Sch 3, para 22	4.35, 4.117, 4.201, 4.212
Sch 3, para 23	4.223
Sch 3, para 24	4.235
Sch 3, para 24, c 42	9.05
Sch 3, para 24A	4.244
Sch 3, para 25	4.163, 4.172, 4.181, 4.190, 4.181, 4.190
Sch 3, para 26	6.73, 6.81
Sch 3, para 27	7.30, 7.38, 7.46, 7.54, 7.129, 7.137, 7.144, 7.151
Sch 3, para 29B	8.63
Sch 3, para 32	6.55
Sch 3, para 35	5.83
Sch 3, para 29	8.36
Sch 3, para 29A	8.50
Sch 3, para 29B	8.63
Sch 3, para 29C	8.77
Sch 3, para 30	11.42
Sch 3, para 31	11.50, 11.58
Sch 3, para 32	6.55, 6.63
Sch 3, para 33	10.28
Sch 3, para 34	10.39
Sch 3, para 34A	10.47, 10.47
Sch 3, para 35	5.83, 10.56, 10.56
Sch 3, para 35A	9.54
Sch 3, para 35B	9.45
Sch 3, para 35C	4.254
Sch 3, para 94	5.59
Sch 3, para 94A(a)	14.02, 14.29, 16.07, 16.71–16.73, 16.75
Sch 3, para 94A(b)	14.02, 14.29, 16.07, 16.71–16.73, 16.75
Sch 3, para 94AA	14.02, 14.29, 16.07, 16.71–16.73, 16.76
Sch 4	14.22
Sch 5	2.13, 3.09, 4.55, 4.65, 5.24, 5.30, 5.40, 5.123, 5.130, 6.13, 6.21, 6.38, 7.17, 7.169, 7.175, 8.27, 8.85, 8.103, 8.109, 8.116, 8.123, 8.130, 8.137, 8.197, 10.20, 11.10, 11.17, 11.25, 11.33, 12.225, 16.02, 16.07, 16.15, 16.74, 16.76–16.91
Sch 5, para 4A	10.13
Sch 5, para 62	8.36

Sch 5, para 63............7.184, 7.192, 8.95,
          8.145, 8.156, 8.163, 8.170, 8.180
Sch 5, para 172 ....16.78–16.79, 16.90
Sch 5, para 172A..........16.78–16.79, 16.90
Sch 5, para 173A................16.78–16.79
Sch 5, para 173(a).....16.07, 16.76, 16.78–16.91
Sch 5, para 173(b).....16.07, 16.76, 16.78–16.91
Sch 5, para 173A........16.07, 16.78–16.91
Sch 7.........................7.120, 7.121
Sch 7, para 1, c 42 .... 16.01
Sch 15B 12.118
Sch 15, Pt II App A p 513
Sexual Offences (Amendment)Act
    1976 (SO(A)A 1976) 2.26–2.27, 3.25
    s 1(1)..........................2.01, 2.38
    s 1(2)..........................2.27, 2.38
    s 7(2).........................3.10, 3.25
Sexual Offences (Amendment)
    Act 1992 (SO(A)A 1992).......15.01, 15.05
    s 1 ....15.06, 15.23
    s 1(1) 15.01
    s 1(3A) 15.02
    s 2(1)(da) 15.05
    s 3(1)............................. 15.06
    s 3(2)............................. 15.06
    s 3(3)............................. 15.06
    s 3(4)............................. 15.06
    s 4(2)............................. 15.04
    s 4(3)............................. 15.04
    s 4(4)............................. 15.04
    s 4(5)............................. 15.04
    s 4(6)............................. 15.04
    s 4(7)............................. 15.04
    s 5(2)............................. 15.06
    s 5(3)............................. 15.06
Sexual Offences (Amendment)Act
    2000 (SO(A)A 2000) 4.141, 4.147
    s 1 ....5.08, 5.127
    s 1(1).........................5.04, 14.22
    s (1)(a) 5.43
    s 2 .... 5.127
    s 3 .... 1.27, 1.61, 4.144, 4.152,
              12.49, 12.221, 14.29, 16.72
    s 3(1)............................. 4.148
    s 3(2)............................. 4.145
    s 3(2)(b) 4.147
    s 3(2)(c) 4.147
    s 3(3)............................. 4.147
    s 3(4)(b) 4.150
    s 4 ....4.146, 4.152
Street Offences Act 1959 (StOA 1959)
    s 1 ....8.95
    s 4 .... 8.101
Taking of Hostages Act 1982
    s 1 .... 16.82

Theft Act 1968 (TA 1968)............... 16.81
    s 1 .... 16.81
    s 8 .... 16.81
    s 9 ....1.27, 12.49, 12.166, App A p 515
    s 9(1)............................. 11.27
    s 9(1)(a) 1.61, 11.30, 12.221, 16.81
    s 9(2)............................. 11.34
    s 9(3)(a) 11.32
    s 9(3)(b) 11.32
    s 10 .... 16.81
    s 12A............................. 16.81
Town Police Clauses Act 1847
    s 28, c 89......................1.27, 12.49
UK Borders Act 2007 .... 12.246
    ss 23–39 .... 12.242
    s 31(4)............................ 8.152
    s 32 .... 12.242
Vagrancy Act 1824 (VA 1824)........... 10.01
    s 4 ....1.27, 10.15, 10.19, 12.49
    s 5 .... 10.19
Vagrancy Act 1898 (VA 1898)
    s 1 ....8.01, 12.221
Violent Crime Reduction Act 2006
    (VCRA 2006)
    s 55 ....1.27, 12.44, 12.45, 12.48
    s 55(1)........................1.27, 12.46
    s 55(2)........................1.27, 12.49
    s 55(3)............................1.28
    s 55(5)........................1.27, 12.50
Voyeurism (Offences) Act 2019 ....1.61
    c 2 s 1(2)......................... 10.03
    s a 10.40
    s 1A.............................. 10.32
Youth Justice and Criminal Evidence
    Act 1999 (YJCEA 1999)...... 13.01, 13.31,
                                   13.33, 15.07
    s 16 ....13.01, 13.26
    s 16(1)............................ 13.29
    s 16(1)(a) 13.02
    s 16(1)(a)(i) 13.02
    s 16(1)(b).......................... 13.02
    s 16(1)(a))(i) 13.02
    s 16(1)(b).......................... 13.02
    s 16(2)(a))(ii)...................... 13.02
    s 16(3)............................ 13.04
    s 16(5)........................13.03, 13.13
    s 17 .... 13.01
    s 17(1)........................13.14, 13.29
    s 17(2)............................ 13.14
    s 17(3)............................ 13.14
    s 17(4).......................13.42–13.43
    s 19(1)........................13.17, 13.29
    s 19(2)............................ 13.04
    s 21 .... 13.04
    s 21(2)............................ 13.06

s 21(3)	13.05	s 45(5)	15.28
s 21(3)(a)	13.05	s 45(6)	15.27, 15.29
s 21(3)(b)	13.05	s 45(8)	15.27
s 21(4)(a)	13.07	s 45(10)	15.30, 15.36
s 21(4)(b)	13.07	s 45A(11)	15.36
s 21(4)(ba)	13.08	s 45A(12)	15.37
s 21(4)(c)	13.07	s 45A(13)	15.38
s 21(4A)	13.09	s 45A(14)	15.39
s 21(4B)(a)	13.09	s 46	15.08, 15.11
s 21(4B)(b)	13.09	s 46(1)	15.08
s 21(4C)	13.08	s 46(2)	15.09
s 22	13.04	s 46(4)	15.10
s 22(1)(a)	13.02, 13.04	s 46(5)	15.10
s 22A(2)	13.16	s 46(6)	15.15
s 22A(3)	13.16	s 46(7)	15.15
s 22A(4)	13.16	s 46(9)	15.16
s 22A(7)	13.16	s 46(11)	15.18
s 22A(8)	13.16	s 49	15.08, 15.31
s 23	13.09, 13.27	s 49(1)(a)	15.22, 15.24
s 24	13.05, 13.27	s 49(1A)	15.31
s 25	13.27	s 49(5)	15.22, 15.24
s 26	13.27		
s 27	13.05, 13.27		
s 27(2)	13.07, 13.16		

STATUTORY INSTRUMENTS

s 28	13.25–13.27, 13.38–13.74
s 28(4)	13.70
ss 28–30	13.25
s 29	13.27
s 30	13.27
s 33A	13.29
s 33A(4)	13.30
s 33A(5)	13.31
s 33A(5)(a)	13.31
ss 33BA–33BB	13.32
s 33BA(5)	13.32
s 33BA(6)	13.32
s 41	13.61, 13.63
s 44	15.20–15.23
s 44(2)	15.20
s 44(4)	15.20
s 44(6)	15.20
s 44(7)	15.21
s 44(8)	15.21
s 44(10)	15.21
s 44(11)	15.21
s 45	15.19, 15.24–15.30
s 45A	15.31–15.39
s 45A(2)	15.31, 15.35
s 45A(4)	15.35
s 45A(5)	15.32
s 45A(6)	15.33
s 45A(7)	15.33
s 45A(8)	15.33
s 45(3)	15.27
s 45(4)	15.28

Channel Tunnel (Security) Order 1994 (SI 2004/570) 16.89
Crime (Sentences)Act(Commencement No 2 and Transitional Provisions) Order 1997(SI 1997/2200) 4.18
Criminal Justice Act 1988 (Reviews of Sentencing) Order 2019 .... 12.248
Criminal Justice Act 2003 (Commencement No 2 and Saving Provisions) Order 2004/ 81 .... 10.09
Criminal Justice Act 2003 (Commencement No 8 and Transitional and SavingProvisions) Order 2005 (SI 2005/950) 12.44
Criminal Justice (Children) (Northern Ireland) Order 1988 (SI 1988/9)
  Sch 1 .... 8.151
Criminal Justice and Immigration Act 2008 (Commencement No 2 and Transitional and Savings Provisions) Order 2008 (SI 2008/1586) 17.02
Criminal Justice and Public Order Act 1994 (Commencement No 5 and Transitional Provisions) Order 1995 (SI 1995/127) 9.05, 9.25, 11.05, 11.12, 11.20
Criminal Procedure Rules 2005 (SI 2005/384)
  r 14.2(2) 1.12

Criminal Procedure Rules 2015 . . . . .1.01
Criminal Procedure Rules
   (CrimPR) 2020 . . . . 1.01, 13.27
   Pt 10 . . . . 1.13, 1.25
   Pt 18 . . . . 13.17
   Pt 41 . . . . 12.250
   r 3.8(4)(d) .13.61, 13.63
   r 3.9. . . . . 13.28
   r 3.31. . . . . 12.17
   r 3.31(4) 12.17
   r 6.2(1) 15.14
   r 6.2(2) 15.14
   r 6.2(3) 15.14
   r 6.4. . . . . 15.11, 15.26, 15.34
   r 6.4(2) 15.11
   r 6.4(c) 15.11
   r 6.4(d) 15.11
   r 6.4(f) 15.11
   r 6.4(3)
   r 6.7. . . . . 15.13
   r 10.2. . . . . .1.40
   r 10.18. . . . . 13.17
   r 14.2. . . . . 1.36, 1.40
   r 14.2(2) 1.12
   r 18.1. . . . . 13.33
   r 18.3. . . . . .13.19, 13.34
   r 18.4. . . . . 13.21
   r 18.4(3) 13.36
   r 18.5(1)(a). 13.22
   r 18.5(1)(b) 13.22
   r 18.5(2) 13.22
   r 18.8. . . . . 13.21
   r 18/9 . . . . 13.23
   r 18.10. . . . . 13.17
   r 18.13. . . . . 13.20
   r 18.14. . . . . 13.36
   r 18.17. . . . . 13.35
   r 28(3). 12.218, 12.231, 14.04
   r 31.3(5)(a). 16.08
Criminal Procedure (Amendment)
   Rules 2007 (SI 2007/699). 1.11
   Sch 2, para 9. . . . . .1.12
Human Fertilisation and Embryology
   (Parental Orders) Regulations 2018
   (SI 2018 No 1412)
   Sch 4. . . . . 6.49, 6.57
Indictment Rules 1971 (SI 1971/3) 1.01
Modern Slavery Act 2015 (Consequential
   Amendments) Regulations 2016/244
   Pt 2 reg 24(c) 4.248
Protection of Children (Northern Ireland)
   Order (SI 1978/1047)
   Art 3 (1)(a). 8.151
Safeguarding Vulnerable Groups
   Act 2006 (Commencement No. 8 and
   Saving) Order 2012
   (SI 2012/2231). 12.217, 16.59
Safeguarding Vulnerable Groups
   Act 2006 (Prescribed Criteria and
   Miscellaneous Provisions) Regulations
   2009 (SI 2009 No 37)
   Pt 2 . . . . 2.13, 2.25, 2.55, 3.09, 3.23, 3.32,
               3.46, 3.54, 3.65, 4.19, 4.35, 4.48,
               4.55, 4.65, 4.86, 4.97, 4.106, 4.117,
               4.128, 4.151, 4.163, 4.172, 4.181, 4.190,
               4.201, 4.212, 4.223, 4.235, 4.244, 4.254,
               5.24, 5.30, 5.47, 5.54, 5.59, 5.67, 5.83,
               5.89, 5.99, 5.111, 5.123, 5.130, 6.13,
               6.21, 6.30, 6.38, 6.46, 6.55, 6.63, 6.73,
               6.81, 7.17, 7.30, 7.38, 7.46, 7.54, 7.67,
               7.75, 7.84, 7.92, 7.100, 7.108, 7.120,
               7.129, 7.137, 7.144, 7.151, 7.169, 7.175,
               7.184, 7.192, 8.20, 8.27, 8.36, 8.50, 8.63,
               8.77, 8.85, 8.93, 8.103, 8.109, 8.116, 8.123,
               8.130, 8.137, 8.145, 8.156, 8.163, 8.170,
               8.180, 8.189, 8.197, 9.24, 9.37, 9.45,
               9.54, 9.66, 9.75, 10.13, 10.20, 10.28,
               10.39, 10.47, 10.56, 11.10, 11.17,
               11.25, 11.33, 11.42, 11.50, 11.58
   reg 3 . . . . 12.220
   reg 4 . . . . 12.221
   reg 5 . . . . 12.222
   reg 6 . . . . 12.223
   Sch 1, para 1. . . . . . . .2.55, 3.46, 4.48, 4.55, 4.75,
               4.106, 4.128, 4.244, 5.83, 5.123, 6.55,
               7.30, 7.38, 7.46, 7.54, 7.75, 7.84, 7.92,
               7.100, 7.108, 7.129, 7.137, 7.144, 7.151,
               8.123, 8.137 8.197, 10.47, 10.56, 12.220
   Sch 1, para 2. . . . . . .2.55, 3.09, 3.32, 3.46, 3.54,
               3.65, 4.19, 4.35, 4.65, 4.86, 4.117,
               4.151, 4.163, 4.172, 4.181, 4.190,
               4.201, 4.212, 4.223, 4.235, 4.244 5.24,
               5.30, 5.40, 5.47, 5.54, 5.59, 5.67, 5.83,
               5.89, 5.99, 5.111, 5.123, 5.130, 6.13,
               6.21, 6.30, 6.38, 6.46, 6.55, 6.73, 6.81,
               7.17, 7.30, 7.38, 7.46, 7.54, 7.75, 7.84,
               7.92, 7.100, 7.108, 7.120, 7.129, 7.137,
               7.144, 7.151, 7.169, 7.175, 7.184, 7.192,
               8.20, 8.27, 8.36, 8.50, 8.63, 8.77, 8.85,
               8.93, 8.103, 8.109, 8.116, 8.123, 8.137,
               8.145, 8.156, 8.163, 8.170, 8.180, 8.189,
               8.197, 9.24, 9.45, 9.54, 10.13, 10.20, 10.28,
               10.39, 10.47, 10.56, 11.10, 11.17, 11.25,
               11.33, 11.42, 11.50, 11.58, 12.221
   Sch 1, para 3. . . . . .4.244, 5.83, 5.123,
               6.55, 7.30, 7.38, 7.46, 7.54, 7.84, 7.92,
               7.100, 7.108, 7.129, 7.137, 7.144, 7.151,
               8.123, 8.137, 8.197, 10.47, 10.56, 12.221
   Sch 1, para 4. . . . . 2.55, 3.09, 3.32, 3.46,
               3.54, 3.65, 4.19, 4.35, 4.48, 4.55, 4.65,

4.75, 4.86, 4.106, 4.117, 4.128, 4.151,
    4.163, 4.172, 4.181, 4.190, 4.201,
    4.212, 4.223, 4.235, 4.244, 5.24, 5.47,
    5.54, 5.59, 5.67, 5.83, 5.89, 5.99, 5.111,
    5.123, 5.130, 6.13, 6.21, 6.30, 6.38, 6.46,
    6.55, 6.73, 6.81, 7.17, 7.75, 7.120, 7.169,
    7.175, 7.184, 7.192, 8.20, 8.27, 8.36, 8.50,
    8.63, 8.77, 8.85, 8.93, 8.103, 8.109,
    8.116, 8.123, 8.137, 8.145, 8.156, 8.163,
    8.170, 8.180, 8.189, 8.197, 9.24, 9.45,
    9.54, 10.13, 10.20, 10.28, 10.39, 10.47,
    10.56, 11.10, 11.17, 11.25, 11.33,
    11.42, 11.50, 11.58, 12.221
Safeguarding Vulnerable Groups Act 2006
    (Commencement No 8 and Saving)
    Order 2012 No 2231) 12.217–12.218
    Pt 2 . . . . 12.218
Serious Crime Act 2015 Regulations
    2017 (SI 2017/ 451). 4.236
Sexual Offences Act 2003 (Commencement)
    Order 2004 (SI 2004/874) 5.71

Sexual Offences Act 2003 (Notification
    Requirements) (England and Wales)
    Regulations 2012 (SI 2012/1876) 14.15
    reg 9 . . . . 14.13
    reg 10 . . . . 14.11
    reg 11 . . . . 14.12
    reg 12 . . . . 14.11
    reg 13 . . . . 14.12
    reg 14 . . . . .14.11, 14.12
Sexual Offences (Amendment)
    Act 2000 (Commencement No 1)
    Order (SI 2000/3303). 5.04, 5.70
Violent Crime Reduction Act 2006
    (Commencement No 1)
    Order 2007 (SI 2007/74)
    Art 2(c). 12.45
Youth Justice and Criminal Evidence Act
    1999 (Commencement No 10)
    (England and Wales) Order 2004
    (SI 2004/2428)
    Art 2(a) 15.08

LIST OF ABBREVIATIONS

AA 1976	Adoption Act 1976
AGO	Attorney General's Office
AMA 1929	Age of Marriage Act 1929
CA 1989	Children Act 1989
CAA 1981	Criminal Attempts Act 1981
CAA 1985	Criminal Attempts Act 1985
CAJA 2009	Coroners and Justice Act 2009
CDA 1988	Crime and Disorder Act 1988
CJA 1948	Criminal Justice Act 1948
CJA 1988	Criminal Justice Act 1988
CJA 1991	Criminal Justice Act 1991
CJA 2003	Criminal Justice Act 2003
CJCA	Criminal Justice and Courts Act
CJCSA 2000	Criminal Justice and Courts Services Act 2000
CJPOA 1994	Criminal Justice and Public Order Act 1994
CJS	Criminal Justice System
CJSM	Criminal Justice System eMail
CLA 1967	Criminal Law Act 1967
CLA 1977	Criminal Law Act 1977
CLAA 1885	Criminal Law Amendment Act 1885
CLAA 1922	Criminal Law Amendment Act 1922
CO	Community Order
CO	Confiscation Order
CPA 1851	Criminal Procedure Act 1851
CPD	Consolidated Criminal Practice Directions
CPIA 1996	Criminal Procedure and Investigations Act 1996
CPR 2013	Criminal Procedure Rules 2013
CPS	Crown Prosecution Service
CrimPR	Criminal Procedure Rules
CRO	Conditional Release Order
C(S)A 1997	Crime (Sentences) Act 1997
CYPA 1933	Children and Young Persons Act 1933
DBS	Disclosure and Barring Service
DCS	Digital Case System
DPP	Director of Public Prosecutions
DTO	Detention and Training Order
DVCVA 2004	Domestic Violence, Crime and Victims Act 2004
ECAT	Council of Europe Convention on Action against Human Trafficking
ECHR	European Convention on Human Rights
FP	Forensic Physician
FRO	Financial Reporting Order
FTO	Foreign Travel Order
GRH	Ground Rules Hearing

LIST OF ABBREVIATIONS

IPP	Imprisonment for the Protection of the Public
ISA	Independent Safeguarding Authority
ISS	Intensive Supervision and Surveillance
ISVA	Independent Sexual Violence Advisor
IwCA 1960	Indecency with Children Act 1960
LASPO 2012	Legal Aid and Punishment of Offenders Act 2012
MA 1949	Marriage Act 1949
MCA 1980	Magistrates' Courts Act 1980
MDA 1913	Mental Deficiency Act 1913
MHA 1959	Mental Health Act 1959
MSA	Modern Slavery Act 2015
NCA	National Crime Agency
NRM	National Referral Mechanism
OAPA 1861	Offences Against the Person Act 1861
OPA 1959	Obscene Publications Act 1959
OPA 1964	Obscene Publications Act 1964
ORA 2014	Offender Rehabilitation Act 2014
PCA 1978	Protection of Children Act 1978
PCA 2002	Protection of Children Act 2002
PCC(S)A 2000	Powers of Criminal Courts (Sentencing) Act 2000
PCMH	Plea and Case Management Hearing
PFA 2012	Protection of Freedoms Act 2012
PIA 1908	Punishment of Incest Act 1908
PII	public interest immunity
POA 1986	Public Order Act 1986
POCA 2002	Proceeds of Crime Act 2002
PTPH	Plea and Trial Preparation Hearing
RSHO	Risk of Sexual Harm Order
SA	Sentencing Act
SARC	Sexual Assault Referral Centre
SC	Sentencing Council
SCA	Serious Crime Act 2007
SCPO	Serious Crime Prevention Order
SGC	Sentencing Guidance Council
SHPO	Sexual Harm Prevention Order
SI	Statutory Instrument
SOA 1956	Sexual Offences Act 1956
SOA 1967	Sexual Offences Act 1967
SOA 2003	Sexual Offences Act 2003
SO(A)A 1976	Sexual Offences (Amendment) Act 1976
SOA 1985	Sexual Offences Act 1985
SOA 1993	Sexual Offences Act 1993
SOA 2000	Sexual Offences Act 2000
SOA 2003	Sexual Offences Act 2003
SOCPA 2005	Serious Organised Crime and Police Act 2005
SOPO	Sexual Offences Prevention Order
SOTP	Sex Offender Treatment Programme
SSO	Suspended Sentence Order

StOA 1959	Street Offences Act 1959
STPO	Slavery and Trafficking Prevention Order
STRO	Slavery and Trafficking Risk Order
SVGA 2006	Safeguarding and Vulnerable Groups Act 2006
TA 1968	Theft Act 1968
ULS	Unduly Lenient Sentence
USI	unlawful sexual intercourse
VA 1824	Vagrancy Act 1824
VA 1898	Vagrancy Act 1898
VCRA 2006	Violent Crime Reduction Act 2006
VPS	Victim Personal Statement
YJCEA 1999	Youth Justice and Criminal Evidence Act 1999
YOI	Young Offender Institution
YOT	Youth Offending Team
YRO	Youth Rehabilitation Orders

INDEX TO INDICTMENTS/CHARGES

Chapter 2 Rape

Offence	Period	Provision	Maximum Penalty	Para Reference
RAPE 'Unlawful carnal knowledge of a woman without her consent by force, fear or fraud'	Pre-1.1.1957	Contrary to common law	LIFE	2.06
RAPE 'Sexual intercourse with a woman without her consent'	1.1.1957–21.12.1976	SOA 1956, s 1(1)	LIFE	2.19
RAPE 'Sexual intercourse with a woman without consent or recklessness as to consent'	22.12.1976–2.11.1993	SOA 1956, s 1(1)	LIFE	2.29
RAPE 'Sexual intercourse with a male or female without consent or recklessness as to consent'	3.11.1994–30.4.2004	SOA 1956, s 1(1)	LIFE	2.38
RAPE 'Intentional penetration of the vagina/anus/mouth of another who did not consent to the penetration without reasonable belief as to consent'	1.5.2004 to date	SOA 2003, s 1(1)	LIFE	2.50

Chapter 3 Sexual Assaults

Offence	Period	Provision	Maximum Penalty	Para Reference
Indecent assault	1.11.1861–31.12.1956	OAPA 1861, s 52	2 years	3.06
Indecent assault on a woman	1.1.1957–30.4.2004	SOA 1956, s 14	2 years or 5 years after 2.7.1960 if complainant under 13. 10 years if after 16.9.1985	3.17

Offence	Period	Provision	Maximum Penalty	Para Reference
Indecent assault on a man	1.1.1957–30.4.2004	SOA 1956, s 15(1)	10 years	3.27
Assault by penetration	1.5.2004 to date	SOA 2003, s 2(1)	LIFE	3.40
Sexual assault	1.5.2004 to date	SOA 2003, s 3(1)	10 years	3.48
Causing a person to engage in sexual activity	1.5.2004	SOA 2003, s 4(1)	10 years	3.58
Causing a person to engage in penetrative sexual activity	1.5.2004	SOA 2003, s 4(1) and (4)	LIFE	3.59

Chapter 4 Offences Involving Children

Offence	Period	Provision	Maximum Penalty	Para Reference
Indecency with a child [D commits act with/towards C]	2.7.1960–30.4.2004	IwCA 1960, s 1	2 years until 1.10.1997, thereafter 10 years	4.12
Indecency with a child [D incites C to commit act]	2.7.1960–30.4.2004	IwCA 1960, s 1	2 years until 1.10.1997, thereafter 10 years	4.13
Causing/inciting a child to engage in sexual activity [Non-penetrative, D over 18]	1.5.2004 to date	SOA 2003, s 10(1)	14 years	4.24
Causing/inciting a child to engage in sexual activity [Penetrative, D over 18]	1.5.2004 to date	SOA 2003, s 10(1) and (2)	14 years	4.25
Causing/inciting a child to engage in sexual activity [Non-penetrative, D under 18]	1.5.2004 to date	SOA 2003, s 13 and s 10(1)	5 years	4.26
Causing/inciting a child to engage in sexual activity [Penetrative, D under 18]	1.5.2004 to date	SOA 2003, s 13 and s 10(2)	5 years	4.27
Causing/inciting a child under 13 to engage in sexual activity [Non-penetrative]	1.5.2004 to date	SOA 2003, s 8(1)	14 years	4.38
Causing/inciting a child under 13 to engage in sexual activity [Penetrative]	1.5.2004 to date	SOA 2003, s 8(1) and (2)	LIFE	4.39

Offence	Period	Provision	Maximum Penalty	Para Reference
Carnal knowledge of a girl under 13	1.1.1886–31.12.1956	CLAA 1885, s 4	LIFE (D over 16) Not less than 3 years (D under 16)	4.49
Carnal knowledge of a girl [13–16]	1.1.1886–31.12.1956	CLAA 1885, s 5	2 years	4.59
Sexual intercourse with a girl under 13	1.1.1957–30.4.2004	SOA 1956, s 5	LIFE	4.68
Sexual intercourse with a girl under 16	1.1.1957–30.4.2004	SOA 1956, s 6	2 years	4.79
Rape of a child under 13	1.5.2004 to date	SOA 2003, s 5(1)	LIFE	4.92
Assault by penetration of a child under 13	1.5.2004 to date	SOA 2003, s 6(1)	LIFE	4.100
Sexual activity with a child [Penetrative, D over 18]	1.5.2004 to date	SOA 2003, s 9(1) and (2)	14 years	4.110
Sexual activity with a child [Penetrative, D under 18]	1.5.2004 to date	SOA 2003, ss 13 and 9(1) and (2)	5 years	4.111
Sexual assault of a child under 13	1.5.2004 to date	SOA 2003, s 7(1)	14 years	4.122
Sexual activity with a child [Non penetrative, D over 18]	1.5.2004 to date	SOA 2003, s 9(1)	14 years	4.132
Sexual activity with a child [Non penetrative, D under 18]	1.5.2004 to date	SOA 2003, ss 13 and 9(1)	5 years	4.134
Abuse of position of trust	8.1.2001–30.4.2004	SO(A)A 2000, s 3(1)	5 years	4.146
Sexual activity with a child by a person in a position of trust	1.5.2004 to date	SOA 2003, s 16	5 years	4.156
Causing a child to engage in sexual activity by a person in a position of trust	1.5.2004 to date	SOA 2003, s 17	5 years	4.165
Engaging in sexual activity in the presence of a child by a person in a position of trust	1.5.2004 to date	SOA 2003, s 18	5 years	4.174
Causing a child to watch a sexual act by a person in a position of trust	1.5.2004 to date	SOA 2003, s 19	5 years	4.183
Engaging in sexual activity in the presence of a child [D over 18]	1.5.2004 to date	SOA 2003, s 11(1)	10 years	4.194
Engaging in sexual activity in the presence of a child [D under 18]	1.5.2004 to date	SOA 2003, s 13 and 11(1)	5 years	4.195
Causing a child to watch a sexual act [D over 18]	1.5.2004 to date	SOA 2003, s 12(1)	10 years	4.205

Offence	Period	Provision	Maximum Penalty	Para Reference
Causing a child to watch a sexual act [D under 18]	1.5.2004 to date	SOA 2003, s 13 and s 12(1)	5 years	4.206
Arranging or facilitating the commission of a child sex offence	1.5.2004 to date	SOA 2003, s 14(1)	14 years	4.215
Meeting a child following sexual grooming	1.5.2004 to date	SOA 2003, s 15(1)	10 years	4.227 4.228 4.229
Sexual communication with a child	3.4.2017 to date	SOA 2003, s.15A	2 years	4.215
Possession of a paedophile manual	3.5.2015 to date	SCA 2015, s.69(1)	3 years	4.247

Chapter 5 Buggery and Offences of Indecency

Offence	Period	Provision	Maximum Penalty	Para Reference
Buggery	1.11.1861–31.12.1956	OAPA, s 61	LIFE (dependent on facts)	5.14
Assault with intent to commit buggery	1.11.1861–31.12.1956	OAPA 1861, s 62	10 years	5.28
Indecent assault upon a male person	1.11.1861–31.12.1956	OAPA 1861, s 62	10 years	5.36
Gross indecency	1.1.1885–31.12.1956	CLAA 1885, s 11	2-5 years (dependent on facts)	5.44
Buggery	1.1.1957–2.11.1994	SOA 1956, s 12(1)	2 years to LIFE (dependent on facts)	5.51
Buggery	3.11.1994–30.4.2004	SOA 1956, s 12(1)	2 years to LIFE (dependent on facts)	5.64
Intercourse with an animal	1.5.2004 to date	SOA 2003, s 69(1)	2 years	5.75
Assault with intent to commit buggery	1.1.1957–30.4.2004	SOA 1956, s 16(1)	10 years	5.78
Indecent assault upon a male person	1.1.1957–30.4.2004	SOA 1956, s 15(1)	10 years	5.87
Gross indecency	1.1.1957–30.4.2004	SOA 1956, s 13	5 years (dependent on facts)	5.96

Offence	Period	Provision	Maximum Penalty	Para Reference
Sexual activity in a public lavatory	1.5.2004 to date	SOA 2003, s 71	Summary only 6 months	5.111
Procuring an act of buggery	27.7.1967–30.4.2004	SOA 1967, s 4(1)	2 years	5.110

Chapter 6 Familial Offences

Offence	Period	Provision	Maximum Penalty	Para Reference
Incest by a male person	1.1.1909–31.12.1956	PIA 1908, s 1(1)	LIFE where C under 13 years otherwise 3-7 years	6.10
Incest by a female person	1.1.1909–31.12.1956	PIA 1908, s 2	3–7 years	6.18
Incest by a male person	1.1.1957–30.4.2004	SOA 1956, s 10(1)	LIFE where Complainant under 13, otherwise 7 years	6.26
Incest by a female person	1.1.1957–30.4.2004	SOA 1956, s 11(1)	7 years	6.35
Incitement of a girl under 16 to commit incest	8.9.1977–30.4.2004	CLA 1977, s 54	2 years	6.44
Penetrative sexual activity with an adult relative	1.5.2004 to date	SOA 2003, s 64(1)	2 years	6.51
Consenting to penetrative sex with an adult relative	1.5.2004 to date	SOA 2003, s 65(1)	2 years	6.59
Penetrative sexual activity with a child family member	1.5.2004 to date	SOA 2003, s 25(1) and (6)	14 years where Defendant is 18 or over, otherwise 5 years	6.68
Non-penetrative sexual activity with a child family member	1.5.2004 to date	SOA 2003, s 25(1)	5 years	6.69
Inciting a child family member to engage in penetrative sexual activity	1.5.2004 to date	SOA 2003, s 26(1) and (6)	14 years where Defendant is 18 or over, otherwise 5 years	6.77
Inciting a child family member to engage in non-penetrative sexual activity	1.5.2004 to date	SOA 2003, s 26(1)	14 years where D is 18 or over, otherwise 5 years	6.78

Chapter 7 Offences Involving the Mentally Disordered

Offence	Period	Provision	Maximum Penalty	Para Reference
Carnal knowledge of an idiot/imbecile	Pre - 31.12.1956	CLAA 1885, s 5(2)	2 years	7.07
Intercourse with an idiot/imbecile	1.1.1957–31.10.1960 1.11.1960–1.5.2004	SOA 1956, s 7	2 years	7.14, 7.21, and 7.14
Sexual activity with a person with a mental disorder impeding choice	1.5.2004 to date	SOA 2003, s 30(1)	LIFE (if penetration involved) otherwise 14 years	7.26
Causing/inciting a person with a mental disorder impeding choice to engage in sexual activity	1.5.2004 to date	SOA 2003, s 31(1)	LIFE (if penetration involved) otherwise 14 years	7.33
Engaging in sexual activity in the presence of a person with a mental disorder impeding choice	1.5.2004 to date	SOA 2003, s 32	10 years	7.40
Causing a person with a mental disorder impeding choice to watch a sexual act	1.5.2004 to date	SOA 2003, s 33	10 years	7.47
Intercourse with a mentally defective patient	1.1.1957–31.10.1960	SOA 1956, s 8	2 years	7.60
Unlawful sexual intercourse with a patient	1.11.1960–30.4.2004	MHA 1959, s 128(a)	2 years	7.68
Sexual activity by a care worker with a person with a mental disorder	1.5.2004 to date	SOA 2003, s 38(1)	14 years if penetration involved, otherwise 10 years	7.76
Causing/inciting sexual activity with a person with a mental disorder by a care worker	1.5.2004 to date	SOA 2003, s 39(1) and (3)	14 years if penetration involved, otherwise 10 years	7.83
Sexual activity in the presence of a person with a mental disorder	1.5.2004 to date	SOA 2003, s 40	7 years	7.90
Causing a person with a mental disorder to watch a sexual act by a care worker	1.5.2004 to date	SOA 2003, s 41(1)	7 years	7.97
Procurement of a defective	1.1.1957–30.4.2004	SOA 1956, s 9(1)	2 years	7.109

Offence	Period	Provision	Maximum Penalty	Para Reference
Inducement, threat or deception to procure sexual activity with a person with a mental disorder	1.5.2004 to date	SOA 2003, s 34(1)	LIFE if penetration involved, otherwise 14 years	7.117
Causing a person with a mental disorder to engage in sexual activity	1.5.2004 to date	SOA 2003, s 35(1) and (2)	LIFE if penetration involved, otherwise 14 years	7.124
Engaging in sexual activity in the presence, procured by inducement, threat or deception, of a person with a mental disorder	1.5.2004 to date	SOA 2003, s 36(1)	10 years	7.131
Causing a person with a mental disorder to watch a sexual act by inducement, threat or deception	1.5.2004 to date	SOA 2003, s 37(1)	10 years	7.138
Causing/encouraging prostitution of a defective	1.1.1957–30.4.2004	SOA 1956, s 29	2 years	7.157
Permitting a defective to use premises for intercourse	1.1.1957–30.4.2004	SOA 1956, s 27	2 years	7.163
Causing or inciting prostitution for gain	1.5.2004 to date	SOA 2003, s 52(1)	7 years	7.170
Controlling prostitution for gain	1.5.2004 to date	SOA 2003, s 53(1)	7 years	7.177

Chapter 8 Prostitution and Trafficking

Chapter 9 Obscene Publications

Offence	Period	Provision	Maximum Penalty	Para Reference
Taking making, distributing, publishing etc indecent photographs of a child	20.8.1978 to date	PCA 1978, s 1(1)(a)	3 years increased to 10 years on 11.1.2001	9.08–9.15

lii INDEX TO INDICTMENTS/CHARGES

Offence	Period	Provision	Maximum Penalty	Para Reference
Possession of indecent photograph of a child	29.9.1988 to date	CJA 1988, s 160(1)	6 months, summary only offence. Amended with maximum of 5 years from 11.1.2001	9.22–9.23
Possession of prohibited images of children	6.4.2010 to date	CAJA 2009, ss 62(1) and 6(a)	3 years	9.31
Possession of an extreme photographic image	26.1.2009 to date	CJIA 2008, s 63	2–3 years (dependent on categorization of images)	9.38
Publishing an obscene article	29.8.1959 to date	OPA 1959, s 2(1)	3 years	9.47
Having an obscene article for publication for gain	31.8.1964 to date	OPA 1959, s 2(1)	3 years	9.48
Disclosing a private sexual photograph or film	13.4.2015 to date	CJCA 2015, s 33(1)	2 years	9.56

Chapter 10 Offences Against Public Decency

Offence	Period	Provision	Maximum Penalty	Para Reference
Outraging public decency	1.1.1950 to date	Contrary to Common Law	LIFE	10.10
Indecent exposure	1.5.2004 to date	SOA 2003, s 66(1)	2 years	10.25
Voyeurism	1.5.2004 to date	SOA 2003, s 67(1)(a) SOA 2003, s 67(1)(b) SOA 2003, s 67(1)(c) SOA 2003, s 67(1)(d)	2 years	10.36
Upskirting	12.4.2019 to date	SOA 2003, s 67A(1) SOA 2003, s 67A(2)	2 years	10.44
Sexual penetration of a corpse	1.5.2004 to date	SOA 2003, s 70(1)	2 years	10.38

Chapter 11 Preparatory Offences

Offence	Period	Provision	Maximum Penalty	Para Reference
Procurement of a woman by threats	1.1.1957–30.4.2004	SOA 1956, s 2(1)	2 years	11.07
Procurement of a woman by false pretences or representations	1.1.1957–30.4.2004	SOA 1956, s 3(1)	2 years	11.14
Administering drugs to obtain or facilitate intercourse	1.1.1957–30.4.2004	SOA 1956, s 4(1)	2 years	11.22
Burglary with intent to commit rape	1.1.1969–30.4.2004	TA 1968, s 9(1)(a)	14 years if building a dwelling, otherwise 10 years	11.30
Administering a substance with intent	1.5.2004 to date	SOA 2003, s 61(1)	10 years	11.38
Committing an offence with intent to commit a sexual offence	1.5.2004 to date	SOA 2003, s 62(1)	LIFE if kidnapping or false imprisonment, otherwise 10 years	11.46
Trespass with intent to commit a sexual offence	1.5.2004 to date	SOA 2003, s 63(1)	10 years	11.54

1
INDICTMENTS

A. Introduction	1.01	I. Offenders of Particular Concern: Drafting Historic Counts to which Schedule 13 Applies	1.41
B. Particularizing Counts	1.06		
C. Duplicity and Multiple Incident Counts	1.11	J. Alternative Verdicts	1.43
		1. The Principle in *Courtie*	1.45
D. Drafting a Multiple Incident Count: The Practicalities	1.16	K. Offences of Attempt	1.49
E. Proving Counts without a Jury	1.21	L. Familial Offences under the Sexual Offences Act 2003	1.53
F. Offences Straddling Implementation Dates of Different Acts	1.26	M. Defendant under 18: Offences under the Sexual Offences Act 2003, s 13	1.54
G. Drafting Counts where an Allegation Straddles Legislation: The Practicalities	1.29	N. Procedure when Either Way or Summary Only Offences Remain on an Indictment	1.55
H. Defective Counts: Effect of Drafting a Count under the Wrong Act	1.35	O. Quashing Indictments	1.58
		1. Delay	1.60

A. INTRODUCTION

1.01 This chapter is intended to provide some helpful tips on drafting indictments in sex cases, although some of the advice will apply generally. As long as the Indictment Rules are not offended, the contents of an indictment are largely a matter of style; this obviously will apply more to the Particulars. The law in relation to indictments is primarily set out in the Indictments Act 1915, which Act is expanded upon by Part 10, Criminal Procedure Rules (CrimPR) 2020.[1] Part 10 itself is supplemented by the 2015 Consolidated Criminal Practice Directions (CPD). The CrimPR 2020 and the Consolidated Criminal Practice Directions should be read together.

1.02 It remains the ultimate responsibility of prosecution counsel, once instructed, to ensure that the indictment is in a proper form.[2] In cases involving many counts, perhaps over several years, which are frequently seen in cases involving sexual offences, the style adopted should be carefully considered in order to assist those using it as a working document. A carefully drawn indictment in such a case will take time to draft but be invaluable for all involved in a trial. It should provide the starting point for preparation of the prosecution opening and clarity of the prosecution case for defence lawyers, judge and jury.

---

[1] SI 20/20/759 in force from 5 October 2020. The 2020 Criminal Procedure Rules replace the 2015 Criminal Procedure Rules and consolidate the rules made in 2015 with the 11 sets of amendments made to those rules.
[2] *R v Newland* (1988) 87 C. App R.

1.03 It is important that an indictment covering multiple allegations over a period of time is carefully balanced to ensure that whilst it properly reflects the criminality alleged, it is not overloaded, though sufficient counts should be included to establish the offending period.[3]

1.04 The drafting should make clear where counts are specimen or multiple incident counts, otherwise the Court will be limited to sentencing for one offence in respect of each count.[4]

1.05 The Court of Appeal, constituted as a 5-judge court, in the case of *R v Forbes* [2016][5] reiterated the importance of specifying the criminality alleged in the counts on the indictment and taking care in framing charges. The prosecution must consider the ingredients of the offence with particular diligence and check that the offences charged are correctly laid, otherwise, on conviction, the judge could be faced with insufficient sentencing powers to reflect the criminality, or in other cases result in convictions being quashed or different offences substituted.

B. PARTICULARIZING COUNTS

1.06 Although there is no requirement to aver for example the place of an offence, when indicting in a case involving numerous allegations over a period of time it is necessary to be as precise as possible in particularizing counts so that the act alleged is clear to all on the face of the document. CrimPR 2020, rule 10.2(1)(b) requires 'such particulars of the conduct constituting the commission of the offence as to make clear what the prosecutor alleges against the defendant'.

1.07 In *Rackham*[6] the Court of Appeal, quashing the convictions, ruled that the trial judge should have acceded to a defence request for better identification by the prosecution of the specific incidents upon which the different counts were based. The court held that the indictment should be drawn with as much particularity as the circumstances of the case would permit and that a difficulty in being precise in every respect is not a reason for not being precise when it is possible to be so.

1.08 It is therefore suggested that a prudent prosecutor will include details which are apparent from the statements over and above simply the time frame; for example, the details of the assault, the place where the act occurred (if that will help to identify it), the day of the week, and so on. This should be possible within the Particulars but if it is felt to be too cumbersome by the drafter, sometimes (where there is no objection taken) a short summary is added below a count, for example in italics.

1.09 If during trial, on an indictment containing specimen counts, the complainant gives evidence identifying specific occasions alleged to be part of a pattern of conduct and there is evidence before the jury which could cause a reasonable jury to acquit on the specimen charge but convict on the particularized occasion or vice versa. The prosecutor should apply

---

[3] *R v Tovey and Smith* [2005] EWCA Crim 530.
[4] *R v Younas* [2017] EWCA Crim 1.
[5] *R v Forbes* [2016] EWCA Crim 1388; [2016] 2 Cr App R (S) 44.
[6] [1997] 2 Cr App R 222.

to amend the indictment and add the particular incident or incidents as separate counts on the indictment.[7]

It is essential to aver a child's age when that is a material particular affecting sentence. Failure to do so will result in the lower maximum sentence being applied.[8] See individual chapters for relevant offences.

1.10

C. DUPLICITY AND MULTIPLE INCIDENT COUNTS

The Criminal Procedure (Amendment) Rules 2007[9] brought about an important change to the rule against particularizing a series of like offences within a single count, meaning that it is no longer essential for a count to relate to a single act. Of all the amendments introduced on 2.4.2007, this is likely to have the greatest impact upon indicting cases involving allegations of repeated sexual abuse.

1.11

Rule 14.2(2) of the Criminal Procedure Rules 2005[10] was a revision of what is often called the 'rule against duplicity'.[11] Rule 14.2(2), now rule 10.2(2) under the 2020 CrimPR, allows a prosecutor in certain circumstances to bring a single charge against a defendant even though that includes more than one incident of the offence alleged. An example of when this will apply is given by the Criminal Procedure Rules Committee in its guidance note to the Rules, and is typical of many sex cases; when, for example, a defendant is alleged to have repeatedly assaulted the same victim in the same way over a period of time. The intention of the Committee in creating this new rule was to take account, among other things, of the potential under the old rules for a perceived unfairness to a victim of multiple offending where, out of many alleged offences, only a few are prosecuted as examples, giving the impression that the victim's distress has been underestimated, or that he or she has not been believed.[12]

1.12

Part 10 of the Criminal Procedure Rules permits more than one incident of the same offence to be charged in one count. This means that an indictment may be drafted in order to reflect a continuing course of conduct rather than single incidents. Therefore, instead of drafting a series of specimen/sample counts,[13] it is now proper to draft a single count covering a series of similar allegations.

1.13

Consideration will still need to be given as to whether this is the correct approach in each particular case. It is most likely to be appropriate when a complainant cannot differentiate between many occasions over a period of time, making a broad allegation without more detail of, for example, several years of regular and repeated acts; but where, for example, there are differences within the evidence creating the possibility of different verdicts dependent upon dates or other factors, it is less likely to be. An indictment can of course contain

1.14

---

[7] *R v Hobson* [2013] EWCA Crim 819, at [24].
[8] *R v SG and DG* [2009] EWCA Crim 2241; *R v R (Paul Brian)* [1993] Crim LR 541.
[9] SI 2007/699.
[10] As amended by para 9 Sch 2 of the Criminal Procedure (Amendment) Rules 2007.
[11] The original text of Rule 14.2(2) remains unamended within the current Criminal Procedure Rules.
[12] Reprinted with kind permission of the Department for Constitutional Affairs; taken from the note prepared by the Secretariat to the Committee, 27.3.2007, published with the Guide to the Rules.
[13] As to which see *R v Smith and Tovey* [2005] EWCA Crim 530.

specific counts reflecting specific incidents as well as multiple incident counts reflecting a course of conduct over a period of time; in many cases this will be the best approach.

1.15 A multiple incident count has the advantage of enabling the sentencing judge to reflect the true criminality in a case involving a series of similar offences which sample counts do not provide.[14] It was encouraged in *R v Forbes* [2016][15] that those who draft indictments should consider the use of multiple incident counts, to avoid the difficulty of sentencers being left with insufficient sentencing powers, when a prolonged course of conduct involving similar abuse is alleged.

D. DRAFTING A MULTIPLE INCIDENT COUNT: THE PRACTICALITIES

1.16 It will still be necessary to draft separate counts to reflect each type of assault both in order for the jury to differentiate between types of assault alleged and for the sentencing judge to properly reflect the overall criminality revealed by the evidence in the total sentence.

1.17 A multiple incident count is only appropriate when not only the precise allegation, but also the defendant's case in respect of it, are the same. If the evidence reveals these to be different, separate counts should be left to the jury.

1.18 Unlike a sample count, which can be left to a jury on the basis that they are sure the alleged offence occurred at least once, a multiple incident count should only be left on the basis that the jury are sure the alleged offence occurred at least twice and should specify a sufficient minimum number of occasions[16] ('On not less than … occasions between …', etc). For this reason, as well as to ensure clarity for the sentence, it is wise for any indictment containing a multiple incident count to also have a single incident count to reflect the same alleged offence occurring on one occasion within the same time frame ('On an occasion between…', etc).

1.19 The Consolidated Criminal Practice Directions give guidance as to when a 'multiple incident' count under rule 10.2(2) may be appropriate. This provides the framework for drafting such a count:

> Multiple offending: count charging more than one incident
>
> 10A.10 CrimPR 10.2(2) allows a single count to allege more than one incident of the commission of an offence in certain circumstances. Each incident must be of the same offence. The circumstances in which such a count may be appropriate include, but are not limited to, the following:
>
> (a) the victim on each occasion was the same, or there was no identifiable individual victim as, for example, in a case of the unlawful importation of controlled drugs or of money laundering;

---

[14] *R v Canavan, Kidd and Shaw* [1998] 1 Cr App R 79; a defendant can only be sentenced for that of which he has been convicted. Also, *R v Hartley* [2011] EWCA Crim 1299.
[15] *R v Forbes* [2016] EWCA Crim 1388; [2016] 2 Cr App R (S) 44 at para [30].
[16] *R v A* [2015] EWCA Crim 177 and *R v Forbes* [2016] EWCA Crim 1388; [2016] 2 Cr App R (S) 44 at para [32].

(b) the alleged incidents involved a marked degree of repetition in the method employed or in their location, or both;

(c) the alleged incidents took place over a clearly defined period, typically (but not necessarily) no more than about a year;

(d) in any event, the defence is such as to apply to every alleged incident without differentiation. Where what is in issue differs between different incidents, a single 'multiple incidents' count will not be appropriate, though it may be appropriate to use two or more such counts according to the circumstances and to the issues raised by the defence.

10A.11 Even in circumstances such as those set out above, there may be occasions on which a prosecutor chooses not to use such a count, in order to bring the case within section 75(3)(a) of the Proceeds of Crime Act 2002 (criminal lifestyle established by conviction of three or more offences in the same proceedings): for example, because section 75(2)(c) of that Act does not apply (criminal lifestyle established by an offence committed over a period of at least 6 months). Where the prosecutor proposes such a course, it is unlikely that CrimPR Part 1 (the overriding objective) will require an indictment to contain a single 'multiple incidents' count in place of a larger number of counts, subject to the general principles set out at paragraph 140A.3.

10A.12 For some offences, particularly sexual offences, the penalty for the offence may have changed during the period over which the alleged incidents took place. In such a case, additional 'multiple incidents' counts should be used so that each count only alleges incidents to which the same maximum penalty applies.

10A.13 In other cases, such as sexual or physical abuse, a complainant may be in a position only to give evidence of a series of similar incidents without being able to specify when or the precise circumstances in which they occurred. In these cases, a 'multiple incidents' count may be desirable. If on the other hand, the complainant is able to identify particular incidents of the offence by reference to a date or other specific event, but alleges that in addition there were other incidents which the complainant is unable to specify, then it may be desirable to include separate counts for the identified incidents and a 'multiple incidents' count or counts alleging that incidents of the same offence occurred 'many' times. Using a 'multiple incidents' count may be an appropriate alternative to using 'specimen' counts in some cases where repeated sexual or physical abuse is alleged. The choice of count will depend on the particular circumstances of the case and should be determined bearing in mind the implications for sentencing set out in *R v Canavan; R v Kidd; R v Shaw* [1998] 1 WLR 604, [1998] 1 Cr App R 79, [1998] 1 Cr App R (S) 243.

1.20 Note also the guidance provided in *R v Hartley*[17] and *R v A*[18] in drafting indictments containing multiple incident count(s).

E. PROVING COUNTS WITHOUT A JURY

1.21 Sections 17–21 of the Domestic Violence, Crime and Victims Act 2004 provides that where a defendant is convicted by the jury on a sample of other counts to be tried in the

---

[17] [2011] EWCA Crim 1299.
[18] [2015] EWCA Crim 177 at para 47

proceedings, those other counts can then be tried by a judge alone. In practice, this is rarely used. Section 18(1) of the Act and CrimPR rule 3.22 impose a mandatory requirement on the prosecution to apply for a preparatory hearing (under rule 3.23) to determine the application for a trial by judge alone.

1.22 If such an application is made and the judge is satisfied that the following three conditions are fulfilled, he may make an order for the trial to take place on the basis that the trial of some, but not all, of the counts included in the indictment may be conducted without a jury.

1.23 The three conditions to be satisfied are set out in s 17:

- The number of counts included in the indictment is likely to mean that a trial by jury involving all of those counts would be impracticable.
- If an order under subsection (2) were made, each count or group of counts which would accordingly be tried with a jury can be regarded as a sample of counts which could accordingly be tried without a jury.
- It is in the interests of justice for an order under s 17(2) to be made.

1.24 Section 17 further provides:

- In deciding whether or not to make an order under s 17(2), the judge must have regard to any steps which might reasonably be taken to facilitate a trial by jury.
- Step is not to be regarded as reasonable if it could lead to the possibility of a defendant in the trial receiving a lesser sentence than would be the case if that step were not taken.
- An order under s 17(2) must specify the counts which may be tried without a jury.

1.25 Form of Indictment for use where an order is made under s 17(2) of the Domestic Violence, Crime and Victims Act 2004:

(Criminal Procedure Rules, Part 10)

Indictment

IN THE CROWN COURT AT ....
THE QUEEN v ....
charged as follows: -

PART 1

Count 1

STATEMENT OF OFFENCE

PARTICULARS

Count 2

STATEMENT OF OFFENCE

PARTICULARS

Count 3

STATEMENT OF OFFENCE

PARTICULARS

etc.

PART 2

Section 1: counts associated with Count 1 in Part 1 of this indictment.

Count 1.1

STATEMENT OF OFFENCE

PARTICULARS

Count 1.2

STATEMENT OF OFFENCE

PARTICULARS

Count 1.3

STATEMENT OF OFFENCE

PARTICULARS

etc.

Section 2: counts associated with Count 2 in Part 1 of this indictment.

Count 2.1

STATEMENT OF OFFENCE

PARTICULARS

Count 2.2

STATEMENT OF OFFENCE

PARTICULARS

Count 2.3

STATEMENT OF OFFENCE

PARTICULARS

etc.

Section 3: counts associated with Count 3 in Part 1 of this indictment.

Count 3.1

STATEMENT OF OFFENCE

PARTICULARS

Count 3.2

STATEMENT OF OFFENCE

PARTICULARS

1. INDICTMENTS

> Count 3.3
>
> STATEMENT OF OFFENCE
>
> PARTICULARS
>
> Etc.
>
> Date............................
>
> ....Crown Court Officer

F. OFFENCES STRADDLING IMPLEMENTATION DATES OF DIFFERENT ACTS

1.26 It is essential that indictments reflecting allegations which potentially or actually straddle two different statutes are carefully drawn to avoid the problems which may arise if a count runs through a commencement date. Those problems were identified by the then Lord Chief Justice Lord Judge in *R v Harries*.[19]

1.27 A lacuna was created by the failure to enact transitional provisions, despite the provision for such power created by s 141 of the Sexual Offences Act (SOA) 2003. This meant that if there was doubt as to whether a sexual offence occurred before or after the implementation of the SOA 2003, the prosecution failed only because it could not prove under which SOA the offence was committed. That lacuna was addressed by the implementation of s 55 of the Violent Crime Reduction Act 2006 on 12.2.2007.

Section 55 provides:

> (1) This section applies where, in any proceedings—
>   (a) person ('the defendant') is charged in respect of the same conduct both with an offence under the Sexual Offences Act 2003 ('the 2003 Act offence') and with an offence specified in subsection (2) ('the pre-commencement offence');
>   (b) the only thing preventing the defendant from being found guilty of the 2003 Act offence is the fact that it has not been proved beyond a reasonable doubt that the time when the conduct took place was after the coming into force of the enactment providing for the offence; and
>   (c) the only thing preventing the defendant from being found guilty of the pre-commencement offence is the fact that it has not been proved beyond a reasonable doubt that that time was before the coming into force of the repeal of the enactment providing for the offence.
> (2) The offences referred to in subsection (1)(a) are—
>   (a) any offence under the Sexual Offences Act 1956 (c. 69);
>   (b) an offence under section 4 of the Vagrancy Act 1824 (c. 83) (obscene exposure);
>   (c) an offence under section 28 of the Town Police Clauses Act 1847 (c. 89) (indecent exposure);

---

[19] *R v Michael Harries and Others* [2007] EWCA Crim 1622.

G. DRAFTING COUNTS WHERE AN ALLEGATION STRADDLES LEGISLATION

(d) an offence under section 61 or 62 of the Offences against the Person Act 1861 (c. 100) (buggery etc.);
(e) an offence under section 128 of the Mental Health Act 1959 (c. 72) (sexual intercourse with patients);
(f) an offence under section 1 of the Indecency with Children Act 1960 (c. 33) (indecency with children);
(g) an offence under section 4 or 5 of the Sexual Offences Act 1967 (procuring an man to commit buggery and living on the earnings of male prostitution);
(h) an offence under section 9 of the Theft Act 1968 (c. 60) (burglary, including entering premises with intent to commit rape);
(i) an offence under section 54 of the Criminal Law Act 1977 (c. 45) (incitement of girl under 16 to commit incest);
(j) an offence under section 1 of the Protection of Children Act 1978 (c. 37) (indecent photographs of children);
(k) an offence under section 3 of the Sexual Offences (Amendment) Act 2000 (c. 44) (abuse of position of trust);
(l) an offence under section 145 of the Nationality, Immigration and Asylum Act 2002 (c. 41) (traffic in prostitution).

Note: offences of incitement, conspiracy and attempt to commit any of the above offences including those under the SOA 2003 are included (s 55(5)).

In such circumstances it will be conclusively presumed, for the purpose of determining guilt, that the time when the conduct occurred was under the old law if the maximum penalty for it was lower then; if it is not lower, then it will be presumed that the conduct occurred under the new law; s 55(3).

1.28

G. DRAFTING COUNTS WHERE AN ALLEGATION STRADDLES LEGISLATION: THE PRACTICALITIES

Where an allegation straddles the implementation dates of two different Acts, typically but not exclusively the 1956 and 2003 Sexual Offences Acts, the trial indictment should contain two counts to reflect that one allegation; one under each Act alleging the offence either side of the implementation date of the new Act. That is, one count covering the period up to the day before the commencement date and the other starting on the commencement date. For s 55 to have effect, both the SOA 2003 and the earlier legislation must be pleaded in the alternative: *Chaney* [2009].[20] The practice amongst some prosecutors in sex cases, especially in a case where the indictment is already necessarily lengthy, to draft a single count by adopting the device of putting the Particulars of Offence under both the old and new law in the same count has been disapproved by the Court of Appeal in *Marshall* (2.12.2009)[21] and appears to have mostly fallen out of use. Such a count would be duplicitous and would impede the proper working of s 55; directions to the jury would be difficult, if not impossible.

1.29

---

[20] *R v Chaney* [2009] EWCA Crim 52.
[21] Unreported, Woolwich CC.

1.30 This will apply equally to a single incident count where the date is in dispute (as in *Cairns*)[22] as to multiple incidents or sample counts where an alleged course of conduct straddles the relevant legislation.

1.31 If, by the time the evidence has closed, there is still no clarity as to which time frame the allegation occurred in, then the count which should be left to the jury for its consideration is that which attracts the lowest maximum sentence for the offence alleged; this will usually be under the earlier Act. The second, alternative count should be withdrawn from the jury.

1.32 Care must be taken even if a guilty plea is known to be intended upon arraignment; *where the dates of an allegation straddle the commencement date of new legislation* this will affect the sentencing powers for the offence. There should therefore never be a single count which runs through the commencement date; otherwise, the sentencer is faced with a single count for which two different sentences are possible.[23]

1.33 Failure to consider this is likely to result in the sentencing tribunal being restricted to the lower sentencing maxima of the two sets of legislation (unless the evidence unequivocally reveals that the offence occurred after the implementation of the new Act) *R v R (Paul Brian)*.[24]

1.34 See para 12.36 for sentencing under the dangerousness provisions where counts span the provisions.

H. DEFECTIVE COUNTS: EFFECT OF DRAFTING A COUNT UNDER THE WRONG ACT

1.35 Where an indictment straddles periods covered for example by the SOA 1956 and the SOA 2003, it is important to check that each count is drafted under the correct Act.

1.36 In *Stocker* [2013][25] the appellant was convicted of rape, contrary to s 1(1) of the SOA 1956. The offence was committed in 2008 and so the relevant statutory provision had been wrongly identified: it should have been s 1(1) of the SOA 2003. The question for the Court of Appeal was whether this was a purely technical defect or whether the count was fundamentally flawed because it breached rule 14(2) of the applicable Criminal Procedure Rules by failing to identify accurately the legislation contravened. From the beginning to the end of the process the charge was, in substance, one of rape under the 2003 Act. The error could have been cured easily by an amendment at any time. The Court of Appeal did not accept that an error in the date of the statute on these facts was so fundamental as to render the proceedings a nullity, or that the draftsman of rule 14(2) would have intended such an outcome for a breach of this kind. Nothing had occurred during the trial to render the indictment a nullity or the conviction unsafe.

---

[22] *R v Cairns* [1998] Crim LR 141.
[23] *R v Cairns* [1998] Crim LR 141.
[24] *R v R (Paul Brian)* [1993] Crim LR 541. See also para 12.18.
[25] [2013] EWCA Crim 1993.

H. DEFECTIVE COUNTS: EFFECT OF DRAFTING A COUNT UNDER THE WRONG ACT

Stocker was 'clearly distinguishable' from *MC* [2012]:[26] in *R v MC*, there was not simply a technicality which had caused no prejudice to the appellant. In *Stocker*, the court observed that there is a clear judicial and legislative steer away from quashing an indictment and allowing appeals on the basis of a purely technical defect. The position in *MC* was different; the appellant was charged with sexual offences against his natural daughter. The matters were alleged to have occurred some time ago and an additional count under s 14(1) of the SOA 1956 was added by a late amendment to the indictment. The particulars alleged that the offence had taken place at a time when the 1956 Act had long since been repealed and replaced by the 2003 Act. On appeal it was submitted that it was open to the court to substitute a conviction under s 9 of the SOA 2003. The Court of Appeal rejected this argument because it did not pay sufficient attention to the requirement in s 3 of the Criminal Appeal Act 1968 that the jury could on the indictment have found the appellant guilty of some other offence. The offence which the respondents sought to argue could be substituted under s 3 was not a known offence. The words 'on the indictment' were important because in order to find a person guilty of an alternative offence, the allegations in the indictment had to amount to or include an allegation of that other offence: *R v Graham and Others*.[27]

1.37

It follows that the court concluded that s 3 of the Criminal Appeal Act did not allow the court to substitute a verdict under s 9 of the 2003 Act in respect of the jury's verdict on the defective count. The allegation did not expressly or impliedly amount to or include an allegation under s 9. In addition, and more fundamentally, the allegation of an offence under the SOA 1956 could not sensibly be said to amount to an offence under the 2003 Act, which superseded and repealed the 1956 Act.

1.38

There followed, after *Stocker*, a series of judgments from the Court of Appeal Criminal Division on the issue of defective indictments in historical sex offence cases.[28] The issue was once again addressed in the case of *R v Walker; R v Coatman*[29] in which LJ Hallet (Vice President) observed that despite the fact that 'over the last few years this court has issued repeated warnings about the dangers of poor drafting of indictments in cases of alleged historic sexual abuse. We have two more examples before us.' Mr Walker and Mr Coatman were both charged and convicted with offences of gross indecency. The counts on the indictment were defective as the statement of offence erroneously pleaded an offence contrary to s 13 of the Sexual Offences Act 1956 (SOA 1956), which was time-barred.

1.39

The Court went on to consider a line of authorities on the point, including the comprehensive review on the effect of defects in an indictment conducted in *R v Stocker* (above), *R v Forbes*[30] and *R v AD*[31] and extracted the following principles:

1.40

(i) the test for the court remains one of safety of the conviction;
(ii) there is 'a clear judicial and legislative steer away from quashing an indictment and allowing appeals on the basis of a purely technical defect. The overriding objective

---

[26] [2012] EWCA Crim 213.
[27] [1997] 1 Cr App R(S) 302.
[28] See for example: *R v White* [2014] EWCA Crim 714; *R v Clarke* [2015] EWCA Crim 350; *R v Silverwood and Chapman* [2015] EWCA Crim 2401; *R v Boateng* [2016]; *R v AD* [2016] EWCA Crim 454; *R v Forbes* [2016] EWCA 1388.
[29] [2018] 1 Cr App R 19.
[30] *R v Forbes* [2016] EWCA 1388.
[31] *R v AD* [2016] EWCA Crim 454

of the criminal justice system is to do justice—to ensure the acquittal of the innocent and the conviction of the guilty. To that end, procedural and technical points should be taken at the time of the trial when they can be properly and fairly addressed' (Stocker at [42]);

(iii) the question for the court is whether the error in the indictment is a purely technical defect or whether the count itself is fundamentally flawed because it breaches r 14.2 [now r 10.2] of the Criminal Procedure Rules in that it fails to identify sufficiently the legislation allegedly contravened. The clear purpose of the relevant parts of r 14.2 is to ensure that an accused has sufficient information to know the case he had to meet and for all parties to know which statutory provisions applied (Stocker at [43]);

(iv) the determination of which defects are properly to be categorized as 'fundamentally flawed' rather than amounting to 'a mere drafting or clerical error' is, 'a particularly fact sensitive issue' (AD at [22]); and

(v) it is necessary to discern the true intention of the draftsman and the effect of the error upon the conduct of the trial (AD at [23] and [24] and Forbes at [56]–[59]).

I. OFFENDERS OF PARTICULAR CONCERN: DRAFTING HISTORIC COUNTS TO WHICH SCHEDULE 13 APPLIES

1.41 On the 13 April 2015 provisions relating to 'special custodial sentences for certain offenders of particular concern' were introduced by a new s 236A in the Criminal Justice Act 2003.[32] Offenders convicted of offences specified in Schedule 18A of the CJA 2003 were subject to a new mandatory sentencing regime. On 1 December 2020 the codifying Sentencing Act 2020, known as the Sentencing Code, subsequently incorporated those provisions into ss 265 (for offenders aged 18–21) and 278 (for offenders aged over 21) and Schedule 13 of the 2020 Act. Schedule 13 of the Sentencing Code includes child sexual offences under ss 5 and 6 of the SOA 2003 (rape or penetration of a child under 13), accessory and inchoate offences and 'relevant 'abolished offences'[33] namely any offence which: (a) was abolished before 13.4.2015;[34] and (b) if committed on the day on which the offender was convicted of the offence, would have constituted an offence under ss 5 or 6 SOA 2003.

1.42 In order to ensure that abolished offences to which ss 265 and 278 apply are identified for the purposes of sentencing (which will include, for example; offences contrary to the 1956 Act under s 5 (sexual intercourse with a girl under 13), ss 14 and 15 (indecent assault on female or male), and s 1 (rape), s 12 (buggery), practitioners should ensure the counts are drafted so as to identify relevant threshold ages of defendants and complainants, and when relevant penetration occurred.[35] See Chapter 12.

---

[32] Inserted by the Criminal Justice and Courts Act 2015 (13.4.2015).
[33] Sch 13, paras 6, 7, and 9. Abolished means the same as repealed (*R v L.F.* [2016] EWCA Crim 561).
[34] The date the original section (s 236A) came into force.
[35] See *R v L.F.* [2016] EWCA Crim 561.

J. ALTERNATIVE VERDICTS

Rather than relying on alternatives included within the legislation, prosecutors would be well advised to draft alternatives expressly on the indictment where appropriate or to apply to add counts where the evidence given at trial reveals an alternative offence. **1.43**

Under the SOA 2003 a number of offences contain essential ingredients which are identical to but less in number than other, more serious offences. There will therefore often be occasions on which if the offence charged is not proved in one or more of its elements, the defendant will be guilty of a lesser offence. An obvious example of this would be those offences of penetrative assault where the evidence at trial falls short on the issue of penetration. In addition, some offences under the SOA 2003 carry different sentences depending upon the precise factual ingredients proved, for example whether penetration has occurred; following the principle in *Courtie*,[36] these are separate offences, meaning yet more offences are created. It will therefore be particularly important for charges and indictments to be carefully drafted in order to accurately reflect the prosecution case. **1.44**

1. The Principle in *Courtie*

In *Courtie*,[37] the House of Lords was dealing with an offence under the SOA 1967 which, like the SOA 2003, created a number of specific offences for which the maximum punishment prescribed varied upon a descending scale, according to the existence or absence of particular factual ingredients. **1.45**

The House of Lords held that where a statute provides for different maximum sentences dependent upon the prosecution's ability to successfully prove a particular factual ingredient, two distinct offences are created by the Act. It was further held that where a not guilty plea is entered, it is the jury's function to determine the facts upon which a person is guilty; it is therefore essential that the indictment correctly sets out those facts, if necessary in separate counts, so that in the event that the difference in a finding of fact will affect the maximum sentence available, the verdict(s) reflect that difference. It is also simpler for the judge to sum the case up to the jury and for the jury to immediately see what alternatives are open to them. **1.46**

The SOA 2003 creates over 50 offences, some carrying different maximum sentences depending upon the facts proved. Under the principle in *Courtie* this means yet more offences[38] are created. An illustration of this would be one of the number of offences where if the sexual activity alleges penetration, the charge is both indictable only and carries a higher maximum sentence than a non-penetrative allegation under the same section; as such, they are separate offences. The indictment should therefore be properly particularized, to set out the facts upon which the elements of the offence relied upon by the prosecution are based. **1.47**

---

[36] [1984] AC 463.
[37] [1984] AC 463.
[38] Over 70 when the subcategories of offences are included.

1. INDICTMENTS

1.48 Careful thought must be given to how many offences are in fact revealed by the evidence: see *R v Grout*,[39] a case involving offences under s 8 of the SOA 2003. Section 8 creates four separate offences applying *Courtie*. The Court of Appeal quashed the conviction, ruling that the indictment should have included more than one count to clearly set out the different offences alleged. This is of course necessary to both ensure clarity for the jury and, upon conviction, provide the correct maximum sentence(s).

K. OFFENCES OF ATTEMPT

1.49 The premise that alternative counts should be added rather than read into an indictment will also apply when an attempt to commit the full offence is an obvious alternative from the outset; indeed, it is thought preferable to have a count added in the event that an alternative of attempt to commit the full offence is to be left to the jury after evidence has been heard.

1.50 Where a count of attempt is to be drafted,[1] it should be indicted under the common law until 27.8.1981[2] and thereafter under the Criminal Attempts Act 1985.

1.51 It is clearer and more helpful to also aver the relevant section of the Act, so that all parties can immediately identify the substantive offence and refer to the appropriate elements, sentence, etc; this course was approved by The Court of Appeal in *Reed & Others* [2021];[3] (following *Privett*) added a postscript to its judgment; Per Fulford LJ, Vice_President:

Postscript: The form of the indictment or charge sheet

> 85. The six cases we have considered in this conjoined appeal offer an opportunity to give guidance on best practice in drafting the statement of offence. It will assist judges and others, not least when it comes to identifying the relevant Sentencing Guideline, if the statement of offence, even in the case of a criminal attempt, in future identifies the substantive offence lying behind the attempt. This is likely to be of considerable assistance in any case of attempt, and not only when there is sexual offending. However, it is particularly valuable in these cases, because of the large number of crimes defined by the Sexual Offences Act, and the potential confusion or even ambiguity which may follow from a lack of precision.
> 86. All the statements of offence in these six cases were technically correct, but some of them were clearer and more explicit than others.
> 87. The model we favour and encourage was the form of the indictment in the case of Matthew Millen. The Statement of Offence on his indictment read:
> 'Attempting to pay for the sexual services of a child, contrary to section 1(1) Criminal Attempts Act 1981 and section 47(1) of the Sexual Offences Act 2003.'
> 88. This identified the substantive offence under section 47(1) as well as stating that the charge was an attempt.
> 89. The Statement of Offence in the indictment of Mark Bennett, on the other hand, read:
> 'Attempting to incite a girl under 16 to engage in sexual activity (penetrative), contrary to section 1(1) of the Criminal Attempts Act 1981.'

---

[39] [2011] EWCA Crim 299.

90. This is not incorrect, but it does not clearly identify the underlying offence. More information would have been provided by a Statement of Offence in the form:
'Attempting to incite a girl under 16 to engage in sexual activity (penetrative), contrary to section 10(1) of the Sexual Offences Act 2003 and section 1(1) of the Criminal Attempts Act 1981.'

91. Although the word 'penetrative' is not strictly necessary, we agree with Mr Jarvis for the Crown that it is an important component, because it affects the maximum sentence.

92. Similarly, the Statement of Offence on the indictment of Alistair Reed was:
'Attempting to cause a child to engage in sexual activity, contrary to section 1(1) of the Criminal Attempts Act 1981.'

93. It would have been better to specify the statutory sexual offence, using a form such as:
'Attempting to cause a child to engage in sexual activity, contrary to section 10(1) of the Sexual Offences Act 2003 and section 1(1) of the Criminal Attempts Act 1981.'

94. This point does not apply only to indictments. There was no indictment in the case of Lee Crisp because he pleaded guilty to the charges against him and was committed to the Crown Court for sentence. His charge sheet read (taking one example):
'Attempt to cause / incite a female child aged under 13 to engage in sexual activity—no penetration between 14/07/2018 and 16/07/2018 attempted to incite "SASHA" a girl aged 12, to engage in sexual activity of a non-penetrative nature, that is to take a photograph of herself naked and forward that photograph to him.
Contrary to section 1(1) of the Criminal Attempts Act 1981.'

95. We would have preferred to see an explicit reference to the substantive offence in section 8(1) (Causing or inciting a child under 13 to engage in sexual activity), not least to avoid confusion with the less serious offence under section 10(1) (Causing or inciting a child under 16 to engage in sexual activity). The charge sheet might then read:
'Attempt to cause / incite a female child aged under 13 to engage in sexual activity—no penetration between 14/07/2018 and 16/07/2018 attempted to incite "SASHA" a girl aged 12, to engage in sexual activity of a non-penetrative nature, that is to take a photograph of herself naked and forward that photograph to him.
Contrary to section 8(1) of the Sexual Offences Act 2003 and section 1(1) of the Criminal Attempts Act 1981.'

96. We agree with Mr Jarvis for the Crown that *'bearing in mind that charges and indictments need to be understood not just by lawyers but by defendants, the public and the press, clarity as to the offence attempted is essential.'* We hope that following this guidance will achieve that necessary goal.

The attempt should be averred in both the Statement and Particulars of Offence. **1.52**

L. FAMILIAL OFFENCES UNDER THE SEXUAL OFFENCES ACT 2003

In drafting indictments generally for a familial offence it is important to remember the following: **1.53**

(i) The maximum penalties such offences attract are usually significantly lower than the equivalent offence drafted outside the familial bracket because they are intended to reflect circumstances where there is consent. Where the complainant is under 13, however, it is suggested that it will be appropriate to indict a non-familial offence or to simply draft, for example, a count of rape of a child under 13 (life) rather than sexual activity with a child family member (5 years where the defendant is under 18 even when the child is under 13). This is the clear intention of Parliament and underpins the current Crown Prosecution Service guidance for indicting such offences.

(ii) Where possible, counts should relate to a specific incident. Where that is impossible because of, for example, several years of regular and repeated acts, it is now appropriate to draft a single multiple-incident count relating to repeated similar offences against the same complainant, preferably using 12-month periods as breaks in the overall timespan (provided the defence is the same to all allegations reflected by the single count). See paras 1.08–1.17 in this chapter.

(iii) If both parties to the sexual act are charged, it is possible for a guilty verdict against one only to stand; one party might be unaware of the relationship or there might not be true consent by the party alleged to have consented to the act.[40]

M. DEFENDANT UNDER 18: OFFENCES UNDER THE SEXUAL OFFENCES ACT 2003, S 13

1.54 When indicting offences under s 13, that is those offences under ss 9–12 for which a defendant under 18 can be charged, it is suggested that it will be good practice to indict both sections, so that the offence to which the indictment relates is obvious. It is suggested that s 13 be indicted first, followed by the relevant section and that the particulars make the act alleged clear. See paras 4.26, 4.27, 4.111, 4.195, and 4.206 for sample indictments.

N. PROCEDURE WHEN EITHER WAY OR SUMMARY ONLY OFFENCES REMAIN ON AN INDICTMENT

1.55 Circumstances may arise where an indictment is amended or otherwise altered to remove indictable only matters which leave only matters triable either way or summarily before the Crown Court; for example, either on a successful application for severance or dismissal of the indictable only charges following the sending of a case to the Crown Court under the Crime and Disorder Act (CDA) 1988, s 51.[41] In such an event, in the case of either way offences the correct course is for the Crown Court to adopt a procedure akin to that used in the magistrates' court to determine mode of trial.[42] Schedule 3 of the CDA 1988, paras 7–13, set out the procedure to be followed for summary and either way offences. However,

---

[40] *R v Gordon* (1927) 19 Cr App R 20 CA; brother and sister both charged in same indictment but tried separately. She was acquitted; that did not make his conviction bad.
[41] S 51A in relation to children and young persons.
[42] Sections 17A to 17C Magistrates' Court Act 1980.

failure to do so will no longer necessarily render the proceedings a nullity; the Court of Appeal in *R v Thwaites* [2006],[43] upholding *R v Ashton* [2006][44] ruled:

> Where a court was confronted by failure to take a required step, properly or at all, before a power was exercised it should first ask itself whether the intention of the legislature was that any act done following that procedural failure should be invalid. If the answer was no, then the court should go on to consider the interests of justice generally, and in particular whether there was a real possibility that either the prosecution or the defence might suffer prejudice on account of the procedural failure.

Following on from *R v Thwaites* and *R v Ashton*, the Court of Appeal has rejected a series of technical procedural arguments in relation to nullity. In R. v Williams [2017][45] Lord Thomas of Cwmgiedd CJ expressed the following general view: **1.56**

> [W]e would hope that in the future the court would take the view that the highly technical law in relation to nullity is an outdated concept that should no longer prevail, that a modern approach should be taken, which is to decide on the fairness of the trial, the prejudice to a defendant and the safety of the conviction. [33]

Note a Crown Court Judge's power to sit as a District Judge during the course of Crown Court proceedings in order to deal with summary matters.[46] **1.57**

O. QUASHING INDICTMENTS

It is proper for two indictments to exist at the same time as long as both are not proceeded with.[47] In the event that an indictment is heavily amended and so preferred as a new indictment, it will be prudent not to apply to quash the existing indictment until after trial. This is in order to ensure that if, for example, the new indictment were invalid for some reason, the only valid indictment is not quashed, leaving the proceedings a nullity. However, see paras 1.48–1.49 for the Court of Appeal's general approach to procedural nullity and *R v MJ* [2019][48] in relation to procedural irregularities in relation to indictments. **1.58**

Equally, a prudent prosecutor when accepting a guilty plea to lesser alternative counts will not proceed to 'offer no evidence' until after sentence has been passed in order to ensure that no application to vacate the plea is made in the interim; counts not intended to be proceeded with should lie on the court file until then. **1.59**

---

[43] *R v Thwaites* [2006] EWCA Crim 3235.
[44] *R v Ashton (John)* [2006] EWCA Crim 794, [2007] 1 WLR 181.
[45] *R v Williams* EWCA Crim 281.
[46] Section 66 Courts Act 2003.
[47] *R v Poole* [1961] AC 223.
[48] *R v MJ* [2019] 1 Cr App R (S) 10.

1. Delay

1.60 The question of delay in an historic sex case is likely to be considered, at least by the prosecutor, prior to the drafting of an indictment. This is, however, a convenient point at which to draw the reader's attention to the authorities on this subject. *R v F* [2011][49] provides guidance on abuse of process applications from a five-Judge Court of Appeal led by the then Lord Chief Justice, Lord Judge. Since then, appeals following conviction based on significant periods of delay have been considered and repeatedly rejected on their facts: *R v PS* [2013][50] (delay of 34 years; provides guidance as to directing the jury on delay); *R v RD* [2013][51] (delays of between 39 and 63 years). It must now be considered that delay of itself, absent an exceptional consequence, is no longer an arguable basis for a stay. See for example *R v Hewitt* [2020] (delay of 37 years and loss of relevant material). For the effects of delay on sentence, see para 12.13 et seq.

1.61 Table of Changes in Sexual Offences Legislation

Table 1.1 Table of Changes in Sexual Offences Legislation

Act	Commencement Date	Cessation Date	Explanatory Note
CAJA 2009, s 62	6.4.2010	In force	Section enacted by SI 2010 No 816
CAA 1981	27.8.1981	In force	Commenced by s 11(1) of Act
CJA 1988, s 160	29.9.1988	In force	Commenced by s 171(6) of Act
CJIA 2008, s 63	26.1.2009	In force	Section enacted by SI 2008 No 2993
CJCA 2015 S 33	13.4.2015	In force	Section enacted by SI 2015 No 778
CLA 1977, s 54	8.9.1977	1.5.2004	Section enacted by SI 1977 No 1365. Section repealed by SOA 2003
CLAA 1885	14.8.1885	1.1.1957	Act repealed by SOA 1956
IwCA 1960	2.7.1960	1.5.2004	Act repealed by SOA 2003
MDA 1913	1.4.1914	1.11.1960	Act repealed by SI 1960 No 1698
MHA 1959, s 128	1.11.1960	1.5.2004	Section enacted by SI 1960 No 1698 Section repealed by SOA 2003
MSA 2015, s 2	31.7.2015	In force	Section enacted by SI 2015 No 1476
OPA 1959, s 2	29.8.1959	In force	Commenced by s 9(3) of Act
OAPA 1861, s 52 s 61 s 62	1.11.1861 1.11.1861 1.11.1861	1.1.1957 1.1.1957 1.1.1957	Sections repealed by SOA 1956
PCA 1978, s 1	20.8.1978	In force	
PIA 1908	1.1.1909	1.1.1957	Act repealed by SOA 1956
SOA 1956	1.1.1957	1.5.2004	Act repealed by SOA 2003

---

[49] EWCA Crim 1844.
[50] [2013] EWCA Crim 1592.
[51] RD [2013] EWCA Crim 1592.

Table 1.1 Continued

Act	Commencement Date	Cessation Date	Explanatory Note
SOA 1967 s 4 s 5	27.7.1967 27.7.1967	1.5.2004 1.5.2004	Sections repealed by SOA 2003
SOA 2003	1.5.2004	In force save for various repealed sections.	Section 53A added by Policing and Crime Act 2009 on 1.4.2010. Sections 57, 58, and 59 repealed and replaced with s 59A as of 6.4.2013 Section 59A repealed by the Modern Slavery Act 2015 on 31.7.2015 Section 15A inserted by Serious Crime Act 2015 on 3.4.3017. Sections 67A inserted by Voyeurism (Offences) Act 2019 on 12.4.2019
SO(A)A 2000, s 3	8.1.2001	1.5.2004	Section enacted by SI 2001 No 452 Act repealed by SOA 2003
SCA, s 69	3.5.2015	In force	Section enacted by SI 2015 No 820
TA 1968, s 9(1)(a)	1.1.1969	1.5.2004*	*Only sexual element of offence repealed by SOA 2003. The substantive offence remains in force.

Note: the authors wish to thank Lucy Luttman, Barrister, for researching, creating, and updating this table.

2
RAPE

A. Introduction	2.01	D. Offences Committed between 22.12.1976 and 2.11.1993	2.26
B. Offences Committed Pre-1.1.1957	2.02		
1. Definition	2.03	E. Offences Committed between 3.11.1994 and 30.4.2004	2.37
C. Offences Committed between 1.1.1957 and 21.12.1976	2.14	F. Offences Committed from 1.5.2004 to date	2.46
		1. Sexual Offences Act 2003	2.46

A. INTRODUCTION

2.01 The offence of rape, originally a common law offence, became a statutory offence in 1957,[1] and was later defined by statute in 1976.[2] The offence was extended in 1992 so that a husband could be convicted of raping his wife. The House of Lords in *R v R* [1992][3] said the marital exemption was a common law misconception (which had been followed for years); *R v R* simply clarified the law. In 1994 the definition of rape was extended to include non-consensual anal intercourse upon a male or female.[4] The SOA 2003 extends the definition further. Most notably, non-consensual penile penetration of the mouth is now defined by s 1 as rape.

B. OFFENCES COMMITTED PRE-1.1.1957

Rape was originally an offence at common law. **2.02**

1. Definition

Unlawful carnal knowledge of a woman without her consent by force, fear or fraud.[5] **2.03**

---

[1] SOA 1956, s 1, commencement date 1.1.1957.
[2] SO(A)A 1976, s 1(1), commencement date 22.12.1976.
[3] *R v R* [1992] 1 AC 599.
[4] Criminal Justice and Public Order Act (CJPOA) 1994, s 142, commencement date 3.11.1994.
[5] East PC 434.

2. RAPE

Proof

2.04
(i) Carnal knowledge: penile penetration of the vagina, even the slightest penetration was sufficient (proof of hymenal damage is not required). Proof of ejaculation is not necessary.[6]
(ii) Lack of consent: even if the girl was under 16[7] her submission is not to be classified as consent.[8] The lack of consent may have been brought about by drink, drugs, sleep, age or mental handicap, so as to render the complainant incapable of giving consent.[9]
(iii) *Mens rea*; proof of intention or recklessness as to consent is required (see para 2.17).

Notes

2.05
(i) Triable only on indictment.
(ii) A boy under 14 was presumed by law to be incapable of committing rape as principal[10] (that is until 1993), but may be guilty of indecent assault[11] (see para 3.03.)
(iii) A boy under 14 could not be convicted of an assault with intent to rape.[12]
(iv) Only a male may be convicted as a principal,[13] but a female may be convicted as an aider and abettor.[14]
(v) If a woman consents to sexual intercourse then changes her mind during intercourse, the male may be convicted if he has the requisite *mens rea*.[15]

Indictment

2.06 RAPE   Pre-1.1.1957

Statement of Offence

RAPE.

Particulars of Offence

D on the ... day of ... had carnal knowledge of C without her consent.

Alternative Offences

Criminal Law Amendment Act 1885

2.07 The following offences constituted alternatives to rape:

(i) CLAA 1885, s 3: procuring defilement of a woman or girl by threats, fraud or under the influence of drugs: **2 YEARS**.

---

[6] *R v Marsden* [1891] 2 QB 149 and later OAPA 1861, s 63.
[7] *R v Harling* (1938) 26 Cr App R 127 CA.
[8] *R v Olugboja* (1981) 73 Cr App R 344 CA.
[9] *R v Malone* (1998) 2 Cr App R 447 CA.
[10] Hale, *The History of Pleas of the Crown*, vol I.
[11] *R v Williams* (1893) 1 QB 320; CLAA 1885, s 9.
[12] *R v Williams* (ibid).
[13] SOA 1956, s 1.
[14] *R v Ram* (1893) 17 Cox CC 609 (in 1893 referred to as principal in second degree).
[15] *R v Kaitamaki* (1985) AC 147 (PC).

(ii) CLAA 1885, s 4: carnal knowledge of a girl aged under 13: LIFE (see paras 4.46–4.53).
(iii) for an attempt to commit this offence: 2 YEARS.
(iv) CLAA 1885, s 5: defilement of a girl aged between 13 and 16 years of age, or an attempt to do the same: 2 YEARS (see paras 4.54–4.63).

Offences Against the Person Act 1861

OAPA 1861, s 52: indecent assault:[16] 2 YEARS (see paras 3.03–3.09). **2.08**

Punishment of Incest Act 1908

PIA 1908, s 4(3): incest: LIFE (see paras 6.12 and 6.20). **2.09**

(i) As defined by common law.
(ii) Attempted rape: fine and/or LIFE.
(iii) Up until 1948 maximum sentence available is LIFE, thereafter it was lowered to 7 YEARS until 1985 when maximum was again increased to LIFE.[17]

Indictment

ATTEMPTED RAPE   until 31.12.1956 **2.10**

Statement of Offence
ATTEMPTED RAPE contrary to Common Law.

Particulars of Offence
D on the ... day of ... attempted to have carnal knowledge of C without her consent.

Sentence

(i) For the full offence: LIFE.[18] **2.11**
(ii) Attempted rape: LIFE.
- This was reduced to 7 YEARS[19] in 1948 but increased again to LIFE imprisonment in 1985.[20]

Sentencing Guidance

See paras 12.13–12.26. **2.12**

---

[16] OAPA 1861, s 52.
[17] SOA 1985, s 3(2), commencement date 16.9.1985.
[18] CJA 1948, s 1.
[19] Attempted Rape Act 1948, s 1.
[20] SOA 1985, s 3(2), commencement date 16.9.1985.

24   2. RAPE

Upon Conviction/Sentence

2.13 (i) Notification not applicable.[21]
(ii) Inclusion in the children's and adults' barred lists not applicable.[22]
(iii) SHPO not applicable.[23]

C. OFFENCES COMMITTED BETWEEN 1.1.1957 AND 21.12.1976

Sexual Offences Act 1956

2.14 (i) This Act consolidated the law with regard to sexual offences in general and to rape—by s 1 and Schedule 1.
(ii) Rape was still a common law offence.

Definition

Sexual Offences Act 1956, s 1(1) and (2)

2.15 (1) It is a felony for a man to rape a woman.
(2) A man who induces a married woman to have sexual intercourse with him by impersonating her husband commits rape.

2.16 The common law definition remained unchanged 'unlawful sexual intercourse with a woman without her consent by force, fear or fraud'.[24]

Proof

2.17 (i) Any penile penetration of the vagina was sufficient, even the slightest, not necessarily proof of ejaculation.[25]
(ii) Lack of consent (as at para 2.04).

Note

2.18 The offence is indictable only.[26]

---

[21] SOA 2003, s 80(1) (not listed in Sch 3); see Chapter 14, Tables 14.2–14.5.
[22] Part 2 of the Safeguarding Vulnerable Groups Act 2006 (Prescribed Criteria and Miscellaneous Provisions) Regulations 2009 (SI 2009 No 37); see Chapter 12, para 12.217.
[23] SA 2020, s 345 (not listed in Sch 3 or Sch 5 SOA 2003); see Chapter 16, para 16.07.
[24] Hale, *The History of Pleas of the Crown*, vol I.
[25] *R v M'Rue* (1838) 8 C & P 641.
[26] SOA 1956, s 37.

Indictment

RAPE   1.1.1957 to 21.12.1976   2.19

> **Statement of Offence**
> RAPE, contrary to section 1(1) of the Sexual Offences Act 1956.
>
> **Particulars of Offence**
> D on the ... day of ... had sexual intercourse with C, without her consent.

Alternative Offences

Sexual Offences Act 1956, s 37, Schedule 2
  (i) s 2 procurement of a woman by threats: **2 YEARS** (see paras 11.04–11.10).   2.20
  (ii) s 3 procurement of a woman by false pretences: **2 YEARS** (see paras 11.11–11.18).
  (iii) s 4 administering drugs to obtain or facilitate intercourse: **2 YEARS** (see paras 11.19–11.26).
  (iv) s 14 indecent assault (on a woman): **2 YEARS** (see paras 3.03–3.09).

However, if the *only* issue is consent, then indecent assault cannot be an alternative,[27] unless the victim is under 16.[28]

The following were available alternatives to an offence of rape from 1956 to 1967[29] (but not   2.21
after 1967):

  (i) s 5 intercourse with a girl under 13: **LIFE** (see paras 4.64–4.74).
  (ii) s 6 intercourse with a girl between 13 and 16: **2 YEARS** (see paras 4.75–4.86).
  (iii) s 7 intercourse with an idiot or imbecile: **2 YEARS** (see paras 7.11–7.21).
  (iv) s 8 intercourse with a defective: **2 YEARS** (see paras 7.57–7.64).
  (v) s 10 incest: **LIFE** if child under 13: **7 YEARS** otherwise (see paras 6.23–6.31).

Indictment

ATTEMPTED RAPE   1.1.1957 – 21.12.1976   2.22

> **Statement of Offence**
> ATTEMPTED RAPE, contrary to section 1(1) of the Sexual Offences Act 1956 and Common Law.
>
> **Particulars of Offence**
> D on the ... day of ... attempted to have sexual intercourse with C, without her consent.

---

[27] *R v Touhey* (1961) 45 Cr App R 23.
[28] See also *R v J* [2004] UKHL 42 in relation to abuse of process and indecent assault as an alternative to a time-barred historic offence.
[29] CLA 1967, s 10.

26   2. RAPE

Sentence

2.23 (i) For the full offence: LIFE.[30]
(ii) Attempted rape: 7 YEARS.[31],[32]

Sentencing Guidance

2.24 The Sentencing Council 'Sexual Offences: Definitive Guideline' contains guidance for sentencing in historic sexual offences. The Guideline applies to all offenders aged 18 and over, sentenced on or after 1 April 2014. When sentencing a defendant who was under 18 at the time of the offence see the 'Sentencing Children and Young Persons—Overarching Principles' and 'Sentencing Children and Young Persons—Sexual Offences' Guidelines which apply to all children and young persons sentenced on or after 1 June 2017. See Chapter 12 para XX. See also *Att.-Gen.'s Reference (R. v O)* [2018][33] where the Court of Appeal held it was correct for the guideline on sentencing children and young people to be applied in relation to an offender who was aged 19 at the time of sentencing, and for the sentence to be that which would have been imposed if he had been convicted at fifteen, rather than to apply the 'approach to sentencing historic sexual offences' detailed in Annex B of the definitive guideline on sexual offences.

Upon Conviction/Sentence

2.25 (i) Notification applies.[34]
(ii) Automatic inclusion in the children's barred list with no right to make representations where the victim was a child. Automatic inclusion in the children's barred list with the right to make representations where the victim was an adult. Automatic inclusion in the adults' barred list with the right to make representations where the victim is an adult.[35]
(iii) SHPO applies.[36]
(iv) Qualifying 'specified sexual offence' in Schedule 18 (Extended Sentences).[37]

D. OFFENCES COMMITTED BETWEEN 22.12.1976 AND 2.11.1993

Sexual Offences (Amendment) Act 1976

2.26 The definition of rape remains (as at para 2.15). Following the decision in *DPP v Morgan*[38] the House of Lords emphasized the requirement of the mental element: the defendant must

---

[30] SOA 1956, s 37, Sch 2 (1)(a).
[31] SOA 1956, s 37, Sch 2(1)(b).
[32] SOA 1985, s 3(2), commencement date 16.9.1985.
[33] *Att.-Gen.'s Reference (R. v O); R. v O* [2018] EWCA Crim 2286, [2019] CrimLR 353, CA.
[34] SOA 2003, s 80(1) and Sch 3, para 1; see Chapter 14, paras 14.1–14.5.
[35] Part 2 of the Safeguarding Vulnerable Groups Act 2006 (Prescribed Criteria and Miscellaneous Provisions) Regulations 2009 (SI 2009 No 37); see Chapter 12, para 12.217.
[36] SA 2020, s 345 and Sch 3 para 1 SOA 2003; see Chapter 16, para 16.07.
[37] SA 2020, s 306, Sch 18, para 29(a); see Chapter 12, para 12.51.
[38] [1976] AC 182, 61 Cr App R 136.

be at least reckless as to whether consent was given. A genuine belief in consent, however unreasonable, provided a defence to the charge.

Following on from this decision, the SO(A)A 1976 was passed,[39] which included a declaration confirming that the jury, in deciding whether the defendant believed in consent, could consider whether reasonable grounds existed for such.[40]

2.27

Definition

Section 1(1) provides that a rape offence consists of:

(i) unlawful sexual intercourse with a woman who at the time of the intercourse does not consent to it;
(ii) at that time he knows that she does not consent to the intercourse or he is reckless as to whether she consents to it.

2.28

Proof

As per Definition.

2.29

Indictment

RAPE   22.12.1976 to 2.11.1993

2.30

Statement of Offence
RAPE, contrary to section 1(1) of the Sexual Offences Act 1956.

Particulars of Offence
D on the ... day of ... 19/20..., had unlawful sexual intercourse with C who at the time of the said intercourse did not consent to it, said D knowing that the said C did not so consent or being reckless as to whether she so consented.
or
D on the ... day of ... raped C.

Alternative Offences

Sexual Offences Act 1956, section 37, Schedule 2
(i) s 2 'procurement of a woman by threats': 2 YEARS (see paras 11.04–11.10).
(ii) s 3 'procurement of a woman by false pretences': 2 YEARS (see paras 11.11–11.18).

2.31

---

[39] Commencement date 22.12.1976.
[40] SO(A)A 1976, s 1(2).

(iii) s 4 'administering drugs to obtain or facilitate intercourse': **2 YEARS** (see paras 11.19–11.26).

(iv) s 14 'indecent assault' (on a woman): **2 YEARS** (see paras 3.12–3.22).

However, if the *only* issue is consent, then indecent assault cannot be an alternative,[41] unless the victim is under 16.

Attempted rape: **7 YEARS** until 15.9.1985. **LIFE** from 16.9.1985.[42] When indicting offences of attempt do so under common law until 26.8.1981, thereafter indict under s 1(1) Criminal Attempts Act 1981. Aver the attempt in both the Statement of Offence and Particulars of Offence. In addition, aver the substantive offence under the relevant Act; see paras 1.51 and 12.157 and *Reed & Others* [2021].[43]

Indictment

2.32 ATTEMPTED RAPE   1.1.1957–26.8.1981

Statement of Offence
ATTEMPTED RAPE, contrary to section 1(1) of the Sexual Offences Act 1956 and Common Law.

Particulars of Offence
D on the ... day of ... 19/20... , attempted to have unlawful sexual intercourse with C who at the time of the said intercourse did not consent to it, said D knowing that the said C did not so consent or being reckless as to whether she so consented.

or

D on the ... day of ... attempted to raped C.

2.33 Before 27.8.1981 when indicting attempted rape follow the model indictments set out at paras 2.10, 2.22, and 2.31). In 1981 the Criminal Attempts Act was passed. Section 1(1) defines a criminal attempt as: 'If with intent to commit an offence to which this section applies, a person does an act which is more than merely preparatory to the commission of the offence, he is guilty of attempting to commit the offence'.

From 27.8.1981 an indictment for attempted rape should be drafted as follows.

---

[41] *R v Touhey* (1961) 45 Cr App R 23. See also *R v J* [2004] UKHL 42 in relation to abuse of process and indecent assault as an alternative to a time-barred historic offence.
[42] As of 16.9.1985; SOA 1985, s 3.
[43] *Reed & Others* [2021] EWCA Crim 572.

Indictment

ATTEMPTED RAPE   27.8.1981 to 30.4.2004   **2.34**

Statement of Offence
ATTEMPTED RAPE, contrary to section 1(1) of the Sexual Offences Act 1956 and section 1(1) of the Criminal Attempts Act 1981.

Particulars of Offence
D on the … day of … 19/20… , attempted to have unlawful sexual intercourse with C who at the time of the said intercourse did not consent to it, said D knowing that the said C did not so consent or being reckless as to whether she so consented.

or

D on the … day of … attempted to rape C.

Sentence

See paras 2.22 and 12.13–12.26.   **2.35**

20.9.1993

As of 20.9.1993 SOA 1993,[44] s 1 abolishes the presumption[45] that a boy under 14 was incapable of sexual intercourse; it remains for offences committed prior to this date. From 20.9.1993 any male aged 10 or over at the time of the offence may be convicted of any sexual offence involving his penetration of the vagina or anus of a female.   **2.36**

E. OFFENCES COMMITTED BETWEEN 3.11.1994 AND 30.4.2004

Introduction

Rape was redefined to include non-consensual anal intercourse with a male or female as of 3.11.1994.[46] The House of Lords in *R v R* [1992][47] said the marital exemption was a common law misconception (which had been followed for years) *R v R* simply clarified the law. This principle has retrospective effect see *R v C (Barry)* [2004].[48]   **2.37**

---

[44] SOA 1993, s 2(2).
[45] Children and Young Persons Act 1933, s 50.
[46] CJPOA 1994, s 142.
[47] *R v R* [1992] 1 AC 599.
[48] *R v C (Barry)* [2004] EWCA Crim 292.

Definition

Sexual Offences Act 1956, s 1

2.38
(1) It is an offence for a man to rape a woman or another man.
(2) A man commits rape if:
   (a) he has sexual intercourse with a person (whether vaginal or anal) who at the time of the intercourse does not consent to it; and
   (b) at the time he knows that the person does not consent to the intercourse or is reckless as to whether that person consents to it.

Section 1(1) of the SO(A)A 1976 only was repealed.[49] Section 1(2) of the SO(A)A 1976 was not repealed (reasonable belief in consent) (see para 2.26).

Proof

2.39 As per Definition.

Notes

2.40
(i) It should be remembered that this change in the law did not have a retrospective effect. Non-consensual anal intercourse pre–3.11.1994 should be charged as 'buggery' and not rape (see paras 5.04–5.06). This is a mistake often made. Indeed, made by all involved in the case of *R v Fowler*,[50] including the Court of Appeal.
(ii) In certain cases it may clarify issues if the particulars aver 'per vaginam' or 'per anum' after the word 'intercourse'. In circumstances where the evidence is unclear as to whether penetration was of the vagina or anus, it is permissible to indict the two as alternatives in one count without offending the rule against duplicity.[51]
(iii) Recklessness/knowledge does not have to be separately averred.[52]

Indictment

2.41 RAPE 3.11.1994–30.4.2004

2.42 See para 2.29. If anal rape is alleged then the Particulars should include 'per anum' after the words 'unlawful sexual intercourse'.

Alternative Offences

2.43 See para 2.30.

---

[49] CJPOA 1994, s 168(3) and Schedule 11.
[50] [2002] EWCA Crim 620, [2002] Crim LR 521.
[51] *R v K (Robert)* [2008] EWCA Crim 1923.
[52] *R v Flitter (Julian)* [2000] 12 WLUK 345.

Sentence

See para 2.22. 2.44

Sentencing Guidance

See paras 2.23 and 2.24. See also Chapter 12, para 12.169. 2.45

F. OFFENCES COMMITTED FROM 1.5.2004 TO DATE

1. Sexual Offences Act 2003

On 1.5.2004 the Sexual Offences Act 2003 came into force. It has created a complete overhaul of the law in relation to sexual offences and the commission of them. 2.46

Section 1 extends the definition of rape to include non-consensual penile penetration of the mouth of a male or female. The Act further seeks to define consent as 'free agreement'.[53] Free agreement has been clarified as covering drunken consent given by a complainant who has consumed even substantial quantities of alcohol, provided that the complainant has not lost the capacity to choose whether to have intercourse.[54] When considering free agreement context is all important:[55] ostensible consent of a vulnerable complainant is to be taken in the context of years of abuse;[56] apparent consent of a complainant from the age of 16 to 25 years is to be taken in the context of sexual abuse by her step-father from the age of 5 years;[57] evidence of grooming will frequently be relevant, although will not necessarily establish an absence of consent.[58] As to deception vitiating consent, if a complainant had not agreed to intercourse if ejaculation were to take place,[59] or intercourse without the use of a condom,[60] or to digital penetration by a female (pretending to be male),[61] then consent was not given. However, an undercover police officer deceiving the complainant as to his employment and environmental beliefs[62] or a defendant's lie about having had a vasectomy[63] was not sufficient to vitiate consent to sexual intercourse. Note that a failure by a party to communicate that he/she has a sexually transmitted disease does not have any 2.47

---

[53] SOA 2003, s 74.
[54] *R v Bree* [2007] EWCA Crim 804, *R v Coates* [2008] 1 Cr App R 52 at [42] and *R v Kamki* [2013] EWCA Crim 2335.
[55] *R v C* [2009] UKHL 42, 'it is difficult to think of an activity which is more person and situation specific than sexual relations'.
[56] *R v PK; R v TK* [2008] EWCA Crim 434.
[57] *R v C* [2012] EWCA Crim 2034.
[58] *R v Robinson* [2011] EWCA Crim 916 and *R v Ali* [2015] EWCA Crim 1279.
[59] *R (F) v DPP* [2013] EWHC 945 (Admin). [2013] Cr App R 21.
[60] *Julian Assange v Swedish Prosecution Authority* [2011] EWHC 2849 (Admin).
[61] *R v McNally (Justine)* [2013] EWCA Crim 1051.
[62] *R (on the application of Monica) v DPP* [2018] EWHC 945 (Admin). The overriding principle to be applied is whether the 'deception which is closely connected with the "nature or purpose of the act", because it relates to sexual intercourse itself rather than the bad circumstances surrounding it is capable of negating a complainant's free exercise of choice for the purposes of section 74 of the 2003 Act' per the LCJ.
[63] *R v Lawrance* [2020] EWCA Crim 971.

32   2. RAPE

bearing on consent, notwithstanding the fact that the complainant would not have consented if he/she had known this fact.[64] Further, the Act introduces a presumption of lack of consent by the complainant in certain specified circumstances.[65] In addition, the defence of honest belief in consent, however unreasonable, has been eradicated by s 1(1)(c), which requires the prosecution to prove an absence of a reasonable belief in consent. An objectively judged unreasonably held belief in consent which arises from conditions such as delusional psychotic illness or personality disorders, is caught by s 1(1)(c),[66] and so does not afford a defence. See para 3.37.

Definition

Sexual Offences Act 2003, s 1

2.48 (1) A person (A) commits an offence if—
  (a) he intentionally penetrates the vagina, anus or mouth of another person (B) with the penis,
  (b) B does not consent to the penetration and
  (c) A does not reasonably believe B consents.
(2) Whether a belief is reasonable is to be determined having regard to all the circumstances, including any steps A has taken to ascertain whether B consents.

Proof

2.49 As per Definition. Further:

  (i) 'Penetration' is a continuing act from entry to withdrawal.[67]
  (ii) Any penetration of the female genitalia, however slight, by the penis of D is sufficient vaginal intercourse for the purposes of rape.[68]
  (iii) 'Vagina' includes vulva.[69]
  (iv) References to a part of the body include references to a part surgically constructed (in particular, through gender reassignment surgery).[70]
  (v) Absence of consent: consent is statutorily defined by section 74 as 'a person consents if he agrees by choice, and has the freedom and capacity to make that choice'. This definition is supplemented by ss 75 and 76 which set out the evidential and conclusive presumptions.
  (vi) A person lacks capacity if s/he lacks the capacity to choose, whether because s/he lacks sufficient understanding of the nature or reasonably foreseeable consequences of what is being done, or for any other reason.[71]

---

[64] *R v B* [2006] EWCA Crim 2945, [2007] 1 WLR 1567.
[65] SOA 2003, ss 75 and 76.
[66] *R v B (MA)* [2013] EWCA Crim 3.
[67] SOA 2003, s 79(2).
[68] *R v J.F.* [2002] Crim 2936.
[69] SOA 2003, s 79(9).
[70] SOA 2003, s 79(3).
[71] *R v A* [2014] EWCA Crim 299, decided in relation to offences under ss 30–33 of the Act.

(vii) Where relied upon, a lack of capacity is to be proven by the Crown to the criminal standard. Expert evidence is permissible but must be sufficiently 'expert' and confined to the issue of capacity.[72]

(ix) Evidential presumptions (section 75)

75 (1) If in proceedings for an offence to which this section applies it is proved—
   (a) that the defendant did the relevant act,
   (b) that any of the circumstances specified in subsection (2) existed, and
   (c) that the defendant knew that those circumstances existed,
   the complainant is to be taken not to have consented to the relevant act unless sufficient evidence is adduced to raise an issue as to whether he consented, and the defendant is to be taken not to have reasonably believed that the complainant consented unless sufficient evidence is adduced to raise an issue as to whether he reasonably believed it.

(2) The circumstances are that—
   (a) any person was, at the time of the relevant act or immediately before it began, using violence against the complainant or causing the complainant to fear that immediate violence would be used against him;
   (b) any person was, at the time of the relevant act or immediately before it began, causing the complainant to fear that violence was being used, or that immediate violence would be used, against another person;
   (c) the complainant was, and the defendant was not, unlawfully detained at the time of the relevant act;
   (d) the complainant was asleep or otherwise unconscious at the time of the relevant act;
   (e) because of the complainant's physical disability, the complainant would not have been able at the time of the relevant act to communicate to the defendant whether the complainant consented;
   (f) any person had administered to or caused to be taken by the complainant, without the complainant's consent, a substance which, having regard to when it was administered or taken, was capable of causing or enabling the complainant to be stupefied or overpowered at the time of the relevant act.

(3) In subsection (2)(a) and (b), the reference to the time immediately before the relevant act began is, in the case of an act which is one of a continuous series of sexual activities, a reference to the time immediately before the first sexual activity began.

(x) Conclusive presumptions (section 76):

76 (1) If in proceedings for an offence to which this section applies it is proved that the defendant did the relevant act and that any of the circumstances specified in subsection (2) existed, it is to be conclusively presumed—
   (a) that the complainant did not consent to the relevant act, and

---

[72] *R v A* [2014] EWCA Crim 299 incorporating the decision of the court in *IM v LM* (Capacity to consent to sexual relations) [2014] EWCA Civ 37: in determining capacity to consent to sexual activity civil and criminal courts should adopt the same test, necessarily informed by the definition and guidance contained in s 2 and s 3 of the 2005 Mental Capacity Act.

(b) that the defendant did not believe that the complainant consented to the relevant act.
(2) The circumstances are that—
(a) the defendant intentionally deceived the complainant as to the nature or purpose of the relevant act;
(b) the defendant intentionally induced the complainant to consent to the relevant act by impersonating a person known personally to the complainant.
(xi) See para 3.37 for intoxication and consent.

Notes

2.50
(i) The offence is indictable only.
(ii) Consideration should be given to alternative specific offences in relation to the mentally disordered, in appropriate circumstances.
(iii) Following the judgment in *R v Heard*[73] a plea of voluntary intoxication is no defence.[74]
(iv) If C consents to sexual intercourse then changes his/her mind during intercourse, D may be convicted if he has the requisite *mens rea*.[75]
(v) There is no requirement that C must demonstrate or communicate their lack of consent.[76]
(vi) It is not fateful to a prosecution that C cannot remember whether she consented or not.[77]
(vii) The issue of whether a defendant had reasonably believed that the complainant was consenting (under s 75) should only be left to the jury if there is some evidence that the defendant's belief was reasonable. The simple fact that the defendant believed the complainant to be consenting is not, without more, sufficient to enable the question to go to the jury.[78]
(viii) Section 76 is to be strictly construed, the cases to which s 76 applies will be rare.[79]
(ix) Mistaken identity is no defence.[80]
(x) In circumstances where the evidence is unclear as to whether penetration was of the vagina or anus, it is permissible to indict the two as alternatives in one count.[81]
(xi) A female may be convicted as an aider and abettor.[82] The secondary party may be convicted even if the principal is acquitted.[83]
(xii) The extended jurisdiction provisions apply to this section where the victim was under 18.[84] See Chapter 17 para 17.01.
(xiii) The s 45 MSA 2015 defence for slavery and trafficking victims who commit an offence does not apply to this offence.[85]

---

[73] [2007] EWCA Crim 125.
[74] Confirmed in *R v Grewal* [2010] EWCA Crim 2448, Elias LJ at [29].
[75] *R v Kaitamaki* (1985) AC 147 (PC).
[76] *R v Malone* [1998] and *R v Hysa* [2007] EWCA Crim 2056.
[77] *R v Tambedou (Seedy)* [2014] EWCA Crim 954.
[78] *R v Ciccarelli* [2011] EWCA Crim 2665.
[79] *R v Bingham* [2013] EWCA Crim 823
[80] *R v Whitta* [2006] EWCA Crim 2626.
[81] *R v K (Robert)* [2008] EWCA Crim 1923.
[82] *R v Ram* (1893) 17 Cox 609 (in 1893 referred to as principal in second degree).
[83] *R v Cogan (John Rodney)* [1976] QB 217.
[84] SOA 2003, s 72; provides for the prosecution within the jurisdiction of a sexual offence committed outside it.
[85] Modern Slavery Act 2015, s 45 and Sch 4, para 33.

F. OFFENCES COMMITTED FROM 1.5.2004 TO DATE

Indictment

RAPE 1.5.2004 to date **2.51**

Statement of Offence

RAPE, contrary to section 1(1) of the Sexual Offences Act 2003

Particulars of Offence

D on the … day of 20 …, intentionally penetrated with his penis the [vagina] or [anus][86] or [mouth] of C who did not consent to the penetration, D not reasonably believing that C consented.

Alternative Offences

(i) Attempted rape: LIFE. Attempt to commit the full offence. When indicting offences **2.52**
of attempt, do so under the CAA 1981.[87] Aver the attempt in both the Statement and Particulars of Offence. In addition, aver the substantive offence under the relevant Act; see paras 1.51 and 12.157 and *Reed & Others* [2021].[88]

Aver the attempt in both the Statement of Offence and Particulars of Offence.

(ii) s 3 sexual assault:[89] **10 YEARS** (see paras 3.45–3.52).
(iii) s 2 sexual assault LIFE (see paras 3.35–3.44).
(iv) s 4 causing a person to engage in sexual activity without consent:[90] LIFE (see paras 3.53–3.64).

Sentence

(i) For the full offence: LIFE.[91] **2.53**
(ii) For an attempt: LIFE.

Sentencing Guidance

The Sentencing Council 'Sexual Offences: Definitive Guideline' contains offence-specific **2.54**
guidelines for s 1 offences. The Guideline applies to all offenders aged 18 and over, sentenced on or after 1 April 2014.

---

[86] Where the evidence is unclear it is permissible to allege penetration of the vagina or anus. The jury must be sure that there was non-consensual penetration of one or the other. *R v K (Robert)* [2009] 1 Cr App R 24 CA.
[87] Implementation date 27.8.1981.
[88] *Reed & Others* [2021] EWCA Crim 572.
[89] SOA 2003, s 3.
[90] SOA 2003, s 1(4).
[91] SOA 2003, s 4.

Upon Conviction/Sentence

2.55
(i) Notification applies.[92]
(ii) Automatic inclusion in the children's barred list with no right to make representations where the victim was a child. Automatic inclusion in the children's barred list with the right to make representations where the victim was an adult. Automatic inclusion in the adults' barred list with the right to make representations.[93]
(iii) SHPO applies.[94]
(iv) Qualifying 'specified sexual offence' in Schedule 18 (Extended Sentences).[95]
(v) Qualifying Schedule 19 offence (Life Sentences).[96]
(vi) Qualifying Schedule 14 offence (Extended Sentences: The Earlier Offence Condition).[97]
(vi) Qualifying 'index' offence (if committed after 3 December 2012) for the purpose of Schedule 15 (Life Sentence for Second Listed Offence).[98]

---

[92] SOA 2003, s 80(1) and Sch 3, para 17; see Chapter 14, paras 14.1–14.5.
[93] Part 2 of the Safeguarding Vulnerable Groups Act 2006 (Prescribed Criteria and Miscellaneous Provisions) Regulations 2009 (SI 2009 No 37) paras 1, 2, and 4; see Chapter 12, para 12.217.
[94] SA 2020, s 345 and SOA 2003, Sch 3, para 17; see Chapter 16, para 16.07.
[95] SA 2020, s 306, Sch 18, para 38(a); see Chapter 12, para 12.51.
[96] SA 2020, s 307, Sch 19, para 20(a); see Chapter 12, para 12.52.
[97] SA 2020, ss 267 and 280, Sch 14, para 9(a); see Chapter 12, para 12.77.
[98] SA 2020, ss 273 and 283, Sch 15, para 9(a); see Chapter 12, para 12.123.

3
SEXUAL ASSAULTS

A. Introduction	3.01	D. Offences committed from 1.5.2004 to date	3.34
B. Offences committed pre-31.12.1956	3.03	1. Introduction	3.34
1. Indecent Assault	3.03	2. Assault by Penetration	3.37
C. Offences committed between 1.1.1957 and 30.4.2004	3.10	3. Sexual Assault	3.47
1. Indecent Assault on a Woman	3.12	4. Causing a Person to Engage in Sexual Activity Without Consent	3.55
2. Indecent Assault on a Man	3.25		
3. Assault with Intent to Commit Buggery	3.33		

A. INTRODUCTION

3.01 Prior to 31.12.1956, the law did not differentiate in relation to genders of the person assaulted. The first section of this chapter therefore applies equally to assaults upon males and females.

3.02 Thereafter, for allegations falling within the period 1.1.1957 to 30.4.2004, the chapter deals first with assaults upon women/girls and then with assaults upon men/boys under the 1956 Act, followed by assaults upon adults of both genders under the 2003 Act (commencement date 1.5.2004), which reverted to there being no differentiation between genders but does categorize offender and complainant.

B. OFFENCES COMMITTED PRE-31.12.1956

1. Indecent Assault

Offences Against the Person Act 1861, s 52

Definition

3.03 An assault, accompanied with circumstances of indecency on the part of the prisoner[1] (towards the person assaulted).[2]

---

[1] Lord Goddard CJ *Beal v Kelley* (1951) 35 Cr App R 128, 130.
[2] Words in parentheses added by the editors of Archbold, 33rd edn, 1954–1959.

38 3. SEXUAL ASSAULTS

Proof

3.04 (i) An assault (any unlawful touching).
(ii) The assault must be either obviously sexual itself or take place in circumstances which make the touching indecent.
(iii) The assault must be directed towards the person assaulted.

Notes

3.05 (i) Triable either way.
(ii) Where the assault is on a girl under 16 that fact should be stated in the indictment,[3] but an indictment is not defective without it.[4]
(iii) Belief that the girl upon whom the assault is committed was 16 years of age or more at the time the offence was committed affords no defence to the person accused.[5]
(iv) A woman may be guilty of an offence under this section.[6]
(v) Consent cannot be a defence where the indecent assault consists of the infliction of blows intended or likely to cause bodily harm,[7] although standards current at the time of the offence must apply. It is likely that current attitudes towards consensual sexual relations differ at different periods of time, according to social norms and therefore the view of injuries which are 'transient or trifling ... calculated to interfere with health or comfort',[8] will reflect those attitudes.[9]
(vi) The Divisional Court held[10] in the case of a man (the respondent) exposing himself to a 9-year-old girl and inviting her to touch his exposed penis, which she did: an invitation to another to touch the invitor could not amount to an assault on the invitee, and therefore there had been no assault and consequently no indecent assault. This lacuna was remedied by the implementation of s 1(1) of the Indecency with Children Act (IwCA) 1960[11] (see paras 4.05–4.17).
(vii) However, where a man asked a boy to handle his (the defendant's) penis and, when the boy refused, pulled the boy towards him before letting him go, it was held to be an indecent act (having the requisite ingredients of an assault in circumstances of indecency even although the act itself was not indecent).[12]
(viii) Indecent assault is an alternative to:
- Rape (see para 2.06).
- Having carnal knowledge of/unlawful sexual intercourse with a girl under 13[13] (see para 4.64).
- Having carnal knowledge of/unlawful sexual intercourse with a girl under 16[14] (see para 4.54).

---

[3] CLAA 1922, s 1.
[4] *R v Stephenson* [1912] 3 KB 341 and Indictments Act 1915.
[5] *R v Maughan* (1934) 24 Cr App R 130 and CLAA 1922, s 1.
[6] *R v Hare* [1934] 1 KB 354.
[7] *R v Brown (1993)* UK HL 19, (1994) 1 AC 212.
[8] *R v Donovan* [1934] 2 KB 498, 509 per Swift J.
[9] *R v Boyea* [1992] Crim LR 574 CA.
[10] *Fairclough v Whipp* (1951) 35 Cr App R 138 CA.
[11] Commencement date 2.7.1960.
[12] *Beal v Kelley* (1951) 35 Cr App R 128.
[13] CLAA 1885, s 4.
[14] CLAA 1885, s 5.

Indictment

INDECENT ASSAULT 1.11.1861 to 31.12.1956   **3.06**

> ### Statement of Offence
> INDECENT ASSAULT, contrary to section 52 of the Offences Against the Person Act 1861.
>
> ### Particulars of Offence
> D, on the … day of … 19/20…, indecently assaulted C.

Alternative Offences

Attempt to commit the full offence. When indicting offences of attempted indecent assault before 27.8.1981,[15] do so under common law. Aver the attempt in both the Statement and Particulars of Offence. In addition, aver the substantive offence under the relevant Act; see paras 1.51 and 12.157 and *Reed & Others* [2021].[16]   **3.07**

Sentence

(i) On indictment: **2 YEARS**.[17]   **3.08**
(ii) Summarily: **6 months**.

Upon Conviction/Sentence

(i) Notification not applicable.[18]   **3.09**
(ii) Automatic inclusion in the children's and adults' barred lists with right to make representations.[19]
(iii) SHPO not applicable.[20]

C. OFFENCES COMMITTED BETWEEN 1.1.1957 AND 30.4.2004

The SOA 1956 consolidated the law with regard to sexual offences. It introduced the specific offence of indecent assault on a man as well as a woman.   **3.10**

> The use in any provision of this Act of the word 'man' without the addition of the word 'boy', or *vice versa*, shall not prevent the provision applying to any person to whom it would have applied if both words had been used, and similarly with the words 'woman' and 'girl'.[21]

---

[15] CAA 1981; implementation date 27.8.1981.
[16] *Reed & Others* [2021] EWCA Crim 572.
[17] OAPA 1861, s 52.
[18] SOA 2003, s 80(1) (not included in Sch 3); see Chapter 14, Tables 14.2–14.5.
[19] Part 2 of the Safeguarding Vulnerable Groups Act 2006 (Prescribed Criteria and Miscellaneous Provisions) Regulations 2009 (SI 2009 No 37) paras 2 and 4; see Chapter 12, para 12.217.
[20] SA 2020, s 345 (not included in Sch 3 or Sch 5 SOA 2003); see Chapter 16, para 16.07.
[21] SOA 1956, s 46.

40   3. SEXUAL ASSAULTS

This applies equally for the purposes of the provisions of the SOA 1967[22] and has effect as if the reference to the SOA 1956 included a reference to the SO(A)A 1976.[23]

3.11 As of 31.12.1956, s 52 of the OAPA 1861 is repealed. From 1.1.1957, s 14 of the SOA 1956 replaces this offence as against a woman or girl. For indecent assault upon a man or boy, see para 3.23.

1. Indecent Assault on a Woman

Sexual Offences Act 1956, s 14

Definition

3.12 An assault, accompanied with circumstances of indecency on the part of the person assaulting towards the person alleged to have been assaulted.[24]

Proof

3.13 (i) An intentional assault (any unlawful touching) by D of C;
(ii) the assault, or the assault and the circumstances accompanying it, are capable of being considered by right-minded persons as indecent, and
(iii) that D intended not just an assault, but an indecent assault.

Notes

3.14 (i) Triable either way.
(ii) Where indecency is clear from the facts of the case there is no difficulty; however, where the circumstances of the assault could be innocent, the jury might be assisted by looking at surrounding factors, such as the relationship if any between D and C and how the assault/touching came about.[25]
(iii) Age must be averred when it will affect the maximum sentence available.[26] For offences which occurred between 2.7.1960 and 15.9.1985 inclusive, it is therefore essential to aver the girl's age if she is/was under 13 for the higher maximum sentence to be available.[27] See also para 1.07.

3.15 Indecent assault on a woman is itself an alternative to the following: rape;[28] unlawful sexual intercourse with a girl under 13; unlawful sexual intercourse with a girl under 16.[29] However, an historic prosecution charging indecent assault as an alternative to unlawful sexual intercourse with a girl under 16 is not possible following the majority opinions of the

---

[22] SOA 1967, s 11(3).
[23] SO(A)A 1976, s 7(2).
[24] R v Court [1989] AC 28 HL; defines and sets out the elements of the offence.
[25] R v Court [1989] AC 28 HL.
[26] R v Hodgson [1973] QB 565 CA, (1973) 57 Cr App R 502.
[27] IwCA 1960, s 2(1) Implementation date 2.7.1960; SOA 1985, s 3(3). Implementation date 16.9.1985.
[28] SOA 1956, s 37 and Sch 2, para 1(a)(ix).
[29] SOA 1956, s 37 and Sch 2, para 2(a).

House of Lords in *J*,[30] as it would circumvent the time-bar then in place for the primary offence. The SOA 2003 abolished any time-bar but it is not retrospective.

Prosecutors must be careful not to charge a s 14 SOA 1956 offence in circumstances where an IWCA offence would be appropriate. In *R v Dunn* [2015][31] Laws LJ made it plain that that inciting a female child to masturbate a male did not amount to an indecent assault. The argument that there could be no real distinction between a D touching a child and the child touching a D did not succeed. Laws LJ confirmed that there could be no indecent assault 'without some form of threat or show of force' to the victim. **3.16**

It follows that prosecutors cannot attempt to circumvent the problem which arises from the fact that a s 1 IWCA offence was not extended to children aged 14–16 until 11.1.2001, by charging an offence under s 14 SOA 1956. See paras 4.07–4.09. **3.17**

It is important that indictments based upon allegations which either potentially or actually straddle any implementation date are carefully drawn so that they do not run through a commencement date and so that a sentencing judge is mindful of the change in the maximum sentence(s) available to him/her.[32] Counts in an indictment which do straddle an implementation date will limit the sentencer to the lower maximum of the two Acts, unless it is obvious from the way in which the case has been conducted that the offences took place after the later Act came into force.[33] See also para 1.23. **3.18**

(i) A girl under the age of 16 cannot in law give any consent which would prevent an act being an assault for the purposes of this section.[34]
(ii) A defence is provided by D's reasonable belief that C is his wife; the fact that the marriage is in fact invalid by virtue of C's age (being under 16)[35] does not make D guilty.[36]
(iii) A woman who is classed as a 'defective' cannot in law give any consent which would prevent an act being an assault for the purposes of this section. However, a person is only to be treated as guilty of an indecent assault on a mentally disordered woman by reason of that incapacity to consent, if that person knew or had reason to suspect her to be a 'defective'.[37]

See Chapter 7 for assaults upon 'defectives'.

Indictment

INDECENT ASSAULT ON A WOMAN 1.1.1957 to 30.4.2004 **3.19**

Statement of Offence
INDECENT ASSAULT, contrary to section 14 of the Sexual Offences Act 1956.

Particulars of Offence
D, on the ... day of ... 19/20... , indecently assaulted C (add C's age if under 13).

---

[30] *R v J* [2004] UKHL 42, Baroness Hale dissenting.
[31] *R v Dunn* [2015] EWCA Crim 724 at para [10].
[32] *R v R (Paul Brian)* [1993] Crim LR 541; no distinction had been drawn when drafting the indictment between the Acts, nor was there any proper citation of age leading to the higher maximum. This gave rise to the sentencing judge passing all sentences under the lower maximum provision and under one Act.
[33] *R v R* [1993] Crim LR 541.
[34] SOA 1956, s 14(2).
[35] Age of Marriage Act (AMA) 1929, ss 1 and 2.
[36] SOA 1956, s 14(3).
[37] SOA 1956, s 14(4).

Alternative Offences

3.20 (i) Attempt to commit the full offence. When indicting offences of attempt, do so under the common law until 26.8.1981;[38] thereafter, under the Criminal Attempts Act 1985. In addition, aver the substantive offence under the relevant Act; see paras 1.51 and 12.157 and *Reed & Others* [2021].[39]

(ii) Common assault; **6 months, fine, or both**[40] although this must now be included in the indictment.[41]

Sentence

3.21 (i) On indictment: **2 YEARS**, or **5 YEARS** after 2.7.1960 if the complainant is a girl under 13 and that fact is averred.[42]

- Note: maximum increased to **10 YEARS** after 16.9.1985;[43] therefore no need to average (for this reason alone) after that date.

(ii) Summarily: **6 months**.

Sentencing Guidance

3.22 (i) Sentencing a charge of indecent assault laid because of the time-bar to unlawful sexual intercourse with a girl under 16 will no longer arise and so the sentencing guidance which existed prior to the decision in *J*[44] is obsolete. However, where the facts of a case include a separate indecent assault (or any other separate offence) common sense dictates—and the House of Lords concurs[45]—that it is perfectly proper to charge that without the unlawful sexual intercourse.

(ii) Sentence must be passed in accordance with the factual basis reflected by a jury's verdict(s).[46]

(iii) The fact that a young person who is indecently assaulted has been sexually abused before may well increase the gravity of the offence and is certainly no mitigation.[47]

(iv) Cases decided before the implementation of an Act which alter the maximum sentences are not to be regarded as authoritative when considering the tariff after the increase.[48]

---

[38] CAA 1981; s 1 commencement date 27.8.1981.
[39] *Reed & Others* [2021] EWCA Crim 572.
[40] *R v Bostock* (1893) 17 Cox 700.
[41] *R v Mearns* (1990) 91 Cr App R 312.
[42] 2.7.1960; IwCA 1960 was implemented, impacting on sentence for indecent assault, in that by s 2(1) it amended the SOA 1956, s 37 and Sch 2, para 17 to increase the sentence to 5 years if the indecent assault was on a girl under 13 years and that fact was stated in the indictment. (Otherwise, the maximum is still 2 years.)
[43] SOA 1985, s 3(3). Implementation date 16.9.1985.
[44] *R v J* [2004] UKHL 42; the House of Lords, overruling the Court of Appeal ruled that substituting indecent assault to circumvent the time-bar was not lawful.
[45] *R v J* [2004] UKHL 42.
[46] *R v Gillespie* [1998] Crim LR 139; *R v Isles* [1998] Crim LR 140.
[47] *A-G's Reference (No 2 of 1995)* [1996] 1 Cr App R(S) 274.
[48] *R v L* [1999] 1 Cr App R 117 CA.

Upon Conviction/Sentence

(i) Notification applies where the other party was under 18 or the offender is sentenced to at least 30 months' imprisonment or admitted to hospital subject to a restriction order.[49] **3.23**
(ii) Automatic inclusion in the children's and adults' barred lists with right to make representations.[50]
(iii) SHPO applies.[51]
(iv) Qualifying 'specified sexual offence' in Schedule 18 (Extended Sentences).[52]

The SOA 2003 repealed this section in full on 30.4.2004. See paras 3.40 and 3.47 for the offences which now cover indecent assault. **3.24**

2. Indecent Assault on a Man

Sexual Offences Act 1956, s 15

Introduction

The SOA 1956 consolidated the law with regard to sexual offences. It introduced the specific offence of indecent assault on a man as well as a woman. **3.25**

> The use in any provision of this Act of the word 'man' without the addition of the word 'boy', or vice versa, shall not prevent the provision applying to any person to whom it would have applied if both words had been used, and similarly with the words 'woman' and 'girl'.[53]

This applies equally for the purposes of the provisions of the SOA 1967[54] and has effect as if the reference to the SOA 1956 included a reference to the SO(A)A 1976.[55]

Definition

An assault, accompanied with circumstances of indecency on the part of the person assaulting towards the person alleged to have been assaulted.[56] **3.26**

Proof

(i) An intentional assault (any unlawful touching) by D of C; **3.27**
(ii) the assault, or the assault and the circumstances accompanying it, are capable of being considered by right-minded persons as indecent; and
(iii) that D intended not just an assault, but an indecent assault.

---

[49] SOA 2003, s 80(1), Sch 3, para 7; see Chapter 14, paras 14.1–14.5.
[50] Part 2 of the Safeguarding Vulnerable Groups Act 2006 (Prescribed Criteria and Miscellaneous Provisions) Regulations 2009 (SI 2009 No 37) paras 2 and 4; see Chapter 12, para 12.217.
[51] SA 2020, s 345 and Sch 3, para 7 SOA 2003; see Chapter 16, para 16.07.
[52] SA 2020, s 306, Sch 18, para 29(j); see Chapter 12, para 12.51.
[53] SOA 1956, s 46.
[54] SOA 1967, s 11(3).
[55] SO(A)A 1976, s 7(2).
[56] *R v Court* [1989] AC 28 HL; defines and sets out the elements of the offence.

Notes

3.28   (i) Triable either way.

(ii) A woman may be guilty of this offence;[57] the sexual touching by a woman of a boy under 16, even as part of or preliminary to an act of sexual intercourse and with his consent, is an offence.[58]

(iii) A boy under the age of 16 cannot in law give any consent which would prevent an act being an assault for the purposes of this section.[59]

(iv) A man who is a 'defective'[60] cannot in law give any consent which would prevent an act being an assault for the purposes of this section, but a person is only to be treated as guilty of an indecent assault on a mentally disordered man by reason of that incapacity to consent, if that person knew or had reason to suspect him to be mentally disordered.[61]

(v) Section 39 of this Act (which makes the spouse of the defendant not competent as a witness) does not apply in the case of this section, except on a charge of indecent assault on a boy under the age of 17.[62]

(vi) Indecent assault on a man is itself an alternative to: buggery; attempt to commit buggery; assault with intent to commit buggery. See paras 5.48–5.91.

Indictment

3.29   INDECENT ASSAULT ON A MALE 1.1.1957 to 30.4.2004

Statement of Offence

INDECENT ASSAULT, contrary to section 15(1) of the Sexual Offences Act 1956.

Particulars of Offence

D, on the ... day of ... 19/20..., indecently assaulted C, a man/boy (where the person is under 16 years add the age).

Alternative Offences

3.30   (i) Attempt to commit the full offence. When indicting offences of attempt, do so under the common law until 26.8.1981;[63] thereafter, under the CAA 1981. See para 1.43. Aver the attempt in both the Statement and Particulars of Offence. In addition, aver the substantive offence under the relevant Act; see paras 1.51 and 12.157 and *Reed & Others* [2021].[64]

(ii) Common assault,[65] **6 months, fine, or both** although this must now be included in the indictment.[66]

---

[57] *R v Hare* [1934] 1 KB 354.
[58] *R v Faulkner v Talbot* (1982) 74 Cr App R 1.
[59] SOA 1956, s 15(2).
[60] 'Defective' is the term used within the SOA 2003 for a mentally disordered person, as it was within the 1956 Act.
[61] SOA 1956, s 15(3).
[62] SOA 1956, s 15(4).
[63] CAA 1981; implementation date 27.8.1981.
[64] *Reed & Others* [2021] EWCA Crim 572.
[65] *R v Bostock* (1893) 17 Cox 700.
[66] *R v Mearns* (1990) 91 Cr App R 312.

Sentence

3.31
(i) On indictment: **10 YEARS**.[67]
(ii) Summarily: **6 months**.[68]

Upon Conviction/Sentence

3.32
(i) Notification applies where the other party was under 18 or the offender is sentenced to at least 30 months' imprisonment or admitted to a hospital subject to a restriction order.[69]
(ii) Automatic inclusion in the children's and adults' barred lists with right to make representations applicable where the other party was under 16 years and did not consent and the offence has not been 'disregarded'[70] (see para 5.01).[71]
(iii) SHPO applies.[72]
(iv) Qualifying 'specified sexual offence' in Schedule 18 (Extended Sentences).[73]

3. Assault with Intent to Commit Buggery

Sexual Offences Act 1956, s 16

See para 5.75 where this offence is set out. **3.33**

D. OFFENCES COMMITTED FROM 1.5.2004 TO DATE

1. Introduction

On 30.4.2004 ss 14 and 15 were repealed. With the implementation of the SOA 2003 on 1.5.2004 came the introduction of a number of new offences and the re-wording of others. Sentences and the notification provisions were also amended. **3.34**

The umbrella offence of 'indecent assault' was replaced by a number of potential alternative offences, breaking down the types of assault and the categories of complainant. The SOA 2003 creates offences based on 'touching' as defined in s 79(8) and further explained in *R v H*.[74] Section 3 sexual assault is an example of this. The shift from 'assault' in 'indecent assault' under the old law as opposed to 'touching' under the new law in 'sexual assault' is significant, and, in some respects, narrows the scope of the offence. See para 3.37. **3.35**

The following section deals only with adult complainants; for sexual assaults upon children see Chapter 4, Part A. **3.36**

---

[67] SOA 1956, s 37(3) and Sch 2, para 18.
[68] SOA 1956, s 37(3) and Sch 2, para 18. Increased to 12 months if CJA 2003, s 282(4) implemented.
[69] SOA 2003, s 80(1), Sch 3, para 8; see Chapter 14, paras 14.1–14.5.
[70] Disregarded conviction or caution within the meaning of Chapter 5 of Pt 5 of the Protection of Freedoms Act 2012.
[71] Part 2 of the Safeguarding Vulnerable Groups Act 2006 (Prescribed Criteria and Miscellaneous Provisions) Regulations 2009 (SI 2009 No 37), Sch 1 paras 2 and 4; see Chapter 12 para 12.217.
[72] SA 2020, s 345 and Sch 3, para 8 SOA 2003; see Chapter 16, para 16.07.
[73] SA 2020, s 306, Sch 18, para 29(k); see Chapter 12, para 12.51.
[74] *R v H* [2005] EWCA Crim 732.

2. Assault by Penetration

Sexual Offences Act 2003, s 2

Definition

3.37 As per Proof.

Proof

3.38 D assaults C by intentional sexual penetration of either the vagina or anus with a part of D's body or anything else when at the time C does not consent and D does not reasonably believe that C consents.

Notes

3.39 (i) Indictable only.
   (ii) 'Sexual' is defined by SOA 2003, s 78:

   'Sexual' touching is sexual if a reasonable person would consider that—(a) whatever its circumstances or any person's purpose in relation to it, it is because of its nature sexual, or (b) because of its nature it may be sexual and because of its circumstances or the purpose of any person in relation to it (or both) it is sexual.

   (iii) R v H[75] is the leading authority: where s 78(b) applied because the nature of the touching concerned was not inevitably sexual, it would be desirable for a judge to identify two distinct questions for the jury:
   - whether they, as 12 reasonable people, considered that, because of its nature, the touching might be sexual;
   - and, if so,
   - whether, in view of the circumstances and/or the purpose of any person in relation to it, the touching was in fact sexual. It was clear from the use of the words 'because of its nature may be sexual', which would otherwise be surplus, that there were two requirements to s 78(b).

   (iv) Consent is defined by the 2003 Act, s 74, to the extent that it provides: 'a person consents if he agrees by choice, and has the freedom and capacity to make that choice.' This definition plainly relates to mental capacity and is important to have in mind when dealing with the often problematic issue of the complainant's lack of capacity through intoxication. The level of intoxication will obviously affect the capability to make a free choice. The government's intention in creating a set of evidential presumptions, was that these would not cover voluntary intoxication leading to incapacity falling short of sleep or a lack of consciousness:

   I have rejected the suggestion that someone who is inebriated could claim they were unable to give consent—as opposed to someone who is unconscious for whatever

---

[75] [2005] EWCA Crim 732, [2005] Crim LR 735.

reason, including because of alcohol—on the ground that we do not want mischievous accusations.[76]

However, following the case of R v Dougal,[77] the government was considering new legislation on this issue: 'Does the law on capacity need to be changed. Should there be a statutory definition of capacity?'[78]

There has been no further legislation and Court of Appeal has since addressed the question in R v Bree [2007].[79] The following extracts are taken from the judgment of the court, delivered by the President of the Queen's Bench Division, Sir Igor Judge:

This appeal required us to address the effect of voluntary heavy alcohol consumption as it applies to the law of rape.

... at the start of the trial the prosecution alleged that the appellant raped M when her level of intoxication was so great that she was effectively unconscious. She lacked the capacity to consent, and therefore did not consent. However, by the end of the evidence, the prosecution case against the appellant had changed. The jury were no longer invited to conclude that M had been unable to consent to intercourse because she was unconscious, rather, the prosecution accepted that the gaps in her recollection were probably the result of intoxication, and lack of memory, rather than unconsciousness. The prosecution case, therefore, was not that the complainant lacked the capacity to consent, but that she did not in fact consent to intercourse. Her ability to resist was hampered by the effects of alcohol, but her capacity to consent remained. She knew what was happening. She knew that she did not want to have sexual intercourse, and so far as she could, made that clear. The appellant's case, as we have indicated, was unchanged from start to finish, that notwithstanding, and perhaps because of drink, M was consenting. He reasonably believed that she was.

... it is clear that for the purposes of the 2003 Act 'capacity' is integral to the concept of 'choice', and therefore to 'consent'.

... Some of the hugely critical discussion arising after Dougal missed the essential point. Neither counsel for the Crown, nor for that matter the judge, was saying or coming anywhere near saying, either that a complainant who through drink is incapable of consenting to intercourse must nevertheless be deemed to have consented to it, or that a man is at liberty to have sexual intercourse with a woman who happens to be drunk, on the basis that her drunkenness deprives her of her right to choose whether to have intercourse or not. Such ideas are wrong in law, and indeed, offensive. All that was being said in Dougal was that when someone who has had a lot to drink is in fact consenting to intercourse, then that is what she is doing, consenting: equally, if after taking drink, she is not consenting, then by definition intercourse is taking place without her consent. This is unexceptionable.

... In our judgment, the proper construction of section 74 of the 2003 Act, as applied to the problem now under discussion, leads to clear conclusions. If, through drink (or for any other reason) the complainant has temporarily lost her capacity to choose whether to have intercourse on the relevant occasion, she is not consenting, and subject to questions about the defendant's state of mind, if intercourse takes

---

[76] Home Office (2002), *Protecting the Public; Strengthening Protection Against Sex Offenders and Reforming the Law on Sexual offences*, Home Office Consultation Paper, Cmnd 5668, November.

[77] [2005] Swansea Crown Court; jury directed to return a verdict of 'not guilty' after prosecution counsel informed him that the Crown did not propose to proceed further because they were unable to prove that the complainant had not given consent because of her level of intoxication.

[78] Government Paper after *R v Dougal; Convicting Rapists and Protecting Victims*.

[79] R v Bree [2007] EWCA Crim 804. See also *R v Evans (Chedwyn)* [2012] Crim 2559 and *R v Kamki* [2013] EWCA Crim 2335.

place, this would be rape. However, where the complainant has voluntarily consumed even substantial quantities of alcohol, but nevertheless remains capable of choosing whether or not to have intercourse, and in drink agrees to do so, this would not be rape. We should perhaps underline that, as a matter of practical reality, capacity to consent may evaporate well before a complainant becomes unconscious. Whether this is so or not, however, is fact specific, or more accurately, depends on the actual state of mind of the individuals involved on the particular occasion.

… Considerations like these underline the fact that it would be unrealistic to endeavour to create some kind of grid system which would enable the answer to these questions to be related to some prescribed level of alcohol consumption. Experience shows that different individuals have a greater or lesser capacity to cope with alcohol than others, and indeed the ability of a single individual to do so may vary from day to day. The practical reality is that there are some areas of human behaviour which are inapt for detailed legislative structures. In this context, provisions intended to protect women from sexual assaults might very well be conflated into a system which would provide patronising interference with the right of autonomous adults to make personal decisions for themselves.

… For these reasons, notwithstanding criticisms of the statutory provisions, in our view the 2003 Act provides a clear definition of 'consent' for the purposes of the law of rape, and by defining it with reference to 'capacity to make that choice', sufficiently addresses the issue of consent in the context of voluntary consumption of alcohol by the complainant. The problems do not arise from the legal principles. They lie with infinite circumstances of human behaviour, usually taking place in private without independent evidence, and the consequent difficulties of proving this very serious offence.

See also paras 2.45, 2.46, and 2.47 re: consent.

(v) Specific intention and defendant's voluntary intoxication: R v Heard:[80]

It is not open to a defendant charged with sexual assault to contend that his voluntary intoxication prevented him from intending to touch. The Judge was accordingly correct, not only to direct the jury that the touching must be deliberate, but also to direct it that the defence that voluntary drunkenness rendered him unable to form the intent to touch was not open to him.[81]

(vi) 'Vagina' includes vulva.[82]
(vii) References to a part of the body include references to a part surgically constructed (in particular, through gender reassignment surgery).[83]
(viii) The ss 75 and 76 presumptions about consent apply to this offence. See para 2.47 (ix) and (x).
(ix) The extended jurisdiction provisions apply to this section where the victim of the offence was under 18.[84] See Chapter 17 para 17.01.
(x) The s 45 MSA 2015 defence for slavery and trafficking victims who commit an offence does not apply to this offence.[85]

---

[80] [2007] EWCA Crim 125.
[81] Per Hughes LJ at para 25.
[82] SOA 2003, s 79(9).
[83] SOA 2003, s 79(3).
[84] SOA 2003, s 72; provides for the prosecution within the jurisdiction of a sexual offence committed outside it.
[85] Modern Slavery Act 2015, s 45 and Sch 4, para 33.

Following the judgment in Heard, it seems that all the sexual offences in the 2003 Act (certainly those in ss 1–4 and 5–15) will be regarded as offences for which a plea of voluntary intoxication is no defence.[86]   **3.40**

Note also the judgment of the Court of Appeal in *R v H*,[87] an expedited prosecution appeal during trial, during which both Bree and Dougal were considered. Per Hallett LJ, delivering the judgment of the full court in allowing the appeal: **3.41**

> Issues of consent and capacity to consent to intercourse in cases of rape should normally be left to a jury to determine. It would be a rare case indeed where it would be appropriate for a judge to stop a case in which, on one view, a 16 year old girl, alone at night and vulnerable through drink, is picked up by a stranger who has sex with her within minutes of meeting her and she says repeatedly she would not have consented to sex in these circumstances.

Indictment

ASSAULT BY PENETRATION 1.5.2004 to date   **3.42**

Statement of Offence
ASSAULT BY PENETRATION, contrary to section 2(1) of the Sexual Offences Act 2003.

Particulars of Offence
D, on the … day of … 20…, intentionally and sexually penetrated the [vagina] *or* [anus] of C with [his finger] *or* [a part of his body, namely his … or with a …], C did not consent to the penetration, and D did not reasonably believe that C was consenting.

Alternative Offences

Attempt to commit the full offence. When indicting offences of attempt, do so under the Criminal Attempts Act 1981. Aver the attempt in both the statement and particulars of offence. In addition, aver the substantive offence under the relevant Act; see paras 1.51 and 12.157 and *Reed & Others* [2021].[88]   **3.43**

Sentence

On indictment: LIFE.   **3.44**

Sentencing Guidance

The Sentencing Council 'Sexual Offences: Definitive Guideline' contains offence-specific guidelines for s2 offences. The Guideline applies to all offenders aged 18 and over, sentenced on or after 1 April 2014.   **3.45**

---

[86] Professor David Ormerod QC CBE, March 2007.
[87] [2007] EWCA Crim 2056.
[88] *Reed & Others* [2021] EWCA Crim 572

50   3. SEXUAL ASSAULTS

Upon Conviction/Sentence

3.46   (i) Notification applies.[89]
(ii) Automatic inclusion in the children's barred list with no right to make representations where the victim was a child. Automatic inclusion in the children's barred list with the right to make representations where the victim was an adult. Automatic inclusion in the adults' barred list with the right to make representations.[90]
(iii) SHPO applies.[91]
(iv) Qualifying 'specified sexual offence' in Schedule 18 (Extended Sentences).[92]
(v) Qualifying Schedule 19 offence (Life Sentences).[93]
(vi) Qualifying Schedule 14 offence (Extended Sentences: The Earlier Offence Condition).[94]
(vii) Qualifying 'index' offence (if committed after 3 December 2012) for the purpose of Schedule 15 (Life Sentence for Second Listed Offence).[95]

3. Sexual Assault

Sexual Offences Act 2003, s 3

Definition

3.47   As per **Proof**.

Proof

3.48   D intentionally and sexually touches C who does not consent to it and D does not reasonably believe that C is consenting.

Notes

3.49   (i) Triable either way.
(ii) 'Sexual' is defined by the SOA 2003, s 78.
(iii) The SOA 2003 creates offences based on 'touching' as defined in s 79(8) and further explained in *R v H*.[96] Section 3 sexual assault is an example of this. The shift from 'assault' in 'indecent assault' under the old law as opposed to 'touching' under the

---

[89] SOA 2003, s 80(1) and Sch 3, para 17; see Chapter 14, paras 14.1–14.5.
[90] Part 2 of the Safeguarding Vulnerable Groups Act 2006 (Prescribed Criteria and Miscellaneous Provisions) Regulations 2009 (SI 2009 No 37) paras 1, 2, and 4; see Chapter 12, para 12.217.
[91] SA 2020, s 345, s 104 and Sch 3, para 17 SOA 2003; see Chapter 16, para 16.07.
[92] SA 2020, s 306, Sch 18, para 38(b); see Chapter 12, para 12.51.
[93] SA 2020, s 307, Sch 19, para 20(b); see Chapter 12, para 12.52.
[94] SA 2020, ss 267 and 280, Sch 14, para 9(b); see Chapter 12, para 12.77.
[95] SA 2020, ss 273 and 283, Sch 15, para 9(b); see Chapter 12, para 12.123.
[96] *R v H* [2005] EWCA Crim 732.

D. OFFENCES COMMITTED FROM 1.5.2004 TO DATE

new law in 'sexual assault' is significant, and, in some respects, narrows the scope of the offence. Examples which might have been an indecent assault, but would not be a sexual assault under the SOA, s 3 as the offence is based on touching include:
- Sexual words alone without touching.
- Defendant walking towards someone with his penis exposed.[97]
- Soaking the complainant's T-shirt without physical contact.[98]
- Touching the complainant's clothing without touching the person.[99]

(iv) *Mens rea*: proof that the offender intended the touching of the complainant to be sexual is not required.[100]
(v) Consent; see **Notes** at para 3.37.
(vi) Defendant's intoxication; see Notes at para 3.37.
(vii) The ss 75 and 76 presumptions about consent apply to this offence. See para 2.47 (ix) and (x).
(viii) The extended jurisdiction provisions apply to this section where the victim of the offence was under 18.[101] See Chapter 17 para 17.01.
(ix) The s 45 MSA 2015 defence for slavery and trafficking victims who commit an offence does not apply to this offence.[102]

Indictment

SEXUAL ASSAULT 1.5.2004 to date   **3.50**

Statement of Offence

SEXUAL ASSAULT, contrary to section 3(1) of the Sexual Offences Act 2003.

Particulars of Offence

D, on the ... day of ... 20..., intentionally and sexually touched C, C did not consent to the touching, and D did not reasonably believe that C consented.

OR:

D, on the ... day of ... 20..., intentionally touched C, the circumstances being that the touching was sexual, C did not consent to the touching, and D did not reasonably believe that C consented.

Alternative Offences

Attempt to commit the full offence. When indicting offences of attempt, do so under the Criminal Attempts Act 1981. Aver the attempt in both the statement and particulars of offence. In addition, aver the substantive offence under the relevant Act; see paras 1.51 and 12.157 and *Reed & Others* [2021].[103]   **3.51**

---

[97] *R v Rolfe* (1952) 36 Cr App R 4.
[98] J.C. Smith and Brian Hogan, *Criminal Law*, 3rd edn (London: Butterworths, 1973), p 614.
[99] *R v H* [2005] EWCA Crim 732 (note para 26) even though V is not being touched through the clothing.
[100] *Attorney General's Reference (No 1 of 2020)* [2020] EWCA Crim 1665, paras [30]–[46] for discussion.
[101] SOA 2003, s 72; provides for the prosecution within the jurisdiction of a sexual offence committed outside it.
[102] Modern Slavery Act 2015, s 45 and Sch 4, para 33.
[103] *Reed & Others* [2021] EWCA Crim 572.

Sentence

3.52   (i) On indictment: **10 YEARS**.
(ii) Summarily: **6 months**.[104]

Sentencing Guidance

3.53   The Sentencing Council 'Sexual Offences: Definitive Guideline' contains offence-specific guidelines for section 3 offences. The Guideline applies to all offenders aged 18 and over, sentenced on or after 1 April 2014.

Note: Where the offence involved a sexual assault on an emergency worker, this must be treated as an aggravating factor and it must be stated in open court that the offence is so aggravated.[105]

Upon Conviction/Sentence

3.54   (i) Notification applies (1) where the offender is under 18 and has been sentenced to imprisonment for a term of at least 12 months or (2) in any other case the victim was under 18 *or* the offender has been sentenced to a term of imprisonment, detained in a hospital or made the subject of a community order of at least 12 months.[106]
(ii) Automatic inclusion in the children's and adults' barred lists with the right to make representations.[107]
(iii) SHPO applies.[108]
(iv) Qualifying 'specified sexual offence' in Schedule 18 (Extended Sentences).[109]

4. Causing a Person to Engage in Sexual Activity Without Consent

Sexual Offences Act 2003, s 4

Introduction

3.55   This is an offence created by the SOA 2003 covering sexual behaviour which has no direct precedent in law. It is included in this chapter for convenience, although it plainly covers activity which does not necessarily involve an assault by D, such as engaging in a conversation or web chat of a sexual nature.[110] There are a number of similar offences without precedent, for example those relating to child complainants, dealt with at Chapter 4 from para 4.189.

---

[104] 12 months if CJA 2003, s 282(4) implemented.
[105] Assaults on Emergency Workers (Offences) Act 2018, s 2.
[106] SOA 2003, s 80(1) and Sch 3, para 18; see Chapter 14, paras 14.1–14.5.
[107] Part 2 of the Safeguarding Vulnerable Groups Act 2006 (Prescribed Criteria and Miscellaneous Provisions) Regulations 2009 (SI 2009 No 37) paras 2 and 4; see Chapter 12, para 12.217.
[108] SA 2020, s 345 and SOA 2003, Sch 3, para 18; see Chapter 16, para 16.07.
[109] SA 2020, s 306, Sch 18, para 38(c); see Chapter 12, para 12.51.
[110] *R v Grout* [2011] EWCA Crim 299, para 29.

Definition

As per Proof. **3.56**

Proof

Section 4(1): D intentionally causes another person (C) to engage in a sexual activity when C is not consenting, and D does not reasonably believe that C is consenting. **3.57**

Penetration; also indict under s 4(4) where the sexual activity involves or includes: **3.58**

(a) penetration of C's anus or vagina;
(b) penetration of C's mouth with a person's (X or Y) penis;
(c) penetration of a person's (X or Y's) anus or vagina with part of C's body or by C with anything else;
(d) penetration of a person's (X or Y's) mouth with C's penis.

Notes

(i) Triable either way if non-penetrative; triable on indictment only if penetration is alleged. **3.59**
(ii) Whether a belief in consent is reasonable is to be determined having regard to all the circumstances, including any steps D has taken to ascertain whether C consents.[111]
(iii) A belief induced by a defendant's mental illness (short of insanity) or personality disorder must be judged by objective standards of reasonableness and not by taking into account the defendant's disorder: *R v B (MA)* at paras 40 and 41.[112] See also para 2.46.
(iv) The evidential and conclusive presumptions (SOA 2003, ss 75 and 76) apply to this section.[113] See paras 2.47 (ix) and (x).
(v) 'Vagina' includes vulva.[114]
(vi) References to a part of the body include references to a part surgically constructed (in particular, through gender reassignment surgery).[115]
(vii) This offence is an alternative to rape.
(viii) The parties to the offence can be of either gender and there is no age restriction but note: if C is under 13 the offence should be charged under s 8 (see para 4.33).
If C is a child aged 13, 14 or 15 the offence should be charged under s 10 (see para 4.18).
If D is aged 18 or over and in a position of trust towards C and C is aged 16 or 17, the offence should be charged under s 17 (see para 4.162).
(ix) The extended jurisdiction provisions apply to this section where the victim of the offence was under 18.[116] See Chapter 17 para 17.01.

---

[111] SOA 2003, s 4(2).
[112] [2013] EWCA Crim 3.
[113] SOA 2003, s 4(3).
[114] SOA 2003, s 79(9).
[115] SOA 2003, s 79(3).
[116] SOA 2003, s 72; provides for the prosecution within the jurisdiction of a sexual offence committed outside it.

(x) The s 45 MSA 2015 defence for slavery and trafficking victims who commit an offence does not apply to this offence.[117]

Indictment

Non-penetrative activity

3.60 CAUSING A PERSON TO ENGAGE IN SEXUAL ACTIVITY WITHOUT CONSENT
1.5.2004 to date

Statement of Offence
CAUSING A PERSON TO ENGAGE IN SEXUAL ACTIVITY WITHOUT CONSENT, contrary to section 4(1) of the Sexual Offences Act 2003.

Particulars of Offence
D, on the … day of … 20… , intentionally caused C to engage in a sexual activity, namely …, when C did not consent to engage in the said activity and D did not reasonably believe that C was consenting.

Penetrative activity

3.61 CAUSING A PERSON TO ENGAGE IN SEXUAL ACTIVITY WITHOUT CONSENT
1.5.2004 to date

Statement of Offence
CAUSING A PERSON TO ENGAGE IN PENETRATIVE SEXUAL ACTIVITY, contrary to sections 4(1) and (4) of the Sexual Offences Act 2003.

Particulars of Offence
D, on the … day of … 20… , intentionally caused C to engage in a sexual activity, [namely …,] involving the penetration of … with … when C did not consent to engaging in the said activity and D did not reasonably believe that C was consenting.

Alternative Offences

3.62 Attempt to commit the full offence. Indict under the Criminal Attempts Act 1981.[118] Aver the attempt in both the Statement and Particulars of Offence. In addition, aver the substantive offence under the relevant Act; see paras 1.51 and 12.157 and *Reed & Others* [2021].[119]

---

[117] Modern Slavery Act 2015, s 45 and Sch 4, para 33.
[118] Implementation date 27.8.1981.
[119] *Reed & Others* [2021] EWCA Crim 572

D. OFFENCES COMMITTED FROM 1.5.2004 TO DATE

Sentence[120]

On indictment: 3.63

(i) Without penetration **10 YEARS**.
(ii) With penetration **LIFE**.

Summarily: **6 months**.[121]

Sentencing Guidance

The Sentencing Council 'Sexual Offences: Definitive Guideline' contains offence-specific guidelines for section 3 offences. The Guideline applies to all offenders aged 18 and over, sentenced on or after 1 April 2014. 3.64

Upon Conviction/Sentence

(i) Notification applies.[122] 3.65
(ii) Automatic inclusion in the children's and adults' barred lists with the right to make representations.[123]
(iii) SHPO applies.[124]
(iv) Qualifying 'specified sexual offence' in Schedule 18 (Extended Sentences).[125]
(v) Qualifying Schedule 19 offence (Life Sentences) where the offender liable to life imprisonment (s 4(1)(a) offence).[126]
(vi) Qualifying Schedule 14 offence (Extended Sentences: The Earlier Offence Condition) where the offender liable to life imprisonment (s 4(1)(a) offence).[127]
(vii) Qualifying 'index' offence (if committed after 3 December 2012) for the purpose of Schedule 15 (Life Sentence for Second Listed Offence) if the offender is liable on conviction on indictment to life imprisonment.[128]

Child Complainants

These are dealt with in Chapter 4, Part A and Chapter 6. The following are the direct alternative offences under the SOA 2003 to indecent assault (of a child): 3.66

(i) Child not related to Defendant and Defendant not in position of trust:
Sexual Activity with a Child; s 9 SOA 2003; see para 4.106.

---

[120] SOA 2003, s 8(3).
[121] 12 months if CJA 2003, s 282(4) implemented.
[122] SOA 2003, s 80(1) and Sch 3, para 19; see Chapter 14, paras 14.1–14.5.
[123] Part 2 of the Safeguarding Vulnerable Groups Act 2006 (Prescribed Criteria and Miscellaneous Provisions) Regulations 2009 (SI 2009 No 37) paras 2 and 4; see Chapter 12, para 12.217.
[124] SA 2020, s 345 and SOA 2003, Sch 3, para 19; see Chapter 16, para 16.07.
[125] SA 2020, s 306, Sch 18, para 38(d); see Chapter 12, para 12.51.
[126] SA 2020, s 307, Sch 19, para 20(c); see Chapter 12, para 12.52.
[127] SA 2020, ss 267 and 280, Sch 14, para 9(c); see Chapter 12, para 12.77.
[128] SA 2020, ss 273 and 283, Sch 15, para 9(c); see Chapter 12, para 12.123.

(ii) Child Complainant related to the Defendant:
Sexual Activity with a Child Family Member; s 25, SOA 2003; see para 6.64.
(iii) Where D is in a position of trust in respect of C:
Abuse of Position of Trust: Sexual Activity with a Child; s 16, SOA 2003; see para 4.153.

4
OFFENCES INVOLVING CHILDREN

A.	Introduction	4.01	J. Offences Committed Between	
	Offences Against Children	4.06	8.1.2001 and 30.4.2004	4.141
B.	Indecent/Sexual Assaults	4.06	1. Abuse of Position of Trust	4.145
	Sexual Behaviour with or Towards a Child	4.07	K. Offences Committed from 1.5.2004	
C.	Offences Committed Between 2.7.1960		to Date	4.152
	and 30.4.2004	4.07	1. Abuse of Position of Trust: Sexual	
	1. Gross Indecency with a Child	4.07	Activity with a Child	4.155
D.	Offences Committed from 30.4.2004		2. Abuse of Position of Trust: Causing/	
	to date	4.21	Inciting a Child to Engage in Sexual	
	1. Causing/Inciting a Child to Engage in		Activity	4.164
	Sexual Activity	4.21	3. Abuse of Position of Trust: Engaging	
	2. Causing or Inciting a Child under 13		in Sexual Activity in the Presence of	
	to Engage in Sexual Activity	4.36	a Child	4.173
	Intercourse with a Person under the Age		4. Abuse of Position of Trust: Causing	
	of Consent	4.49	a Child to Watch a Sexual Act	4.182
E.	Offences Committed Pre-31.12.1956	4.49	L. Offences Without Precedent	4.191
	1. Carnal Knowledge of Girls Aged		1. Engaging in Sexual Activity in the	
	under 13	4.49	Presence of a Child	4.192
	2. Carnal Knowledge of Girls Aged 13 to 16	4.57	2. Causing a Child to Watch a Sexual Act	4.202
F.	Offences Committed Between 1.1.1957		3. Arranging or Facilitating the	
	and 30.4.2004	4.67	Commission of a Child Sex Offence	4.213
	1. Sexual Intercourse with a Girl under 13	4.67	4. Meeting a Child Following Sexual	
	2. Sexual Intercourse with a Girl under 16	4.77	Grooming	4.224
G.	Offences Committed from 1.5.2004		5. Sexual Communication with a Child	4.236
	to date	4.88	6. Possession of a Paedophile Manual	4.245
	1. Rape of a Child under 13	4.89	7. Other Offences Against Children	4.255
	2. Assault of a Child under 13 by		M. Offences Committed by Children or	
	Penetration	4.98	Young Persons	4.256
	3. Penetrative Sexual Activity with a Child	4.107	Presumption and Determination of Age	4.261
	Sexual Assault Upon a Child	4.118	N. *Doli Incapax*	2.261
H.	Offences committed pre-31.12.1956	4.118	O. Presumption that Boys under the Age	
	1. Indecent Assault Upon a Child	4.118	of 14 are Incapable of Vaginal or Anal	
I.	Offences Committed Between 1.1.1957		Intercourse	4.262
	and 30.4.2004	4.119	P. Determination of Age	4.264
	1. Sexual Assault of a Child under 13	4.120	Q. Proving Age	4.268
	2. Non-penetrative Sexual Activity with		R. Discretion to Remit Cases from the	
	a Child	4.129	Adult Magistrates' Court to the	
	Offences Involving Abuse of a Position		Youth Court	4.269
	of Trust	4.141		

A. INTRODUCTION

4.01 This chapter includes offences committed both against and by children or young persons. Offences committed by those under 18 appear in this chapter together with the offence as set out for an adult defendant, with amended particulars for indictments and information on maximum sentences available. The notification requirements for a child/young person convicted of a sexual offence also differ from those for adults; these are set out in Chapter 14.

4.02 Where offences cover the same behaviour, notwithstanding that they are called something different, they appear together as a type of offence from 1950 to date; for example, carnal knowledge of a girl, unlawful sexual intercourse with a girl (under 13 and under 16), sexual assault of a child by penetration under 13, and sexual activity with a child involving penetration. Some offences involving children appear in separate chapters, for example where a child is related to the defendant the offence will appear within Chapter 6.

4.03 The SOA 2003 introduced eight offences in respect of which according to current interpretation of the statute neither consent nor belief in consent are defences (although see footnote 1). Four (ss 5–8 inclusive) relate to victims under 13 and four to offences where the child victim is aged between 13 and 16 (ss 9–13).

4.04 There will be situations where a decision has to be taken as to which is the correct section to charge on the facts or whether to charge alternative sections. The case of *R v G*[1] reinforces the point that s 5 is a strict liability offence. The CPS Guidance, in cases where a defendant admits sexual activity with a child under 13 but states that the victim consented, is that the proper course is to charge a s 5 offence (rape of a child under 13) and invite the court to hold a Newton hearing. It is stated that on no account should a s 1 rape count be added as an alternative. That Guidance also reflects the clear intention of Parliament that judges should decide the issue of consent when it arises in this way. Notwithstanding that, it could be argued that in appropriate circumstances the fundamental issue of consent ought to be tried by a jury, and a s 1 offence added to the indictment for that sole purpose. It is suggested that an example of such circumstances might be a 12-year-old girl who alleges wholly non-consensual intercourse whereas the defendant in his mid-teens asserts consensual intercourse, albeit with a girl who is in law unable to give consent.

See also para 4.88 *et seq*.

4.05 The Serious Crime Act 2015 introduced two new offences against or involving children. Section 67 inserted a new s 15A into the SOA 2003. The 15A offence criminalizes a person aged 18 years or over who communicates with a child under 16 (who the adult does not reasonably believe to be 16 or over), if the communication is sexual or if it is intended to elicit from the child a communication which is sexual. Section 69 makes it an offence to be

---

[1] *R v G* [2008] UKHL 37; and the HL decision rejecting a challenge to the decision: *G v UK* [2012] CLR 46.

in possession a 'paedophile manual', that is any item containing advice or guidance about abusing children sexually.

OFFENCES AGAINST CHILDREN

B. INDECENT/SEXUAL ASSAULTS

Offences of indecent assault upon a child up to 1.1.1957 (see paras 3.03–3.09   **4.06**
Offences of indecent assault upon a child 1.1.1957 to 30.4.2004 (see paras 3.10–3.30)
Offences of sexual assault upon a child 1.5.2005 to date (see paras 4.119–4.151)

SEXUAL BEHAVIOUR WITH OR TOWARDS A CHILD

C. OFFENCES COMMITTED BETWEEN 2.7.1960 AND 30.4.2004

1. Gross Indecency with a Child

Indecency with Children Act 1960, s 1

Until the implementation of the IwCA 1960, there was no offence covering a situation where a defendant caused a child to touch him (D) or another in a sexual manner or committed a sexual act in the presence of a child for his (D's) own sexual gratification.   **4.07**

The IwCA 1960 provides for the offence of gross indecency with/towards a child or incitement of a child to commit an act of gross indecency with D or another (X).   **4.08**

Definition

For offences committed up until 11.1.2001: D committed an act of gross indecency with or towards a child under 14 or incited a child under 14 to commit such an act with D or another (X).   **4.09**

For offences committed from 11.1.2001:[2] D committed an act of gross indecency with or towards a child *under 16* or incited a child *under 16* to commit such an act with D or another (X).   **4.10**

Proof

As per Definition; note that the age of the child is an essential ingredient about which the jury must be satisfied and unless it is admitted between the parties as a fact, requires a   **4.11**

---

[2] Word substituted by Criminal Justice and Court Services Act 2000 s 39 (11.1. 2001).

4. OFFENCES INVOLVING CHILDREN

judicial direction.[3] In *R v Dunn* [2015][4] Laws LJ made it plain that that inciting a female child to masturbate a male did not amount to an indecent assault. The argument that there could be no real distinction between a D touching a child and the child touching a D, did not succeed. Laws LJ confirmed that there could be no indecent assault 'without some form of threat or show of force' to the victim.

4.12 It follows that prosecutors cannot attempt to circumvent the problem which arises from the fact that a s 1 IWCA offence was not extended to children aged 14–16 until 11.1.2001, by charging an offence under s 14 SOA 1956. See para 3.16.

Notes

4.13
(i) Triable either way.
(ii) Consent of DPP not required, despite being offence involving 'gross indecency'.[5]
(iii) A genuine belief that C was 16 or over will afford D with a defence.[6]
(iv) It is necessary to specify the exact age of the child; it is an essential ingredient of the offence[7] and unless admitted requires a judicial direction.[8]
(v) 'With or towards' is to be read as a phrase, not separately.[9]
(vi) The act must be directed towards C, with D at least deriving sexual satisfaction from knowing C is watching him.[10]
(vii) Allowing a young child's hand to remain on D's penis for 5 minutes without more, amounts to an 'invitation' to continue the indecent activity;[11] this invitation is therefore sufficient to be an 'act'.

Indictment

Where D commits an act with or towards C

4.14 INDECENCY WITH A CHILD 2.7.1960 to 30.4.2004

Statement of Offence

INDECENCY WITH A CHILD, contrary to section 1(1) of the Indecency with Children Act 1960.

Particulars of Offence

D, on the ... day of ... , ... , committed an act of gross indecency with or towards C, a child of the age of ... years (in that he/by ...).

---

[3] *R v Goss and Goss* (1990) 90 Cr App R 400 CA.
[4] *R v Dunn* [2015] EWCA Crim 724 at para [10].
[5] CJA 1972, s 48.
[6] *B (A Minor) v DPP* [2000] 2 AC 428 HL.
[7] *R v Goss and Goss* (1990) 90 Cr App R 400 CA.
[8] *R v Radcliffe* [1990] Crim LR 524 CA.
[9] *DPP v Burgess* [1971] QB 432.
[10] *R v Francis* (1989) 88 Cr App R 127 CA.
[11] *R v Speck* (1977) 65 Cr App R 161 CA; *R v B* [1999] Crim LR 594 CA.

C. OFFENCES COMMITTED BETWEEN 2.7.1960 AND 30.4.2004

Where D incites C to commit an act

INDECENCY WITH A CHILD 2.7.1960 to 30.4.2004   **4.15**

Statement of Offence

INDECENCY WITH A CHILD, contrary to section 1(1) of the Indecency with Children Act 1960.

Particulars of Offence

D, on the ... day of ... , ... , incited C, a child of the age of ... years, to commit an act of gross indecency with him, the said D/with D (by ...).

It may be desirable to specify the act alleged, particularly where there are a number of counts on the indictment, hence the option in brackets '(by ...)'. Aver the child's precise age (see Notes at para 4.10).   **4.16**

Alternative Offences

(i) Attempt to commit the full offence. When indicting offences of attempted indecent assault before 27.8.1981,[12] do so under common law, thereafter indict under s 1(1) Criminal Attempts Act 1981. Aver the attempt in both the Statement and Particulars of Offence. In addition, aver the substantive offence under the relevant Act; see paras 1.51 and 12.157 and *Reed & Others* [2021].[13]   **4.17**

(ii) Outraging public decency; indict under common law: sentence at large, see para 10.03.

Sentence

(i) On indictment: **4.18**
- Until 1.10.1997: **2 YEARS**.[14]
- From 1.10.1997:[15] **10 YEARS**.[16]

(ii) Summarily: **6 months**.[17]

Upon Conviction/Sentence

(i) Notification applies.[18]   **4.19**

---

[12] CAA 1981; implementation date 27.8.1981.
[13] *Reed & Others* [2021] EWCA Crim 572.
[14] IwCA 1960, s 1(1).
[15] C(S)A 1997 (Commencement No 2 and Transitional Provisions) Order 1997 (SI 1997 No 2200).
[16] IwCA 1960, s 1(1) as amended by C(S)A 1997, s 52.
[17] 12 months if CJA 2003, s 282(4) implemented.
[18] SOA 2003, s 80(1) and Sch 3, para 11; see Chapter 14 Tables 14.1–14.5.

4. OFFENCES INVOLVING CHILDREN

    (ii) Automatic inclusion in the children's and adults' barred lists with the right to make representations.[19]

    (iii) SHPO applies.[20]

    (iv) Qualifying 'specified sexual offence' in Schedule 18 (Extended Sentences).[21]

4.20 As of 30.4.2004 s 1 of the IwCA 1960 is repealed. From 1.5.2004 s 10 of the SOA 2003 covers this offence.

D. OFFENCES COMMITTED FROM 30.4.2004 TO DATE

1. Causing/Inciting a Child to Engage in Sexual Activity

Sexual Offences Act 2003, s 10

Introduction

4.21 This offence is intended to cover situations where the defendant (D) is using a child either alone or together with a third party (X) for D's sexual gratification. It will include circumstances where D is obtaining sexual gratification from merely observing C and X (and others) rather than taking an active role in the sexual activity (as long as he has caused or incited its happening).

4.22 See notes at para 4.23 in respect of the duplication of s 10 and the effects of charging under this section where C is under 13 (covered under s 8 at para 4.33 *et seq*).

4.23 Note: although s 10 relates to defendants over 18, this is one of the four offences for which a defendant under 18 can be prosecuted by virtue of s 13[22] and so that option is set out here as well.

Definition

4.24 As per Proof. The definition of 'sexual' as set out in s 78 applies (see para 3.37).

Proof

4.25 (i) D, aged 18 or over, intentionally cause/incites C to engage in a sexual activity when C is either under 16 (and D does not reasonably believe that C is 16 or over) or C is under 13.

    (ii) Penetration; also indict under s 10(2) where the sexual activity involves or includes:
- penetration of C's anus or vagina;
- penetration of C's mouth with another person's (X or Y's) penis;

---

[19] Part 2 of the Safeguarding Vulnerable Groups Act 2006 (Prescribed Criteria and Miscellaneous Provisions) Regulations 2009 (SI 2009 No 37) paras 2 and 4; see Chapter 12 para 12.217.

[20] SA 2020, s 345 and SOA 2003 Sch 3, para 11; see Chapter 16 para 16.07.

[21] SA 2020, s 306, Sch 18, para 31; see Chapter 12 para 12.51.

[22] SOA 2003, s 13 provides for the prosecution of anything which would be an offence under ss 9–12 inclusive if the defendant were aged 18; the maximum sentence is 5 years on indictment under s 13.

D. OFFENCES COMMITTED FROM 30.4.2004 TO DATE

- penetration of a person's (X or Y's) anus or vagina with a part of C's body or by C with anything else;
- penetration of a person's (X or Y's) mouth with C's penis.

(iii) Where D is under 18 and so liable by virtue of s 13:
- Identical, except in respect of D's age.

Notes

(i) Triable either way if non-penetrative; triable on indictment only if penetration is alleged. **4.26**
(ii) The type of activity is not specified, save that it must be 'sexual' as per the SOA 2003, s 78.
(iii) This offence is an alternative to rape (SOA 2003, s 1; see para 2.47).
(iv) Neither consent nor belief in consent is a defence to this offence.
(v) A belief on the defendant's part that the child is aged 16 or over will afford him a defence, provided that the belief is reasonable.
(vi) Following the judgment in *R v Heard*,[23] it seems that all the sexual offences in the 2003 Act (certainly those in ss 1–4 and 5–15) will be regarded as offences for which a plea of voluntary intoxication is no defence.[24]
(vii) This section duplicates s 8 (causing/inciting a child under 13 to engage in sexual activity) where C is under 13. Where the defendant is 18 or over, it will be appropriate when charging/indicting in such a case to use s 8; s 8 is simpler to indict and explain to a jury, is indictable only reflecting the seriousness of the offence, and has a higher maximum sentence. (Note: s 8 is not available under s 13 when D is under 18.)
(viii) The extended jurisdiction provisions apply to this section.[25] See Chapter 17 para 17.01.
(ix) The s 45 MSA 2015 defence for slavery and trafficking victims who commit an offence does not apply to this offence.[26]

Indictment

Non-penetrative activity where D is over 18

CAUSING (OR INCITING) A CHILD TO ENGAGE IN SEXUAL ACTIVITY 1.5.2004 to date **4.27**

Statement of Offence

CAUSING (OR INCITING) A CHILD TO ENGAGE IN SEXUAL ACTIVITY, contrary to section 10(1) of the Sexual Offences Act 2003.

Particulars of Offence

D, a person of or over the age of 18 years, on the … day of … 20 … , intentionally caused [or incited] C to engage in an activity, namely … the circumstances being such that the activity was sexual [C was aged under 16 years (namely … , years) and D did not reasonably believe that C was of or over the age of 16 years] *or* [C was under 13 years].

---

[23] [2007] EWCA Crim 125. Principle adopted and followed, for example, in the case of *R v Grout* [2011] EWCA Crim 299 (in relation to s 8 offence).
[24] Professor David Ormerod QC CBE, March 2007.
[25] SOA 2003, s 72; provides for the prosecution within the jurisdiction of a sexual offence committed outside it.
[26] Modern Slavery Act 2015, s 45 and Sch 4, para 33.

4. OFFENCES INVOLVING CHILDREN

Penetrative activity where D is over 18

4.28 CAUSING (OR INCITING) A CHILD TO ENGAGE IN SEXUAL ACTIVITY 1.5.2004 to date

Statement of Offence
CAUSING (OR INCITING) A CHILD TO ENGAGE IN SEXUAL ACTIVITY, contrary to sections 10(1) and (2) of the Sexual Offences Act 2003.

Particulars of Offence
D, a person of or over the age of 18 years, on the … day of … 20 … , intentionally caused [*or* incited] C to engage in an activity, namely … involving the penetration of … with … , the circumstances being such that the activity was sexual [C was aged under 16 years (namely … years) and D did not reasonably believe that C was of or over the age of 16] *or* [C was under 13 years].

Non-penetrative where D is under 18

4.29 CAUSING (OR INCITING) A CHILD TO ENGAGE IN SEXUAL ACTIVITY 1.5.2004 to date

Statement of Offence
CAUSING (OR INCITING) A CHILD TO ENGAGE IN SEXUAL ACTIVITY, contrary to sections 13(1) and 10(1) of the Sexual Offences Act 2003.

Particulars of Offence
D, a person under the age of 18 years, on the … day of … 20 … , intentionally caused [*or* incited] C to engage in an activity, namely … , the circumstances being such that the activity was sexual [C was aged under 16 or 13 years (namely … years) and D did not reasonably believe that C was of or over the age of 16 years] *or* [C was under 13 years].

Penetrative where D is under 18

4.30 CAUSING (OR INCITING) A CHILD TO ENGAGE IN SEXUAL ACTIVITY 1.5.2004 to date

Statement of Offence
CAUSING (OR INCITING) A CHILD TO ENGAGE IN SEXUAL ACTIVITY, contrary to sections 13(1), 10(1) and 10(2) of the Sexual Offences Act 2003.

Particulars of Offence
D, a person under the age of 18 years, on the … day of … 20 … , intentionally caused [*or* incited] C to engage in a sexual activity, (namely …), involving the penetration of … with … , when [C was aged under 16/13 years (namely … years) and D did not reasonably believe that C was of or over the age of 16 years] *or* [C was under 13 years].

D. OFFENCES COMMITTED FROM 30.4.2004 TO DATE

Alternative Offences

4.31 Attempt to commit the full offence. When indicting offences of attempt, do so under s 1(1) Criminal Attempts Act 1981.[27] Aver the attempt in both the Statement and Particulars of Offence. In addition, aver the substantive offence under the relevant Act; see paras 1.51 and 12.157 and *Reed & Others* [2021].[28]

4.32 The SOA 2003 has created a number of possible alternatives which are self-evident; where to prove a particular offence requires elements which are identical to but fewer than another, usually more serious, offence. This will include those offences of assault which do not include penetration as possible alternatives to penetrative offences, if that is evidentially an appropriate course. There will therefore often be occasions on which if the offence charged is not proved in one or more of its elements, the defendant will be guilty of a lesser offence. An obvious example of this would be those offences of penetrative assault where the evidence at trial falls short on the issue of penetration. Prosecutors would be well advised to draft alternatives on the indictment where appropriate, or to apply to add counts where the evidence given at trial reveals an alternative offence, rather than rely on included offences.

Sentence

4.33
(i) Where D is 18 or over (s 10):
- On indictment: **14 YEARS**.
- Summarily: **6 months**.[29]

(ii) Where D is under 18 (s 13):
- On indictment: **5 YEARS**.
- Summarily: **6 months**.[30]

Sentencing Guidance

4.34 For adult offenders: The Sentencing Council 'Sexual Offences: Definitive Guideline' contains offence-specific guidelines. The Guideline applies to all offenders aged 18 and over, sentenced on or after 1 April 2014. For children and young persons: the 'Sentencing Children and Young Persons—Overarching Principles' and 'Sentencing Children and Young Persons—Sexual Offences' Guidelines apply to all children and young persons sentenced on or after 1 June 2017. When sentencing an Offender who has committed a sexual offence with, or in respect of, a person who is, or who the Offender believes to be, a child and no sexual activity occurs refer to *R v Reed and Others* [2021],[31] see Chapter 12 para 12.176.

---

[27] Implementation date 27.8.1981.
[28] *Reed & Others* [2021] EWCA Crim 572.
[29] 12 months if CJA 2003, s 282(4) implemented.
[30] 12 months if CJA 2003, s 282(4) implemented.
[31] *Reed & Others* [2021] EWCA Crim 572.

Upon Conviction/Sentence

4.35 (i) Notification applies to s 10 offences.[32] Notification applies to s 13 offences if D sentenced to 12 months or more imprisonment.[33] The notification period is halved for under 18s.

(ii) Section 10 offence: automatic inclusion in the children's and adults' barred lists with the right to make representations.[34]

(iii) SHPO applies.[35]

(iv) Section 10 and Section 13 offences: Qualifying 'specified sexual offences' in Schedule 18 (Extended Sentences).[36]

(v) Section 10 offence: Qualifying Schedule 14 offence (Extended Sentences: The Earlier Offence Condition).[37]

(vii) Section 10 offence: Qualifying 'index' offence (if committed after 3 December 2012) for the purpose of Schedule 15 (Life Sentence for Second Listed Offence).[38]

2. Causing or Inciting a Child under 13 to Engage in Sexual Activity

Sexual Offences Act 2003, s 8

Introduction

4.36 It is suggested that this is the appropriate section under which to charge/indict a defendant where he (D) is using a child under 13, either alone or together with a third party for D's sexual gratification; see notes at para 4.37 for its duplication and the effects of charging under the correct section where C is under 13. It is interesting to note that under s 8, D can be under 18 but will be liable to a maximum of life imprisonment, higher than the identical offence under s 10 and far higher than the 5-year maximum penalty for young offenders convicted of offences under ss 9–12 by virtue of s 13.

4.37 In *Grout*[39] the Court of Appeal held that s 8 creates four offences, each of which must be carried out intentionally. The first is causing penetrative sexual activity; the second is inciting such activity; the third is causing non-penetrative sexual activity and the fourth is inciting such activity. It is therefore important that the charge or indictment specifies which of these offences is being alleged (para 27).

> [T]he offences created by section 8 are directed towards a defendant who intentionally causes or incites *the child*, that is (B) himself or herself, to engage in 'sexual activity'. The offence is not concerned with whether the defendant engages in sexual activity (para 28).

---

[32] SOA 2003, s 80(1) and Sch 3, para 21; see Chapter 14 paras 14.1–14.5.
[33] SOA 2003, s 80(1) and Sch 3, para 22; see Chapter 14 paras 14.1–14.5.
[34] Part 2 of the Safeguarding Vulnerable Groups Act 2006 (Prescribed Criteria and Miscellaneous Provisions) Regulations 2009 (SI 2009 No 37) paras 2 and 4; see Chapter 12 para 12.217.
[35] SA 2020, s 345 and SOA 2003 Sch 3, paras 21 and 22; see Chapter 16 para 16.07.
[36] SA 2020, s 306, Sch 18, paras 38(j) and (m); see Chapter 12 para 12.51.
[37] SA 2020, ss 267 and 280, Sch 14, para 9(i); see Chapter 12 para 12.77.
[38] SA 2020, ss 273 and 283, Sch 15, para 9(i); see Chapter 12 para 12.123.
[39] *R v Grout* [2011] EWCA Crim 299.

D. OFFENCES COMMITTED FROM 30.4.2004 TO DATE   67

In *Jones*[40] it was made clear that the offence was concerned with incitement of a child and not the effect upon the child.

Definition

As per Proof. **4.38**

Proof

(i) Section 8(1): D intentionally causes or incites another person (C) to engage in a sexual activity and C is under 13. **4.39**
(ii) Penetration; also indict under s 8(2) where the sexual activity involves or includes:
- penetration of C's anus or vagina;
- penetration of C's mouth with a person's (X or Y's) penis;
- penetration of a person's (X or Y's) anus or vagina with part of C's body by C with anything else;
- penetration of a person's (X or Y's) mouth with C's penis.

Notes

(i) Triable either way if non-penetrative; triable on indictment only if penetration is alleged. **4.40**
(ii) This section duplicates s 10 (causing/inciting a child to engage in sexual activity) where C is either under 16 or 13. It will be appropriate when charging/indicting in such a case to use s 8; s 8 is simpler to indict and explain to a jury, is indictable only reflecting the seriousness of the offence, and has a higher maximum sentence.
(iii) Neither consent nor belief in consent is a defence to this offence.
(iv) Following the judgment in R v Heard,[41] it seems that all the sexual offences in the 2003 Act (certainly those in ss 1–4 and 5–15) will be regarded as offences for which a plea of voluntary intoxication is no defence.[42]
(v) This offence is an alternative to rape.
(vi) The extended jurisdiction provisions[43] apply to this section. See Chapter 17 para 17.01.
(vii) The s 45 MSA 2015 defence for slavery and trafficking victims who commit an offence does not apply to this offence.[44]

Indictment

Non-penetrative

CAUSING (OR INCITING) A CHILD UNDER 13 TO ENGAGE IN SEXUAL ACTIVITY **4.41**
1.5.2004 to date

---

[40] *R v Jones (Ian)* [2007] EWCA Crim 1118, para 16.
[41] [2007] EWCA Crim 125.
[42] Professor David Ormerod QC CBE, March 2007.
[43] SOA 2003, s 72; provides for the prosecution within the jurisdiction of a sexual offence committed outside it. See Chapter 17.
[44] Modern Slavery Act 2015, s 45 and Sch 4, para 33.

> **Statement of Offence**
> CAUSING (OR INCITING) A CHILD UNDER 13 TO ENGAGE IN SEXUAL ACTIVITY, contrary to section 8(1) of the Sexual Offences Act 2003.
>
> **Particulars of Offence**
> D, on the … day of … 20 … , intentionally caused *or* [incited] C to engage in a sexual activity, namely … , when C was aged under 13 years (namely … years).

Penetrative

4.42 CAUSING (OR INCITING) A CHILD UNDER 13 TO ENGAGE IN SEXUAL ACTIVITY
1.5.2004 to date

> **Statement of Offence**
> CAUSING (OR INCITING) A CHILD UNDER 13 TO ENGAGE IN SEXUAL ACTIVITY, contrary to sections 8(1) and (2) of the Sexual Offences Act 2003.
>
> **Particulars of Offence**
> D, on the … day of … 20 … , intentionally caused *or* [incited] C to engage in a sexual activity, (namely … ,) involving the penetration of … with … when C was aged under 13 years (namely … years).

Alternative Offences

4.43 Attempt to commit the full offence. When indicting offences of attempt, do so under the CAA 1981.[45] Aver the attempt in both the Statement and Particulars of Offence. In addition, aver the substantive offence under the relevant Act; see paras 1.51 and 12.157 and *Reed & Others* [2021].[46]

4.44 The SOA 2003 has created a number of possible alternatives which are self-evident; where to prove a particular offence requires elements which are identical to but less than another, usually more serious, offence. This will include those offences of assault which do not include penetration as possible alternatives to penetrative offences if that is evidentially an appropriate course. There will therefore often be occasions on which if the offence charged is not proved in one or more of its elements, the defendant will be guilty of a lesser offence. An obvious example of this would be those offences of penetrative assault where the evidence at trial falls short on the issue of penetration.

4.45 Prosecutors would be well advised to draft alternatives on the indictment where appropriate, or to apply to add counts where the evidence given at trial reveals an alternative offence, rather than rely on included offences.

---

[45] Implementation date 27.8.1981.
[46] *Reed & Others* [2021] EWCA Crim 572.

E. OFFENCES COMMITTED PRE-31.12.1956   69

Sentence

4.46
(i) On indictment:
- With penetration: **LIFE**.[47]
- Without penetration: **14 YEARS**.[48]

(ii) Summarily: **6 months**.[49]

Sentencing Guidance

The Sentencing Council 'Sexual Offences: Definitive Guideline' contains offence-specific guidelines. The Guideline applies to all offenders aged 18 and over, sentenced on or after 1 April 2014. When sentencing an Offender who has committed a sexual offence with, or in respect of, a person who is, or who the Offender believes to be, a child and no sexual activity occurs refer to *R v Reed and Others* [2021],[50] see Chapter 12 para 12.176.   **4.47**

Upon Conviction/Sentence

4.48
(i) Notification applies.[51]
(ii) Automatic inclusion in the children's barred list with no right to make representations. Automatic inclusion in the adults' barred list with the right to make representations.[52]
(iii) SHPO applies.[53]
(iv) Qualifying 'specified sexual offence' in Schedule 18 (Extended Sentences).[54]
(v) Qualifying Schedule 19 offence (Life Sentences) where liable on conviction on indictment to life imprisonment.[55]
(vi) Qualifying Schedule 14 offence (Extended Sentences: The Earlier Offence Condition).[56]
(vii) Qualifying 'index' offence (if committed after 3 December 2012) for the purpose of Schedule 15 (Life Sentence for Second Listed Offence).[57]

Intercourse with a Person under the Age of Consent

E. OFFENCES COMMITTED PRE-31.12.1956

1. Carnal Knowledge of Girls Aged under 13

Criminal Law Amendment Act 1885, s 4

---

[47] SOA 2003, s 8(2).
[48] SOA 2003, s 8(3).
[49] 12 months if CJA 2003, s 282(4) implemented.
[50] *Reed & Others* [2021] EWCA Crim 572.
[51] SOA 2003, s 80(1) and Sch 3, para 21 SOA 2003; see Chapter 14 paras 14.1–14.5.
[52] Part 2 of the Safeguarding Vulnerable Groups Act 2006 (Prescribed Criteria and Miscellaneous Provisions) Regulations 2009 (SI 2009 No 37) paras 1 and 4; see Chapter 12 para 12.217.
[53] SA 2020, s 345 and SOA 2003 Sch 3, para 21; see Chapter 16 para 16.07.
[54] SA 2020, s 306, Sch18, para 38(h); see Chapter 12 para 12.51.
[55] SA 2020, s 307, Sch 19, para 20(f); see Chapter 12 para 12.52.
[56] SA 2020, ss 267 and 280, Sch 14, para 9(g); see Chapter 12 para 77.
[57] SA 2020, ss 273 and 283, Sch 15, para 9(g); see Chapter 12 para 12.123.

70   4. OFFENCES INVOLVING CHILDREN

Definition

4.49 Any person who unlawfully and carnally knows any girl under the age of 13 years ... [58]

Proof

4.50 (i) Unlawful sexual intercourse. For 'sexual intercourse', any degree of penetration is sufficient[59] and ejaculation is not required.[60]
(ii) With a girl aged under 13 at the time of the offence.
(iii) Consent is immaterial.

Notes

4.51 (i) Triable only on indictment.
(ii) The irrebuttable presumption[61] at the time that a boy under 14 was incapable of sexual intercourse applies to this offence; he could, however, be convicted of indecent assault.[62]
(iii) It is no defence to a charge under s 4 that the defendant made a mistake as to the girl's age, even if that is based on reasonable grounds.[63]
(iv) There is no limitation of time in respect of prosecuting a s 4 offence.
(v) Consent is immaterial,[64] although where a girl under 13 does not consent a count of rape should be preferred.[65]
(vi) This offence is an alternative to rape.

Indictment

4.52 CARNAL KNOWLEDGE OF A GIRL UNDER 13 Pre-31.12.1956

Statement of Offence
CARNAL KNOWLEDGE OF A GIRL UNDER 13, contrary to section 4 of the Criminal Law Amendment Act 1885.

---

[58] CLAA 1885, s 4.
[59] *R v Russen* 1 East PC.
[60] *R v Jennings* 4 C&P 249.
[61] *R v Phillips* 8 C&P 736.
[62] *R v Williams* [1893] 1 QB 320.
[63] *R v Prince* [1875] LR 2 CCR 154.
[64] *R v Beale* 10 Cox 157.
[65] *R v Dicken* 14 Cox 8.

E. OFFENCES COMMITTED PRE-31.12.1956   71

> **Particulars of Offence**
>
> D, on the … day of … 19 …, had carnal knowledge of or sexual intercourse with C, a girl of the age of … (specify age under 13).

Alternative Offences

(i) Attempt to commit the full offence.[66] When indicting offences of attempt do so under common law. Aver the attempt in both the Statement of Offence and Particulars of Offence. In addition, aver the substantive offence under the relevant Act; see paras 1.51 and 12.157 and *Reed & Others* [2021].[67]   **4.53**

(ii) Indecent assault;[68] **2 YEARS**[69] (see para 3.03).

(iii) Carnal knowledge of 'idiot or imbecile'[70] **2 YEARS** (see paras 7.04–7.10).

Sentence

On indictment:[71]   **4.54**

- Defendant over 16: **LIFE**.
- Defendant under 16: **Not less than 3 YEARS**.[72]
- Attempt at any age: **2 YEARS**.

Upon Conviction/Sentence

(i) Notification not applicable.[73]   **4.55**

(ii) Automatic inclusion in the children's barred list with no right to make representations. Automatic inclusion in the adults' barred list with the right to make representations.[74]

(iii) SHPO not applicable.[75]

As of 31.12.1956, s 4 of the CLAA 1885 is repealed. From 1.1.1957 s 5 (see paras 4.64–4.74) of the SOA 1956 replaces this offence.   **4.56**

---

[66] Criminal Procedure Act (CPA) 1851, s 9; CLAA 1885, s 4.
[67] *Reed & Others* [2021] EWCA Crim 572.
[68] By virtue of CLAA 1885, s 9.
[69] OAPA 1861, s 52.
[70] The words used in drafting the Act.
[71] CLAA 1885, s 4.
[72] *R v Cawthron* [1913] 3 KB 168.
[73] SOA 2003, s 80(1) (not listed in Sch 3); see Chapter 14 Tables 14.2–14.5.
[74] Part 2 of the Safeguarding Vulnerable Groups Act 2006 (Prescribed Criteria and Miscellaneous Provisions) Regulations 2009 (SI 2009 No 37) paras 1 and 4; see Chapter 12 para 12.217.
[75] SA 2020, s 345 (not listed in Sch 3 or Sch 5 SOA 2003); see Chapter 16 para 16.07.

72 4. OFFENCES INVOLVING CHILDREN

2. Carnal Knowledge of Girls Aged 13 to 16

Criminal Law Amendment Act 1885, s 5

Definition

4.57 Any person who unlawfully and carnally knows or attempts to have unlawful carnal knowledge of a girl over the age of 13 years[76] and under the age of 16 years ...

Proof

4.58 (i) Unlawful sexual intercourse; for 'sexual intercourse' any degree of penetration is sufficient[77] and ejaculation is not required;[78]
(ii) with a girl aged over 13 and under 16[79] at the time of the offence.
(iii) Consent is immaterial.

Notes

4.59 A prosecution under s 5(1) (for the full offence or an attempt) cannot be brought more than 12 months after the offence has been committed.[80] In practice, therefore, the offence under this section will no longer appear on an indictment.

4.60 It is no longer permissible to charge indecent assault as a substitute when the time-bar for an offence under s 5 makes it impossible to charge.[81] A defence is provided to s 5(1) if D is 23 or under, believed C was over 16 and there was reasonable cause[82] to believe that C was over 16 at the time, and it is the first occasion on which he is charged with a s 5 offence.[83] A defence is provided to s 5(1) to prove that at the time when the offence was allegedly committed D had reasonable cause to believe that C was his wife (notwithstanding that a marriage where either party is under 16 shall be void).[84]

4.61 The presumption at the time that a boy under 14 was incapable of sexual intercourse applies to this offence; he could, however, be convicted of indecent assault.[85]

---

[76] CLAA 1885, s 5.
[77] *R v Russen* 1 East PC.
[78] *R v Jennings* 4 C&P 249.
[79] *R v Shott* 3 C&K 206; when the girl is under 13 there cannot be a conviction.
[80] CLAA 1928, s 1 and SOA 1956, s 37 Sch 2 (10)(a) and (b).
[81] *R v J* [2004] UKHL 42.
[82] *R v Banks* [1916] 2 KB 621.
[83] CLAA 1922, s 2, enacted 4.8.1922.
[84] Age of Marriage Act 1929, s 1(1) and Marriage Act (MA) 1949, s 2.
[85] *R v Williams* [1893] 1 QB 320; 20.9.1993; presumption abolished by SOA 1993, s 1.

E. OFFENCES COMMITTED PRE-31.12.1956   73

Indictment

CARNAL KNOWLEDGE OF A GIRL Pre-31.12.1956   **4.62**

Statement of Offence
CARNAL KNOWLEDGE OF A GIRL, contrary to section 5(1) of the Criminal Law Amendment Act 1885.

Particulars of Offence
D on the ... day of ... 19 ..., had carnal knowledge of C, a girl of the age of ... (specify age between 13–16).

Alternative Offences

(i) Attempt to commit the full offence.[86] When indicting offences of attempt do so under common law. Aver the attempt in both the Statement of Offence and Particulars of Offence. In addition, aver the substantive offence under the relevant Act; see paras 1.51 and 12.157 and *Reed & Others* [2021].[87]   **4.63**

(ii) Indecent assault:[88] 2 YEARS[89] (should be added to the indictment as an alternative.

(iii) Common assault: at common law, sentence at large, unless C consented.[90]

Sentence

On indictment: full offence and attempt: 2 YEARS.   **4.64**

Upon Conviction/Sentence

(i) Notification not applicable.[91]   **4.65**

(ii) Automatic inclusion in the children's and adults' barred lists with the right to make representations.[92]

(iii) SHPO not applicable.[93]

---

[86] CLAA 1885, s 5.
[87] *Reed & Others* [2021] EWCA Crim 572.
[88] CLAA 1885, s 9.
[89] OAPA 1861, s 52.
[90] *R v Bostock* 17 Cox 700.
[91] SOA 2003, s 80(1) (not listed in Sch 3); see Chapter 14 Tables 14.2–14.5.
[92] Part 2 of the Safeguarding Vulnerable Groups Act 2006 (Prescribed Criteria and Miscellaneous Provisions) Regulations 2009 (SI 2009 No 37) paras 2 and 4; see Chapter 12 para 12.217.
[93] SA 2020, s 345 (not listed in Sch 3 or Sch 5 SOA 2003); see Chapter 16 para 16.07.

74   4. OFFENCES INVOLVING CHILDREN

4.66   As of 31.12.1956 s 5 of the CLAA 1885 is repealed. From 1.1.1957 s 6 (see para 4.75) of the SOA 1956 replaces this offence.

F. OFFENCES COMMITTED BETWEEN 1.1.1957 AND 30.4.2004

1. Sexual Intercourse with a Girl under 13

Sexual Offences Act 1956, s 5

Introduction

4.67   Also known as unlawful sexual intercourse (or USI) with a girl under 13.

The offence remains essentially the same as under the CLAA 1885: that D had unlawful sexual intercourse with C, she being a girl under 13 at the time of the offence. Sexual intercourse remains as defined at para 4.47 (penetration is sufficient, ejaculation unnecessary).

Definition

4.68   It is an offence for a man[94] to have unlawful sexual intercourse with a girl under the age of 13.[95]

Proof

4.69   (i) Unlawful sexual intercourse. For 'sexual intercourse' any degree of penetration is sufficient and ejaculation is not required.[96]
(ii) With a girl aged under 13 at the time of the offence.
(iii) Consent is immaterial.

Notes

4.70   (i) Triable only on indictment.
(ii) Neither consent nor belief in consent is a defence to this offence.

---

[94] SOA 1956, s 46; 'man' and 'boy' are interchangeable—no need to aver both.
[95] SOA 1956, s 5.
[96] SOA 1956, s 44.

F. OFFENCES COMMITTED BETWEEN 1.1.1957 AND 30.4.2004

(iii) It is no defence to a charge under s 5 that D made a mistake as to C's age, even if that is based on reasonable grounds.[97]
(iv) There is no limitation of time in respect of prosecuting a s 5 offence.
(v) The irrebuttable presumption at the time that a boy under 14 was incapable of sexual intercourse applies to this offence;[98] he could, however, be convicted of indecent assault.[99]

Indictment

SEXUAL INTERCOURSE WITH A GIRL UNDER 13 1.1.1957 to 30.4.2004   **4.71**

Statement of Offence

SEXUAL INTERCOURSE WITH A GIRL UNDER 13, contrary to section 5 of the Sexual Offences Act 1956.

Particulars of Offence

D, on the ... day of ... 20 ... , had sexual intercourse with C, a girl under the age of 13 years (namely ... years).

Alternative Offences

(i) Attempt to commit the full offence. When indicting offences of attempt do so under common law until 26.8.1981, thereafter indict under s 1(1) Criminal Attempts Act 1981. Aver the attempt in both the Statement of Offence and Particulars of Offence. In addition, aver the substantive offence under the relevant Act; see paras 1.51 and 12.157 and *Reed & Others* [2021].[100]   **4.72**
(ii) Indecent assault:[101] **5 YEARS** to 15.9.1985[102] if fact of age stated in the indictment (otherwise **2 YEARS** for a female over 13), thereafter **10 YEARS** (see para 3.19).[103]
(iii) The offence is itself an alternative to rape: **LIFE** (see para 2.22).

---

[97] *R v Prince* [1875] LR 2 CCR 154.
[98] SOA 1993, s 1 abolished the presumption for acts on or after 20.9.1993.
[99] *R v Williams* [1893] 1 QB 320.
[100] *Reed & Others* [2021] EWCA Crim 572.
[101] By virtue of CLAA 1885, s 9.
[102] SOA 1956, s 37 and Sch 37, as amended by SOA 1985, s 3(3).
[103] See para 3.17. *R v Hodgson* (1973) 57 Cr App R 502.

76   4. OFFENCES INVOLVING CHILDREN

Sentence

4.73   On indictment:

- For the full offence: **LIFE**.[104]
- For an attempt: **7 YEARS**.[105]

4.74   Sentencing Guidance

See the Sentencing Council 'Sexual Offences: Definitive Guideline' for the correct approach to sentencing in historic cases.

Upon Conviction/Sentence

4.75   (i) Notification applicable.[106]
(ii) Automatic inclusion in the children's barred list with no right to make representations. Automatic inclusion in the adults' barred list with the right to make representations.[107]
(iii) SHPO applicable.[108]
(iv) Qualifying 'specified sexual offence' in Schedule 18 (Extended Sentences).[109]

4.76   The SOA 2003 repealed this section in full. Two new offences in this area are created; rape of a child under 13 (SOA 2003, s 5) (see para 4.88), assault of a child under 13 by penetration (SOA 2003, s 6).

2. Sexual Intercourse with a Girl under 16

Sexual Offences Act 1956, s 6

Introduction

4.77   Also known as unlawful sexual intercourse (or USI) with a girl under 16.

The offence remains essentially the same as under the CLAA 1885: that D had unlawful sexual intercourse with C, she being a girl aged between 13 and 16 at the time of the offence.

---

[104] SOA 1956, s 37(3) and Sch 2(2)(a).
[105] SOA 1956, s 37(3) and Sch 2(2)(b).
[106] SOA 2003, s 80(1) and Sch 3, para 2; see Chapter 14 paras 14.1–14.5.
[107] Part 2 of the Safeguarding Vulnerable Groups Act 2006 (Prescribed Criteria and Miscellaneous Provisions) Regulations 2009 (SI 2009 No 37) paras 1 and 4; see Chapter 12 para 12.217.
[108] SA 2020, s 345 and SOA 2003, Sch 3, para 2; see Chapter 16 para 16.07.
[109] SA 2020, s 306, Sch 18, para 29(e); see Chapter 12 para 12.51.

F. OFFENCES COMMITTED BETWEEN 1.1.1957 AND 30.4.2004

Sexual intercourse remains as defined at para 4.47 (penetration is sufficient, ejaculation unnecessary). Consent is immaterial but if she was not consenting a count of rape should be preferred; unlawful sexual intercourse is a proper alternative to rape and so both can be put before the jury in appropriate circumstances. The only difference between proving this offence and rape is that consent is immaterial here.

Definition

4.78 It is an offence for a man[110] to have unlawful sexual intercourse with a girl ... under the age of 16.[111]

Proof

4.79
(i) Unlawful sexual intercourse. For 'sexual intercourse' any degree of penetration is sufficient and ejaculation is not required.[112]
(ii) With a girl aged under 16 at the time of the offence.
(iii) Consent is immaterial.

Notes

4.80
(i) Triable either way.
(ii) A prosecution under s 6 (for either the full offence or an attempt) cannot be brought more than 12 months after the offence has been committed.[113] In practice, therefore, the offence under this section will no longer appear on an indictment or be the subject of a charge.
(iii) It will depend on the facts of the case as to whether it would be an abuse of process to charge indecent assault when the time-bar for an offence under s 5 makes it impossible to charge.[114] Where that is done, however, the court should bear in mind the two-year maximum s 6 USI would have attracted and the sentencing guidelines for s 6 USI.
(iv) A defence is afforded to D if he is under 24, believed C was over 16[115] and there was reasonable cause to believe that C was over 16 at the time, and it is the first occasion on which he is charged with a like offence. Here, a 'like offence' means one under the same section/an attempt, or one under the CLAA 1885, s 5(1) (which s 6 replaced).[116]

---

[110] SOA 1956, s 46; 'man' and 'boy' are interchangeable—no need to aver both.
[111] SOA 1956, s 6(1).
[112] SOA 1956, s 44.
[113] CLAA 1928, s 1 and SOA 1956, s 37 and Sch 2, para 10(a) and (b); *R v West* [1898] 1 QB 174.
[114] *R v J* [2004] UKHL 42.
[115] SOA 1956, s 6(3) and *R v Banks* [1916] 2 KB 621, 12 Cr App R 74.
[116] SOA 1956, s 6(3).

4. OFFENCES INVOLVING CHILDREN

(v) A defence[117] is also provided to s 6(1) by proof that at the time when the offence was allegedly committed D had reasonable cause to believe that C was his wife (notwithstanding that a marriage where either party is under 16 shall be void).[118]

(vi) This offence is an alternative to rape.

Indictment

4.81 SEXUAL INTERCOURSE WITH A GIRL UNDER 16 1.1.1957 to 30.4.2004

> ### Statement of Offence
> SEXUAL INTERCOURSE WITH A GIRL UNDER 16, contrary to section 6 of the Sexual Offences Act 1956.
>
> ### Particulars of Offence
> D on the ... day of ... 20 ..., had sexual intercourse with C, a girl under the age of 16 years (namely ... years).

4.82 It is not necessary to aver the specific age of the girl over and above being under 16, but, depending upon the complexity of the prosecution case, it is good practice to particularize the counts as fully as possible,[119] hence the option contained within brackets.

Alternative Offences

4.83 (i) Attempt to commit the full offence. When indicting offences of attempt do so under common law until 26.8.1981, thereafter indict under s 1(1) Criminal Attempts Act 1981. Aver the attempt in both the Statement of Offence and Particulars of Offence. In addition, aver the substantive offence under the relevant Act; see paras 1.51 and 12.157 and *Reed & Others* [2021].[120]

(ii) Indecent assault:[121] **2 YEARS** to 15.9.1985[122] thereafter **10 YEARS** (see para 3.19).

(iii) The offence is an alternative to rape: **LIFE** (see para 2.35).

Sentence

4.84 (i) On indictment:[123]
- For the full offence: **2 YEARS**.
- For an attempt: **2 YEARS**.

---

[117] SOA 1956, s 6(2).
[118] AMA 1929, s 1(1) and MA 1949, s 2.
[119] See Indictments, para 1.10.
[120] *Reed & Others* [2021] EWCA Crim 572.
[121] SOA 1956, s 14.
[122] SOA 1956, s 37 and Sch 2, para 17 as amended by SOA 1985, s 3(3) (16.8.1985).
[123] SOA 1956, s 37(3) and Sch 2, para 10(a) and (b).

(ii) Summarily:
- 6 months.[124]

Sentencing Guidance

See the Sentencing Council 'Sexual Offences: Definitive Guideline' for the correct approach to sentencing in historic cases. **4.85**

Upon Conviction/Sentence

(i) Notification applicable where offender 20 years or over.[125] **4.86**
(ii) Automatic inclusion in the Children and Adult barred lists with the right to make representations.[126]
(iii) SHPO applicable.[127]
(iv) Qualifying 'specified sexual offence' in Schedule 18 (Extended Sentences).[128]

The SOA 2003 repealed the SOA 1956, s 6. Within the umbrella offence of the SOA 2003, s 9, s 9(2)(a) (see para 4.224) specifically replaces the old offence of USI with a girl under 16. In addition, the SOA 2003, s 9(2) expands the ambit of sexual activity with a girl under 16 to include penetrative sexual activity beyond vaginal or anal penetration. In keeping with the rest of the Act, s 9 includes both genders rather than only female children as potential complainants. **4.87**

G. OFFENCES COMMITTED FROM 1.5.2004 TO DATE

The SOA 2003 (implementation date 1.5.2004) substituted the following two offences under s 5 (rape of a child under 13) and s 6 (assault of a child under 13 by penetration) (see para 4.64 for the old offence of USI with a girl under 13 under the SOA 1956). **4.88**

1. Rape of a Child under 13

Sexual Offences Act 2003, s 5

---

[124] 12 months if CJA 2003, s 282(4) implemented.
[125] SOA 2003, s 80(1) and Sch 3, para 3, SOA 2003; see Chapter 14 paras 14.1–14.5.
[126] Part 2 of the Safeguarding Vulnerable Groups Act 2006 (Prescribed Criteria and Miscellaneous Provisions) Regulations 2009 (SI 2009 No 37) paras 2 and 4; see Chapter 12 para 12.217.
[127] SA 2020, s 345 and SOA 2003, Sch 3, para 3; see Chapter 16 para 16.07.
[128] SA 2020, s 306, Sch 18, para 29(f); see Chapter 12 para 12.51.

4. OFFENCES INVOLVING CHILDREN

Introduction

4.89 This offence is arguably one of the replacement offences for the old offence of s 5 USI because consent is not an ingredient of it; a child under 13 is presumed to be unable to give consent. The purpose of the 2003 legislation is to protect children under 13 from themselves as well as from others. However, where the child did in fact consent it is likely to affect sentence, especially where the defendant is also young.[129]

See para 4.04.

Definition

4.90 As per Proof.

Proof

4.91
(i) D intentionally penetrated;
(ii) C's vagina/anus/mouth with his penis and
(iii) at the time C was under 13.
(iv) Consent is no defence.

Notes

4.92
(i) The offence is triable only on indictment.
(ii) This offence is an alternative to rape (see para 4.04 for commentary in respect of charging these as alternatives). However, CPS guidance makes clear that in circumstances where the defendant admits sexual activity but says the child consented, on no account should a s 1 rape offence be added as an alternative. The correct course is to invite the court to hold a Newton hearing.[130] See para 2.46 for s 1 rape. It is also an alternative to attempted rape (para 2.51), assault by penetration (para 3.35), s 7 sexual assault of a child under 13 (para 4.119), and s 9(2) penetrative sexual activity with a child (para 4.107).
(iii) Neither consent nor belief in consent are defences to this offence. Mistake as to the age of the victim is not a defence to a charge under s 5, making this element one of strict liability.[131] Where it is a defence, the SOA 2003 sets that fact out specifically. Following the judgment in R v Heard,[132] it seems that all the sexual offences in the

---

[129] *A-G's Ref (Nos 11 and 12 of 2012)* [2012] EWCA Crim 1119; *Cleverley* [2010] EWCA Crim 1842; *A-G's Ref (Nos 74 and 83 of 2007)* [2007] EWCA 2550.
[130] See online guidance: <http://www.CPS.gov.uk>.
[131] *R v G* [2006] EWCA Crim 821.
[132] [2007] EWCA Crim 125.

G. OFFENCES COMMITTED FROM 1.5.2004 TO DATE

2003 Act (certainly those in ss 1–4 and 5–15) will be regarded as offences for which a plea of voluntary intoxication is no defence.[133]
(iv) The extended jurisdiction provisions apply to this section.[134] See Chapter 17 para 17.01.
(v) Section 73 provides a defence to an offence of aiding abetting or counselling the commission of an offence under this section where he acts for the purpose of;
   (a) protecting the child from sexually transmitted infection,
   (b) protecting the physical safety of the child,
   (c) preventing the child from becoming pregnant, or
   (d) promoting the child's emotional well-being by the giving of advice,
      and not for the purpose of obtaining sexual gratification or for the purpose of causing or encouraging the activity constituting the offence or the child's participation in it.
(vi) The s 45 MSA 2015 defence for slavery and trafficking victims who commit an offence does not apply to this offence.[135]

Indictment

RAPE OF A CHILD UNDER 13 1.5.2004 to date   4.93

Statement of Offence
RAPE OF A CHILD UNDER 13, contrary to section 5(1) of the Sexual Offences Act 2003.

Particulars of Offence
D, on the … day of … 20 … , intentionally penetrated the [vagina] or [anus] or [mouth] of C, a person under the age of 13 years (namely … years), with his penis.

Alternative Offences

(i) Attempt to commit the full offence. When indicting offences of attempt do so under   4.94
s 1(1) Criminal Attempts Act 1981.[136] Aver the attempt in both the Statement of Offence and Particulars of Offence. In addition, aver the substantive offence under the relevant Act; see paras 1.51 and 12.157 and *Reed & Others* [2021].[137]
(ii) Sexual assault of a child under 13 (s 7) (see para 4.119).
(iii) Penetrative sexual activity with a child (s 9(2)) (see para 4.107). Note if the elements of a s 5 offence are made out, the prosecution should not charge a s 9 offence instead.[138]

---

[133] Professor David Ormerod QC CBE, March 2007.
[134] SOA 2003, s 72; provides for the prosecution within the jurisdiction of a sexual offence committed outside it.
[135] Modern Slavery Act 2015, s 45 and Sch 4, para 33.
[136] Implementation date 27.8.1981.
[137] *Reed & Others* [2021] EWCA Crim 572.
[138] *Tolhurst v DPP* [2008] EWHC 2976 (Admin).

82   4. OFFENCES INVOLVING CHILDREN

Sentence

4.95 On indictment: LIFE.[139]

Sentencing Guidance

4.96 (i) The Sentencing Council 'Sexual Offences: Definitive Guideline' contains offence-specific guidelines. The Guideline applies to all offenders aged 18 and over, sentenced on or after 1 April 2014. When sentencing an Offender who has committed a sexual offence with, or in respect of, a person who is, or who the Offender believes to be, a child and no sexual activity occurs refer to *R v Reed and Others* [2021],[140] see Chapter 12 para 12.176

(ii) Where a defendant under 18 is charged under this section rather than under a s 13[141] offence, the court cannot offend Article 8 if it passes an appropriate sentence.[142]

Upon Conviction/Sentence

4.97 (i) Notification applicable.[143]

(ii) Automatic inclusion in the children's barred list with no right to make representations. Automatic inclusion in the adults' barred list with the right to make representations.[144]

(iii) SHPO applicable.[145]

(iv) Qualifying 'specified sexual offence' in Schedule 18 (Extended Sentences).[146]

(v) Qualifying Schedule 19 offence (Life Sentences).[147]

(vi) Qualifying offence for the purpose of Schedule 13 (Offenders of Particular Concern).[148]

(vii) Qualifying Schedule 14 offence (Extended Sentences: The Earlier Offence Condition).[149]

(viii) Qualifying 'index' offence (if committed after 3 December 2012) for the purpose of Schedule 15 (Life Sentence for Second Listed Offence).[150]

---

[139] SOA 2003, s 5(2).
[140] *Reed & Others* [2021] EWCA Crim 572.
[141] Section 13 governs the prosecution of defendants under 18 who but for their age would commit an offence under ss 9–12; it provides a maximum sentence of 5 years.
[142] *R v G* [2006] EWCA Crim 821.
[143] SOA 2003, s 80(1) and Sch 3, para 19; see Chapter 14 paras 14.1–14.5.
[144] Part 2 of the Safeguarding Vulnerable Groups Act 2006 (Prescribed Criteria and Miscellaneous Provisions) Regulations 2009 (SI 2009 No 37) paras 1 and 4; see Chapter 12 para 12.217.
[145] SA 2020, s 345 and SOA 2003 Sch 3, para 19; see Chapter 16 para 16.07.
[146] SA 2020, s 306, Sch 18, para 38(e); see Chapter 12 para 12.51.
[147] SA 2020, s 307, Sch 19, para 20(d); see Chapter 12 para 12.52.
[148] SA 2020, ss 265 and 278 and Sch 13, para 6(a); Chapter 12 para 12.101.
[149] SA 2020, ss 267 and 280, Sch 14, para 9(d); see Chapter 12 para 12.77.
[150] SA 2020, ss 273 and 283, Sch 15, para 9(d); see Chapter 12 para 12.123.

2. Assault of a Child under 13 by Penetration

Sexual Offences Act 2003, s 6

Definition

Intentional sexual penetration by a person (D) of another's (C's) vagina or anus with either a part of his body or anything else when that other person (C) was under 13. **4.98**

Proof

(i) Intentional sexual penetration by a person (D) of another's (C's) vagina or anus; **4.99**
(ii) with either a part of his body or anything else; and
(iii) at the time C was under 13.

Notes

(i) Triable only on indictment. **4.100**
(ii) Although the umbrella offence under s 9 (Sexual Activity with a Child) also covers the elements of this offence, it is suggested that s 6 is the appropriate charge/count where the allegation is sexual intercourse with a girl under 13; s 6 is simpler to indict and explain to a jury, is indictable only, reflecting the seriousness of the offence, and has a higher maximum sentence.
(iii) Neither consent nor belief in consent is a defence to this offence.
(iv) Following the judgment in R v Heard,[151] it seems that all the sexual offences in the 2003 Act (certainly those in ss 1–4 and 5–15) will be regarded as offences for which a plea of voluntary intoxication is no defence.[152]
(v) The offence is itself an alternative to rape (specifically, rape of a child under 13); see para 4.88.
(vi) The extended jurisdiction provisions[153] apply to this section. See Chapter 17 para 17.01.
(vii) Section 73 provides a defence to an offence of aiding abetting or counselling the commission of an offence under this section where he acts for the purpose of;
    (a) protecting the child from sexually transmitted infection,
    (b) protecting the physical safety of the child,
    (c) preventing the child from becoming pregnant, or
    (d) promoting the child's emotional well-being by the giving of advice,

---

[151] [2007] EWCA Crim 125.
[152] Professor David Ormerod QC, CBE, March 2007.
[153] SOA 2003, s 72; provides for the prosecution within the jurisdiction of a sexual offence committed outside it.

84   4. OFFENCES INVOLVING CHILDREN

and not for the purpose of obtaining sexual gratification or for the purpose of causing or encouraging the activity constituting the offence or the child's participation in it.

(viii) The s 45 MSA 2015 defence for slavery and trafficking victims who commit an offence does not apply to this offence.[154]

Indictment

4.101 ASSAULT BY PENETRATION OF A CHILD UNDER 13 1.5.2004 to date

> **Statement of Offence**
> ASSAULT BY PENETRATION OF A CHILD UNDER 13, contrary to section 6(1) of the Sexual Offences Act 2003.
>
> **Particulars of Offence**
> D, on the ... day of ... 20 ... , intentionally penetrated the [vagina] *or* [anus] of C, a person under the age of 13 years (namely ... years).

4.102 It is not strictly necessary to aver the specific age of the complainant over and above being under 13 but, depending upon the complexity of the prosecution case, its inclusion would help to clarify it in particularizing several counts on an indictment; hence the option contained within brackets.[155]

Alternative Offences

4.103 (i) Attempt to commit the full offence. When indicting offences of attempt do so under s 1(1) Criminal Attempts Act 1981.[156] Aver the attempt in both the Statement of Offence and Particulars of Offence. In addition, aver the substantive offence under the relevant Act; see paras 1.51 and 12.157 and *Reed & Others* [2021].[157]

(ii) Sexual assault of a child under 13; 14 YEARS; see para 4.119.

Sentence

4.104 On indictment: LIFE.[158]

---

[154] Modern Slavery Act 2015, s 45 and Sch 4, para 33.
[155] *R v Rackham* [1997] 2 Cr App R 222.
[156] Implementation date 27.8.1981.
[157] *Reed & Others* [2021] EWCA Crim 572.
[158] SOA 2003, s 6(2).

G. OFFENCES COMMITTED FROM 1.5.2004 TO DATE

Sentencing Guidance

4.105 The Sentencing Council 'Sexual Offences: Definitive Guideline' contains offence-specific guidelines. The Guideline applies to all offenders aged 18 and over, sentenced on or after 1 April 2014. When sentencing an Offender who has committed a sexual offence with, or in respect of, a person who is, or who the Offender believes to be, a child and no sexual activity occurs refer to *R v Reed and Others* [2021],[159] see Chapter 12 para 12.176.

Upon Conviction/Sentence

4.106
(i) Notification applicable.[160]
(ii) Automatic inclusion in the children's barred list with no right to make representations. Automatic inclusion in the adults' barred list with the right to make representations.[161]
(iii) SHPO applicable.[162]
(iv) Qualifying 'specified sexual offence' in Schedule 18 (Extended Sentences).[163]
(v) Qualifying Schedule 19 offence (Life Sentences).[164]
(vi) Qualifying offence for the purpose of Schedule 13 (Offenders of Particular Concern).[165]
(vii) Qualifying Schedule 14 offence (Extended Sentences: The Earlier Offence Condition).[166]
(viii) Qualifying 'index' offence (if committed after 3 December 2012) for the purpose of Schedule 15 (Life Sentence for Second Listed Offence).[167]

3. Penetrative Sexual Activity with a Child

Sexual Offences Act 2003, s 9(1) and (2)

Introduction

4.107 A defendant under 18 may be prosecuted for this offence under s 13. Within the umbrella offence of s 9 (see para 4.129 for non-penetrative assaults under s 9), s 9(2)(a) covers the old offence of USI with a girl under 16. Section 9(2) in general expands the ambit of such offences beyond sexual intercourse to include other penetrative sexual activity.

---

[159] *Reed & Others* [2021] EWCA Crim 572.
[160] SOA 2003, s 80(1) and Sch 3, para 19, SOA 2003; see Chapter 14 paras 14.1–14.5.
[161] Part 2 of the Safeguarding Vulnerable Groups Act 2006 (Prescribed Criteria and Miscellaneous Provisions) Regulations 2009 (SI 2009 No 37) paras 1 and 4; see Chapter 12 para 12.217.
[162] SA 2020, s 345 and SOA 2003 Sch 3, para 19; see Chapter 16 para 16.07.
[163] SA 2020, s 306, Sch 18, para 38(f); see Chapter 12 para 12.51.
[164] SA 2020, s 307, Sch 19, para 20(e); see Chapter 12 para 12.52.
[165] SA 2020, ss 265 and 278 and Sch 13, para 6(b); Chapter para 12.101.
[166] SA 2020, ss 267 and 280, Sch 14, para 9(e); see Chapter 12 para 12.77.
[167] SA 2020, ss 273 and 283, Sch 15, para 9(e); see Chapter 12 para 12.123.

4. OFFENCES INVOLVING CHILDREN

See para 4.128 for non-penetrative sexual activity with a child.

Definition

4.108 As per Proof.

Proof

4.109
(i) Intentional sexual touching by D of C;
(ii) when C is either under 16 (and D does not reasonably believe that C is 16 or over) or C is under 13;
(iii) which involves any of the following:
- penetration of C's anus or vagina with part of D's body or anything else;
- penetration of C's mouth with D's penis;
- penetration of D's anus or vagina with part of C's body;
- penetration of C's mouth with D's penis.

Notes

4.110
(i) A penetrative offence under s 9(2) is indictable only.
(ii) The offence under s 9(2) is itself an alternative to rape (of a child under 13 where appropriate).
(iii) Neither consent nor belief in consent is a defence to this offence.
(iv) Following the judgment in R v Heard,[168] it seems that all the sexual offences in the 2003 Act (certainly those in ss 1–4 and 5–15) will be regarded as offences for which a plea of voluntary intoxication is no defence.[169]
(v) The extended jurisdiction provisions apply to this section.[170] See Chapter 17 para 17.01.
(vii) Section 73 provides a defence to an offence of aiding abetting or counselling the commission of an offence under s 9 and s 13 (which would be an offence under s 9 if the offender were aged 18) where he acts for the purpose of;
  (a) protecting the child from sexually transmitted infection,
  (b) protecting the physical safety of the child,
  (c) preventing the child from becoming pregnant, or
  (d) promoting the child's emotional well-being by the giving of advice,
    and not for the purpose of obtaining sexual gratification or for the purpose of causing or encouraging the activity constituting the offence or the child's participation in it.
(viii) The s 45 MSA 2015 defence for slavery and trafficking victims who commit an offence does not apply to this offence.[171]

---

[168] [2007] EWCA Crim 125.
[169] Professor David Ormerod QC CBE, March 2007.
[170] SOA 2003, s 72; provides for the prosecution within the jurisdiction of a sexual offence committed outside it.
[171] Modern Slavery Act 2015, s 45 and Sch 4, para 33.

G. OFFENCES COMMITTED FROM 1.5.2004 TO DATE

Indictment

Defendant is over 18

PENETRATIVE SEXUAL ACTIVITY WITH A CHILD 1.5.2004 to date **4.111**

Statement of Offence
PENETRATIVE SEXUAL ACTIVITY WITH A CHILD, contrary to ss 9(1) and (2) of the Sexual Offences Act 2003.

Particulars of Offence
D, a person of at least 18 years, on the … day of … 20 … , intentionally and sexually touched C and that touching involved penetration of C's [mouth] *or* [vagina] *or* [anus] with D's penis, (in that he/she …), when C was aged under 16 years (namely … years) and [D did not reasonably believe that C was of or over the age of 16 years] *or* [C was under 13 years].

Defendant is under 18

PENETRATIVE SEXUAL ACTIVITY WITH A CHILD 1.5.2004 to date **4.112**

Statement of Offence
PENETRATIVE SEXUAL ACTIVITY WITH A CHILD, contrary to sections 13, 9(1) and (2) of the Sexual Offences Act 2003.

Particulars of Offence
D, a person under the age of 18 years *or* (of … years), on the … day of … 20 … , intentionally and sexually touched C and the touching involved penetration of C's [mouth] *or* [vagina] *or* [anus] with D's penis, (in that he/she …), when C was aged under 16 years (namely … years) and [D did not reasonably believe that C was of or over the age of 16 years] *or* [C was under 13 years].

Where the offence is a penetrative offence under s 9(2), it is necessary to aver the age of the complainant and it may be useful to aver the exact age. Also, depending upon the complexity of the prosecution case, it is good practice where possible to particularize the count(s) as fully as possible, hence the options contained within brackets 'in that he/she … '.[172] **4.113**

Alternative Offences

(i) Attempt to commit the full offence. When indicting offences of attempt do so under s 1(1) Criminal Attempts Act 1981.[173] Aver the attempt in both the Statement of **4.114**

---

[172] *R v Rackham* [1997] 2 Crim App R 222.
[173] Implementation date 27.8.1981.

88   4. OFFENCES INVOLVING CHILDREN

Offence and Particulars of Offence. In addition, aver the substantive offence under the relevant Act; see paras 1.51 and 12.157 and *Reed & Others* [2021].[174]

(ii) Sexual assault of a child under **13 YEARS**; see para 4.119.

Sentence

4.115   On indictment:

- where defendant is 18 or over: **14 YEARS**.[175]
- where defendant is under 18: **5 YEARS**.[176]

Sentencing Guidance

4.116   For adult offenders: The Sentencing Council 'Sexual Offences: Definitive Guideline' contains offence-specific guidelines. The Guideline applies to all offenders aged 18 and over, sentenced on or after 1 April 2014.

For children and young persons: The 'Sentencing Children and Young Persons—Overarching Principles' and 'Sentencing Children and Young Persons—Sexual Offences' Guidelines apply to all children and young persons sentenced on or after 1 June 2017. When sentencing an Offender who has committed a sexual offence with, or in respect of, a person who is, or who the Offender believes to be, a child and no sexual activity occurs refer to *R v Reed and Others* [2021],[177] see Chapter 12 para 12.176.

Upon Conviction/Sentence

4.117   Section 9 and s 13 offences: notification applies.[178] The notification period is halved for under 18s.

(ii) Section 9 offence: Automatic inclusion in the children's and adults' barred lists with the right to make representations applicable.[179]
(iii) Section 9 and s 13 offences: SHPO applicable.[180]
(iv) Section 9 and 13 offences: Qualifying 'specified sexual offence' in Schedule 18 (Extended Sentences).[181]
(v) Section 9 offence: Qualifying Schedule 14 offence (Extended Sentences: The Earlier Offence Condition).[182]

---

[174] *Reed & Others* [2021] EWCA Crim 572.
[175] SOA 2003, s 9(2).
[176] SOA 2003, s 13(2).
[177] *Reed & Others* [2021] EWCA Crim 572.
[178] SOA 2003, s 80(1) and Sch 3, paras 21 and 22 SOA 2003; see Chapter 14 paras 14.01–14.05.
[179] Part 2 of the Safeguarding Vulnerable Groups Act 2006 (Prescribed Criteria and Miscellaneous Provisions) Regulations 2009 (SI 2009 No 37) paras 2 and 4; see Chapter 12 para 12.217.
[180] SA 2020, s 345 and SOA 2003, Sch 3, para 19; see Chapter 16 para 16.07.
[181] SA 2020, s 306, Sch 18, paras 38(i) and (m); see Chapter 12 para 12.51.
[182] SA 2020, ss 267 and 280, Sch 14, para 9(h); see Chapter 12 para 12.77.

(vi) Section 9 offence: Qualifying 'index' offence (if committed after 3 December 2012) for the purpose of Schedule 15 (Life Sentence for Second Listed Offence).[183]

Sexual Assault Upon a Child

H. OFFENCES COMMITTED PRE-31.12.1956

1. Indecent Assault Upon a Child

Offences Against the Person Act 1861, s 52

Definition

See paras 3.01–3.09. **4.118**

I. OFFENCES COMMITTED BETWEEN 1.1.1957 AND 30.4.2004

Sexual Offences Act 1956

Definition

See paras 3.10–3.30. **4.119**

1. Sexual Assault of a Child under 13

Sexual Offences Act 2003, s 7

Definition

As per Proof. **4.120**

Proof

(i) D intentionally touches C. **4.121**

---

[183] SA 2020, ss 273 and 283, Sch 15, para 9(h); see Chapter 12 para 12.123.

4. OFFENCES INVOLVING CHILDREN

(ii) The touching is sexual.
(iii) C is under 13.

Notes

4.122 (i) Triable either way.

(ii) This offence is an alternative to a number of offences, including: s 5 rape of a child under 13 (para 4.88), s 6 assault of a child under 13 by penetration (para 4.97), s 9 sexual activity with a child (paras 4.107 and 4.129).

(iii) Neither consent nor belief in consent is a defence to this offence.

(iv) Following the judgment in R v Heard,[184] it seems that all the sexual offences in the 2003 Act (certainly those in ss 1–4 and 5–15) will be regarded as offences for which a plea of voluntary intoxication is no defence.[185]

(v) The extended jurisdiction provisions[186] apply to this section. See Chapter 17 para 17.01.

(vi) Section 73 provides a defence to an offence of aiding abetting or counselling the commission of an offence under this section where he acts for the purpose of;
   (a) protecting the child from sexually transmitted infection,
   (b) protecting the physical safety of the child,
   (c) preventing the child from becoming pregnant, or
   (d) promoting the child's emotional well-being by the giving of advice,
   and not for the purpose of obtaining sexual gratification or for the purpose of causing or encouraging the activity constituting the offence or the child's participation in it.

(v) The s 45 MSA 2015 defence for slavery and trafficking victims who commit an offence does not apply to this offence.[187]

Indictment

4.123 SEXUAL ASSAULT OF A CHILD UNDER 13 1.5.2004 to date

Statement of Offence

SEXUAL ASSAULT OF A CHILD UNDER 13, contrary to section 7(1) of the Sexual Offences Act 2003.

Particulars of Offence

D, on the ... day of ... 20 ... , intentionally touched C, a girl/boy under 13 (namely ... years), in that he/she ... eg masturbated C, the circumstances being that the touching was sexual.

---

[184] [2007] EWCA Crim 125.
[185] Professor David Ormerod QC CBE, March 2007.
[186] SOA 2003, s 72; provides for the prosecution within the jurisdiction of a sexual offence committed outside it.
[187] Modern Slavery Act 2015, s 45 and Sch 4, para 33.

It is not necessary to aver the particular act alleged or to specify the age of the complainant over and above being under 13, but depending upon the nature and complexity of the prosecution case it is good practice, and sometimes essential, to particularize the counts as fully as possible, hence the options contained within brackets.[188]

4.124

Alternative Offences

(i) Attempt to commit the full offence. When indicting offences of attempt do so under s 1(1) Criminal Attempts Act 1981.[189] Aver the attempt in both the Statement of Offence and Particulars of Offence. In addition, aver the substantive offence under the relevant Act; see paras 1.51 and 12.157 and *Reed & Others* [2021].[190]

(ii) Section 3 Sexual Assault: **10 YEARS** (see para 3.42).

4.125

Sentence

(i) On indictment: **14 YEARS**.[191]
(ii) Summarily: **6 months**.[192]

4.126

Sentencing Guidance

The Sentencing Council 'Sexual Offences: Definitive Guideline' contains offence-specific guidelines. The Guideline applies to all offenders aged 18 and over, sentenced on or after 1 April 2014. When sentencing an Offender who has committed a sexual offence with, or in respect of, a person who is, or who the Offender believes to be, a child and no sexual activity occurs refer to *R v Reed and Others* [2021],[193] see Chapter 12 para 12.176

4.127

Upon Conviction/Sentence

(i) Notification applies where the offender was 18 or over or is sentenced to at least 12 months' custody.[194]
(ii) Automatic inclusion in the children's barred list with no right to make representations. Automatic inclusion in the adults' barred list with right to make representations.[195]

4.128

---

[188] *R v Rackham* [1997] 2 Cr App R 222; see also Indictments, para 1.09.
[189] Implementation date 27.8.1981.
[190] *Reed & Others* [2021] EWCA Crim 572.
[191] SOA 2003, s 7(2).
[192] SOA 2003, s 7(2). CJA 2003, s 282(2), s 7(3); to be applied for offences committed after 1.5.2004.
[193] *Reed & Others* [2021] EWCA Crim 572.
[194] SOA 2003, s 80(1) and Sch 3, para 20 SOA 2003; see Chapter 14 paras 14.01–14.05.
[195] Part 2 of the Safeguarding Vulnerable Groups Act 2006 (Prescribed Criteria and Miscellaneous Provisions) Regulations 2009 (SI 2009 No 37) paras 1 and 4; see Chapter 12 para 12.217.

4. OFFENCES INVOLVING CHILDREN

(iii) SHPO applies.[196]
(iv) Qualifying 'specified sexual offence' in Schedule 18 (Extended Sentences).[197]
(v) Qualifying Schedule 14 offence (Extended Sentences: The Earlier Offence Condition).[198]
(vi) Qualifying 'index' offence (if committed after 3 December 2012) for the purpose of Schedule 15 (Life Sentence for Second Listed Offence).[199]

2. Non-penetrative Sexual Activity with a Child

Sexual Offences Act 2003, s 9(1)

4.129 A defendant under 18 may be charged with this offence under s 13. See para 4.106 for penetrative sexual activity with a child.

Definition

4.130 As per Proof.

Proof

4.131
(i) D intentionally touches C sexually when:
(ii) either:
- C is under 16 and D does not reasonably believe C is 16 or over; or
- C is under 13.

Notes

4.132
(i) Either way when penetration not averred.
(ii) Neither consent nor belief in consent are defences to this offence.
(iii) Following the judgment in R v Heard,[200] it seems that all the sexual offences in the 2003 Act (certainly those in ss 1–4 and 5–15) will be regarded as offences for which a plea of voluntary intoxication is no defence.[201]
(iv) The extended jurisdiction provisions[202] apply to this section. See Chapter 17 para 17.01.
(v) Section 73 provides a defence to an offence of aiding abetting or counselling the commission of an offence under this section where he acts for the purpose of;
   (a) protecting the child from sexually transmitted infection,
   (b) protecting the physical safety of the child,

---

[196] SA 2020, s 345 and SOA 2003, Sch 3, para 20; see Chapter 16 para 16.07.
[197] SA 2020, s 306, Sch 18, para 38(f); see Chapter 12 para 12.51.
[198] SA 2020, ss 267 and 280, Sch 14, para 9(f); see Chapter 12 para 12.77.
[199] SA 2020, ss 273 and 283, Sch 15, para 9(f); see Chapter 12 para 12.123.
[200] [2007] EWCA Crim 125.
[201] Professor David Ormerod QC CBE, March 2007.
[202] SOA 2003, s 72 provides for the prosecution within the jurisdiction of a sexual offence committed outside it.

I. OFFENCES COMMITTED BETWEEN 1.1.1957 AND 30.4.2004

(c) preventing the child from becoming pregnant, or
(d) promoting the child's emotional well-being by the giving of advice,
and not for the purpose of obtaining sexual gratification or for the purpose of causing or encouraging the activity constituting the offence or the child's participation in it.
(vi) The s 45 MSA 2015 defence for slavery and trafficking victims who commit an offence does not apply to this offence.[203]

Indictment

Defendant over 18

SEXUAL ACTIVITY WITH A CHILD 1.5.2004 to date   4.133

Statement of Offence
SEXUAL ACTIVITY WITH A CHILD, contrary to section 9(1) of the Sexual Offences Act 2003.

Particulars of Offence
D, a person aged 18 years or over, … on the … day of … 20 … , intentionally touched C sexually in that he/she … e.g. masturbated C, at a time when C was under 16 (namely … years) and [D did not reasonably believe that C was 16 or over] *or* [C was under 13 years].

Defendant under 18

SEXUAL ACTIVITY WITH A CHILD 1.5.2004 to date   4.134

Statement of Offence
SEXUAL ACTIVITY WITH A CHILD, contrary to section 13 and section 9(1) of the Sexual Offences Act 2003.

Particulars of Offence
D, a person under the age of 18 years … , on the … day of … 20 … , intentionally touched C sexually in that he/she … e.g. masturbated C/digitally penetrated C's vagina, at a time when C was under 16 (namely … years) and [D did not reasonably believe that C was 16 or over] *or* [C was under 13 years].

Note indict contrary to ss 13 and 9(1).[204] Note also the s 45 MSA 2015 defence for slavery and trafficking victims who commit an offence does not apply to s 13 offences.[205]   4.135

---

[203] Modern Slavery Act 2015, s 45 and Sch 4, para 33.
[204] See Indictments, para 1.46.
[205] Modern Slavery Act 2015, s 45 and Sch 4, para 33.

94 4. OFFENCES INVOLVING CHILDREN

Alternative Offences

4.136 (i) Attempt to commit the full offence. When indicting offences of attempt do so under s 1(1) Criminal Attempts Act 1981.[206] Aver the attempt in both the Statement of Offence and Particulars of Offence. In addition, aver the substantive offence under the relevant Act; see paras 1.51 and 12.157 and *Reed & Others* [2021].[207]

(ii) Section 3 Sexual Assault: **10 YEARS** see para 3.51; other offences under the SOA 2003 may also be alternatives depending on the factual elements such as age of the child and whether there was penetration or not.

Sentence

4.137 Defendant 18 or over:[208]

(i) On indictment: **14 YEARS**.[209]
(ii) Summarily: 6[210] months.[211]

4.138 Defendant under 18:[212]

(i) On indictment: **5 YEARS**.
(ii) Summarily: 6[213] months.[214]

Sentencing Guidance

4.139 See para 4.115

Upon Conviction/Sentence

4.140 See para 4.116

OFFENCES INVOLVING ABUSE OF A POSITION OF TRUST

J. OFFENCES COMMITTED BETWEEN 8.1.2001 AND 30.4.2004

4.141 The SO(A)A 2000 created an offence of Abuse of Trust (ss 3 and 4 govern it). This covers sexual relationships between teacher and pupil as well as others in a caring/supervisory position in relation to under 18s.

---

[206] Implementation date 27.8.1981.
[207] *Reed & Others* [2021] EWCA Crim 572.
[208] SOA 2003, s 9(2).
[209] SOA 2003, s 9(3)(b).
[210] CJA 2003, s 282(2), s 9(3); to be applied for offences committed after 1.5.2004.
[211] SOA 2003, s 9(3).
[212] SOA 2003, s 13(2).
[213] CJA 2003, s 282(2), s 7(3); to be applied for offences committed after 1.5.2004.
[214] SOA 2003, s 9(3).

J. OFFENCES COMMITTED BETWEEN 8.1.2001 AND 30.4.2004

'Position of Trust' is defined[215] thus; briefly, it covers where D is 18 or over and looks after people under 18, and C is such a person in D's care being either: **4.142**

(i) cared for in a hospital, children's care home, residential home or similar, nursing home, mental health nursing home or other similar residential accommodation, or
(ii) in receipt of full-time education at an educational institution.

D 'looks after' if he is regularly involved in caring for, training, supervising, or being in sole charge.

Any such act also constitutes an offence if committed in Scotland or Northern Ireland.[216] **4.143**

It is proposed, by the Police, Crime, Sentencing and Courts Bill that further, defined positions of trust will be added and a new offence created to reflect this under s 22A of the SOA 2003. **4.144**

The new further positions of trust will be defined by reference to the activity which D is carrying out in relation to C, namely, coaching, teaching, training, supervising or instructing in a sport or a religion, as defined. It is intended two further requirements will need to be met:

that D carries out the activity 'on a regular basis'.
D knows that s/he carries out that activity on a regular basis in relation to C.

The Police Bill defines 'sport' as 'using games in which physical skill is the predominant factor and those which are engaged in for the purpose of competition or display'. 'Religion' is defined to capture 'those involved in a religion that holds a belief in one or more gods, and those involved in a religion that do not hold a belief in a god'.

Note, spouses and civil partners are exempt from these offences.[217] In addition sexual relationships that pre-date the position of trust are also not encompassed within these offences.[218]

1. Abuse of Position of Trust

Sexual Offences (Amendment) Act 2000, s 3

Definition

As per Proof. **4.145**

Proof

(i) D, aged 18 or over; **4.146**
(ii) was in a position of trust[219] in respect of C;

---

[215] SOA(A) 2000, s 4, SOA 2003 s 21.
[216] S20 SOA 2003.
[217] SOA 2003, s 23.
[218] SOA 2003, s 24. It is for the defendant to prove that such a relationship existed before 8.1.2001.
[219] See Introductory note at para 4.142; see SO(A)A 2000, s 4 for full definition.

4. OFFENCES INVOLVING CHILDREN

(iii) when he had sexual intercourse (vaginal/anal) with C or engaged in any other sexual activity with or directed towards C; and

(iv) C was under 18 at the time.

Notes

4.147 (i) Triable either way.

(ii) Note: statutory defences:
- actual and reasonable lack of knowledge in respect of either C's age[220] or the position of trust;[221]
- and C were lawfully married at the time.[222]
- If the position of trust and sexual relationship between D and C already existed before the commencement of the SO(A)A 2000.[223]

Indictment

4.148 ABUSE OF POSITION OF TRUST 8.1.2001 to 30.4.2004

Statement of Offence

ABUSE OF A POSITION OF TRUST, contrary to section 3(1) of the Sexual Offences (Amendment) Act 2000.

Particulars of Offence

D, on the … day of … 20 … , being a person of at least 18 years, had sexual intercourse with C, s/he being a person under the age of 18 years, and being at the time in a position of trust in relation to C, in that he looked after persons under the age of 18 years who …

For example:

were resident on the children's ward at … hospital and C was at the time a residential/in-patient receiving such care at … hospital

or

were in receipt of full-time education at … school and C was at the time receiving such education at … school (D being her English teacher).

Alternative Offences

4.149 Attempt to commit the full offence. When indicting offences of attempt do so under s 1(1) Criminal Attempts Act 1981.[224] Aver the attempt in both the Statement of Offence and Particulars of Offence. In addition, aver the substantive offence under the relevant Act; see paras 1.51 and 12.157 and *Reed & Others* [2021].[225]

---

[220] SOA 2000, s 3(2)(a).
[221] SO(A)A 2000, s 3(2)(b).
[222] SO(A)A 2000, s 3(2)(c).
[223] SO(A)A 2000, s 3(3).
[224] Implementation date 27.8.1981.
[225] *Reed & Others* [2021] EWCA Crim 572.

Sentence

(i) On indictment: 5 YEARS.[226] **4.150**
(ii) Summarily: 6 months.[227]

Upon Conviction/Sentence

(i) Notification applies if the offender was 20 or over.[228] **4.151**
(ii) Automatic inclusion in the children's and adults' barred lists with the right to make representations.[229]
(iii) SHPO applies.[230]

K. OFFENCES COMMITTED FROM 1.5.2004 TO DATE

Introduction

The SOA 2003 repealed ss 3 and 4 of the SO(A)A 2000. Section 16 of the SOA 2003 replaces this offence but widens its ambit beyond intercourse to include any intentional sexual touching. In addition, three new offences by persons in a position of trust are created; Causing/Inciting Child to Engage in Sexual Activity (s 17; see para 4.162), Sexual Activity in Presence of Child (s 18; see para 4.171) and Causing a Child to Watch a Sexual Act (s 19; see para 4.180). **4.152**

These four offences under the 2003 Act essentially mirror the child sex offences under ss 9–12 in terms of elements to be proved, except that the age of the child afforded protection is under 18 rather than under 16 and there is the additional factor of the position of trust the defendant is said to be in. Interestingly, the maximum sentence each of the abuse of trust offences attracts is 5 years, rather than the 14-year maximum attracted by ss 9–12. No doubt those behind the drafting of the 2003 Act intended these offences to reflect situations where consent is not an issue but where young people need to be protected from those taking advantage of them and indeed from themselves in not being able to form a fully mature perspective on such a relationship, hence the lower maximum sentences; it has, however, provided an odd anomaly as between similar sections of the Act. **4.153**

Section 21[231] of the 2003 Act defines those in a position of trust; s 22[232] interprets those definitions. Section 23[233] exempts spouses and civil partners[234] from these offences. Section 24 exempts a defendant where the sexual relationship pre-dated the position of trust. **4.154**

---

[226] SO(A)A 2000, s 3(4)(b).
[227] SOA(A)A 2000, s 3(4)(a). Increased to 12 months if CJA 2003, s 282(4) implemented.
[228] SOA 2003, s 80(1) and Sch 3, para 16; see Chapter 14 paras 14.01–14.05.
[229] Part 2 of the Safeguarding Vulnerable Groups Act 2006 (Prescribed Criteria and Miscellaneous Provisions) Regulations 2009 (SI 2009 No 37) paras 2 and 4; see Chapter 12 para 12.217.
[230] SA 2020, s 345 and SOA 2003, Sch 3, para 16; see Chapter 16 para 16.07.
[231] As amended.
[232] As amended.
[233] As amended.
[234] Civil partners inserted from 5.5.2005.

1. Abuse of Position of Trust: Sexual Activity with a Child

Sexual Offences Act 2003, s 16

Definition

4.155   As per Proof.

Proof

4.156
(i) D, aged 18 or over;
(ii) intentionally touches another person (C) sexually;
(iii) when D is in a position of trust in relation to C, who is either under 18 (and D does not reasonably believe that C is 18 or over), or under 13.

Notes

4.157
(i) Triable either way.
(ii) Statutory defences exist in relation to D's knowledge of both C's age and the position of trust but there is in relation to all these latest sexual offences of abuse of trust an evidential burden on D to raise 'sufficient evidence' to show that he either did not know that C was under 18[235] or did not know of the relationship of trust between them[236] (or both, if that is his case). Once D has raised the issue(s) through sufficient evidence, it will be for the prosecution to disprove to the criminal standard.
(iii) The extended jurisdiction provisions[237] apply to this section. See Chapter 17 para 17.01.
(iv) Section 73 provides a defence to an offence of aiding abetting or counselling the commission of an offence under this section where C is under 16 and where D acts for the purpose of;
  (a) protecting the child from sexually transmitted infection,
  (b) protecting the physical safety of the child,
  (c) preventing the child from becoming pregnant, or
  (d) promoting the child's emotional well-being by the giving of advice,
  and not for the purpose of obtaining sexual gratification or for the purpose of causing or encouraging the activity constituting the offence or the child's participation in it.
(v) The s 45 MSA 2015 defence for slavery and trafficking victims who commit an offence does not apply to this offence.[238]

---

[235] SOA 2003, s 16(3).
[236] SOA 2003, s 16 (4).
[237] SOA 2003, s 72; provides for the prosecution within the jurisdiction of a sexual offence committed outside it.
[238] Modern Slavery Act 2015, s 45 and Sch 4, para 33.

Indictment

SEXUAL ACTIVITY WITH A CHILD BY A PERSON IN A POSITION OF TRUST **4.158**
1.5.2004 to date

Statement of Offence
SEXUAL ACTIVITY WITH A CHILD BY A PERSON IN A POSITION OF TRUST, contrary to section 16(1) and 21(5) of the Sexual Offences Act 2003.

Particulars of Offence
D, a person of at least 18 years, on the ... day of ... 20 ..., intentionally touched C sexually (in that he ...), when [C was under 18 years and D did not reasonably believe that s/he was of or over the age of 18] or [C was under 13] and when D was in a position of trust in relation to C, in that whilst D looked after persons receiving education at ... school, C was a pupil receiving education there and D could reasonably be expected to know of the circumstances by virtue of which s/he was in a position of trust in relation to C (in that s/he was C's physical education teacher).

Note: section 21(5) provides for circumstances where C is receiving education at an institution where D is in a position of trust towards C, hence its addition to the facts of this sample indictment. **4.159**

Alternative Offences

(i) Attempt to commit the full offence. When indicting offences of attempt do so under s 1(1) Criminal Attempts Act 1981.[239] Aver the attempt in both the Statement of Offence and Particulars of Offence. In addition, aver the substantive offence under the relevant Act; see paras 1.51 and 12.157 and *Reed & Others* [2021].[240] **4.160**

(ii) Attempt to commit the corresponding offence under s 9 if there is concern over the proof of D's position of trust, although the higher sentence under s 9 makes that a more attractive primary count to a prosecutor.[241]

Sentence

(i) On indictment: **5 YEARS**.[242] **4.161**
(ii) Summarily: **6 months**.[243]

---

[239] Implementation date 27.8.1981.
[240] *Reed & Others* [2021] EWCA Crim 572.
[241] Note, however, that any 'excessive sentence' could offend Article 8.
[242] SOA 2003, s 16(5)(b).
[243] SOA 2003, s 16(5)(a). Increased to 12 months if CJA 2003, s 282(4) implemented.

Sentencing Guidance

4.162 The Sentencing Council 'Sexual Offences: Definitive Guideline' contains offence-specific guidelines. The Guideline applies to all offenders aged 18 and over, sentenced on or after 1 April 2014.

Upon Conviction/Sentence

4.163
(i) Notification applies if the offender is sentenced to a term of imprisonment; detained in hospital or made the subject of a community sentence for 12 months or more.[244]
(ii) Automatic inclusion in the children's and adults' barred lists with the right to make representations.[245]
(iii) SHPO applies.[246]
(iv) Qualifying 'specified sexual offence' in Schedule 18 (Extended Sentences).[247]

2. Abuse of Position of Trust: Causing/Inciting a Child to Engage in Sexual Activity

Sexual Offences Act 2003, s 17

Definition

4.164 As per Proof.

Proof

4.165
(i) D, aged 18 or over;
(ii) intentionally causes/incites C to engage in a sexual activity; and
(iii) when D is in a position of trust in relation to C, who is either under 18 (and D does not reasonably believe that C is 18 or over), or under 13; and
(iv) where subsection (2) applies, D knows or could reasonably be expected to know of the circumstances by virtue of which he is in a position of trust in relation to C.

Notes

4.166
(i) Triable either way.
(ii) Statutory defences exist in relation to D's knowledge of both C's age and the position of trust but there is in relation to all these latest sexual offences of abuse of trust an

---

[244] SOA 2003, s 80(1) and Sch 3, para 25; see Chapter 14 paras 14.01–14.05.
[245] Part 2 of the Safeguarding Vulnerable Groups Act 2006 (Prescribed Criteria and Miscellaneous Provisions) Regulations 2009 (SI 2009 No 37) paras 2 and 4; see Chapter 12 para 12.217.
[246] SA 2020, s 345 and SOA 2003, Sch 3, para 25; see Chapter 16 para 16.07.
[247] SA 2020, s 306, Sch 18, para 38(q); see Chapter 12 para 12.51.

evidential burden on D to raise 'sufficient evidence' to show that he either did not know that C was under 18[248] or did not know of the relationship of trust between them[249] (or both, if that is his case). Once D has raised the issue(s) through sufficient evidence, it will be for the prosecution to disprove to the criminal standard.

(iii) The extended jurisdiction provisions[250] apply to this section. See Chapter 17 para 17.01.

(iv) The s 45 MSA 2015 defence for slavery and trafficking victims who commit an offence does not apply to this offence.[251]

Indictment

CAUSING A CHILD TO ENGAGE IN SEXUAL ACTIVITY BY A PERSON IN A POSITION OF TRUST 1.5.2004 to date **4.167**

Statement of Offence

CAUSING A CHILD TO ENGAGE IN SEXUAL ACTIVITY BY A PERSON IN A POSITION OF TRUST, contrary to section 17(1) and 21(4)(a) of the Sexual Offences Act 2003.

Particulars of Offence

D, a person of at least 18 years, on the ... day of ... 20 ..., intentionally caused [or incited] C to engage in a sexual activity, namely ..., when [C was under 18 years and D did not reasonably believe that s/he was of or over the age of 18] *or* [C was under 13] and when D was in a position of trust in relation to C, in that whilst D looked after persons receiving treatment at ... hospital, C was an in-patient staying and receiving treatment there and D could reasonably be expected to know of the circumstances by virtue of which s/he was in a position of trust in relation to C (in that s/he was C's ward sister).

Note: section 21(4) provides for circumstances where C is being cared for and accommodated at an institution such as a hospital (subsection 4(a)) or care home where D is in a position of trust towards C), hence its addition to the facts of this sample indictment. **4.168**

Alternative Offences

(i) Attempt to commit the full offence. When indicting offences of attempt do so under s 1(1) Criminal Attempts Act 1981.[252] Aver the attempt in both the Statement of **4.169**

---

[248] SOA 2003, s 17(3).
[249] SOA 2003, s 17(4).
[250] SOA 2003, s 72; provides for the prosecution within the jurisdiction of a sexual offence committed outside it.
[251] Modern Slavery Act 2015, s 45 and Sch 4, para 33.
[252] Implementation date 27.8.1981.

102   4. OFFENCES INVOLVING CHILDREN

Offence and Particulars of Offence. In addition, aver the substantive offence under the relevant Act; see paras 1.51 and 12.157 and *Reed & Others* [2021].[253]

(ii) Attempt to commit the corresponding offence under s 10 if there is concern over the proof of D's position of trust, although the higher sentence under s 10 makes that a more attractive primary count to a prosecutor.[254] See para 4.18.

Sentence

4.170
(i) On indictment: **5 YEARS**.[255]
(ii) Summarily: **6 months**.[256]

Sentencing Guidance

4.171 The Sentencing Council 'Sexual Offences: Definitive Guideline' contains offence-specific guidelines. The Guideline applies to all offenders aged 18 and over, sentenced on or after 1 April 2014.

Upon Conviction/Sentence

4.172
(i) Notification applies if the offender is sentenced to a term of imprisonment; detained in hospital or made the subject of a community sentence for 12 months or more.[257]
(ii) Automatic inclusion in the children's and adults' barred lists with the right to make representations.[258]
(iii) SHPO applies.[259]
(iv) Qualifying 'specified sexual offence' in Schedule 18 (Extended Sentences).[260]

3. Abuse of Position of Trust: Engaging in Sexual Activity in the Presence of a Child

Sexual Offences Act 2003, s 18

Definition

4.173 As per Proof.

---

[253] *Reed & Others* [2021] EWCA Crim 572.
[254] Note, however, that any 'excessive sentence' could offend Article 8.
[255] SOA 2003, s 17(5)(b).
[256] SOA 2003, s 17(5)(a). 12 months if CJA 2003, s 282(4) implemented.
[257] SOA 2003, s 80(1) and Sch 3, para 25; see Chapter 14 paras 14.01–14.05.
[258] Part 2 of the Safeguarding Vulnerable Groups Act 2006 (Prescribed Criteria and Miscellaneous Provisions) Regulations 2009 (SI 2009 No 37) paras 2 and 4; see Chapter 12 para 12.217.
[259] SA 2020, s 345 and SOA 2003, Sch 3, para 25; see Chapter 16 para 16.07.
[260] SA 2020, s 306, Sch 18, para 38(r); see Chapter 12 para 12.51.

K. OFFENCES COMMITTED FROM 1.5.2004 TO DATE 103

Proof

(i) D, aged 18 or over;
(ii) intentionally engages in a sexual activity for the purpose of obtaining sexual gratification;
(iii) when C is either present or in a place from which D can be observed; and
(iv) knowing or believing that C is aware, or intending that C should be aware, that he is engaging in it;
(v) when D is in a position of trust in relation to C, who is either under 18 (and D does not reasonably believe that C is 18 or over), or under 13; and
(vi) where subsection (2) applies, D knows or could reasonably be expected to know of the circumstances by virtue of which he is in a position of trust in relation to C.

4.174

Notes

(i) Triable either way.
(ii) Statutory defences exist in relation to D's knowledge of both C's age and the position of trust but there is in relation to all these latest sexual offences of abuse of trust an evidential burden on D to raise 'sufficient evidence' to show that he either did not know that C was under 18[261] or did not know of the relationship of trust between them[262] (or both, if that is his case). Once D has raised the issue(s) through sufficient evidence, it will be for the prosecution to disprove to the criminal standard.
(iii) The extended jurisdiction provisions[263] apply to this section. See Chapter 17 para 17.01.
(iv) The s 45 MSA 2015 defence for slavery and trafficking victims who commit an offence does not apply to this offence.[264]

4.175

Indictment

ENGAGING IN SEXUAL ACTIVITY IN THE PRESENCE OF A CHILD 1.5.2004 to date   4.176

Statement of Offence
ENGAGING IN SEXUAL ACTIVITY IN THE PRESENCE OF A CHILD, contrary to section 18(1) and 21(4)(d) of the Sexual Offences Act 2003.

Particulars of Offence
D, a person of at least 18 years, on the … day of … 20 … , for the purpose of obtaining sexual gratification, intentionally engaged in sexual activity when C was present/in a place from which D could be observed, when [C was under 18 years and D did not reasonably believe that s/he was of or over the age of 18] *or* [C was under 13] and when D

---

[261] SOA 2003, s 18(3).
[262] SOA 2003, s 18(4).
[263] SOA 2003, s 72; provides for the prosecution within the jurisdiction of a sexual offence committed outside it.
[264] Modern Slavery Act 2015, s 45 and Sch 4, para 33.

4. OFFENCES INVOLVING CHILDREN

> was in a position of trust in relation to C, in that whilst D looked after persons living in a children's home, namely … when C was a child cared for and accommodated there and D could reasonably be expected to know of the circumstances by virtue of which s/he was in a position of trust in relation to C (in that s/he was the home's matron).

4.177 Note: section 21(4) provides for circumstances where C is being cared for and accommodated at an institution such as a children's home (subsection 4(d)), hospital, or care home where D is in a position of trust towards C, hence its addition to the facts of this sample indictment.

Alternative Offences

4.178 (i) Attempt to commit the full offence. When indicting offences of attempt do so under s 1(1) Criminal Attempts Act 1981.[265] Aver the attempt in both the Statement of Offence and Particulars of Offence. In addition, aver the substantive offence under the relevant Act; see paras 1.51 and 12.157 and *Reed & Others* [2021].[266]
(ii) The corresponding offence under s 11 if there is concern over the proof of D's position of trust, although the higher sentence under s 11 makes that a more attractive primary count to a prosecutor.[267] See para 4.191.

Sentence

4.179 (i) On indictment: 5 YEARS.[268]
(ii) Summarily: **6 months**.[269]

Sentencing Guidance

4.180 The Sentencing Council 'Sexual Offences: Definitive Guideline' contains offence-specific guidelines. The Guideline applies to all offenders aged 18 and over, sentenced on or after 1 April 2014.

Upon Conviction/Sentence

4.181 (i) Notification applies if the offender is sentenced to a term of imprisonment; detained in hospital or made the subject of a community sentence for 12 months or more.[270]
(ii) Automatic inclusion in the children's and adults' barred lists with the right to make representations.[271]

---

[265] Implementation date 27.8.1981.
[266] *Reed & Others* [2021] EWCA Crim 572.
[267] Note, however, that any 'excessive sentence' could offend Article 8.
[268] SOA 2003, s 18(5)(b).
[269] SOA 2003, s 18(5)(a). Increased to 12 months if CJA 2003, s 282(4) implemented.
[270] SOA 2003, s 80(1) and Sch 3, para 25; see Chapter 14 paras 14.01–14.05.
[271] Part 2 of the Safeguarding Vulnerable Groups Act 2006 (Prescribed Criteria and Miscellaneous Provisions) Regulations 2009 (SI 2009 No 37) paras 2 and 4; see Chapter 12 para 12.217.

K. OFFENCES COMMITTED FROM 1.5.2004 TO DATE 105

(iii) SHPO applies.[272]
(iv) Qualifying 'specified sexual offence' in Schedule 18 (Extended Sentences).[273]

4. Abuse of Position of Trust: Causing a Child to Watch a Sexual Act

Sexual Offences Act 2003, s 19

Definition

As per Proof. 4.182

Proof

(i) D, aged 18 or over; 4.183
(ii) for the purpose of obtaining sexual gratification;
(iii) intentionally causes (C) to either watch a third person (X) engaging in a sexual activity, or to look at an image of any person engaging in a sexual activity;
(iv) when D is in a position of trust in relation to C, who is either under 18 (and D does not reasonably believe that C is 18 or over), or under 13; and
(v) where subsection (2) applies, D knows or could reasonably be expected to know of the circumstances by virtue of which he is in a position of trust in relation to C.

Notes

(i) Triable either way. 4.184
(ii) Statutory defences exist in relation to D's knowledge of both C's age and the position of trust but there is in relation to all these latest sexual offences of abuse of trust an evidential burden on D to raise 'sufficient evidence' to show that he either did not know that C was under 18[274] or did not know of the relationship of trust between them[275] (or both, if that is his case). Once D has raised the issue(s) through sufficient evidence, it will be for the prosecution to disprove to the criminal standard.
(iii) The extended jurisdiction provisions apply.[276] See Chapter 17 para 17.01.
(iv) The s 45 MSA 2015 defence for slavery and trafficking victims who commit an offence does not apply to this offence.[277]

Indictment

CAUSING A CHILD TO WATCH A SEXUAL ACT BY A PERSON IN A POSITION OF TRUST 1.5.2004 to date 4.185

---

[272] SA 2020, s 345 and SOA 2003, Sch 3, para 25; see Chapter 16 para 16.07.
[273] SA 2020, s 306, Sch 18, para 38(s); see Chapter 12 para 12.51.
[274] SOA 2003, s 19(3).
[275] SOA 2003, s 19 (4).
[276] SOA 2003, s 72; provides for the prosecution within the jurisdiction of a sexual offence committed outside it.
[277] Modern Slavery Act 2015, s 45 and Sch 4, para 33.

> ### Statement of Offence
> CAUSING A CHILD TO WATCH A SEXUAL ACT BY A PERSON IN A POSITION OF TRUST, contrary to section 19(1) and 21(5) of the Sexual Offences Act 2003.
>
> ### Particulars of Offence
> D, a person of at least 18 years, on the ... day of ... 20 ... , for the purpose of obtaining sexual gratification, intentionally caused C to watch X engaging in a sexual activity *or* [look at an image of a person engaging in a sexual activity], C was under 18 years at the time and the said D did not reasonably believe that s/he was of or over the age of 18, *or* [C was under 13] and the said D was in a position of trust in relation to C in that whilst D looked after persons receiving education at ... school, C was a pupil receiving education there and the said D could reasonably be expected to know of the circumstances by virtue of which s/he was in a position of trust in relation to C (in that s/he was the head teacher).

4.186 Note: section 21(5) provides for circumstances where C is being cared for and taught at an institution such as a school where D is not receiving education and so is in a position of trust towards C, hence its addition to the facts of this sample indictment.

Alternative Offences

4.187 (i) Attempt to commit the full offence. When indicting offences of attempt do so under s 1(1) Criminal Attempts Act 1981.[278] Aver the attempt in both the Statement of Offence and Particulars of Offence. In addition, aver the substantive offence under the relevant Act; see paras 1.51 and 12.157 and *Reed & Others* [2021].[279]

(ii) The corresponding offence under s 12 if there is concern over the proof of D's position of trust, although the higher sentence under s 12 makes that a more attractive primary count to a prosecutor.[280] See para 4.202.

Sentence

4.188 (i) On indictment: **5 YEARS**.[281]
(ii) Summarily: **6 months**.[282]

Sentencing Guidance

4.189 The Sentencing Council 'Sexual Offences: Definitive Guideline' contains offence-specific guidelines. The Guideline applies to all offenders aged 18 and over, sentenced on or after 1 April 2014.

---

[278] Implementation date 27.8.1981.
[279] *Reed & Others* [2021] EWCA Crim 572.
[280] Note, however, that any 'excessive sentence' could offend Art 8.
[281] SOA 2003, s 19(5)(b).
[282] SOA 2003, s 19(5)(a). Increased to 12 months if CJA 2003, s 282(4) implemented.

Upon Conviction/Sentence

(i) Notification applies if the offender is sentenced to a term of imprisonment; detained in hospital or made the subject of a community sentence for 12 months or more.[283]   **4.190**
(ii) Automatic inclusion in the children's and adults' barred lists with the right to make representations.[284]
(iii) SHPO applies.[285]
(iv) Qualifying 'specified sexual offence' in Schedule 18 (Extended Sentences).[286]

L. OFFENCES WITHOUT PRECEDENT

The SOA 2003 created a number of offences covering sexual behaviour in relation to children either not previously the subject of criminal charges or duplicated at least in part by other offences. From 3.4.2017 two additional offences were incorporated into the 2003 Act: sexual communication with a child (s 15A) and possession of a paedophile manual (s 69).   **4.191**

1. Engaging in Sexual Activity in the Presence of a Child

Sexual Offences Act 2003, s 11

A defendant under 18 may be prosecuted for this offence under s 13.   **4.192**

Definition

As per Proof.   **4.193**

Proof

(i) D aged 18 or over;   **4.194**
(ii) intentionally engages in a sexual activity for the purpose of obtaining sexual gratification; and
(iii) he engages in it when another person (C) is present or is in a place from which D can be observed; and
(iv) D knows or believes that C is aware, or intends that C should be aware, that he is engaging in it; and
(v) either:
  - C is under 16 and D does not reasonably believe that C is 16 or over; or
  - C is under 13.
(vi) Where D is under 18:
  - identical except for D's age.

---

[283] SOA 2003, s 80(1) and Sch 3, para 25; see Chapter 14 paras 14.01–14.05.
[284] Part 2 of the Safeguarding Vulnerable Groups Act 2006 (Prescribed Criteria and Miscellaneous Provisions) Regulations 2009 (SI 2009 No 37) paras 2 and 4; see Chapter 12 para 12.217.
[285] SA 2020, s 345 and SOA 2003, Sch 3, para 25; see Chapter 16 para 16.07.
[286] SA 2020, s 306, Sch 18, para 38(t); see Chapter 12 para 12.51.

108   4. OFFENCES INVOLVING CHILDREN

Notes

4.195
(i) Triable either way.
(ii) Neither consent nor belief in consent is a defence to this offence.
(iii) Following the judgment in *R v Heard*,[287] it seems that all the sexual offences in the 2003 Act (certainly those in ss 1–4 and 5–15) will be regarded as offences for which a plea of voluntary intoxication is no defence.[288]
(iv) 'For the purpose of sexual gratification': the prosecution has to prove a link between that purpose and the presence or observation of the child.[289]
(v) 'Observed': References to observation (however expressed) are to observation whether direct or by looking at an image.[290]
(vi) The extended jurisdiction provisions apply to this section.[291] See Chapter 17 para 17.01.
(vii) The s 45 MSA 2015 defence for slavery and trafficking victims who commit an offence is available for an offence under this section, provided it was committed on or after 31.7.2015.[292]

Indictment

When D is 18 or over

4.196   ENGAGING IN SEXUAL ACTIVITY IN THE PRESENCE OF A CHILD 1.5.2004 to date

Statement of Offence
ENGAGING IN SEXUAL ACTIVITY IN THE PRESENCE OF A CHILD, contrary to section 11(1) of the Sexual Offences Act 2003.

Particulars of Offence
D, a person of or over the age of 18 years, on the …, day of … 20 …, for the purpose of obtaining sexual gratification, intentionally engaged in sexual activity when C, a person under the age of 16 years *or* [under the age of 13 years], was present, in a place from which D could be observed, D knowing or believing that C was aware *or* [intending that C should be aware] that he was engaging in such activity, and not reasonably believing that C was aged 16 years or over.

When D is under 18

4.197   ENGAGING IN SEXUAL ACTIVITY IN THE PRESENCE OF A CHILD 1.5.2004 to date

Statement of Offence
ENGAGING IN SEXUAL ACTIVITY IN THE PRESENCE OF A CHILD, contrary to sections 13 and 11(1) of the Sexual Offences Act 2003.

---

[287] [2007] EWCA Crim 125.
[288] Professor David Ormerod QC CBE, March 2007.
[289] *R v B [2018]* EWCA Crim 1439 at [25].
[290] SOA 2003, s 79(5).
[291] SOA 2003, s 72; provides for the prosecution within the jurisdiction of a sexual offence committed outside it.
[292] Modern Slavery Act 2015, s 45 commencement date 31.7.2015 (SI 2015/1476). This offence is not an excluded offence in Sch 4 of the Act. The s 45 defence is not retrospective, see *R v Joseph (Verna Sermanfure)* [2017] EWCA Crim 36.

L. OFFENCES WITHOUT PRECEDENT

> **Particulars of Offence**
>
> D, a person aged under 18 years, on the ... day of ... 20 ..., for the purpose of obtaining sexual gratification, intentionally engaged in sexual activity when C a person under the age of 16 years *or* [under the age of 13 years], was present, in a place from which D could be observed, D knowing *or* believing that C was aware, *or* [intending that C should be aware], that he was engaging in such activity, and not reasonably believing that C was aged 16 years or over.

Alternative Offences

Attempt to commit the full offence. When indicting offences of attempt do so under s 1(1) Criminal Attempts Act 1981.[293] Aver the attempt in both the Statement of Offence and Particulars of Offence. In addition, aver the substantive offence under the relevant Act; see paras 1.51 and 12.157 and *Reed & Others* [2021].[294] **4.198**

Note that the s 45 MSA 2015 defence for slavery and trafficking victims who commit offences does not apply to s 13 offences but it is not excluded from s 11 offences.[295]

Sentence

(i) Where defendant is over 18: **4.199**
- On indictment: **10 years**; summarily: **6 months**.[296]

(ii) Where defendant is under 18:
- On indictment: **5 years**; summarily: **6 months**.[297]

Sentencing Guidance

For adult offenders: The Sentencing Council 'Sexual Offences: Definitive Guideline' contains offence-specific guidelines. The Guideline applies to all offenders aged 18 and over, sentenced on or after 1 April 2014. For children and young persons: The 'Sentencing Children and Young Persons—Overarching Principles' and 'Sentencing Children and Young Persons—Sexual Offences ' Guideline applies to all children and young persons sentenced on or after 1 June 2017. When sentencing an Offender who has committed a sexual offence with, or in respect of, a person who is, or who the Offender believes to be, a child and no sexual activity occurs refer to *R v Reed and Others* [2021],[298] see Chapter 12 para 12.176. **4.200**

Upon Conviction/Sentence

(i) Section 11 and 13 offences: Notification applies.[299] The notification period is halved for under 18s. **4.201**

---

[293] Implementation date 27.8.1981.
[294] *Reed & Others* [2021] EWCA Crim 572.
[295] Modern Slavery Act 2015, s 45 and Sch 4, para 33.
[296] SOA 2003, s 11(2).
[297] SOA 2003, s 11(2).
[298] *Reed & Others* [2021] EWCA Crim 572.
[299] SOA 2003, Sch 3 paras 21 and 22. SOA 2003; see Chapter 14 para Tables 14.1–14.5.

110   4. OFFENCES INVOLVING CHILDREN

(ii) Section 11 offence: Automatic inclusion in the Children and Adult barred lists with the right to make representations.[300]
(iii) Section 11 and 13 offences: SHPO applies.[301]
(iv) Section 11 and 13 offences: Qualifying 'specified sexual offence' in Schedule 18 (Extended Sentences).[302]
(v) Section 11 offence: Qualifying Schedule 14 offence (Extended Sentences: The Earlier Offence Condition).[303]
(vi) Section 11 offence: Qualifying 'index' offence (if committed after 3 December 2012) for the purpose of Schedule 15 (Life Sentence for Second Listed Offence).[304]

2. Causing a Child to Watch a Sexual Act

Sexual Offences Act 2003, s 12

Introduction

4.202 In *R v Abdullahi*[305] the Court of Appeal (CA) held that this must be done 'for the purpose of obtaining sexual gratification' but the gratification need not be contemporaneous; so D is guilty if this is done in order to 'groom' a child with a view to sexual activity later. D caused the 13-year-old complainant, whom he plied with drink and drugs, to watch a pornographic film depicting heterosexual and homosexual sexual activity. Subsequently, in his room, he touched the complainant's penis. He was charged with offences under the SOA 2003, ss 12 and 14. It was sufficient that D showed the images for the purpose of obtaining sexual gratification, either by enjoying seeing the complainant looking at the images or with a view to putting him in the mood to provide sexual gratification to D later.

4.203 A defendant under 18 may be prosecuted for this offence under s 13.

Definition

4.204 As per Proof.

Proof

4.205 (i) D, aged 18 or over;
(ii) for the purpose of obtaining sexual gratification;[306]

---

[300] Part 2 of the Safeguarding Vulnerable Groups Act 2006 (Prescribed Criteria and Miscellaneous Provisions) Regulations 2009 (SI 2009 No 37) paras 2 and 4; see Chapter 12 para 12.217.
[301] SA 2020, s 345 and SOA 2003, Sch 3 paras 21 and 22; see Chapter 16 para 16.07.
[302] SA 2020, s 306, Sch 18, paras 38(k) and (m); see Chapter 12 para 12.51.
[303] SA 2020, ss 267 and 280, Sch 14, para 9(j); see Chapter 12 para 12.77.
[304] SA 2020, ss 273 and 283, Sch 15, para 9(j); see Chapter 12 para 12.123.
[305] [2006] EWCA Crim 2060.
[306] *R v Abdullahi* [2006] EWCA Crim 2060.

L. OFFENCES WITHOUT PRECEDENT

(iii) intentionally causes C to watch a third person engaging in a sexual activity, or to look at an image of any person engaging in a sexual activity; and
(iv) either:
- C is under 16 and D does not reasonably believe that C is 16 or over; or
- C is under 13.
(v) Where D is under 18:
- identical except for D's age.

Notes

(i) Triable either way.[307] 4.206
(ii) Neither consent nor belief in consent is a defence to this offence.
(iii) Following the judgment in *R v Heard*,[308] it seems that all sexual offences in the 2003 Act (certainly those in ss 1-4 and 5-15) will be regarded as offences for which a plea of voluntary intoxication is no defence.[309]
(iv) *R v Abdullahi*;[310] the gratification which must be proved need not be contemporaneous. This could therefore be charged in respect of activity which is part of sexual 'grooming'.
(v) 'Image': means a moving or still image and includes an image produced by any means and, where the context permits, a three-dimensional image.[311]
(vi) The extended jurisdiction provisions apply to this section.[312] See Chapter 17 para 17.01.
(vii) The s 45 MSA 2015 defence for slavery and trafficking victims who commit an offence is available for an offence under this section, provided it was committed on or after 31.7.2015.[313]

Indictment

When D is 18 or over

CAUSING A CHILD TO WATCH A SEXUAL ACT 1.5.2004 to date 4.207

Statement of Offence

CAUSING A CHILD TO WATCH A SEXUAL ACT, contrary to section 12(1) of the Sexual Offences Act 2003.

---

[307] SOA 2003, s 2(2).
[308] [2007] EWCA Crim 125.
[309] Professor David Ormerod QC CBE, March 2007.
[310] [2006] EWCA Crim 2060.
[311] SOA 2003, s 79(4).
[312] SOA 2003, s 72 provides for the prosecution within the jurisdiction of a sexual offence committed outside it.
[313] Modern Slavery Act 2015, s 45 commencement date 31.7.2015 (SI 2015/1476). This offence is not an excluded offence in Sch 4 of the Act. The s 45 defence is not retrospective, see *R v Joseph (Verna Sermanfure)* [2017] EWCA Crim 36.

112   4. OFFENCES INVOLVING CHILDREN

Particulars of Offence

D, a person of or over the age of 18 years, on the ... day of ... 20 ..., for the purpose of obtaining sexual gratification, intentionally caused C, a person under the age of 16 years or [a person under 13 years] (namely ... years), to watch X engaging in a sexual activity or [look at an image of a person engaging in a sexual activity], D not reasonably believing that C was aged 16 years or over.

When D is under 18

4.208   CAUSING A CHILD TO WATCH A SEXUAL ACT 1.5.2004 to date

---

Statement of Offence

CAUSING A CHILD TO WATCH A SEXUAL ACT, contrary to sections 13 and 12(1) of the Sexual Offences Act 2003.

Particulars of Offence

D, a person under the age of 18 years, on the ... day of ... 20 ..., for the purpose of obtaining sexual gratification, intentionally caused C, a person under the age of 16 years or [a person under 13 years] (namely ... years), to watch X engaging in a sexual activity or [look at an image of a person engaging in a sexual activity], D not reasonably believing that C was aged 16 years or over.

Alternative Offences

4.209   Attempt to commit the full offence. When indicting offences of attempt do so under s 1(1) Criminal Attempts Act 1981.[314] Aver the attempt in both the Statement of Offence and Particulars of Offence. In addition, aver the substantive offence under the relevant Act; see paras 1.51 and 12.157 and *Reed & Others* [2021].[315]

Note that the s 45 MSA 2015 defence for slavery and trafficking victims who commit offences does not apply to s 13 offences but it is not excluded from s 12 offences.[316]

Sentence

4.210
(i) On indictment:
- Where defendant is over 18: **10 YEARS**.[317]
- Where defendant is under 18: **5 YEARS**.[318]

(ii) Summarily:
- Where defendant is over 18: **6 months**.[319]
- Where defendant is under 18: **6 months**.[320]

---

[314] Implementation date 27.8.1981.
[315] *Reed & Others* [2021] EWCA Crim 572.
[316] Modern Slavery Act 2015, s 45 and Sch 4, para 33.
[317] SOA 2003, s 12(b).
[318] SOA 2003, s 13(b).
[319] SOA 2003, s 12(a).
[320] SOA 2003, s 13(a).

Sentencing Guidance

For adult offenders: The Sentencing Council 'Sexual Offences: Definitive Guideline' contains offence-specific guidelines. The Guideline applies to all offenders aged 18 and over, sentenced on or after 1 April 2014. For children and young persons: The 'Sentencing Children and Young Persons—Overarching Principles' and 'Sentencing Children and Young Persons—Sexual Offences' Guideline applies to all children and young persons sentenced on or after 1 June 2017. When sentencing an Offender who has committed a sexual offence with, or in respect of, a person who is, or who the Offender believes to be, a child and no sexual activity occurs refer to *R v Reed and Others* [2021],[321] see Chapter 12 para 12.176.

4.211

Upon Conviction/Sentence

(i) Section 12 and 13 offences: Notification applies.[322] The notification period is halved for under 18s.
(ii) Section 12 offence: Automatic inclusion in the children's and adults' barred lists with the right to make representations.[323]
(iii) Section 12 and 13 offences: SHPO applies.[324]
(iv) Section 12 and 13 offences: Qualifying 'specified sexual offence' in Schedule 18 (Extended Sentences).[325]
(v) Section 12 offence: Qualifying Schedule 14 offence (Extended Sentences: The Earlier Offence Condition).[326]
(vi) Section 12 offence: Qualifying 'index' offence (if committed after 3 December 2012) for the purpose of Schedule 15 (Life Sentence for Second Listed Offence).[327]

4.212

3. Arranging or Facilitating the Commission of a Child Sex Offence

Sexual Offences Act 2003, s 14

Introduction

This section makes it an offence for someone to arrange or facilitate the commission of the offences within ss 9–13 either within or outside the jurisdiction; the offence may be committed anywhere in the world. As s 13 provides for the prosecution of a defendant under 18 who has committed one of the ss 9–12 offences, this offence covers all age ranges. Note, however, that s 14 provides no difference in sentencing maxima for young defendants.

4.213

Section 14 The Police, Crime, Sentencing and Courts Bill 2021 sets out the government's intention to include under the umbrella of s14 those child sex offences where the victim/intended victim is aged 13 or under (ss 5–8 SOA 2003). In relation to sentence, the maximum

4.214

---

[321] *Reed & Others* [2021] EWCA Crim 572.
[322] SOA 2003, s 80(1) and Sch 3 paras 21 and 22. SOA 2003; see Chapter 14 paras 14.01–14.05.
[323] Part 2 of the Safeguarding Vulnerable Groups Act 2006 (Prescribed Criteria and Miscellaneous Provisions) Regulations 2009 (SI 2009 No 37) paras 2 and 4; see Chapter 12 para 12.217.
[324] SA 2020, s 345 and SOA 2003 Sch 3 paras 21 and 22; see Chapter 16 para 16.07.
[325] SA 2020, s 306, Sch 18, paras 38(l) and (m); see Chapter 12 para 12.51.
[326] SA 2020, ss 267 and 280, Sch 14, para 9(k); see Chapter 12 para 12.77.
[327] SA 2020, ss 273 and 283, Sch 15, para 9(k); see Chapter 12 para 12.123.

114   4. OFFENCES INVOLVING CHILDREN

sentence under s 14 (on Indictment, 14 years) will be increased to the maximum sentence applicable to the offence arranged or facilitated (ss 5 and 6 attract life imprisonment).

Definition

4.215   As per Proof.

Proof

4.216
(i) D intentionally arranges or facilitates something that he intends to do, intends another person to do, or believes that other person will do;
(ii) in any part of the world; and
(iii) doing it will involve the commission of an offence under any of ss 9–13.

Notes

4.217
(i) Triable either way.
(ii) Statutory defences as set out in s 14(2) and (3) protect those working, for example, in the field of sexual health who act for the protection of a child knowing that, for example, the person they are supplying contraceptives to is either under 16 themselves, or an adult in a sexual relationship with someone who is under 16.
(iii) Where the offence involves a fictional child, the substantive offence should be charged; it is unnecessary to charge an attempt.[328]
(iv) The extended jurisdiction provisions apply to this section.[329] See Chapter 17 para 17.01.
(v) The s 45 MSA 2015 defence for slavery and trafficking victims who commit an offence does not apply to ss 13 or 14 offences.[330]

Indictment

4.218   ARRANGING OR FACILITATING THE COMMISSION OF A CHILD SEX OFFENCE
1.5.2004 to date

Statement of Offence
ARRANGING OR FACILITATING THE COMMISSION OF A CHILD SEX OFFENCE, contrary to section 14(1) of the Sexual Offences Act 2003.

Particulars of Offence
D, on the … day of … 20.. (on or about the day of / between the … day of … , and the … day of … , …), intentionally arranged or facilitated the doing of an act, which he intended to do *or* [intended X to do] *or* [believed X would do], the doing of which

---

[328] See CPS Guidance on Rape and Sexual Offences, Chapter 7: Charging Practice for section 14 offences (Effective November 2020) and *Reed and Others* [2021] EWCA Crim 572 at para [13].
[329] SOA 2003, s 72 provides for the prosecution within the jurisdiction of a sexual offence committed outside it.
[330] Modern Slavery Act 2015, s 45 and Sch 4, para 33.

L. OFFENCES WITHOUT PRECEDENT 115

> act would involve the commission of an offence of sexual activity with a child, contrary to section ... [9/10/11/12 or 13] of the Sexual Offences Act 2003, in that he ... (set out briefly the act of arrangement/facilitation; this could simply be done by setting out the particular offence under ss 9–12).

Add s 13 to the statement of offence if D is under 18 (see paras 4.112 and 4.206 for examples). **4.219**

Alternative Offences

Attempt to commit the full offence. When indicting offences of attempt do so under s 1(1) Criminal Attempts Act 1981.[331] Aver the attempt in both the Statement of Offence and Particulars of Offence. In addition, aver the substantive offence under the relevant Act; see paras 1.51 and 12.157 and *Reed & Others* [2021].[332] **4.220**

Sentence

(i) On indictment: **14 YEARS**.[333]
(ii) Summarily: **6 months**.[334]
4.221

Sentencing Guidance

For adult offenders: The Sentencing Council 'Sexual Offences: Definitive Guideline' contains relevant offence-specific guidelines. The Guideline applies to all offenders aged 18 and over, sentenced on or after 1 April 2014. When sentencing an Offender who has committed a sexual offence with, or in respect of, a person who is, or who the Offender believes to be, a child and no sexual activity occurs refer to *R v Reed and Others* [2021],[335] see Chapter 12 para 12.176. **4.222**

Upon Conviction/Sentence

(i) Notification applies if the offender was 18 or over or is sentenced to imprisonment for a term of at least 12 months.[336]
(ii) Automatic inclusion in the children's and adults' barred lists with the right to make representations.[337]
(iii) SHPO applies.[338]
4.223

---

[331] Implementation date 27.8.1981.
[332] *Reed & Others* [2021] EWCA Crim 572.
[333] SOA 2003, s 14(4)(b).
[334] SOA 2003, s 14(4)(a). Increased to 12 months if CJA 2003, s 282(4) implemented.
[335] *Reed & Others* [2021] EWCA Crim 572.
[336] SOA 2003, s 80(1), Sch 3 para 23; SOA 2003; see Chapter 14 paras 14.01–14.05.
[337] Part 2 of the Safeguarding Vulnerable Groups Act 2006 (Prescribed Criteria and Miscellaneous Provisions) Regulations 2009 (SI 2009 No 37) paras 2 and 4; see Chapter 12 para 12.217.
[338] SA 2020, s 345 and SOA 2003 para 23; see Chapter 16 para 16.07.

(iv) Qualifying 'specified sexual offence' in Schedule 18 (Extended Sentences).[339]
(v) Qualifying Schedule 14 offence (Extended Sentences: The Earlier Offence Condition).[340]
(vi) Qualifying 'index' offence (if committed after 3 December 2012) for the purpose of Schedule 15 (Life Sentence for Second Listed Offence).[341]
(vii) Lifestyle offence for purposes of POCA 2002.[342]
(viii) Serious Crime Prevention Order applicable for offences convicted after 6 April 2008.[343]

4. Meeting a Child Following Sexual Grooming

Sexual Offences Act 2003, s 15

4.224 This offence may be committed anywhere in the world. It will be commonly used to deal with situations where a defendant sets up a meeting in order to commit sexual offences upon a child under 16 instigated by D after internet communication, for example in a 'chat room' where his age and identity are easily disguised. This is intended to protect children from themselves as well as from others. The wording of s 15 has been amended several times, consequently the wording of the indictment will subtly differ depending on the date on which the offence occurred. The precondition in relation to the number of occasions D met or communicated with D (s 15(1)(a)) was amended from 'at least two earlier occasions' to 'at least two occasions' on 14.7.2008, then to 'one or more occasions' on 13.4.2015. Consequently, if D met or communicated with D only once prior to 13.4.2015 it will not be an offence under this section. Prior to 14.7.2008 the ways in which the offence could be committed were limited to D meeting C, or D travelling to meet C, this was subsequently extended to include C travelling to meet D.

Definition

4.225 1.5.2004 to 13.7.2008[344]

(1) A person aged 18 or over (A) commits an offence if—
   (a) having met or communicated with another person (B) on at least two earlier occasions, he—
      (i) intentionally meets B, or
      (ii) travels with the intention of meeting B in any part of the world,
   (b) at the time, he intends to do anything to or in respect of B, during or after the meeting and in any part of the world, which if done will involve the commission by A of a relevant offence,

---

[339] SA 2020, s 306, Sch 18, para 38(n); see Chapter 12 para 12.51.
[340] SA 2020, ss 267 and 280, Sch 14, para 9(l); see Chapter 12 para 12.77.
[341] SA 2020, ss 273 and 283, Sch 15, para 9(l); see Chapter 12 para 12.123.
[342] POCA 2002, Sch2, para 8(2)(a).
[343] SCA 2007, s 19 and Sch 1, para 4; see Chapter 12 para 12.240.
[344] Section as enacted (1.5.2004).

L. OFFENCES WITHOUT PRECEDENT 117

  (c) B is under 16, and
  (d) A does not reasonably believe that B is 16 or over.
 (2) In subsection (1)—
  (a) the reference to A having met or communicated with B is a reference to A having met B in any part of the world or having communicated with B by any means from, to or in any part of the world;

14.7.2008 to 12.4.2015[345]

 (1) A person aged 18 or over (A) commits an offence if—
  (a) *A has met or communicated with another person (B) on at least two occasions and subsequently—*
   (i) *A intentionally meets B,*
   (ii) *A travels with the intention of meeting B in any part of the world or arranges to meet B in any part of the world, or*
   (iii) *B travels with the intention of meeting A in any part of the world,*
  (b) *A intends to do anything to or in respect of B, during or after the meeting mentioned in paragraph (a)(i) to (iii) and in any part of the world, which if done will involve the commission by A of a relevant offence.*[346]
  (c) B is under 16, and
  (d) A does not reasonably believe that B is 16 or over.
 (2) In subsection (1)—
  (a) the reference to A having met or communicated with B is a reference to A having met B in any part of the world or having communicated with B by any means from, to or in any part of the world.

13.4.2015 to present[347]

 (1) A person aged 18 or over (A) commits an offence if—
  (a) A has met or communicated with another person (B) *on one or more occasions*[348] and subsequently—
   (i) A intentionally meets B,
   (ii) A travels with the intention of meeting B in any part of the world or arranges to meet B in any part of the world, or
   (iii) B travels with the intention of meeting A in any part of the world,
  (b) A intends to do anything to or in respect of B, during or after the meeting mentioned in paragraph (a)(i) to (iii) and in any part of the world, which if done will involve the commission by A of a relevant offence.
  (c) B is under 16, and
  (d) A does not reasonably believe that B is 16 or over.

---

[345] Section as amended (14.7.2008).
[346] Wording substituted by Criminal Justice and Immigration Act 2008, Sch 15 para 1 (14.7.2008).
[347] Section as amended (13.4.2015).
[348] Wording substituted by Criminal Justice and Courts Act 2015, s 36(1) (13.4.2015) SI 2015/778.

4. OFFENCES INVOLVING CHILDREN

(2) In subsection (1)—
   (a) the reference to A having met or communicated with B is a reference to A having met B in any part of the world or having communicated with B by any means from, to or in any part of the world.

Proof

4.226 As per definitions above. The following reflects the current enactment of the section:

(i) D, aged 18 or over;[349]
(ii) D having met or communicated with C on one or more occasions;[350]
(iii) D subsequently: (a) intentionally meets C (b) D travels with the intention of meeting C in any part of the world or (c) C travels with the intention of meeting D in any part of the world.[351]
(iii) D intends to do anything to or in respect of C during or after meeting and in any part of the world, which if done will involve the commission by D of a 'relevant' offence.[352]
(iv) At the time C must be under 16, and D not reasonably believe that C was 16 or over.[353]
(v) The communication need not have been sexual in nature.[354]
(vi) Section 15(2)(a) states that the reference to D having met or communicated with C is a reference to D having met C in any part of the world or having communicated with C by any means from, to or in any part of the world.
(vii) 'Relevant offence'[355] means any of the following:
an offence under this Part (that is, an offence under SOA 2003, ss 1–79; this in fact covers all the offences within the Act);
anything done outside England and Wales and Northern Ireland which is not an offence within subparagraph (i) or(ii) but would be an offence within subparagraph (i) if done in England and Wales.[356] This is intended to cover offences abroad which are not named under the SOA 2003 but the elements of which constitute an offence within it.

Notes

4.227 (i) Triable either way.[357]
(ii) Prior to 13.4.2015 it would not be an offence if D had simply met C once before the relevant event; the requirement before that date was meeting on at least 2 occasions.

---

[349] SOA 2003, s 15(1).
[350] SOA 2003, s 15(1)(a).
[351] SOA 2003, s 15(1)(i) to (iii).
[352] SOA 2003, s 15(1)(b).
[353] SOA 2003, s 15(1)(c) and (d).
[354] *R v Gavrina* [2010] EWCA Crim 1693, para 16.
[355] SOA 2003, s 15(2)(b).
[356] References in the section to Northern Ireland and NI sexual offences in paras 61–92 of Sch 3) in the Act were repealed on 2.2.2009; SI 2008/1769 and SI 2008/1779.
[357] SOA 2003. s 15(4).

L. OFFENCES WITHOUT PRECEDENT   119

(iii) Following the judgment in *R v Heard*,[358] it seems that all the sexual offences in the 2003 Act (certainly those in ss 1–4 and 5–15) will be regarded as offences for which a plea of voluntary intoxication is no defence.[359]

(iv) The extended jurisdiction provisions apply to this section.[360] See Chapter 17 para 17.01.

(v) The s 45 MSA 2015 defence for slavery and trafficking victims who commit an offence does not apply to this offence.[361]

Indictment

MEETING A CHILD FOLLOWING SEXUAL GROOMING 1.5.2004 to 13.7.2008   **4.228**

Statement of Offence

MEETING A CHILD FOLLOWING SEXUAL GROOMING, contrary to section 15(1) of the Sexual Offences Act 2003.

Particulars of Offence

D, a person of *or* [over] 18 years, having met or communicated with C on at least two earlier occasions, on the … day of … 20 …, [intentionally met] *or* [travelled with the intention of meeting] C, a person under the age of 16 years (namely … years), D not reasonably believing that C was aged 16 years, and [intending to do anything to] *or* [in respect] of C, [either during] *or* [after the meeting], which if done would involve the commission by D of a relevant offence (namely …).

MEETING A CHILD FOLLOWING SEXUAL GROOMING 14.7.2008 to 12.4.2014   **4.229**

Statement of Offence

MEETING A CHILD FOLLOWING SEXUAL GROOMING, contrary to section 15(1) of the Sexual Offences Act 2003.

Particulars of Offence

D, a person of *or* [over] 18 years, having met or communicated with C on at least two occasions, on the … day of … 20 …, [intentionally met C] *or* [travelled with the intention of meeting C] *or* [C travelled with the intention of meeting D in any part of the world], C being a person under the age of 16 years (namely … years), D not reasonably believing that C was aged 16 years, and [intending to do anything to] *or* [in respect of] C, [either during] *or* [after the meeting], which if done would involve the commission by D of a relevant offence (namely …).

---

[358] [2007] EWCA Crim 125.
[359] Professor David Ormerod QC CBE, March 2007.
[360] SOA 2003, s 72 provides for the prosecution within the jurisdiction of a sexual offence committed outside it. See Chapter 17.
[361] Modern Slavery Act 2015, s 45 and Sch 4, para 33.

120 4. OFFENCES INVOLVING CHILDREN

4.230 MEETING A CHILD FOLLOWING SEXUAL GROOMING 13.4.2014 to date

> ### Statement of Offence
> MEETING A CHILD FOLLOWING SEXUAL GROOMING, contrary to section 15(1) of the Sexual Offences Act 2003.
>
> ### Particulars of Offence
> D, a person of *or* [over] 18 years, having met or communicated with C on one or more occasions, on the ... day of ... 20 ... , [intentionally met] *or* [travelled with the intention of meeting C] *or* [C travelled with the intention of meeting D], C being a person under the age of 16 years (namely ... years), D not reasonably believing that C was aged 16 years, and [intending to do anything to] *or* [in respect of] C, [either during] *or* [after the meeting], which if done would involve the commission by D of a relevant offence (namely ...).

4.231 It is not strictly necessary to aver C's specific age but it is a useful addition and may clarify matters. If there is clear evidence of what the specific offence intended is you may wish to include it, as with the number of occasions on which D communicated with or met C prior to the intended meeting.

Alternative Offences

4.232 Attempt to commit the full offence. When indicting offences of attempt do so under s 1(1) Criminal Attempts Act 1981.[362] Aver the attempt in both the Statement of Offence and Particulars of Offence. In addition, aver the substantive offence under the relevant Act; see paras 1.51 and 12.157 and *Reed & Others* [2021].[363]

Sentence

4.233 (i) On indictment: **10 YEARS**.[364]
(ii) Summarily: **6 months**.[365]

Sentencing Guidance

4.234 The Sentencing Council 'Sexual Offences: Definitive Guideline' contains relevant offence-specific guidelines. The Guideline applies to all offenders aged 18 and over,

---

[362] Implementation date 27.8.1981.
[363] *Reed & Others* [2021] EWCA Crim 572.
[364] SOA 2003, s 15(4).
[365] SOA 2003, s 15(4). 12 months if CJA 2003, s 282(4) implemented.

L. OFFENCES WITHOUT PRECEDENT   121

sentenced on or after 1 April 2014. When sentencing an Offender who has committed a sexual offence with, or in respect of, a person who is, or who the Offender believes to be, a child and no sexual activity occurs refer to *R v Reed and Others* [2021],[366] see Chapter 12 para 12.176.

Upon Conviction/Sentence

(i) Notification applies.[367] **4.235**
(ii) Automatic inclusion in the children's and adults' barred lists with the right to make representations.[368]
(iii) SHPO applies.[369]
(iv) Qualifying 'specified sexual offence' in Schedule 18 (Extended Sentences).[370]
(v) Qualifying Schedule 14 offence (Extended Sentences: The Earlier Offence Condition).[371]
(vi) Qualifying 'index' offence (if committed after 3 December 2012) for the purpose of Schedule 15 (Life Sentence for Second Listed Offence).[372]

5. Sexual Communication with a child

Sexual Offences Act 2003, s 15A
Section 15A was inserted on 3 April 2017 by the Serious Crime Act 2015[373] creating a new **4.236**
offence criminalizing sexual communication with a child. The offence is widely drafted to include all forms of online and offline communication, for example text messages, social media, emails, calls and letters. The offence is not retrospective.

Definition

(1) A person aged 18 or over (A) commits an offence if— **4.237**
    (a) for the purpose of obtaining sexual gratification, A intentionally communicates with another person (B),
    (b) the communication is sexual or is intended to encourage B to make (whether to A or to another) a communication that is sexual, and
    (c) B is under 16 and A does not reasonably believe that B is 16 or over.

---

[366] *Reed & Others* [2021] EWCA Crim 572.
[367] SOA 2003, s 80(1), Sch 3 para 24. SOA 2003; see Chapter 14 para Tables 14.1–14.5.
[368] Part 2 of the Safeguarding Vulnerable Groups Act 2006 (Prescribed Criteria and Miscellaneous Provisions) Regulations 2009 (SI 2009 No 37) paras 2 and 4; see Chapter 12 para 12.217.
[369] SA 2020, s 345 and SOA 2003, Sch 3 para 24; see Chapter 16 para 16.07.
[370] SA 2020, s 306, Sch 18, para 38(o); see Chapter 12 para 12.51.
[371] SA 2020, ss 267 and 280, Sch 14, para 9(m); see Chapter 12 para 12.77.
[372] SA 2020, ss 273 and 283, Sch 15, para 9(m); see Chapter 12 para 12.123.
[373] SCA 2015, s 67, SI 2017/451 (3.4.2017).

122 4. OFFENCES INVOLVING CHILDREN

(2) For the purposes of this section, a communication is sexual if—
  (a) any part of it relates to sexual activity, or
  (b) a reasonable person would, in all the circumstances but regardless of any person's purpose, consider any part of the communication to be sexual;
  and in paragraph (a) 'sexual activity' means an activity that a reasonable person would, in all the circumstances but regardless of any person's purpose, consider to be sexual.

Proof

4.238 As per definition.

Notes

4.239
(i) Triable either way.[374]
(ii) 'Sexual' has the definition ascribed by subsection (2). The s 78 definition does not apply.
(v) The s 45 MSA 2015 defence for slavery and trafficking victims who commit an offence is available for an offence under this section, provided it was committed on or after 31.7.2015.[375]

Indictment

4.240 SEXUAL COMMUNICATION WITH A CHILD 3.4.2017 to date

Statement of Offence

SEXUAL COMMUNICATION WITH A CHILD, contrary to section 15A(1) of the Sexual Offences Act 2003.

Particulars of Offence

D, aged 18 or [over], on the ... day of ... 20.. , for the purpose of obtaining sexual gratification intentionally communicated with C, a person aged under 16 and whom D did not reasonably believe to be 16 or over, and the communication was sexual or [and the communication was intended to encourage C to make a sexual communication].

---

[374] SOA 2003, s 15A(3).
[375] Modern Slavery Act 2015, s 45 commencement date 31.7.2015 (SI 2015/1476). This offence is not an excluded offence in Sch 4 of the Act. The s 45 defence is not retrospective, see *R v Joseph (Verna Sermanfure)* [2017] EWCA Crim 36.

L. OFFENCES WITHOUT PRECEDENT 123

Alternative Offences

4.241 Attempt to commit the full offence. When indicting offences of attempt do so under s 1(1) Criminal Attempts Act 1981.[376] Aver the attempt in both the Statement of Offence and Particulars of Offence. In addition, aver the substantive offence under the relevant Act; see paras 1.51 and 12.157 and *Reed & Others* [2021].[377]

Sentence

4.242
(i) On indictment: **2 YEARS**.[378]
(ii) Summarily: **6 months**.[379]

Sentencing Guidance

4.243 There are currently no Sentencing Council guidelines applicable to this offence. When sentencing offences for which there is no specific sentencing guideline the Sentencing Council, 'General Guideline: Overarching Principles' applies to all individual offenders aged 18 and older sentenced on or after 1 October 2019. When sentencing an Offender who has committed a sexual offence with, or in respect of, a person who is, or who the Offender believes to be, a child and no sexual activity occurs refer to *R v Reed and Others* [2021],[380] see Chapter 12 para 12.176.

Upon Conviction/Sentence

4.244
(i) Notification applies.[381]
(ii) Automatic inclusion in the children's and adults' barred lists not applicable.[382]
(iii) SHPO applies.[383]
(iv) Qualifying 'specified sexual offence' in Schedule 18 (Extended Sentences).[384]

6. Possession of a Paedophile Manual

Serious Crime Act 2015, s69

4.245 Section 69 of the Serious Crime Act 2015 was enacted on 3 May 2015[385] and prohibits the possession of a 'paedophile manual'.

---

[376] Implementation date 27.8.1981.
[377] *Reed & Others* [2021] EWCA Crim 572.
[378] SOA 2003, s 15A(3).
[379] SOA 2003, s 15A(3). Increased to 12 months if CJA 2003, s 282(4) implemented.
[380] *Reed & Others* [2021] EWCA Crim 572.
[381] SOA 2003, s 80(1), Sch 3 para 24A; see Chapter 14 paras 14.01–14.05.
[382] Part 2 of the Safeguarding Vulnerable Groups Act 2006 (Prescribed Criteria and Miscellaneous Provisions) Regulations 2009 (SI 2009 No 37) not included in paras 1, 2, 3, or 4; see Chapter 12 para 12.217.
[383] SA 2020, s 345 and SOA 2003, Sch 3 para 24A; see Chapter 16 para 16.07.
[384] SA 2020, s 306, Sch 18, para 38(p); see Chapter 12 para 12.51.
[385] SI 2015/820.

4. OFFENCES INVOLVING CHILDREN

Definition

4.246 69(1) It is an offence to be in possession of any item that contains advice or guidance about abusing children sexually.

Proof

4.247 As per definition. Further:

(i) 'abusing children sexually' means doing anything that constitutes an offence: (a) under sections 1 to 71 of the SOA 2003 and equivalent offences under Northern Irish legislation, in relation to under 16 year olds; (b) under section 1 of the Protection of Children Act 1978, or equivalent offence under Northern Irish legislation (but not pseudo-photographs); or (c) under section 2 of the Modern Slavery Act 2015 (human trafficking) committed with a view to exploitation that consists of or includes behaviour within section 3(3) of that Act (sexual exploitation),[386] or doing anything outside England and Wales or Northern Ireland that would constitute such an offence if done in England and Wales or Northern Ireland.[387]

(ii) 'item' includes anything in which information of any description is recorded.[388]

Notes

4.248
(i) Triable either way.[389]
(ii) Consent of the DPP required to prosecute.[390]
(iii) Subsection (2) creates three statutory defences. The burden lies on the defendant to prove, to the civil standard, that either:
   (a) D had a legitimate reason for being in possession of the item.
   (b) D had not read, viewed or (as appropriate) listened to the item, and did not know, and had no reason to suspect, that it contained advice or guidance about abusing children sexually.
   (c) the item was sent to D without any request made by D or on D's behalf, and D did not keep it for an unreasonable time.
(iv) The inclusion in s 69(2) of offences under section 2 MSA 2015 was added from 17.3.2016.[391]

---

[386] Para (c) added 17 March 2016.
[387] SCA 2015, s 69(8).
[388] SCA 2015, s 69(8).
[389] SCA 2015, s 69(3).
[390] SCA 2015, s 69(4)(a).
[391] Added by Modern Slavery Act 2015 (Consequential Amendments) Regulations 2016/244 Pt 2 reg 24(c) (17.3.2016).

(v) The s 45 MSA 2015 defence for slavery and trafficking victims who commit an offence is available for an offence under this section, provided it was committed on or after 31.7.2015.[392]

Indictment

POSSESSION OF A PAEDOPHILE MANUAL 3.5.2015 to date   4.249

Statement of Offence

POSSESSION OF A PAEDOPHILE MANUAL, contrary to section 69(1) of the Serious Crime Act 2015.

Particulars of Offence

D, on the … day of … 20 …, had in his possession an item [entitled], that contained advice or guidance as to how to abuse children sexually.

Alternative Offences

Attempt to commit the full offence. When indicting offences of attempt do so under s 1(1) Criminal Attempts Act 1981.[393] Aver the attempt in both the Statement of Offence and Particulars of Offence. In addition, aver the substantive offence under the relevant Act; see paras 1.51 and 12.157 and *Reed & Others* [2021].[394]   4.250

Sentence

(i) On indictment: **3 YEARS**.[395]   4.251
(ii) Summarily: **6 months**.[396]

Sentencing Guidance

There are currently no Sentencing Council guidelines applicable to this offence. When sentencing offences for which there is no specific sentencing guideline the Sentencing Council, 'General Guideline: Overarching Principles' applies to all individual offenders aged 18 and older sentenced on or after 1 October 2019.   4.252

---

[392] Modern Slavery Act 2015, s 45 commencement date 31.7.2015 (SI 2015/1476). This offence is not an excluded offence in Sch 4 of the Act. The s 45 defence is not retrospective, see *R v Joseph (Verna Sermanfure)* [2017] EWCA Crim 36.
[393] Implementation date 27.8.1981.
[394] *Reed & Others* [2021] EWCA Crim 572.
[395] SCA 2015, s 69(3)(a).
[396] SCA 2015, s 69(3)(c). Increased to 12 months if CJA 2003, s 282(4) implemented.

126   4. OFFENCES INVOLVING CHILDREN

4.253 However, note the comment of Edis J (then), when sentencing Jon Venables in 2018: 'A manual of this kind is different from images and films because its purpose is to inspire actual offending. It is probably not designed to excite or to achieve sexual gratification simply by being looked at, but to give practical advice. It is extremely important that possession of this kind of thing should be clearly punished.'[397]

Upon Conviction/Sentence

4.254 (i) Notification applies where D is 18 or over and sentenced to 12 months' imprisonment or more,[398]
(ii) Automatic inclusion in the children's and adults' barred lists not applicable.[399]
(iii) SHPO applies.[400]
(iv) Forfeiture under s 69(5)(b) SCA 2015.7.

7. Other Offences Against Children

4.255 Not covered within this chapter but set out elsewhere:

(i) Incest/offences within the family (Familial Offences, Chapter 6).
(ii) Child prostitution (Prostitution and Trafficking, Chapter 8).
(iii) Indecent photographs of children (Obscene Publications, Chapter 9).

M. OFFENCES COMMITTED BY CHILDREN OR YOUNG PERSONS

4.256 The age of both the complainant and the defendant can make a difference to the maximum sentence. As such, the principle as enunciated in *R v Courtie*[401] applies.

When indicting such offences under the SOA 2003, consider the advantages and disadvantages of undertaking more elements to prove. In terms of sentence, an offence committed by a defendant under 18 will often attract higher maximum penalties if the sections specifying child offences are not used. For example, an allegation of sexual touching by a young man aged 17 on a complainant aged 12 will attract a maximum of 14 years if pleaded simply under s 7 (sexual assault); it would however only attract a 5-year maximum (even if the assault were penetrative) under s 13 (ss 9–12 committed by a defendant under 18).

4.257 By virtue of the SOA 2003, s 13 a person under the age of 18 who does an act which amounts to committing any of the following offences:

(i) sexual activity with a child (s 9);

---

[397] As referenced in the sentencing appeal *R v Durrant (Andrew)* [2018] EWCA Crim 2400, at para [15].
[398] SOA 2003, s 80(1) and Sch 3, para 35C. SOA 2003; see Chapter 14 paras 14.01–14.05.
[399] Part 2 of the Safeguarding Vulnerable Groups Act 2006 (Prescribed Criteria and Miscellaneous Provisions) Regulations 2009 (SI 2009 No 37); see Chapter 12 para 12.217.
[400] SA 2020, s 345 and SOA 2003, Sch 3 para 35C; see Chapter 16 para 16.07.
[401] [1984] AC 463; see para 1.38 (Indictments).

(ii) causing or inciting a child to engage in sexual activity (s 10);
(iii) engaging in sexual activity in the presence of a child (s 11);
(iv) causing a child to watch a sexual act (s 12), is liable to conviction but will attract a lower maximum sentence on indictment: **5 YEARS** (summarily; still **6 months/ fine/both**).

These appear in this chapter together with the corresponding offence as set out for an adult defendant with amended particulars of indictments and information on available sentences, orders, etc. **4.258**

Note that in relation to these offences, neither consent nor belief in consent are defences. Note that in relation to s 13 offences:

the extended jurisdiction provisions apply to this section.[402] See Chapter 17 para 17.01.
the s 73 defence (exceptions to aiding abetting and counselling) applies to an offence under s 13 which would be an offence under ss 9 if the offender were aged under 18.
(ii) The s 45 MSA 2015 defence for slavery and trafficking victims who commit an offence does not apply.[403] But note the anomaly between adult and youth offenders in relation to ss 11 and 12 offences (see paras 4.196 and 4.207).

Indictments: when indicting, it is suggested that it will be safer to aver both sections; both can be read together to establish the relevant age. It is also suggested that it will be better practice to aver s 13 first, as the principal section under which the count is averred or the charge brought. **4.259**

Youth Court Powers: the maximum available sentence available to the Youth Court is 2 years; however the PCC(S)A 2000, s 91 has been amended by the SOA 2003[404] to allow youths (who have not committed a 'grave crime') to be committed to the Crown Court for trial, where the youth has been charged with an offence under the SOA 2003, s 3, 13, 25, or 26.[405] It is therefore possible for a youth charged under s 13 of the SOA 2003, to be committed to the Crown Court and receive a sentence of up to 5 years' imprisonment. **4.260**

IV. Presumption and Determination of Age

N. *DOLI INCAPAX*

At common law there was a rebuttable presumption that a child aged not less than 10 but under 14 years was *doli incapax*; that is, incapable of committing a crime. The presumption **4.261**

---

[402] SOA 2003, s 72; provides for the prosecution within the jurisdiction of a sexual offence committed outside it.
[403] Modern Slavery Act 2015, s 45 and Sch 4, para 33.
[404] Section 91(1)(b)–(e) substituted for s. 91(1)(b)(c) (1.5.2004) by Sexual Offences Act 2003. Following Magistrates' Courts Act (MCA) 1980, s 24.
[405] PCC(S)A 2000, s 91(1)(b)–(e).

was rebutted only if the prosecution proved beyond reasonable doubt, not only that the child caused an actus reus with *mens rea*, but also that he knew that the particular act was not merely naughty or mischievous, but 'seriously wrong'. This presumption was abolished on 30.9.1998 by the CDA 1998, s 34.[406] This was intended to put children aged 10 and above on the same footing as adults from the time of the implementation of s 34. The presumption still applies to historic abuse cases pre-dating the implementation of s 34.[407] However, the presumption is rebuttable by evidence that the child knew its actions were 'seriously wrong'.[408]

O. PRESUMPTION THAT BOYS UNDER THE AGE OF 14 ARE INCAPABLE OF VAGINAL OR ANAL INTERCOURSE

4.262 Section 1 of the SOA 1993 abolished this presumption as from 20.9.1993. It follows that rape cannot be proved against a boy under 14 before 20.9.1993. This change was not retrospective.[409] However, the evidence of penetration can be adduced, and the case can be dealt with as an indecent assault.

4.263 Note: *R v Claydon*;[410] conviction for buggery quashed on retrospective basis because D was under 14 (13 years old).

P. DETERMINATION OF AGE

4.264 By s 99(1) of the Children and Young Persons Act (CYPA) 1933 and now s 405 of the Sentencing Code, where a person, whether charged with an offence or not, is brought before a court other than for the purpose of giving evidence, and it appears to the court that he is a child or young person, the court must make 'due inquiry' as to the age of that person. In so doing, the court shall take such evidence as may be forthcoming at the hearing of the case.[411]

4.265 Any order or judgment of the court is not invalidated by subsequent proof that the person's age was incorrectly stated.[412] The age of a defendant that is presumed or declared by the court shall, for the purposes of the CYPA 1933, apply.

4.266 Therefore, if subsequent information comes to light, that information has no effect on orders and determinations of the court.

4.267 A similar provision exists for determinations under the MCA 1980.[413]

---

[406] *R v JTB* [2009] UKHL 20. Confirms that the presumption and defence are abolished by s 34.
[407] CDA 1998 Sch 9 para 1 'nothing in section 34 shall apply in relation to anything done before [its] commencement'. *Fethney* [2011] EWCA Crim 3096.
[408] *Bevan* [2011] EWCA Crim 654.
[409] *Fethney* [2011] EWCA Crim 3096.
[410] [2005] EWCA Crim 2827.
[411] CYPA 1933, s 99(1). SA 2002, s 405(2).
[412] CYPA 1933, s 99(1).
[413] MCA 1980, s 150(4).

Q. PROVING AGE

Age can be proven by testimony of someone present at the time of birth. If a birth certificate is produced to prove age, evidence must also be adduced to positively identify the person as the person named in the certificate.[414]

4.268

R. DISCRETION TO REMIT CASES FROM THE ADULT MAGISTRATES' COURT TO THE YOUTH COURT

Adult magistrates' courts that have begun the trial of a defendant believing him to be over 18 have discretion to remit the case to the Youth Court or to continue the hearing in the adult court (if that belief is discovered to be incorrect).[415] The same discretion exists during Youth Court trials.

4.269

---

[414] *R v Rogers* (1914) 10 Cr App R 276.
[415] CYPA 1933, s 46(1).

5

BUGGERY AND OFFENCES OF INDECENCY

A. Introduction	5.01	E. Intercourse with an Animal, 30.4.2004 to date	5.75
B. Buggery: Categories of Offences and Related Sentences up to 30.4.2004	5.02	F. Assault with Intent to Commit Buggery, 1.1.1957 to 30.4.2004	5.84
1. Is it Rape or Buggery?	5.04	1. Assault with Intent to Commit Buggery 3.11.1994 to 30.4.2004	5.90
2. Buggery Offences (pre-dating the Sexual Offences Act 2003) which can still be charged	5.05	2. Indecent Assault on a Man	5.92
C. Offences Committed Pre-1.1.1957	5.10	G. Gross Indecency with Another Man, 1.1.1957 to 30.4.2004	5.101
1. Buggery	5.10	1. Attempted Gross Indecency 1.1.1961	5.112
2. Bestiality	5.18	2. Attempted Gross Indecency 1.5.2004	5.113
3. Assault with Intent to Commit Buggery	5.25	H. Sexual Activity in a Public Lavatory, 30.4.2004 to date	5.115
4. Indecent Assault upon a Male Person, pre-1.1.1957	5.32	I. Procuring Others to Commit Buggery, 27.7.1967 to 30.4.2004	5.124
5. Gross Indecency between Males, pre-1.1.1957	5.41	1. Procuring Others to Commit Buggery	5.124
D. Offences Committed between 1.1.1957 and 30.4.2004	5.48		
1. Buggery	5.48		

A. INTRODUCTION

Over the years the offences of buggery, assault with intent to commit buggery, gross indecency and procurement have been the subject of review and gradual reform which has resulted in considerable limitation, in line with changes in public opinion. Most importantly, with the passing of the SOA 2000, homosexual acts in private between consenting adults over 16 no longer constitute an offence. The passing of the SOA 2003 repealed the offences featured in this chapter, and extinguished the offence of buggery. One effect of this has been the right of people previously subject to notification to be removed from the register upon application. From 1 October 2012, those convicted or cautioned for offences of buggery or gross indecency between males (under ss 12 and 13 of the SOA 1956 or corresponding earlier offences under s 61 OAPA 1861 and s 11 CLAA 1885) when the other party to the act had consented and was aged 16 or over, and the act would not now be an offence of sexual activity in a public lavatory (s 71A SOA 2003) can apply to the Secretary of State for the offence to be 'disregarded' under s 92 of the Protection of Freedoms Act 2012. The Policing and Crime Act 2017 went further; those convicted of offences under ss 12 and 13 SOA 1956 (and similar specified offences under earlier Acts and corresponding service offences), who have since died, are posthumously pardoned by virtue of s 164 of the Act. Pardon is subject to conditions that (a) the other party to the act had consented and was aged 16 or over, and

5.01

(b) any such conduct at the time the section came into force (31.1.2017) would not be an offence of sexual activity in a public lavatory (s 71A SOA 2003).

B. BUGGERY: CATEGORIES OF OFFENCES AND RELATED SENTENCES UP TO 30.4.2004

5.02 The implementation of the SOA 1967 heralded major retrospective changes to the offence of buggery, with its abolition of the criminalization of acts of private and consensual buggery between males over 21. Thereafter, piecemeal amendments to the law have taken place. This has resulted in there being a variety of ways in which the offence is made out, with criteria changing over the years and largely, since 1967, not being retrospective. As a result, a list of offences that may still be prosecuted has been compiled, uniquely for this chapter. See paras 5.07–5.08.

5.03 A separate sentencing table has been included in this book, see paras 5.07–5.08. It is important to charge the correct factual scenario (specifying age/whether in private and/or consent was given) in order to attract the appropriate maximum sentence.

1. Is it Rape or Buggery?

5.04 When considering charge the following key points should be considered:

(i) Male rape ought to be charged as buggery[1] until, and including 2.11.1994, and only as rape thereafter (from 3.11.1994).

(ii) From 27.7.1967[2] private and consensual acts of buggery between males over 21 were decriminalized. This change in the law was retrospective. Acts of consensual buggery by a male upon a female remained an offence up until, and including, 2.11.1994; thereafter no offence was committed. If there was no consent, rape should be charged.

(iii) The age of consent for males was later reduced to 18 in 1994,[3] and then to 16 in 2001.[4] These changes were not retrospective. It follows therefore that consenting 20-year-olds committing acts of buggery and gross indecency in private can still be said to have committed the offence of buggery until 1994, just as two consenting 17-year-old males can be said to have committed the offence of buggery or gross indecency until 2001. However, neither of these offences can be prosecuted as they are time-barred (see paras 5.43 and 5.62).

(iv) Consent to prosecute must be obtained from the DPP for offences of buggery, or for aiding or abetting, counselling or procuring its commission where either of those men were at the time under the age of consent, which by the year 2001 was reduced to 16 (SOA 1967, s 8 as amended by SO(A)A 2000, s 1(1)).

---

[1] Sexual Offences Act 1956, s 12.
[2] Sexual Offences Act 1967, s 1, commencement date 27.7.1967.
[3] CJPOA 1994, s 145, commencement date 3.11.94.
[4] SO(A)A 2000, s 1(1); commencement date 8.1.2001. SO(A)A 2000 (Commencement No 1) Order (SI 2000 No 3303).

(v) Offences of gross indecency[5] and consensual buggery between males over 16 may not be prosecuted if 12 months or more has expired since the date of the offence.[6]

Notwithstanding its unlikely application for these offences, the s 45 defence applies these offences if committed on or after 31.7.2015.[7]

2. Buggery Offences (pre-dating the Sexual Offences Act 2003) which can still be charged

This list must be read in conjunction with para 5.04.

(i) Buggery by a male aged 16 and over, with a boy or girl under 16 (where the other party consents), in public or in private.[8,9]   **5.05**
(ii) Buggery by a male aged 16 or over, of a boy or girl under 16 (where there is no consent by the other party) in public or in private.[10]
From 3.11.1994 on the basis of the same fact charge **rape**.
(iii) Buggery by a male aged 16 or over, of a man or woman over 16 without his or her consent, whether or not in private.
From 3.11.1994, on the basis of the same fact charge **rape**.
(iv) Buggery by a male aged under 16, of a person under 16 in public and in private.[11,12]
(v) Buggery of a male or female of any age, otherwise than in private.
(vi) Buggery of an animal (bestiality).
(vii) Buggery of a female over 16, with her consent, in private or public, until 2.11.1994.

After 2.11.1994 if the act is in private and the female consents, no offence is committed. However, if the female does not consent, **rape** ought to be charged.

In practical terms offences most commonly prosecuted before the change in the law (extending the offence of rape) on 3.11.1994 are (i) to (iii). (See paras 5.10, 5.48, 5.60, 5.63).   **5.06**

Sentences

The punishment for buggery was defined by statute: 'penal servitude for life'—maximum.[13]   **5.07**
In 1967 sentences were revised, these changes being retrospective.[14]   **5.08**

---

[5] SOA 1967, s 13.
[6] SOA 1967, s 7.
[7] Modern Slavery Act 2015, s 45 commencement date 31.7.2015 (SI 2015/1476). This offence is not an excluded offence in Sch 4 of the Act. The s 45 defence is not retrospective, see *R v Joseph (Verna Sermanfure)* [2017] EWCA Crim 36.
[8] Consent of DPP required.
[9] If the defendant believes that the victim is 16 or over, then he has a defence. *R v Kumar* [2005] Crim LR CLR 470, [2004] EWCA Crim 3207.
[10] Consent of DPP required.
[11] Note that before 20.9.1993 males under 14 were presumed incapable of committing this offence. (SOA 1993, ss 1 and 2). Thereafter the presumption of incapability reverts to the age of 10 years (CYPA 1933, s 50). If committed upon a girl or boy under 14, the perpetrator alone is liable. (1 Hale 670; 3 Co Inst 59, 1 East PC 480).
[12] Consent of DPP required.
[13] OAPA 1861, s 61.
[14] SOA 1967, ss 3 and 10.

5. BUGGERY AND OFFENCES OF INDECENCY

Table 5.1 Sentencing

Offence	Date	Max. sentence
Buggery with a boy under 16 (with his consent, whether or not in private)	1.1.1950–30.4.2004	LIFE
Buggery with a boy under 16 (without his consent)	1.1.1950–2.11.1994	LIFE
Buggery with a boy under 16 (without his consent)	3.11.1994–30.4.2004	Charge as rape:[a] LIFE
Bestiality	1.1.1950–30.4.2004	LIFE
Buggery of a female with or without her consent, in private or public	1.1.1950–2.11.1994	LIFE
Buggery of a female without her consent	3.11.1994–30.4.2004	Charge as rape:[b] LIFE
Buggery with a male aged 16 or over without his consent (whether or not in private)	1.1.1950–2.11.1994	10 YEARS
Buggery with a male aged 16 or over without his consent (whether or not in private)	3.11.1994–30.4.2004	Charge as rape: LIFE
Buggery if the accused is over 21 and the other party, male or female, is aged 16–20	1.1.1950–2.11.1994	5 YEARS
Buggery, where the accused is over 21 and the other male is aged 16–18	3.11.1994–30.4.2004	5 YEARS
Buggery, if the accused is under 21 and the other party, male or female, is aged 16–20 and consented (whether in public or private)	1.1.1950–2.11.1994	2 YEARS
Buggery committed between two males over the age of consent, otherwise than in private[c]	1.1.1950–30.4.2004 (offence is time-barred 12 months after commission)[d]	2 YEARS

[a] SOA 1994, s 1.
[B] SOA 1994, s 1.
[c] The age of consent reducing to 18 on 3.11.1994 (CJPOA 1994, s 145), and 16 on 8.1.2001 (SO(A)A 2000, s 1).
[d] SOA 1967, s 7.

Sentencing Guidance

5.09 Sentences of between 3 to 5 years' imprisonment for homosexual offences against boys,[15] 'when there are neither aggravating nor mitigating factors. The place in the bracket will depend on age, intelligence and education'.[16] The Court of Appeal identified aggravating features:

- physical injury;
- emotional and psychological damage;
- moral corruption;
- abuse of authority or trust;

and in mitigation:

(i) mental imbalance or personality disorders;
(ii) emotional stress.

---

[15] Under the age of consent.
[16] R v Willis (1974) 60 Cr App R 146, [1975] 1 WLR 292 CA.

C. OFFENCES COMMITTED PRE-1.1.1957

1. Buggery

Offences Against the Person Act 1861, s 61

Definition

To commit buggery 'with mankind or with any animal'.   **5.10**

The essential elements of the offence were governed by common law. Buggery at common law is defined as sexual intercourse per anum: **5.11**

(i) by a man, with a man;[17]
(ii) by a man with a woman;[18]
(iii) by a man or woman with an animal. An offence is committed if the animal is the perpetrator (the 'agent') or the other party (the 'patient') and need not be per anum.[19]

Proof

As per Definition.   **5.12**

Notes

    5.13

(i) Trial on indictment only.
(ii) Consent was no defence.[20] Both the perpetrator and the other party (if consenting) were equally guilty.
(iii) However, the SOA 1967 limited the offence substantially, in that buggery between consenting males over the age of 21 was de-criminalized, provided that the act takes place in private.[21] The changes were retrospective.[22]
(iv) It follows that once the Act was passed, such activity was no longer an offence, even if the act of buggery took place before 1967.[23]
(v) The act does not take place in private if more than two people take part or are present, or the act takes place in a lavatory to which the public have or are permitted to have access, whether on payment or otherwise.[24]
(vi) This limitation did not apply to homosexual acts on United Kingdom merchant ships by crew members, until 1994.[25]

---

[17] *R v Jacobs* (1817) Russ & Ry 331.
[18] Including husband on wife, *R v Wiseman* (1718) Fortes KB 91.
[19] *R v Bourne* (1952) 36 Cr App R 125.
[20] *R v Jellyman* 8 C&P 604.
[21] SOA 1967, s 1(1) and (2).
[22] SOA 1967, s 10.
[23] SOA 1967, s 10.
[24] SOA 1967, s 1(1) and (2).
[25] SOA 1967, s 2, CJPOA 1994, s 146(2).

136 5. BUGGERY AND OFFENCES OF INDECENCY

(vii) Consent to such acts cannot be given by a man who is suffering from a severe mental handicap,[26] unless the accused proves that he did not know and had no reason to suspect that man to be suffering from such abnormality.

Indictment

5.14 BUGGERY Pre-1.1.1957

> **Statement of Offence**
> BUGGERY, contrary to section 61 of the Offences against the Person Act 1861.
> **Particulars of Offence**
> D, a person of or over the age of 21 years on the … , day of … , … (in a public place, namely …) committed buggery with C (a male person under the age of 21 years, namely of the age of … years) or with X, a woman with/without X's consent.

5.15 The particulars should clarify which factual category of offence is charged and so should include the bracketed material above as appropriate, i.e.:

(i) ages of parties where relevant;[27]
(ii) whether or not the offence was otherwise than in private;
(iii) whether or not with consent (prior to 1994).

5.16 This is important in order to ensure that the offence attracts the appropriate sentence.[28] See paras 5.07–5.08.

5.17 Separate counts ought to be drafted catering for the relevant combination of factual ingredients which might attract a different maximum punishment. (See para 5.05 for alternative offences.)

2. Bestiality

5.18 An indictment for bestiality follows the previous example (excluding the bracketed material), but needs to specify in the particulars the type of animal involved. This offence was repealed by the SOA in 2004; a new offence of intercourse with an animal was created (new maximum penalty 2 years' imprisonment).

Alternative Offences

5.19 There are distinct categories for this offence; if the jury are not satisfied in relation to one category they could convict of another. The indictment should contain specific and if necessary separate counts to cater for this.[29] See para 5.05.

---

[26] As defined by SOA 1967, s 3A, as a state of arrested or incomplete development of mind which includes severe impairment of intelligence and social functioning.
[27] *R v D* [1993] Crim LR 542.
[28] CLA 1967, s 6; *R v Reakes* [1974] Crim LR 615 CA; *R v Courtie* [1984] AC 463.
[29] CLA 1967, s 6; *R v Reakes, R v Courtie* ibid.

If the entire charge is not made out then attempted buggery may be charged.[30] This offence is also triable only on indictment. **5.20**

The maximum sentence is **10 YEARS** if with an animal, a female or a boy under 16.[31] Otherwise the same maximum as for the full offence applies.[32] **5.21**

ATTEMPTED BUGGERY Pre-1.1.57 **5.22**

Statement of Offence
ATTEMPTED BUGGERY, contrary to section 62 of the Offences against the Person Act 1861.

Particulars of Offence
D, on the … day of. … attempted to commit buggery with C.

Sentence

See para 5.21. **5.23**

Upon Conviction/Sentence

(i) Notification not applicable.[33] **5.24**
(ii) Automatic inclusion in the children's and adults' barred lists with right to make representations applicable where the other party was under 16 years and did not consent.[34]
(iii) SHPO not applicable[35]

3. Assault with Intent to Commit Buggery

Offences Against the Person Act 1861, s 62

Definition

To '… commit any assault with intent to commit the same …' (that is, buggery). **5.25**

Proof

As per Definition. **5.26**

---

[30] OAPA 1861, s 62.
[31] SOA 1967, s 3(4)(b).
[32] CLA 1967, s 7(2) and CAA 1981, s 4(5).
[33] SOA 2003, s 80(1) (not listed in Sch 3); see Chapter 14 Tables 14.2–14.5.
[34] Part 2 of the Safeguarding Vulnerable Groups Act 2006 (Prescribed Criteria and Miscellaneous Provisions) Regulations 2009 (SI 2009 No 37); Sch1, paras 2 and 4; see Chapter 12 para 12.217.
[35] SA 2020, s 345 (not listed in Sch 3 or Sch 5 SOA 2003); see Chapter 16 para 16.07.

Notes

5.27 This offence is triable only on indictment.

Indictment

5.28 ASSAULT WITH INTENT TO COMMIT BUGGERY Pre-1.1.1957

Statement of Offence
ASSAULT WITH INTENT TO COMMIT BUGGERY, contrary to section 62 of the Offences against the Person Act 1861.

Particulars of Offence
D on the … day of … assaulted C with intent to commit buggery with the said C.

Sentence

5.29 On indictment: **10 YEARS**.

Upon Conviction/Sentence

5.30 (i) Notification not applicable.[36]
(ii) Automatic inclusion in the children's barred list with right to make representations applicable where the other party was under 16 years and did not consent.[37]
(iii) SHPO not applicable[38]

5.31 The SOA 1956 came into force on 1.1.1957. Section 16(1) covers this offence.

4. Indecent Assault upon a Male Person, pre-1.1.1957

Offences Against the Person Act 1861, s 62

Definition

5.32 Any indecent assault upon any male person.

5.33 This offence is defined by common law, as an assault in circumstances of indecency.[39]

---

[36] SOA 2003, s 80(1) (not listed in Sch 3); see Chapter 14 Tables 14.2–14.5.
[37] Part 2 of the Safeguarding Vulnerable Groups Act 2006 (Prescribed Criteria and Miscellaneous Provisions) Regulations 2009 (SI 2009 No 37), Sch 1 para 2; see Chapter 12 para 12.217.
[38] SA 2020, s 345 (not listed in Sch 3 or Sch 5 SOA 2003); see Chapter 16 para 16.07.
[39] *Beal v Kelley* (1951) 35 Cr App R 128. See para 3.05.

C. OFFENCES COMMITTED PRE-1.1.1957

Proof

There was held to be an indecent assault in circumstances where a male forcibly pulled a boy's hand towards his penis,[40] but not when a young girl touched the penis of a male at his invitation.[41,42]

5.34

Notes

(i) The offence is triable either way.
(ii) An indecent assault under s 62 could be committed by a woman.[43]
(iii) Consent is a defence,[44] unless the male is under 16.[45]

5.35

Indictment

INDECENT ASSAULT UPON A MALE PERSON Pre-1.1.1957

5.36

Statement of Offence

INDECENT ASSAULT UPON A MALE PERSON, contrary to section 62 of the Offences against the Person Act 1861.

Particulars of Offence

D, on the … day of … indecently assaulted C, a male person (under the age of 16 years).

Alternative Offences

(i) When indicting offences of attempt do so under common law. Aver the attempt in both the Statement of Offence and Particulars of Offence. In addition, aver the substantive offence under the relevant Act; see paras 1.51 and 12.157 and *Reed & Others* [2021]:[46] **10 YEARS.**[47]
(ii) Common assault.[48] This must be charged on the indictment.[49]

5.37

ATTEMPTED INDECENT ASSAULT UPON A MALE Pre-26.8.1981

5.38

---

[40] *Beal v Kelley* (1951) 35 Cr App R 128.
[41] *Fairclough v Whipp* (1951) 35 Cr App R 138.
[42] Later the IwCA 1960 provides that this would be an offence under s 1. See paras 4.07–4.10.
[43] *R v Hare* [1934] 1 KB 354, 24 Cr App R 108.
[44] *R v Wollaston* 12 Cox CCR.
[45] CLAA 1922, s 1.
[46] *Reed & Others* [2021] EWCA Crim 572.
[47] OAPA 1861, s 62.
[48] *R v Bostock* (1893) 17 Cox 700.
[49] *R v Mearns* (1990) 91 Cr App R 312.

140 5. BUGGERY AND OFFENCES OF INDECENCY

Statement of Offence

ATTEMPTED INDECENT ASSAULT UPON A MALE, contrary to section 62 of the Offences against the Person Act 1861 and common law.

Particulars of Offence

D, on the … day of. … attempted to indecently assault C, a male person (under the age of 16 years).

Sentence

5.39 (i) On indictment: **10 YEARS**.[50]
(ii) Summarily: **6 months**.

Upon Conviction/Sentence

5.40 (i) Notification not applicable.[51]
(ii) Automatic inclusion in the children's barred list with right to make representations applicable where the other party was under 16 years and did not consent.[52]
(iii) SHPO not applicable.[53]

5. Gross Indecency between Males, pre-1.1.1957

Criminal Law Amendment Act 1885, s 11

Definition

5.41 Any male person who, in public or private, commits or is a party to the commission of, or who procures or attempts to procure the commission by any male person of, any act of gross indecency with another male person.

Proof

5.42 The offence is committed in one of two ways:

(i) committing an act of gross indecency;
(ii) procuring the commission by a man of an act of gross indecency.

Gross indecency is not defined by statute or common law, but would usually cover intercrural (leg or thigh) contact, mutual masturbation or oral–genital contact.[54] The behaviour has to be 'directed towards' or 'against' the other person.[55]

---

[50] OAPA 1861, s 62.
[51] SOA 2003, s 80(1) (not listed in Sch 3); see Chapter 14, Tables 14.2–14.5.
[52] Part 2 of the Safeguarding Vulnerable Groups Act 2006 (Prescribed Criteria and Miscellaneous Provisions) Regulations 2009 (SI 2009 No 37), Sch 1 para 2; see Chapter 12, para 12.217.
[53] SA 2020, s 345 (not listed in Sch 3 or Sch 5 SOA 2003); see Chapter 16, para 16.07.
[54] As recommended in the Wolfenden Committee Report.
[55] *R v Hall* [1964] 1 QB 273, 47 Cr App R 253; *R v Preece and Howells* (1977) QB 370, 63 Cr App R 28 CA.

Notes

(i) These offences (gross indecency and procuring an offence of gross indecency) are triable either way.[56]

(ii) Historically, before the passing of the SOA 1967 consent of the other party was no defence and both parties were liable. However, the SOA 1967 limited the offence substantially, in that where the act takes place in private between consenting males over the age of 21, it is no longer an offence, nor is it an offence in those circumstances to procure the commission of the said act.[57] The changes were retrospective. No male can now be charged with the offence if it took place before 1967.

(iii) Either party is liable for conviction, but for both to be convicted it must be proved that one party committed the act with the other and that they both were acting in concert to behave in a grossly indecent manner (viewed from an objective point of view), even though there has been no physical contact.[58]

(iv) See para 5.13 for the definition of 'private'.

(v) See para 5.04 for restrictions on the defence of consent. This was later reduced to 18 in 1994[59] and 16 in 2001;[60] although these two amendments are not retrospective.

(vi) It follows that consenting 20 year olds committing acts of gross indecency in private can still be said to have committed such an offence until 1994, just as two consenting 17-year-old males can be said to have committed an offence until 2001.

(vii) However these offences cannot be prosecuted as all offences of gross indecency over the age of 16 are time-barred; proceedings must be instituted within 12 months.[61]

(viii) Consent to prosecute must be obtained from the DPP where either of those two men were over the age of consent, which by 2001 had been reduced to 16.[62]

5.43

Indictment

GROSS INDECENCY Pre-1.1.1957

5.44

Statement of Offence

GROSS INDECENCY, contrary to section 11 of the Criminal Law Amendment Act 1885.

Particulars of Offence

D, a male person, committed or was party to the commission of or procured or attempted to procure the commission of an act of gross indecency with C (a male person under the age of 21, namely ...).

---

[56] MCA 1980, s 17 and Sch 1.
[57] SOA 1967, ss 1 and 4(3).
[58] *R v Hunt* 34 Cr App R 135 CCA.
[59] CJPOA 1994, s 143(1) (3.11.1994).
[60] SO(A)A 2000, s (1)(a) (8.1.2001).
[61] SOA 1967, s 7.
[62] SOA 1967, s 8.

142   5. BUGGERY AND OFFENCES OF INDECENCY

Alternative Offences

Sexual Offences Act 1956, s 15

5.45   Indecent assault, where there is no consent: **10 YEARS**. See para 3.29.

Procurement of gross indecency. Examples of when a charge of procuring (or attempting to procure) an act of gross indecency would be appropriate are where:

(i)   a male persuaded, or attempted to persuade, a young boy to touch his penis;[63]
(ii) two individuals were talking about their desire to act indecently together.[64]

Sentence

5.46   On indictment:

(i)   an act of gross indecency by a male over the age of 21 with another male under the age of consent: **5 YEARS**;[65]
(ii) procuring or attempting to procure the commission by a male of gross indecency under the age of consent: **5 YEARS**;[66]
(iii) otherwise for an act of gross indecency (or attempting to procure the same) between males over the age of consent: **2 YEARS**;[67]
(iv) attempting to commit an act of gross indecency; as points (i) and (iii) .[68]

Upon Conviction/Sentence

5.47   (i)   Notification applies where the other party was under 18 or the offender is sentenced to at least 30 months' imprisonment or admitted to a hospital subject to a restriction order.[69]
(ii) Automatic inclusion in the children's and adults' barred lists with right to make representations applicable where the other party was under 16 years and did not consent and the offence has not been 'disregarded'[70] (see para 5.01).[71]
(iii) SHPO applies.[72]
(iv) Qualifying 'specified sexual offence' in Schedule 18 (Extended Sentences).[73]

---

[63] *R v Burrows* 35 Cr App R 180.
[64] *R v Miskell* 37 Cr App R 214.
[65] SOA 1956, s 37, CJPOA 1994, s 144.
[66] SOA 1956, s 37, CJPOA 1994, s 144.
[67] SOA 1956, s 37, CJPOA 1994, s 144.
[68] CAA 1981, ss 1 and 4.
[69] SOA 2003, s 80(1), Sch 3, para 8; see Chapter 14 paras 14.01–14.05.
[70] Disregarded conviction or caution within the meaning of Chapter 5 of Pt 5 of the Protection of Freedoms Act 2012.
[71] Part 2 of the Safeguarding Vulnerable Groups Act 2006 (Prescribed Criteria and Miscellaneous Provisions) Regulations 2009 (SI 2009 No 37), Sch 1 paras 2 and 4; see Chapter 12 para 12.217.
[72] SA 2020, s 345 and Sch 3, para 8 SOA 2003; see Chapter 16 para 16.07.
[73] SA 2020, s 306, Sch 18, para 29(k); see Chapter 12 para 12.51.

D. OFFENCES COMMITTED BETWEEN 1.1.1957 AND 30.4.2004

1. Buggery

Sexual Offences Act 1956, s 12

The SOA 1956 consolidated the law with regard to sexual offences and repealed s 61 of the OAPA 1861. **5.48**

Section 12 of the SOA 1956 is substituted.[74]

Definition

It is an offence for a person to commit buggery with another person or with an animal. **5.49**

Proof

As per Definition; also see paras 5.02–5.06. **5.50**

Indictment

BUGGERY 1.1.1957 to 21.7.1967 **5.51**

Statement of Offence
BUGGERY, contrary to section 12(1) of the Sexual Offences Act 1956.

Particulars of Offence
D a person of or over the age of 21 years on the ... day of ... committed buggery with C (in a public place, namely ...) or with C, a male person under the age of 21 years (namely of the age of ... years), or with C, a male person, with/without his consent, or with C, a woman.

Alternative Offences

Attempted buggery. From 1.1.1957 until 26.8.1981 to indict an offence of attempted buggery; the Statement of Offence should read 'Attempted Buggery' and the particulars as above with the addition of the word 'attempted'. In addition, aver the substantive offence under the relevant Act; see paras 1.51 and 12.157 and *Reed & Others* [2021].[75] **5.52**

The maximum sentence is **10 YEARS**.

---

[74] SOA 1956, s 51 and Sch 4, commencement date 1.1.57.
[75] *Reed & Others* [2021] EWCA Crim 572.

Sentence

5.53 See para 5.08.

Upon Conviction/Sentence

5.54 (i) Notification applies where the offender was aged over 20 years and the other party was aged under 18.[76]
(ii) Automatic inclusion in the children's and adults' barred lists with right to make representations applicable where the other party was under 16 years and did not consent and the offence has not been 'disregarded'.[77,78]
(iii) SHPO applies.[79]

Buggery 22.7.1967 to 2.11.1994

Notes

5.55 For indictments during this period, the model for 1.1.1957 onwards (see para 5.51) should be used. In addition, the following might be added at the end of the Statement of Offence: 'and section 3(1)(a) of the Sexual Offences Act 1967'.

Alternative Offences

5.56 Attempted Buggery. Pursuant to the enactment of the CAA 1981 (27.8.1981)[80] an attempted buggery ought to be framed as below from 27.8.1981 to 30.4.2004. In addition, aver the substantive offence under the relevant Act; see paras 1.51 and 12.157 and *Reed & Others* [2021].[81]

5.57 ATTEMPTED BUGGERY 27.8.1981 to 30.4.2004

Statement of Offence

ATTEMPTED BUGGERY, contrary to section 12(1) of the Sexual Offences Act 1956 and section 1(1) of the Criminal Attempts Act 1981.

Particulars of Offence

D on the ... day of ... attempted to commit buggery with C (in a public place, namely ...) or with C, a male person under the age of 21 years (namely of the age of ... years), or with C, a woman.

Sentence

5.58 As per maximum for full offence, see para 5.08.

---

[76] SOA 2003, s 80(1) and Sch 3, para 5; see Chapter 14 paras 14.01–14.05.
[77] Disregarded conviction or caution within the meaning of Chapter 5 of Pt 5 of the Protection of Freedoms Act 2012.
[78] Part 2 of the Safeguarding Vulnerable Groups Act 2006 (Prescribed Criteria and Miscellaneous Provisions) Regulations 2009 (SI 2009 No 37), Sch 1, paras 2 and 4; see Chapter 12 para 12.217.
[79] SA 2020, s 345 and SOA 2003, Sch 3, para 5; see Chapter 16 para 16.07.
[80] CAA 1981, s 11(1).
[81] *Reed & Others* [2021] EWCA Crim 572.

D. OFFENCES COMMITTED BETWEEN 1.1.1957 AND 30.4.2004

Upon Conviction/Sentence

(i) Notification applies where the offender was aged over 20 years and the other party was aged 18 or over.[82] **5.59**

(ii) Automatic inclusion in the children's and adults' barred lists with right to make representations applicable where the other party was under 16 years and did not consent and the offence has not been 'disregarded'.[83],[84]

(iii) SHPO applies.[85]

Buggery 3.11.1994 to 7.1.2001

Definition

See para 5.49. **5.60**

Proof

See paras 5.02–5.06. **5.61**

Notes

The CJPOA 1994 (as of 3.11.94) reduced the age of consent for homosexual acts to 18.[86] This was not retrospective. However, acts of consensual buggery committed between males aged 18–20 before 3.11.1994, are time-barred after one year. **5.62**

Further, non-consensual acts of buggery are from 1994 defined as rape.[87] If there is a lack of consent then rape ought to be alleged. There is no longer any power for a judge to sentence an offence of buggery on the basis of there being a lack of consent.[88] **5.63**

Indictment

BUGGERY 3.11.1994 to 7.1.2001 **5.64**

Statement of Offence

BUGGERY, contrary to section 12(1) of the Sexual Offences Act 1956.

Particulars of Offence

D (a person of, or over the age of 21) on the … day of …, committed buggery with C (a person under the age of 18 years, namely …) (in a public place, namely …) or with C, a woman.

---

[82] SOA 2003, s 80(1) and Sch 3, paras 5 and 94; see Chapter 14 paras 14.01–14.05.
[83] Disregarded conviction or caution within the meaning of Chapter 5 of Pt 5 of the Protection of Freedoms Act 2012.
[84] Part 2 of the Safeguarding Vulnerable Groups Act 2006 (Prescribed Criteria and Miscellaneous Provisions) Regulations 2009 (SI 2009 No 37), Sch 1, paras 2 and 4; see Chapter 12 para 12.217.
[85] SA 2020, s 345 and SOA 2003, Sch 3, paras 5 and 94; see Chapter 16 para 16.07.
[86] Section 143(1) and (3) insert paras (1A) to (1C) into SOA 1956, s 12. As such, the charge does not need to state the 1967 Act.
[87] SOA 1956, s 1 as amended by CJPOA 1994, s 142.
[88] *R v Davies* [1998] 1 Cr App R(S) 380 CA.

Alternative Offences

5.65 See para 5.56.

Sentence

5.66 See para 5.08.

Upon Conviction/Sentence

5.67 (i) Notification applies where the offender was aged over 20 years and the other party was aged 18 or over.[89]
(ii) Automatic inclusion in the children and adult barred lists with right to make representations applicable where the other party was under 16 years and did not consent and the offence has not been 'disregarded'.[90],[91]
(iii) SHPO applies.[92]

8.1.2001 to 30.4.2004

Definition

5.68 See para 5.49.

Proof

5.69 See paras 5.02–5.06.

Notes

5.70 The SOA 2000 reduced the age of consent to 16.[93] This was not retrospective. However, acts of buggery between 16–17-year-old males before 3.11.1994 cannot be prosecuted as they are time-barred by one year.

From 1.5.2004

5.71 As of 1.5.2004 the SOA 2003 came into force.[94] This Act modernizes the law in relation to sexual offences and represents a complete overhaul of the law.

---

[89] SOA 2003, s 80(1) and Sch 3, para 5; see Chapter 14 paras 14.01–14.05.
[90] Disregarded conviction or caution within the meaning of Chapter 5 of Pt 5 of the Protection of Freedoms Act 2012.
[91] Part 2 of the Safeguarding Vulnerable Groups Act 2006 (Prescribed Criteria and Miscellaneous Provisions) Regulations 2009 (SI 2009 No 37), Sch 1, paras 2 and 4; see Chapter 12 para 12.217.
[92] SA 2020, s 345 and SOA 2003, Sch 3, para 5; see Chapter 16 para 16.07.
[93] SOA 2000, s 1(1), commencement date 8.1.2001; SO(A)A 2000 (Commencement No 1) Order 2000 (SI 2000 No 3303).
[94] (Commencement) Order 2004 (SI 2004 No 874).

5.72 Two offences under the old law no longer exist, that is consensual anal intercourse otherwise than in private,[95] and procuring a man to commit buggery in private.[96] For the former, depending on the facts, the common law offence of committing an act outraging public decency may be charged. See paras 10.03–10.13.

5.73 Buggery of a child under the age of consent[97] is now covered by both:

(i) SOA 2003, s 5—rape of a child under 13 (see paras 4.88–4.96).
(ii) SOA 2003, s 1—rape per anum (see paras 2.47–2.54).

5.74 Bestiality[98] is now covered by the SOA 2003, s 69—intercourse with an animal.

Section 69 SOA 2003 extends the old offence to include penetration of a vagina and to include female offenders.

E. INTERCOURSE WITH AN ANIMAL, 30.4.2004 TO DATE

Sexual Offences Act 2003 s 69

5.75 For offences committed before 31.12.1957 see para 5.18. For offences committed between 1.1.1957 and 30.4.2004 see para 5.51.

Definition

5.76
(1) A person commits an offence if—
   (a) he intentionally performs an act of penetration with his penis,
   (b) what is penetrated is the vagina or anus of a living animal, and
   (c) he knows that, or is reckless as to whether, that is what is penetrated.
(2) A person (D) commits an offence if—
   (a) D intentionally causes, or allows, D's vagina or anus to be penetrated,
   (b) the penetration is by the penis of a living animal, and
   (c) D knows that, or is reckless as to whether, that is what D is being penetrated by.

Proof

5.77 As per definition.

Notes

5.78
(i) The offence is triable either way.[99]
(ii) The s 69(1) offence can only be committed by a male person, whereas a male or female can commit a s 69(2) offence.

---

[95] SOA 1956, s 12.
[96] SOA 1956, s 4.
[97] SOA 1956, s 12.
[98] SOA 1956, s 12.
[99] SOA 2003, s 69(3).

148 5. BUGGERY AND OFFENCES OF INDECENCY

(iii) Penetration is a continuing act from entry to withdrawal.[100]
(iv) 'Vagina' includes vulva.[101]
(v) References to a part of the body include references to a part surgically constructed (in particular, through gender reassignment surgery).[102]
(vi) Section 79(10) of the SOA 2003 defines vagina or anus as to include references to 'any similar part' in relation to an animal. The Defendant must know or be reckless as to whether that is what was penetrated.
(vii) Offences committed before 1.5.2004 are prosecuted as offences of Buggery under s 61 OAPA 1861 (pre 31.12.1957) and the s 12 SOA 1956 (between 1.1.57 and 1.5.2003).
(v) The s 45 MSA 2015 defence for slavery and trafficking victims who commit an offence is available for an offence under this section, provided it was committed on or after 31.7.2.15.[103]

Indictment

5.79 INTERCOURSE WITH AN ANIMAL 1.5.2004 to date.

> ### Statement of Offence
> INTERCOURSE WITH AN ANIMAL, contrary to section 69(1) of the Sexual Offences Act 2003.
>
> ### Particulars of Offence
> D on the … day of 20…, intentionally penetrated the anus of a living animal with his penis, namely a …, D knowing that, or being reckless as to whether, that is what was penetrated.

Alternative Offences

5.80 Attempt to commit the full offence. When indicting offences of attempt do so under s 1(1) Criminal Attempts Act 1981.[104] Aver the attempt in both the Statement of Offence and Particulars of Offence. In addition, aver the substantive offence under the relevant Act; see paras 1.51 and 12.157 and *Reed & Others* [2021].[105]

Sentence

5.81 (i) On indictment: **2 YEARS**.
(ii) Summarily: **6 months** and/or an unlimited fine.[106]
(iii) Attempt: the same.

---

[100] SOA 2003, s 79(2).
[101] SOA 2003, s 79(9).
[102] SOA 2003, s 79(3).
[103] Modern Slavery Act 2015, s 45 commencement date 31.7.2015 (SI 2015/1476). This offence is not an excluded offence in Sch 4 of the Act. The s 45 defence is not retrospective, see *R v Joseph (Verna Sermanfure)* [2017] EWCA Crim 36.
[104] Implementation date 27.8.1981.
[105] *Reed & Others* [2021] EWCA Crim 572.
[106] S 69(3) SOA 2003.

Sentencing Guidance

The Sentencing Council 'Sexual Offences: Definitive Guideline' does not cover this offence. The Sentencing Guidelines Council's Guideline (May 2007), gave a starting point of a community order, and the range was 'an appropriate non-custodial sentence'. The guidance listed 'recording activity and circulating pictures/video' an aggravating feature and listed one mitigating feature; 'symptom of isolation, rather than depravity'. **5.82**

Upon Conviction/Sentence

(i) Notification applies:[107] **5.83**
   (a) where the offender was under 18, he is or has been sentenced in respect of the offence to imprisonment for a term of at least 12 months;
   (b) in any other case, the offender, in respect of the offence or finding, is or has been (i) sentenced to a term of imprisonment, or (ii) detained in a hospital.

Automatic inclusion in the children's and adults' barred lists not applicable.[108]

SHPO applies.[109]
Qualifying 'specified sexual offence' in Schedule 18 (Extended Sentences).[110]

F. ASSAULT WITH INTENT TO COMMIT BUGGERY, 1.1.1957 TO 30.4.2004

Sexual Offences Act 1956, s 16(1)

Definition

To 'assault another person with intent to commit buggery'. **5.84**

Proof

As per Definition. **5.85**

Notes

(i) This offence is triable only on indictment. **5.86**
(ii) The SOA 1956 consolidated the law with regard to sexual offences (as of 1.1.1957). OAPA 1861, s 62 was repealed and SOA 1956, s 16 substituted.

---

[107] SOA 2003, s 80(1) and Sch 3, para 35, see Chapter 14 paras 14.01–14.05.
[108] Part 2 of the Safeguarding Vulnerable Groups Act 2006 (Prescribed Criteria and Miscellaneous Provisions) Regulations 2009 (SI 2009 No 37) not included in paras 1, 2, 3, and 4; see Chapter 12, para 12.217.
[109] SA 2020, s 345 and SOA 2003, Sch 3, para 35; see Chapter 16, para 16.07.
[110] SA 2020, s 306, Sch 18, para 38(az); see Chapter 12, para 12.51.

150   5. BUGGERY AND OFFENCES OF INDECENCY

Indictment

5.87 ASSAULT WITH INTENT TO COMMIT BUGGERY 1.1.1957 to 30.4.2004

> **Statement of Offence**
> ASSAULT WITH INTENT TO COMMIT BUGGERY, contrary to section 16(1) of the Sexual Offences Act 1956.
>
> **Particulars of Offence**
> D on the ... day of ... assaulted C with intent to commit buggery with the said C.

Sentence

5.88 On indictment: **10 YEARS**.

Upon Conviction/Sentence

5.89 (i) Notification applicable where the other party was under 18.[111]
 (ii) Automatic inclusion in the children's and adults' barring lists with the right to make representations.[112]
 (iii) SHPO applicable.[113]
 (iv) Qualifying 'specified sexual offence' in Schedule 18 (Extended Sentences).[114]

1. Assault with Intent to Commit Buggery 3.11.1994 to 30.4.2004

5.90 Once the CJPOA 1994 was passed, classifying non-consensual buggery as rape, an anomaly occurs. This offence was not re-classified to cover assault with intent to commit anal rape.[115] It is therefore an offence to assault another with intent to bugger, which includes the offence of anal rape post-1994. For offences committed after 3.11.1994 the offence would rarely in practice be charged. The sentence remained at 10 years' imprisonment.

5.91 *The SOA 2003 repeals this offence in its entirety.*

2. Indecent Assault on a Man

Sexual Offences Act 1956, s 15(1)

5.92 The SOA 1956 consolidated the law with regard to sexual offences and repealed the OAPA 1861, s 62. The SOA 1956, s 15(1) was substituted (as of 1.1.1957).

---

[111] SOA 2003, s 80(1) and Sch 3, para 9; see Chapter 14 paras 14.01–14.05.
[112] Part 2 of the Safeguarding Vulnerable Groups Act 2006 (Prescribed Criteria and Miscellaneous Provisions) Regulations 2009 (SI 2009 No 37), Sch 1, paras 2 and 4; see Chapter 12 para 12.217.
[113] SA 2020, s 345 and SOA 2003, Sch 3, para 9; see Chapter 16 para 16.07.
[114] SA 2020, s 306, Sch 18, para 29(l); see Chapter 12 para 12.51.
[115] The common law offence of assault with intent to rape had fallen into disuse and OAPA 1861, s 38, which defined an offence of assault with intent to rape, had been abolished in 1967.

F. ASSAULT WITH INTENT TO COMMIT BUGGERY, 1.1.1957 TO 30.4.2004

Definition

To make an indecent assault on a man.   **5.93**

Proof

Section 15(2) provided that a boy under 16 cannot give consent. However, if the defendant has a genuine belief that the victim is over 16 then, if the boy was in fact consenting or the defendant believed that he was, then there is no criminal liability.[116]   **5.94**

Notes

(i) This offence is triable either way.   **5.95**
(ii) Section 15(3) provided that a mentally disordered person cannot give consent and that the perpetrator would be guilty if he knew or had reason to suspect the person to be mentally disordered. See para 7.01.

Indictment

INDECENT ASSAULT UPON A MALE PERSON 1.1.1957 to 30.4.2004   **5.96**

Statement of Offence
INDECENT ASSAULT ON A MALE PERSON, contrary to section 15(1) of the Sexual Offences Act 1956.
Particulars of Offence
D on the ... day of ... indecently assaulted C, a male person (aged under 16 years).

Alternative Offences

Attempted indecent assault upon a male person. When indicting offences of attempt do so under common law until 26.8.1981, thereafter indict under s 1(1) Criminal Attempts Act 1981. Aver the attempt in both the Statement of Offence and Particulars of Offence. In addition, aver the substantive offence under the relevant Act; see paras 1.51 and 12.157 and *Reed & Others* [2021].[117] If the victim is aged under 16 then the age is usually averred.   **5.97**

Sentence

(i) On indictment: **10 YEARS**.[118]   **5.98**
(ii) Summarily: **6 months**.

---

[116] *R v K* [2002] 1 AC 462 HL; *R v Fernandez* [2002] The Times 26 June.
[117] *Reed & Others* [2021] EWCA Crim 572.
[118] SOA 1956, s 37 and Sch 2, para 18(i) and 19(i).

152   5. BUGGERY AND OFFENCES OF INDECENCY

Upon Conviction/Sentence

5.99 (i) Notification applicable where the other party is under 18, or the offender is or has been sentenced to a term of imprisonment of at least 30 months or made subject to a restriction order.[119]
(ii) Automatic inclusion in the children's and adults' barring lists with the right to make representations.[120]
(iii) SHPO applicable.[121]
(iv) Qualifying 'specified sexual offence' in Schedule 18 (Extended Sentences).[122]

5.100 For offences after 1.5.2004: see paras 3.45–3.52.

G. GROSS INDECENCY WITH ANOTHER MAN, 1.1.1957 to 30.4.2004

Sexual Offences Act 1956, s 13

5.101 The SOA 1956 consolidated the law in relation to sexual offences. Section 11 of the CLAA 1885 was repealed. Section 13 of the SOA 1956 was substituted (as of 1.1.1957).

Definition

5.102 … to commit an act of gross indecency with another man, whether in public or private, or to be a party to the commission by a man of an act of gross indecency with another man.

Proof

5.103 As per Definition.

Notes

5.104 After 1960 offences involving children (under 14) are best charged as offences under the IwCA 1960. See para 4.05.

Indictment

5.105 GROSS INDECENCY 1.1.1957 to 30.4.2004

---

[119] SOA 2003, s 80(1) and Sch 3, para 8; see Chapter 14 paras 14.01–14.05.
[120] Part 2 of the Safeguarding Vulnerable Groups Act 2006 (Prescribed Criteria and Miscellaneous Provisions) Regulations 2009 (SI 2009 No 37), Sch 1, paras 2 and 4; see Chapter 12 para 12.217.
[121] SA 2020, s 345 and SOA 2003, Sch 3, para 8; see Chapter 16 para 16.07.
[122] SA 2020, s 306, Sch 18, para 29(k); see Chapter 12 para 12.51.

> **Statement of Offence**
> GROSS INDECENCY, contrary to section 13 of the Sexual Offences Act 1956.
>
> **Particulars of Offence**
> D, on the ... day of ... being a male person (over the age of 21 years/under the age of 21 years), committed/was party to the commission of/procured the commission of an act of gross indecency with C, a man (under the age of 16 years, namely ...) (in a public place, namely ...).

In addition if one of the parties is under the age of 21 then the age should be averred, in order to attract the appropriate maximum sentence.[123] **5.106**

Alternative Offences

An attempt to commit the full offence. Sentence as per the full offence, see para 5.08. **5.107**

ATTEMPTED GROSS INDECENCY 1.1.1957 to 26.8.1981

> **Statement of Offence**
> ATTEMPTED GROSS INDECENCY, contrary to section 13 of the Sexual Offences Act 1956 and common law.
>
> **Particulars of Offence**
> D, on the ... day of. ... , being a male person (over the age of 21 years/under the age of 21 years) attempted to commit an act of gross indecency with C, a man (under the age of 21 years namely ...).

If one of the parties is under the age of 21 then this ought to be averred in order to attract the appropriate maximum sentence.[124] **5.108**

When indicting offences of attempt do so under common law until 26.8.1981, thereafter indict under s 1(1) Criminal Attempts Act 1981. Aver the attempt in both the Statement of Offence and Particulars of Offence. In addition, aver the substantive offence under the relevant Act; see paras 1.51 and 12.157 and *Reed & Others* [2021].[125] **5.109**

Sentence

See para 5.46. **5.110**

Upon Conviction/Sentence

(i) Notification applicable where the offender was over 20 and the other party was under 18.[126] **5.111**
(ii) Automatic inclusion in the children's and adults' barred lists with right to make representations applicable where the other party was under 16 years and

---

[123] SOA 1956, s 3(4).
[124] SOA 1967, s 3(2).
[125] *Reed & Others* [2021] EWCA Crim 572.
[126] SOA 2003, s 80(1) and Sch 3, para 6; see Chapter 14 paras 14.01–14.05.

did not consent and the offence has not been 'disregarded'[127,128] (iii) SHPO applicable.[129]

1. Attempted Gross Indecency 1.1.1961

5.112 The IwCA 1960, s 1(1) creates a separate offence of committing or inciting an act of gross indecency with or towards a child under 14 (the maximum sentence is 2 years, until 1.10.97 when the offence was extended to include children under 16 and the sentence was increased to 10 years.[130] (See para 4.05.)

2. Attempted Gross Indecency 1.5.2004

5.113 The offences of gross indecency[131] and procuring a man to commit buggery in private[132] were both repealed by the SOA 2003. Thereafter, s 4 SOA 2003 created an offence of causing an adult to engage in sexual activity (see paras 3.58–3.59) and ss 8 and 10 of the SOA 2003 created offences of causing/inciting a child to engage in sexual activity (see paras 4.24–4.39).

5.114 Section 71 SOA 2003 created a summary offence of sexual activity in a Public Lavatory.

H. SEXUAL ACTIVITY IN A PUBLIC LAVATORY, 1.5.2004 TO DATE

Sexual Offences Act 2003, s 71

5.115 This summary only offence covers consensual sexual activity between adults.

Definition

5.116 (1) A person (D) commits an offence if—

(a) D is in a lavatory to which at the least a section of the public has/is permitted to
(b) he intentionally engages in an activity, and
(c) the activity is sexual.
(2) For the purposes of this section, an activity is sexual if a reasonable person would, in all the circumstances but regardless of any person's purpose consider it be sexual.

Proof

5.117 As per definition.

---

[127] Part 2 of the Safeguarding Vulnerable Groups Act 2006 (Prescribed Criteria and Miscellaneous Provisions) Regulations 2009 (SI 2009 No 37), Sch 1 paras 2 and 4; see Chapter 12 Para 12.217.
[128] Disregarded conviction or caution within the meaning of Chapter 5 of Pt 5 of the Protection of Freedoms Act 2012.
[129] SA 2020, s 345 and SOA 2003, Sch 3, para 6; see Chapter 16 para 16.07.
[130] C(S)A 1997, s 52.
[131] SOA 1956, s 13.
[132] SOA 1967, s 4.

H. SEXUAL ACTIVITY IN A PUBLIC LAVATORY, 1.5.2004 TO DATE

Notes

5.118

(i) The offence is summary only.
(ii) The definition of sexual is objective for the purposes of this section.
(iii) D must intentionally engage in sexual activity in a lavatory to which the public, is permitted access either by payment or otherwise.
(iv) The s 45 MSA 2015 defence for slavery and trafficking victims who commit an offence is available for an offence under this section, provided it was committed on or after 31.7.2.15.[133]

Charge 1.5.2004 to date

D, on the … day of … was in a lavatory to which at the least a section of the public has/is permitted to enter, and intentionally engaged in a sexual activity, contrary to section 71 Sexual Offences Act 2003.

5.119

Alternative Offence

Attempt to commit the full offence. When charging offences of attempt do so under s 1(1) Criminal Attempts Act 1981.[134] Aver the attempt in the charge wording. In addition, aver the substantive offence legislation in addition to the CAA 1981, adopting the principle in *Reed & Others* [2021].[135] See paras 1.51 and 12.157.

5.120

Sentence

6 months' imprisonment and/or an unlimited fine.[136]

5.121

This offence is not included in the Sentencing Council Sexual Offences Definitive Guideline, but see the Magistrates' Court Sentencing Guideline which applies to all offenders aged 18 and older, who are sentenced on or after 24 April 2017.

5.122

Upon Conviction/Sentence

5.123

(i) Notification not applicable.[137]
(ii) Automatic inclusion in the children's and adults' barred lists with the right to make representations not applicable.[138]
(iii) SHPO not applicable.[139]

---

[133] Modern Slavery Act 2015, s 45 commencement date 31.7.2015 (SI 2015/1476). This offence is not an excluded offence in Sch 4 of the Act. The s 45 defence is not retrospective, see *R v Joseph (Verna Sermanfure)* [2017] EWCA Crim 36.
[134] Implementation date 27.8.1981.
[135] *Reed & Others* [2021] EWCA Crim 572.
[136] S71(3) SOA 2003.
[137] SOA 2003 (not in Sch 3), s 80(1); see Chapter 14 Tables 14.2–14.5.
[138] Part 2 of the Safeguarding Vulnerable Groups Act 2006 (Prescribed Criteria and Miscellaneous Provisions) Regulations 2009 (SI 2009 No 37) not included in paras 1, 2, 3, and 4; see Chapter 12 para 12.217.
[139] SA 2020, s 345 (not in Sch 3 or Sch 5 SOA 2003); see Chapter 16 para 16.07.

156   5. BUGGERY AND OFFENCES OF INDECENCY

I. PROCURING OTHERS TO COMMIT BUGGERY, 27.7.1967 TO 30.4.2004

1. Procuring Others to Commit Buggery

Sexual Offences Act 1967, s 4(1)

Definition

5.124   A man who procures another man to commit with a third man an act of buggery…

Proof

5.125   Procurement requires a positive act, and that the defendant brought about a course of conduct which would not otherwise necessarily have been embarked upon.[140]

5.126   The prosecution have to prove that the defendant:

(i) procured the second man to commit the offence of buggery;
(ii) was aware that he was procuring the second male to commit an act of buggery with a third male;
(iii) this offence can only be committed if one of the parties to the buggery is under 16 or otherwise than in private, or with two or more present.[141]

Notes

5.127   (i) The offence is triable either way.[142]
(ii) The various amendments to the offence of buggery since 1967 apply; the age of consent was reduced to 18 in 1994,[143] and 16 in 2000[144] (see para 5.04).
(iii) The extension of the offence of rape to include anal intercourse in 1994,[145] meant that from then on an offence of procurement is committed only if one of the parties to the buggery is under the age of consent or the buggery takes place otherwise than in private or more than two people are present.
(iv) This offence was repealed by the SOA 2003.

Indictment

5.128   PROCURING AN ACT OF BUGGERY 27.7.1967 to 30.4.2004

---

[140] *R v Broadfoot* 64 Cr App R 71.
[141] SOA 1967, ss 1 and 4(1).
[142] MCA 1980, s 17(1).
[143] CJPOA 1994, s 143, from 3.11.1994.
[144] SO(A)A 2000, ss 1 and 2, as from 1.5.2004.
[145] CJPOA 1994, s 142.

I. PROCURING OTHERS TO COMMIT BUGGERY, 27.7.1967 TO 30.4.2004

Statement of Offence

PROCURING AN ACT OF BUGGERY, contrary to section 4(1) of the Sexual Offences Act 1967.

Particulars of Offence

D on the ... day of ... procured another man (namely) to commit with a third man (namely) an act of buggery.

Sentence

(i) On indictment: **2 YEARS**.
(ii) Summarily: **6 months**.

5.129

Upon Conviction/Sentence

(i) Notification not applicable.[146]
(ii) Automatic inclusion in the children's and adults' barring lists not applicable.[147]
(iii) SHPO not applicable.[148]

5.130

---

[146] SOA 2003, s 80(1) (not listed in Sch 3); see Chapter 14 Tables 14.2–14.5.
[147] Part 2 of the Safeguarding Vulnerable Groups Act 2006 (Prescribed Criteria and Miscellaneous Provisions) Regulations 2009 (SI 2009 No 37) paras 2 and 4; see Chapter 12 para 12.217.
[148] SA 2020, s 345 (not listed in Sch 3 or Sch 5 SOA 2003); see Chapter 16 para 16.07.

6

FAMILIAL OFFENCES

A. Introduction	6.01	1. Incitement of Girls under 16 to have Incestuous Intercourse	6.41
B. Offences Committed Pre-1.1.1957	6.07	E. Offences Committed from 1.5.2004 to date	6.48
1. Incest by Males	6.07	1. Penetrative Sex with an Adult Relative	6.48
2. Incest by Females	6.15	2. Consenting to Penetrative Sex with an Adult Relative	6.56
C. Offences Committed between 1.1.1957 and 30.4.2004	6.23	3. Sexual Activity with a Child Family Member	6.64
1. Incest by Males	6.23	4. Inciting a Child Family Member to Engage in Sexual Activity	6.74
2. Incest by Females	6.32		
D. Offences Committed between 8.9.1977 and 30.4.2004	6.41		

A. INTRODUCTION

6.01 Before the passing of the Punishment of Incest Act (PIA) 1908, incest was punishable in England and Ireland only by proceedings in the ecclesiastical courts. The 1908 Act created the offence of incest, which covered sexual intercourse with an immediate blood relative or half-sibling. It included offences by males upon females and females permitting with their consent a male blood relative to have sexual relations with them.

6.02 Offences under the SOA 1956 had the same parameters. Again the all-important factor was blood relationships. Section 10(1) provided for it to be an offence for a man to have sexual intercourse with a woman whom he knew to be his granddaughter, daughter, sister or mother. Section 11(1) provided for it to be an offence for a woman aged 16 or over to permit a man whom she knew to be her grandfather, father, brother or son to have sexual intercourse with her by her consent. Section 54(1) of the CLA 1977 created an additional offence for a male to incite a girl under the age of 16 to have incestuous intercourse.

6.03 The SOA 2003 made significant changes. It created two new gender-neutral offences designed to capture the sexual abuse and exploitation of children within the concept of the modern 'family unit'. Section 25 creates an offence of sexual activity with a child family member, whilst s 26 covers inciting a child family member to engage in sexual activity. The scope of the proscribed sexual activity is extended to any form of touching, whilst the child 'family' member must be under 18. The Act also widens the category of family who can commit such offences by extending prohibited family relationships beyond blood relationships to include adoptive relationships, as well as past and present step-parents and foster parents. Although not specifically mentioned within s 27, adoptive parents who are in the role of parents who care for and live with the child will be included by virtue of their falling within the ambit of s 27(2). Adoptive parents are to be treated as being on a par with biological parents. This is in keeping with the intention of the Sexual Offences Review in making its recommendations for changes to the law in this area, in stating that 'the kind of definition linked to bloodlines (alone) ... was no longer tenable'.[1] Also included are cases where both parties live in the same household, and cases where a person is regularly involved in caring for, training, supervising or being in sole charge of the complainant. Excluded will be those related by adoption where there is no caring role falling within the terms of s 27(4), for example adoptive siblings over 18 who are not themselves related by blood. These new familial sex offences (that is, under ss 25 and 26) include all acts which would have been incest under the old law where the complainant is/was under 18.

6.04 In addition, the 2003 Act also created two offences to cover the situation where a person aged 16 or over sexually penetrates a relative aged 18 or over (s 64) or allows that adult relative to penetrate them (s 65). Penetration means penetration of another person's vagina or anus by any part of the defendant's body or with 'anything else', and penetration of another's mouth with his penis. In contrast to the familial offences, these offences (under ss 64 and 65) cover a limited circle of blood relationships, that is, parent, child, grandchild, brother, sister, half-brother, half-sister, uncle, aunt, nephew or niece. For the first time, uncles and aunts are included.

6.05 It should be borne in mind that the offences under ss 25 and 26 include within their ambit situations of sexual intercourse between an adult and a child too young to be able to give true consent, notwithstanding that the protection of such young people from both themselves and others must be the very purpose of a legislative minimum age of consent.

6.06 In drafting indictments generally for a familial offence it is important to remember the following:

(i) The maximum penalties such offences attract are usually significantly lower than the equivalent offence drafted outside the familial bracket because they are intended to reflect circumstances where there is consent. Where C is under 13, however, it will be appropriate to indict the non-familial offence either as the primary count with a familial offence in the alternative or to simply draft, for example, a count of rape of a child under 13 (life) rather than sexual activity with a child family member (5 years where the defendant is under 18 even when the child is under 13). This is the clear intention of Parliament and underpins the current CPS guidance for indicting such offences.

(ii) Where possible, counts should relate to a specific incident with each count drafted to make clear what is alleged by giving sufficient detail. Where that is impossible because of, for example, several years of regular and repeated acts, multiple incident counts should be included in an indictment to both reflect the course of conduct and found a basis for sentencing on the full facts rather than for a single specimen. See Chapter 1 paras 1.08–1.17.

---

[1] *Setting the Boundaries: Reforming the Law on Sex Offences* (Home Office, 2000), para 5.5.11.

(iii) If both parties to the sexual act are charged, it is possible for a guilty verdict against one only to stand; one party might be unaware of the relationship or there might not be true consent by the party alleged to have consented to the act.[2]

B. OFFENCES COMMITTED PRE-1.1.1957

1. Incest by Males

Punishment of Incest Act 1908, s 1

Definition

Carnal knowledge[3] by any male person of a female person, who is to his knowledge his grand-daughter, daughter, sister or mother.   **6.07**

Proof

(i) Carnal knowledge (that is, penetration of vagina by penis; ejaculation unnecessary);[4]   **6.08**
(ii) by any male person of his mother, sister, daughter or granddaughter. The term 'sister' includes a half-sibling.[5]
(iii) Consent is immaterial.[6] It is the blood relationship which is key; proof of lawful marriage linking D and C is not required.[7]

Notes

(i) Triable on indictment only.[8]   **6.09**
(ii) Prosecution for any offence under the PIA had to be sanctioned prior to commencement by the Attorney General unless brought by the DPP,[9] similar to the current position.
(iii) For penetration of the anus, indict the offence as buggery (see para 5.10).
(iv) Where it is alleged that the female complainant is aged under 13 years that must be specifically alleged on the indictment in order for the higher sentencing power to be invoked.[10]

---

[2] *R v Gordon* (1927) 19 Cr App R 20 CA; brother and sister both charged in same indictment but tried separately; she was acquitted—that did not make his conviction bad.
[3] That is, vaginal sexual intercourse.
[4] OAPA 1861, s 63.
[5] PIA 1908, s 3.
[6] PIA 1908, s 1(2).
[7] PIA 1908, s 3.
[8] PIA 1908, s 4(2).
[9] PIA 1908, s 6.
[10] PIA 1908, s 1(1).

Indictment

6.10 INCEST BY A MALE PERSON Pre-1.1.1957

Statement of Offence

INCEST, contrary to section 1(1) of the Punishment of Incest Act 1908.

Particulars of Offence

D, being a male person, on the … day of … 19 … , had carnal knowledge of C, who is and was to his knowledge his granddaughter/daughter/(half-)sister/mother (if she was under 13 years at the time, add C's age).

Alternative Offences

6.11 (i) Attempt to commit the full offence. When indicting offences of attempt do so under common law. Aver the attempt in both the Statement of Offence and Particulars of Offence. In addition, aver the substantive offence under the relevant Act; see paras 1.51 and 12.157 and *Reed & Others* [2021].[11]

(ii) Indecent assault: **2 YEARS** (see para 3.19).

Sentence

6.12 (i) On indictment for the full offence:
- when averred and proved that C is under 13 **LIFE**, or not less than **3 YEARS**.[12]
- Otherwise, not less than **3 YEARS** and not exceeding **7 YEARS**.[13]

(ii) For an attempt: **2 YEARS**.[14]

Upon Conviction/Sentence

6.13 (i) Notification not applicable.[15]

(ii) Automatic inclusion in the children's barred list with the right to make representations if the offence was committed against a child. Automatic inclusion in the adults' barred list with the right to make representations if the offence was committed against a child or the other party to the act did not consent.[16]

---

[11] *Reed & Others* [2021] EWCA Crim 572.
[12] PIA 1908, s 1(1) and CLAA 1885, s 4.
[13] PIA 1908, s 1(1) and section 1(1) Criminal Justice Act 1948.
[14] PIA 1908, s 1(3).
[15] SOA 2003, s 80(1) (not listed in Sch 3); see Chapter 14, Tables 14.2–14.5.
[16] Part 2 of the Safeguarding Vulnerable Groups Act 2006 (Prescribed Criteria and Miscellaneous Provisions) Regulations 2009 (SI 2009 No 37) paras 2 and 4; see Chapter 12, para 12.217.

(iii) SHPO not applicable[17] as not in Schedules 3 or 5 although the court had power under the 1908 Act where the girl/woman was under 21 to 'divest the defendant of all control over her and if he was her guardian to remove her from his guardianship and appoint another guardian'.[18]

As of 1.1.1957 PIA, s 1 is repealed. From the 1.1.1957 SOA 1956, s 10 covers this offence (see para 6.23). **6.14**

2. Incest by Females

Punishment of Incest Act 1908, s 2

Definition

Permitting with her consent by any female person of or above the age of 16 by her grandfather, father, brother or son to have carnal knowledge[19] of her, knowing him to be her grandfather, father, brother or son as the case may be. **6.15**

Proof

(i) A female over 16 years permitting with consent (not simply submitting to); **6.16**
(ii) her grandfather, father, brother or son (the term 'brother' includes a half-sibling);[20]
(iii) to have carnal knowledge of her (that is, penetration of vagina by penis; ejaculation unnecessary).[21]

Notes

(i) Triable on indictment only.[22] **6.17**
(ii) Prosecution for any offence under the PIA must be sanctioned prior to commencement by the Attorney General unless brought by the DPP.[23]
(iii) Proof of lawful marriage linking D and C is not required.[24]

---

[17] SA 2020, s 345 (not listed in Sch 3 or Sch 5 SOA 2003); see Chapter 16 para 16.07.
[18] PIA 1908, s 1(4).
[19] Sexual intercourse.
[20] PIA 1908, s 3.
[21] OAPA 1861, s 63.
[22] PIA 1908, s 4(2).
[23] PIA 1908, s 6.
[24] PIA 1908, s 3.

164   6. FAMILIAL OFFENCES

Indictment

6.18   INCEST BY A FEMALE PERSON Pre-1.1.1957

> ### Statement of Offence
> INCEST, contrary to section 2 of the Punishment of Incest Act 1908.
>
> ### Particulars of Offence
> D, being a female person of the age of 16 or over, on the … day of … 19 … , with her consent permitted C who is and was to her knowledge her grandfather/father/(half-)brother/son, to have carnal knowledge of her.

Alternative Offences

6.19   Section 2 of the PIA does not provide for the offence of attempt, perhaps not surprisingly, as it is difficult to envisage circumstances in which it would be charged. If, however, you are indicting an offence of attempt, do so under common law. Aver the attempt in both the Statement and Particulars of Offence. In addition, aver the substantive offence under the relevant Act; see paras 1.51 and 12.157 and *Reed & Others* [2021].[25]

Sentence

6.20   On indictment: not less than 3 YEARS and not exceeding 7 YEARS.[26]

Upon Conviction/Sentence

6.21   (i) Notification not applicable.[27]
(ii) Automatic inclusion in the children's barred list with the right to make representations if the offence was committed against a child. Automatic inclusion in the adults' barred list with the right to make representations if the offence was committed against a child or the other party to the act did not consent.[28]
(iii) SHPO not applicable[29]

---

[25] *Reed & Others* [2021] EWCA Crim 572.
[26] PIA 1908, s 2 and s 1(1) Criminal Justice Act 1948.
[27] SOA 2003, s 80(1) (not listed in Sch 3); see Chapter 14, Tables 14.2–14.5.
[28] Part 2 of the Safeguarding Vulnerable Groups Act 2006 (Prescribed Criteria and Miscellaneous Provisions) Regulations 2009 (SI 2009 No 37) paras 2 and 4; see Chapter 12, para 12.217.
[29] SA 2020, s 345 (not listed in Sch 3 or Sch 5 SOA 2003); see Chapter 16, para 16.07.

6.22 As of 1.1.1957 PIA, s 2 is repealed. From 1.1.1957 SOA 1956, s 11 covers this offence (see para 6.32).

C. OFFENCES COMMITTED BETWEEN 1.1.1957 AND 30.4.2004

1. Incest by Males

Sexual Offences Act 1956, s 10

Definition

6.23 For a man to have sexual intercourse with a woman or girl whom he knows to be his granddaughter, daughter, sister or mother.

Proof

6.24
(i) Sexual intercourse (that is, penetration of vagina by penis; ejaculation unnecessary);[30]
(ii) by any male person with his granddaughter, daughter, sister or mother. The term 'sister' includes a half-sibling.[31]
(iii) Consent is immaterial.

Notes

6.25
(i) Triable on indictment only.
(ii) Prosecution for this offence, or an attempt to commit it, may not be commenced except with the consent of, or by, the DPP.[32]
(iii) A genuine mistake as to the identity of the woman provides D with a defence.[33]
(iv) For offences committed after the commencement of the SOA 1993,[34] a boy of 14 or over can be charged as the presumption of incapacity was abolished.[35]
(v) It is the blood relationship which is key; proof of lawful marriage linking D and C is not required.[36]

---

[30] SOA 1956, s 44.
[31] SOA 1956, s 10(2).
[32] SOA 1956, s 37(2) and Sch 2 14(a) and (b).
[33] *R v Baillie-Smith* (Raymond) (1977) 64 Cr App R 76 CA.
[34] Commencement date 20.9.1993.
[35] SOA 1993, ss 1, 2(2), and 3.
[36] SOA 1956, s 10(2).

166   6. FAMILIAL OFFENCES

(vi) The legal adoption of the woman to another family does not provide the blood relative with a defence.[37]

Indictment

6.26 INCEST BY A MALE PERSON 1.1.1957 to 30.4.2004

> **Statement of Offence**
> INCEST, contrary to section 10(1) of the Sexual Offences Act 1956.
>
> **Particulars of Offence**
> D, being a male person, on the … day of … 19/20……, had sexual intercourse with C, whom he knew to be his grand-daughter, daughter, (half-)sister or mother (add C's age if under 13 at the time).

Alternative Offences

6.27 (i) Attempt to commit the full offence. When indicting offences of attempt do so under common law until 26.8.1981, thereafter indict under s 1(1) Criminal Attempts Act 1981.[38] Aver the attempt in both the Statement of Offence and Particulars of Offence. In addition, aver the substantive offence under the relevant Act; see paras 1.51 and 12.157 and *Reed & Others* [2021].[39]

(ii) Unlawful sexual intercourse with a girl under 13: LIFE (see para 4.70) (or under 16, 2 YEARS; that will be academic on an historic offence, as prosecution is time-barred however, after 12 months on an offence under the SOA 1956, s 6).

(iii) Where C is under 16, indecent assault, even if not specifically averred; indecent assault is a specified alternative to ss 5 and 6 (the USI offences):[40] **2, 5 or 10 YEARS** (see paras 3.19 and 3.29).

Sentence

6.28 (i) On indictment:
- if C is under 13 years: LIFE.
- Otherwise **7 YEARS**.[41]

(ii) An attempt attracts the same maximum.

---

[37] Adoption Act (AA) 1976, s 47(1).
[38] Implementation date 27.8.1981.
[39] *Reed & Others* [2021] EWCA Crim 572.
[40] SOA 1956, s 37(5) and Sch 2.
[41] SOA 1956, s 37(3) and Sch 2, para 14(a) and (b).

C. OFFENCES COMMITTED BETWEEN 1.1.1957 AND 30.4.2004

Sentencing Guidance

6.29 Guidance is to be found in *A-G's Reference (No 1 of 1989)*[42] re father with daughter, giving assistance divided by her various potential age ranges and setting out aggravating features. It should be read subject to the Practice Statement (Crime: Sentencing).[43]

Upon Conviction/Sentence

6.30
(i) Notification applies if the victim or other party was under 18.[44]
(ii) Automatic inclusion in the children's barred list with the right to make representations if the offence was committed against a child. Automatic inclusion in the adult's barred list with the right to make representations if the offence was committed against a child or the other party to the act did not consent.[45]
(iii) SHPO applies.[46]
(iv) Qualifying 'specified sexual offence' in Schedule 18 (Extended Sentences).[47]

6.31 As of 1.5.2004, SOA 1956, s 10 is repealed. From 1.4.2004 SOA 2003, ss 64 and 25 cover this offence (see para 6.48).

2. Incest by Females

Sexual Offences Act 1956, s 11

Definition

6.32 Sexual intercourse with her permission and consent between a man and a woman of 16 years or over, she knowing that he is her grandfather, father, brother, or son. 'Brother' includes a half-sibling.

Proof

6.33
(i) A female over 16 years permitting with consent (not simply submitting to);
(ii) her grandfather, father, brother or son (the term 'brother' includes a half-sibling);[48]

---

[42] [1989] 3 WLR 1117.
[43] [1992] 1 WLR 948.
[44] SOA 2003, s 80(1) and Sch 3, para 4; see Chapter 14 paras 14.01–14.05.
[45] Part 2 of the Safeguarding Vulnerable Groups Act 2006 (Prescribed Criteria and Miscellaneous Provisions) Regulations 2009 (SI 2009 No 37) paras 2 and 4; see Chapter 12, para 12.217.
[46] SA 2020, s 345 and SOA 2003, Sch 3, para 4; see Chapter 16, para 16.07.
[47] SA 2020, s 306, Sch 18, para 29(i); see Chapter 12, para 12.51.
[48] SOA 1956, s 11(2).

168 6. FAMILIAL OFFENCES

(iii) to have sexual intercourse with her (that is, penetration of vagina by penis; ejaculation unnecessary).[49]

Notes

6.34
(i) Triable only on indictment.
(ii) Prosecution for this offence, or an attempt to commit it, may not be commenced except with the consent of or by the DPP.[50]
(iii) The common law presumption of incapacity is a boy of under 14 had no application where a woman was charged with incest.[51]
(iv) The legal adoption of either party to another family does not provide a defence; the criminality is in the fact of and knowledge of the blood relationship.[52]
(v) Proof of lawful marriage linking D and C is not required.[53]

Indictment

6.35 INCEST BY A FEMALE PERSON 1.1.1957 to 30.4.2004

Statement of Offence
INCEST, contrary to section 11(1) of the Sexual Offences Act 1956.

Particulars of Offence
D, being a female person of the age of ... , on the ... day of ... 19/20 ... , with her consent permitted C, whom she knew to be her grandfather/father/(half-)brother/son, to have sexual intercourse with her.

Alternative Offences

6.36 Attempt to commit the full offence. When indicting offences of attempt do so under common law until 26.8.1981, thereafter indict under s 1(1) Criminal Attempts Act 1981.[54] Aver the attempt in both the Statement of Offence and Particulars of Offence. In addition, aver the substantive offence under the relevant Act; see paras 1.51 and 12.157 and *Reed & Others* [2021].[55]

---

[49] OAPA 1861, s 63.
[50] SOA 1956, s 37(2) and Sch 2.
[51] *R v Pickford* [1995] 1 Cr App R 420 CA.
[52] AA 1976, s 47(1).
[53] SOA 1956, s 11(2).
[54] Implementation date 27.8.1981.
[55] *Reed & Others* [2021] EWCA Crim 572.

Sentence

6.37
(i) The full offence on indictment: maximum **7 YEARS**.[56]
(ii) Attempt on indictment: **2 YEARS**.[57]

Upon Conviction/Sentence

6.38
(i) Notification not applicable.[58]
(ii) Automatic inclusion in the children's barred list with the right to make representations if the offence was committed against a child. Automatic inclusion in the adults' barred list with the right to make representations if the offence was committed against a child or the other party to the act did not consent.[59]
(iii) SHPO not applicable.[60]
(iv) Qualifying 'specified sexual offence' in Schedule 18 (Extended Sentences).[61]

6.39 As of 30.4.2004, SOA 1956, s 11 is repealed. From 1.5.2004 SOA 2003, s 65 covers this offence directly (see para 6.56). Note, however, that the scope for familial offences by women is widened to include penetration by a woman using an object on another of either gender under s 64 because the section is gender non-specific.

6.40 The SOA 2003 creates four offences of sexual activity either with a child within the 'family' or with adult relatives. Although the former category holds higher maximum sentences than the latter, they are still not as high as some other equivalent non-familial offences. See para 6.03.

D. OFFENCES COMMITTED BETWEEN 8.9.1977 AND 30.4.2004

1. Incitement of Girls under 16 to have Incestuous Intercourse

Criminal Law Act 1977, s 54

Definition

6.41 … a man to incite to have sexual intercourse with him a girl under the age of sixteen whom he knows to be his granddaughter, daughter or sister.[62]

---

[56] SOA 1956, s 37(3) and Sch 2, para 15(a).
[57] SOA 1956, s 37(3) and Sch 2, para 15(b).
[58] SOA 2003, s 80(1) (not listed in Sch 3); see Chapter 14 Tables 14.2–14.5.
[59] Part 2 of the Safeguarding Vulnerable Groups Act 2006 (Prescribed Criteria and Miscellaneous Provisions) Regulations 2009 (SI 2009 No 37) paras 2 and 4; see Chapter 12 para 12.217.
[60] SA 2020, s 345 (not listed in Sch 3 or Sch 5 SOA 2003); see Chapter 16 para 16.07.
[61] SA 2020, s 306, Sch 18, para 29(i); see Chapter 12 para 12.51.
[62] CLA 1977, s 54(1).

170   6. FAMILIAL OFFENCES

Proof

6.42   (i) Incitement or encouragement by D;
(ii) of his granddaughter, daughter, sister or half-sister;[63]
(iii) who is/was aged under 16 at the time;
(iv) to have sexual intercourse with him.

Notes

6.43   (i) This offence is triable either way.[64]
(ii) This section applies even if the relationship between the parties cannot be traced through lawful wedlock.[65]

Indictment

6.44   INCITEMENT OF A GIRL UNDER 16 TO COMMIT INCEST 8.9.1977 to 30.4.2004

Statement of Offence

INCITEMENT OF A GIRL UNDER 16 TO COMMIT INCEST, contrary to section 54 of the Criminal Law Act 1977.

Particulars of Offence

D, a boy/man, on the ... day of ... incited C, a girl under the age of 16, whom he knows to be his grand-daughter/daughter/(half-)sister, to have sexual intercourse with him.

Sentence

6.45   (i) On indictment: **2 YEARS**.[66]
(ii) Summarily: **6 months**.[67]

Upon Conviction/Sentence

6.46   (i) Notification applies.[68]

---

[63] CLA 1977, s 54(2).
[64] CLA 1977, s 54(4).
[65] CLA 1977, s 54 (2).
[66] CLA 1977, s 54(4)(b).
[67] CLA 1977, s 54(4)(a).
[68] SOA 2003, s 80(1) and Sch 3, para 12; see Chapter 14 paras 14.01–14.05.

(ii) Automatic inclusion in the children's and adults' barred lists with the right to make representations.[69]
   (iii) SHPO applies.[70]
   (iv) Qualifying 'specified sexual offence' in Schedule 18 (Extended Sentences).[71]

6.47 As of 1.5.2004, CLA 1977, s 54 is repealed. From 1.5.2004, SOA 2003, s 26 covers this offence (see para 6.74). Note the increase in the maximum sentence from 2 years' to 14 years' imprisonment, as of 1.5.2004.

E. OFFENCES COMMITTED FROM 1.5.2004 TO DATE

1. Penetrative Sex with an Adult Relative

Sexual Offences Act 2003, s 64

Definition

6.48 As per Proof.

Proof

6.49
   (i) Intentional sexual[72] penetration of C's vagina[73] or anus by D's penis or by D using anything else, or penetration of C's mouth by D's penis.
   (ii) D is 16 years or over (unless the offence relates to D's adopted child or child by parental order,[74] in which case D is 18 years or over).[75]
   (iii) C is 18 years or over.
   (iv) C is D's child, parent, grandchild, grandparent, brother, sister, half-brother, half-sister, niece, nephew, uncle or aunt. (Uncle/aunt has the ordinary meaning of brother/sister of a person's parent; likewise, niece/nephew means the child of a person's brother or sister.)[76] This now includes adoptive parents and relationships arising by virtue of a

---

[69] Part 2 of the Safeguarding Vulnerable Groups Act 2006 (Prescribed Criteria and Miscellaneous Provisions) Regulations 2009 (SI 2009 No 37) paras 2 and 4; see Chapter 12, para 12.217.
[70] SA 2020, s 345 and Sch 3, para 12; see Chapter 16, para 16.07.
[71] SA 2020, s 306, Sch 18, para 34; see Chapter 12, para 12.51.
[72] SOA 2003, s 78 defines 'sexual'; either because of the nature of the act or its circumstances/purpose or both. See also *R v H* [2005] 2 All ER 859 CA for the two-stage approach required.
[73] 'Vagina' includes vulva, SOA 2003, s 79.
[74] As per Human Fertilisation and Embryology Act 2008 as amended by Human Fertilisation and Embryology (Parental Orders) Regulations 2018 (SI 2010 No 1412) Sch 4.
[75] SOA 2003, s 64 (3A), section added by Criminal Justice and Immigration Act 2008 Schedule 15 para 5(4) (8.7.2008).
[76] SOA 2003, s 64(3).

172   6. FAMILIAL OFFENCES

parental order (baby born to surrogate mother treated as child of couple whom one of them has contributed to the embryo).[77]
  (v) D knows or could reasonably be expected to know that that he is related to C in that way.[78]
  (vi) Where the blood relationship is proved, D is to be taken to have known or to have been reasonably expected to have known of it unless sufficient evidence is adduced to raise an issue as to whether he knew or could reasonably have been expected to know that he was.[79]

Notes

6.50   (i) Triable either way.
  (ii) This offence could be committed by a woman penetrating either a male or female's body using an object; this is a change from the previous legislation, which only contemplated penetration by males, but in keeping with the ambit of such offences under the SOA 2003.
  (iii) 'Penetration' is a continuing act from entry to withdrawal.[80]
  (iv) 'Vagina' includes vulva.[81]
  (v) References to a part of the body include references to a part surgically constructed (in particular, through gender reassignment surgery).[82]
  (vi) The s 45 MSA 2015 defence for slavery and trafficking victims who commit an offence does not apply to this offence.[83]

Indictment

6.51   PENETRATIVE SEXUAL ACTIVITY WITH AN ADULT RELATIVE 1.5.2004 to date

Statement of Offence
SEX WITH AN ADULT RELATIVE, contrary to section 64(1) of the Sexual Offences Act 2003.

Particulars of Offence
D, being a person of [or over] the age of 16 [or 18] years, on the … day of … 20 … , intentionally and sexually penetrated the anus/vagina/mouth of C with his [penis] or [anything else if vagina/anus (name object)], C was aged … /18 years or over at the time

---

[77] Human Fertilisation and Embryology Act 2008 as amended by Human Fertilisation and Embryology (Parental Orders) Regulations 2018 (SI 2018 No 1412) Sch 4.
[78] SOA 2003, s 64(1)(e).
[79] SOA 2003, s 64(4).
[80] SOA 2003, s 79(2).
[81] SOA 2003, s 79(9).
[82] SOA 2003, s 79(3).
[83] Modern Slavery Act 2015, s 45 and Sch 4, para 33.

E. OFFENCES COMMITTED FROM 1.5.2004 TO DATE

and the relationship of D to C was that of son/daughter/mother/father/grandson/granddaughter/grandfather/grandmother/
(half-)brother/(half-)sister/niece/nephew/uncle/aunt, and the said D knew or could reasonably be expected to know that he was so related to C
An example of this might be:

Particulars of Offence

D, being a person then aged 17 years, on the ... day of ... 20 ..., intentionally and sexually penetrated the anus of C with his penis, C was then aged (e.g. 19) years and the relationship of D to C was that of half-brother and the said D knew or could reasonably be expected to know that he was so related to C.

Alternative Offences

Attempt to commit the full offence. When indicting offences of attempt do so under s1(1) Criminal Attempts Act 1981.[84] Aver the attempt in both the Statement of Offence and Particulars of Offence. In addition, aver the substantive offence under the relevant Act; see paras 1.51 and 12.157 and *Reed & Others* [2021].[85]

6.52

Sentence

(i) On indictment: **2 YEARS**.[86]
(ii) Summarily: **6 months** or **fine** or **both**.[87]

6.53

Sentencing Guidance

The Sentencing Council 'Sexual Offences: Definitive Guideline' contains offence-specific guidelines for section 64 offences. The Guideline applies to all offenders aged 18 and over, sentenced on or after 1 April 2014.

6.54

Upon Conviction/Sentence

(i) Notification applies where D is either under 18 and has been sentenced to 12 months or more, or D is over 18 and has been sentenced either to a term of imprisonment or to be detained in a hospital.[88]

6.55

---

[84] Implementation date 27.8.1981.
[85] *Reed & Others* [2021] EWCA Crim 572.
[86] SOA 2003, s 64(5)(b).
[87] SOA 2003, s 64(5)(a), 12 months if CJA 2003, s 282(4) implemented.
[88] SOA 2003, s 80(1) and Sch 3, para 32; see Chapter 14 paras 14.01–14.05.

174   6. FAMILIAL OFFENCES

(ii) Automatic inclusion in the children's and adults' barred lists not applicable.[89]
(iii) SHPO applies.[90]
(iv) Qualifying 'specified sexual offence' in Schedule 18 (Extended Sentences).[91]

2. Consenting to Penetrative Sex with an Adult Relative

Sexual Offences Act 2003, s 65

Definition

6.56   As per Proof.

Proof

6.57   (i) Consensual sexual[92] penetration of D's vagina[93] or anus by C's penis or by C using anything else, or penetration of D's mouth by C's penis.
(ii) D is 16 years or over, unless the offence relates to D's adopted child or child by parental order,[94] in which case D is 18 years or over.[95]
(iii) C is 18 years or over.
(iv) D is C's child, parent, grandchild, grandparent, brother, sister, half-brother, half-sister, niece, nephew, uncle or aunt. (Uncle/aunt has the ordinary meaning of brother/sister of a person's parent; likewise, niece/nephew means the child of a person's brother or sister.)[96] This now includes adoptive parents and relationships arising by virtue of a parental order (baby born to surrogate mother treated as child of couple whom one of them has contributed to the embryo).[97]
(v) D knows or could reasonably be expected to know that that he is related to C in that way.[98]
(vi) Where the blood relationship is proved, D is to be taken to have known or to be been reasonably expected to have known of it unless sufficient evidence is adduced to raise

---

[89] Part 2 of the Safeguarding Vulnerable Groups Act 2006 (Prescribed Criteria and Miscellaneous Provisions) Regulations 2009 (SI 2009 No 37) not included in paras 1, 2, 3, or 4; see Chapter 12 para 12.217.
[90] SA 2020, s 345 and Sch 3, para 32 SOA 2003; see Chapter 16 para 16.07.
[91] SA 2020, s 306, Sch 18, para 38(av); see Chapter 12 para 12.51.
[92] SOA 2003, s 78 defines 'sexual'; either because of the nature of the act or its circumstances/purpose or both. See also *R v H* [2005] 2 All ER 859 CA for the two-stage approach required.
[93] 'Vagina' includes vulva, SOA 2003, s 79.
[94] As per Human Fertilisation and Embryology Act 2008 as amended by Human Fertilisation and Embryology (Parental Orders) Regulations 2018 (SI 2018 No 1412) Schedule 4.
[95] SOA 2003, s 65 (3A), section added by Criminal Justice and Immigration Act 2008 Sch 15 para 5(4) (8.7.2008).
[96] SOA 2003, s 65(3).
[97] Human Fertilisation and Embryology Act 2008 as amended by Human Fertilisation and Embryology (Parental Orders) Regulations 2018 (SI 2018 No 1412) Sch 4).
[98] SOA 2003, s 64(1)(e).

an issue as to whether he knew or could reasonably have been expected to know that he was a blood relation.[99]

Notes

(i) Triable either way.
(ii) 'Penetration' is a continuing act from entry to withdrawal.[100]
(iii) 'Vagina' includes vulva.[101]
(iv) References to a part of the body include references to a part surgically constructed (in particular, through gender reassignment surgery).[102]
(v) The s 45 MSA 2015 defence for slavery and trafficking victims who commit an offence does not apply to this offence.[103]

Indictment

CONSENTING TO PENETRATIVE SEX WITH AN ADULT RELATIVE 1.5.2004 to date

6.58

6.59

Statement of Offence
CONSENTING TO SEX WITH AN ADULT RELATIVE, contrary to section 65(1) of the Sexual Offences Act 2003

Particulars of Offence
D, being a person of [or over] the age of 16 [or 18] years, on the ... day of ... 20 ..., consented to the sexual penetration of her vagina by C with his penis when A was 18 years or over, the relationship of D to C was that of son/daughter/mother/father/grandson/grand-daughter/grandfather/grandmother/(half-)brother/(half-)sister/niece/nephew/uncle/aunt and the said D knew or could reasonably have been expected to know that he/she was so related to C.

An example of this might be:

Particulars of Offence

D, being a person of or over the age of 16 years, on the ... day of ... 20 ..., consented to the sexual penetration of her vagina by C with his penis when A was 18 years or over, the

---

[99] SOA 2003, s 65(4).
[100] SOA 2003, s 79(2).
[101] SOA 2003, s 79(9).
[102] SOA 2003, s 79(3).
[103] Modern Slavery Act 2015, s 45 and Sch 4, para 33.

relationship of D to C was that of niece and the said D knew or could reasonably have been expected to know that she was so related to C.

Alternative Offences

6.60 Attempt to commit the full offence. When indicting offences of attempt do so under s1(1) Criminal Attempts Act 1981.[104] Aver the attempt in both the Statement of Offence and Particulars of Offence. In addition, aver the substantive offence under the relevant Act; see paras 1.51 and 12.157 and *Reed & Others* [2021].[105]

Sentence

6.61 (i) On indictment: **2 YEARS**.[106]
(ii) Summarily: **6 months** or **fine** or **both**.[107]

Sentencing Guidance

6.62 The Sentencing Council 'Sexual Offences: Definitive Guideline' contains offence-specific guidelines for section 65 offences. The Guideline applies to all offenders aged 18 and over, sentenced on or after 1 April 2014.

Upon Conviction/Sentence

6.63 (i) Notification applies where D is either under 18 and has been sentenced to 12 months or more, or D is over 18 and has been sentenced either to a term of imprisonment or to be detained in a hospital.[108]
(ii) Automatic inclusion in the children's and adults' barred lists not applicable.[109]
(iii) SHPO applies.[110]
(iv) Qualifying 'specified sexual offence' in Schedule 18 (Extended Sentences).[111]

---

[104] Implementation date 27.8.1981.
[105] *Reed & Others* [2021] EWCA Crim 572.
[106] SOA 2003, s 65(5).
[107] SOA 2003, s 65(5). 12 months if CJA 2003, s 282(4) implemented. Section 282(4) is not retrospective.
[108] SOA 2003, s 80(1) and Sch 3, para 32; see Chapter 14, paras 14.01–14.05.
[109] Part 2 of the Safeguarding Vulnerable Groups Act 2006 (Prescribed Criteria and Miscellaneous Provisions) Regulations 2009 (SI 2009 No 37); see Chapter 12, para 12.217.
[110] SA 2020, s 345 and Sch 3, para 32; see Chapter 16, para 16.07.
[111] SA 2020, s 306, Sch 18, para 38(aw); see Chapter 12, para 12.51.

3. Sexual Activity with a Child Family Member

Sexual Offences Act 2003, s 25

Definition

As per Proof. **6.64**

Proof

(i) D intentionally and sexually touches C; **6.65**
(ii) the relationship of D to C is within s 27 and;
(iii) D knows or could reasonably be expected to know that and C is either under 18 (and D does not reasonably believe that C is 18 or over) or C is under 13.
(iv) Penetration; also indict under s 25(6) where any of the following are alleged:
- penetration of C's anus or vagina with a part of D's body or anything else;
- penetration of C's mouth with D's penis;
- penetration of D's anus or vagina with a part of C's body; or
- penetration of D's mouth with C's penis.

(v) Note the following:
   (a) Where in proceedings for an offence under this section it is proved that C was under 18, D is to be taken not to have reasonably believed C was 18 or over unless sufficient evidence is adduced to raise an issue as to whether he reasonably believed it.[112]
   (b) Where in proceedings for an offence under this section it is proved that the relation of D to C was of a description falling within s 27 (see para 6.66), it is to be taken that D knew or could reasonably have been expected to know that his relation to C was of that description unless sufficient evidence is adduced to raise an issue as to whether he knew or could reasonably have been expected to know that it was.[113]
   (c) 'Penetration' is a continuing act from entry to withdrawal.[114]
   (d) 'Vagina' includes vulva.[115]
   (e) References to a part of the body include references to a part surgically constructed (in particular, through gender reassignment surgery).[116]
   (f) Touching includes touching—
      (i) with any part of the body,

---

[112] SOA 2003, s 25(2(a)).
[113] SOA 2003, s 25(3).
[114] SOA 2003, s 79(2).
[115] SOA 2003, s 79(9).
[116] SOA 2003, s 79(3).

6. FAMILIAL OFFENCES

   (ii) with anything else,
   (iii) through anything
         and in particular includes touching amounting to penetration.[117]

6.66 Who is a family member is much wider under this section and is separately defined by s 27 for the purposes of this section of the Act. The relation of D to C is within this section if one of the following applies:

   (i) D or C is parent, grandparent, brother, sister, half-brother, half-sister, aunt or uncle to the other.[118]
   (ii) D is or has been C's foster parent.[119]
   (iii) If D and C live or have lived in the same household, or D has been regularly involved in caring for, training, supervising or being in sole charge of C; and[120]
   - one of them is or has been the other's step-parent;
   - D and C are cousins;
   - one of them is or has been the other's stepbrother or stepsister; or
   - the parent or present or former foster parent of one of them is or has been the other's foster parent.
   (iv) If D and C live in the same household and D is regularly caring for, training, supervising or being in sole charge of D.[121]

Notes

6.67
   (i) Triable only on indictment if defendant is over 18 and penetration is alleged; triable either way if non-penetrative.[122]
   (ii) Although it would be possible to prosecute under s 25(6) where C is under 13, it is perhaps more likely that the proper charge for this offence would be one of rape of a child under 13 (s 5 carries maximum of LIFE; see para 4.94). Consideration should perhaps be given to putting a s 5 charge/count as the primary one, with the familial offence as an alternative to it. See introductory remarks and notes at para 6.06.
   (iii) It is not an offence where D is lawfully married to C, or they are civil partners,[123] at the time of the sexual conduct and C is over 16 at the time.[124]
   (iv) A defence is afforded where the relationship is not one of blood relatives and a sexual relationship already existed immediately prior to the existence of the relationship bringing the couple within s 27.[125]
   (v) Adoptive relations are excluded from the definition of family members under s 27. Arguably, however, adoptive parents could fit the description as primary carers living with the child.

---

[117] SOA 2003, s 79(8).
[118] SOA 2003, s 27(2)(a).
[119] SOA 2003, s 27(2)(b). Foster parent is itself defined under s 5(c)(i)(a) and(ii).
[120] SOA 2003, s 27(3)(a)–(d) inclusive.
[121] SOA 2003, s 27(4)(a) and (b).
[122] SOA 2003, s 25(4)–(6).
[123] Civil Partnership Act 2004, s 261(1), Sch 27, para 174.
[124] SOA 2003, s 28(1)(a) and (b).
[125] SOA 2003, s 29.

E. OFFENCES COMMITTED FROM 1.5.2004 TO DATE 179

(vi) Those who have been adopted away from the family are included if they fall into one of the categories in s 27, just as under the old law[126] where a blood relative could not escape prosecution because either party had been adopted away from the family.
(vii) The fact that D is/is not over 18 should be averred; it affects the maximum sentences which can be passed.
(viii) In dealing with a SHPO in respect of a sibling who is not the victim, it may be wise to involve the family court.[127]
(ix) A person is not guilty of aiding, abetting or counselling the commission against a child of an offence under section 25 if he acts for the purpose of:
  (a) protecting the child from sexually transmitted infection,
  (b) protecting the physical safety of the child,
  (c) preventing the child from becoming pregnant, or
  (d) promoting the child's emotional well-being by the giving of advice,
  and not for the purpose of obtaining sexual gratification or for the purpose of causing or encouraging the activity constituting the offence or the child's participation in it.[128]
(x) The extended jurisdiction provisions apply to this section.[129] See Chapter 17 para 17.01.
(xi) The s 45 MSA 2015 defence for slavery and trafficking victims who commit an offence does not apply to this offence.[130]

Indictment

PENETRATIVE SEXUAL ACTIVITY WITH A CHILD FAMILY MEMBER, contrary to s 25(1) and (6) of the Sexual Offences Act 2003 1.5.2004 to date **6.68**

Statement of Offence
SEXUAL ACTIVITY WITH A CHILD FAMILY MEMBER, contrary to section 25(1) and (6) of the Sexual Offences Act 2003.

Particulars of Offence
Examples of this might be:
  D, on the ... day of ... 20 ... , being a person of [*or* over] the age of 18 years, intentionally and sexually touched his foster daughter by penetrating her mouth with his penis, when D either knew or could reasonably have been expected to have known that C was his foster daughter, and [where D did not reasonably believe that C was aged 18 or over at the time] *or* [where C was under 13 at the time].
  Or:
  D, on the ... day of ... 20 ... , being a person of [*or* over] the age of 18 years, intentionally and sexually touched her cousin by digitally penetrating her vagina when D either knew or could reasonably have been expected to have known that C was her cousin, and [where D did not reasonably believe that C was aged 18 or over at the time] *or* [where C was under 13 at the time].

---

[126] SOA 2003, s 27(1)(b).
[127] R v D [2005] EWCA Crim 2951, [2006] CLR 364.
[128] SOA 2003, s73(1) and (2)(d).
[129] SOA 2003, s 72; provides for the prosecution within the jurisdiction of a sexual offence committed outside it.
[130] Modern Slavery Act 2015, s 45 and Sch 4, para 33.

6.69 NON-PENETRATIVE SEXUAL ACTIVITY WITH A CHILD FAMILY MEMBER, contrary to s 25(1) of the Sexual Offences Act 2003 1.5.2004 to date

---

Statement of Offence
SEXUAL ACTIVITY WITH A CHILD FAMILY MEMBER, contrary to section 25(1) of the Sexual Offences Act 2003.

Particulars of Offence
Examples of this might be:

D, on the … day of … 20 … , a person of *or* [over] the age of 18 years, intentionally and sexually touched his daughter by kissing and stroking her breasts, when D either knew or could reasonably have been expected to have known that C was his daughter and where C was under 13 at the time.

Or

D, on the … day of … 20 … , a person of *or* [over] the age of 18 years, intentionally and sexually touched her brother by performing oral sex upon him, when D either knew or could reasonably have been expected to have known that C was her brother and where D did not reasonably believe that C was aged 18 or over at the time.

Alternative Offences

6.70 Attempt to commit the full offence. When indicting offences of attempt do so under s1(1) Criminal Attempts Act 1981.[131] Aver the attempt in both the Statement of Offence and Particulars of Offence. In addition, aver the substantive offence under the relevant Act; see paras 1.51 and 12.157 and *Reed & Others* [2021].[132]

Sentence

6.71 (i) On indictment:
- When D is over 18: **14 YEARS**.[133]
- In all other cases: **5 YEARS**.[134]

(ii) Summarily: **6 months**.[135]

Sentencing Guidance

6.72 See para 12.133; The Sentencing Council 'Sexual Offences: Definitive Guideline' contains offence-specific guidelines for section 25 offences. The Guideline applies to all offenders aged 18 and over, sentenced on or after 1 April 2014.

---

[131] Implementation date 27.8.1981.
[132] *Reed & Others* [2021] EWCA Crim 572.
[133] SOA 2003, s 25(4)(a) and 25(4)(b)(ii).
[134] SOA 2003, s 25(5)(b).
[135] SOA 2003, ss 25 (4)(b)(i) and (5)(a); 12 months if CJA 2003, s 282(4) implemented.

E. OFFENCES COMMITTED FROM 1.5.2004 TO DATE   181

Upon Conviction/Sentence

(i) Notification applies if D was over 18 at the time or is/has been sentenced to 12 months or more.[136]   **6.73**
(ii) Automatic inclusion in the children's and adults' barred lists with the right to make representations.[137]
(iii) SHPO applies.[138] In dealing with SHPO in respect of a sibling who is not the victim, it may be wise to involve the family court.[139]
(iv) Qualifying 'specified sexual offence' in Schedule 18 (Extended Sentences).[140]
(v) Qualifying Schedule 14 offence where the offender was 18 or over at the time of the offence (Extended Sentences: The Earlier Offence Condition).[141]
(vi) Qualifying 'index' offence (if committed after 3 December 2012) for the purpose of Schedule 15 (Life Sentence for Second Listed Offence) where the offender was 18 or over at the time of the offence.[142]

4. Inciting a Child Family Member to Engage in Sexual Activity

Sexual Offences Act 2003, s 26

Definition

As per Proof.   **6.74**

Proof

(i) C intentionally incites D to sexually touch him (C) or allows himself (D) to be sexually touched by C;   **6.75**
(ii) the relationship of D to C is within s 27 and;
(iii) D knows or could reasonably be expected to know that and C is either under 18 (and D does not reasonably believe that C is 18 or over) or C is under 13.
(iv) Penetration; also indict under s 26(6) where any of the following are alleged:
  - penetration of D's anus or vagina[143] with a part of C's body or anything else;
  - penetration of C's mouth with D's penis;
  - penetration of D's anus or vagina[144] with a part of C's body; or
  - penetration of D's mouth with C's penis.
(v) Note the following:
  (a) Where in proceedings for an offence under this section it is proved that C was under 18, D is to be taken not to have reasonably believed C was 18 or over unless

---

[136] SOA 2003, s 80(1) and Sch3, para 26; see Chapter 14 paras 14.01–14.05.
[137] Part 2 of the Safeguarding Vulnerable Groups Act 2006 (Prescribed Criteria and Miscellaneous Provisions) Regulations 2009 (SI 2009 No 37) paras 2 and 4; see Chapter 12 para 12.217.
[138] SA 2020, s 345 and SOA 2003, Sch 3, para 26; see Chapter 16 para 16.07.
[139] *R v D* [2005] EWCA Crim 2951, [2006] CLR 364.
[140] SA 2020, s 306, Sch 18, para 38(u); see Chapter 12 para 12.51.
[141] SA 2020, ss 267 and 280, Sch 14, para 9(n); see Chapter 12 para 12.77.
[142] SA 2020, ss 273 and 283, Sch 15, para 9(n); see Chapter 12 para 12.123.
[143] 'Vagina' includes vulva, SOA 2003, s 79.
[144] 'Vagina' includes vulva, SOA 2003, s 79.

sufficient evidence is adduced to raise an issue as to whether he reasonably believed it.[145]

(b) Where in proceedings for an offence under this section it is proved that the relation of D to C was of a description falling within s 27 (set out under s 25 at para 6.64 *et seq*), it is to be taken that D knew or could reasonably have been expected to know that his relation to C was of that description unless sufficient evidence is adduced to raise an issue as to whether he knew or could reasonably have been expected to know that it was.[146]

(c) 'Penetration' is a continuing act from entry to withdrawal.[147]

(d) 'Vagina' includes vulva.[148]

(e) References to a part of the body include references to a part surgically constructed (in particular, through gender reassignment surgery).[149]

(f) Touching includes touching—
   (i) with any part of the body,
   (ii) with anything else,
   (iii) through anything
   and in particular includes touching amounting to penetration.[150]

Notes

6.76

(i) Triable only on indictment if D is 18 or over and penetration is alleged; triable either way if penetration is not alleged and if D is under 18 irrespective of whether penetration is alleged or not.

(ii) Although it would be possible to prosecute under s 26(6) where C is under 13 and the activity is penetrative, it is perhaps more likely that the proper charge for this offence would be one of sexual activity with a child under 13 (s 8 carries maximum of **life**; see para 4.43). Consideration should at least be given to putting a s 8 charge/count as the primary one, with the familial offence as an alternative to it.

(iii) There is an exception for a defendant who is lawfully married to or the civil partner[151] of D at the time of the sexual conduct and D is over 16 at the time.[152]

(iv) Those who have been adopted away from the family are included if they fall into one of the categories in s 27, just as under the old law[153] where a blood relative could not escape prosecution because either party had been adopted away from the family.

(v) Adoptive parents are to be viewed as on a par with biological parents.[154]

(vi) The fact that D is/is not over 18 should be averred; it affects the maximum sentences which can be passed.

---

[145] SOA 2003, s 26(2).
[146] SOA 2003, s 26(3).
[147] SOA 2003, s 79(2).
[148] SOA 2003, s 79(9).
[149] SOA 2003, s 79(3).
[150] SOA 2003, s 79(8).
[151] Civil Partnership Act 2004, s 261(1) and Schedule 27(174) implemented on 5.12.2005.
[152] SOA 2003, s 28(1)(a) and (b).
[153] SOA 2003, s 27(1)(b).
[154] *Setting the Boundaries*, para 5.6.1.

(vii) The extended jurisdiction provisions apply to this section.[155] See Chapter 17 para 17.01.
(viii) The s 45 MSA 2015 defence for slavery and trafficking victims who commit an offence does not apply to this offence.[156]

Indictment

6.77 INCITING A CHILD FAMILY MEMBER TO ENGAGE IN PENETRATIVE SEXUAL ACTIVITY contrary to s 26(1) and (6) of the Sexual Offences Act 2003 1.5.2004 to date

---

Statement of Offence

INCITING A CHILD FAMILY MEMBER TO ENGAGE IN PENETRATIVE SEXUAL ACTIVITY, contrary to section 26(1) and (6) of the Sexual Offences Act 2003.

Particulars of Offence

D, on the ... day of ... 20 ..., being a person of ... years, intentionally incited C to sexually touch D/allow himself to be touched by D by encouraging or permitting her to perform oral sex upon him, where D either knew or could reasonably have been expected to have known that C was his daughter/granddaughter (anyone within s 27), and [where D did not reasonably believe that C was aged 18 or over at the time] *or* [where C was under 13 at the time].

6.78 INCITING A CHILD FAMILY MEMBER TO ENGAGE IN NON-PENETRATIVE SEXUAL ACTIVITY contrary to s 26(1) of the Sexual Offences Act 2003 1.5.2004 to date

---

Statement of Offence

INCITING A CHILD FAMILY MEMBER TO ENGAGE IN SEXUAL ACTIVITY, contrary to section 26(1) of the Sexual Offences Act 2003.

Particulars of Offence

D, on the ... day of ... 20 ..., being a person of ... years, intentionally incited C to sexually touch D by encouraging her to masturbate him, where D either knew or could reasonably have been expected to have known that C was his daughter/granddaughter (anyone within s 27), and [where D did not reasonably believe that C was aged 18 or over at the time] *or* [where C was under 13 at the time].

---

[155] SOA 2003, s 72; provides for the prosecution within the jurisdiction of a sexual offence committed outside it. See Chapter 17.
[156] Modern Slavery Act 2015, s 45 and Sch 4, para 33.

Alternative Offences

6.79 Attempt to commit the full offence. When indicting offences of attempt do so under s1(1) Criminal Attempts Act 1981.[157] Aver the attempt in both the Statement of Offence and Particulars of Offence. In addition, aver the substantive offence under the relevant Act; see paras 1.51 and 12.157 and *Reed & Others* [2021].[158]

Sentence

6.80 (i) On indictment where D is 18 or over: **14 YEARS**,[159] summarily **6 months**.[160]
(ii) On indictment where D is under 18: **5 YEARS**, summarily **6 months**.[161]

Upon Conviction/Sentence

6.81 (i) Notification applies if D was over 18 at the time or is/has been sentenced to 12 months or more.[162]
(ii) Automatic inclusion in the children's and adults' barred lists with the right to make representations.[163]
(iii) SHPO applies.[164] In dealing with SHPO in respect of a sibling who is not the victim, it may be wise to involve the family court.[165]
(iv) Qualifying 'specified sexual offence' in Schedule 18 (Extended Sentences).[166]
(v) Qualifying Schedule 14 offence where the offender was 18 or over at the time of the offence (Extended Sentences: The Earlier Offence Condition).[167]
(vi) Qualifying 'index' offence (if committed after 3 December 2012) for the purpose of Schedule 15 (Life Sentence for Second Listed Offence) where the offender was 18 or over at the time of the offence.[168]

---

[157] Implementation date 27.8.1981.
[158] *Reed & Others* [2021] EWCA Crim 572.
[159] SOA 2003, s 26(4)(a) and 26(4)(b)(ii).
[160] SOA 2003, s 26(5).
[161] The fact of penetration does not alter the maximum sentence.
[162] SOA 2003, s 80(1) and Sch 3, para 26; see Chapter 14 paras 14.01–14.05.
[163] Part 2 of the Safeguarding Vulnerable Groups Act 2006 (Prescribed Criteria and Miscellaneous Provisions) Regulations 2009 (SI 2009 No 37) paras 2 and 4; see Chapter 12 para 12.217.
[164] SA 2020, s 345 and SOA 2003, Sch 3, para 26; see Chapter 16 para 16.07.
[165] *R v D* [2005] EWCA Crim 2951, [2006] CLR 364.
[166] SA 2020, s 306, Sch 18, para 38(v); see Chapter 12 para 12.51.
[167] SA 2020, ss 267 and 280, Sch 14, para 9(o); see Chapter 12 para 12.77.
[168] SA 2020, ss 273 and 283, Sch 15, para 9(o); see Chapter 12 para 12.123.

7

OFFENCES INVOLVING THE MENTALLY DISORDERED

A. Introduction		
Sexual Assaults Upon the Mentally Disordered	7.04	
B. Offences committed pre-31.12.1956	7.04	
1. Carnal Knowledge of a Mentally Disordered Female	7.04	
C. Offences Committed Between 1.1.1957 and 30.4.2004		
1. Intercourse with an Idiot/Imbecile Woman	7.11	
D. Offences Committed from 1.5.2004 to date	7.22	
1. Sexual Activity with a Person with Mental Disorder Impeding Choice	7.23	
2. Causing or Inciting a Person with a Mental Disorder Impeding Choice to Engage in Sexual Activity	7.31	
3. Engaging in Sexual Activity in the Presence of a Person with a Mental Disorder Impeding Choice	7.39	
4. Causing a Person with a Mental Disorder Impeding Choice to Watch a Sexual Act	7.47	
Abuse of the Mentally Disordered, as Patients or by Those Certain Responsibility for Them	7.55	
E. Offences Committed between 1.11.1913 and 31.12.1956	7.55	
1. Carnal Knowledge of Female under Care/Treatment	7.55	
F. Offences Committed between 1.1.1957 and 31.10.1960	7.61	
1. Intercourse with Defectives Receiving Treatment	7.61	
G. Offences Committed between 1.11.1960 and 30.4.2004	7.69	
1. Intercourse with a Mentally Disordered Patient	7.69	
H. Offences Committed from 1.5.2004 to date	7.76	
1. Sexual Activity with a Person who has a Mental Disorder by a Care Worker	7.77	
2. Care Workers: Causing or Inciting Sexual Activity with a Person with a Mental Disorder	7.85	
3. Care Workers: Sexual Activity in the Presence of a Person with a Mental Disorder	7.93	
4. Care Workers: Causing a Person with a Mental Disorder to Watch a Sexual Act	7.101	
Offences Designed to Protect the Mentally Disordered from Procuration	7.109	
I. Offences Committed pre-31.12.1956	7.109	
1. Procuring a Female to have Carnal Connection	7.109	
2. Procurement of a Defective 1.1.1957 to 30.4.2004	7.117	
J. Offences Committed from 1.5.2004 to date	7.121	
1. Procuring by Inducement, Threat, or Deception Sexual Activity with a Mentally Disordered Person	7.122	
2. Causing a Person with a Mental Disorder to Engage in Sexual Activity by Inducement, Threat, or Deception	7.130	
3. Engaging in Sexual Activity in the Presence, Procured by Inducement, Threat, or Deception, of a Person with a Mental Disorder	7.138	
4. Causing a Person with a Mental Disorder to Watch a Sexual Act by Inducement, Threat, or Deception	7.145	
Offences Protecting the Mentally Disordered from Prostitution or Abuse upon Premises		
K. Offences committed pre-1.1.1957	7.152	
1. Causing or Encouraging Prostitution of a Defective	7.153	
2. Permitting Premises to be Used for Sexual Intercourse with a Female Defective	7.157	
L. Offences Committed between 1.1.1957 to 30.4.2004	7.161	
1. Causing or Encouraging the Prostitution of any Woman or Girl who is a Defective	7.164	
2. Permitting a Defective to Use Premises for Intercourse	7.170	
M. Offences Committed from 1.5.2004 to date	7.176	
1. Causing or Inciting Prostitution for Gain	7.177	
2. Controlling Prostitution for Gain	7.185	

7. OFFENCES INVOLVING THE MENTALLY DISORDERED

A. INTRODUCTION

7.01 This chapter deals principally with offences upon women. Mentally disordered males have in the past been provided with some protection (see paras 5.86 and 7.65[1]), but not extensively so, until the SOA 2003 was passed.

7.02 The SOA 2003 consolidated the law and provided offences against both mentally disordered males and females.

7.03 Before the passing of the SOA 1956 (commencement date 1.1.1957) there were several statutes dealing with offences against the mentally disordered. In each there was a separate definition of individuals, currently described as mentally disordered. In the main, terms used are offensive to the modern reader. They nevertheless have been included in order to cover the rare occasions that such a case (pre-dating 1957) would be prosecuted. However, judicial discretion may allow for an indictment to contain the term 'mental disorder' instead of 'idiot/imbecile/defective'.

Sexual Assaults Upon the Mentally Disordered

B. OFFENCES COMMITTED PRE-31.12.1956

1. Carnal Knowledge of a Mentally Disordered Female

Criminal Law Amendment Act 1885, s 5(2)

Definition

7.04 Any person who 'unlawfully and carnally knows, (that is, has vaginal intercourse with) or attempts to have unlawful carnal knowledge of any female idiot or imbecile woman or girl' in any circumstances not amounting to rape.

Proof

7.05 (i) Carnal knowledge, that is penetration of vagina by the penis, proof of ejaculation not necessary;[2]
(ii) that the woman was an 'idiot or imbecile' as defined;
(iii) that the defendant knew the woman was an 'idiot or imbecile'.[3]

---

[1] Indecent Assaults upon Males. SOA 1956, s 15(3) and Mental Health Act (MHA) 1959, s 128.
[2] *R v Marsden* [1891] 2 QB 149, and later OAPA 1861, s 63.
[3] CLAA 1885, s 5(2).

Notes

7.06

(i) The offence is triable only on indictment.
(ii) An 'imbecile' was defined (by common law) as a woman incapable of appreciating the nature and quality of the act in question, or incapable of exercising an act of her own will in giving or withholding her consent; this incapacity must arise from want of understanding.[4]
(iii) An 'idiot' was defined as a person who has 'no mind' (whether or not from birth).[5]
(iv) Proof of consent is not required.

Indictment

CARNAL KNOWLEDGE OF AN 'IDIOT/IMBECILE' Pre-31.12.1956

7.07

Statement of Offence

CARNAL KNOWLEDGE OF AN IMBECILE WOMAN, contrary to section 5(2) of the Criminal Law Amendment Act 1885.

Particulars of Offence

D on a day between ... had unlawful carnal knowledge of C, an imbecile woman, in circumstances not amounting to rape, knowing that the said C is an imbecile/idiot woman/girl.

Alternative Offences

Attempt to commit the full offence. When indicting offences of attempt do so under common law. Aver the attempt in both the Statement of Offence and Particulars of Offence. In addition, aver the substantive offence under the relevant Act; see paras 1.51 and 12.157 and *Reed & Others* [2021].[6]

7.08

Sentence

On indictment: **2 YEARS**.

7.09

As of 1.1.1957, SOA 1956, s 7 covers this offence.[7]

7.10

---

[4] *R v Turner* [1886] CCC Sess Papers.
[5] *R v F* 74 JP 384.
[6] *Reed & Others* [2021] EWCA Crim 572.
[7] The CLAA 1885 was repealed.

188 7. OFFENCES INVOLVING THE MENTALLY DISORDERED

C. OFFENCES COMMITTED BETWEEN 1.1.1957 AND 30.4.2004

1. Intercourse with an Idiot/Imbecile Woman

Sexual Offences Act 1956, s 7

Definition

7.11   ... unlawful sexual intercourse with a woman whom he knows to be an idiot or imbecile.

Proof

7.12   (i) Sexual intercourse—proof of penetration will suffice.[8]
(ii) For the common law definition of 'imbecile' and 'idiot' see para 7.06.
(iii) That the defendant knew the female to be an 'idiot/imbecile'.

Notes

7.13   (i) The offence is triable only on indictment.[9]
(ii) Consent to prosecute must be obtained from the DPP.[10]
(iii) If the maximum sentence of 2 years' imprisonment would not accurately reflect the gravity of the offence, and the complainant is not mentally capable of consenting, then a charge of rape would be appropriate (see para 2.04).
(iv) Severe impairment is to be measured as against the standard of ordinary persons, without any impairment.[11]
(v) Expert evidence as to impairment, whilst admissible, is not essential.[12]
(vi) The defendant is afforded a statutory defence, if he can prove that he did not believe, and had no reason to believe, that the complainant was a 'defective'.[13]
(vii) SOA 1956, s 7 provides a statutory alternative to:
  (a) rape;[14]
  (b) intercourse with a girl under 13;[15]
  (c) incest.[16]

---

[8] SOA 1956, s 44.
[9] SOA 1956, s 37 and Sch 2, para 11(a).
[10] MHA 1959, s 128(4).
[11] *Hall* (1987) 86 Cr App R 159.
[12] *Hall* (1987) 86 Cr App R 162.
[13] SOA 1956, s 7(2) and SOA 1956, s 47.
[14] SOA 1956, s 37 and Sch 2, para 1.
[15] SOA 1956, s 37 and Sch 2, para 2.
[16] SOA 1957, s 37 and Sch 2, para 14.

C. OFFENCES COMMITTED BETWEEN 1.1.1957 AND 30.4.2004

Indictment

INTERCOURSE WITH AN 'IDIOT/IMBECILE' 1.1.1957 to 31.10.1960   **7.14**

Statement of Offence

INTERCOURSE WITH AN IDIOT/IMBECILE, contrary to section 7 of the Sexual Offences Act 1956.

Particulars of Offence

D on the … day of … 19… , had unlawful sexual intercourse with a woman whom he knew to be an idiot/imbecile.

Alternative Offences

Attempt to commit the full offence. When indicting offences of attempt do so under common law until 26.8.1981, thereafter indict under s 1(1) Criminal Attempts Act 1981.[17] Aver the attempt in both the Statement of Offence and Particulars of Offence. In addition, aver the substantive offence under the relevant Act; see paras 1.51 and 12.157 and *Reed & Others* [2021].[18]   **7.15**

Sentence

(i) On indictment: **2 YEARS**.[19]
(ii) An attempt attracts the same sentence.   **7.16**

Upon Conviction/Sentence

(i) Notification not applicable.[20]
(ii) Automatic inclusion in the children's and adults' barred lists with the right to make representations.[21]
(iii) SHPO not applicable.[22]
(iv) Specified sexual offence in Schedule 18 (Extended Sentence).[23]   **7.17**

1.11.1960 to 30.4.2004

---

[17] Implementation date 27.8.1981.
[18] *Reed & Others* [2021] EWCA Crim 572
[19] SOA 1956, s 37 and Sch 2, para 11(b).
[20] SOA 2003 (not in Sch 3), s 80(1); see Chapter 14 para Tables 14.2–14.5.
[21] Part 2 of the Safeguarding Vulnerable Groups Act 2006 (Prescribed Criteria and Miscellaneous Provisions) Regulations 2009 (SI 2009 No 37) paras 2 and 4; see Chapter 12 para 12.217.
[22] SA 2020, s 345 (not in Sch 3 or Sch 5 SOA 2003); see Chapter 16 para 16.07.
[23] SA 2020, s 306, Sch 18, para 29(g); see Chapter 12 para 12.51.

Definition

7.18 See para 7.11.

Proof

7.19 See para 7.12.

Notes

7.20 (i) The term 'idiot/imbecile' was abandoned in 1960,[24] the term 'defective' was substituted. This was defined as 'a person suffering from severe subnormality within the meaning of the Mental Health Act 1959'.[25]

(ii) This was soon after amended to 'a person suffering from a state of arrested or incomplete development of mind which includes severe impairment of intelligence and social functioning', by the Mental Health (Amendment) Act 1982.[26]

Indictment

7.21 As at para 7.14, except substitute 'defective' for 'idiot/imbecile'.

D. OFFENCES COMMITTED FROM 1.5.2004 TO DATE

7.22 The SOA 2003 repealed the SOA 1956, s 7 in full. SOA 2003, s 30—sexual activity with a person with a mental disorder impeding choice covers this offence. Additional offences have been created, including: inciting a person with a mental disorder impeding choice to engage in sexual activity,[27] engaging in sexual activity in the presence of such persons[28] or causing them to watch.[29]

1. Sexual Activity with a Person with Mental Disorder Impeding Choice

Sexual Offences Act 2003, s 30

---

[24] MHA 1959, s 127. Commencement date 1.11.1960 (SI 1960/1698).
[25] MHA 1959, s 127(1)(b) (SOA 1956, s 45 substituted).
[26] MH(A)A 1982 Sch 3.
[27] SOA 2003, s 31.
[28] SOA 2003, s 32.
[29] SOA 2003, s 33.

Definition

(1) A person (A) commits an offence if—   **7.23**
   (a) he intentionally touches another person (B),
   (b) the touching is sexual,
   (c) B is unable to refuse because of, or for a reason related to, a mental disorder, and
   (d) A knows or could reasonably be expected to know that B has a mental disorder and that because of it, or for a reason related to it, B is likely to be unable to refuse.

Proof

(i) See indictment particulars for elements of the offence.   **7.24**
(ii) Of particular note: for offences under ss 30–33 inclusive the prosecution must prove that C is unable to refuse because of, or for a reason related to, a mental disorder, and is unable to choose because he/she lacks the capacity to choose, whether because he/she lacks sufficient understanding of the nature or reasonably foreseeable consequences of what is being done, or for any other reason[30] or he/she is unable to communicate his/her choice to D.[31]
(iii) 'Mental disorder' has the meaning given by section 1 Mental Health Act 1983.[32]
(iv) The case of *Cooper*[33] makes three key points:
   (a) the inability to communicate choice must be linked to a mental and not physical disability;
   (b) the capacity to choose is person and situation specific;
   (c) a complainant may be robbed of the capacity to choose even though s/he can understand the information relevant to making the choice;
(iv) where the complainant's inability to communicate choice not to consent to the sexual act is due to a physical disability, the ordinary offences in ss 1–4 apply; where the inability to communicate choice is due to a mental disorder, the special offences in ss 30–33 apply[34] (per Lord Roger).
(v) 'Touching' includes touching:
   (a) with any part of the body,
   (b) with anything else,
   (c) through anything,
   and in particular includes touching amounting to penetration.[35]

---

[30] These encompass a wide range of circumstances, including irrational fears, delusions and phobias (para 25) linked to a 'disorder, such as those which drive a person to refuse a life-saving injection or to refuse food in anorexia'. *Cooper* [2009] UKHL 42.
[31] SOA 2003, ss 30(2), 31(2), 32(2), 33(2).
[32] SOA 2003, s 79(6).
[33] *Cooper* [2009] UKHL 42.
[34] *Cooper* [2009] UKHL 42, para 7.
[35] SOA 2003, s 79(8).

7. OFFENCES INVOLVING THE MENTALLY DISORDERED

(vi) 'Sexual': Penetration, touching or any other activity is sexual if a reasonable person would consider that (a) whatever its circumstances or any person's purpose in relation to it, it is because of its nature sexual, or (b) because of its nature it may be sexual and because of its circumstances or the purpose of any person in relation to it (or both) it is sexual.[36]

Notes

7.25 (i) If penetration is involved the offence is indictable only, except penetration of A's anus or vagina with an object.[37]

(ii) If penetration is not involved then the offence is triable either way.[38]

(iii) Penetration is a continuing act from entry to withdrawal.[39]

(iv) References to a part of the body include references to a part surgically constructed (in particular, through gender reassignment surgery.[40] 'Vagina' includes vulva.[41]

(v) If the offence alleged falls within subsection (3), this ought to be averred in the indictment.

(vi) A woman suffering from cerebral palsy with a mental age well below that of her contemporaries, although able to speak, was held to be unable to communicate her choice as to sexual touching, as compared to the ability to do so of a woman the same age, not suffering from her disabilities.[42]

(vii) Section 73 provides a defence to an offence of aiding abetting or counselling the commission of an offence under this section against a person under 16, where he acts for the purpose of;

(a) protecting the child from sexually transmitted infection,
(b) protecting the physical safety of the child,
(c) preventing the child from becoming pregnant, or
(d) promoting the child's emotional well-being by the giving of advice,
and not for the purpose of obtaining sexual gratification or for the purpose of causing or encouraging the activity constituting the offence or the child's participation in it.

The extended jurisdiction provisions apply to this section where the victim of the offence was under 18.[43] See Chapter 17 para 17.01.

The s 45 MSA 2015 defence for slavery and trafficking victims who commit an offence does not apply to this offence.[44]

---

[36] SOA 2003, s 78.
[37] SOA 2003, s 30(3)(c).
[38] SOA 2003, s 30(4).
[39] SOA 2003, s 79(1).
[40] SOA 2003, s 79(2).
[41] SOA 2003, s 79(9).
[42] *Hulme v DPP* [2006] EWHC 1347 (Admin).
[43] SOA 2003, s 72; provides for the prosecution within the jurisdiction of a sexual offence committed outside it.
[44] Modern Slavery Act 2015, s 45 and Sch 4, para 33.

D. OFFENCES COMMITTED FROM 1.5.2004 TO DATE

Indictment

SEXUAL ACTIVITY WITH MENTALLY DISORDERED PERSON IMPEDING CHOICE 1.5.2004 to date **7.26**

Statement of Offence
SEXUAL ACTIVITY WITH A PERSON WITH A MENTAL DISORDER IMPEDING CHOICE, contrary to section 30(1) of the Sexual Offences Act 2003.

Particulars of Offence
D on the … day of … of 20… , intentionally touched C, by penetrating her mouth with his penis in sexual circumstances where C was unable to refuse because of or for a reason related to a mental disorder, and D knew or could reasonably be expected to know that C had a mental disorder and that because of it or for a reason related to it C was likely to be unable to refuse.

Alternative Offences

Attempt to commit the full offence. When indicting offences of attempt do so under s 1(1) Criminal Attempts Act 1981.[45] Aver the attempt in both the Statement of Offence and Particulars of Offence. In addition, aver the substantive offence under the relevant Act; see paras 1.51 and 12.157 and *Reed & Others* [2021].[46] **7.27**

Sentence

(i) On indictment: **7.28**
- If penetration is involved: **LIFE**.[47]
- If no penetration is involved: **14 YEARS**.[48]

(ii) Summarily: **6 months**.[49]

The Sentencing Council 'Sexual Offences: Definitive Guideline' contains offence-specific guidelines for s 30 offences. The Guideline applies to all offenders aged 18 and over, sentenced on or after 1 April 2014. **7.29**

---

[45] Implementation date 27.8.1981.
[46] *Reed & Others* [2021] EWCA Crim 572.
[47] SOA 2003, s 30(3).
[48] SOA 2003, s 30(4)(b).
[49] SOA 2003, s 30(4)(a), 12 months if CJA 2003, s 282(2) implemented.

Upon Conviction/Sentence

7.30

Notification applies.[50]

Automatic inclusion in the children's barred list with no right to make representations where the offence committed against a child; with representations where the offence committed against an adult. Automatic inclusion in the adults' barred list with no right to make representations.[51]

SHPO applies.[52]

Qualifying 'specified sexual offence' in Schedule 18 (Extended Sentences).[53]

Qualifying Schedule 19 offence (Life Sentences) where offender liable on conviction on indictment to life imprisonment.[54]

Qualifying Schedule 14 offence (Extended Sentences: The Earlier Offence Condition) where offender liable on conviction on indictment to life imprisonment.[55]

Qualifying 'index' offence (if committed after 3 December 2012) for the purpose of Schedule 15 (Life Sentence for Second Listed Offence) where liable on conviction on indictment to imprisonment for life.[56]

2. Causing or Inciting a Person with a Mental Disorder Impeding Choice to Engage in Sexual Activity

Sexual Offences Act 2003, s 31

Definition

7.31

(1) A person (A) commits an offence if—
   (a) he intentionally causes or incites another person (B) to engage in activity,
   (b) the activity is sexual,
   (c) B is unable to refuse because of or for a reason related to a mental disorder, and
   (d) A knows or could reasonably be expected to know that B has a mental disorder and that because of it or for a reason related to it B is likely to be unable to refuse.

---

[50] SOA 2003, s 80(1) and Sch 3, para 27; see Chapter 14 paras 14.01–14.05.
[51] Part 2 of the Safeguarding Vulnerable Groups Act 2006 (Prescribed Criteria and Miscellaneous Provisions) Regulations 2009 (SI 2009 No 37) paras 1, 2, and 3; see Chapter 12 para 12.217.
[52] SA 2020, s 345 and Sch 3, para 27 SOA 2003; see Chapter 16 para 16.07.
[53] SA 2020, s 306, Sch 18, para 38(w); see Chapter 12 para 12.51.
[54] SA 2020, s 307, Sch 19, para 20(g); see Chapter 12 para 12.52.
[55] SA 2020, ss 267 and 280, Sch 14, para 9(p); see Chapter 12 para 12.77.
[56] SA 2020, ss 273 and 283, Sch 15, para 9(p); see Chapter 12 para 12.123.

Proof

See Definition for elements of offence. 7.32

Notes

(i) If penetration is involved the offence is indictable only.[57] 7.33
(ii) If penetration is not involved then the offence is triable either way.[58] See also para 7.25(iii).
(iii) If the offence falls within subsection (3) then this ought to be averred in the indictment.
(iv) For definitions of 'mental disorder' and 'sexual' see para 7.24.
(iv) The extended jurisdiction provisions apply to this section where the victim of the offence was under 18.[59] See Chapter 17 para 17.01.
(v) The s 45 MSA 2015 defence for slavery and trafficking victims who commit an offence does not apply to this offence.[60]

Indictment

CAUSING/INCITING A PERSON WITH A MENTAL DISORDER IMPEDING CHOICE TO ENGAGE IN SEXUAL ACTIVITY 1.5.2004 to date 7.34

Statement of Offence

CAUSING/INCITING A PERSON, WITH A MENTAL DISORDER IMPEDING CHOICE TO ENGAGE IN SEXUAL ACTIVITY, contrary to section 31(1) of the Sexual Offences Act 2003.

Particulars of Offence

D on the ... day of ... intentionally caused/incited C, to engage in a sexual activity, namely ..., and C was unable to refuse because of or for a reason related to a mental disorder, and D knew or could reasonably have been expected to have known that C had a mental disorder and that because of it or for a reason related to it C is likely to be unable to refuse.

---

[57] SOA 2003, s 31(3).
[58] SOA 2003, s 31(4).
[59] SOA 2003, s 72; provides for the prosecution within the jurisdiction of a sexual offence committed outside it.
[60] Modern Slavery Act 2015, s 45 and Sch 4, para 33.

Alternative Offences

7.35 Attempt to commit the full offence. When indicting offences of attempt do so under s 1(1) Criminal Attempts Act 1981.[61] Aver the attempt in both the Statement of Offence and Particulars of Offence. In addition, aver the substantive offence under the relevant Act; see paras 1.51 and 12.157 and *Reed & Others* [2021].[62]

Sentence

7.36 (i) On indictment:
- If penetration is involved: **LIFE**.[63]
- If no penetration is involved: **14 YEARS**.[64]

(ii) Summarily: **6 months**.[65]

7.37 The Sentencing Council 'Sexual Offences: Definitive Guideline' contains offence-specific guidelines for s 31 offences. The Guideline applies to all offenders aged 18 and over, sentenced on or after 1 April 2014.

Upon Conviction/Sentence

7.38 Notification applies.[66]

Automatic inclusion in the children's barred list without representations where a child was caused or incited to engage in sexual activity; with representations where an adult was caused or incited to engage in sexual activity. Automatic inclusion in the adults' barred list without representations.[67]

SHPO applies.[68]

Qualifying 'specified sexual offence' in Schedule 18 (Extended Sentences).[69]

Qualifying Schedule 19 offence (Life Sentences) where offender liable on conviction on indictment to life imprisonment.[70]

Qualifying Schedule 14 offence (Extended Sentences: The Earlier Offence Condition) where offender liable on conviction on indictment to life imprisonment.[71]

---

[61] Implementation date 27.8.1981.
[62] *Reed & Others* [2021] EWCA Crim 572.
[63] SOA 2003, s 31(3).
[64] SOA 2003, s 31(4).
[65] SOA 2003, s 31(4). 12 months if CJA 2003, s 282(2) implemented.
[66] SOA 2003, s 80(1) and Sch 3, para 27; see Chapter 14 paras 14.01–14.05.
[67] Part 2 of the Safeguarding Vulnerable Groups Act 2006 (Prescribed Criteria and Miscellaneous Provisions) Regulations 2009 (SI 2009 No 37), paras 1, 2, and 3; see Chapter 12 para 12.217.
[68] SA 2020, s 345 and Sch 3, para 27 SOA 2003; see Chapter 16 para 16.07.
[69] SA 2020, s 306, Sch 18, para 38(x); see Chapter 12 para 12.51.
[70] SA 2020, s 307, Sch 19, para 20(h); see Chapter 12 para 12.52.
[71] SA 2020, ss 267 and 280, Sch 14, para 9(q); see Chapter 12 para 12.77.

3. Engaging in Sexual Activity in the Presence of a Person with a Mental Disorder Impeding Choice

Sexual Offences Act 2003, s 32

Definition

(1) A person (A) commits an offence if—   **7.39**
   (a) he intentionally engages in an activity,
   (b) the activity is sexual,
   (c) for the purpose of obtaining sexual gratification, he engages in it—
      (i) when another person (B) is present or is in a place from which A can be observed, and
      (ii) knowing or believing that (B) is aware, or intending that B should be aware, that he is engaging in it,
   (d) B is unable to refuse because of or for a reason related to a mental disorder, and
   (e) A knows or could reasonably be expected to know that B has a mental disorder and that because of it or for a reason related to it B is likely to be unable to refuse.

Proof

See Definition for elements of the offence.   **7.40**

Notes

(i) The offence is triable either way.[73]   **7.41**
(ii) For definitions of 'mental disorder' and 'sexual' see para 7.24.
(iii) References to observation (however expressed) are to observation whether direct or by looking at an image.[74]
(iii) The extended jurisdiction provisions apply to this section where the victim of the offence was under 18.[75] See Chapter 17 para 17.01.

---

[72] SA 2020, ss 273 and 283, Sch 15, para 9(q); see Chapter 12 para 12.123.
[73] SOA 2003, s 32(3).
[74] SOA 2003, s 79(7).
[75] SOA 2003, s 72; provides for the prosecution within the jurisdiction of a sexual offence committed outside it.

(iii) The s 45 MSA 2015 defence for slavery and trafficking victims who commit an offence does not apply to this offence.[76]

Indictment

7.42 ENGAGING IN SEXUAL ACTIVITY IN THE PRESENCE OF A PERSON WITH A MENTAL DISORDER IMPEDING CHOICE 1.5.2004 to date

> **Statement of Offence**
> ENGAGING IN SEXUAL ACTIVITY IN THE PRESENCE OF A PERSON WITH A MENTAL DISORDER IMPEDING CHOICE, contrary to section 32 of the Sexual Offences Act 2003.
>
> **Particulars of Offence**
> D on the … day of … for the purpose of obtaining sexual gratification, intentionally engaged in sexual activity when C was [present] *or* [in a place from which D can be observed] and C being unable to refuse because of or for a reason related to a mental disorder, D [knowing or believing that C is aware] *or* [intending that C should be aware], that he was engaging in such activity, and where D knew or could reasonably have been expected to know that C had a mental disorder.

Alternative Offences

7.43 Attempt to commit the full offence. When indicting offences of attempt do so under s 1(1) Criminal Attempts Act 1981.[77] Aver the attempt in both the Statement of Offence and Particulars of Offence. In addition, aver the substantive offence under the relevant Act; see paras 1.51 and 12.157 and *Reed & Others* [2021].[78]

Sentence

7.44 (i) On indictment: **10 YEARS**.[79]
(ii) Summarily: **6 months**.[80]

7.45 The Sentencing Council 'Sexual Offences: Definitive Guideline' contains offence-specific guidelines for section 32 offences. The Guideline applies to all offenders aged 18 and over, sentenced on or after 1 April 2014.

---

[76] Modern Slavery Act 2015, s 45 and Sch 4, para 33.
[77] Implementation date 27.8.1981.
[78] *Reed & Others* [2021] EWCA Crim 572.
[79] SOA 2003, s 32(3)(b).
[80] SOA 2003, s 32(3)(a), 12 months if CJA 2003, s 282(2) implemented.

D. OFFENCES COMMITTED FROM 1.5.2004 TO DATE   199

Upon Conviction/Sentence   7.46

Notification applies.[81]

Automatic inclusion in the children's barred list without representations where a child was present at, or observed the offence; with representations where an adult was present at or observed the offence. Automatic inclusion in the adults' barred list without representations.[82]

SHPO applies.[83]

Qualifying 'specified sexual offence' in Schedule 18 (Extended Sentences).[84]

4. Causing a Person with a Mental Disorder Impeding Choice to Watch a Sexual Act

Sexual Offences Act 2003, s 33

Definition

(1) A person (A) commits an offence if—   7.47
   (a for the purpose of obtaining sexual gratification, he intentionally causes another person (B) to watch a third person engaging in an activity, or to look at an image of any person engaging in an activity.
   (b) The activity is sexual,
   (c) B is unable to refuse because of or for a reason related to a mental disorder, and
   (d) A knows or could reasonably be expected to know that B has a mental disorder and that because of it or for a reason related to it B is likely to be unable to refuse.

Proof

See Definition for elements of the offence.   7.48

Notes

(i) This offence is triable either way.[85]   7.49
(ii) For definitions of 'mental disorder' and 'sexual' see para 7.24.

---

[81] SOA 2003, s 80(1) and Sch 3, para 27; see Chapter 14 paras 14.01–14.05.
[82] Part 2 of the Safeguarding Vulnerable Groups Act 2006 (Prescribed Criteria and Miscellaneous Provisions) Regulations 2009 (SI 2009 No 37), paras 1, 2, and 3; see Chapter 12 para 12.217.
[83] SA 2020, s 345 and Sch 3, para 27 SOA 2003; see Chapter 16 para 16.07.
[84] SA 2020, s 306, Sch 18, para 38(y); see Chapter 12 para 12.51.
[85] SOA 2003, s 33(3).

7. OFFENCES INVOLVING THE MENTALLY DISORDERED

(iii) 'Image' means a moving or still image and includes an image produced by any means and, where the context permits, a three-dimensional image.[86] References to an image of a person include references to an image of an imaginary person.[87]

(ii) The extended jurisdiction provisions apply to this section where the victim of the offence was under 18.[88] See Chapter 17 para 17.01.

(iii) The s 45 MSA 2015 defence for slavery and trafficking victims who commit an offence does not apply to this offence.[89]

Indictment

7.50 CAUSING A PERSON WITH A MENTAL DISORDER IMPEDING CHOICE TO WATCH A SEXUAL ACT 1.5.2004 to date

---

Statement of Offence

CAUSING A PERSON WITH A MENTAL DISORDER IMPEDING CHOICE, TO WATCH A SEXUAL ACT, contrary to section 33 of the Sexual Offences Act 2003.

Particulars of Offence

D on the … day of … for the purpose of obtaining sexual gratification, intentionally caused C [to watch X engaging in a sexual activity] *or* [to look at an image of a person engaging in a sexual activity], and C being unable to refuse because of or for a reason related to a mental disorder, and where D knew or could reasonably have been expected to know that C had a mental disorder.

Alternative Offences

7.51 Attempt to commit the full offence. When indicting offences of attempt do so under s 1(1) Criminal Attempts Act 1981.[90] Aver the attempt in both the Statement of Offence and Particulars of Offence. In addition, aver the substantive offence under the relevant Act; see paras 1.51 and 12.157 and *Reed & Others* [2021].[91]

Sentence

7.52 (i) On indictment: **10 YEARS**.[92]
(ii) Summarily: **6 months**.[93]

---

[86] SOA 2003, s 79(4).
[87] SOA 2003, s 79(5).
[88] SOA 2003, s 72; provides for the prosecution within the jurisdiction of a sexual offence committed outside it.
[89] Modern Slavery Act 2015, s 45 and Sch 4, para 33.
[90] Implementation date 27.8.1981.
[91] *Reed & Others* [2021] EWCA Crim 572.
[92] SOA 2003, s 33(3)(b).
[93] SOA 2003, s 33(3)(a), 12 months if CJA 2003, s 282(2) implemented.

E. OFFENCES COMMITTED BETWEEN 1.11.1913 AND 31.12.1956   201

The Sentencing Council 'Sexual Offences: Definitive Guideline' contains offence-specific guidelines for section 33 offences. The Guideline applies to all offenders aged 18 and over, sentenced on or after 1 April 2014. **7.53**

Upon Conviction/Sentence **7.54**

Notification applies.[94]
Automatic inclusion in the children's barred list without representations where a child was caused to watch the sexual activity; with representations where an adult was caused to watch the sexual activity. Automatic inclusion in the adults' barred list without representations.[95]
SHPO applies.[96]
Qualifying 'specified sexual offence' in Schedule 18 (Extended Sentences).[97]

Abuse of the Mentally Disordered, as Patients or by Those with Certain Responsibility for Them

E. OFFENCES COMMITTED BETWEEN 1.11.1913 AND 31.12.1956

1. Carnal Knowledge of Female under Care/Treatment

Mental Deficiency Act 1913, s 56

Definition

Any person: **7.55**

1(a) who unlawfully and carnally knows or attempts to have carnal knowledge of, any woman or girl under care or treatment in an institution or certified house or approved home, or whilst placed out on licence therefrom or under guardianship under this Act

or ...

(e) who with intent that any woman or girl who is a defective should be unlawfully and carnally known by any man whether such carnal knowledge is intended to be with

---

[94] SOA 2003, s 80(1) and Sch 3, para 27; see Chapter 14 paras 14.01–14.05.
[95] Part 2 of the Safeguarding Vulnerable Groups Act 2006 (Prescribed Criteria and Miscellaneous Provisions) Regulations 2009 (SI 2009 No 37), paras 1, 2, and 3; see Chapter 12 para 12.217.
[96] SA 2020, s 345 and Sch 3, para 27 SOA 2003; see Chapter 16 para 16.07.
[97] SA 2020, s 306, Sch 18, para 38(z); see Chapter 12 para 12.51.

7. OFFENCES INVOLVING THE MENTALLY DISORDERED

any particular man or generally, takes or causes to be taken such woman or girl out of the possession and against the will of her parent, or any other person having the lawful care or charge of her.

Proof

7.56 As per Definition. Note the following:

(i) Carnal knowledge is defined as 'proof of penetration'—without necessarily ejaculation.[98]

(ii) The defendant must be proven either not to have known or not to have had reason to suspect that the woman or girl was a defective.[99]

(iii) Defective is defined as a female idiot, imbecile, feeble minded or moral imbecile.[100]

Notes

7.57 (i) The offence is triable only on indictment.[101]

(ii) This offence may be an alternative to an offence of rape.[102]

Alternative Offences

7.58 Section 56(1)(e): an attempt to commit the full offence. When indicting offences of attempt do so under common law. Aver the attempt in both the Statement of Offence and Particulars of Offence. In addition, aver the substantive offence under the relevant Act; see paras 1.51 and 12.157 and *Reed & Others* [2021].[103]

Sentence

7.59 On indictment: **2 YEARS**.[104]

7.60 As of 1.1.1957 the MDA 1913, s 56 is repealed. Separate offences are created by ss 8, 9, 21, 27 and 29 of the SOA 1956.[105]

---

[98] *R v Marsden* [1891] 2 QB 149; OAPA 1861, s 63.
[99] *R v Marsden* [1891] 2 QB 149; OAPA 1861, s 63, MDA 1913, s 56(1)(e).
[100] MDA 1913, s 1.
[101] MDA 1913, s 56(4).
[102] MDA 1913, s 56(5).
[103] *Reed & Others* [2021] EWCA Crim 572.
[104] MDA 1913, s 56(1)(e).
[105] As of 1.1.1957.

F. OFFENCES COMMITTED BETWEEN 1.1.1957 AND 31.10.1960

1. Intercourse with Defectives Receiving Treatment

Sexual Offences Act 1956, s 8

Definition

(1) ... unlawful sexual intercourse with a woman who is under care or treatment in an institution, certified house or approved home within the meaning of the Mental Deficiency Act 1913, or placed out on licence therefrom or under guardianship under that Act. [106]

7.61

Proof

As per Definition. In addition note:

7.62

(i) Meaning of defective: '... mental defectiveness means a condition of arrested or incomplete development of mind existing before the age of 18, whether arising from inherent causes or induced by disease or injury'.[107]
(ii) Meaning of care or treatment: that the woman is under the care or treatment in an institution, certified house or approved home, or placed out on licence.[108] If the female has breached the terms of the licence, or run away, the offence is still committed.[109]

Notes

(i) The offence is triable only on indictment.[110]

7.63

(ii) The defendant is afforded a defence if he can prove that he did not believe and had no reason to believe that the woman was mentally disordered.[111]
(iii) This offence is an alternative to an offence of rape.

---

[106] Repealed 1.11.1960 (SI 1960/1698).
[107] SOA 1956, s 45(1).
[108] SOA 1956, s 8.
[109] *R v Balderstone* (1955) 39 Cr App R 97 CCA.
[110] SOA 1956, s 37 and Sch 2, para 12.
[111] SOA 1956, s 47, s 8(1)(2).

Indictment

7.64 INTERCOURSE WITH A MENTALLY DEFECTIVE PATIENT 1.1.1957 to 31.10.1960

> **Statement of Offence**
> INTERCOURSE WITH A DEFECTIVE, contrary to section 8 of the Sexual Offences Act 1956.
>
> **Particulars of Offence**
> D on the … day of … had unlawful sexual intercourse with C, a female [under the care/treatment in an institution/certified house/approved home within the meaning of the Mental Deficiency Act 1913] *or* [placed out on licence from … an institution/certified house/approved home within the meaning of the Mental Deficiency Act 1913] *or* [under guardianship of the Mental Deficiency Act 1913].

Alternative Offences

7.65 Attempt to commit the full offence. When indicting offences of attempt do so under common law. Aver the attempt in both the Statement of Offence and Particulars of Offence. In addition, aver the substantive offence under the relevant Act; see paras 1.51 and 12.157 and *Reed & Others* [2021].[112]

Sentence

7.66 (i) On indictment: 2 YEARS.[113]
(ii) For an attempt the maximum is the same.[114]

Upon Conviction/Sentence

7.67 (i) Notification not applicable.[115]
(ii) Automatic inclusion in the children's and adults' barred lists not applicable.[116]
(iii) SHPO not applicable.[117]

7.68 *As of 1.11.1960 the MHA 1959, s 128(1) repealed SOA 1956, s 8.*

---

[112] *Reed & Others* [2021] EWCA Crim 572
[113] SOA 1956, s 37 and Sch 2, para 12(a).
[114] SOA 1956, s 37 and Sch 2, para 12(b).
[115] SOA 2003, s 80(1) (not in Sch 3); see Chapter 14 Tables 14.2–14.5.
[116] Part 2 of the Safeguarding Vulnerable Groups Act 2006 (Prescribed Criteria and Miscellaneous Provisions) Regulations 2009 (SI 2009 No 37); see Chapter 12 para 12.217.
[117] SA 2020, s 345 (not in Sch 3 or Sch 5); see Chapter 16 para 16.07.

G. OFFENCES COMMITTED BETWEEN 1.11.1960 AND 30.4.2004

1. Intercourse with a Mentally Disordered Patient

Mental Health Act 1959, s 128(1)

Definition

It is an offence: 7.69

(a) for a man who is an officer on the staff or is otherwise employed in, or is one of the managers of, a hospital or nursing home, to have unlawful sexual intercourse with a woman who is for the time being receiving treatment for mental disorder in that hospital or home, or to have such intercourse on the premises of which the hospital or home forms part with a woman who is for the time being receiving such treatment there as an outpatient;

(b) for a man to have unlawful sexual intercourse with a woman who is a mentally disordered patient and is subject to his guardianship under this Act or is otherwise in his custody or care under this Act or in pursuance of arrangements under the National Health Service Act 1946 or Part III of the National Assistance Act 1948, or as a resident in a residential home for mentally disordered persons within the meaning of Part III of this Act.

Proof

As per Definition. 7.70

Note:

(i) Sexual intercourse must be proved (penile penetration of the vagina, without necessarily proof of ejaculation).[118]

(ii) This offence also covers buggery of such a female patient, or an act of gross indecency upon another man.[119] This is retrospective.[120]

(iii) It is a complete defence if the defendant proves that he did not know and had no reason to suspect that the complainant was a mentally disordered patient.[121]

---

[118] SOA 1956, s 44.
[119] SOA 1967, s 1(4).
[120] SOA 1967, s 10(1).
[121] MHA 1959, s 128; SOA 1956, s 47(2).

Notes

7.71
(i) This offence is triable only on indictment.
(ii) Consent to prosecute must be obtained from the DPP.[122]

Indictment

7.72 INTERCOURSE WITH A MENTALLY DISORDERED PATIENT 1.11.1960 to 30.4.2004

> ### Statement of Offence
> UNLAWFUL SEXUAL INTERCOURSE WITH A PATIENT, contrary to section 128(a) Mental Health Act 1959.
>
> ### Particulars of Offence
> D, a man who is an officer on the staff/employed in/a manager of … the … Hospital/ the … mental nursing home, on the … day of … had unlawful sexual intercourse with C, a woman receiving treatment at the said … Hospital/ … mental nursing home.

Alternative Offences

7.73 Attempt to commit the full offence. When indicting offences of attempt do so under common law until 26.8.1981, thereafter indict under s 1(1) Criminal Attempts Act 1981.[123] Aver the attempt in both the Statement of Offence and Particulars of Offence. In addition, aver the substantive offence under the relevant Act; see paras 1.51 and 12.157 and *Reed & Others* [2021].[124]

Sentence

7.74 On indictment:

(i) For the full offence: **2 YEARS**.[125]
(ii) For an attempt: **2 YEARS**.

Upon Conviction/Sentence

7.75 (i) Notification not applicable.[126]

---

[122] MHA 1959, s 128(4).
[123] Implementation date 27.8.1981.
[124] *Reed & Others* [2021] EWCA Crim 572
[125] MHA 1959, s 128(3).
[126] SOA 2003, s 80(1) (not in Sch 3); see Chapter 14 Tables 14.2–14.5.

(ii) Automatic inclusion in the children's barred list without representations where offence committed against a child otherwise inclusion in the children's and adults' barred lists with the right to make representations.[127]
(iii) SHPO not applicable.[128]
(iv) Specified sexual offence in Schedule 18 (Extended Sentence).[129]

H. OFFENCES COMMITTED FROM 1.5.2004 TO DATE

The SOA 2003 repealed the MHA 1959, s 128 in full. SOA 2003, s 38 sexual activity with a person with a mental disorder, now covers this offence. Additional offences are created including causing/inciting sexual activity,[130] sexual activity in the presence of a person with a mental disorder[131] or causing a person with a mental disorder to watch a sexual act.[132] **7.76**

1. Sexual Activity with a Person who has a Mental Disorder by a Care Worker

Sexual Offences Act 2003, s 38

Definition

(1) A person (A) commits an offence if— **7.77**
　(a) he intentionally touches another person (B),
　(b) the touching is sexual,
　(c) B has a mental disorder,
　(d) A knows or could reasonably be expected to know that B has a mental disorder, and
　(e) A is involved in B's care in a way that falls within section 42.

Proof

(i) See Definition for elements of the offence. **7.78**
(ii) In relation to ss 38–41 of the SOA 2003, once the prosecution have proved that the complainant had a mental disorder, it is to be taken that the defendant knew or could reasonably have been expected to have known that the complainant had such disorder, unless he adduces sufficient evidence to raise an issue in this regard.

---

[127] Part 2 of the Safeguarding Vulnerable Groups Act 2006 (Prescribed Criteria and Miscellaneous Provisions) Regulations 2009 (SI 2009 No 37), paras 1, 2, and 4; see Chapter 12 para 12.217.
[128] SA 2020, s 345 (not in Sch 3 or Sch 5); see Chapter 16 para 16.07.
[129] SA 2020, Sch 18, para 30; see Chapter 12 para 12.51.
[130] SOA 2003, s 39.
[131] SOA 2003, s 40.
[132] SOA 2003, s 41.

(ii) For definitions of 'mental disorder', 'sexual' and 'touching' see para 7.24.
(iii) Section 42 SOA 2003 defines care worker:
   (1) For the purposes of sections 38–41, a person (A) is involved in the care of another person (B) in a way that falls within this section if any of subsections (2) to (4) applies.
   (2) This subsection applies if–
      (a) B is accommodated and cared for in a care home, community home, voluntary home, children's home, or premises in Wales at which a secure accommodation service is provided, and
      (b) A has functions to perform in the course of employment in the home or the premises which have brought him or are likely to bring him into regular face to face contact with B.
   (3) This subsection applies if B is a patient for whom services are provided—
      (a) by a National Health Service body or an independent medical agency;
      (b) in an independent hospital; or
      (c) in Wales, in an independent clinic,
      and A has functions to perform for the body or agency or in the hospital or clinic in the course of employment which have brought A or are likely to bring A into regular face to face contact with B
   (4) This subsection applies if A—
      (a) is, whether or not in the course of employment, a provider of care, assistance or services to B in connection with B's mental disorder, and
      (b) as such, has had or is likely to have regular face to face contact with B.
   (5) In this section 'care home' means—
      (a) an establishment in England which is a care home for the purposes of the Care Standards Act 2000 (c. 14); and
      (b) a place in Wales at which a care home service, within the meaning of Part 1 of the Regulation and Inspection of Social Care (Wales) Act 2016 is provided wholly or mainly to persons aged 18 or over
      'children's home' —
      (a) has the meaning given by section 1 of the Care Standards Act 2000 in relation to a children's home in England, and
      (b) means a place in Wales at which a care home service within the meaning of Part 1 of the Regulation and Inspection of Social Care (Wales) Act 2016 is provided wholly or mainly to persons under the age of 18;
      'community home' has the meaning given by section 53 of the Children Act 1989 (c. 41);
      'employment' means any employment, whether paid or unpaid and whether under a contract of service or apprenticeship, under a contract for services, or otherwise than under a contract;
      'independent clinic' has the meaning given by section 2 of the Care Standards Act 2000;
      'independent hospital'—
      (a) in England, means—
         (i) a hospital as defined by section 275 of the National Health Service Act 2006 that is not a health service hospital as defined by that section; or

(ii) any other establishment in which any of the services listed in section 22(6) are provided and which is not a health service hospital as so defined; and

(b) in Wales, has the meaning given by section 2 of the Care Standards Act 2000;

'independent medical agency' means an undertaking (not being an independent hospital, or in Wales an independent clinic) which consists of or includes the provision of services by medical practitioners;

'National Health Service body' means—

(a) a Local Health Board,
(b) a National Health Service trust,
(ba) the Secretary of State in relation to the exercise of functions under section 2A or 2B of, or paragraph 7C, 8 or 12 of Schedule 1 to, the National Health Service Act 2006,
(bb) a local authority in relation to the exercise of functions under section 2B or 111 of, or any of paragraphs 1 to 7B, or 13 of Schedule 1 to, the National Health Service Act 2006, or
(d) a Special Health Authority;

'secure accommodation service' has the meaning given in Part 1 of the Regulation and Inspection of Social Care (Wales) Act 2016;

'voluntary home' has the meaning given by section 60(3) of the Children Act 1989.

(6) In subsection (5), in the definition of 'independent medical agency', 'undertaking' includes any business or profession and—

(a) in relation to a public or local authority, includes the exercise of any functions of that authority; and
(b) in relation to any other body of persons, whether corporate or unincorporate, includes any of the activities of that body

Notes

(i) If penetration is involved the offence is indictable only,[133] save when penetration of A's anus or vagina with an object is alleged in which case it is triable either way.[134] See para 7.25(iii) and (iv) for 'penetration' and references to 'parts of the body'.

(ii) Sections 38–41 are all subject to two exceptions: (a) if the parties are aged 16 or over and are civil partners[135] and (b) if the parties were in a lawful sexual relationship before one of them became the carer.[136]

(iii) Where the offence falls within subsection (3), then this ought to be alleged in the indictment.

7.79

---

[133] SOA 2003, s 38(3).
[134] SOA 2003, s 38(3)(c).
[135] SOA 2003, s 43.
[136] SOA 2003, s 44.

(vi) In these cases, questions of the complainant's reliability will often be crucial to the case. If so, this is a question to be decided by a jury, in general.[137]

Section 73 provides a defence to an offence of aiding abetting or counselling the commission of an offence under this section against a person under 16, where he acts for the purpose of;

(a) protecting the child from sexually transmitted infection,
(b) protecting the physical safety of the child,
(c) preventing the child from becoming pregnant, or
(d) promoting the child's emotional well-being by the giving of advice,

and not for the purpose of obtaining sexual gratification or for the purpose of causing or encouraging the activity constituting the offence or the child's participation in it.

The extended jurisdiction provisions apply to this section where the victim of the offence was under 18.[138] See Chapter 17 para 17.01.

The s 45 MSA 2015 defence for slavery and trafficking victims who commit an offence does not apply to this offence.[139]

Indictment

7.80 SEXUAL ACTIVITY BY A CARE WORKER WITH A PERSON WITH A MENTAL DISORDER 1.5.2004 to date

Statement of Offence
SEXUAL ACTIVITY WITH A PERSON WITH A MENTAL DISORDER BY A CARE WORKER, contrary to section 38(1) [and (3)] of the Sexual Offences Act 2003.

Particulars of Offence
D on the ... day of ... intentionally touched C, a person with a mental disorder, [by penetrating her mouth with his penis, in circumstances where the touching was sexual, where D knew or could reasonably have been expected to know that C had a mental disorder, and where D was a person involved in C's care in a way falling within section 42 of the Sexual Offences Act 2003.

Alternative Offences

7.81 Attempt to commit the full offence. When indicting offences of attempt do so under s 1(1) Criminal Attempts Act 1981.[140] Aver the attempt in both the Statement of Offence and Particulars of Offence. In addition, aver the substantive offence under the relevant Act; see paras 1.51 and 12.157 and *Reed & Others* [2021].[141]

---

[137] *R v Watts (James Michael)* [2010] EWCA Crim 1824, [2011] CLR 68.
[138] SOA 2003, s 72; provides for the prosecution within the jurisdiction of a sexual offence committed outside it.
[139] Modern Slavery Act 2015, s 45 and Sch 4, para 33.
[140] Implementation date 27.8.1981.
[141] *Reed & Others* [2021] EWCA Crim 572.

Sentence

(i) On indictment: **7.82**
- If penetration is involved: **14 YEARS**.[142]
- If no penetration is involved: **10 YEARS**.[143]

(ii) Summarily: **6 months**.[144]

(iii) Attempt: the same maximum.

The Sentencing Council 'Sexual Offences: Definitive Guideline' contains offence-specific guidelines for s 38 offences. The Guideline applies to all offenders aged 18 and over, sentenced on or after 1 April 2014. **7.83**

Upon Conviction/Sentence

(i) Notification applicable where the offender under 18 and has been sentenced to at least 12 months' imprisonment, in any other case, the offender has been sentenced to a term of imprisonment, a hospital order or made subject to community order of at least 12 months.[145] **7.84**

(ii) Automatic inclusion in the children's barred list without representations where offence committed against a child; with representations where offence committed against an adult. Automatic inclusion in the adults' barred list without representations.[146]

(iii) SHPO applicable.[147]

(iv) Specified sexual offence in Schedule 18 (Extended Sentence).[148]

2. Care Workers: Causing or Inciting Sexual Activity with a Person with a Mental Disorder

Sexual Offences Act 2003, s 39

Definition

(1) A person (A) commits an offence if— **7.85**
   (a) he intentionally causes or incites another person (B) to engage in an activity,
   (b) the activity is sexual,
   (c) B has a mental disorder,

---

[142] SOA 2003, s 38(3).
[143] SOA 2003, s 38(4)(b).
[144] SOA 2003, s 38(4)(a), 12 months if CJA 2003, s 282(2) implemented.
[145] SOA 2003, s 80(1), Sch 3, para 28; see Chapter 14 paras 14.01–14.05.
[146] Part 2 of the Safeguarding Vulnerable Groups Act 2006 (Prescribed Criteria and Miscellaneous Provisions) Regulations 2009 (SI 2009 No 37), paras 1, 2, and 3; see Chapter 12 para 12.217.
[147] SA 2020, s 345, Sch 3, para 28; see Chapter 16 para 16.07.
[148] SA 2020, Sch 18, para 38(ae); see Chapter 12 para 12.51.

7. OFFENCES INVOLVING THE MENTALLY DISORDERED

(d) A knows or could reasonably be expected to know that B has a mental disorder, and
(e) A is involved in B's care in a way that falls within section 42.

Proof

7.86 See Definition for elements of the offence.

Notes

7.87 (i) If the offence involves penetration then it is triable only on indictment.[149] If penetration is not alleged then the offence is triable either way.[150]
(ii) Sections 38–41 are all subject to two exceptions: (a) if the parties are aged 16 or over and are civil partners[151] and (b) if the parties were in a lawful sexual relationship before one of them became the carer.[152]
(iii) Where the offence falls within subsection (3), then this ought to be alleged in the indictment.
(iv) For definitions of 'mental disorder', 'sexual' and see para 7.24.
(v) For s 42 definition of care worker see para 7.74 (iii).
(vi) The extended jurisdiction provisions apply to this section where the victim of the offence was under 18.[153] See Chapter 17 para 17.01.
(vii) The s 45 MSA 2015 defence for slavery and trafficking victims who commit an offence does not apply to this offence.[154]

Indictment

7.88 CAUSING/INCITING SEXUAL ACTIVITY WITH A PERSON WITH A MENTAL DISORDER BY A CARE WORKER 1.5.2004 to date

> **Statement of Offence**
> CAUSING OR INCITING SEXUAL ACTIVITY WITH A PERSON WITH A MENTAL DISORDER BY A CARE WORKER, contrary to section 39(1) [and (3)] of the Sexual Offences Act 2003.
>
> **Particulars of Offence**
> D on the … day of … intentionally caused/incited C, a person with a mental disorder, to engage in sexual activity, [which involved penetration of C's. …..with Z's. ….,] where

---

[149] SOA 2003, s 39(3).
[150] SOA 2003, s 39(4).
[151] SOA 2003, s 43.
[152] SOA 2003, s 44.
[153] SOA 2003, s 72; provides for the prosecution within the jurisdiction of a sexual offence committed outside it.
[154] Modern Slavery Act 2015, s 45 and Sch 4, para 33.

> D knew or could reasonably be expected to know that C had a mental disorder, and where D was a person involved in C's care in a way falling within section 42 of the Sexual Offences Act 2003.

Alternative Offences

7.89 Attempt to commit the full offence. When indicting offences of attempt do so under s 1(1) Criminal Attempts Act 1981.[155] Aver the attempt in both the Statement of Offence and Particulars of Offence. In addition, aver the substantive offence under the relevant Act; see paras 1.51 and 12.157 and *Reed & Others* [2021].[156]

Sentence

7.90
(i) On indictment:
- If penetration involved: **14 YEARS**.[157]
- If no penetration: **10 YEARS**.[158]
(ii) Summarily: **6 months**.[159]
(iii) An attempt attracts the same sentences.

7.91 The Sentencing Council 'Sexual Offences: Definitive Guideline' contains offence-specific guidelines for s 39 offences. The Guideline applies to all offenders aged 18 and over, sentenced on or after 1 April 2014.

Upon Sentence/Conviction

7.92
(i) Notification applicable: where the offender under 18 and has been sentenced to at least 12 months' imprisonment, in any other case, the offender has been sentenced to a term of imprisonment, a hospital order or made subject to community order of at least 12 months.[160]
(ii) Automatic inclusion in the children's barred list without representations where offence committed against a child; with representations where offence committed against an adult. Automatic inclusion in the adults' barred list without representations.[161]
(iii) SHPO applicable.[162]
(iv) Specified sexual offence in Schedule 18 (Extended Sentence).[163]

---

[155] Implementation date 27.8.1981.
[156] *Reed & Others* [2021] EWCA Crim 572.
[157] SOA 2003, s 39(3).
[158] SOA 2003, s 39(4)(b).
[159] SOA 2003, s 39(4)(a), 12 months if CJA 2003, s 282(3) implemented.
[160] SOA 2003, s 80(1), Sch 3, para 28; see Chapter 14 paras 14.01–14.05.
[161] Part 2 of the Safeguarding Vulnerable Groups Act 2006 (Prescribed Criteria and Miscellaneous Provisions) Regulations 2009 (SI 2009 No 37), paras 1, 2, and 3; see Chapter 12 para 12.217.
[162] SA 2020, s 345, Sch 3, para 28; see Chapter 16 para 16.07.
[163] SA 2020, Sch 18, para 38(af); see Chapter 12 para 12.51.

3. Care Workers: Sexual Activity in the Presence of a Person with a Mental Disorder

Sexual Offences Act 2003, s 40

Definition

7.93 (1) A person (A) commits an offence if—
  (a) he intentionally engages in an activity,
  (b) the activity is sexual,
  (c) for the purpose of obtaining sexual gratification, he engages in it—
    (i) when another person (B) is present or in a place from which A can be observed, and
    (ii) knowing or believing that B is aware, or intending that B should be aware, that he is engaging in it,
  (d) B has a mental disorder,
  (e) A knows or could reasonably be expected to know that B has a mental disorder, and
  (f) A is involved in B's care in a way that falls within section 42.

Proof

7.94 See Definition for elements of offence.

Notes

7.95 (i) This offence is triable either way.[164]
  (ii) For definitions of 'mental disorder' and 'sexual' and see para 7.24.
  (iv) References to observation (however expressed) are to observation whether direct or by looking at an image.[165]
  (iii) For s 42 definition of care worker see para 7.74 (iii).
  (iv) Sections 38–41 are all subject to two exceptions: (a) if the parties are aged 16 or over and are civil partners[166] and (b) if the parties were in a lawful sexual relationship before one of them became the carer.[167]
  (iii) The extended jurisdiction provisions apply to this section where the victim of the offence was under 18.[168] See Chapter 17 para 17.01.

---

[164] SOA 2003, s 40(3).
[165] SOA 200 3, s 79(7).
[166] SOA 2003, s 43.
[167] SOA 2003, s 44.
[168] SOA 2003, s 72; provides for the prosecution within the jurisdiction of a sexual offence committed outside it.

H. OFFENCES COMMITTED FROM 1.5.2004 TO DATE   215

(iv) The s 45 MSA 2015 defence for slavery and trafficking victims who commit an offence does not apply to this offence.[169]

Indictment

SEXUAL ACTIVITY IN THE PRESENCE OF A PERSON WITH A MENTAL DISORDER 1.5.04 to date   **7.96**

Statement of Offence
SEXUAL ACTIVITY IN THE PRESENCE OF A PERSON WITH A MENTAL DISORDER, contrary to section 40 of the Sexual Offences Act 2003.

Particulars of Offence
D on the ... day of ... for the purpose of obtaining sexual gratification, intentionally engaged in a sexual activity when C, who has a mental disorder [was present] *or* [was in a place from which D could be observed], [knowing or believing that C was aware] *or* [intending that C should be aware] that he was engaging in such activity, and where D knew or could reasonably be expected to have known that C had a mental disorder, and where D was a person involved in C's care in a way falling within section 42 of the Sexual Offences Act 2003.

Alternative Offences

Attempt to commit the full offence. When indicting offences of attempt do so under s 1(1) Criminal Attempts Act 1981.[170] Aver the attempt in both the Statement of Offence and Particulars of Offence. In addition, aver the substantive offence under the relevant Act; see paras 1.51 and 12.157 and *Reed & Others* [2021].[171]   **7.97**

Sentence

(i) On indictment: **7 YEARS**.[172]   **7.98**
(ii) Summarily: **6 months**.[173]
(iii) Attempt: the same.

The Sentencing Council 'Sexual Offences: Definitive Guideline' contains offence-specific guidelines for s 40 offences. The Guideline applies to all offenders aged 18 and over, sentenced on or after 1 April 2014.   **7.99**

---

[169] Modern Slavery Act 2015, s 45 and Sch 4, para 33.
[170] Implementation date 27.8.1981.
[171] *Reed & Others* [2021] EWCA Crim 572.
[172] SOA 2003, s 40(3)(b).
[173] SOA 2003, s 40(3)(a), 12 months if CJA 2003, s 282(2) implemented.

Upon Conviction/Sentence

7.100
(i) Notification applicable: where the offender under 18 and has been sentenced to at least 12 months' imprisonment, in any other case, the offender has been sentenced to a term of imprisonment, a hospital order or made subject to community order of at least 12 months.[174]
(ii) Automatic inclusion in the children's barred list without representations where a child was present at or observed the offence; with representations where an adult was present at or observed the offence. Automatic inclusion in the adults' barred list without representations.[175]
(iii) SHPO applicable.[176]
(iv) Specified sexual offence in Schedule 18 (Extended Sentence).[177]

4. Care Workers: Causing a Person with a Mental Disorder to Watch a Sexual Act

Sexual Offences Act 2003, s 41

Definition

7.101
(1) A person (A) commits an offence if—
   (a) for the purpose of obtaining sexual gratification, he intentionally causes another person (B) to watch a third person engaging in an activity, or to look at an image of any person engaging in an activity,
   (b) the activity is sexual,
   (c) B has a mental disorder,
   (d) A knows or could reasonably be expected to know that B has a mental disorder, and
   (e) A is involved in B's care in a way that falls within section 42.

Proof

7.102 See Definition for elements of the offence.

---

[174] SOA 2003, s 80(1), Sch 3, para 28; see Chapter 14 paras 14.01–14.05.
[175] Part 2 of the Safeguarding Vulnerable Groups Act 2006 (Prescribed Criteria and Miscellaneous Provisions) Regulations 2009 (SI 2009 No 37), paras 1, 2, and 3; see Chapter 12 para 12.217.
[176] SA 2020, s 345, Sch 3, para 28; see Chapter 16 para 16.07.
[177] SA 2020, Sch 18, para 38(ag); see Chapter 12 para 12.51.

H. OFFENCES COMMITTED FROM 1.5.2004 TO DATE

Notes

7.103

(i) This offence is triable either way.[178]
(ii) Sections 38–41 are all subject to two exceptions:
 (a) if the parties are aged 16 or over and are civil partners;[179] and
 (b) if the parties were in a lawful sexual relationship before one of them became the carer.[180]
(ii) For definitions of 'mental disorder' and 'sexual' see para 7.24.
(iii) 'Image' means a moving or still image and includes an image produced by any means and, where the context permits, a three-dimensional image.[181] References to an image of a person include references to an image of an imaginary person.[182]
(iv) For a s 42 definition of care worker see para 7.74 (iii).
(v) The extended jurisdiction provisions apply to this section where the victim of the offence was under 18.[183] See Chapter 17 para 17.01.
(vi) The s 45 MSA 2015 defence for slavery and trafficking victims who commit an offence does not apply to this offence.[184]

Indictment

CAUSING A PERSON WITH A MENTAL DISORDER TO WATCH A SEXUAL ACT BY A CARE WORKER 1.5.2004 to date

7.104

Statement of Offence

CAUSING A PERSON WITH A MENTAL DISORDER TO WATCH A SEXUAL ACT BY A CARE WORKER, contrary to section 41(1) of the Sexual Offences Act 2003.

Particulars of Offence

D on the … day of 20 … for the purpose of obtaining sexual gratification, intentionally caused C, a person with a mental disorder, [to watch a third person engaging in a sexual activity] *or* [to look at an image of any person engaging in a sexual activity] where D knew or could reasonably be expected to have known that C had a mental disorder, and where D was a person involved in C's care in a way falling within section 42 of the Sexual Offences Act 2003.

---

[178] SOA 2003, s 41(3).
[179] SOA 2003, s 43.
[180] SOA 2003, s 44.
[181] SOA 2003, s 79(4).
[182] SOA 2003, s 79(5).
[183] SOA 2003, s 72; provides for the prosecution within the jurisdiction of a sexual offence committed outside it.
[184] Modern Slavery Act 2015, s 45 and Sch 4, para 33.

218   7. OFFENCES INVOLVING THE MENTALLY DISORDERED

Alternative Offences

7.105 Attempt to commit the full offence. When indicting offences of attempt do so under s 1(1) Criminal Attempts Act 1981.[185] Aver the attempt in both the Statement of Offence and Particulars of Offence. In addition, aver the substantive offence under the relevant Act; see paras 1.51 and 12.157 and *Reed & Others* [2021].[186]

Sentence

7.106 (i) On indictment: **7 YEARS**.[187]
(ii) Summarily: **6 months**.[188]
(iii) Attempt: the same.

7.107 The Sentencing Council 'Sexual Offences: Definitive Guideline' contains offence-specific guidelines for section 41 offences. The Guideline applies to all offenders aged 18 and over, sentenced on or after 1 April 2014.

Upon Conviction/Sentence

7.108 (i) Notification applicable: where the offender under 18 and has been sentenced to at least 12 months' imprisonment, in any other case, the offender has been sentenced to a term of imprisonment, a hospital order or made subject to community order of at least 12 months.[189]
(ii) Automatic inclusion in the children's barred list without representations where a child was caused to watch the sexual activity; with representations where an adult was caused to watch the sexual activity. Automatic inclusion in the adults' barred list without representations.[190]
(iii) SHPO applicable.[191]
(iv) Specified sexual offence in Schedule 18 (Extended Sentence).[192]

---

[185] Implementation date 27.8.1981.
[186] *Reed & Others* [2021] EWCA Crim 572.
[187] SOA 2003, s 41(3)(b).
[188] SOA 2003, s 41(3)(a), 12 months if CJA 2003, s 282(2) implemented.
[189] SOA 2003, s 80(1), Sch 3, para 28; see Chapter 14 paras 14.01–14.05.
[190] Part 2 of the Safeguarding Vulnerable Groups Act 2006 (Prescribed Criteria and Miscellaneous Provisions) Regulations 2009 (SI 2009 No 37), paras 1, 2, and 3; see Chapter 12 para 12.217.
[191] SA 2020, s 345, Sch 3, para 28; see Chapter 16 para 16.07.
[192] SA 2020, Sch 18, para 38(ah); see Chapter 12 para 12.51.

Offences Designed to Protect the Mentally Disordered from Procuration

I. OFFENCES COMMITTED PRE-31.12.1956

1. Procuring a Female to have Carnal Connection

Mental Deficiency Act 1913, s 56

Definition

Any person who '… 1(b) who procures, or attempts to procure any woman or girl who is a defective to have unlawful carnal connection whether within or without the King's dominions, with any person or persons'. **7.109**

Proof

As per Definition, in addition the prosecution must prove: **7.110**

(i) sexual intercourse (penile penetration of the vagina), without necessarily ejaculation;[193]
(ii) that the female was defective within the definition (see para 7.52);
(iii) that the defendant knew or had reason to suspect that the woman or girl was a defective.[194]

Notes

(i) The offence is triable only on indictment.[195] **7.111**
(ii) This offence may be an alternative to an offence of rape.[196]

---

[193] *R v Marsden* [1891] 2 QB 149; and later OAPA 1861, s 63.
[194] *R v Marsden* [1891] 2 QB 149; OAPA 1861, s 63, MDA 1913, s 56(1)(e).
[195] MDA 1913, s 56(4).
[196] MDA 1913, s 56(5).

7. OFFENCES INVOLVING THE MENTALLY DISORDERED

Sentence

7.112 On indictment: **2 YEARS**.[197]

7.113 *As of 1.1.1957, s 56 of the MDA 1913 is repealed. From 1.1.1957 s 9 of the SOA 1956 covers this offence.*

1.1.1957 to 30.4.2004

2. Procurement of a Defective

Sexual Offences Act 1956, s 9

Definition

7.114 (1) ... to procure a woman who is a defective to have unlawful sexual intercourse in any part of the world.

Proof

7.115 (i) Procuration is proved by showing that the defendant 'set about to see that it [unlawful sexual intercourse] happens, and takes the appropriate steps to produce it happening'.[198]
(ii) See para 7.58 for definition of mental defective.[199]
(iii) See para 7.66 for definition of sexual intercourse.[200]
(iv) The defendant is afforded a defence if he can prove that he did not know and had no reason to suspect that the female was defective.[201]

Notes

7.116 (i) Triable only on indictment.[202]
(ii) The offence may be committed by a male or female upon a female.

---

[197] MDA 1913, s 56(1)(e).
[198] *AG's Reference (No 1 of 1975)* [1975] QB 773, 61 Cr App R 118 CA.
[199] SOA 1956, s 45.
[200] SOA 1956, s 44.
[201] SOA 1956, s 9(2) and s 47.
[202] SOA 1956, s 37 and Sch 2, para 13.

I. OFFENCES COMMITTED PRE-31.12.1956   221

Indictment

2. Procurement of a Defective 1.1.1957 to 30.4.2004

Statement of Offence   7.117
PROCUREMENT OF A DEFECTIVE TO HAVE UNLAWFUL SEXUAL INTERCOURSE, contrary to section 9(1) of the Sexual Offences Act 1956.

Particulars of Offence
D on the … day of … procured C, a woman who is a defective, to have unlawful sexual intercourse.

Alternative Offences

Attempt to commit the full offence. When indicting offences of attempt do so under   7.118
common law until 26.8.1981, thereafter indict under s 1(1) Criminal Attempts Act 1981.[203] Aver the attempt in both the Statement of Offence and Particulars of Offence. In addition, aver the substantive offence under the relevant Act; see paras 1.51 and 12.157 and *Reed & Others* [2021].[204]

Sentence

(i) On indictment: 2 YEARS.[205]   7.119
(ii) An attempt carries the same maximum.[206]

Upon Conviction/Sentence

(i) Notification not applicable.[207]   7.120
(ii) Automatic inclusion in the children's and adults' barred lists with the right to make representations.[208]

---

[203] Implementation date 27.8.1981.
[204] *Reed & Others* [2021] EWCA Crim 572.
[205] SOA 1956, s 37 and Sch 2, para 13(a).
[206] SOA 1956, s 37 and Sch 2, para 13(b).
[207] SOA 2003, s 80(1) (not included in Sch 3); see Chapter 14 Tables 14.2–14.5.
[208] Part 2 of the Safeguarding Vulnerable Groups Act 2006 (Prescribed Criteria and Miscellaneous Provisions) Regulations 2009 (SI 2009 No 37) paras 2 and 4; see Chapter 12 para 12.217.

7. OFFENCES INVOLVING THE MENTALLY DISORDERED

(iii) SHPO not applicable.[209]

(iv) Specified sexual offence in Schedule 18 (Extended Sentence).[210]

J. OFFENCES COMMITTED FROM 1.5.2004 TO DATE

7.121 The SOA 2003, Schedule 7 repealed the SOA 1956, s 9(1) in full. A number of new offences in this area are created. These include procuring by inducement, threat, or deception sexual activity with a mentally disordered person,[211] causing a person with a mental disorder to engage in or agree to engage in sexual activity by inducement, threat, or deception,[212] engaging in sexual activity in the presence, procured by inducement, threat, or deception of a mentally disordered person[213] or causing a mentally disordered person to watch sexual activity by inducement, threat, or deception.[214]

1. Procuring by Inducement, Threat, or Deception Sexual Activity with a Mentally Disordered Person

Sexual Offences Act 2003, s 34

Definition

7.122 (1) A person (A) commits an offence if—

(a) with the agreement of another person (B) he intentionally touches that person,
(b) the touching is sexual,
(c) A obtains B's agreement by means of an inducement offered or given, a threat made or a deception practised by A for that purpose,
(d) B has a mental disorder, and
(e) A knows or could reasonably be expected to know that B has a mental disorder.

Proof

7.123 See Definition for elements of offence.

---

[209] SA 2020, s 345 (not included in Sch 3 or Sch 5 SOA 2003); see Chapter 16 para 16.07.
[210] SA 2020, Sch 18, para 29(h); see Chapter 12 para 12.51.
[211] SOA 2003, s 34.
[212] SOA 2003, s 35.
[213] SOA 2003, s 36.
[214] SOA 2003, s 37.

Notes

(i) If penetration is involved the offence is indictable only,[215] except penetration of A's anus or vagina with an object.[216] If penetration is not alleged then the offence is triable either way.[217] See para 7.25(iii) and (iv) for 'penetration' and references to 'parts of the body'.

(ii) Where the offence falls within subsection (2), then this ought to be alleged in the indictment.

(iii) For definitions of 'touching', 'sexual' and 'mental disorder' see para 7.24.

(iv) Section 73 provides a defence to an offence of aiding abetting or counselling the commission of an offence under this section against a person under 16, where he acts for the purpose of;

   (a) protecting the child from sexually transmitted infection,
   (b) protecting the physical safety of the child,
   (c) preventing the child from becoming pregnant, or
   (d) promoting the child's emotional well-being by the giving of advice,

   and not for the purpose of obtaining sexual gratification or for the purpose of causing or encouraging the activity constituting the offence or the child's participation in it.

(v) The extended jurisdiction provisions apply to this section where the victim of the offence was under 18.[218] See Chapter 17 para 17.01.

(vi) The s 45 MSA 2015 defence for slavery and trafficking victims who commit an offence does not apply to this offence.[219]

Indictment

INDUCEMENT, THREAT, OR DECEPTION TO PROCURE SEXUAL ACTIVITY WITH A PERSON WITH A MENTAL DISORDER 1.5.2004 to date   **7.125**

Statement of Offence

SEXUAL ACTIVITY WITH A PERSON WITH A MENTAL DISORDER WHOSE AGREEMENT THERTO IS PROCURED BY INDUCEMENT THREAT, OR DECEPTION, contrary to section 34(1) and (2) of the Sexual Offences Act 2003.

Particulars of Offence

D on the … day of 20…, intentionally touched C, a person with a mental disorder, by penetrating her mouth with his penis, in circumstances where the touching was sexual, where C agreed to the touching, where D had obtained her agreement by [giving her an inducement] *or* [making a threat] or [practising deception], (namely …) and where D knew or could reasonably have been expected to know that C had a mental disorder.

---

[215] SOA 2003, s 34(2).
[216] SOA 2003, s 34(2)(c).
[217] SOA 2003, s 34(3).
[218] SOA 2003, s 72; provides for the prosecution within the jurisdiction of a sexual offence committed outside it.
[219] Modern Slavery Act 2015, s 45 and Sch 4, para 33.

Alternative Offences

7.126 Attempt to commit the full offence. When indicting offences of attempt do so under s 1(1) Criminal Attempts Act 1981.[220] Aver the attempt in both the Statement of Offence and Particulars of Offence. In addition, aver the substantive offence under the relevant Act; see paras 1.51 and 12.157 and *Reed & Others* [2021].[221]

Sentence

7.127   (i) On indictment:
- If penetration is involved: **LIFE**.[222]
- If no penetration is involved: **14 YEARS**.[223]

   (ii) Summarily: **6 months**.[224]
   (iii) Attempt: the same.

7.128 The Sentencing Council 'Sexual Offences: Definitive Guideline' contains offence-specific guidelines for s 34 offences. The Guideline applies to all offenders aged 18 and over, sentenced on or after 1 April 2014.

Upon Conviction/Sentence

7.129   (i) Notification applicable.[225]
   (ii) Automatic inclusion in the children's barred list without representations where victim was a child; inclusion with representations where the victim was an adult. Automatic inclusion in the adults' barred list without representations.[226]
   (iii) SHPO applicable.[227]
   (iv) Specified sexual offence in Schedule 18 (Extended Sentence).[228]
   (v) Qualifying Schedule 19 offence (Life Sentences) where offender liable on conviction on indictment to life imprisonment.[229]
   (vi) Qualifying Schedule 14 offence (Extended Sentences: The Earlier Offence Condition) where offender liable on conviction on indictment to life imprisonment.[230]

---

[220] Implementation date 27.8.1981.
[221] *Reed & Others* [2021] EWCA Crim 572.
[222] SOA 2003, s 34(2).
[223] SOA 2003, s 34(3)(b).
[224] SOA 2003, s 34(3)(a). 12 months if CJA 2003, s 282(2) is implemented.
[225] SOA 2003, s 80(1) and Sch 3, para 27; see Chapter 14 paras 14.01–14.05.
[226] Part 2 of the Safeguarding Vulnerable Groups Act 2006 (Prescribed Criteria and Miscellaneous Provisions) Regulations 2009 (SI 2009 No 37), paras 1, 2, and 3; see Chapter 12 para 12.217.
[227] SA 2020, s 345 and Sch 3, para 27; see Chapter 16 para 16.07.
[228] SA 2020, Sch 18, para 38(aa); see Chapter 12 para 12.51.
[229] SA 2020, s 307, Sch 19, para 20(i); see Chapter 12 para 12.52.
[230] SA 2020, ss 267 and 280, Sch 14, para 9(r); see Chapter 12 para 12.77.

J. OFFENCES COMMITTED FROM 1.5.2004 TO DATE

(vii) Qualifying 'index' offence (if committed after 3 December 2012) for the purpose of Schedule 15 (Life Sentence for Second Listed Offence) where liable on conviction on indictment to imprisonment for life.[231]

2. Causing a Person with a Mental Disorder to Engage in Sexual Activity by Inducement, Threat, or Deception

Sexual Offences Act 2003, s 35

Definition

(1) A person (A) commits an offence if—   **7.130**
    (a) by means of an inducement offered or given, a threat made or a deception practised by him for this purpose, he intentionally causes another person (B) to engage in, or to agree to engage in, an activity,
    (b) the activity is sexual,
    (c) B has a mental disorder, and
    (d) A knows or could reasonably be expected to know that B has a mental disorder.

Proof

See Definition for elements of the offence.   **7.131**

Notes

(i) If the offence involves penetration then it is triable only on indictment.[232] If penetration is not alleged then the offence is triable either way.[233] See para 7.25(iii) and (iv) for 'penetration' and references to 'parts of the body'.   **7.132**
(ii) Where the offence falls within subsection (2), then this ought to be alleged in the indictment.
(iii) For definitions of 'sexual' and 'mental disorder' see para 7.24.
(iv) The extended jurisdiction provisions apply to this section where the victim of the offence was under 18.[234] See Chapter 17 para 17.01.
(v) The s 45 MSA 2015 defence for slavery and trafficking victims who commit an offence does not apply to this offence.[235]

---

[231] SA 2020, ss 273 and 283, Sch 15, para 9(r); see Chapter 12 para 12.123.
[232] SOA 2003, s 35(2).
[233] SOA 2003, s 35(3).
[234] SOA 2003, s 72; provides for the prosecution within the jurisdiction of a sexual offence committed outside it.
[235] Modern Slavery Act 2015, s 45 and Sch 4, para 33.

226   7. OFFENCES INVOLVING THE MENTALLY DISORDERED

Indictment

7.133 CAUSING A PERSON WITH A MENTAL DISORDER TO ENGAGE IN SEXUAL ACTIVITY 1.5.2004 to date

---

Statement of Offence
CAUSING A PERSON WITH A MENTAL DISORDER TO ENGAGE IN OR AGREE TO ENGAGE IN SEXUAL ACTIVITY BY INDUCEMENT, THREAT, OR DECEPTION, contrary to section 35(1) and (2) of the Sexual Offences Act 2003.

Particulars of Offence
D on the … day of 20 intentionally caused C to [engage in] *or* [agree to engage in] the penetration of D's mouth/anus/vagina with C's penis a sexual activity, where C [agreed to the activity] *or* [engaged in the activity] and D had obtained her agreement by [giving her an inducement] *or* [making a threat] *or* [practising a deception] (namely …) and where D knew or could reasonably have been expected to know that C had a mental disorder.

Alternative Offences

7.134 Attempt to commit the full offence. When indicting offences of attempt do so under s 1(1) Criminal Attempts Act 1981.[236] Aver the attempt in both the Statement of Offence and Particulars of Offence. In addition, aver the substantive offence under the relevant Act; see paras 1.51 and 12.157 and *Reed & Others* [2021].[237]

Sentence

7.135 (i) On indictment:
- If penetration is involved: **LIFE**.[238]
- If no penetration is involved: **14 YEARS**.[239]

(ii) Summarily: **6 months**.[240]

(iii) Attempt: the same.

7.136 The Sentencing Council 'Sexual Offences: Definitive Guideline' contains offence-specific guidelines for s 35 offences. The Guideline applies to all offenders aged 18 and over, sentenced on or after 1 April 2014.

---

[236] Implementation date 27.8.1981.
[237] *Reed & Others* [2021] EWCA Crim 572.
[238] SOA 2003, s 35(2).
[239] SOA 2003, s 35(3)(b).
[240] SOA 2003, s 35(3)(a). 12 months if CJA 2003, s 282(2) implemented.

Upon Conviction/Sentence

(i) Notification applicable.[241]

(ii) Automatic inclusion in the children's barred list without representations where person induced, threatened or deceived was a child; inclusion with representations where person induced, threatened or deceived was an adult. Automatic inclusion in the adults' barred list without representations.[242]

(iii) SHPO applicable.[243]

(iv) Specified sexual offence in Schedule 18 (Extended Sentence).[244]

(v) Qualifying Schedule 19 offence (Life Sentences) where offender liable on conviction on indictment to life imprisonment.[245]

(vi) Qualifying Schedule 14 offence (Extended Sentences: The Earlier Offence Condition) where offender liable on conviction on indictment to life imprisonment.[246]

(vi) Qualifying 'index' offence (if committed after 3 December 2012) for the purpose of Schedule 15 (Life Sentence for Second Listed Offence) where liable on conviction on indictment to imprisonment for life.[247]

7.137

3. Engaging in Sexual Activity in the Presence, Procured by Inducement, Threat, or Deception, of a Person with a Mental Disorder

Sexual Offences Act 2003, s 36

Definition

(1) A person (A) commits an offence if—

(a) he intentionally engages in an activity,

(b) the activity is sexual,

(c) for the purpose of obtaining sexual gratification, he engages in it—

   (i) when another person (B) is present or is in a place from which A can be observed, and

   (ii) knowing or believing that B is aware, or intending that B should be aware, that he is engaging in it,

(d) B agrees to be present or in the place referred to in paragraph (c)(i) because of an inducement offered or given, a threat made or a deception practised by A for the purpose of obtaining that agreement,

7.138

---

[241] SOA 2003, s 80(1) and Sch 3, para 27; see Chapter 14 paras 14.01–14.05.
[242] Part 2 of the Safeguarding Vulnerable Groups Act 2006 (Prescribed Criteria and Miscellaneous Provisions) Regulations 2009 (SI 2009 No 37), paras 1, 2, and 3; see Chapter 12 para 12.217.
[243] SA 2020, s 345 and Sch 3, para 27; see Chapter 16 para 16.07.
[244] SA 2020, s 306, Sch 18, para 38(ab); see Chapter 12 para 12.51.
[245] SA 2020, s 307, Sch 19, para 20(j); see Chapter 12 para 12.52.
[246] SA 2020, ss 267 and 280, Sch 14, para 9(s); see Chapter 12 para 12.77.
[247] SA 2020, ss 273 and 283, Sch 15, para 9(s); see Chapter 12 para 12.123.

(e) B has a mental disorder, and
(f) A knows or could reasonably be expected to know that B has a mental disorder.

Proof

7.139 See Definition for elements of offence.

Notes

7.140
(i) This offence is triable either way.[248]
(ii) For definitions of 'sexual' and 'mental disorder' see para 7.24.
(iii) References to observation (however expressed) are to observation whether direct or by looking at an image.[249]
(iv) The extended jurisdiction provisions apply to this section where the victim of the offence was under 18.[250] See Chapter 17 para 17.01.
(v) The s 45 MSA 2015 defence for slavery and trafficking victims who commit an offence does not apply to this offence.[251]

Indictment

7.141 ENGAGING IN SEXUAL ACTIVITY IN THE PRESENCE, PROCURED BY INDUCEMENT, THREAT, OR DECEPTION, OF A PERSON WITH A MENTAL DISORDER 1.5.2004 to date

---

Statement of Offence
ENGAGING IN SEXUAL ACTIVITY IN THE PRESENCE, PROCURED BY INDUCEMENT, THREAT, OR DECEPTION, OF A PERSON WITH A MENTAL DISORDER, contrary to section 36(1) of the Sexual Offences Act 2003.

Particulars of Offence
D on the … day of 20… , for the purpose of obtaining sexual gratification, intentionally engaged in an activity and that activity was sexual, [when C was present] or [in a place from which D could be observed], [knowing or believing that C was aware] *or* [intending that C be aware] that he is engaging in it, and D had obtained C's agreement by [giving her an inducement] *or* [making a threat] *or* [a deception practised by D] for the purpose of obtaining that agreement, and where D knew or could reasonably have been expected to know that C had a mental disorder.

---

[248] SOA 2003, s 36(2).
[249] SOA 2003, s 79(7).
[250] SOA 2003, s 72; provides for the prosecution within the jurisdiction of a sexual offence committed outside it.
[251] Modern Slavery Act 2015, s 45 and Sch 4, para 33.

Alternative Offences

Attempt to commit the full offence. When indicting offences of attempt do so under s 1(1) Criminal Attempts Act 1981.[252] Aver the attempt in both the Statement of Offence and Particulars of Offence. In addition, aver the substantive offence under the relevant Act; see paras 1.51 and 12.157 and *Reed & Others* [2021].[253]

7.142

Sentence

(i) On indictment: **10 YEARS**.[254]
(ii) Summarily: **6 months**.[255]
(iii) Attempt: the same.

7.143

Upon Conviction/Sentence

(i) Notification applicable.[256]
(ii) Automatic inclusion in the children's barred list without representations where the person present or observing was a child; inclusion with representations where the person present or observing was an adult. Automatic inclusion in the adults' barred list without representations.[257]
(iii) SHPO applicable.[258]
(iv) Specified sexual offence in Schedule 18 (Extended Sentence).[259]

7.144

4. Causing a Person with a Mental Disorder to Watch a Sexual Act by Inducement, Threat, or Deception

Sexual Offences Act 2003, s 37

Definition

(1) A person (A) commits an offence if—
  (a) for the purpose of obtaining sexual gratification, he intentionally causes another person (B) to watch a third person engaging in an activity, or to look at an image of any person engaging in an activity,

7.145

---

[252] Implementation date 27.8.1981.
[253] *Reed & Others* [2021] EWCA Crim 572.
[254] SOA 2003, s 36(2)(b).
[255] SOA 2003, s 36(2)(a). 12 months if CJA 2003, s 282(2) implemented.
[256] SOA 2003, s 80(1) and Sch 3, para 27; see Chapter 14 paras 14.01–14.05.
[257] Part 2 of the Safeguarding Vulnerable Groups Act 2006 (Prescribed Criteria and Miscellaneous Provisions) Regulations 2009 (SI 2009 No 37), paras 1, 2, and 3; see Chapter 12 para 12.217.
[258] SA 2020, s 345 and Sch 3, para 27; see Chapter 16 para 16.07.
[259] SA 2020, s 306, Sch 18, para 38(ac); see Chapter 12 para 12.51.

230   7. OFFENCES INVOLVING THE MENTALLY DISORDERED

    (b) the activity is sexual,
    (c) B agrees to watch or look because of an inducement offered or given, a threat made or a deception practised by A for the purpose of obtaining that agreement,
    (d) B has a mental disorder, and
    (e) A knows or could reasonably be expected to know that B has a mental disorder.

Proof

7.146 See Definition for elements of offence.

Notes

7.147
(i) This offence is triable either way.[260]
(ii) For definitions of 'sexual' and 'mental disorder' see para 7.24.
(iii) 'Image' means a moving or still image and includes an image produced by any means and, where the context permits, a three-dimensional image.[261] References to an image of a person include references to an image of an imaginary person.[262]
(iv) The extended jurisdiction provisions apply to this section where the victim of the offence was under 18.[263] See Chapter 17 para 17.01.
(v) The s 45 MSA 2015 defence for slavery and trafficking victims who commit an offence does not apply to this offence.[264]

Indictment

7.148 CAUSING A PERSON WITH A MENTAL DISORDER TO WATCH A SEXUAL ACT BY INDUCEMENT, THREAT, OR DECEPTION 1.5.2004 to date

Statement of Offence
CAUSING A PERSON WITH A MENTAL DISORDER TO WATCH A SEXUAL ACT BY INDUCEMENT, THREAT, OR DECEPTION, contrary to section 37(1) of the Sexual Offences Act 2003.

---

[260] SOA 2003, s 37(2).
[261] SOA 2003, s 79(4).
[262] SOA 2003, s 79(5).
[263] SOA 2003, s 72; provides for the prosecution within the jurisdiction of a sexual offence committed outside it.
[264] Modern Slavery Act 2015, s 45 and Sch 4, para 33.

J. OFFENCES COMMITTED FROM 1.5.2004 TO DATE

> **Particulars of Offence**
>
> D on the ... day of 20..., for the purpose of sexual gratification, intentionally caused C, a person with a mental disorder, [to watch X engaging in a sexual activity] *or* [to look at an image of any person engaging in sexual activity], and D had obtained C's agreement by [giving her an inducement] *or* [making a threat] *or* [a deception practised by D] for the purpose of obtaining that agreement, and where D knew or could reasonably have been expected to know that C had a mental disorder.

Alternative Offences

7.149 Attempt to commit the full offence. When indicting offences of attempt do so under s 1(1) Criminal Attempts Act 1981.[265] Aver the attempt in both the Statement of Offence and Particulars of Offence. In addition, aver the substantive offence under the relevant Act; see paras 1.51 and 12.157 and *Reed & Others* [2021].[266]

Sentence

7.150
(i) On indictment: **10 YEARS**.[267]
(ii) Summarily: **6 months**.[268]
(iii) Attempt: the same.

Upon Conviction/Sentence

7.151
(i) Notification applicable.[269]
(ii) Automatic inclusion in the children's barred list without representations where the person induced, threatened or deceived was a child; inclusion with representations where the person induced, threatened or deceived was an adult. Automatic inclusion in the adults' barred list without representations.[270]
(iii) SHPO applicable.[271]
(iv) Specified sexual offence in Schedule 18 (Extended Sentences).[272]

---

[265] Implementation date 27.8.1981.
[266] *Reed & Others* [2021] EWCA Crim 572
[267] SOA 2003, s 37(2)(b).
[268] SOA 2003, s 37(2)(a). 12 months if CJA 2003, s 282(2) is implemented.
[269] SOA 2003, s 80(1) and Sch 3, para 27; see Chapter 14 paras 14.01–14.05.
[270] Part 2 of the Safeguarding Vulnerable Groups Act 2006 (Prescribed Criteria and Miscellaneous Provisions) Regulations 2009 (SI 2009 No 37), paras 1, 2, and 3; see Chapter 12 para 12.217.
[271] SA 2020, s 345 and Sch 3, para 27; see Chapter 16 para 16.07.
[272] SA 2020, s 306, Sch 18, para 38(ad); see Chapter 12 para 12.51.

Offences Protecting the Mentally Disordered from Prostitution or Abuse Upon Premises

K. OFFENCES COMMITTED PRE-1.1.1957

7.152 Section 56(1) of the Mental Deficiency Act 1913 created two offences.

  (i) Section 56(1)(c): causing or encouraging prostitution of a defective.
  (ii) Section 56(1)(d): being the owner/occupier of premises used for sexual activity with a defective.

1. Causing or Encouraging Prostitution of a Defective

Mental Deficiency Act 1913, s 56(1)(c)

Definition

7.153 Any person who '… causes or encourages prostitution whether within or without the King's dominions of any woman or girl who is defective'.

Proof

7.154
  (i) As per Definition.
  (ii) See para 7.52 for definition of defective.
  (iii) The prosecution must prove that he did not know or have reason to suspect that the woman or girl was a defective.[273]

Notes

7.155
  (i) The offence is triable only on indictment.[274]
  (ii) This offence may be an alternative to an offence of rape.[275]

---

[273] MDA 1913, s 56(1)(e).
[274] MDA 1913, s 56(4).
[275] MDA 1913, s 56(5).

K. OFFENCES COMMITTED PRE-1.1.1957

Sentence

(i) On indictment: **2 YEARS**.[276]
(ii) Attempt: the same.

7.156

2. Permitting Premises to be Used for Sexual Intercourse with a Female Defective

Mental Deficiency Act 1913, s 56(1)(d)

Definition

Any person '… being the owner or occupier of any premises, or having or acting or assisting in the management or control thereof, induces or knowingly suffers any woman or girl who is a defective to resort to or be in or upon such premises for the purpose of being unlawfully and carnally known by any man whether such carnal knowledge is intended to be with any particular man or generally'.

7.157

Proof

As per Definition. Of note is:

7.158

(i) Carnal knowledge is defined as penile penetration of the vagina, without necessarily ejaculation.[277]
(ii) The prosecution must prove that the defendant knew or had reason to suspect that the woman or girl was a defective.[278]

Notes

(i) The offence is triable only on indictment.[279]
(ii) This offence may be an alternative to an offence of rape.[280]

7.159

Sentence

On indictment: **2 YEARS**.[281]

7.160

---

[276] MDA 1913, s 56(1)(e).
[277] *R v Marsden* (1891) 2 QB 149; and later OAPA 1861, s 63.
[278] MDA 1913, s 56(1)(e).
[279] MDA 1913, s 56(4).
[280] MDA 1913, s 56(5).
[281] MDA 1913, s 56(1(e).

L. OFFENCES COMMITTED BETWEEN 1.1.1957 TO 30.4.2004

7.161 As of 1.1.1957 the MDA 1913, s 56 was repealed. Two offences were created.

7.162 The SOA 1956, s 29 covers the offence of causing or encouraging the prostitution of any woman or girl who is a defective.

7.163 The SOA 1956, s 27 covers the offence of permitting a defective to use premises for intercourse.

1. Causing or Encouraging the Prostitution of any Woman or Girl who is a Defective

Sexual Offences Act 1956, s 29

Definition

7.164 ... to cause or encourage the prostitution in any part of the world of any woman or girl who is a defective.

Proof

7.165
(i) As per Definition.
(ii) See para 7.58 for definition of mental defective.
(iii) It is a defence for the defendant to prove that he did not know and had no reason to suspect the female to be a defective.[282]

Notes

7.166 This offence is triable only on indictment.[283]

Indictment

7.167 CAUSING/ENCOURAGING PROSTITUTION OF A DEFECTIVE 1.1.1957 to 30.4.2004

---

[282] SOA 1956, s 29(2).
[283] SOA 1956, s 37 and Sch 2, para 39.

L. OFFENCES COMMITTED BETWEEN 1.1.1957 TO 30.4.2004

> **Statement of Offence**
>
> CAUSING/ENCOURAGING PROSTITUTION OF A DEFECTIVE, contrary to section 29 of the Sexual Offences Act 1956.
>
> **Particulars of Offence**
>
> D on the … day of … caused/encouraged the prostitution of C, a woman who is a defective.

Sentence

(i) On indictment: 2 YEARS.
(ii) Attempt: the same.

7.168

Upon Conviction/Sentence.[284]

(i) Notification not applicable.[285]
(ii) Automatic inclusion in the children's and adults' barred lists with the right to make representations.[286]
(iii) SHPO not applicable.[287]
(iv) Specified sexual offence in Schedule 18 (Extended Sentence).[288]

7.169

2. Permitting a Defective to Use Premises for Intercourse

Sexual Offences Act 1956, s 27

Definition

… a person who is the owner or occupier of any premises, or who has or acts or assists in the management or control of any premises, to induce or knowingly suffer a woman who is a defective to resort to or be on those premises for the purpose of having unlawful sexual intercourse with men or with a particular man.

7.170

Proof

(i) See Definition.

7.171

---

[284] SOA 1956, s 37 and Sch, para 29.
[285] SOA 2003 (not in Sch 3), s 80(1); see Chapter 14 Tables 14.2–14.5.
[286] Part 2 of the Safeguarding Vulnerable Groups Act 2006 (Prescribed Criteria and Miscellaneous Provisions) Regulations 2009 (SI 2009 No 37) paras 2 and 4; see Chapter 12 para 12.217.
[287] SA 2020, s 345 (not in Sch 3 or Sch 5 SOA 2003); see Chapter 16 para 16.07.
[288] SA 2020, s 306, Sch 18, para 29(x); see Chapter 12 para 12.51.

7. OFFENCES INVOLVING THE MENTALLY DISORDERED

(ii) See para 7.58 for definition of mental defective.

(iii) It is a defence for the defendant to prove that he did not know nor had reason to suspect her to be defective.[289]

Notes

7.172 The offence is triable only on indictment.[290]

Indictment

7.173 PERMITTING A DEFECTIVE TO USE PREMISES FOR INTERCOURSE 1.1.1957 to 30.4.2004

Statement of Offence
PERMITTING A DEFECTIVE TO USE PREMISES FOR INTERCOURSE, contrary to section 27 of the Sexual Offences Act 1956.

Particulars of Offence
D, being an [owner/occupier of any premises] *or* [a person who acts/assists in the management/control of premises] namely … , on the … day of … , induced/knowingly suffered C, a woman who is a defective, to resort to/to be on those premises for the purpose of having unlawful sexual intercourse with men/a man.

Sentence

7.174 On indictment: **2 YEARS**.[291]

Upon Conviction/Sentence

7.175 (i) Notification not applicable.[292]

(ii) Automatic inclusion in the children's and adults' barred lists with the right to make representations.[293]

---

[289] SOA 1956, s 27(2) and s 47.
[290] SOA 1956, s 37 and Sch 2, para 27.
[291] SOA 1956, s 37 and Sch 2, para 27.
[292] SOA 2003 (not in Sch 3), s 80(1); see Chapter 14 Tables 14.2-14.5.
[293] Part 2 of the Safeguarding Vulnerable Groups Act 2006 (Prescribed Criteria and Miscellaneous Provisions) Regulations 2009 (SI 2009 No 37) paras 2 and 4; see Chapter 12 para 12.217.

(iii) SHPO not applicable.[294]
(iv) Specified sexual offence in Schedule 18 (Extended Sentence).[295]

M. OFFENCES COMMITTED FROM 1.5.2004 TO DATE

The SOA 2003 repealed the SOA 1956, ss 27 and 29. Section 52 covers the offence of causing or inciting prostitution for gain. Section 53 covers the offence of controlling prostitution for gain. In each case there is no requirement that the prostitution involved is that of a mentally disordered person.   7.176

1. Causing or Inciting Prostitution for Gain

Sexual Offences Act 2003, s 52

Definition

Any person who   7.177

(a) ... intentionally causes or incites another person to become a prostitute in any part of the world, and
(b) he does so for or in the expectation of gain for himself or a third person.

Proof

(i) As per Definition.   7.178
(ii) For proof of causing see para 8.37.
(iii) For proof of inciting see para 8.37.
(iv) 'gain' includes any financial advantage, including the discharge of an obligation to pay or the provision of goods or services (including sexual services) gratuitously or at a discount; or the goodwill of any person which is or appears likely, in time, to bring financial advantage.[296]
(v) Prostitution covers the offer of sexual services to another in return for payment or promise of payment.[297]

---

[294] SA 2020, s 345 (not in Sch 3 or Sch 5 SOA 2003); see Chapter 16 para 16.07.
[295] SA 2020, s 306, Sch 18, para 29(v); see Chapter 12 para 12.51.
[296] SOA 2003, s 54(1).
[297] SOA 2003, ss 51(2) and 54(2).

238   7. OFFENCES INVOLVING THE MENTALLY DISORDERED

Notes

7.179   (i) This offence is triable either way.[298]

(ii) The s 45 MSA 2015 defence for slavery and trafficking victims who commit an offence is available for an offence under this section, provided it was committed on or after 31.7.2015.[299]

Indictment

7.180   CAUSING OR INCITING PROSTITUTION FOR GAIN 1.5.2004 to date

---

Statement of Offence
CAUSING OR INCITING PROSTITUTION FOR GAIN, contrary to section 52(1) of the Sexual Offences Act 2003.

Particulars of Offence
D on the … of 20… , intentionally caused/incited C to become a prostitute and did so for or in the expectation of gain for himself or of a third person.

Alternative Offences

7.181   Attempt to commit the full offence. When indicting offences of attempt do so under s 1(1) Criminal Attempts Act 1981.[300] Aver the attempt in both the Statement of Offence and Particulars of Offence. In addition, aver the substantive offence under the relevant Act; see paras 1.51 and 12.157 and *Reed & Others* [2021].[301]

Sentence

7.182   (i) On indictment: **7 YEARS**.[302]

(ii) Summarily: **6 months**.[303]

(iii) Attempt: the same.

7.183   The Sentencing Council 'Sexual Offences: Definitive Guideline' contains offence-specific guidelines for s 52 offences. The Guideline applies to all offenders aged 18 and over, sentenced on or after 1 April 2014.

---

[298] SOA 2003, s 52(2).
[299] Modern Slavery Act 2015, s 45 commencement date 31.7.2015 (SI 2015/1476). This offence is not an excluded offence in Sch 4 of the Act. The s 45 defence is not retrospective, see *R v Joseph (Verna Sermanfure)* [2017] EWCA Crim 36.
[300] Implementation date 27.8.1981.
[301] *Reed & Others* [2021] EWCA Crim 572.
[302] SOA 2003, s 5(2)(b).
[303] SOA 2003, s 52(2)(a). 12 months if CJA 2003, s 282(2) is implemented.

Upon Conviction/Sentence

(i) Notification not applicable.[304] 7.184
(ii) Automatic inclusion in the children's and adults' barred lists with the right to make representations.[305]
(iii) SHPO applicable.[306]
(iv) Qualifying 'specified sexual offence' in Schedule 18 (Extended Sentences).[307]
(v) Lifestyle offence for purposes of POCA 2002.[308]
(vi) Serious Crime Prevention Order applicable for offences convicted after 6 April 2008.[309]

2. Controlling Prostitution for Gain

Sexual Offences Act 2003, s 53(1)

Definition

Any person who 7.185

(a) ... intentionally controls any of the activities of another person relating to that person's prostitution in any part of the world, and
(b) he does so for or in the expectation of gain for himself or a third person.

Proof

As per definition. Further: 7.186

(i) Control may cover such activities as the price charged, venue, diary, travel, bookings—even through a third party. See para 7.176(ii).
(ii) Prostitution covers the offer of sexual services to another in return for payment or promise of payment.[310]
(iii) 'Gain' includes any financial advantage, including the discharge of an obligation to pay or the provision of goods or services (including sexual services) gratuitously or at a discount; or goodwill likely to bring financial advantage.[311]

---

[304] SOA 2003, s 80(1) (not listed in Sch 3); see Chapter 14 Tables 14.2–14.5.
[305] Part 2 of the Safeguarding Vulnerable Groups Act 2006 (Prescribed Criteria and Miscellaneous Provisions) Regulations 2009 (SI 2009 No 37) paras 2 and 4; see Chapter 12 para 12.217.
[306] SA 2020, s 345 and Sch 5, para 63 SOA 2003; see Chapter 16 para 16.07.
[307] SA 2020, s 306, Sch 18, para 38(am); see Chapter 12 para 12.51.
[308] POCA 2002, Sch 2.
[309] SCA 2007, s 19 and Sch 1, para 4; see Chapter 12 para 12.240.
[310] SOA 2003, ss 51(2) and 54(2).
[311] SOA 2003, s 54(1).

240   7. OFFENCES INVOLVING THE MENTALLY DISORDERED

Notes

7.187   (i) This offence is triable either way.
(ii) Control is to be given its ordinary English usage and covers instructing or directing a person to carry out the relevant activity or to do it in a certain way. The person may agree for a variety of reasons including even the simple hope of a better life. It does not require force or coercion.[312]
(iii) Article 26 of the Council of Europe Convention on Action against Human Trafficking 2005 (ECAT) requires careful consideration be given to whether public policy calls for a prosecution and punishment of victims of trafficking who have been compelled to become involved in unlawful activities.[313] Following the ratification of ECAT the National Referral Mechanism was established. The National Referral Mechanism (NRM) is the framework for identifying victims of human trafficking and ensuring they receive the appropriate protection and support.
(iv) The s 45 MSA 2015 defence for slavery and trafficking victims who commit an offence is available for an offence under this section, provided it was committed on or after 31.7.2015.[314]

Indictment

7.188   CONTROLLING PROSTITUTION FOR GAIN 1.5.2004 to date

Statement of Offence

CONTROLLING PROSTITUTION FOR GAIN, contrary to section 53(1) of the Sexual Offences Act 2003.

Particulars of Offence

D on the ... day of ... intentionally controlled C's activities in relation to C's prostitution, in the expectation of gain for himself or a third person.

Alternative Offences

7.189   Attempt to commit the full offence, charge under s 1(1) of the CAA 1981. Aver the attempt in the Statement and Particulars of Offence.

---

[312] *Massey* [2007] EWCA Crim 2664.
[313] *R v LM* [2010] EWCA Crim 2327.
[314] Modern Slavery Act 2015, s 45 commencement date 31.7.2015 (SI 2015/1476). This offence is not an excluded offence in Sch 4 of the Act. The s 45 defence is not retrospective, see *R v Joseph (Verna Sermanfure)* [2017] EWCA Crim 36.

Sentence

(i) On indictment: **7 YEARS**.[315] 7.190
(ii) Summarily: **6 months**.[316]
(iii) Attempt: the same.

The Sentencing Council 'Sexual Offences: Definitive Guideline' contains offence-specific 7.191
guidelines for s 53 offences. The Guideline applies to all offenders aged 18 and over, sentenced on or after 1 April 2014.

Upon Conviction/sentence

(i) Notification not applicable.[317] 7.192
(ii) Automatic inclusion in the children's and adults' barred lists with the right to make representations.[318]
(iii) SHPO applicable.[319]
(iv) Qualifying 'specified sexual offence' in Schedule 18 (Extended Sentences).[320]
(v) Lifestyle offence for purposes of POCA 2002.[321]
(vi) Serious Crime Prevention Order applicable for offences convicted after 6 April 2008.[322]

---

[315] SOA 2003, s 53(2)(b).
[316] SOA 2003, s 53(2)(a). 12 months if CJA 2003, s 282(2) implemented.
[317] SOA 2003, s 80(1) (not listed in Sch 3); see Chapter 14 Tables 14.2–14.5.
[318] Part 2 of the Safeguarding Vulnerable Groups Act 2006 (Prescribed Criteria and Miscellaneous Provisions) Regulations 2009 (SI 2009 No 37) paras 2 and 4; see Chapter 12 para 12.217.
[319] SA 2020, s 345 and Sch 5, para 63 SOA 2003); see Chapter 16 para 16.07.
[320] SA 2020, s 306, Sch 18, para 38(an); see Chapter 12 para 12.51.
[321] POCA 2002, Sch 2.
[322] SCA 2007, s 19 and Sch 1, para 4; see Chapter 12 para 12.240.

8
PROSTITUTION AND TRAFFICKING

A.	Introduction	8.01	G. Offences Committed between	
	Causing or Encouraging Prostitution		1.1.1957 and 30.4.2004	8.94
	of Young Women or Girls	8.07	1. Man Living on Earnings of Prostitution	8.96
B.	Offences Committed		2. Women Exercising Control over	
	pre-31.12.1956	8.07	Prostitute	8.104
	1. Procuration of Women under 21 into		3. Detention of a Woman in a Brothel or	
	Prostitution	8.07	other Premises	8.110
C.	Offences Committed between		4. Soliciting by Men for Immoral Purposes	8.117
	1.1.1957 and 30.4.2004	8.13	H. Offences Committed between	
	1. Causing or Encouraging Prostitution		27.7.1967 and 30.4.2004	8.124
	of a Girl under 16	8.14	1. Living on the Earnings of Male	
	2. Procuring a Girl under 21 to have		Prostitution	8.124
	Unlawful Sexual Intercourse	8.21	I. Offences Committed from	
D.	Offences Committed from		1.5.2004 to Date	8.131
	1.5.2004 to Date	8.28	1. Keeping a Brothel Used for Prostitution	8.131
	1. Paying for Sexual Services of a Child	8.29	2. Controlling Prostitution for Gain	8.138
	2. Causing or Inciting Child Prostitution		**Trafficking for Sexual Exploitation**	8.145
	or Inciting Child Pornography	8.37	J. Offences Committed between	
	3. Controlling a Child Prostitute or		1.1.1957 and 30.4.2004	8.146
	a Child Involved in Pornography	8.51	K. Offences Committed from	
	4. Arranging or Facilitating Child		1.5.2004 to 5.4.2013	8.149
	Prostitution or Pornography	8.64	1. Trafficking into the UK for Sexual	
Procuring Prostitution of Women		8.78	Exploitation	8.150
E.	Offences Committed between		2. Trafficking within the UK for Sexual	
	1.1.1957 and 30.4.2004	8.78	Exploitation	8.157
	1. Causing Prostitution of Women	8.79	3. Trafficking out of the UK for Sexual	
F.	Offences Committed from		Exploitation	8.164
	1.5.2004 to Date	8.87	4. Trafficking People for Sexual	
	1. Causing or Inciting Prostitution		Exploitation	8.172
	for Gain	8.87	5. Human Trafficking	8.181
Living on the Earnings of Prostitution		8.94	**Paying for the Sexual Services of a**	
			Prostitute Subjected to Force etc	8.190

A. INTRODUCTION

Before the SOA 1956 was passed, several offences relating to prostitution and trading in prostitution existed, in particular under the Vagrancy Act 1898.[1] Taking into account the rarity of these pre-1.1.1957 offences being prosecuted, only one, procuration of women under 21 into prostitution, has been included.[2]

8.01

---

[1] Vagrancy Act (VA) 1898, s 1: living off the earnings of prostitution. Commencement date 12.10.1898.
[2] CLAA 1885, s 2.

8.02 After 1.1.1957 a great number of offences were created to deal with prostitution and the exploitation of prostitutes.

8.03 Until the passing of the SOA 2003 there were few statutory offences dealing with the exploitation of male prostitutes. Such offences as did exist dealt primarily with adult males/females living off the earnings of male prostitution[3] (except the offence of Solicitation by Men, contrary to the SOA 1956, s 32; see paras 8.96–8.102).

8.04 It was only after 1.5.2004 that the offences of procuring or causing prostitution of males were made offences.[4] Further, summary only offences of kerb crawling and soliciting were extended to cover male and female prostitutes.[5]

8.05 See paras 7.143–7165 for the following offences involving prostitution and the mentally disordered:

> Causing or encouraging prostitution of a defective
> Permitting premises to be used for sexual intercourse with a female defective
> Causing or encouraging the prostitution of any women or girl who is defective
> Permitting premises to be used for sexual intercourse with a female defective

8.06 These offences have been dealt with chronologically, in their categories:

A. Causing or encouraging prostitution of young women
B. Causing prostitution of women
C. Living on the earnings of prostitution
D. Trafficking of prostitutes

Causing or Encouraging Prostitution of Young Women or Girls

B. OFFENCES COMMITTED PRE-31.12.1956

1. Procuration of Women under 21 into Prostitution

Criminal Law Amendment Act 1885, s 2

Definition

8.07 Procures or attempts to procure any girl or woman under 21 years of age to have unlawful carnal connection, either within or without the Queen's dominions with any other person or persons; or

---

[3] SOA 1967, s 5.
[4] SOA 2003, ss 52 and 53.
[5] SOA 2003, s 56 and Sch 1.

(1) Procures or attempts to procure any woman or girl to become, either within or without the Queen's dominions, a common prostitute; or
(2) Procures or attempts to procure any woman or girl to leave the United Kingdom with intent that she may become an inmate of a brothel elsewhere; or
(3) Procures or attempts to procure any woman or girl to leave her usual place of abode in the United Kingdom (such place not being a brothel) with intent that she may, for the purposes of prostitution, become an inmate of or frequent a brothel within or without the Queen's dominions.

Proof

As per Definition. 8.08

In addition:

(i) 'common prostitute' covers the offer by a woman of her body for acts of 'lewdness' for payment in return.[6] The female has to be prepared to make such an offer to 'all and sundry' for any one who might hire her for that purpose, not just on one occasion.[7]

Notes

Triable on indictment only. 8.09

Indictment

PROCURING A WOMAN UNDER 21 TO BECOME A COMMON PROSTITUTE 8.10
Pre-31.12.1956

Statement of Offence
PROCURING A WOMAN TO BECOME A COMMON PROSTITUTE, contrary to section 2(1) of the Criminal Law Amendment Act 1885.

Particulars of Offence
D on the … day of … procured C, a woman, not being a common prostitute, aged under 21 years, to become a common prostitute.

---

[6] *R v De Munck* 13 Cr App R 113 CCA, [1918–19] All ER Rep 499.
[7] *R v Morris-Lowe* [1985] 1 All ER 400.

Alternative Offences

8.11 An attempt to commit the full offence. When indicting offences of attempt do so under common law. Aver the attempt in both the Statement of Offence and Particulars of Offence. In addition, aver the substantive offence under the relevant Act; see paras 1.51 and 12.157 and *Reed & Others* [2021].[8]

Sentence

8.12 On indictment: 2 YEARS.

C. OFFENCES COMMITTED BETWEEN 1.1.1957 AND 30.4.2004

8.13 From 1.1.1957 the CLAA 1898, s 2 is repealed. Sections 28 (procuration of a girl under 16) and 23 (procuration of a girl under 21) of the SOA 1956 cover the offence previously covered by s 2 of the CLAA 1898. Other offences were created, including; causing prostitution,[9] detention of a woman in a brothel,[10] man living off the earnings of prostitution,[11] woman exercising control over a prostitute[12] and brothel keeping.[13]

1. Causing or Encouraging Prostitution of a Girl under 16

Sexual Offences Act 1956, s 28(1)

Definition

8.14 (1) To cause or encourage the prostitution of, or the commission of unlawful sexual intercourse with, or of an indecent assault on, a girl under the age of 16 for whom he is responsible.

(2) Where a girl has become a prostitute, or has had unlawful sexual intercourse, or has been indecently assaulted, a person shall be deemed to have caused or encouraged it, if he knowingly allowed her to consort with, or to enter or to continue in the employment of, any prostitute or person of known immoral character.

---

[8] *Reed & Others* [2021] EWCA Crim 572.
[9] SOA 1956, s 22. See paras 8.57–8.65.
[10] SOA 1956, s 24. See paras 8.89–8.95.
[11] SOA 1956, s 30. See paras 8.75–8.82.
[12] SOA 1956, s 31. See paras 8.83–8.88.
[13] SOA 1956, s 33–36.

Proof

As per Definition. In addition: 8.15

(i) It is sufficient for proof of causing/encouraging, to prove that the defendant does nothing to prevent the act when he is in a position to do so.[14]
(ii) Proof of those defined as responsible; this includes: a parent, legal guardian, any person with 'possession or control' of her (this was later amended to parental responsibility for)[15] or any person who has care for her.[16] A babysitter has been held to fall into this category.[17]
(iii) The definition of prostitute covers the offer of her body for lewdness for payment.[18] This includes passive acts of sexual activity; no physical contact is necessary, where the woman offers herself as a participant in physical acts of indecency for the sexual gratification of men.[19]
(iv) For unlawful sexual intercourse see para 7.12; for indecent assault see para 3.12.
(v) If the girl appears to have been under the age of 16 at the time, she is presumed to have been so, unless the contrary is proved.[20]

Notes

(i) Triable on indictment only. 8.16
(ii) Both males and females can commit this offence. The complainant must be female and under 16.[21]

Indictment

CAUSING OR ENCOURAGING PROSTITUTION OF A GIRL UNDER 16 1.1.1957 to 30.4.2004 8.17

Statement of Offence
CAUSING/ENCOURAGING PROSTITUTION OF A GIRL UNDER THE AGE OF 16, contrary to section 28(1) of the Sexual Offences Act 1956.

---

[14] *Ralphs* (1913) 9 Cr App Rep 86 CCA.
[15] Children Act (CA) 1989, s 108(4) and Sch 12, para 14 (commencement date 16.11.1989). The parent is not to be treated as responsible if any residence order under the CA 1989 does not name him or her as the person with whom the child is to live, or if there is a care order in existence.
[16] SOA 1956, s 28(3).
[17] *R v Drury* (1975) 60 Cr App R 195 CA.
[18] *R v De Munck* 13 Cr App R 113 CCA.
[19] *R v Webb* [1964] 1 QB 357, [1963] 3 All ER 177 CCA.
[20] SOA 1956, s 28(5).
[21] SOA 1956, s 28(1).

248   8. PROSTITUTION AND TRAFFICKING

> **Particulars of Offence**
>
> D on the … day of … caused/encouraged [the prostitution of] *or* [commission of unlawful sexual intercourse on] *or* [indecent assault on] C, a girl under the age of 16 for whom he/she is responsible.

Alternative Offences

8.18 An attempt to commit the full offence. When indicting offences of attempt do so under common law until 26.8.1981, thereafter indict under s 1(1) Criminal Attempts Act 1981.[22] Aver the attempt in both the Statement of Offence and Particulars of Offence. In addition, aver the substantive offence under the relevant Act; see paras 1.51 and 12.157 and *Reed & Others* [2021].[23]

Sentence

8.19 On indictment: 2 YEARS.

Upon Conviction/Sentence

8.20 (i) Notification applies.[24]
(ii) Automatic inclusion in the children's and adults' barred lists with the right to make representations.[25]
(iii) SHPO applies.[26]
(iv) Qualifying 'specified sexual offence' in Schedule 18 (Extended Sentences).[27]

2. Procuring a Girl under 21 to have Unlawful Sexual Intercourse

Sexual Offences Act 1956, s 23

---

[22] Implementation date 27.8.1981.
[23] *Reed & Others* [2021] EWCA Crim 572.
[24] SOA 2003, s 80(1), Sch 3, para 10; see Chapter 14, paras 14.01–14.05.
[25] Part 2 of the Safeguarding Vulnerable Groups Act 2006 (Prescribed Criteria and Miscellaneous Provisions) Regulations 2009 (SI 2009 No 37) paras 2 and 4; see Chapter 12, para 12.217.
[26] SA 2020, s 345 and SOA 2003 Sch 3, para 10; See Chapter 16, para 16.07.
[27] SA 2020, s 306, Sch 18, para 29(w); see Chapter 12, para 12.51.

Definition

(1) to procure a girl under the age of 21 to have unlawful sexual intercourse in any part of the world with a third person.   8.21

Proof

(i) To procure, that is to bring about a course of conduct, which the woman would not have embarked upon on her own;[28]   8.22
(ii) a girl under 21;
(iii) to have unlawful sexual intercourse;
(iv) in any part of the world;
(v) that the accused intended that she would have intercourse with another man, and did not genuinely believe that the victim was 21 or over.[29]

Notes

(i) The offence is triable on indictment only.   8.23
(ii) Unlawful sexual intercourse means 'illicit sexual intercourse', outside the bond of marriage.[30]
(iii) The offence may be committed by a male or female as principal.
(iv) The third person may not be tried as a party to the offence, but as a conspirator.
(v) Sexual intercourse with another party must take place.[31]

Indictment

PROCURING A GIRL UNDER 21 TO HAVE UNLAWFUL SEXUAL INTERCOURSE   8.24
1.1.1957 to 30.4.2004

Statement of Offence
PROCURING A GIRL UNDER THE AGE OF 21 TO HAVE UNLAWFUL SEXUAL INTERCOURSE, contrary to section 23(1) of the Sexual Offences Act 1956.

Particulars of Offence
D on the … day of … procured C, a girl under the age of 21 years, and knowing that the said girl was under the age of 21, to have unlawful sexual intercourse with Z.

---

[28] *R v Broadfoot* (1977) 64 Cr App R 71 CA.
[29] *R v B (A Minor) v DPP* [2000] 2 Cr App R 65; *R v K* [2001] 3 All ER 897.
[30] *R v Chapman* 42 Cr App R 257 CCA.
[31] *R v Mackenzie and Higginson* (1910) 6 Cr App R 64 CCA.

250   8. PROSTITUTION AND TRAFFICKING

Alternative Offences

8.25 An attempt to commit the full offence. When indicting offences of attempt do so under common law until 26.8.1981, thereafter indict under s 1(1) Criminal Attempts Act 1981.[32] Aver the attempt in both the Statement of Offence and Particulars of Offence. In addition, aver the substantive offence under the relevant Act; see paras 1.51 and 12.157 and *Reed & Others* [2021].[33]

Sentence

8.26 (i) On indictment: **2 YEARS**.
(ii) An attempt carries the same maximum.

Upon Conviction/Sentence

8.27 (i) Notification not applicable.[34]
(ii) Automatic inclusion in the children's and adults' barred lists with the right to make representations.[35]
(iii) SHPO not applicable[36]
(iv) Qualifying 'specified sexual offence' in Schedule 18 (Extended Sentences).[37]

D. OFFENCES COMMITTED FROM 1.5.2004 TO DATE

8.28 The SOA 2003 repealed ss 23 and 28 of the SOA 1956 in full. Several offences relating to child prostitution are created: paying for sexual services of a child[38] (see para 8.29), causing or inciting child prostitution or pornography[39] (see para 8.36), controlling a child prostitute or a child involved in pornography[40] (see para 8.43).

1. Paying for Sexual Services of a Child

Sexual Offences Act 2003, s 47(1)

---

[32] Implementation date 27.8.1981.
[33] *Reed & Others* [2021] EWCA Crim 572.
[34] SOA 2003, s 80(1) (not listed in Sch 3). See Chapter 14 Tables 14.2–14.5.
[35] Part 2 of the Safeguarding Vulnerable Groups Act 2006 (Prescribed Criteria and Miscellaneous Provisions) Regulations 2009 (SI 2009 No 37) paras 2 and 4; see Chapter 12 para 12.217.
[36] SA 2020, s 345 (not listed in Sch 3 or Sch 5 SOA 2003); see Chapter 16 para 16.07.
[37] SA 2020, s 306, Sch 18, para 29(r); see Chapter 12 para 12.51.
[38] SOA 2003, s 47.
[39] SOA 2003, s 48.
[40] SOA 2003, s 49.

D. OFFENCES COMMITTED FROM 1.5.2004 TO DATE

Definition

(1) A person (A) commits an offence if—   **8.29**
    (a) he intentionally obtains for himself the sexual services of another person (B),
    (b) before obtaining those services he has made or promised payment for those services to B or a third person, or knows that another person has made or promised such a payment, and
    (c) either—
        (i) B is under 18, and A does not reasonably believe that B is 18 or over, or
        (ii) B is under 13.

Proof

As per Definition.   **8.30**

Notes

(i) If the offence is committed against a person under 16 and penetration is involved, the offence is triable only on indictment, otherwise triable either way.[41]   **8.31**
(ii) 'payment' means any financial advantage, including the discharge of an obligation to pay or the provision of goods and services (including sexual services) gratuitously or at a discount.[42]
(iii) Sexual services covers a wide variety of activities within the definition of 'sexual' under the SOA 2003, s 78.
(iv) Where the child is under 13 or under 16, this ought to be averred in the particulars. In addition, if penetration is involved, as per subsection (6), this ought to be averred.
(v) The extended jurisdiction provisions apply to this section.[43] See Chapter 17 para 17.01.
(vi) The s 45 Modern Slavery Act (MSA) 2015 defence for slavery and trafficking victims who commit an offence does not apply to this offence.[44]

Indictment

PAYING FOR SEXUAL SERVICES OF A CHILD 1.5.2004 to date   **8.32**

---

[41] SOA 2003, s 47(3)–(6).
[42] SOA 2003, s 47(2).
[43] SOA 2003, s 72; provides for the prosecution within the jurisdiction of a sexual offence committed outside it.
[44] Modern Slavery Act 2015, s 45 and Sch 4, para 33.

252   8. PROSTITUTION AND TRAFFICKING

> ### Statement of Offence
> PAYING FOR SEXUAL SERVICES OF A CHILD, contrary to section 47(1) of the Sexual Offences Act 2003.
>
> ### Particulars of Offence
> D, on the … day of … intentionally obtained for himself the sexual services of C, the said C being aged under 18 years, and the said D not reasonably believing that she was of or over the age of 18 years, and, before obtaining those services, the said D [promised payment for those services to C or another person X] *or* [knew that Y had made payment for those services to the said C or another person X].

Alternative Offences

8.33 If the payment or promise thereof is not proved under this section, then the following offences (carrying similar maximum sentences) may provide alternatives:

  (i) SOA 2003, s 5: rape of child under 13, see paras 4.88–4.96.
  (ii) SOA 2003, s 6: assault of child under 13 by penetration, see paras 4.97–4.105.
  (iii) SOA 2003, s 7: sexual assault of child under 13, see paras 4.119–4.127.
  (iv) SOA 2003, s 9: sexual activity with a child, see paras 4.106–4.116.

Sentence

8.34   (i) On indictment:
  - where penetration involved, and the child is under 13: **LIFE**;[45]
  - where penetration involved and the child is aged 13–16: **14 YEARS**;[46]
  - where penetration is not involved and the child is under 16: **14 YEARS**;[47]
  - in any other case: **7 YEARS**.[48]

  (ii) Summarily:
  - **6 months** or a fine not exceeding the statutory maximum or **both**.[49]

8.35 The Sentencing Council 'Sexual Offences: Definitive Guideline' contains offence-specific guidelines for s 47 offences. The Guideline applies to all offenders aged 18 and over, sentenced on or after 1 April 2014. The Guideline should be used only where the victim is aged 16 or 17 years old. If the victim is under 13 refer to the Guideline for 'rape of a child under 13', 'assault by penetration of a child under 13', 'sexual assault of a child under 13', or 'causing or inciting a child under 13 to engage in sexual activity', depending on the activity involved

---

[45] SOA 2003, s 47(3).
[46] SOA 2003, s 47(4)(a).
[47] SOA 2003, s 47(4)(b).
[48] SOA 2003, s 47(5)(b).
[49] 12 months if CJA 2003, s 282(4) implemented. Such cases not requiring proof of penetration of any sort.

in the offence. If the victim is aged 13–15 refer to the <u>sexual activity with a child</u> Guideline. When sentencing an Offender who has committed a sexual offence with, or in respect of, a person who is, or who the Offender believes to be, a child and no sexual activity occurs refer to *R v Reed and Others* [2021],[50] see Chapter 12 para 12.176.

Upon Conviction/Sentence 8.36

(i) Notification applies if the victim was under 16 *and* (a) the offender was 18 or over *or* (b) is sentenced to at least 12 months' imprisonment.[51]
(ii) Automatic inclusion in the children's and adults' barred lists with the right to make representations.[52]
(iii) SHPO applies.[53]
(iv) Qualifying 'specified sexual offence' in Schedule 18 (Extended Sentences).[54]
(v) Qualifying Schedule 19 offence (Life Sentences).[55]
(vi) Qualifying Schedule 14 offence (Extended Sentences: The Earlier Offence Condition).[56]
(vii) Qualifying 'index' offence (if committed after 3 December 2012) for the purpose of Schedule 15 (Life Sentence for Second Listed Offence) if the offence is against a person aged under 16.[57]

2. Causing or Inciting Child Prostitution or Inciting Child Pornography

Sexual Offences Act 2003, s 48(1)

Definition

(1) A person commits an offence if— 8.37
   (a) he intentionally causes or incites another person (B) to become a prostitute, or to be involved in pornography, in any part of the world, and
   (b) either—
      (i) B is under 18, and A does not reasonably believe that B is 18 or over, or
      (ii) B is under 13.

---

[50] *Reed & Others* [2021] EWCA Crim 572
[51] SOA 2003, s 80(1), Sch 3, para 29; see Chapter 14 paras 14.01–14.05.
[52] Part 2 of the Safeguarding Vulnerable Groups Act 2006 (Prescribed Criteria and Miscellaneous Provisions) Regulations 2009 (SI 2009 No 37) paras 2 and 4; see Chapter 12 para 12.217.
[53] SA 2020, s 345 and Sch 3, para 29 and Sch 5, para 62 SOA 2003; see Chapter 16 para 16.07.
[54] SA 2020, s 306, Sch 18, para 38(ai); see Chapter 12 para 12.51.
[55] SA 2020, s 307, Sch 19, para 20(k); see Chapter 12 para 12.52.
[56] SA 2020, ss 267 and 280, Sch 14, para 9(t); see Chapter 12 para 12.77.
[57] SA 2020, ss 273 and 283, Sch 15, para 9(t); see Chapter 12 para 12.123.

254 8. PROSTITUTION AND TRAFFICKING

Proof

8.38 As per Definition, in addition:

(i) 'prostitute'—is defined as a person (A) who on at least one occasion offers or provides sexual services in return for payment or promise of payment to A or a third person;[58]
(ii) 'payment' means any financial advantage, including an obligation to pay or the provision of goods or services gratuitously, or at a discount;[59]
(iii) 'involvement in pornography' if an indecent image of that person is recorded;[60]
(iv) 'causing'—the defendant must contemplate or desire that the act would ensue on his/her authority and as a result of his/her control/influence over the other person;
(v) 'inciting'—covers a suggestion, proposal, persuasion, inducement, threats or pressure.[61]

Notes

8.39
(i) Triable either way.[62]
(ii) The offence may be committed where the sexual activity does not for any reason take place.
(iii) The extended jurisdiction provisions apply to this section.[63] See Chapter 17 para 17.01.
(iv) The s 45 MSA 2015 defence for slavery and trafficking victims who commit an offence does not apply to this offence.[64]

Indictment

8.40 CAUSING OR INCITING CHILD PROSTITUTION OR PORNOGRAPHY 1.5.2004 to 2.5.2015

Statement of Offence
CAUSING OR INCITING CHILD PROSTITUTION/PORNOGRAPHY, contrary to section 48(1) of the Sexual Offences Act 2003.

Particulars of Offence
D on the … day of … intentionally incited C, a person under the age of [18 years, the said D not reasonably believing that C was aged 18 years or over] *or* [13 years], to become a prostitute.

---

[58] SOA 2003, s 51(2).
[59] SOA 2003, s 51(3).
[60] SOA 2003, s 51(1).
[61] *R v Fitzmaurice* [1983] QB 1083; *Invicta Plastics Ltd v Clare* [1976] RTR 251.
[62] SOA 2003, s 49(2).
[63] SOA 2003, s 72; provides for the prosecution within the jurisdiction of a sexual offence committed outside it.
[64] MSA 2015, s 45 and Sch 4, para 33.

Alternative Offences

An attempt to commit the full offence. When indicting offences of attempt do so under s 1(1) Criminal Attempts Act 1981.[65] Aver the attempt in both the Statement of Offence and Particulars of Offence. In addition, aver the substantive offence under the relevant Act; see paras 1.51 and 12.157 and *Reed & Others* [2021].[66] **8.41**

From 3.5.2015[67] the s 48 offence was updated and the references to 'prostitute' and 'pornography' were removed and replaced with 'sexually exploited'. From 31.3.2017[68] the reference to a recorded image was extended to include streamed or transmitted images. **8.42**

Definition

(1) A person (A) commits an offence if— **8.43**
 (a) he intentionally causes or incites another person (B) to be sexually exploited, in any part of the world, and
 (b) either—
  (i) B is under 18, and A does not reasonably believe that B is 18 or over, or
  (ii) B is under 13.

Proof

As per Definition, in addition: **8.44**

(i) 'sexually exploited'—defined as (a) a person (A) who on at least one occasion offers or provides sexual services in return for payment or promise of payment to A or a third person;[69] or (b) if an indecent image of that person is recorded, or streamed or otherwise transmitted;[70]
(ii) 'payment' means any financial advantage, including an obligation to pay or the provision of goods or services gratuitously, or at a discount;[71]
(iv) 'causing'—the defendant must contemplate or desire that the act would ensue on his/her authority and as a result of his/her control/influence over the other person;
(v) 'inciting'—covers a suggestion, proposal, persuasion, inducement, threats or pressure.[72]

---

[65] Implementation date 27.8.1981.
[66] *Reed & Others* [2021] EWCA Crim 572.
[67] Words substituted by Serious Crime Act 2015 c 9 Pt 5 s 68(3)(a), (3.5.2015).
[68] Policing and Crime Act 2017, s 176 (31.3.2017).
[69] SOA 2003, s 51(2).
[70] SOA 2003, s 51(1). The words 'or streamed or otherwise transmitted' inserted by the Policing and Crime Act 2017, s 176 (31.3.2017).
[71] SOA 2003, s 51(3).
[72] *R v Fitzmaurice* [1983] QB 1083; *Invicta Plastics Ltd v Clare* [1976] RTR 251.

256 8. PROSTITUTION AND TRAFFICKING

Notes

8.45
(i) Triable either way.[73]
(ii) The offence may be committed where the sexual activity does not for any reason take place.
(iii) The extended jurisdiction provisions apply to this section.[74] See Chapter 17 para 17.01.
(iv) The s 45 MSA 2015 defence for slavery and trafficking victims who commit an offence does not apply to this offence.[75]

Indictment

8.46 CAUSING OR INCITING SEXUAL EXPLOITATION OF A CHILD 3.5.2015 to date

> ### Statement of Offence
> CAUSING OR INCITING SEXUAL EXPLOITATION OF A CHILD, contrary to section 48(1) of the Sexual Offences Act 2003.
>
> ### Particulars of Offence
> D on the ... day of ... intentionally incited C, a person under the age of [18 years, the said D not reasonably believing that C was aged 18 years or over] *or* [13 years], to be sexually exploited.

Alternative Offences

8.47 An attempt to commit the full offence. When indicting offences of attempt do so under s 1(1) Criminal Attempts Act 1981.[76] Aver the attempt in both the Statement of Offence and Particulars of Offence. In addition, aver the substantive offence under the relevant Act; see paras 1.51 and 12.157 and *Reed & Others* [2021].[77]

Sentence

8.48
(i) On indictment: **14 YEARS**.[78]
(ii) Summarily: **6 months** or a **fine** not exceeding the statutory maximum or **both**.[79]

---

[73] SOA 2003, s 49(2).
[74] SOA 2003, s 72 provides for the prosecution within the jurisdiction of a sexual offence committed outside it.
[75] Modern Slavery Act 2015, s 45 and Sch 4, para 33.
[76] Implementation date 27.8.1981.
[77] *Reed & Others* [2021] EWCA Crim 572.
[78] SOA 2003, s 48(2)(b).
[79] SOA 2003, s 48(2)(a). 12 months if CJA 2003, s 282(4) implemented.

D. OFFENCES COMMITTED FROM 1.5.2004 TO DATE

The Sentencing Council 'Sexual Offences: Definitive Guideline' contains offence-specific guidelines for s 48 offences. The Guideline applies to all offenders aged 18 and over, sentenced on or after 1 April 2014. When sentencing an Offender who has committed a sexual offence with, or in respect of, a person who is, or who the Offender believes to be, a child and no sexual activity occurs refer to *R v Reed and Others* [2021],[80] see Chapter 12 para 12.176.   **8.49**

Upon Conviction/Sentence

(i) Notification applies if the offender was 18 or over *or* is sentenced to at least 12 months' imprisonment.[81]   **8.50**
(ii) Automatic inclusion in the children's and adults' barred lists with the right to make representations.[82]
(iii) SHPO applies.[83]
(iv) Qualifying 'specified sexual offence' in Schedule 18 (Extended Sentences).[84]
(v) Qualifying Schedule 14 offence (Extended Sentences: The Earlier Offence Condition).[85]
(vi) Qualifying 'index' offence (if committed after 3 December 2012) for the purpose of Schedule 15 (Life Sentence for Second Listed Offence).[86]
(vii) Lifestyle offence for purposes of POCA 2002.[87]
(viii) Serious Crime Prevention Order applicable for offences convicted after 6 April 2008.[88]

3. Controlling a Child Prostitute or a Child Involved in Pornography

Sexual Offences Act 2003, s 49(1)

Definition

(1) A person (A) commits an offence if—   **8.51**
　　(a) he intentionally controls any of the activities of another person (B) relating to B's prostitution or involvement in pornography in any part of the world, and

---

[80] *Reed & Others* [2021] EWCA Crim 572.
[81] SOA 2003, s 80(1), Sch 3, para 29A; see Chapter 14 paras 14.01–14.05.
[82] Part 2 of the Safeguarding Vulnerable Groups Act 2006 (Prescribed Criteria and Miscellaneous Provisions) Regulations 2009 (SI 2009 No 37) paras 2 and 4; see Chapter 12 para 12.217.
[83] SA 2020, s 345 and SOA 2003 Sch 3, para 29A; see Chapter 16 para 16.07.
[84] SA 2020, s 306, Sch 18, para 38(aj); see Chapter 12 para 12.51.
[85] SA 2020, ss 267 and 280, Sch 14, para 9(u); see Chapter 12 para 12.77.
[86] SA 2020, ss 273 and 283, Sch 15, para 9(u); see Chapter 12 para 12.123.
[87] POCA 2002, Sch 2.
[88] SCA 2007, s 19 and Sch 1, para 4; see Chapter 12 para 12.240.

258   8. PROSTITUTION AND TRAFFICKING

(b) either—
   (i) B is under 18, and A does not reasonably believe that B is 18 or over, or
   (ii) B is under 13.

Proof

8.52 As per Definition. In addition:

(i) For proof of prostitution see para 8.37.
(ii) For proof of the term 'payment' see para 8.37.
(iii) For proof of the term 'involved in pornography' see para 8.37.

Notes

8.53 (i) Triable either way.
(ii) The extended jurisdiction provisions apply to this section.[89] See Chapter 17 para 17.01.
(iii) The s 45 MSA 2015 defence for slavery and trafficking victims who commit an offence does not apply to this offence.[90]

Indictment

8.54 CONTROLLING CHILD PROSTITUTION/PORNOGRAPHY 1.5.2004 to 2.5.2015

Statement of Offence
CONTROLLING A CHILD PROSTITUTE OR A CHILD INVOLVED IN PORNOGRAPHY, contrary to section 49(1) of the Sexual Offences Act 2003.

Particulars of Offence
D on the … day of … intentionally controlled the activities of C relating to the said C's prostitution or involvement in pornography, [the said C being a person under the age of 18 years, and the said D not reasonably believing that the said C was aged 18 years or over] *or* [the said C being a person under the age of 13 years].

Alternative Offences

8.55 An attempt to commit the full offence. When indicting offences of attempt do so under s 1(1) Criminal Attempts Act 1981.[91] Aver the attempt in both the Statement of Offence and

---

[89] SOA 2003, s 72; provides for the prosecution within the jurisdiction of a sexual offence committed outside it.
[90] Modern Slavery Act 2015, s 45 and Sch 4, para 33.
[91] Implementation date 27.8.1981.

Particulars of Offence. In addition, aver the substantive offence under the relevant Act; see paras 1.51 and 12.157 and *Reed & Others* [2021].[92]

From 3.5.2015[93] the s 49 offence was updated and the references to 'prostitute' and 'pornography' were removed and replaced with 'sexually exploited'. From 31.3.2017[94] the reference to a recorded image was extended to include streamed or transmitted images. **8.56**

Definition

(1) A person (A) commits an offence if—
    (a) he intentionally controls any of the activities of another person (B) relating to B's sexual exploitation in any part of the world, and
    (b) either—
        (i) B is under 18, and A does not reasonably believe that B is 18 or over, or
        (ii) B is under 13.

Proof

As per Definition. In addition: **8.57**

(i) For proof of 'sexual exploitation'[95] see para 8.44.
(ii) For proof of the term 'payment'[96] see para 8.37.

Notes

(i) Triable either way. **8.58**
(ii) The extended jurisdiction provisions apply to this section.[97]
(iii) The s 45 MSA 2015 defence for slavery and trafficking victims who commit an offence does not apply to this offence.[98]

Indictment

CONTROLLING A CHILD IN RELATION TO SEXUAL EXPLOITATION 3.5.2015 to date **8.59**

---

[92] *Reed & Others* [2021] EWCA Crim 572.
[93] Words substituted by Serious Crime Act 2015 c 9 Pt 5 s 68(3)(a), (3.5.2015).
[94] Policing and Crime Act 2017, s 176 (31.3.2017).
[95] SOA 2003, s 51(1).
[96] SOA 2003, s 51(3).
[97] SOA 2003, s 72; provides for the prosecution within the jurisdiction of a sexual offence committed outside it. See Chapter 17.
[98] Modern Slavery Act 2015, s 45 and Sch 4, para 33.

> ### Statement of Offence
> CONTROLLING A CHILD IN RELATION TO SEXUAL EXPLOITATION, contrary to section 49(1) of the Sexual Offences Act 2003.
>
> ### Particulars of Offence
> D on the … day of … intentionally controlled the activities of C relating to the said C's sexual exploitation, [the said C being a person under the age of 18 years, and the said D not reasonably believing that the said C was aged 18 years or over] *or* [the said C being a person under the age of 13 years].

Alternative Offences

8.60 An attempt to commit the full offence. When indicting offences of attempt do so under s 1(1) Criminal Attempts Act 1981.[99] Aver the attempt in both the Statement of Offence and Particulars of Offence. In addition, aver the substantive offence under the relevant Act; see paras 1.51 and 12.157 and *Reed & Others* [2021].[100]

Sentence

8.61 (i) On indictment: **14 YEARS**.[101]
(ii) Summarily: **6 months** or a **fine** not exceeding the statutory maximum or **both**.[102]

8.62 The Sentencing Council 'Sexual Offences: Definitive Guideline' contains offence-specific guidelines for s 49 offences. The Guideline applies to all offenders aged 18 and over, sentenced on or after 1 April 2014. When sentencing an Offender who has committed a sexual offence with, or in respect of, a person who is, or who the Offender believes to be, a child and no sexual activity occurs refer to *R v Reed and Others* [2021],[103] see Chapter 12 para 12.176.

Upon Conviction/Sentence

8.63 (i) Notification applies if the offender was 18 or over *or* is sentenced to at least 12 months' imprisonment.[104]

---

[99] Implementation date 27.8.1981.
[100] *Reed & Others* [2021] EWCA Crim 572.
[101] SOA 2003, s 49(2)(b).
[102] SOA 2003, s 48(2)(a). 12 months if CJA 2003, s 282(4) implemented.
[103] *Reed & Others* [2021] EWCA Crim 572.
[104] SOA 2003, s 80(1), Sch 3, para 29B; see Chapter 14 paras 14.01–14.05.

(ii) Automatic inclusion in the children's and adults' barred lists with the right to make representations.[105]
(iii) SHPO applies.[106]
(iv) Qualifying 'specified sexual offence' in Schedule 18 (Extended Sentences).[107]
(v) Qualifying Schedule 14 offence (Extended Sentences: The Earlier Offence Condition).[108]
(vi) Qualifying 'index' offence (if committed after 3 December 2012) for the purpose of Schedule 15 (Life Sentence for Second Listed Offence).[109]
(vii) Lifestyle offence for purposes of POCA 2002.[110]
(viii) Serious Crime Prevention Order applicable for offences convicted after 6 April 2008.[111]

4. Arranging or Facilitating Child Prostitution or Pornography

Sexual Offences Act 2003, s 50(1)

Definition

(1) A person (A) commits an offence if— **8.64**
   (a) he intentionally arranges or facilitates the prostitution or involvement in pornography in any part of the world of another person (B), and
   (b) cither—
      (i) B is under 18, and A does not reasonably believe that B is 18 or over, or
      (ii) B is under 13.

Proof

As per Definition. In addition: **8.65**

(i) For proof of prostitution see para 8.37.
(ii) For proof of the term 'payment' see para 8.37.
(iii) For proof of the term 'involved in pornography' see para 8.37.

---

[105] Part 2 of the Safeguarding Vulnerable Groups Act 2006 (Prescribed Criteria and Miscellaneous Provisions) Regulations 2009 (SI 2009 No 37) paras 2 and 4; see Chapter 12 para 12.217.
[106] SA 2020, s 345 and SOA 2003 Sch 3, para 29B; see Chapter 16 para 16.07.
[107] SA 2020, s 306, Sch 18, para 38(ak); see Chapter 12 para 12.51.
[108] SA 2020, ss 267 and 280, Sch 14, para 9(v); see Chapter 12 para 12.77.
[109] SA 2020, ss 273 and 283, Sch 15, para 9(v); see Chapter 12 para 12.123.
[110] POCA 2002, Sch 2.
[111] SCA 2007, s 19 and Sch 1, para 4; see Chapter 12 para 12.240.

Notes

8.66
(i) Triable either way.
(ii) The extended jurisdiction provisions apply to this section.[112] See Chapter 17 para 17.01.
(iii) The s 45 MSA 2015 defence for slavery and trafficking victims who commit an offence does not apply to this offence.[113]

Indictment

8.67 ARRANGING/FACILITATING CHILD PROSTITUTION OR PORNOGRAPHY 1.5.2004 to 2.5.2015

> **Statement of Offence**
> ARRANGING (FACILITATING) CHILD PROSTITUTION (PORNOGRAPHY), contrary to section 50(1) of the Sexual Offences Act 2003.
>
> **Particulars of Offence**
> D on the ... day of ... intentionally arranged or facilitated the [prostitution *or* involvement in pornography of C], the said C being a person under the age of [18 years *or* 13 years], and the said D not reasonably believing that the said C was aged 18 years or over.

Alternative Offences

8.68 An attempt to commit the full offence. When indicting offences of attempt do so under s 1(1) Criminal Attempts Act 1981.[114] Aver the attempt in both the Statement of Offence and Particulars of Offence. In addition, aver the substantive offence under the relevant Act; see paras 1.51 and 12.157 and *Reed & Others* [2021].[115]

8.69 From 3.5.2015[116] the s 49 offence was updated and the references to 'prostitute' and 'pornography' were removed and replaced with 'sexually exploited'. From 31.3.2017[117] the reference to a recorded image was extended to include streamed or transmitted images.

---

[112] SOA 2003, s 72; provides for the prosecution within the jurisdiction of a sexual offence committed outside it.
[113] Modern Slavery Act 2015, s 45 and Sch 4, para 33.
[114] Implementation date 27.8.1981.
[115] *Reed & Others* [2021] EWCA Crim 572.
[116] Words substituted by Serious Crime Act 2015 c. 9 Pt 5 s 68(3)(a), (3.5.2015).
[117] Policing and Crime Act 2017, s 176 (31.3.2017).

Definition

(1) A person (A) commits an offence if— 8.70
   (a) he intentionally arranges or facilitates the sexual exploitation in any part of the world of another person (B), and
   (b) either—
      (i) B is under 18, and A does not reasonably believe that B is 18 or over, or
      (ii) B is under 13.

Proof

As per Definition. In addition: 8.71

(i) For proof of 'sexual exploitation'[118] see para 8.44.
(ii) For proof of the term 'payment'[119] see para 8.37.

Notes

(i) Triable either way. 8.72
(ii) The extended jurisdiction provisions apply to this section.[120] See Chapter 17 para 17.01.
(iii) The s 45 MSA 2015 defence for slavery and trafficking victims who commit an offence does not apply to this offence.[121]

Indictment

ARRANGING OR FACILITATING SEXUAL EXPLOITATION OF A CHILD PROSTITUTION OR PORNOGRAPHY 3.5.2015 to date 8.73

Statement of Offence
ARRANGING OR FACILITATING SEXUAL EXPLOITATION OF A CHILD, contrary to section 50(1) of the Sexual Offences Act 2003.

Particulars of Offence
D on the ... day of ... intentionally arranged or facilitated the sexual exploitation of C in ..., the said C being a person under the age of [18 years and the said D not reasonably believing that the said C was aged 18 years or over *or* 13 years].

---

[118] SOA 2003, s 51(1).
[119] SOA 2003, s 51(3).
[120] SOA 2003, s 72 provides for the prosecution within the jurisdiction of a sexual offence committed outside it.
[121] Modern Slavery Act 2015, s 45 and Sch 4, para 33.

Alternative Offences

8.74 An attempt to commit the full offence. When indicting offences of attempt do so under s 1(1) Criminal Attempts Act 1981.[122] Aver the attempt in both the Statement of Offence and Particulars of Offence. In addition, aver the substantive offence under the relevant Act; see paras 1.51 and 12.157 and *Reed & Others* [2021].[123]

Sentence

8.75 (i) On indictment: **14 YEARS**.[124]
(ii) Summarily: **6 months** or a **fine** not exceeding the statutory maximum or **both**.[125]

8.76 The Sentencing Council 'Sexual Offences: Definitive Guideline' contains offence specific guidelines for s 50 offences. The Guideline applies to all offenders aged 18 and over, sentenced on or after 1 April 2014. When sentencing an Offender who has committed a sexual offence with, or in respect of, a person who is, or who the Offender believes to be, a child and no sexual activity occurs refer to *R v Reed and Others* [2021],[126] see Chapter 12 para 12.176.

Upon Conviction/Sentence

8.77 (i) Notification applies if the offender was 18 or over *or* is sentenced to at least 12 months' imprisonment.[127]
(ii) Automatic inclusion in the children's and adults' barred lists with the right to make representations.[128]
(iii) SHPO applies.[129]
(iv) Qualifying 'specified sexual offence' in Schedule 18 (Extended Sentences).[130]
(v) Qualifying Schedule 14 offence (Extended Sentences: The Earlier Offence Condition).[131]
(vi) Qualifying 'index' offence (if committed after 3 December 2012) for the purpose of Schedule 15 (Life Sentence for Second Listed Offence).[132]

---

[122] Implementation date 27.8.1981.
[123] *Reed & Others* [2021] EWCA Crim 572.
[124] SOA 2003, s 50(2)(b).
[125] SOA 2003, s 50(2)(a). 12 months if CJA 2003, s 282(4) implemented.
[126] *Reed & Others* [2021] EWCA Crim 572.
[127] SOA 2003, s 80(1), Sch 3, para 29C; see Chapter 14 paras 14.01–14.05.
[128] Part 2 of the Safeguarding Vulnerable Groups Act 2006 (Prescribed Criteria and Miscellaneous Provisions) Regulations 2009 (SI 2009 No 37) paras 2 and 4; see Chapter 12, para 12.217.
[129] SA 2020, s 345 and SOA 2003 Sch 3, para 29C; see Chapter 16 para 16.07.
[130] SA 2020, s 306, Sch 18, para 38(al); see Chapter 12 para 12.51.
[131] SA 2020, ss 267 and 280, Sch 14, para 9(w); see Chapter 12 para 12.77.
[132] SA 2020, ss 273 and 283, Sch 15, para 9(w); see Chapter 12 para 12.123.

(vii) Lifestyle offence for purposes of POCA 2002.[133]
(viii) Serious Crime Prevention Order applicable for offences convicted after 6 April 2008.[134]

Procuring Prostitution of Women

E. OFFENCES COMMITTED BETWEEN 1.1.1957 AND 30.4.2004

See paras 7.154–7.159 for the SOA 1956, s 29; causing prostitution of a defective. **8.78**

1. Causing Prostitution of Women

Sexual Offences Act 1956, s 22(1)

Definition

(a) to procure a woman to become, in any part of the world, a common prostitute; or **8.79**
(b) to procure a woman to leave the United Kingdom, intending her to become an inmate of or frequent a brothel elsewhere; or
(c) to procure a woman to leave her usual place of abode in the United Kingdom, intending her to become an inmate of or frequent a brothel in any part of the world for the purposes of prostitution.

Proof

(i) To procure, that is to bring about a course of conduct, which the woman in question would not have embarked upon of her own volition;[135] **8.80**
(ii) a woman (this cannot apply to procuration of a male);
(iii) into becoming a common prostitute.
(iv) For s 22(1)(a) the defendant has to believe that the woman was not a prostitute before he procured her.[136]

---

[133] POCA 2002, Sch 2.
[134] SCA 2007, s 19 and Sch 1, para 4; see Chapter 12 para 12.240.
[135] *R v Broadfoot* 64 Cr App R 71 CA, *A-G's Reference (No 1 of 1975)*.
[136] *R v Brown* [1984] 3 All ER 1013.

Notes

8.81 (i) Triable on indictment only.[137]

(ii) A female who is already a prostitute cannot be procured for the purposes of this offence.[138]

(iii) The term 'common prostitute' covers the offer of a woman's body commonly for acts of lewdness for payment, on more than one occasion.[139]

Indictment

8.82 PROCURING PROSTITUTION OF WOMEN 1.1.1957 to 30.4.2004

Statement of Offence

PROCURING A WOMAN TO BECOME A COMMON PROSTITUTE, contrary to section 22(1) of the Sexual Offences Act 1956.

Particulars of Offence

D on the … day of … at … procured C, a woman, to become a common prostitute.

Alternative Offences

8.83 An attempt to commit the full offence. When indicting offences of attempt do so under common law until 26.8.1981, thereafter indict under s 1(1) Criminal Attempts Act 1981.[140] Aver the attempt in both the Statement of Offence and Particulars of Offence. In addition, aver the substantive offence under the relevant Act; see paras 1.51 and 12.157 and *Reed & Others* [2021].[141]

Sentence

8.84 (i) On indictment: 2 YEARS.[142]

(ii) An attempt attracts the same maximum.

---

[137] SOA 1956, s 37(2) and Sch 2, para 23.
[138] SOA 1956. *R v Brown* [1984] 3 All ER 1013.
[139] *R v Morris-Lowe* [1985] 1 All ER 40.
[140] Implementation date 27.8.1981.
[141] *Reed & Others* [2021] EWCA Crim 572.
[142] SOA 1956, s 37(2) and Sch 2, para 23.

Upon Conviction/Sentence

(i) Notification not applicable.[143] **8.85**
(ii) Automatic inclusion in the children's and adults' barred lists with the right to make representations.[144]
(iii) SHPO not applicable.[145]
(iv) Qualifying 'specified sexual offence' in Schedule 18 (Extended Sentences).[146]
From 1.5.2004 SOA 2003, s 52 covers this offence. **8.86**

F. OFFENCES COMMITTED FROM 1.5.2004 TO DATE

1. Causing or Inciting Prostitution for Gain

Sexual Offences Act 2003, s 52(1)

Definition

(1) A person (A) commits an offence if— **8.87**
 (a) he intentionally causes or incites another person to become a prostitute in any part of the world, and
 (b) he does so for or in the expectation of gain for himself or a third person.

Proof

As per Definition. **8.88**

(i) For proof of causing see para 8.37.
(ii) For proof of inciting see para 8.37.
(iii) For proof of prostitute see para 8.37.
(iv) 'gain' includes any financial advantage, including the discharge of an obligation to pay or the provision of goods or services (including sexual services) gratuitously or at a discount; or the goodwill of any person which is or appears likely, in time, to bring financial advantage.[147]

---

[143] SOA 2003, s 80(1) (not listed in Sch 3); see Chapter 14 Tables 14.2 -14.5.
[144] Part 2 of the Safeguarding Vulnerable Groups Act 2006 (Prescribed Criteria and Miscellaneous Provisions) Regulations 2009 (SI 2009 No 37) paras 2 and 4; see Chapter 12 para 12.217.
[145] SA 2020, s 345 (not listed in Sch 3 or Sch 5 SOA 2003); see Chapter 16 para 16.07.
[146] SA 2020, s 306, Sch18, para 29(q); see Chapter 12 para 12.51.
[147] SOA 2003, s 54(1).

268   8. PROSTITUTION AND TRAFFICKING

Notes

8.89   (i) This offence is triable either way.[148]
(ii) The s 45 MSA 2015 defence for slavery and trafficking victims who commit an offence is available for an offence under this section, provided it was committed on or after 31.7.2.15.[149]

Indictment

8.90   CAUSING/INCITING PROSTITUTION FOR GAIN 1.5.2004 to date

---

Statement of Offence

CAUSING OR INCITING PROSTITUTION FOR GAIN, contrary to section 52(1) of the Sexual Offences Act 2003.

Particulars of Offence

D on the … day of … intentionally caused/incited C to become a prostitute in … in the expectation of gain for himself or a third person.

Alternative Offences

8.91   An attempt to commit the full offence. When indicting offences of attempt do so under s 1(1) Criminal Attempts Act 1981.[150] Aver the attempt in both the Statement of Offence and Particulars of Offence. In addition, aver the substantive offence under the relevant Act; see paras 1.51 and 12.157 and *Reed & Others* [2021].[151]

Sentence

8.92   (i) On indictment: **7 YEARS**.[152]
(ii) Summarily: **6 months** or a **fine** not exceeding the statutory maximum or **both**.[153]

---

[148] SOA 2003, s 52(2).
[149] MSA 2015, s 45 commencement date 31.7.2015 (SI 2015/1476). This offence is not an excluded offence in Sch 4 of the Act. The s 45 defence is not retrospective, see *R v Joseph (Verna Sermanfure)* [2017] EWCA Crim 36.
[150] Implementation date 27.8.1981.
[151] *Reed & Others* [2021] EWCA Crim 572.
[152] SOA 2003, s 52(2)(b).
[153] SOA 2003, s 52(2)(a). 12 months if CJA 2003, s 282(4) implemented.

G. OFFENCES COMMITTED BETWEEN 1.1.1957 AND 30.4.2004

Upon Conviction/Sentence

(i) Notification not applicable.[154]   **8.93**
(ii) Automatic inclusion in the children's and adults' barred lists with the right to make representations.[155]
(iii) SHPO applicable.[156]
(iv) Qualifying 'specified sexual offence' in Schedule 18 (Extended Sentences).[157]
(v) Lifestyle offence for purposes of POCA 2002.[158]
(vi) Serious Crime Prevention Order applicable for offences convicted after 6 April 2008.[159]

Living on the Earnings of Prostitution

G. OFFENCES COMMITTED BETWEEN 1.1.1957 AND 30.4.2004

The SOA 1956, ss 33–36 created three summary offences, covering the keeping of brothels or allowing premises to be so used. These summary only offences are not included. However, the SOA 2003, s 55 amends the SOA 1956, s 33 and so creates a triable either way offence of brothel keeping[160] which has been included.   **8.94**

Other summary only offences of loitering,[161] soliciting (kerb crawling)[162] and persistent soliciting,[163] are not included in the text.   **8.95**

1. Man Living on Earnings of Prostitution

Sexual Offences Act 1956, s 30(1)

Definition

(1) For a man knowingly to live wholly or in part on the earnings of prostitution.   **8.96**
(2) For the purposes of this section a man who lives wholly or is habitually in the company of a prostitute, or who exercises control, direction, or influence over a prostitute's

---

[154] SOA 2003, s 80(1) (not listed in Sch 3); see Chapter 14 Tables 14.2 -14.5.
[155] Part 2 of the Safeguarding Vulnerable Groups Act 2006 (Prescribed Criteria and Miscellaneous Provisions) Regulations 2009 (SI 2009 No 37) paras 2 and 4; see Chapter 12 para 12.217.
[156] SA 2020, s 345 and Sch 5, para 63 SOA 2003; see Chapter 16 para 16.07.
[157] SA 2020, s 306, Sch 18, para 38(am); see Chapter 12 para 12.51.
[158] POCA 2002, Sch 2.
[159] SCA 2007, s 19 and Sch 1, para 4; see Chapter 12 para 12.240.
[160] SOA 1956, s 33A. In force 1.5.2004.
[161] Street Offences Act (StOA) 1959, s 1.
[162] SOA 1985, s 1.
[163] SOA 1985, s 2.

270   8. PROSTITUTION AND TRAFFICKING

movements in a way which shows he is aiding, abetting, or compelling her prostitution with others, shall be presumed to be knowingly living on the earnings of prostitution, unless he proves the contrary.

Proof

8.97 As per Definition. In addition:

(i) Man covers man or boy.[164]
(ii) It must be proved that the woman on whose earnings the man was living was a prostitute; for proof of prostitute see paras 8.15.
(iii) Control, direction or influence.
(iv) Living on the earnings of prostitution covers payments received, not necessarily from the prostitutes themselves, for goods/services supplied to them for the purposes of prostitution.[165]
(v) The prosecution must prove that the defendant knew the female to be a prostitute, and knew that he was in part living on her earnings.

Notes

8.98
(i) This offence is triable either way.
(ii) If the prosecution proves that the defendant was either living with a prostitute, habitually in her company or exercising control, direction or influence over her movements which showed that he was aiding, abetting, compelling her prostitution, then the presumption in s 30(2) applies, that is, he is knowingly living on her earnings.[166]
(iii) Examples of living on the earnings of prostitution include selling a directory of prostitutes for which they pay to be included.[167] Letting premises for prostitution where the prostitute and the lessor are in the business of prostitution together.[168]
(iv) This offence may only be committed by a male as principal.
(v) The charge may relate to the commission of the offence on one day only, although evidence of their relations before or after the specified date may be adduced.[169]

Indictment

8.99 MAN LIVING ON EARNINGS OF PROSTITUTION 1.1.1957 to 30.4.2004

---

[164] SOA 1956, s 46.
[165] *Shaw v DPP* [1961] 2 All ER 446 HL.
[166] *R v Clarke* 63 Cr App R 16 CA.
[167] *Shaw v DPP* [1962] AC 220 HL.
[168] *Stewart v DPP* (1986) 83 Cr App R 327 CA.
[169] *R v Hill* 10 Cr App R 56 CCA.

G. OFFENCES COMMITTED BETWEEN 1.1.1957 AND 30.4.2004

Statement of Offence
LIVING ON PROSTITUTION, contrary to section 30(1) of the Sexual Offences Act 1956.

Particulars of Offence
D, a man, on the … day of … knowingly lived wholly or in part on the earnings of the prostitution of C.

Alternative Offences

There are a number of alternatives ways included within the definition of s 30(2), see para 8.75. **8.100**

Sentence

(i) On indictment: **7 YEARS**.[170] **8.101**
(ii) Summarily: **6 months**.[171]

Sentencing Guidance

If there has been no element of coercion or corruption of the prostitute, then a sentence of **2 years** would be appropriate.[172] **8.102**

Upon Conviction/Sentence

(i) Notification not applicable.[173] **8.103**
(ii) Automatic inclusion in the children's and adults' barred lists with the right to make representations.[174]
(iii) SHPO not applicable.[175]

---

[170] SOA 1956, s 37(3) and Sch 2, para 30(i). The maximum of 2 years was increased on 16.8.1959 by StOA 1959, s 4.
[171] SOA 1956, s 37(3) and Sch 2, para 30(ii).
[172] *R v Farrugia and Others* (1979) 69 Cr App R 108 CA.
[173] SOA 2003, s 80(1) (not listed in Sch 3); see Chapter 14 Tables 14.2–14.5.
[174] Part 2 of the Safeguarding Vulnerable Groups Act 2006 (Prescribed Criteria and Miscellaneous Provisions) Regulations 2009 (SI 2009 No 37) paras 2 and 4; see Chapter 12 para 12.217.
[175] SA 2020, s 345 (not listed in Sch 3 or Sch 5 SOA 2003); see Chapter 16 para 16.07.

2. Women Exercising Control over Prostitute

Sexual Offences Act 1956, s 31

Definition

8.104 ... for a woman, for purposes of gain, to exercise control, direction or influence over a prostitute's movements in a way which shows she is aiding, abetting, or compelling her prostitution.

Proof

8.105 As per Definition. In addition:

(i) See para 8.15 for the meaning of prostitution.
(ii) Only a woman/girl may commit this offence upon a female prostitute.[176]
(iii) For proof of living on the earnings see paras 8.76.
(iv) For *mens rea* see para 8.76.

Notes

8.106 The offence is triable either way.[177]

Indictment

8.107 WOMEN EXERCISING CONTROL/DIRECTION/INFLUENCE OVER A PROSTITUTE
1.1.1957 to 30.4.2004

Statement of Offence

EXERCISING CONTROL/DIRECTION/INFLUENCE OVER A PROSTITUTE, contrary to section 31 of the Sexual Offences Act 1956.

Particulars of Offence

D a woman/girl,[178] on the ... day of ... exercised control/direction/influence over the movements of C, a prostitute, for purposes of gain, in a way which shows she is aiding, abetting or compelling her prostitution.

---

[176] The terms 'woman/girl' are interchangeable (SOA 1956, s 46).
[177] MCA 1980, s 17(1) and Sch 1.
[178] The terms 'woman/girl' are interchangeable (SOA 1956, s 46).

Sentence

(i) On indictment: **7 YEARS**.[179] **8.108**
(ii) Summarily: **6 months**.[180]

Upon Conviction/Sentence

(i) Notification not applicable.[181] **8.109**
(ii) Automatic inclusion in the children's and adults' barred lists with the right to make representations.[182]
(iii) SHPO not applicable.[183]

3. Detention of a Woman in a Brothel or other Premises

Sexual Offences Act 1956, s 24

Definition

(1) … to detain a woman against her will on any premises with the intention that she shall **8.110**
have unlawful sexual intercourse with men or with a particular man, or to detain a woman against her will in a brothel.
(2) Where a woman is on any premises for the purpose of having unlawful sexual intercourse or is in a brothel, a person shall be deemed … to detain her there if, with the intention of compelling or inducing her to remain there, he either withholds from her, her clothes or any other property belonging to her or threatens her with legal proceedings in the event of her taking away clothes provided for her by him or on his directions.

Proof

(i) As per Definition. **8.111**
(ii) For unlawful sexual intercourse see para 2.17.
(iii) For the definition of brothel see para 8.112.

---

[179] SOA 2003, s 37(3) and Sch 2, para 31(i).
[180] SOA 2003, s 37(3) and Sch 2, para 31(ii).
[181] SOA 2003, s 80(1) (not listed in Sch 3); see Chapter 14 Tables 14.2–14.5.
[182] Part 2 of the Safeguarding Vulnerable Groups Act 2006 (Prescribed Criteria and Miscellaneous Provisions) Regulations 2009 (SI 2009 No 37) paras 2 and 4; see Chapter 12 para 12.217.
[183] SA 2020, s 345 (not listed in Sch 3 or Sch 5 SOA 2003); see Chapter 16 para 16.07.

274   8. PROSTITUTION AND TRAFFICKING

(iv) In addition, proof that the accused intended to detain the woman at the brothel/premises so that she would have unlawful sexual intercourse with a man/men.

Notes

8.112
(i) The offence is triable only on indictment.
(ii) The detained woman who has taken clothes in order to leave these premises will not be liable to any legal proceedings.[184]
(iii) Both males and females may commit this offence.
(iv) The offence may be committed upon a girl, the words 'woman' and 'girl' are interchangeable.[185]

Indictment

8.113 DETENTION OF A WOMAN IN A BROTHEL OR OTHER PREMISES 1.1.1957 to 30.4.2004

> ### Statement of Offence
> DETAINING A WOMAN AGAINST HER WILL FOR UNLAWFUL SEXUAL INTERCOURSE (IN A BROTHEL), contrary to section 24(1) of the Sexual Offences Act 1956.
>
> ### Particulars of Offence
> D on the ... day of ... [detained C, a woman, against her will at ... intending her to have unlawful sexual intercourse with men/with X, a man] or [detained C, a woman, against her will at, ... a brothel].

Alternative Offences

8.114
(i) An attempt to commit the full offence. When indicting offences of attempt do so under common law until 26.8.1981, thereafter indict under s 1(1) Criminal Attempts Act 1981.[186] Aver the attempt in both the Statement of Offence and Particulars of Offence. In addition, aver the substantive offence under the relevant Act; see paras 1.51 and 12.157 and *Reed & Others* [2021].[187]
(ii) CYPA 1933, s 3—allowing a child aged between the ages of 4 and 16 of whom they have custody, care or control to reside in or frequent a brothel. A summary offence only. Maximum: **6 months**.

---

[184] SOA 1956, s 24(3).
[185] SOA 1956, s 46.
[186] Implementation date 27.8.1981.
[187] *Reed & Others* [2021] EWCA Crim 572.

Sentence

(i) On indictment: **2 YEARS**.[188]
(ii) An attempt carries the same maximum.

8.115

Upon Conviction/Sentence

(i) Notification not applicable.[189]
(ii) Automatic inclusion in the Children and Adult barred lists with the right to make representations.[190]
(iii) SHPO not applicable.[191]
(iv) Qualifying 'specified sexual offence' in Schedule 18 (Extended Sentences).[192]

8.116

4. Soliciting by Men for Immoral Purposes

Sexual Offences Act 1956, s 32

Definition

For a man persistently to solicit or importune in a public place for immoral purposes.

8.117

Proof

(i) Proof of 'persistently' requires at least two approaches.
(ii) 'Solicit' and 'importune' mean the same, that is, to allure and tempt for the purposes of sexual activity.[193]
(iii) The soliciting has to take place in a street or public place;
(iv) and must be done for the purposes of prostitution.

8.118

Notes

(i) The offence is triable either way.

8.119

---

[188] SOA 1956, s 37(3) and Sch 2, para 25.
[189] SOA 2003, s 80(1) (not listed in Sch 3); see Chapter 14 Tables 14.2 -14.5.
[190] Part 2 of the Safeguarding Vulnerable Groups Act 2006 (Prescribed Criteria and Miscellaneous Provisions) Regulations 2009 (SI 2009 No 37) paras 2 and 4; see Chapter 12 para 12.217.
[191] SA 2020, s 345 (not listed in Sch 3 or Sch 5 SOA 2003); see Chapter 16 para 16.07.
[192] SA 2020, s 306, Sch 18, para 29(s); see Chapter 12 para 12.51.
[193] *Behrendt v Burridge* (1976) 63 Cr App R 202 DC.

(ii) Only males may be prosecuted for this offence. The person solicited may be male or female.[194]

(iii) Street and public place are widely defined[195] to include, for example, a passage, or any place to which the public have access.

Indictment

8.120 SOLICITATION FOR IMMORAL PURPOSES 1.1.1957 to 30.4.2004

Statement of Offence
SOLICITATION FOR IMMORAL PURPOSES, contrary to section 32 of the Sexual Offences Act 1956.

Particulars of Offence
D, a male, on … persistently solicited and importuned in a public place, namely … for immoral purposes.

Alternative Offences

8.121 An attempt to commit the full offence. When indicting offences of attempt do so under common law until 26.8.1981, thereafter indict under s 1(1) Criminal Attempts Act 1981.[196] Aver the attempt in both the Statement of Offence and Particulars of Offence. In addition, aver the substantive offence under the relevant Act; see paras 1.51 and 12.157 and *Reed & Others* [2021].[197]

Sentence

8.122 (i) On indictment: **2 YEARS**.[198]
(ii) Summarily: **6 months**.[199]

Upon Conviction/Sentence

8.123 (i) Notification not applicable.[200]

---

[194] *R v Goddard* (1990) 92 Cr App R 185 CA.
[195] SOA 1959, s 1(4).
[196] Implementation date 27.8.1981.
[197] *Reed & Others* [2021] EWCA Crim 572.
[198] SOA 1956, s 37(3) and Sch 2, para 32(i).
[199] SOA 1956, s 37(3) and Sch 2, para 32(ii).
[200] SOA 2003, s 80(1) (not listed in Sch 3); see Chapter 14 Tables 14.2–14.5.

(ii) Automatic inclusion in the children's and adults' barred lists not applicable.[201]
(iii) SHPO not applicable.[202]
(iv) Qualifying 'specified sexual offence' in Schedule 18 (Extended Sentences).[203]

H. OFFENCES COMMITTED BETWEEN 27.7.1967 AND 30.4.2004

1. Living on the Earnings of Male Prostitution

Sexual Offences Act 1967, s 5

Definition

A man or woman who knowingly lives wholly or in part on the earnings of prostitution of another man. **8.124**

Proof

As per definition. See para 8.15 for definition of prostitution. **8.125**

Notes

There is no presumption in this Act in relation to living on earnings.[204] See para 8.77. **8.126**

Indictment

LIVING ON THE EARNINGS OF MALE PROSTITUTION 27.7.1967 to 30.4.2004 **8.127**

Statement of Offence

LIVING ON PROSTITUTION, contrary to section 5 of the Sexual Offences Act 1967.

Particulars of Offence

D on the ... day of ... knowingly lived (in part) on the earnings of the prostitution of C, a male.

---

[201] Part 2 of the Safeguarding Vulnerable Groups Act 2006 (Prescribed Criteria and Miscellaneous Provisions) Regulations 2009 (SI 2009 No 37) not included in paras 1, 2, 3, or 4; see Chapter 12 para 12.217.
[202] SA 2020, s 345 (not listed in Sch 3 or Sch 5 SOA 2003); see Chapter 16 para 16.07.
[203] SA 2020, s 306, Sch 18, para 29(y); see Chapter 12 para 12.51.
[204] As in SOA 1956, s 30(2).

278   8. PROSTITUTION AND TRAFFICKING

Alternative Offences

8.128   An attempt to commit the full offence. When indicting offences of attempt do so under common law until 26.8.1981, thereafter indict under s 1(1) Criminal Attempts Act 1981.[205] Aver the attempt in both the Statement of Offence and Particulars of Offence. In addition, aver the substantive offence under the relevant Act; see paras 1.51 and 12.157 and *Reed & Others* [2021].[206]

Sentence

8.129   (i) On indictment: **7 YEARS**.[207]
(ii) Summarily: **6 months**.[208]

Upon Conviction/Sentence

8.130   (i) Notification not applicable.[209]
(ii) Automatic inclusion in the Children and Adult barred lists with the right to make representations.[210]
(iii) SHPO not applicable.[211]
(iv) Qualifying 'specified sexual offence' in Schedule 18 (Extended Sentences).[212]

I. OFFENCES COMMITTED FROM 1.5.2004 TO DATE

1. Keeping a Brothel Used for Prostitution

Sexual Offences Act 1956, s 33A[213]

Definition

8.131   … to keep or to manage, or act or assist in the management of, a brothel to which people resort for practices involving prostitution (whether or not also for other practices).

---

[205] Implementation date 27.8.1981.
[206] *Reed & Others* [2021] EWCA Crim 572.
[207] SOA 1967, s 5(1)(b).
[208] SOA 1967, s 5(1)(a).
[209] SOA 2003, s 80(1) (not listed in Sch 3); see Chapter 14 Tables 14.2–14.5.
[210] Part 2 of the Safeguarding Vulnerable Groups Act 2006 (Prescribed Criteria and Miscellaneous Provisions) Regulations 2009 (SI 2009 No 37); see Chapter 12 para 12.217.
[211] SA 2020, s 345 (not listed in Sch 3 or Sch 5 SOA 2003); see Chapter 16 para 16.07.
[212] SA 2020, s 306, Sch 18, para 32(b); see Chapter 12 para 12.51.
[213] *Abbott v Smith* [1965] 2 QB 662, [1964] 3 All ER 762.

I. OFFENCES COMMITTED FROM 1.5.2004 TO DATE

Proof

8.132
(i) For 'keeping a brothel' some significant control over the premises must be proved; or
(ii) for 'managing a brothel' the same must be proved, and evidence of an active part in the running of the business as a business;[214] or
(iii) for 'acting or assisting in the management of' duties that are more than menial must be proved.
(iv) That the premises was a brothel.

Notes

8.133
(i) This offence is triable either way.
(ii) Proof that joint use of premises by a team of women for the purposes of prostitution is sufficient, even where one was using it on a given day.[215]
(iii) This offence was created by virtue of an amendment of the SOA 1956, s 33.[216] Before 1.5.2004 it could be tried summarily only (s 33 offence).
(iv) 'Prostitution' has the meaning given by section 51(2) of the Sexual Offences Act 2003.[217]

Indictment

KEEPING A BROTHEL USED FOR PROSTITUTION 1.5.2004 to date **8.134**

Statement of Offence
KEEPING A BROTHEL USED FOR PROSTITUTION, contrary to section 33A(1) of the Sexual Offences Act 1956

Particulars of Offence
D on the ... day of ... kept/managed/acted/assisted in the management of a brothel to which people resorted for practices involving prostitution.

Alternative Offences

Attempt to commit the full offence. When indicting offences of attempt do so under s 1(1) Criminal Attempts Act 1981.[218] Aver the attempt in both the Statement of Offence and **8.135**

---

[214] *Stevens v Christy* 85 Cr App R 249 DC, [1987] Crim LR 503.
[215] SOA 2003, s 55.
[216] As amended by s 55(1) and (2) SOA.
[217] SOA 1956, s 33A(2).
[218] Implementation date 27.8.1981.

280   8. PROSTITUTION AND TRAFFICKING

Particulars of Offence. In addition, aver the substantive offence under the relevant Act; see paras 1.51 and 12.157 and *Reed & Others* [2021].[219]

Sentence

8.136 (i) On indictment: **7 YEARS**.
(ii) Summarily: **6 months**.[220]

Upon Conviction/Sentence

8.137 (i) Notification not applicable.[221]
(ii) Automatic inclusion in the children's and adults' barred lists not applicable.[222]
(iii) SHPO not applicable.[223]
(iv) Qualifying 'specified sexual offence' in Schedule 18 (Extended Sentences).[224]
(v) Serious Crime Prevention Order applicable for offences convicted after 6 April 2008.[225]

2. Controlling Prostitution for Gain

Sexual Offences Act 2003, s 53(1)

Definition

8.138 (1) A person commits an offence if—
(a) he intentionally controls any of the activities of another person relating to that person's prostitution in any part of the world, and
(b) he does so for or in the expectation of gain for himself or a third person.

Proof

8.139 As per Definition.

(i) Control may cover such activities as the price charged, venue, diary, travel, bookings—even through a third party. See para 7.176(ii).

---

[219] *Reed & Others* [2021] EWCA Crim 572.
[220] 12 months if CJA 2003, s 282(4) implemented.
[221] SOA 2003, s 80(1) (not listed in Sch 3); see Chapter 14 Tables 14.2–14.5.
[222] Part 2 of the Safeguarding Vulnerable Groups Act 2006 (Prescribed Criteria and Miscellaneous Provisions) Regulations 2009 (SI 2009 No 37) not listed in paras 1, 2, 3, or 4; see Chapter 12 para 12.217.
[223] SA 2020, s 345 (not listed in Sch 3 or Sch 5 SOA 2003); see Chapter 16 para 16.07.
[224] SA 2020, s 306, Sch 18, para 29(z); see Chapter 12 para 12.51.
[225] SCA 2007, s 19 and Sch 1, para 4; see Chapter 12 para 12.240.

(ii) For proof of prostitution see para 8.37.
(iii) 'gain' includes any financial advantage, including the discharge of an obligation to pay or the provision of goods or services (including sexual services) gratuitously or at a discount; or goodwill likely to bring financial advantage.[226]

Notes

(i) This offence is triable either way. 8.140
(ii) This offence is more restricted than the old offence of living on the earnings of prostitution under the SOA 1956, s 30. See para 8.117 for requisite knowledge.
(iii) Article 26 of the Council of Europe Convention on Action against Human Trafficking 2005 (ECAT) requires careful consideration be given to whether public policy calls for a prosecution and punishment of victims of trafficking who have been compelled to become involved in unlawful activities.[227] Following the ratification of ECAT the National Referral Mechanism was established. The National Referral Mechanism (NRM) is the framework for identifying victims of human trafficking and ensuring they receive the appropriate protection and support.
(iv) The s 45 MSA 2015 defence for slavery and trafficking victims who commit an offence is available for an offence under this section, provided it was committed on or after 31.7.2.15.[228]

Indictment

CONTROLLING PROSTITUTION FOR GAIN 1.5.2004 to date 8.141

Statement of Offence
CONTROLLING PROSTITUTION FOR GAIN, contrary to section 53(1) of the Sexual Offences Act 2003.

Particulars of Offence
D on the ... day of ... intentionally controlled C's activities in relation to C's prostitution, in the expectation of gain for himself or a third person.

Alternative Offences

Attempt to commit the full offence. When indicting offences of attempt do so under s 1(1) Criminal Attempts Act 1981.[229] Aver the attempt in both the Statement of Offence and 8.142

---

[226] SOA 2003, s 54(1).
[227] *R v LM* [2010] EWCA Crim 2327.
[228] MSA 2015, s 45 commencement date 31.7.2015 (SI 2015/1476). This offence is not an excluded offence in Sch 4 of the Act. The s 45 defence is not retrospective, see *R v Joseph (Verna Sermanfure)* [2017] EWCA Crim 36.
[229] Implementation date 27.8.1981.

Particulars of Offence. In addition, aver the substantive offence under the relevant Act; see paras 1.51 and 12.157 and *Reed & Others* [2021].[230]

Sentence

8.143 (i) On indictment: **7 YEARS**.[231]
(ii) Summarily: **6 months** or a **fine** not exceeding the statutory maximum or **both**.[232]

8.144 The Sentencing Council 'Sexual Offences: Definitive Guideline' contains offence- specific guidelines for s 53 offences. The Guideline applies to all offenders aged 18 and over, sentenced on or after 1 April 2014.

Upon Conviction/Sentence

8.145 (i) Notification not applicable.[233]
(ii) Automatic inclusion in the children's and adults' barred lists with the right to make representations.[234]
(iii) SHPO applicable.[235]
(iv) Qualifying 'specified sexual offence' in Schedule 18 (Extended Sentences).[236]
(v) Lifestyle offence for purposes of POCA 2002.[237]
(vi) Serious Crime Prevention Order applicable for offences convicted after 6 April 2008.[238]

Trafficking for Sexual Exploitation

J. OFFENCES COMMITTED BETWEEN 1.1.1957 AND 30.4.2004

8.146 The SOA 1956 created a number of offences that were later used (with varying degrees of success) to prosecute those involved in people trafficking, dealt with in other sections of the book.

---

[230] *Reed & Others* [2021] EWCA Crim 572.
[231] SOA 2003, s 53(2)(b).
[232] SOA 2003, s 52(2)(a); 12 months if CJA 2003, s 282 implemented.
[233] SOA 2003, s 80(1) (not listed in Sch 3); see Chapter 14 Tables 14.2–14.5.
[234] Part 2 of the Safeguarding Vulnerable Groups Act 2006 (Prescribed Criteria and Miscellaneous Provisions) Regulations 2009 (SI 2009 No 37) paras 2 and 4; see Chapter 12 para 12.217.
[235] SA 2020, s 345 and Sch 5, para 63 SOA 2003; see Chapter 16 para 16.07.
[236] SA 2020, s 306, Sch 18, para 38(an); see Chapter 12 para 12.51.
[237] POCA 2002, Sch 2.
[238] SCA 2007, s 19 and Sch 1, para 4; see Chapter 12 para 12.240.

These include: **8.147**

- SOA 1956, s 2: procurement of a woman by threats. See paras 11.04–11.10.
- SOA 1956, s 3: procurement of a woman by false pretences. See paras 11.11–11.18.
- SOA 1956, s 22: causing prostitution of women in any part of the world. See paras 8.58–8.65.
- SOA 1956, s 24: detention of a woman in a brothel. See paras 8.89–8.95.
- SOA 1956, s 28: causing prostitution of a girl under 16. See paras 8.14–8.20.
- SOA 1956, s 30: man living on the earnings of prostitution. See paras 8.75–8.82.
- SOA 1956, s 31: woman exercising control over a prostitute. See paras 8.83–8.88.

The SOA 2003 clarifies the position as to which offences ought to be charged. **8.148**

K. OFFENCES COMMITTED FROM 1.5.2004 TO 5.4.2013

The SOA 2003 created three specific offences: **8.149**

(i) s 57: trafficking into the UK for sexual exploitation;
(ii) s 58: trafficking within the UK for sexual exploitation;
(iii) s 59: trafficking out of the UK for sexual exploitation.

Note these have been repealed as of 6.4.2013.[239]

1. Trafficking into the UK for Sexual Exploitation

Sexual Offences Act 2003, s 57

Definition

(1) A person commits an offence if he intentionally arranges or facilitates the arrival in **8.150** the United Kingdom of another person (B) and either—
  (a) he intends to do anything to or in respect of B, after B's arrival but in any part of the world, which if done will involve the commission of a relevant offence, or
  (b) he believes that another person is likely to do something to or in respect of B, after B's arrival but in any part of the world, which if done will involve the commission of a relevant offence.

---

[239] Sections 57–59 repealed by Protection of Freedoms Act 2012 (6.4.2013) and replaced by s 59A.

Proof

8.151 As per Definition. In addition:

(i) Relevant offences include:
- SOA 2003, ss 1–79;
- PCA 1978, s 1(1)(a) (taking, permitting to be taken or making an indecent photograph or pseudo-photograph of a child under 18);
- an offence listed in Criminal Justice (Children) (Northern Ireland) Order 1988, Schedule 1;
- an offence under the Protection of Children (Northern Ireland) Order 1978, Art 3(1)(a); or
- anything done outside England, Wales, Northern Ireland which is not an offence within paras (a)–(d) but would be if done in England and Wales or Northern Ireland.

(ii) 'Arranges or facilitates' may cover the provision of a ticket, or providing false papers.[240]

(iii) The facilitation or arrangement must be intentional, and the accused must have the necessary intention or belief in relation to s 57(1)(a) or (b).

Notes

8.152
(i) The offence is triable either way.
(ii) The accused and the victim may be male or female.
(iii) If the victim is under 18, a charge under the SOA 2003, s 50 (causing or inciting child prostitution or pornography) may be appropriate, see paras 8.36–8.42.
(iv) This section applies to anything done in the UK, and to anything done outside it by a body incorporated under the law of a part of the UK or by:
- a British citizen;
- a British Overseas Territories citizen;
- a British national (Overseas);
- a British overseas citizen;
- a person who is a British subject under the British Nationality Act 1981; or
- a British protected person within the meaning given by s 50(1) of that Act.

After 30.1.2008 this was simplified. Sections 57–59 apply to anything done whether inside or outside the United Kingdom.[241]

---

[240] Cf Hansard, vol 648, col 210 (13.5.2003).
[241] UK Borders Act 2007, s 31(4).

Indictment

TRAFFICKING INTO THE UK FOR SEXUAL EXPLOITATION 1.5.2004 to 5.4.2013   **8.153**

Statement of Offence
TRAFFICKING INTO THE UNITED KINGDOM FOR SEXUAL EXPLOITATION, contrary to section 57(1)(a) of the Sexual Offences Act 2003.

Particulars of Offence
D on the … day of … intentionally arranged/facilitated the arrival in the United Kingdom of C, D intending to do anything to or in respect of the said C, after C's arrival but in any part of the world which would involve the commission of a relevant offence, namely (…).

Alternative Offences

An attempt to commit the full offence. When indicting offences of attempt do so under   **8.154**
s 1(1) Criminal Attempts Act 1981.[242] Aver the attempt in both the Statement of Offence and Particulars of Offence. In addition, aver the substantive offence under the relevant Act; see paras 1.51 and 12.157 and *Reed & Others* [2021].[243]

Sentence

(i) On indictment: **14 YEARS**.[244]   **8.155**
(ii) Summarily: **6 months** or a **fine** not exceeding the statutory maximum or **both**.[245]

Upon Conviction/Sentence

(i) Notification not applicable.[246]   **8.156**
(ii) Automatic inclusion in the children's and adults' barred lists with the right to make representations.[247]
(iii) SHPO applicable.[248]

---

[242] Implementation date 27.8.1981.
[243] *Reed & Others* [2021] EWCA Crim 572.
[244] SOA 2003, s 57(2)(b).
[245] 12 months if CJA 2003, s 282(4) implemented.
[246] SOA 2003, s 80(1) (not listed in Sch 3); see Chapter 14 Tables 14.2–14.5.
[247] Part 2 of the Safeguarding Vulnerable Groups Act 2006 (Prescribed Criteria and Miscellaneous Provisions) Regulations 2009 (SI 2009 No 37) paras 2 and 4; see Chapter 12 para 12.217.
[248] SA 2020, s 345 and Sch 5, para 63 SOA 2003; see Chapter 16 para 16.07.

(iv) Qualifying 'specified sexual offence' in Schedule 18 (Extended Sentences).[249]
(v) Lifestyle offence for purposes of POCA 2002.[250]
(vi) From 12.2.2007: forfeiture of a relevant vehicle, ship or aircraft.[251]
(vi) Serious Crime Prevention Order applicable for offences convicted after 6 April 2008.[252]

2. Trafficking within the UK for Sexual Exploitation

Sexual Offences Act 2003, s 58

Definition

8.157 (1) A person commits an offence if he intentionally arranges or facilitates travel within the United Kingdom by another person (B) and either—
   (a) he intends to do anything to or in respect of B, during or after the journey and in any part of the world, which if done will involve the commission of a relevant offence, or
   (b) he believes that another person is likely to do something to or in respect of B during or after the journey and in any part of the world, which if done will involve the commission of a relevant offence.

Proof

8.158 As per Definition. In addition:

(i) See para 8.128 for 'arranges or facilitates'.
(ii) See para 8.128 for the definition of 'relevant offence'.
(iii) See para 8.128 for jurisdiction.
(iv) The facilitation or arrangement must be intentional, and the accused must have the necessary intention or belief within s 58(1)(a) or (b).

Notes

8.159 The offence is triable either way.

---

[249] SA 2020, s 306, Sch 18, para 38(ao); see Chapter 12 para 12.51.
[250] POCA 2002, Sch 2.
[251] SOA 2003, s 60A, in force from 12.2.2007.
[252] SCA 2007, s 19 and Sch 1, para 2; see Chapter 12 para 12.240.

K. OFFENCES COMMITTED FROM 1.5.2004 TO 5.4.2013   287

Indictment

TRAFFICKING WITHIN THE UK FOR SEXUAL EXPLOITATION 1.5.2004 to 5.4.2013   **8.160**

Statement of Offence
TRAFFICKING WITHIN THE UNITED KINGDOM FOR SEXUAL EXPLOITATION, contrary to section 58(1)(a) of the Sexual Offences Act 2003.

Particulars of Offence
D on the … day of … intentionally arranged/facilitated travel within the United Kingdom by C, D intending to do anything to or in respect of C, during or after the journey in any part of the world, which would involve the commission of a relevant offence, namely (…).

Alternative Offences

An attempt to commit the full offence. When indicting offences of attempt do so under s 1(1) Criminal Attempts Act 1981.[253] Aver the attempt in both the Statement of Offence and Particulars of Offence. In addition, aver the substantive offence under the relevant Act; see paras 1.51 and 12.157 and *Reed & Others* [2021].[254]   **8.161**

Sentence

(i) On indictment: **14 YEARS**.[255]
(ii) Summarily: **6 months** or a fine not exceeding the statutory maximum or **both**.[256]   **8.162**

Upon Conviction/Sentence

(i) Notification not applicable.[257]
(ii) Automatic inclusion in the children's and adults' barred lists with the right to make representations.[258]
(iii) SHPO applicable.[259]
(iv) Qualifying 'specified sexual offence' in Schedule 18 (Extended Sentences).[260]   **8.163**

---

[253] Implementation date 27.8.1981.
[254] *Reed & Others* [2021] EWCA Crim 572.
[255] SOA 2003, s 58(2)(b).
[256] 12 months if CJA 2003, s 282(4) implemented.
[257] SOA 2003, s 80(1) (not listed in Sch 3); see Chapter 14 Tables 14.2–14.5.
[258] Part 2 of the Safeguarding Vulnerable Groups Act 2006 (Prescribed Criteria and Miscellaneous Provisions) Regulations 2009 (SI 2009 No 37) paras 2 and 4; see Chapter 12 para 12.217.
[259] SA 2020, s 345 and Sch 5, para 63 SOA 2003; see Chapter 16 para 16.07.
[260] SA 2020, s 306, Sch 18, para 38(ap); see Chapter 12 para 12.51.

288   8. PROSTITUTION AND TRAFFICKING

(v) Lifestyle offence for purposes of POCA 2002.[261]
(vi) From 12.2.2007: forfeiture of a relevant vehicle, ship or aircraft.[262]
(vi) Serious Crime Prevention Order applicable for offences convicted after 6 April 2008.[263]

3. Trafficking out of the UK for Sexual Exploitation

Sexual Offences Act 2003, s 59(1)

Definition

8.164 A person commits an offence if he intentionally engages or facilitates the departure from the United Kingdom of another person (B) and either—

(a) he intends to do anything to or in respect of B, after B's departure but in any part of the world, which if done will involve the commission of a relevant offence, or
(b) he believes that another person is likely to do something to or in respect of B, after B's departure but in any part of the world, which if done will involve the commission of a relevant offence.

Proof

8.165
(i) As per Definition. In addition:
(ii) See para 8.128 for arranges or facilitates.
(iii) See para 8.128 for the definition of 'relevant offence'.
(iv) See para 8.128 for jurisdiction.
(v) The facilitation or arrangement must be intentional and the accused must have the necessary intention or belief within s 59(1)(a) or (b).

Notes

8.166 The offence is triable either way.

Indictment

8.167 TRAFFICKING OUT OF THE UK FOR SEXUAL EXPLOITATION 1.5.2004 to 5.4.2013.

---

[261] POCA 2002, Sch 2.
[262] SOA 2003, s 60A, in force from 12.2.2007.
[263] SCA 2007, s 19 and Sch 1, para 2; see Chapter 12 para 12.240.

Statement of Offence

TRAFFICKING OUT OF THE UNITED KINGDOM FOR SEXUAL EXPLOITATION, contrary to section 59(1)(a) of the Sexual Offences Act 2003.

Particulars of Offence

D on the ... day of ... intentionally arranged/facilitated the departure from the United Kingdom by C, D intending to do anything to or in respect of C, after C's departure but in any part of the world, which would involve the commission of a relevant offence, namely (...).

Alternative Offences

An attempt to commit the full offence. When indicting offences of attempt do so under s 1(1) Criminal Attempts Act 1981.[264] Aver the attempt in both the Statement of Offence and Particulars of Offence. In addition, aver the substantive offence under the relevant Act; see paras 1.51 and 12.157 and *Reed & Others* [2021].[265]

8.168

Sentence

(i) On indictment: **14 YEARS**.[266]
(ii) Summarily: **6 months** or a **fine** not exceeding the statutory maximum or **both**.[267]

8.169

Upon Conviction/Sentence

(i) Notification not applicable.[268]
(ii) Automatic inclusion in the children's and adults' barred lists with the right to make representations.[269]
(iii) SHPO applicable.[270]
(iv) Qualifying 'specified sexual offence' in Schedule 18 (Extended Sentences).[271]
(v) Lifestyle offence for purposes of POCA 2002.[272]
(vi) From 12.2.2007: forfeiture of a relevant vehicle, ship or aircraft.[273]

8.170

---

[264] Implementation date 27.8.1981.
[265] *Reed & Others* [2021] EWCA Crim 572.
[266] SOA 2003, s 59(2)(b).
[267] 12 months if CJA 2003, s 282(4) implemented.
[268] SOA 2003, s 80(1) (not listed in Sch 3); see Chapter 14 Tables 14.2–14.5.
[269] Part 2 of the Safeguarding Vulnerable Groups Act 2006 (Prescribed Criteria and Miscellaneous Provisions) Regulations 2009 (SI 2009 No 37) paras 2 and 4; see Chapter 12 para 12.217.
[270] SA 2020, s 345 and Sch 5, para 63 SOA 2003; see Chapter 16 para 16.07.
[271] SA 2020, s 306, Sch 18, para 38(aq); see Chapter 12 para 12.51.
[272] POCA 2002, Sch 2.
[273] SOA 2003, s 60A, in force from 12.2.2007.

(vi) Serious Crime Prevention Order applicable for offences convicted after 6 April 2008.[274]

8.171 The Sentencing Council 'Sexual Offences: Definitive Guideline' contains offence-specific guidelines in relation to s 59A offences. Section 59A has since been repealed. However the Guideline states: 'This Guideline (s 59A) also applies to offences, committed before 6 April 2013, of trafficking into/within/out of the UK for sexual exploitation contrary to sections 57 to 59 of the Sexual Offences Act 2003. The Guideline applies to all offenders aged 18 and over, sentenced on or after 1 April 2014.'

4. Trafficking People for Sexual Exploitation

Sexual Offences Act 2003, s 59A

Definition

8.172 Section 59A:[275]

(1) A person (A) commits an offence if A intentionally arranges or facilitates—
  (a) the arrival in, or entry into, the United Kingdom or another country of another person (B),
  (b) the travel of B within the United Kingdom or another country, or
  (c) the departure of B from the United Kingdom or another country, with a view to the sexual exploitation of B.

8.173 (2) For the purposes of subsection (1)(a) and (c), A's arranging or facilitating is with a view to the sexual exploitation of B if, and only if—
  (a) A intends to do anything to or in respect of B, after B's arrival, entry or (as the case may be) departure but in any part of the world, which if done will involve the commission of a relevant offence, or
  (b) A believes that another person is likely to do something to or in respect of B, after B's arrival, entry or (as the case may be) departure but in any part of the world, which if done will involve the commission of a relevant offence.

(3) For the purposes of subsection (1)(b) A's arranging or facilitating is with a view to the sexual exploitation of B if, and only if—
  (a) A intends to do anything to or in respect of B, during or after the journey and in any part of the world, which if done will involve the commission of a relevant offence, or
  (b) A believes that another person is likely to do something to or in respect of B, during or after the journey and in any part of the world, which if done will involve the commission of a relevant offence.

---

[274] SCA 2007, s 19 and Sch 1, para 2; see Chapter 12 para 12.240.
[275] Section inserted by the Protection of Freedoms Act 2012, s 109(1) and (2).

Proof

8.174 A person who is a UK national commits an offence under this section regardless of—

(a) where the arranging or facilitating takes place, or
(b) which country is the country of arrival, entry, travel or (as the case may be) departure.

8.175 A person who is not a UK national commits an offence under this section if—

(a) any part of the arranging or facilitating takes place in the United Kingdom, or
(b) the United Kingdom is the country of arrival, entry, travel or (as the case may be) departure.
- 'country' includes any territory or other part of the world;
- 'relevant offence' means—
(a) any offence under the law of England and Wales which is an offence under this Part or under section 1(1)(a) of the Protection of Children Act 1978, or
(b) anything done outside England and Wales which is not an offence within paragraph (a) but would be if done in England and Wales;
- 'UK national' means—
(a) a British citizen,
(b) a person who is a British subject by virtue of Part 4 of the British Nationality Act 1981 and who has the right of abode in the United Kingdom, or
(c) a person who is a British Overseas Territories citizen by virtue of a connection with Gibraltar.

Notes

8.176
(i) The offence is triable either way.
(ii) This offence was short-lived. Having been implemented on 6.4.2013 it was repealed on 31.7.2015 by the Modern Slavery Act 2015 and replaced with an offence under s 2 of that Act.

Indictment

TRAFFICKING PEOPLE FOR SEXUAL EXPLOITATION 6.4.2013 to 30.7.2015   **8.177**

Statement of Offence

TRAFFICKING PEOPLE FOR SEXUAL EXPLOITATION contrary to section 59A(1)(a) of the Sexual Offences Act 2003

Particulars of Offence

A on a day between ... and the ... day of ... intentionally arranged or facilitated the arrival in, or entry into the United Kingdom (or another country) of B with a view to the sexual exploitation of the said B, in that the said A intending to do anything to the said B after her arrival in the United Kingdom, which, if done, would involve the commission of a relevant offence.

292   8. PROSTITUTION AND TRAFFICKING

Sentence

8.178 (i) On indictment: **14 YEARS**.
(ii) Summarily: **12 months** or a **fine** not exceeding the statutory maximum or **both**;

8.179 The Sentencing Council 'Sexual Offences: Definitive Guideline' contains offence-specific guidelines for section 59A offences. The Guideline applies to all offenders aged 18 and over, sentenced on or after 1 April 2014.

Upon Conviction/Sentence

8.180 (i) Notification not applicable.[276]
(ii) Automatic inclusion in the children's and adults' barred lists with the right to make representations.[277]
(iii) SHPO applicable.[278]
(iv) Qualifying 'specified sexual offence' in Schedule 18 (Extended Sentences).[279]
(v) Lifestyle offence for purposes of POCA 2002.[280]
(vi) From 12.2.2007: forfeiture of a relevant vehicle, ship or aircraft; if the convicted person was the driver, owner or the director, manager or secretary of a company that owned the property or was in possession of the vehicle under a hire-purchase agreement.[281]
(vi) Serious Crime Prevention Order applicable for offences convicted after 6 April 2008.[282]

5. Human Trafficking

Modern Slavery Act 2015, s 2

8.181 Section 59A was repealed by the Modern Slavery Act[283] on 31 July 2015. The Modern Slavery Act 2015 consolidated existing slavery and trafficking offences into two offences under ss 1 and 2. The s 2 offence of 'Human Trafficking' replaced the existing trafficking offences. The s 2 offence covers exploitation committed in one or more of the following five specified forms: slavery; servitude and forced or compulsory labour; sexual exploitation; removal of organs; securing services etc by force, threats or deception; and securing services etc from children and vulnerable persons. This section deals only with sexual exploitation.

---

[276] SOA 2003, s 80(1) (not listed in Sch 3); see Chapter 14 Tables 14.2–14.5.
[277] Part 2 of the Safeguarding Vulnerable Groups Act 2006 (Prescribed Criteria and Miscellaneous Provisions) Regulations 2009 (SI 2009 No 37) paras 2 and 4; see Chapter 12 para 12.217.
[278] SA 2020, s 345 and Sch 5, para 63 SOA 2003; see Chapter 16 para 16.07.
[279] SA 2020, s 306, Sch 18, para 38(ar); see Chapter 12 para 12.51.
[280] POCA 2002, Sch 2.
[281] SOA 2003, s 60A, in force from 12.2.2007.
[282] SCA 2007, s 19 and Sch 1, para 2; see Chapter 12 para 12.240.
[283] Repealed by Modern Slavery Act 2015 (31.7.2015) The repeal has effect as SI 2015/1476 subject to transitional provisions and savings specified in SI 2015/1476 art. 3.

Definition

A person commits an offence if the person arranges or facilitates the travel of another person (B) with a view to B being exploited.[284] **8.182**

Proof

As per definition. Further: **8.183**

(i) 'Arranges or facilitates' B's travel; a person may in particular arrange or facilitate B's travel by recruiting B, transporting or transferring B, harbouring or receiving B, or transferring or exchanging control over B.[285] Travel means: arriving in, or entering, any country; departing from any country, and travelling within any country.[286]

(ii) With a 'view to B being exploited'; A person arranges or facilitates B's travel with a view to B being exploited only if: (a) the person intends to exploit B (in any part of the world) during or after the travel, or (b) the person knows or ought to know that another person is likely to exploit B (in any part of the world) during or after the travel.[287]

(ii) Exploited; a person is exploited only if one of more of the following apply to the person (1) slavery, servitude and forced or compulsory labour; (2) sexual exploitation; (3) removal of organs; (4) securing services etc. by force, threats or deception; or (5) securing services etc. from children and vulnerable persons.[288]

(iii) Sexual exploitation is defined as something is done to or in respect of the person (a) which involves the commission of an offence under: (i) section 1(1)(a) of the Protection of Children Act 1978 (indecent photographs of children), or (ii) Part 1 of the Sexual Offences Act 2003 (sexual offences), as it has effect in England and Wales; or (b) which would involve the commission of such an offence if it were done in England and Wales.[289]

Notes

(i) The offence is triable either way. **8.184**
(ii) Consent of C to travel is not relevant.[290]
(iii) Travel: walking, for instance, between adjacent rooms, or other journeys involving truly minimal distances (for instance of a few feet or yards) may well be outside

---

[284] MSA 2015, s 2(1).
[285] MSA 2015, s 2(3).
[286] MSA 2015, s 2(5).
[287] MSA 2015, s 2(4).
[288] MSA, s 3.
[289] MSA 2015, s 3(3).
[290] MSA 2015, s 2(2).

the ambit of this provision because there is a clear geographical element to the offence. Substantive journeys took place involving a number of miles do fall within the provision.[291]

(vi) Jurisdiction: A person who is a UK national commits an offence under this section regardless of: (a) where the arranging or facilitating takes place, or (b) where the travel takes place. A person who is not a UK national commits offence under this section if: (a) any part of the arranging or facilitating takes place in the United Kingdom, or (b) the travel consists of arrival in or entry into, departure from, or travel within, the United Kingdom.[292]

(iv) The NRM[293] referral should have already been made for trafficking victims who are identified at an early stage. Note the s 45 defence for slavery or trafficking victims who commit offences does not apply to offences under s 2 MSA 2015.[294]

Indictment

8.185 HUMAN TRAFFICKING FOR SEXUAL EXPLOITATION 31.7.2015 to date

---
Statement of Offence
HUMAN TRAFFICKING contrary to section 2(1) Modern Slavery Act 2015

Particulars of Offence
D on the … day of … arranged or facilitated the travel of another, C, with the intention that C would be sexually exploited by D [or knew or ought to have known that C would be sexually exploited by another] during or after the travel.

Alternative Offences

8.186 (i) An attempt to commit the full offence. When indicting offences of attempt do so under s 1(1) Criminal Attempts Act 1981.[295] Aver the attempt in both the Statement of Offence and Particulars of Offence. In addition, aver the substantive offence under the relevant Act; see paras 1.51 and 12.157 and *Reed & Others* [2021].[296]

(ii) Section 4 creates an offence of committing any offence with the intention to commit an offence of human trafficking under section 2. Section 4 is widely drafted and will include an offence committed by aiding, abetting, counselling or procuring an offence under section 2.

---

[291] *R v Ali (Yasir)* [2015] EWCA Crim 1279 at [80].
[292] MSA 2015, s 2(6).
[293] National Referral Mechanism.
[294] MSA 2014, s 45 and Sch 4, para 36.
[295] Implementation date 27.8.1981.
[296] *Reed & Others* [2021] EWCA Crim 572.

K. OFFENCES COMMITTED FROM 1.5.2004 TO 5.4.2013   295

Sentence

(i) On indictment: **LIFE**.[297] 8.187
(ii) Summarily: **6 months** or a **fine** not exceeding the statutory maximum or **both**.[298]

There are no Sentencing Council Guidelines for offences under the Modern Slavery Act 2015. However, interim explanatory guidance for sentencing offences of sexual exploitation under s 2 of the MSA 2015 has now been included in the Sexual Offences Guidelines, pending the future publication of full guidance. The s 59A offence (now repealed) Guideline may still be of use for sentencing cases of sexual exploitation prosecuted under s 2 of the MSA 2015. But note the different maximum sentences: 14 years for s 59A whereas the maximum for a s 2 offence is life. 8.188

Note: Consultation Guidelines were published on 15 October 2020.

Upon Conviction/Sentence

(i)   Notification not applicable.[299] 8.189
(ii)   Automatic inclusion in the children's and adults' barred lists with the right to make representations.[300]
(iii) SHPO applicable.[301]
(iv)   Qualifying 'specified sexual offence' in Schedule 18 where involves sexual exploitation (Extended Sentences).[302]
(v)   Qualifying Schedule 19 offence (Life Sentences).[303]
(vi)   Qualifying Schedule 14 offence (Extended Sentences: The Earlier Offence Condition).[304]
(vii) Qualifying 'index' offence (if committed after 3 December 2012) for the purpose of Schedule 15 (Life Sentence for Second Listed Offence).[305]
(viii) Slavery and Trafficking Prevention Order applicable.[306]
(ix)   Power to make Slavery and Trafficking Reparation Order applies.[307]
(x)   Forfeiture of land, ship, vehicle, ship of aircraft used in connection with the offence.[308]
(vi)   Serious Crime Prevention Order applicable for offences convicted after 6 April 2008.[309]

---

[297] MSA 2015, s 5(1)(a).
[298] MSA 2015, s 5(1)(b). The Act refers to 12 months' imprisonment, the 12 months will only apply if CJA 2003, s 282(4) implemented.
[299] SOA 2003, s 80(1) (not in Sch 3); see Chapter 14 para Tables 14.2–14.5.
[300] Part 2 of the Safeguarding Vulnerable Groups Act 2006 (Prescribed Criteria and Miscellaneous Provisions) Regulations 2009 (SI 2009 No 37) paras 2 and 4; see Chapter 12 para 12.217.
[301] SA 2020, s 345 (not in Sch 3) included in Sch 5, para 63B; SOA 2003; see Chapter 16 para 16.07.
[302] SA 2020, s 306, Sch 18, para 39; see Chapter 12 para 12.51.
[303] SA 2020, s 307, Sch 19, para 22(b); see Chapter 12 para 12.52.
[304] SA 2020, ss 267 and 280, Sch 14, para 12(b); see Chapter 12 para 12.77.
[305] SA 2020, ss 273 and 283, Sch 15, para 12(b); see Chapter 12 para 12.123.
[306] Slavery and Trafficking Prevention Order (STPO), s 14 MSA 2015.
[307] MSA 2015, s 8.
[308] SA 2020 s 160(1) and MSA 2015, s 11.
[309] SCA 2007, s 19 and Sch 1, para 2; see Chapter 12 para 12.240.

Paying for the Sexual Services of a Prostitute Subjected to Force etc

Sexual Offences Act 2003, s 53A(1) 1.4.2010 to date

8.190 Section 53A was inserted into the SOA 2003 with effect from 1.4.2010.[310] The new section creates a strict liability offence which is committed by the person who pays or promises payment for the sexual services of a prostitute who has been subject to exploitative conduct by a third party, of a kind likely to induce or encourage the provision of sexual services. The third party responsible for the exploitative conduct must have been acting for or in the expectation of gain for himself/herself or another (but not for D or for the prostitute).

Definition

8.191 (1) A person (D) commits an offence if—
  (a) D makes or promises payment for the sexual services of a prostitute (C),
  (b) a third person (X) has engaged in exploitative conduct of a kind likely to induce or encourage C to provide the sexual services for which D has made or promised payment, and
  (c) X engaged in that conduct for or in the expectation of gain for X or another person (apart from D or C).

Proof

8.192 As per definition.

Notes

8.193 (i) the offence is summary only.
  (ii) X engages in exploitative conduct if (a) X uses force, threats (whether or not relating to violence) or any other form of coercion;[311] or (b) X practices any form of deception.[312]
  (iii) 'Gain' means (a) any financial advantage, including the discharge of an obligation to pay or the provision of goods or services (including sexual services) gratuitously or at a discount;[313] or (b) the goodwill of any person which is or appears likely, in time, to bring financial advantage.[314]
  (iv) 'Prostitute' means a person C who, on at least one occasion and whether or not compelled to do so, offers or provides sexual services to another person in return for

---

[310] Section 53A inserted by Policing and Crime Act 2009 (SI 2010/507).
[311] SOA 2003, s 53A(3)(a).
[312] SOA 2003, s 53A(3)(b).
[313] SOA 2003, s 54(1)(a).
[314] SOA 2003, s 54(1)(b).

payment or a promise of payment to D or a third person. 'Prostitution' is to be interpreted accordingly.[315]
(v) 'Payment' means any financial advantage, including the discharge of an obligation to pay or the provision of goods or services (including sexual services) gratuitously or at a discount.[316]
(v) It is irrelevant where in the world the sexual services are to be provided and whether those services are provided.[317]
(vi) The offence is one of strict liability and no mental element is required in respect of D's knowledge that the prostitute was forced, threatened, coerced or deceived.[318]

Charge 1.4.2010 to date

D, on the … day of ….made or promised payment to C, a prostitute, for sexual services, C having been likely induced or encouraged to provide said sexual services by the exploitative conduct of X, acting in the expectation of gain for himself/herself or another, contrary to section 53A Sexual Offences Act 2003. **8.194**

Sentence

Fine not exceeding Level 3 (currently £1,000) on the standard scale.[319] **8.195**

This offence is not included in the SC Magistrates' Court Sentencing Guidelines. **8.196**

Upon Conviction/Sentence

(i) Notification not applicable.[320] **8.197**
(ii) Automatic inclusion in the children's and adults' barred lists with the right to make representations not applicable.[321]
(iii) SHPO applicable.[322]

---

[315] SOA 2003, s 54(2).
[316] SOA 2003, s 53A(3).
[317] SOA 2003, s 53A(2)(a).
[318] SOA 2003, s 53A(2)(b).
[319] SOA 2003, s 53A(4).
[320] SOA 2003, s 80(1) (not in Sch 3): see Chapter 14 Tables 14.2–14.5.
[321] Part 2 of the Safeguarding Vulnerable Groups Act 2006 (Prescribed Criteria and Miscellaneous Provisions) Regulations 2009 (SI 2009 No 37) not included in paras 1, 2, 3, and 4; see Chapter 12 para 12.217.
[322] SA 2020, s 345 (not in Sch 3 or Sch 5 SOA 2003); see Chapter 16 para 16.07.

9

INDECENT IMAGES/OBSCENE PUBLICATIONS

A. Introduction	9.01	1. Possession of a Prohibited Image of a Child	9.38
1. Obscene Publications	9.03	2. Possession of an Extreme Pornographic Image, 26.1.2009 to date	9.46
B. Child Pornography	9.05		
1. Offences Committed from 20.8.1978 to date	9.05	D. Obscene Publications	9.55
2. Offences Committed from 29.9.1988 to date	9.25	1. Publishing an Obscene Article or Having an Obscene Article for Publication for Gain	9.58
C. Possession of Prohibited and Extreme Pornographic Images of Children	9.38	E. Other Offences	9.67
		1. Disclosing Private Sexual Photographs or Films, 13.4.2015 to date	9.67

A. INTRODUCTION

The Protection of Children Act (PCA) 1978 consolidated the law on child pornography, essentially legislating against the taking, showing, distribution and publishing of indecent photographs of children under 16. Before 1978 these categories of offences were prosecuted under obscenity laws, customs and excise legislation, offences of indecent assault and gross indecency with children. This Act is still in force. Section 160 of the CJA 1988 extended the PCA 1978 offences to include an offence of simple possession of such a photograph. The Criminal Justice and Public Order Act (CJPOA) 1994 extended these offences to computer data and computerized images of children. The SOA 2003 increased the age limit under the definition of 'child' to include those aged 16 and 17[1] (except those who are married or co-habiting). 9.01

New offences created by the SOA 2003 include: SOA 2003, s 48—causing or inciting child prostitution or pornography (see para 8.36), SOA 2003, s 49—controlling a child involved in child pornography (see para 8.43), and s 50—arranging child pornography (see para 8.50). 9.02

---

[1] Section 7(6) PCA 1978, as amended by SOA 2003 (1.5.2004).

1. Obscene Publications

9.03 For the readers of this book, the most common usages of these charges will be to cover the retail distribution of obscene material: in shops or by mail order. The Obscene Publications Act (OPA) 1959 and the extended offence under the OPA 1964 are still in force. The offence is time-barred (that is, there may be no prosecution under these sections more than 2 years after the commission of the offence).[2] The topic is not dealt with in its historical context.

9.04 Section 2 of the OPA 1959 creates the offence of publication of an obscene article. In 1964,[3] the offence was extended to possessing an obscene article for gain.

B. CHILD PORNOGRAPHY

1. Offences Committed from 20.8.1978 to date

Taking, making, distributing, publishing etc photographs of children

Protection of Children Act 1978, s 1

Definition

9.05 1(1) [Subject to sections 1A and 1B][4] it is an offence for a person—
   (a) to take, or permit to be taken [or to make],[5] any indecent photograph [or pseudo-photograph] of a child; or
   (b) to distribute or show such indecent photographs [or pseudo-photographs]; or
   (c) to have in his possession such indecent photographs [or pseudo-photographs], with a view to their being distributed or shown by himself or others; or
   (d) to publish or cause to be published any advertisement likely to be understood as conveying that the advertiser distributes or shows such indecent photographs [or pseudo-photographs] or intends to do so.

Proof

9.06 (i) 'Photograph' includes a film, copy of a photograph (negative or positive) or film, and a photograph comprised in a film.[6] Film includes any form of video recording.[7] As from 3.2.1994, this definition is extended to include data stored on a computer disk or by other electronic means capable of conversion to a photograph.[8]

---

[2] OPA 1959, s 2(3).
[3] OPA 1964, s 1.
[4] Words inserted by Sexual Offences Act 2003 c 42 Sch 6 para 24 (1.5.2004).
[5] Amendments in brackets in force from 3.2.1995. PCA 1978, s 1(1) as amended by CJPOA 1994 (commencement date 3.2.1995, SI 1995/127).
[6] PCA 1978, s 7(2).
[7] PCA 1978, s 7(5).
[8] PCA 1978, s 7(4). Substituted by CJPOA 1994.

B. CHILD PORNOGRAPHY 301

(ii) As from 3.2.1995: 'pseudo-photograph'[9] is defined as an image, whether made by computer graphics or otherwise, which appears to be a photograph.[10] This term includes a copy of a pseudo-photograph, and data stored on a computer disk or by other electronic means which is capable of conversion into a pseudo-photograph.[11] It is sufficient if the predominant impression given by the pseudo-photograph is that the person shown is a child.[12] This section covers the position where the image is created by computer graphics and gives the impression that the person shown is a child.[13]

(iii) References to photograph also include:
   (a) a tracing or other image, whether made by electronic or other means (of whatever nature)—
      (i) which is not itself a photograph or pseudo-photograph, but
      (ii) which is derived from the whole or part of a photograph or pseudo-photograph (or a combination of either or both); and
   (b) data stored on a computer disc or by other electronic means which is capable of conversion into an image within (a);
      and subsection (8) applies in relation to such an image as it applies in relation to a pseudo-photograph.[14]

(iv) 'Indecent' is not defined in the Act, and is a matter for the tribunal of fact alone. The jury ought to be directed that they decide whether it would be considered indecent by right-thinking people.[15] The photograph itself and the age of the child may be taken into account, but not the circumstances of the taking of the photograph or the defendant's motives for taking it.[16] If photographs show children and are indecent then they are indecent photographs.[17] This includes photographs of adults behaving in a highly indecent manner in which a child appears.[18]

(iv) Section 1(1)(a): as from 3.2.1995: 'to make' covers the following:
   - downloading an image from the internet onto a computer or disk;[19]
   - printing off an image downloaded from the internet;[20]
   - opening an image attached to an e-mail;[21]
   - storing an image on a computer directory;[22]
   - accessing sites knowing the likelihood that pop-ups of illegal material would occur.[23]

   The act of making or taking the photograph has to be deliberate and intentional, made in the knowledge that the image is or is likely to be indecent.[24] The

---

[9] 'Pseudo-photograph' inserted by CJPOA 1994, s 84(1) and (2).
[10] PCA 1978, s 7(7).
[11] PCA 1978, s 7(9).
[12] PCA 1978, s 7(8).
[13] PCA 1978, s 7(7).
[14] Section 7(4A) (inserted by s 69 Criminal Justice and Immigration Act 2008) (8.7.2008).
[15] R v Smethurst [2002] 1 Cr App R 6 CA.
[16] R v Owen [1988] 1 WLR 134 and R v Graham-Kerr [1988] 1 WLR 1098.
[17] PCA 1978, s 7(3), as amended by CJPOA 1994, s 84(1)(3) from 3.2.1995.
[18] R v Owen [1988] 1 WLR 134 at page 295.
[19] R v Smith; R v Jayson [2003] 1 Cr App R 13.
[20] R v Bowden [2002] 2 Cr App R 438 CA.
[21] R v Smith; R v Jayson [2003] 1 Cr App R 13.
[22] Atkins v DPP; Goodland v DPP [2000] 2 Cr App R 248 CA.
[23] Harrison [2007] EWCA Crim 2976.
[24] R v Smith; R v Jayson [2003] 1 Cr App R 13.

prosecution do not have to prove that the defendant intended the photograph or pseudo-photograph to be for an indecent purpose.[25]

(v) 'permit to be taken' covers the allowing of such photographs to be taken, being in a position to forbid it.[26]

(vi) Section 1(1)(b): 'distribute or show', a person is to be regarded as distributing an indecent photograph [or pseudo-photograph] if he parts with possession of it to, or exposes or offers it for acquisition by, another person.[27] Images kept on a computer and made available to people on the internet is sufficient.[28] Note the statutory defence: s 1(4), see (xi).

(vii) Section 1(1)(c): 'possession with a view to their being distributed or shown' requires some degree of control over the article in question, and knowledge of possession of the article (but not necessarily knowledge that the photograph or pseudo-photograph is of a child).[29] It is a matter for the jury to decide whether images may have been beyond the defendant's control. Lack of computer skills, or necessary software, may be relevant.[30] There is a specific requirement of intention; mere knowledge that others could or were likely to see them is not enough.[31] 'Shown' means to a third party, possession with a view to showing it to oneself is an offence contrary to the CJA 1988, s 160 but not under PCA 1978, s 1(1)(c)[32] (see para 9.18). A person who stores indecent photographs on their computer and enables others to view them via the internet using a password does possess them with a view to them being shown.[33] Note the statutory defence: PCA 1978, s 1(4); see (xi).

(viii) Section 1(1)(d): 'publishing': the prosecution must prove that the defendant published the material intentionally. The statutory defence under s 1(4)(b) does not apply.

(ix) 'Causing to be published': the prosecution must prove *mens rea*; where a statute creates an offence of causing something to be done, it is not to be construed as an absolute offence but as one requiring proof of the appropriate *mens rea*.[34]

(x) 'Child' is defined by the PCA 1978, s 1(1)(a) and (2), as a person under the age of 16. This was later amended by the SOA 2003 to increase the age to those aged 16 and 17[35] (unless married or living together; see (xiv)). In cases where the age of the child is unknown the question is one for the jury based on all evidence in the case. Although *R v Land*[36] is regarded as authority for the principle that expert evidence (tendered by either side) as to whether a person depicted a photograph is a child is inadmissible, see now *R v RT & MAM*[37] in which Bean LJ considering *Land* stated 'The passage beginning with the observation that "in any event such expert evidence tendered by either side would be inadmissible" is obiter, though from a judge of great criminal

---

[25] *R v Smethurst* [2002] 1 Cr App R 6 CA.
[26] *Thompson v Lodwick* [1983] RTR 76.
[27] PCA 1978, s 1(2).
[28] *R v Fellows and Arnold* [1997] Cr App R 244 CA. *Dooley* [2005] EWCA Crim 3093.
[29] *R v Land* [1999] QB 65.
[30] *R v Porter* [2006] EWCA Crim 560.
[31] *R v Dooley* [2006] 1 Cr App R 21.
[32] *R v ET* 163 JP 349, CA.
[33] *R v Fellows and Arnold* [1997] Cr App R 244 CA.
[34] *Ross Hillman Ltd v Bond* [1974] QB 435 DC.
[35] PCA 1978, s 2, as amended by SOA 2003, s 45(2).
[36] *R v Land* [1999] I Cr App R 301; QB 65.
[37] *R v RT & MAM* [2020] EWCA Crim 1343 at [29].

experience. It is not easy to construe. Judge LJ cannot have meant that expert evidence about the age of an individual is always inadmissible.'

In cases before the 2003 Act was passed, prosecutors could rely on the rebuttable presumption in the CYPA 1933, s 99(2), based on appearance that a child be under 16. After 1.5.2004, s 2(3) creates a similar presumption in relation to those under 18.

(xi) It is a defence to an offence under the PCA 1978, s 1(1)(b) or (c) if the defendant proves that he either had legitimate reasons for possessing, distributing or showing these photographs or pseudo-photographs,[38] or did not know or have cause to suspect them to be indecent.[39] The question of legitimate reason is one for the jury.

(xii) Section 1A (as amended on 1.5.2004)[40] provides a defence to offences under s 1(a), (b) or (c), where the image is a photograph or a pseudo-photograph[41] and the child is proved, by the defendant, to be aged 16 or over.

(xiii) Section 1(a) (taking or making): a defence is provided under s 1A if the defendant proves they were married, in a civil partnership or living together in an enduring family relationship at the time;[42] and
- there is sufficient to raise the question that she consented, or he had a reasonable belief in her consent;[43] and
- the child was either alone or with the defendant.[44] This defence does not apply to permitting.

(xiv) Section 1(1)(b) (distributing or showing): a defence is provided under s 1A if the defendant proves they were married, in a civil partnership or living together in an enduring family relationship at the time;[45] and the photograph shows only the child or the child and the defendant.[46] The prosecution must prove that the showing or distribution was to someone other than the child.[47]

(xv) Section 1(1)(c) (possessing with a view): a defence is provided under s 1A if the defendant proves that they were married, in a civil partnership or living together in an enduring family relationship at the time;[48] and the photograph shows only the child or the child alone or with the defendant.[49] There also has to be sufficient evidence adduced to raise (a) the child's consent or the defendant's reasonable belief in consent; and (b) as to whether the defendant had the image in their possession with a view to it being distributed to anyone other than the child.[50]

(xvi) Section 1B provides a defence to s 1(1)(a) where it can be proved that it was necessary for the defendant to make the images for the purpose of any criminal proceedings, or the prevention, detection or investigation of crime, or that he was a member of the Security Service[51] or the Secret Intelligence

---

[38] PCA 1978, s 1(4)(a).
[39] PCA 1978, s 1(4)(b).
[40] SOA 2003, ss 45(1)(3) and 46(1).
[41] Pseudo-photograph inserted by Coroners and Justice Act 2009 (6.4.2010).
[42] PCA 1978, 1A(1). This does not include a 'one night stand'. *R v M* [2011] EWCA Crim 252.
[43] PCA 1978, s 1A(4).
[44] PCA 1978, s 1A(3).
[45] PCA 1978, 1A(1). This does not include a 'one night stand'. *R v M* [2011] EWCA Crim 252.
[46] PCA 1978, s 1A(3).
[47] PCA 1978, s 1A(5).
[48] PCA 1978, 1A(1). This does not include a 'one night stand'. *R v M* [2011] EWCA Crim 252.
[49] PCA 1978, s 1A(3).
[50] PCA 1978, s 1A(6).
[51] PCA 1978, s 1B(1)(b).

Service[52] or GCHQ[53] and it was necessary to make the photograph or pseudo-photograph.[54] Whether honest research into child pornography constitutes a 'legitimate reason' for possession (or making) it is a question of fact in each case. The courts 'are plainly entitled to bring a measure of scepticism to bear upon such an enquiry... they should not too readily accept that the defence is made out'.[55]

Notes

9.07
(i) Triable either way.[56]
(ii) DPP consent is required.[57]
(iii) This offence may be committed by a male, female or a corporation. Where the offence has been committed by a body corporate with the consent of, connivance or neglect by any director, manager, secretary or officer (and any person purporting to be such)[58] that person shall be liable to prosecution.
(iv) The extended jurisdiction provisions apply to this section.[59] See Chapter 17 para 17.01.
(v) The s 45 MSA 2015 defence for slavery and trafficking victims who commit an offence is available for an offence under this section, provided it was committed on or after 31.7.2015.[60]

Indictment

9.08 TAKING OR PERMITTING TO BE TAKEN INDECENT PHOTOGRAPHS OF A CHILD 20.8.1978 to 2.2.1995

Statement of Offence
TAKING or [PERMITTING TO BE TAKEN] INDECENT PHOTOGRAPHS OF A CHILD, contrary to section 1(1)(a) of the Protection of Children Act 1978.

Particulars of Offence
X on the ... day of ... [took or permitted to be taken] an indecent photograph of a child, (image reference ...).

Note: Child defined as under 16.

---

[52] Inserted into s 1B(1)(b) by Criminal Justice and Immigration Act 2008 (8.7.2008).
[53] PCA 1978, s 1B(1)(c).
[54] PCA 1978, s 1B(1)(a).
[55] *Atkins v DPP; Goodland v DPP* [2000] EWHC Admin 302.
[56] PCA 1978, s 6(1).
[57] PCA 1978, s 1(3).
[58] PCA 1978, s 3.
[59] SOA 2003, s 72(1)(d)(i); provides for the prosecution within the jurisdiction of a sexual offence committed outside it.
[60] Modern Slavery Act 2015, s 45 commencement date 31.7.2015 (SI 2015/1476). This offence is not an excluded offence in Sch 4 of the Act. The s 45 defence is not retrospective, see *R v Joseph (Verna Sermanfure)* [2017] EWCA Crim 36.

TAKING/PERMITTING TO BE TAKEN/MAKING INDECENT PHOTOGRAPHS/ **9.09**
PSEUDO-PHOTOGRAPHS OF A CHILD 3.2.1995 to date

> ### Statement of Offence
> TAKING *or* [PERMITTING TO BE TAKEN *or* MAKING] INDECENT PHOTOGRAPHS [*or* PSEUDO-PHOTOGRAPHS] OF A CHILD, contrary to section 1(1)(a) of the Protection of Children Act 1978.
>
> ### Particulars of Offence
> D on the ... day of ... took *or* [permitted to be taken *or* made] an indecent photograph [pseudo-photograph] of a child, (*image reference* ...).
>
> Note: Child defined as under 16 until 30.04.2004. From 1.5.2004 child defined as under 18.

DISTRIBUTE OR SHOW INDECENT PHOTOGRAPHS OF A CHILD 20.8.1978 to **9.10**
2.2.1995

> ### Statement of Offence
> DISTRIBUTING *or* [SHOWING] INDECENT PHOTOGRAPHS OF A CHILD, contrary to section 1(1)(b) of the Protection of Children Act 1978.
>
> ### Particulars of Offence
> D on the ... day of ... distributed *or* [showed] an indecent photograph of a child, (*image reference* ...).
>
> Note: Child defined as under 16.

DISTRIBUTE OR SHOW INDECENT PHOTOGRAPHS/ PSEUDO-PHOTOGRAPH OF **9.11**
A CHILD 3.2.1995 to date

> ### Statement of Offence
> DISTRIBUTING *or* [SHOWING] INDECENT PHOTOGRAPHS *or* [PSEUDO-PHOTOGRAPHS] OF A CHILD, contrary to section 1(1)(b) of the Protection of Children Act 1978.
>
> ### Particulars of Offence
> D on the ... day of ... distributed *or* [showed] an indecent photograph [*or* pseudo-photograph] of a child, (*image reference* ...)
>
> Note: Child defined as under 16 until 30.04.2004. From 1.5.2004 child defined as under 18.

9.12 POSSESSION OF AN INDECENT PHOTOGRAPH OF A CHILD WITH A VIEW TO IT BEING DISTRIBUTED OR SHOWN 20.8.1978 to 2.2.1995

Statement of Offence
POSSESSION OF AN INDECENT PHOTOGRAPH OF A CHILD WITH A VIEW TO IT BEING DISTRIBUTED OR SHOWN BY HIMSELF OR OTHERS, contrary to section 1(1)(c) of the Protection of Children Act 1978.

Particulars of Offence
D on the … day of … had in his possession an indecent photograph (*image reference …*) with a view to it being distributed or shown by himself or others.

Note: Child defined as under 16.

9.13 POSSESSION OF AN INDECENT PHOTOGRAPH/PSEUDO-PHOTOGRAPH OF A CHILD WITH A VIEW TO IT BEING DISTRIBUTED OR SHOWN 3.2.1995 to date

Statement of Offence
POSSESSION OF AN INDECENT PHOTOGRAPH *or* [PSEUDO-PHOTOGRAPH] OF A CHILD WITH A VIEW TO IT BEING DISTRIBUTED OR SHOWN BY HIMSELF OR OTHERS, contrary to section 1(1)(c) of the Protection of Children Act 1978.

Particulars of Offence
D on the … day of … had in his possession an indecent photograph *or* [pseudo-photograph] (*image reference …*) with a view to it being distributed or shown by himself or others.

Note: Child defined as under 16 until 30.04.2004. From 1.5.2004 child defined as under 18.

9.14 PUBLISHING OR CAUSING TO BE PUBLISHED AN ADVERTISMENT TO DISTRIBUTE OR SHOW INDECENT PHOTOGRAPHS OF A CHILD 20.8.1978 to 2.2.1995

Statement of Offence
PUBLISH OR CAUSE TO BE PUBLISHED AN ADVERTISMENT TO DISTRIBUTE OR SHOW INDECENT PHOTOGRAPHS OF A CHILD OR INTENDS TO DISTRIBUTE OR SHOW INDECENT PHOTOGRAPHS OF A CHILD, contrary to section 1(1)(d) of the Protection of Children Act 1978.

Particulars of Offence
D on the … day of … published or caused to be published an advertisement likely to be understood as conveying that the advertiser distributes or shows indecent photographs of children or intends to distribute or show indecent photographs of children.

Note: Child defined as under 16.

9.15 PUBLISHING OR CAUSING TO BE PUBLISHED AN ADVERTISEMENT TO DISTRIBUTE OR SHOW INDECENT PHOTOGRAPHS/PSEUDO-PHOTOGRAPHS OF A CHILD 3.2.1995 to date

> **Statement of Offence**
>
> PUBLISH OR CAUSE TO PUBLISH AN ADVERTISEMENT TO DISTRIBUTE OR SHOW INDECENT PHOTOGRAPHS *or* [PSEUDO-PHOTOGRAPHS] OF A CHILD OR INTENDS TO DISTRIBUTE OR SHOW INDECENT PHOTOGRAPHS *or* [PSEUDO-PHOTOGRAPHS] OF A CHILD, contrary to section 1(1)(d) of the Protection of Children Act 1978.
>
> **Particulars of Offence**
>
> D on the … day of … published or caused to be published an advertisement likely to be understood as conveying that the advertiser distributes or shows indecent photographs *or* [pseudo-photographs] of children or intends to distribute or show indecent photographs *or* [pseudo-photographs] of children.
>
> Note: Child defined as under 16 until 30.04.2004. From 1.5.2004 child defined as under 18.

9.16 Where there are a large number of photographs or pseudo-photographs involved, the indictment should include:

- specific counts to reflect a broad range of images (see sentencing at paras 9.13 and 12.03–12.12), these counts should clarify whether the image is a photograph or pseudo-photograph with an identifying reference eg J-peg or M-peg file, or exhibit reference. If there is a dispute, alternative counts ought to be averred;
- a comprehensive count covering the remainder.

9.17 There ought to be agreement if possible as to the number of images at each level (see sentencing at paras 9.13 and 12.03–12.12) and the estimated age of the child in the images.[61] Where the defendant sends images to others a specific count ought to be included in the indictment.[62]

Alternative Offences

9.18
(i) Attempt to commit the full offence. When indicting offences of attempt do so under s 1(1) Criminal Attempts Act 1981.[63] Aver the attempt in both the Statement of Offence and Particulars of Offence. In addition, aver the substantive offence under the relevant Act; see paras 1.51 and 12.157 and *Reed & Others* [2021].[64]
(ii) Conspiracy (by A) with another (B) to distribute indecent photographs to himself (ie A) (CLA 1977, s 1): the indictment particulars must make it clear that the distribution is to A, in these circumstances.[65]

---

[61] *Thompson (Richard)* [2004] 2 Cr App R 262.
[62] *Wild* [2002] 1 Cr App R(S) 156.
[63] Implementation date 27.8.1981.
[64] *Reed & Others* [2021] EWCA Crim 572.
[65] *Barker* (unreported), 27 March 1998 CA (No 9705014 Z5).

(iii) Incitement to distribute indecent photographs of children: does not require proof that the person incited intended to distribute the photographs.[66]

Sentence

9.19 (i) On indictment: **3 YEARS**. This was increased to **10 YEARS** on 11.1.2001.[67]
(ii) Summarily: **6 months**.[68]

Sentencing Guidance

9.20 For offences before 14.5.2007 the guideline case was *Oliver, Hartrey and Baldwin*.[69]

9.21 For offences sentenced between 14.5.2007 and 1.4.2014 the Sentencing Guidelines Council Sexual Offences Act 2003 Definitive Guidelines applied.

9.22 For historic offences see the Sentencing Council 'Sexual Offences' Definitive Guideline which outlines the approach to historic cases.

9.23 The Sentencing Council, 'Sexual Offences' Definitive Guideline contains offence-specific guidelines for s 1 offences; the Guideline classifies images by reference to three categories of seriousness:

- Category A—Images involving penetrative sexual activity, sexual activity with an animal or sadism.
- Category B—Images involving non-penetrative sexual activity.
- Category C—Indecent images not falling within categories A or B.

The Guideline applies in relation to offenders aged 18, sentenced on or after 1 April 2014.

Note: for the purposes of categorization in accordance with the SC Guidelines, the production of images is not necessarily confined to making or taking images at source, some images may be properly categorized as a hybrid of possession or production, the two are not mutually exclusive. See *R v Bateman* [2020][70] (involving an adult pornography image with a child's head superimposed) for the correct approach to categorization in such cases.

Upon Conviction/Sentence

9.24 (i) Notification applies where the photograph/pseudo-photographs show persons under 16 and (a) the conviction/finding or caution was before 1.5.2004 *or* (b)(i) the offender was 18 or over *or* (ii) is sentenced to imprisonment of at least 12 months.[71]

---

[66] *DPP v Armstrong* [2000] Crim LR 379.
[67] Criminal Justice and Courts Services Act (CJCSA) 2000, s 41(1) commencement date 11.1.2001 (SI 2000 No 3302).
[68] 12 months if CJA 2003, s 282(4) implemented.
[69] [2003] 1 Cr App R 28.
[70] *R v Bateman (Paul Michael)* [2020] EWCA Crim 1333.
[71] SOA 2003, s 80(1) and Sch 3, para 13; see Chapter 14 paras 14.01–14.05.

(ii) Automatic inclusion in the children's and adults' barred lists with the right to make representations.[72]
(iii) SHPO applies.[73]
(iv) Qualifying 'specified sexual offence' in Schedule 18 (Extended Sentences).[74]
(v) Qualifying Schedule 14 offence (Extended Sentences: The Earlier Offence Condition).[75]
(vi) Qualifying 'index' offence (if committed after 3 December 2012) for the purpose of Schedule 15 (Life Sentence for Second Listed Offence).[76]

2. Offences Committed from 29.9.1988 to date

Possession of indecent photograph of a child

Criminal Justice Act 1988, s 160

9.25 The CJA 1988, s 160(1) was designed to supplement provisions in the PCA 1978 in order to provide for the simple possession of indecent photographs of children. The offence was similarly extended to computerized data and pseudo-photographs in 1995.[77] This offence was originally summary only until 11.1.2001.[78] On 1.5.2003 the definition of child was extended to include a child aged 16 or 17 subject to exceptions.[79]

Definition

9.26 It is an offence for a person to have an indecent photograph or pseudo-photograph[80] of a child in his possession.

Proof

9.27
(i) For the definition of photograph (and pseudo-photograph)[81] see para 9.06.
(ii) For the definition of indecent see para 9.06.
(iii) For the definition of child see para 9.06.[82]
(iv) The issue of possession (in relation to s 160 and possession of extreme images) was revisited in *R v Okoro* [2018][83] in which it was upheld that two elements had to be made out in order for an individual to have possession:
(1) the images must have been within the defendant's custody or control, ie so that he was capable of accessing them; and

---

[72] Part 2 of the Safeguarding Vulnerable Groups Act 2006 (Prescribed Criteria and Miscellaneous Provisions) Regulations 2009 (SI 2009 No 37) paras 2 and 4; see Chapter 12, para 12.217.
[73] SA 2020, s 345 and SOA 2003, Sch 3, para 13; see Chapter 16, para 16.07.
[74] SA 2020, s 306, Sch 18, para 35; see Chapter 12, para 12.51.
[75] SA 2020, ss 267 and 280, Sch 14, para 6; see Chapter 12, para 12.77.
[76] SA 2020, ss 273 and 283, Sch 15, para 9(6); see Chapter 12, para 12.123.
[77] CJPOA 1994, s 84(4), commencement date 03.2.1995 (SI 1995 No 127).
[78] CJCSA 2000, s 41(3) (SI 2000 No 3302).
[79] SOA 2003, s 45(2).
[80] Amended by CJPOA 1994, s 84(1) and (2) and commencement date 3.2.1995.
[81] CJA 1988, s 160(1) and (4).
[82] CJA 1988, s 160(1) and (4).
[83] *R v Okoro* [2018] EWCA Crim 1929.

(2) he must have known that he possessed an image or a group of images. It is clear that knowledge of the content of those images is not required to make out the basic ingredients of the offence; instead that issue is dealt with by the statutory defences. [46]

In relation to deleted images: if a person cannot retrieve or gain access to an image then he no longer has custody or control of it.[84]

(v) Section 160(2) provides a defence if the defendant had a legitimate reason for possession of the image (s 160(2)(a), or had not seen it and did not know or have cause to suspect it to be indecent[85] (s 160(2)(b)), or that it had been sent to him without request and had not been kept for an unreasonable length of time (s 160(2)(c)).

(vi) Section 160A (as amended)[86] provides a statutory defence for offences committed after 1.5.2004[87] if the defendant proves that the child was 16 or over at the time the photograph was taken and at they were married, in a civil partnership or living together in an enduring family relationship at the time.[88] This defence applies only if the photograph shows the child alone or with the defendant.[89]

(vii) If the defendant adduces sufficient evidence of consent or reasonable belief in consent, the prosecution must prove that the child did not consent and that the defendant did not reasonably believe that the child consented.[90]

Notes

9.28
(i) Summary only until 10.1.2001, thereafter triable either way.[91]
(ii) DPP consent is required.[92]
(iii) This offence may be committed by a male, female or a corporation.[93]
(iv) The extended jurisdiction provisions apply to this section.[94] See Chapter 17 para 17.01.
(v) The s 45 MSA 2015 defence for slavery and trafficking victims who commit an offence is available for an offence under this section, provided it was committed on or after 31.7.2015.[95]

---

[84] *R v Porter* [2006] 2 Cr App R 25.
[85] See *R v Collier (Edward John)* [2004] EWCA Crim 1411.
[86] 'Pseudo-photograph' inserted by the Coroners and Justice Act 2009 (6.4.2010). 'Civil partnership' added by Civil Partnership Act 2004 (5.12. 2005).
[87] Section 160A inserted by SOA 2003 (1.5.2004).
[88] CJA 1988, s160A(1).
[89] CJA 1988, s 160A(3).
[90] CJA 1988, s 160A(4).
[91] CJA 1988, s 160(2A) and (3), as amended by CJCSA 2000, s 41(3).
[92] CJA 1988, s 160(4).
[93] CJA 1988, s 160(4).
[94] SOA 2003, s 72(1)(d)(ii); provides for the prosecution within the jurisdiction of a sexual offence committed outside it. See Chapter 17.
[95] Modern Slavery Act 2015, s 45 commencement date 31.7.2015 (SI 2015/1476). This offence is not an excluded offence in Sch 4 of the Act. The s 45 defence is not retrospective, see *R v Joseph (Verna Sermanfure)* [2017] EWCA Crim 36.

Indictment

POSSESSION OF INDECENT PHOTOGRAPH OF A CHILD 29.9.1988 to 2.3.1995   9.29

> ### Statement of Offence
> POSSESSION OF AN INDECENT PHOTOGRAPH OF A CHILD, contrary to section 160(1) of the Criminal Justice Act 1988.
>
> ### Particulars of Offence
> D on a day between ... and ... was in possession of an indecent photograph of a child (image ...).
>
> Note: Child defined as under 16.

POSSESSION OF INDECENT PHOTOGRAPH/PSEUDO-PHOTOGRAPHS OF A CHILD 3.3.1995 to date   9.30

> ### Statement of Offence
> POSSESSION OF AN INDECENT PHOTOGRAPH *or* [PSEUDO-PHOTOGRAPH] OF A CHILD, contrary to section 160(1) of the Criminal Justice Act 1988.
>
> ### Particulars of Offence
> D on a day between ... and ... was in possession of an indecent photograph *or* [pseudo-photograph] of a child, (image ...).
>
> Note: Child defined as under 16 until 30.04.2004. From 1.5.2004 child defined as under 18.

Where there are a large number of photographs or pseudo-photographs involved, the indictment should include: 9.31

- specific counts to reflect a broad range of images (see sentencing at paras 9.13 and 12.03–12.12), these counts should clarify whether the image is a photograph or pseudo-photograph with an identifying reference eg J-peg or M-peg file, or exhibit reference. If there is a dispute, alternative counts ought to be averred;
- a comprehensive count covering the remainder.

There ought to be agreement if possible, as to the number of images and their level of indecency (see sentencing at para 9.20) and the estimated age of the child in the images.[96]   9.32

Where an image has been deleted, absent cogent evidence of the requisite knowledge and skill to retrieve deleted images, it is often more appropriate to indict an offence contrary to s 1 PCA 1978, provided there is evidence of the act of making and *mens rea*.   9.33

---

[96] *Thompson (Richard)* [2004] 2 Cr App R 262.

312   9. INDECENT IMAGES/OBSCENE PUBLICATIONS

Alternative Offences

9.34 Attempt to commit the full offence. When indicting offences of attempt do so under s 1(1) Criminal Attempts Act 1981.[97] Aver the attempt in both the Statement of Offence and Particulars of Offence. In addition, aver the substantive offence under the relevant Act; see paras 1.51 and 12.157 and *Reed & Others* [2021].[98]

Sentence

9.35 The Sentencing Council, 'Sexual Offences' Definitive Guideline contains offence-specific guidelines for s 160 offences; the Guideline classifies images by reference to three categories of seriousness:

- Category A—Images involving penetrative sexual activity, sexual activity with an animal or sadism.
- Category B—Images involving non-penetrative sexual activity.
- Category C—Indecent images not falling within categories A or B.

The Guideline applies in relation to offenders aged 18 or over, sentenced on or after 1.4.2014.

Note: for the purposes of categorization in accordance with the SC Guidelines, the production of images is not necessarily confined to making or taking images at source. Some images may be properly categorized as a hybrid of possession or production; the two are not mutually exclusive. See *R v Bateman* [2020][99] (involving an adult pornography image with a child's head superimposed) for the correct approach to categorization in such cases.

See paras 9.20–9.22 for historic sentencing and paras 12.03–12.12 for sentencing multiple offences.

9.36 From 11.1.2001:[100]

(i) On indictment: **5 YEARS**.
(ii) Summarily: **6 months**.

Upon Conviction/Sentence

9.37 (i) Notification applies where the photograph/pseudo-photographs show persons under 16 *and* (a) the conviction/finding or caution was before 1.5.2004 *or* (b)(i) the offender was 18 or over *or* (ii) is sentenced to imprisonment of at least 12 months.[101]
(ii) Automatic inclusion in the children's and adults' barred lists with the right to make representations.[102]
(iii) SHPO applies.[103]
(iv) Qualifying 'specified sexual offence' in Schedule 18 (Extended Sentences).[104]

---

[97] Implementation date 27.8.1981.
[98] *Reed & Others* [2021] EWCA Crim 572.
[99] *R v Bateman (Paul Michael)* [2020] EWCA Crim 1333.
[100] Previously summary only.
[101] SOA 2003, s 80(1) and Sch 3, para 15; see Chapter 14 paras 14.01–14.05.
[102] Part 2 of the Safeguarding Vulnerable Groups Act 2006 (Prescribed Criteria and Miscellaneous Provisions) Regulations 2009 (SI 2009 No 37); see Chapter 12, para 12.217.
[103] SA 2020, s 345 and SOA 2003, Sch 3, para 15; see Chapter 16 para 16.07.
[104] SA 2020, s 306, Sch 18, para 7; see Chapter 12, para 12.51.

C. POSSESSION OF PROHIBITED AND EXTREME PORNOGRAPHIC IMAGES OF CHILDREN

1. Possession of a Prohibited Image of a Child

Coroners and Justice Act 2009, s 62

Definition

9.38 To be in possession[105] of:

(i) a pornographic image;[106]
(ii) that focuses solely or principally on a child's genitals or anal region;[107] or
(iii) that portrays any of the following:[108]
    (a) the performance by a person of an act of intercourse or oral sex with or in the presence of a child;
    (b) an act of masturbation by, of, involving or in the presence of a child;
    (c) an act which involves penetration of the vagina or anus of a child with a part of a person's body or with anything else;
    (d) an act of penetration, in the presence of a child, of the vagina or anus of a person with a part of a person's body or with anything else;
    (e) the performance by a child of an act of intercourse or oral sex with an animal (whether dead or alive or imaginary);
    (f) the performance by a person of an act of intercourse or oral sex with an animal (whether dead or alive or imaginary) in the presence of a child' (For the purposes of (a)—(f) penetration is a continuing act from entry to withdrawal (s 62(8));
(iv) and that is grossly offensive, disgusting or otherwise of an obscene character.[109]

Proof

9.39
(i) A 'child' is a person under 18.[110]
(ii) It also includes pictures of a person over 18 where:[111]
    (a) the impression conveyed by the image is that the person shown is a child; or
    (b) the predominant impression conveyed is that the person shown is a child despite the fact that some of the physical characteristics shown are not those of a child.
(iii) The image can be of an imaginary person or child.[112]

---

[105] Possession has the same meaning as s 160 CJA 1988 and s 1 PCA 1978. See also *R v Okoro* [2018] EWCA Crim 1929 (para 9.27).
[106] CJA 2009, ss 62(2)(a) and (3).
[107] CJA 2009, s 62(2)(b); (6)(a).
[108] CJA 2009, s 62(2)(b); (6)(b); (7).
[109] CJA 2009, s 62(2)(c).
[110] CJA 2009, s 65(5).
[111] CJA 2009, s 65(6).
[112] Sections 65(7) and (8).

9. INDECENT IMAGES/OBSCENE PUBLICATIONS

(iv) 'Image' includes—
  (a) a moving or still image (produced by any means);[113] or
  (b) data (stored by any means) which is capable of conversion into a moving or still image;[114]
  (c) 'Image' does not include an indecent photograph, or indecent pseudo-photograph, of a child.[115]
(v) The image is 'pornographic' if it is produced solely or principally for the purpose of sexual arousal.[116] This must be judged in the context of the whole where it forms part of a series of images.[117]
(vi) Excluded images include images that fall within a 'classified work'[118] such as films that have been issued a classification certificate. The Act expressly excludes from the exemption images extracted from classified works for the purpose of sexual arousal.[119]

Notes

9.40
(i) The offence is triable either way.
(ii) DPP consent is required.[120]
(iii) It is a defence if the person had a legitimate reason for being in possession of the image concerned; had not seen the image concerned and did not know, nor had any cause to suspect, it to be a prohibited image of a child; or that the person was sent the image concerned without any prior request having been made by or on behalf of the person, and did not keep it for an unreasonable time.[121]

Indictment

9.41 Possession of Prohibited Images of Children 6.4.2010 to date

---

Statement of Offence

POSSESSION OF PROHIBITED IMAGES OF CHILDREN, contrary to section 62(1) and (6)(a) of the Coroners and Justice Act 2009.

Particulars of Offence

A on a day between … and the … day of …, was in possession of a pornographic image of a child, which focuses solely or principally on a child's genitals or anal region, the said image being grossly offensive, disgusting or otherwise of an obscene character.

---

[113] Section 65(2)(a).
[114] Section 65(2)(b).
[115] Section 65(3).
[116] Section 62(3).
[117] Section 62(4), (5).
[118] Section 63(7).
[119] Section 63(3)(b).
[120] Section 62(9)(a).
[121] Section 64(1).

Alternative Offences

9.42 Attempt to commit the full offence. When indicting offences of attempt do so under s 1(1) Criminal Attempts Act 1981.[122] Aver the attempt in both the Statement of Offence and Particulars of Offence. In addition, aver the substantive offence under the relevant Act; see paras 1.51 and 12.157 and *Reed & Others* [2021].[123]

Sentence

9.43
(i) On indictment: **3 YEARS**, a fine or both.
(ii) Summarily: **6 months**, a fine or both.[124]

9.44 There are, as at date of publication, no Sentencing Council Guidelines applicable to this offence. When sentencing offences for which there is no specific sentencing guideline the Sentencing Council, General Guideline: Overarching Principles applies to all cases sentenced on or after 1 October 2019.

Upon Conviction/Sentence

9.45
(i) Notification applies if the offender was aged 18 or over and is sentenced to a term of imprisonment of at least 2 years.[125]
(ii) Automatic inclusion in the children's and adults' barred lists with the right to make representations.[126]
(iii) SHPO applies.[127]

2. Possession of an Extreme Pornographic Image, 26.1.2009 to date

Criminal Justice and Immigration Act 2008, s 63[128]

Definition

9.46
(i) To be in possession of an extreme pornographic image.[129]
(ii) An image is 'pornographic' if it is of such a nature that it must reasonably be assumed to have been produced solely or principally for the purpose of sexual

---

[122] Implementation date 27.8.1981.
[123] *Reed & Others* [2021] EWCA Crim 572.
[124] Coroners and Justice Act 2009, s 66.
[125] SOA 2003, s 80(1) and Sch 3, para 35B; see Chapter 14 paras 14.01–14.05.
[126] Part 2 of the Safeguarding Vulnerable Groups Act 2006 (Prescribed Criteria and Miscellaneous Provisions) Regulations 2009 (SI 2009 No 37) paras 2 and 4; see Chapter 12 para 12.217.
[127] SA 2020, s 345 and SOA 2003, Sch 3, para 35B; see Chapter 16 para 16.07.
[128] Section reproduced as amended. Sections 5A, 7A, and 7B inserted by the Criminal Justice and Courts Act 2015 (13.4.2015). SI 2015/778.
[129] CJIA 2008, s 63(1).

9. INDECENT IMAGES/OBSCENE PUBLICATIONS

arousal.[130] This must be judged in the context of the whole where it forms part of a series of images.[131]

(iii) An 'extreme image' is an image which falls within either s 63(7) or s 63(7A)[132] *and* is grossly offensive, disgusting or otherwise of an obscene character;[133] and

Section 63(7): an image if it portrays in an explicit and realistic way, any of the following

(a) an act which threatens a person's life,[134]
(b) an act which results, or is likely to result, in serious injury to a person's anus, breasts or genitals,[135]
(c) an act which involves sexual interference with a human corpse,[136] or
(d) a person performing an act of intercourse or oral sex with an animal (whether dead or alive),[137] and

and a reasonable person looking at the image would think that any such person or animal was real.

Section 63(7A): an image if it portrays in an explicit and realistic way, either of the following:

an act which involves the non-consensual penetration of a person's vagina, anus or mouth by another with the other person's penis, or

an act which involves the non-consensual sexual penetration of a person's vagina or anus by another with a part of the other person's body or anything else.

For the purposes of s 7A, penetration is a continuing act from entry to withdrawal and 'vagina' includes vulva.[138]

Proof

9.47 (i) References to a part of the body include references to a part surgically constructed (in particular through gender reassignment surgery).[139]

(ii) 'Image' means—
(a) a moving or still image (produced by any means); or
(b) data (stored by any means) which is capable of conversion into such an image.[140]

(iii) Section 63 does not apply to excluded images. Excluded images include images that fall within a 'classified work'[141] such as films that have been issued a classification certificate, unless, for the purpose of sexual arousal.[142]

---

[130] CJIA 2008, s 63(3).
[131] CJIA 2008, s 63(4), (5).
[132] CJIA 2008, s 63(5A)(a).
[133] CJIA 2008, s 63(5A)(b).
[134] CJIA 2008, s 63(7)(a).
[135] CJIA 2008, s 63(7)(b).
[136] CJIA 2008, s 63(7)(c).
[137] CJIA 2008, s 63(7)(d).
[138] CJIA 2008, s 63(7B).
[139] CJIA 2008, s 63(9).
[140] CJIA 2008, s 63(8).
[141] CJIA 2008, s 64(7).
[142] CJIA 2008, s 64(3)(b).

Notes

9.48

(i) This offence is triable either way.
(ii) Consent of the DPP is required.
(iii) It is a defence if there is a legitimate reason for being in possession of the image concerned;[143] or if the person had not seen the image concerned and did not know, nor had any cause to suspect, it to be an extreme pornographic image; or that the person was sent the image concerned without any prior request having been made by or on behalf of the person, and did not keep it for an unreasonable time.
(iv) From 13.4.2015[144] subsections (5A) and (7A) were inserted into s 63, extending the offence to include images portraying in an explicit and realistic way non-consensual sexual penetration.
(v) The s 45 MSA 2015 defence for slavery and trafficking victims who commit an offence is available for an offence under this section, provided it was committed on or after 31.7.2015.[145]

Defence: Participation in Consensual Acts: Criminal Justice and Immigration Act 2008, s 66[146]

Where D is charged with an offence under s 63 that relates to an act or acts within s 63(7) (a)–(c) or 7A (but not 63(7)(d)), it is a defence for D to prove— **9.49**

Section 66(A2):
    (a) that D directly participated in the act or any of the acts portrayed, and
    (b) that the act or acts did not involve the infliction of any non-consensual harm on any person, and
    (c) if the image portrays an act within section 63(7)(c), that what is portrayed as a human corpse was not in fact a corpse, and
    (d) if the image portrays an act within s 63(7A), that what is portrayed as non-consensual penetration was in fact consensual.
(3) For the purposes of this section harm inflicted on a person is 'non-consensual' harm if—
    (a) the harm is of such a nature that the person cannot, in law, consent to it being inflicted on himself or herself; or
    (b) where the person can, in law, consent to it being so inflicted, the person does not in fact consent to it being so inflicted.[147]

---

[143] CJIA 2008, s 65(2).
[144] SI 2015 No. 778 (13.4.2015).
[145] Modern Slavery Act 2015, s 45 commencement date 31.7.2015 (SI 2015/1476). This offence is not an excluded offence in Sch 4 of the Act. The s 45 defence is not retrospective, see *R v Joseph (Verna Sermanfure)* [2017] EWCA Crim 36.
[146] Section reproduced as amended. Subsections (A1) and (A2) inserted by the Criminal Justice and Courts Act 2015 (13.4.2015). SI 2015/778 and subsection (2)(d) by the Justice Act (Northern Ireland) 2016 (13.5.2016).
[147] CJIA 2008, s 66(3).

Indictment

9.50 POSSESSION OF AN EXTREME PORNOGRAPHIC IMAGE 26.1.2009 to date

> ### Statement of offence
> POSSESSION OF AN EXTREME PORNOGRAPHIC IMAGE, contrary to section 63(1) [and 63(7)(a) or (b) or from 13.4.2017 63(7A)(a) or (b) as applicable] Criminal Justice and Immigration Act 2008.
>
> ### Particulars of offence
> D on a day between … and … possessed an extreme pornographic image namely an image (*specify type*).

9.51 Note there are differences in sentencing maxima dependent upon whether the image(s) fall within subsections 63(7)(c) and (d) (necrophilia or bestiality), or subsections 63(7)(a) and (b) (life threatening acts or serious injury) and from 13.4.2015 subsections 63(7A)(a) and (b) (explicit and realistic depiction of non-consensual penetration). The indictment should identify the relevant subsections, where applicable, to identify the type of image(s) and therefore the maximum sentence applicable. See para 9.39.

Sentence

9.52 (i) If the offence portrays an act within s 63(7)(a) or (b), or (7A)(a) or (b): summarily **6 months**,[148] on indictment **3 YEARS**.

(ii) If the offence does not portray an act within s 63(7)(a) or (b), or (7A)(a) or (b): summarily 6 months,[149] on indictment 2 YEARS.

9.53 There are currently no Sentencing Council Guidelines applicable to this offence. When sentencing offences for which there is no specific sentencing guideline the Sentencing Council, General Guideline: Overarching Principles applies to all cases sentenced on or after 1 October 2019.

Upon Sentence/Conviction

9.54 (i) Notification applies if the offender was aged 18 or over and is sentenced to a term of imprisonment of at least 2 years.[150]

(ii) Automatic inclusion in the children's and adults' barred lists with the right to make representations.[151]

(iii) SHPO applies.[152]

---

[148] CJIA 2008, s 67(4)(a), Section 67(4)(a) states the relevant period as '12 months', but 12 months is to be read as 6 months unless CJA 2003 s154(1) commenced. S 154(1) is not yet in force.

[149] CJIA 2008, s 67(4)(a), Section 67(4)(a) states the relevant period as '12 months', but 12 months is to be read as 6 months unless CJA 2003 s154(1) commenced. Section 154(1) is not yet in force.

[150] SOA 2003, s 80(1) and Sch 3, para 35A; see Chapter 14 paras 14.01–14.05.

[151] Part 2 of the Safeguarding Vulnerable Groups Act 2006 (Prescribed Criteria and Miscellaneous Provisions) Regulations 2009 (SI 2009 No 37) paras 2 and 4; see Chapter 12, para 12.217.

[152] SA 2020, s 345 and SOA 2003, Sch 3, para 35A; see Chapter 16, para 16.07.

D. OBSCENE PUBLICATIONS

As stated (see Introduction) the most commonly charged offences will relate to the retail distribution of obscene material: in shops or by mail order. The OPA 1959 and the OPA 1964 are still in force. The offence is time-barred (that is, there may be no prosecution under these sections more than 2 years after the commission of the offence).[153] The topic is not dealt with in its historical context. **9.55**

Section 2 of the OPA 1959 created the offence of publishing an obscene article. **9.56**

In 1964,[154] the offence was extended to having obscene articles for gain. **9.57**

1. Publishing an Obscene Article or Having an Obscene Article for Publication for Gain

Obscene Publications Act 1959, s 2

Definition

Any person who, whether for gain or not publishes an obscene article or who has an obscene article for publication for gain[155] (whether gain to himself or to another). **9.58**

Proof

(i) 'Publishes' is defined by statute as the distribution, circulation, selling, hiring, giving, lending or offering for sale or hire,[156] or the showing, playing, projecting (data), an article containing matter to be looked at.[157] This includes the uploading or downloading of a web page, the electronic transmission of data[158] and providing another with a password to enable access to a computer.[159] The publication need only be to one other person.[160] **9.59**

(ii) 'Obscene' is defined as any article which tends to deprave and corrupt persons who are likely, having regard to all relevant circumstances, to read, see or hear the matter contained or embodied in it.[161]

(iii) 'Article' is defined as any description or article containing or embodying matter to be read or looked at or both, any sound record and any film or other record of a picture or pictures.[162] This includes articles in programmes included in programme

---

[153] OPA 1959, s 2(3).
[154] OPA 1964, s 1.
[155] Wording: 'or who has an obscene article for publication for gain (whether gain to himself or gain to another' inserted by the Obscene Publications Act 1964 (s 1(1)) (31.8.1964).
[156] OPA 1959, s 1(3)(a).
[157] OPA 1959, s 1(3)(b).
[158] *R v Perrin* [2002] 4 Archbold News 2 CA.
[159] *R v Fellows and Arnold* [1997] 1 Cr App R 244 CA.
[160] *R v Smith (Gavin)* [2012] EWCA Crim 398.
[161] OPA 1959, s 1(1).
[162] OPA 1959, s 1(2).

9. INDECENT IMAGES/OBSCENE PUBLICATIONS

services,[163] negatives and anything which is intended to be used (either alone or as one of a set) for the reproduction or manufacture therefrom of articles containing or embodying matter to be read, looked at or listened to,[164] which includes: pictures produced by a video cassette[165] or a computer disk.[166]

(iv) 'Having' an article for publication for gain covers where the defendant has the article in his ownership, possession or control.[167]

Notes

9.60   (i) The offence is triable either way.[168]
(ii) DPP consent is required in certain cases.[169]
(iii) This offence may be committed by a male, female or a corporation.
(iv) 'Deprave' has been held to mean make morally bad, to pervert, to debase or to corrupt morally.[170]
(v) 'Corrupt' has been defined as to render morally unsound or rotten, to destroy the moral purity or chastity, to pervert or ruin a good quality, to debase, to defile.[171]
(vi) Once the prosecution has proved that the article is obscene, if the defence can prove that the publication of the article is justified as being for the public good on the ground that it is in the interest of science, literature, art or learning, or of other objects of general concern, then he/she is afforded a defence (the s 4(1) defence). The s 4(1) defence does not apply where the article in question is a moving picture film or soundtrack. However under s 4(1A) it is a defence (in relation to a film or soundtrack) if proved that publication of the film or soundtrack is justified as being for the public good on the ground that it is in the interests of drama, opera, ballet or any other art, or of literature or learning.
(vii) Expert evidence is admissible on whether the article is in the interest of science, literature, art or learning.[172]
(viii) It is a complete defence to publishing an obscene article, if the defendant proves that he has not examined the article and had no reasonable cause to suspect that it was such that his publication of it would make him liable to be convicted of an offence.[173]
(viii) It is a complete defence of an offence of having an obscene article for publication for gain if the defendant proves that he had not examined the article and had no reasonable cause to suspect that it was such and that his having it would make him liable to be convicted.[174]

---

[163] OPA 1959, s 1(4) as defined by s 1(6). See also s (1)(5) for inclusion as if it were recorded matter.
[164] OPA 1964, s 2.
[165] *A-G Reference (No 5 of 1980)* 72 Cr App R 71 CA.
[166] *R v Fellows and Arnold* [1997] Cr App R 244 CA.
[167] OPA 1964, s 1(2).
[168] OPA 1959, s 2.
[169] OPA 1959, s 2(3A).
[170] *R v Penguin Books Ltd* [1961] Crim LR 176 (the '*Lady Chatterley's Lover* case').
[171] *R v Penguin Books Ltd* [1961] Crim LR 176 at 177.
[172] OPA 1958, s 4(2).
[173] OPA 1959, s 2(5).
[174] OPA 1964, s 1(3).

(ix) Where the essence of the offence is that the material is obscene, the prosecution must prosecute under the OPA 1959, and not charge the common law offence of publishing an obscene libel.[175]

(x) Where; (a) in relation to an exhibition or film or anything said or done in the course of the exhibition or film the essence of the offence is that the exhibition or what was said or done was obscene, indecent, offensive, disgusting or injurious to morality; or (b) in respect of an agreement to give an exhibition or film or to cause anything to be said or done in the course of such an exhibition where the common law offence consists of conspiring to corrupt public morals or to do any act contrary to public morals or decency the prosecution should not charge a common law offence.[176]

Note: the s 2(4) and s 2(4A) defence provisions ensure that the defences available under the OPA 1959 are not evaded by the prosecution. However, the common law offence of outraging public decency (and conspiracy) is not barred by s 2(4).[177] (See paras 10.03–10.13.)

(xi) The offence is time-barred. A prosecution for this offence may only be brought within 2 years of the commission of the offence.[178]

(xii) The s 45 MSA 2015 defence for slavery and trafficking victims who commit an offence is available for an offence under this section, provided it was committed on or after 31.7.2015.[179]

Indictment

PUBLISHING AN OBSCENE ARTICLE 29.8.1959 to date   9.61

Statement of Offence
PUBLISHING AN OBSCENE ARTICLE, contrary to section 2(1) of the Obscene Publications Act 1959.

Particulars of Offence
D on a day between ... and ... [sold] *or* [let on hire or gave or lent] *or* [distributed or circulated] *or* [offered for sale or for letting on hire] an obscene article, namely ... (adding where necessary) the particulars of which are attached to this indictment.

Particulars should specify pages and lines complained of when necessary as in a book which may be in the following form:

Particulars of Obscene Articles Contained in the Book Entitled ...

Count 1 of indictment. A book entitled the ... beginning at ... line ... and ending at ... line ..., with the words ...

---

[175] OPA 1959, s 2(4).
[176] OPA 1959, s 2(4A).
[177] *R v Gibson* [1990] 2 QB 619.
[178] OPA 1959, s 2(3).
[179] Modern Slavery Act 2015, s 45 commencement date 31.7.2015 (SI 2015/1476). This offence is not an excluded offence in Sch 4 of the Act. The s 45 defence is not retrospective, see *R v Joseph (Verna Sermanfure)* [2017] EWCA Crim 36.

9.62 HAVING AN OBSCENE ARTICLE FOR PUBLICATION FOR GAIN 31.8.1964 to date

> **Statement of Offence**
> HAVING AN OBSCENE ARTICLE FOR PUBLICATION FOR GAIN, contrary to section 2(1) of the Obscene Publications Act 1959.
>
> **Particulars of Offence**
> D on a day between the … and … had an obscene article, namely … for publication for gain. (If appropriate on the facts of the case, particulars—as in above example)

Alternative Offences

9.63 Attempt to commit the full offence. When indicting offences of attempt do so under common law until 26.8.1981, thereafter indict under s 1(1) Criminal Attempts Act 1981.[180] Aver the attempt in both the Statement of Offence and Particulars of Offence. In addition, aver the substantive offence under the relevant Act; see paras 1.51 and 12.157 and *Reed & Others* [2021].[181]

Sentence

9.64 (i) On indictment: **3 YEARS**.[182]
(ii) Summarily: **6 months**.[183]

9.65 As at date of publication there are no Sentencing Council Guidelines applicable to this offence. When sentencing offences for which there is no specific sentencing guideline the Sentencing Council, General Guideline: Overarching Principles applies to all cases sentenced on or after 1 October 2019.

Upon Conviction/Sentence

9.66 (i) Notification not applicable.[184]
(ii) Automatic barring from working with children or vulnerable adults does not apply.[185]
(iii) SHPO not applicable.[186]
(iv) Mandatory forfeiture in specified cases.[187]

---

[180] Implementation date 27.8.1981.
[181] *Reed & Others* [2021] EWCA Crim 572.
[182] OPA 1959, s 2(1)(b).
[183] OPA 1959, s 2(1)(a). Increased to 12 months from commencement of CJA 2003 s154(1).
[184] SOA 2003, s 80(1) (not listed in Schedule 3); see Chapter 14 Tables 14.2–14.5.
[185] Part 2 of the Safeguarding Vulnerable Groups Act 2006 (Prescribed Criteria and Miscellaneous Provisions) Regulations 2009 (SI 2009 No 37); see Chapter 12 para 12.217.
[186] SA 2020, s 345 (not listed in Sch 3 or Sch 5 SOA 2003); see Chapter 16 para 16.07.
[187] OPA 1964(4) Where articles are seized under s 3 of the Obscene Publications Act 1959 (which provides for the seizure and forfeiture of obscene articles kept for publication for gain), and a person is convicted under s 2 of that Act of having them for publication for gain, the court on his conviction shall order the forfeiture of those articles.

E. OTHER OFFENCES

1. Disclosing Private Sexual Photographs or Films, 13.4.2015 to date

Criminal Justice and Courts Act 2015, s 33

Section 33 of the Criminal Justice and Courts Act (CJCA) 2015 created the offence of disclosing private sexual photographs or films; an offence colloquially known as 'revenge porn'. The section came into force on 13.4.2015.[188] **9.67**

Definition

Section 33(1): **9.68**
It is an offence for a person to disclose a private sexual photograph or film if the disclosure is made-

(a) without the consent of an individual who appears in the photograph or film, and
(b) with the intention of causing that individual distress.

Proof

(i) A person 'discloses' something to a person, if by any means, he or she gives or shows it to the person or makes it available to the person.[189] Something that is given, shown or made available to a person is disclosed; (a) whether or not it is given shown or made available for reward, and (b) whether or not it has previously been given shown or made available to that person.[190] 'By any means ... gives or shows' has a wide ambit, this includes uploading images to the internet; sending by text, e-mail or social media; or by any other electronic or physical mechanism. **9.69**

(ii) 'Photograph' or 'film' means a still or moving image in any form that: (a) appears to consist of or include one or more photographed or filmed images; and (b) in fact consists of or includes one or more photographed or filmed images.[191] (including photographed or filmed images that have been altered in any way).[192] A 'photograph or filmed image' means a still or moving image that (a) was originally captured by photography or filming; or (b) is part of an image originally captured by photography or filming.[193] 'Filming' means making a recording, on any medium, from which a moving image may be produced by any means.[194] References to photograph

---

[188] SI 2015/778 art 3, Sch 1 para 27.
[189] CJCA 2015, s 34(2).
[190] CJCA 2015, s 34(3).
[191] CJCA 2015, s 34(4).
[192] CJCA 2015, s 34(5).
[193] CJCA 2015, s 34(6).
[194] CJCA 2015, s 34(7).

9. INDECENT IMAGES/OBSCENE PUBLICATIONS

or film include negatives and data stored by any means which is capable of conversion into an image.[195]

(iii) A photograph or film is 'private' if it shows something that is not of a kind ordinarily seen in public.[196]

(iv) A photograph or film is 'sexual' if; (a) it shows all or part of an individual's exposed genitals or pubic area, (b) it shows something that a reasonable person would consider to be sexual because of its nature, or (c) its content, taken as a whole, is such that a reasonable person would consider it to be sexual.[197]

(v) Consent: consent to a disclosure includes general consent covering the disclosure, as well as consent to the particular disclosure.[198]

(vi) Intention: A person is not to be taken to have intended to cause distress merely because that was the natural and probable consequence of the disclosure.[199]

Notes

9.70   (i) The offence is triable either way.[200]

(ii) A photograph or film will not be private and sexual if: (a) it does not consist of or include a photographed or filmed image that is itself private and sexual, (b) it is only private or sexual by virtue of being altered or combined, or (c) it is only by virtue of alteration or combination that the person is shown as part of, or with, whatever makes the photograph or film private and sexual.[201] An altered or combined photograph or film: (a) consists of or includes a photographed or filmed image that has been altered in any way, (b) combines two or more photographed or filmed images, and (c) combines a photographed or filmed image with something else.[202]

(iii) It is not an offence for the defendant to disclose the photograph or film to the individual who appears in the photograph.[203]

(iv) It is a defence to prove that the defendant reasonably believed that the disclosure was necessary for the purposes of preventing, detecting or investigating crime (section 33(3)).

(v) It is a defence to show that: (a) the disclosure was made in the course of, or with a view to, the publication of journalistic material, and (b) he or she reasonably believed that, in the particular circumstances, the publication of the journalistic material was, or would be, in the public interest (section 33(4)). 'Publication' of journalistic material means disclosure to the public at large or to a section of the public.[204]

(vi). It is a defence to show that: (a) he or she reasonably believed that the photograph or film had previously been disclosed for reward, whether by the person in the

---

[195] CJCA 2015, s 34(8).
[196] CJCA 2015, s 35(2).
[197] CJCA 2015, s 35(3).
[198] CJCA 2015, s 33(7)(a).
[199] CJCA 2015, s 33(8).
[200] CJCA 2015, s 33(9).
[201] CJCA 2015, s 35(5).
[202] CJCA 2015, s 35(4).
[203] CJCA 2015, s 33(2).
[204] CJCA 2015, s 33(7)(b).

E. OTHER OFFENCES 325

photograph or film or another person, and (b) he or she had no reason to believe that the previous disclosure for reward was made without the consent of the person in the photograph or film (section 33(5)).

(vii) The evidential burden is on the defence raise the issue of a defence under sections 33(4) or 33(5). Once raised, it is for the prosecution to disprove.[205]

(viii) Schedule 8 of the Act makes special provision in relation to persons providing information society services.[206]

(ix) The s 45 MSA 2015 defence for slavery and trafficking victims who commit an offence is available for an offence under this section, provided it was committed on or after 31.7.2015.[207]

Indictment

DISCLOSING PRIVATE SEXUAL PHOTOGRAPHS OR FILMS 13.4.2015 to date   9.71

Statement of Offence

DISCLOSING A PRIVATE SEXUAL PHOTOGRAPH *or* [FILM], contrary to section 33(1) of the Criminal Justice and Courts Act 2015.

Particulars of Offence

D on the … day of … disclosed a private sexual photograph *or* [film] [*insert J-peg, M-peg or exhibit reference*] without the consent of C who appears in the [photograph *or* film] with the intention of causing C distress.

When there is more than one photograph or film the J-peg or M-peg file reference or exhibit reference should always be included in the particulars of offence.

Alternative Offences

(i) Attempt to commit the full offence. When indicting offences of attempt do so under 9.72
s 1(1) Criminal Attempts Act 1981.[208] Aver the attempt in both the Statement of Offence and Particulars of Offence. In addition, aver the substantive offence under the relevant Act; see paras 1.51 and 12.157 and *Reed & Others* [2021].[209]

(ii) Where the photograph or film was of a child under 18 at the time taken or filmed, consideration should be given as to whether the more appropriate offence is one under section 1 of the Protection of Children Act 1978 (taking, distributing, possessing or

---

[205] CJCA 2015, s 33(6).
[206] CJCA 2015, s 33(10).
[207] Modern Slavery Act 2015, s 45 commencement date 31.7.2015 (SI 2015/1476). This offence is not an excluded offence in Sch 4 of the Act. The s 45 defence is not retrospective, see *R v Joseph (Verna Sermanfure)* [2017] EWCA Crim 36.
[208] Implementation date 27.8.1981.
[209] *Reed & Others* [2021] EWCA Crim 572.

publishing indecent photographs of a child) or under section 160 of the Criminal Justice Act 1988 (possession of an indecent photograph of a child).

Sentence

9.73 (i) On indictment: **2 YEARS**.[210]
(ii) Summarily: **6 months**.[211]

9.74 The Sentencing Council, 'Intimidatory Offences' Definitive Guideline contains an offence-specific guideline for s 33 offences. The Guidelines apply to all offenders aged 18 and over, who are sentenced on or after 1 October 2018, regardless of the date of the offence.

Upon Conviction/Sentence

9.75 (i) Notification does not apply.[212]
(ii) Automatic barring from working with children or vulnerable adults does not apply.[213]
(iii) SHPO not applicable.[214]

---

[210] CJCA 2015, s 33(9)(a).
[211] CJCA 2015, s 33(9)(b). Increased to 12 months from commencement of CJA 2003 s154(1). This section is not yet in force.
[212] SOA 2003, s 80(1) (not listed in Sch 3); see Chapter 14, Tables 14.2–14.5.
[213] Part 2 of the Safeguarding Vulnerable Groups Act 2006 (Prescribed Criteria and Miscellaneous Provisions) Regulations 2009 (SI 2009 No 37); see Chapter 12, para 12.217.
[214] SA 2020, s 345 (not listed in Sch 3 or Sch 5 SOA 2003); see Chapter 16, para 16.07.

10
OFFENCES AGAINST PUBLIC DECENCY

A. Offences Committed from 1.1.1950 to date	10.04	C. Offences Committed from 1.5.2004 to date	10.22
1. Outraging Public Decency	10.04	1. Exposure	10.22
B. Offences Committed pre-30.4.2004	10.15	2. Voyeurism, 1.5.2004 to date	10.29
1. Indecent Exposure, 22.6.1824 to 30.4.2004	10.15	D. Alternative Offences	10.53

These offences deal with indecent acts which offend public decency. The old common law offence of outraging public decency is the most wide-ranging of offences in this section. This offence was not repealed by the SOA 2003; rather, its use was effectively extended by the CJA 2003, s 320. The offence is no longer indictable only, but triable either way.[1] Offences of indecent exposure and voyeurism created by the SOA 2003 replace and extend certain old offences, in particular under the Vagrancy Act (VA) 1824. **10.01**

New offences such as intercourse with an animal[2] and sexual penetration of a corpse[3] were created: (animal) see paras 5.18 and 5.74–5.75; (corpse) see para 10.34. **10.02**

On 12 April 2019[4] s 79A was added to the Sexual Offences Act 2003 creating 2 new offences to deal with the modern phenomenon of what is colloquially known as 'upskirting'. **10.03**

A. OFFENCES COMMITTED FROM 1.1.1950 TO DATE

1. Outraging Public Decency

This offence is a common law offence and covers lewd, disgusting, or obscene acts performed in public. In practice most cases have tended to involve acts of public masturbation, sexual intercourse in public places and prostitutes advertising in public places. A conviction for this offence was upheld where the defendants had made earrings from dried human foetuses and displayed them, as hanging from a sculpted human head in a gallery.[5] **10.04**

This offence was not repealed by the SOA 2003. New legislation covering sexual activity in a public lavatory,[6] voyeurism,[7] and indecent exposure,[8] will often cover the criminality **10.05**

---

[1] CJA 2003, s 320.
[2] SOA 2003, s 69.
[3] SOA 2003, s 70.
[4] Added by Voyeurism (Offences) Act 2019 c 2 s 1(2).
[5] R v Gibson and Sylveire [1990] 2 QB 619, 91 Cr App R 341 CA.
[6] SOA 2003, s 71.
[7] SOA 2003, ss 67 and 67A.
[8] SOA 2003, s 66.

10. OFFENCES AGAINST PUBLIC DECENCY

alleged. Where a statutory offence covers the conduct in question, that statutory offence should be preferred to the common law.

10.06 This offence will be reserved for offences of a more serious and unusual nature that do not readily fall within other sections of the Act; the maximum sentence is life imprisonment as opposed to, for example, 2 years' imprisonment for cases of exposure.

Definition

10.07 All open lewdness, grossly scandalous, and whatever openly outrages decency or is offensive and disgusting, or is injurious to public morals, by tending to corrupt the mind and destroy the love of decency, morality, and good order[9] (common law).

Proof

10.08 The prosecution must prove:

(i) a deliberate act (it is arguable that the prosecution must also prove that the perpetrator was at least reckless as to whether his act could be seen by two or more[10]);

(ii) that this act was of such a lewd, obscene or disgusting character as constitutes an outrage on public decency. This evidence can be given by a police officer. It is not necessary to prove that the act did disgust or annoy individuals who were present.[11] The test for this is objective.

(iii) This act must be committed in public so that more than one person has the opportunity to have witnessed it. The act (or exposure) does not of itself have to take place in public but must be visible (*or* audible) from a place to which the public have access.[12] It is sufficient for just one person to have witnessed it, as long as at least one other (present) might have witnessed it at the time.[13] Witnessing the act can be by means other than sight, for example hearing it.[14]

Notes

10.09 (i) The offence is triable either way,[15] but not before 20.1.2004;[16] offences of this nature committed before 20.1.2004 are on indictment only.

(ii) The particulars must aver the element of indecency.[17]

---

[9] 2 Russ Cr 12th edn.
[10] *R v Rowley* [1991] Crim LR 785.
[11] *R v Clayton and Halsey* [1963] 1 QB 163, 46 Cr App R 450.
[12] *Walker* [1996] Cr App R 111 CA.
[13] *R v Mayling* [1963] 2 QB 717, 47 Cr App R 102.
[14] *R v Hamilton* [2007] EWCA Crim 2062.
[15] CJA 2003, s 320.
[16] Criminal Justice Act 2003 (Commencement No 2 and Saving Provisions) Order 2004/81.
[17] *R v Clifford* (1988) 8 CL 86.

(iii) This offence can be committed by a male or female upon a male or female.[18]
(iv) The s 45 MSA 2015 defence for slavery and trafficking victims who commit an offence is available for an offence under this section, provided it was committed on or after 31.7.2015.[19]

Indictment

OUTRAGING PUBLIC DECENCY 1.1.1950 to date 10.10

Statement of Offence

Committing an act outraging public decency.

Particulars of Offence

D on the … day of… committed an act of a lewd, obscene and disgusting nature and outraging public decency, by indecently …

Sentence

(i) On indictment: **fine or imprisonment** or both. As this offence is a common law offence there is no maximum sentence, so long as neither is 'inordinate'.[20] 10.11
(ii) On summary conviction: **6 months** or a **fine** not exceeding the prescribed sum or **both**.[21]

Sentencing Guidance

There are, as at date of publication, no Sentencing Council Guidelines applicable to this offence. When sentencing offences for which there is no specific sentencing Guideline, the Sentencing Council 'General Guideline: Overarching Principles' applies to all individual offenders aged 18 and over that are sentenced on or after 1 October 2019. Further, the court should have regard to any applicable sentencing guidelines for equivalent offences under the Sexual Offences Act 2003. See, by way of example, *R v Hardy* [2019][22] in which the offender, who was seen displaying, rubbing, and shaking his penis in a fast food restaurant car park, was sentenced by reference to the s 66 SOA 2003 offence of exposure. 10.12

Upon Conviction/Sentence

(i) Notification not applicable.[23] 10.13

---

[18] *Evans v Ewells* [1972] 2 All ER 22, [1972] 1 WLR 671.
[19] Modern Slavery Act 2015, s 45 commencement date 31.7.2015 (SI 2015/1476). This offence is not an excluded offence in Sch 4 of the Act. The s 45 defence is not retrospective, see *R v Joseph (Verna Sermanfure)* [2017] EWCA Crim 36.
[20] *R v Morris* [1951] 1 KB 394, 34 Cr App R 210.
[21] MCA 1980, s 32(1). Maximum fine £5,000 for offences committed before 12.3.2015, thereafter unlimited fine.
[22] *R v Hardy (James)* [2013] EWCA Crim 2125.
[23] SOA 2003, s 80(1) (not listed in Sch 3) SOA 2003; see Chapter 14 Tables 14.2–14.5.

330 10. OFFENCES AGAINST PUBLIC DECENCY

(ii) Automatic inclusion on the children's and adults' barred lists not applicable.[24]
(iii) SHPO applicable.[25]

10.14 The SOA 2003 did not repeal the common law offence of outraging public decency. However, most offences that might previously have been charged under this Act, will now be now charged as:

(a) exposure:[26] exposure of genitals intending someone to see them and that someone would be caused alarm and distress; maximum 2 years; or
(b) voyeurism:[27] observing someone doing a private act knowing there is no consent, for the purpose of sexual gratification; maximum 2 years; or
(c) threatening behaviour;[28]
(d) disorderly conduct.[29]

B. OFFENCES COMMITTED PRE-30.4.2004

1. Indecent Exposure, 22.6.1824 to 30.4.2004

Vagrancy Act 1824, s 4

10.15 In practice, most cases of indecent exposure are prosecuted under:

(a) VA 1824, s 4 and dealt with summarily (until 2004); or
(b) SOA 2003, s 66.

Definition

10.16 Willfully, openly, lewdly, and obscenely exposing his person with intent to insult any female ...

Proof

10.17 (i) This offence can only be committed by a male, and the exposure has to be of the penis.[30]
(ii) The exposure does not have to take place in public but must be capable of being seen by the public.[31]

---

[24] Part 2 of the Safeguarding Vulnerable Groups Act 2006 (Prescribed Criteria and Miscellaneous Provisions) Regulations 2009 (SI 2009 No 37) paras 2 and 4; see Chapter 12 para 12.217.
[25] SA 2020, s 345. The common law offence is not listed in Sch 3 but is listed in Sch 5, para 4A of the SOA 2003; see Chapter 16 para 16.07.
[26] SOA 2003, s 66.
[27] SOA 2003, s 67.
[28] Public Order Act (POA) 1986, s 4.
[29] POA 1986, s 5.
[30] *Evans v Ewells* [1972] 2 All ER 22.
[31] *Hunt v DPP* [1990] Crim LR 812.

C. OFFENCES COMMITTED FROM 1.5.2004 TO DATE

(iii) The man must have at least been reckless as to whether he was indecently exposing himself.

Notes

10.18
(i) These offences were summary offences only. Accordingly, a 6-month time limit to prosecute applied.
(ii) This offence can only be committed upon a woman. Cases of indecent exposure to a male may be prosecuted summarily under the Town and Police Clauses Act 1847, s 28. The maximum sentence is one of 14 days' imprisonment or a fine on the level 3 standard scale. In such cases the act must take place in public and a person was likely to have been annoyed. This offence was repealed and abolished by the SOA 2003.

Sentence

10.19
(i) Maximum sentence: **3 months** and a fine: level 3 standard scale.[32]
(ii) **12 months** (if further offences under VA 1824, s 4 are committed and the defendant is committed to the Crown Court to be sentenced).[33]

Upon Conviction/Sentence

10.20
(i) Notification requirements not applicable.[34]
(ii) Automatic inclusion on the children's and adults' barred lists not applicable.[35]
(iii) SHPO not applicable.[36]

This offence has been repealed under the SOA 2003. The following offences may now be charged. 10.21

C. OFFENCES COMMITTED FROM 1.5.2004 to date

1. Exposure

Sexual Offences Act 2003, s 66(1)

Definition

10.22
(1) (a) he intentionally exposes his genitals and
(b) intends that someone will see them and be caused alarm or distress.

---

[32] MCA 1980, s 34(3).
[33] VA 1824, s 5.
[34] SOA 2003, s 80(1) (not listed in Schedule 3); see Chapter 14 Tables 14.2–14.5.
[35] Part 2 of the Safeguarding Vulnerable Groups Act 2006 (Prescribed Criteria and Miscellaneous Provisions) Regulations 2009 (SI 2009 No 37) paras 2 and 4; see Chapter 12 para 12.217.
[36] SA 2020, s 345 (not listed in Sch 3 or Sch 5 SOA 2003); see Chapter 16 para 16.07.

332   10. OFFENCES AGAINST PUBLIC DECENCY

Proof

10.23 The prosecution must prove

(i) exposure of the genitalia;
(ii) intention to expose genitals and that someone will see them and be caused harassment, alarm or distress.

Notes

10.24
(i) This offence is triable either way.[37]
(ii) The offence may be committed as principal by males or females.
(iii) The s 45 MSA 2015 defence for slavery and trafficking victims who commit an offence does not apply to this offence.[38]

Indictment

10.25 INDECENT EXPOSURE 1.5.2004 to date

Statement of Offence
EXPOSURE, contrary to section 66(1) of the Sexual Offences Act 2003.

Particulars of Offence
D on the … day of 20…, intentionally exposed his genitals, intending that someone would see them and be caused alarm or distress.

Sentence

10.26
(i) On indictment: **2 YEARS**.[39]
(ii) Summarily: **6 months**[40] or a **fine**[41] or **both**.[42]

Sentencing Guidance

10.27 The Sentencing Council 'Sexual Offences: Definitive Guideline' contains offence-specific guidelines for s 66 offences. The Guideline applies to all offenders aged 18 and over, sentenced on or after 1 April 2014.

---

[37] SOA 2003, s 66(2).
[38] Modern Slavery Act 2015, s 45 and Sch 4, para 33.
[39] SOA 2003, s 66(2).
[40] Increased to 12 months once s 282(4), CJA 2003 implemented.
[41] Maximum fine £5,000 for offences committed before 12.3.2015, thereafter unlimited fine.
[42] SOA 2003, s 66(2).

Upon Conviction/Sentence

(i) Notification applies if (a) the offender under 18 has been sentenced to at least 12 months' imprisonment or (b) in any other case, the victim was under 18 or the offender has been sentenced to a term of imprisonment, detention in a hospital, or to a minimum 12 months' community sentence.[43] **10.28**

(ii) Automatic inclusion in the children's and adults' barred lists if offence committed against a child under 16.[44]

(iii) SHPO applies.[45]

(iv) Qualifying 'specified sexual offence' in Schedule 18 (Extended Sentences).[46]

2. Voyeurism, 1.5.2004 to date

Sexual Offences Act 2003, s 67

Prior to the implementation of s 67 SOA 2003, there was no specific offence of voyeurism. Section 67 introduced four separate voyeurism offences. Section 67(1) is the basic offence of voyeurism. Section 67(2) incorporates the operation of equipment into the offence. Section 67(3) incorporates the recording of the private act. Section 67(4) covers the installation of equipment to commit a voyeurism offence. **10.29**

Definition

(1) A person commits an offence if— **10.30**
   (a) for the purposes of obtaining sexual gratification, he observes another person doing a private act, and
   (b) he knows that the other person does not consent to being observed for his sexual gratification.

(2) A person commits an offence if—
   (a) he operates equipment with the intention of enabling another person to observe, for the purpose of obtaining sexual gratification, a third person (B) doing a private act, and
   (b) he knows that B does not consent to his operating equipment with that intention.

(3) A person commits an offence if—
   (a) he records another person (B) doing a private act,
   (b) he does so with the intention that he or a third person will, for the purpose of obtaining sexual gratification, look at an image of B doing the act, and
   (c) he knows that B does not consent to his recording the act with that intention.

---

[43] SOA 2003, s 80(1), Sch 3, para 33; see Chapter 14 paras 14.01–14.05.
[44] Part 2 of the Safeguarding Vulnerable Groups Act 2006 (Prescribed Criteria and Miscellaneous Provisions) Regulations 2009 (SI 2009 No 37) paras 2 and 4: see Chapter 12 para 12.217.
[45] SA 2020, s 345 and SOA 2003 Sch 3, para 33; see Chapter 16 para 16.07.
[46] SA 2020, s 306, Sch 18, para 38(ax); see Chapter 12 para 12.51.

(4) A person commits an offence if he installs equipment, or constructs or adapts a structure or part of a structure, with the intention of enabling himself or another person to commit an offence under subsection (1).

Proof

10.31 For a section 67(1) offence the prosecution must prove:

(1) D observed another person. As to 'observe', per Aikens LJ

The verb 'observes' is not further defined in the SOA but we think it must connote a deliberate decision on the part of the defendant to look at someone doing a 'private act', as opposed to an accidental perception of someone doing a 'private act'. 'Observes' must also exclude a careless and, we think, reckless perception.[47]

(2) The person was doing a private act. A person is defined as doing a private act if the person is in a place which, in the circumstances, would reasonably be expected to provide privacy, and

   (a) the person's genitals, buttocks, or breasts are exposed or covered only with underwear, ('Breasts' does not extend to the exposed male chest)[48]

   (b) the person is using a lavatory, or

   (c) the person is doing a sexual act that is not of a kind ordinarily done in public.[49]

   Whether a person was doing a private act in a place which, in the circumstances, would reasonably be expected to provide privacy would depend inevitably on the context of the observation.[50] Whether a particular place is such would appear to be an objective test.[51] Issues of whether there was a reasonable expectation of privacy and whether the act of intercourse was private were matters for the jury.[52]

(3) For the purpose of sexual gratification.[53] The purpose of the deliberate observation of the private act by the defendant has to be his own 'sexual gratification', not someone else's sexual gratification. This 'purpose' can only be the result of the defendant's own (subjective) thought process.[54]

(4) D knows that the other person did not consent to them observing the private act for their sexual gratification.[55] This must involve proof of a specific state of mind of the defendant, viz. his actual knowledge that the other person does not consent to being observed (deliberately) by the defendant for the specific purpose of the defendant obtaining sexual gratification from that observation.[56] The sexual gratification does

---

[47] R v B. [M] [2012] EWCA Crim 770 at para [59].
[48] R v Bassett (Kevin) [2008] EWCA Crim 1174.
[49] SOA 2003, s 68(1).
[50] R v Bassett (Kevin) [2008] EWCA Crim 1174.
[51] R v B (M) [2012] EWCA Crim 770 at [59].
[52] R v Richards (Tony) 2020 [EWCA] Crim 95.
[53] SOA 2003, s 67(1)(a).
[54] R v B (M) [2012] EWCA Crim 770 at [60].
[55] SOA 2003, s 67(1)(b).
[56] R v B (M) [2012] EWCA Crim 770 at [61].

not have to be simultaneous, contemporaneous or synchronized with the watching of the act.[57]

For a s 67(2) offence the prosecution must prove: **10.32**

(1) D operated equipment with the intention of enabling another person to observe a third person doing a private act.[58] ('Private act' is as defined as above).[59] Operating equipment includes enabling or securing its activation by another person without that person's knowledge.[60]
(2) For the purpose of the other person obtaining sexual gratification.[61]
(3) D knows that the third person did not consent to them operating the equipment with the requisite intention.[62]

For a s 67(3) offence the prosecution must prove: **10.33**

(1) D recorded another person doing a private act.[63] ('Private act' is as defined as above).[64] For example, a manager of a sports centre recording women using the shower and sunbeds or[65] recording persons using a disabled toilet.[66]
(2) With the intention that D or a third person will, for the purpose of obtaining sexual gratification, look at the image of the person doing the act.[67]
(3) D knows that the third person did not consent to them recording the act with the requisite intention.[68]

For a s 67(4) offence the prosecution must prove: **10.34**

(1) D installed equipment **or** constructed or adapted a structure or part of a structure.[69] Structure includes a tent, vehicle, or vessel or other temporary or moveable structure.[70] For example, installing a video camera in the loft above a bathroom to enable an offender to watch his stepdaughter in the shower[71] or concealing a camera in a toilet paper roll in a neighbour's bathroom.[72]
(2) With the intention of enabling himself or another to commit an offence of voyeurism under s 67(1).[73]

---

[57] *R v Abdullahi (Osmund Mohammed)* [2006] EWCA Crim 2060, case decided in relation to s 12 SOA 2003 offence.
[58] SOA 2003, s 67(2)(a).
[59] SOA 2003, s 68(1).
[60] SOA 2003, s 68(1A). Section 1A added by Voyeurism (Offences) Act 2019 (12.4.2019).
[61] SOA 2003, s 67(2)(a).
[62] SOA 2003, s 67(2)(b).
[63] SOA 2003, s 67(3)(a).
[64] SOA 2003, s 68(1).
[65] *R v Turner (Mark)* [2006] 2 Cr. App. R. (S). 51.
[66] *R v Henderson (Trevor)* [2007] EWCA Crim 3264.
[67] SOA 2003, s 67(3)(b).
[68] SOA 2003, s 67(3)(c).
[69] SOA 2003, s 67(4).
[70] SOA 2003, s 68(2).
[71] *R v IP* [2005] 1 Cr. App. R. 102.
[72] *R v McCann* [2007] 1 Cr App R (S) 4.
[73] SOA 2003, s 67(4).

Notes

10.35 (i) All offences under s 67 are triable either way.[74]

(ii) The s 45 MSA 2015 defence for slavery and trafficking victims who commit an offence does not apply to this offence.[75]

Indictment

10.36 VOYEURISM 1.5.2004 to date

Statement of Offence
VOYEURISM, contrary to section 67(1)(a) of the Sexual Offences Act 2003.

Particulars of Offence
D on the … day of 20.., for the purpose of obtaining sexual gratification, observed C doing a private act, C being in a place which, in the circumstances, would reasonably be expected to provide privacy and [state nature of C's act/state of undress] D knowing that C did not consent to being so observed for D's sexual gratification.

Statement of Offence
VOYEURISM, contrary to section 67(1)(b) of the Sexual Offences Act 2003.

Particulars of Offence
D on the … day of 20… , operated equipment with the intention of enabling another person to observe, for the purpose of obtaining sexual gratification, C doing a private act, C being in a place which, in the circumstances, would reasonably be expected to provide privacy and [state nature of C's act/state of undress], D knowing that C did not consent to D operating the equipment with that intention.

Statement of Offence
VOYEURISM, contrary to section 67(1)(c) of the Sexual Offences Act 2003.

Particulars of Offence
D on the … day of 20… , recorded C doing a private act, C being in a place which, in the circumstances, would reasonably be expected to provide privacy and [state nature of C's act/state of undress] with the intention that D or a third person will, for the purpose of obtaining sexual gratification, look at an image of C doing the act, D knowing that C did not consent to being recorded with that intention.

Statement of Offence
VOYEURISM, contrary to section 67(1)(d) of the Sexual Offences Act 2003.

---

[74] SOA 2003, s 67(5).
[75] Modern Slavery Act 2015, s 45 and Sch 4, para 33.

C. OFFENCES COMMITTED FROM 1.5.2004 TO DATE

> **Particulars of Offence**
>
> D on the … day of 20… , [installed equipment *or* constructed *or* adapted a structure or part of a structure] with the intention of enabling himself or another to commit an offence of voyeurism under section 67(1) of the Sexual Offences Act 2003.

Sentence

For all s 67 offences: **10.37**

(i) On indictment: **2 YEARS**.[76]
(ii) Summarily: **6 months**[77] or a **fine**[78] not exceeding the statutory maximum or both.

Sentencing Guidance

The Sentencing Council 'Sexual Offences: Definitive Guideline' contains offence-specific guidelines for s 67 offences. The Guideline applies to all offenders aged 18 and over, sentenced on or after 1.4.2014.   **10.38**

Upon Conviction/Sentence

(i) Notification applies (a) where the offender under 18 is sentenced to imprisonment of at least 12 months (b) in any other case where victim under 18 *or* the offender has been sentenced to imprisonment, hospital detention or community sentence of at least 12 months.[79]   **10.39**
(ii) Automatic inclusion in the children's and adults' barred lists with the right to make representations where the victim was under 16.[80]
(iii) SHPO applies.[81]
(iv) Qualifying 'specified sexual offence' in Schedule 18 (Extended Sentences).[82]

Sexual Offences Act 2003, s 67A

Section 1 of the Voyeurism (Offences) Act 2019 inserts two new 'upskirting' offences into the SOA 200 under s 67A of operating equipment (s 67A(1)) or recording an image (s 67A(2) under another person's clothing. The new offences came into effect on 12.4.2019 and are not retrospective.   **10.40**

---

[76] SOA 2003.
[77] Increased to 12 months once s 282(4), CJA 2003 implemented.
[78] Maximum fine £5,000 for offences committed before 12.3.2015, thereafter unlimited fine.
[79] SOA 2003, s 80(1) and Sch 3, para 34; see Chapter 14 paras 14.01–14.05.
[80] Part 2 of the Safeguarding Vulnerable Groups Act 2006 (Prescribed Criteria and Miscellaneous Provisions) Regulations 2009 (SI 2009 No 37) paras 2 and 4; see Chapter 12 para 12.217.
[81] SA 2020, s 345 and SOA 2003, Sch 3 para 34; see Chapter 16 para 16.07.
[82] SA 2020, s 306, Sch 18, para 38(ay); see Chapter 12 para 12.51.

338   10. OFFENCES AGAINST PUBLIC DECENCY

Definition

10.41 As set out in the legislation, hence the use of 'A' and 'B' rather than 'D' and 'C' and 'C' for a third party rather than 'X':

(1) A person (A) commits an offence if—
   (a) A operates equipment beneath the clothing of another person (B),
   (b) A does so with the intention of enabling A or another person (C), for a purpose mentioned in subsection (3), to observe—
      (i) B's genitals or buttocks (whether exposed or covered with underwear), or
      (ii) the underwear covering B's genitals or buttocks,
         in circumstances where the genitals, buttocks or underwear would not otherwise be visible, and
   (c) A does so—
      (i) without B's consent, and
      (ii) without reasonably believing that B consents.
(2) A person (A) commits an offence if—
   (a) A records an image beneath the clothing of another person (B),
   (b) the image is of—
      (i) B's genitals or buttocks (whether exposed or covered with underwear), or
      (ii) the underwear covering B's genitals or buttocks,
   in circumstances where the genitals, buttocks or underwear would not otherwise be visible,
   (c) A does so with the intention that A or another person (C) will look at the image for a purpose mentioned in subsection (3), and
   (d) A does so—
      (i) without B's consent, and
      (ii) without reasonably believing that B consents.
(3) The purposes referred to in subsections (1) and (2) are—
   (a) obtaining sexual gratification (whether for A or C);
   (b) humiliating, alarming or distressing B.

Proof

10.42 As per Definition. Further:

(i) Consent: a person consents if he agrees by choice, and has the freedom and capacity to make that choice.[83]
(ii) 'Image' means a moving or still image and includes an image produced by any means and, where the context permits, a three-dimensional image.[84]
(iii) Operating equipment includes enabling or securing its activation by another person without that person's knowledge and so will included automated equipment.[85]
(iv) 'Sexual gratification' see para 10.41 above.

---

[83] SOA 2003, s 74.
[84] SOA 2003, s 79(4).
[85] SOA 2003, s 68(1A).

Notes

10.43

(i) The offence is triable either way.[86]
(v) The s 45 MSA 2015 defence for slavery and trafficking victims who commit an offence is available for an offence under this section, provided it was committed on or after 31.7.2015.[87]

Indictment

VOYEURISM: ADDITIONAL OFFENCES 12.4.2019 to date

10.44

Statement of Offence
OPERATING EQUIPMENT BENEATH CLOTHING ('UPSKIRTING'), contrary to section 67A(1) of the Sexual Offences Act 2003.

Particulars of Offence
D on the ... day of 20..., for the purpose of obtaining sexual gratification *or* [humiliating, alarming or distressing C], operated equipment beneath the clothing of C, with the intention of enabling D or another person to observe C's genitals or buttocks *or* [C's underwear covering C's genitals or buttocks] in circumstances where the genitals, buttocks or underwear would otherwise not be visible, and C did not consent, and D not reasonably believe C consented.

Statement of Offence
RECORDING BENEATH CLOTHING ('UPSKIRTING'), contrary to section 67A(2) of the Sexual Offences Act 2003.

Particulars of Offence
D on the ... day of 20..., recorded an image of C's genitals or buttocks *or* [C's underwear covering C's genitals or buttocks] beneath C's clothing, in circumstances where the genitals, buttocks or underwear would otherwise not be visible, with the intention that D or another would look at the image for the purpose of obtaining sexual gratification *or* [humiliating, alarming or distressing C], and C did not consent, and D did not reasonably believe C consented.

Sentence

10.45

(i) On indictment: **2 YEARS**.[88]
(ii) Summarily: **6 months or a fine**.[89]

---

[86] SOA 2003, s 67A(4).
[87] Modern Slavery Act 2015, s 45 commencement date 31.7.2015 (SI 2015/1476). This offence is not an excluded offence in Sch 4 of the Act. The s 45 defence is not retrospective, see *R v Joseph (Verna Sermanfure)* [2017] EWCA Crim 36.
[88] SOA 2003, 67A(4)(b).
[89] SOA 2003, s 67(4)(a). Increased to 12 months once s 282(4), CJA 2003 implemented.

340   10. OFFENCES AGAINST PUBLIC DECENCY

Sentencing Guidance

10.46 There are currently no Sentencing Council Guidelines for the section 67A offence.

Upon Conviction/Sentence

10.47 (i) Notification applies where the offence was committed under s (3)(a) (for the purpose of sexual gratification) *and* (1) the offender is under 18 and was sentenced to imprisonment of at least 12 months *or* (b) in any other case, the victim was under 18 years *or* the offender was sentenced to imprisonment; detained in hospital or made subject to a community order of at least 12 months.[90]

(ii) Automatic inclusion in the children's and adults' barred lists not applicable.[91]

(iii) SHPO applies.[92]

10.48 Section 70 of the Sexual Offences Act 2003 created the offence of having intercourse with a corpse for which there had been no precedent.

2. Sexual Penetration of a Corpse

Sexual Offences Act 2003, s 70

Definition

10.49 A person (D) commits an offence if—

(a) he intentionally performs an act of penetration with a part of his body or anything else,

(b) what is penetrated is a part of the body of a dead person,

(c) he knows that, or is reckless as to whether, that is what is penetrated, and

(d) the penetration is sexual.

Proof

10.50 As per definition:

(i) The penetration can be by part of the body or an object.

(ii) D must know or be reckless as to whether he is penetrating a part of the body of a dead person.

(iii) The penetration must be sexual.

---

[90] SOA 2003, s 80(1) and Sch 3, para 34A; see Chapter 14 paras 14.01–14.05.
[91] Part 2 of the Safeguarding Vulnerable Groups Act 2006 (Prescribed Criteria and Miscellaneous Provisions) Regulations 2009 (SI 2009 No 37) not included in paras 1, 2, 3, or 4; see Chapter 12 para 12.217.
[92] SA 2020, s 345 and SOA 2003, Sch 3 para 34A; see Chapter 16 para 16.07.

Notes

10.51

(i) This offence is triable either way.
(ii) Penetration is a continuing act from entry to withdrawal.[93]
(iii) The s 45 MSA 2015 defence for slavery and trafficking victims who commit an offence does not apply to this offence.[94]

Indictment

1.5.2004 to date.

10.52

Statement of Offence
SEXUAL PENETRATION OF A CORPSE contrary to section 70(1) of the Sexual Offences Act 2003.

Particulars of Offence
D, on the … day of …, 20 … , intentionally performed an act of penetration of a part of the body of a dead person with a part of his body in circumstances where the penetration was sexual and D knew that that is what was being penetrated, or was reckless in relation thereto.

D. ALTERNATIVE OFFENCES

Attempt to commit the full offence. When indicting offences of attempt do so under s 1(1) Criminal Attempts Act 1981.[95] Aver the attempt in both the Statement of Offence and Particulars of Offence. In addition, aver the substantive offence under the relevant Act; see paras 1.51 and 12.157 and *Reed & Others* [2021].[96]

10.53

Sentence

(i) On indictment: **2 YEARS**
(ii) Summarily: **6 months** and/or an unlimited fine.[97]

10.54

Sentencing Guidance

The Sentencing Council 'Sexual Offences: Definitive Guideline' does not cover this offence. The Sentencing Guidelines Council's Guideline (May 2007), gave a starting point of a community order and the range was 'an appropriate non-custodial sentence'. For repeat offenders the range was 4 weeks' to 18 months' custody, with a starting point of 26 weeks'

10.55

---

[93] SOA 2003, s 79(2).
[94] Modern Slavery Act 2015, s 45 and Sch 4, para 33.
[95] Implementation date 27.8.1981.
[96] *Reed & Others* [2021] EWCA Crim 572.
[97] SOA 2003, s 70(2).

custody. Four aggravating factors were specifically identified; distress caused to the relatives or friends of the deceased, physical damage caused to the body, the corpse was that of a child, and the offence having been committed in a funeral home or mortuary.

Upon Conviction/Sentence

10.56 (i) Notification applies:[98]
  (a) where the offender was under 18, he is or has been sentenced in respect of the offence to imprisonment for a term of at least 12 months;
  (b) in any other case, the offender, in respect of the offence or finding, is or has been: (i) sentenced to a term of imprisonment, or (ii) detained in a hospital.

Automatic inclusion in the children's and adults' barred lists not applicable.[99]

SHPO applies.[100]

Qualifying 'specified sexual offence' in Schedule 18 (Extended Sentences).[101]

---

[98] SOA 2003, s 80(1) and Sch 3, para 35, see Chapter 14, paras 14.01–14.05.
[99] Part 2 of the Safeguarding Vulnerable Groups Act 2006 (Prescribed Criteria and Miscellaneous Provisions) Regulations 2009 (SI 2009 No 37) not included in paras 1, 2, 3, and 4; see Chapter 12, para 12.217.
[100] SA 2020, s 345 and SOA 2003, Sch 3, para 35; see Chapter 16, para 16.07.
[101] SA 2020, s 306, Sch 18, para 38(ba); see Chapter 12, para 12.51.

11

PREPARATORY OFFENCES

A. Introduction	11.01	E. Burglary with Intent to Commit Rape, 1.1.1969 to 30.4.2004	11.27
B. Procurement of a Woman by Threats or Intimidation, 1.1.1957 to 30.4.2004	11.04	F. Administering a Substance with Intent, 1.5.2004 to date	11.35
C. Procurement of Intercourse by False Pretences, 1.1.1957 to 30.4.2004	11.11	G. Committing an Offence with Intent to Commit a Sexual Offence, 1.5.2004 to date	11.43
D. Administering Drugs to Obtain or Facilitate Intercourse, 1.1.1957 to 30.4.2004	11.19	H. Trespass with Intent to Commit a Sexual Offence, 1.5.2004 to date	11.51

A. INTRODUCTION

This chapter includes: **11.01**

(a) offences of procurement (those not dealt with in Chapter 8), and
(b) other preparatory offences.

The SOA 1956 in the main followed earlier legislation, the Criminal Law Amendment Act (CLAA) 1885, which was largely concerned with the 'white slave market'. By the time the SOA 2003 was passed these offences were rarely charged. For this reason the pre-1956 Act offences have not been included. **11.02**

- For SOA 1956, s 22: procuration of a woman to become a prostitute, see para 8.58.
- For SOA 1956, s 23: procurement of girl under 21, see para 8.21.
- For SOA 1967, s 4: procurement to commit homosexual acts, see para 5.106.

Other preparatory offences: **11.03**

- For SOA 1956, s 16: assault with intent to commit buggery, see para 5.75.
- For assault with intent to commit rape (common law offence—fallen into disuse).

B. PROCUREMENT OF A WOMAN BY THREATS OR INTIMIDATION, 1.1.1957 TO 30.4.2004

1. Procurement of a Woman by Threats or Intimidation

Sexual Offences Act 1956, s 2(1)

344   11. PREPARATORY OFFENCES

Definition

11.04 ... to procure a woman by threats or intimidation, to have unlawful sexual intercourse in any part of the world.

Proof

11.05
(i) For definition of procuring, see para 8.22.
(ii) The threats and intimidation must relate to the procuring.
(iii) Until 3.2.1995[1] there was a requirement that sexual intercourse was unlawful, that is, outside marriage; thereafter the word has been deleted from the definition.
(iv) The accused must have an intention to procure the female to have sexual intercourse with him or another man.
(v) The requirement of corroboration was removed as of 3.2.1995.[2]

Notes

11.06
(i) The offence is triable on indictment only.
(ii) The offence can be committed upon a girl or woman
(iii) The sexual intercourse relates to penetration of the vagina by the penis.
(iv) A male or female may commit this offence. The victim can only be female.

Indictment

11.07 PROCUREMENT OF A WOMAN BY THREATS 1.1.1957 to 30.4.2004

Statement of Offence
PROCURATION BY THREATS OR INTIMIDATION, contrary to section 2(1) of the Sexual Offences Act 1956.

Particulars of Offences
D on the ... day of ... procured C, a woman to have (unlawful) sexual intercourse with himself (or another), by threats or intimidation (state the nature of the alleged threats/intimidation).

Alternative Offences

11.08 An attempt to commit this offence. When indicting offences of attempt do so under common law until 26.8.1981, thereafter indict under s 1(1) Criminal Attempts Act 1981.[3]

---

[1] Words repealed by CJPOA 1994, s 168 (1) and (3) and Sch 9, para 2, Sch 11 (implementation date 3.2.1995).
[2] Section 2(2) repealed by CJPOA 1994, Sch 11 para 1, SI 1995/127.
[3] Implementation date 27.8.1981.

Aver the attempt in both the Statement of Offence and Particulars of Offence. In addition, aver the substantive offence under the relevant Act; see paras 1.51 and 12.157 and *Reed & Others* [2021].[4]

Sentence

On indictment: **2 YEARS**.[5]   **11.09**

Upon Conviction/Sentence

(i) Notification not applicable.[6]   **11.10**
(ii) Automatic inclusion in the children's and adults' barred lists with the right to make representations.[7]
(iii) SHPO not applicable.[8]
(iv) Qualifying 'specified sexual offence' in Schedule 18 (Extended Sentences).[9]

C. PROCUREMENT OF INTERCOURSE BY FALSE PRETENCES, 1.1.1957 TO 30.4.2004

Sexual Offences Act 1956, s 3(1)

Definition

… to procure a woman by false pretences or false representations, to have unlawful sexual intercourse in any part of the world.   **11.11**

Proof

(i) For definition of procuring: see para 8.22.   **11.12**
(ii) The false pretences or representations must relate to the procuring.
(iii) Until 3.2.1999[10] there was a requirement that sexual intercourse was unlawful, that is outside marriage; thereafter the word has been deleted from the definition.
(iv) The accused must have an intention to procure the female to have sexual intercourse with him or another man.
(v) The requirement of corroboration was removed as of 3.2.1995.[11]

---

[4] *Reed & Others* [2021] EWCA Crim 572.
[5] SOA 1956, Sch 2, para 8.
[6] SOA 2003, s 80(1) (not listed in Sch 3); see Chapter 14 Tables 14.2–14.5.
[7] Part 2 of the Safeguarding Vulnerable Groups Act 2006 (Prescribed Criteria and Miscellaneous Provisions) Regulations 2009 (SI 2009 No 37) paras 2 and 4; see Chapter 12 para 12.217.
[8] SA 2020, s 345 (not listed in Sch 3 or Sch 5 SOA 2003); see Chapter 16 para 16.07.
[9] SA 2020, s 306, Sch 18, para 29(b); see Chapter 12 para 12.51.
[10] Words repealed by CJPOA 1994, s 168 (1) and (3) and Sch 9, para 2, Sch 11 (implementation date 3.2.1995).
[11] Section 3(2) repealed by CJPOA 1994, Sch 11, para 1, SI 1995/127.

Notes

11.13
(i) The offence is triable on indictment only.
(ii) The offence can be committed upon a girl or woman.
(iii) The sexual intercourse relates to penetration of the vagina by the penis.
(iv) A male or female may commit this offence. The victim can only be female.

Indictment

11.14 PROCUREMENT OF A WOMAN BY FALSE PRETENCES OR REPRESENTATIONS
1.1.1957 to 30.4.2004

Statement of Offence

PROCURATION BY FALSE PRETENCES OR FALSE REPRESENTATIONS, contrary to section 3(1) of the Sexual Offences Act 1956.

Particulars of Offences

D on the … day of … procured C, a woman to have (unlawful) sexual intercourse with himself (or X), by falsely pretending or representing to her that (state the nature of the alleged pretence or representation).

Alternative Offences

11.15 An attempt to commit this offence. When indicting offences of attempt do so under common law until 26.8.1981, thereafter indict under s 1(1) Criminal Attempts Act 1981.[12] Aver the attempt in both the Statement of Offence and Particulars of Offence. In addition, aver the substantive offence under the relevant Act; see paras 1.51 and 12.157 and *Reed & Others* [2021].[13]

Sentence

11.16 On indictment: 2 YEARS.[14]

Upon Conviction/Sentence

11.17
(i) Notification not applicable.[15]
(ii) Automatic inclusion in the children's and adults' barred lists with the right to make representations.[16]
(iii) SHPO not applicable.[17]

---

[12] Implementation date 27.8.1981.
[13] *Reed & Others* [2021] EWCA Crim 572.
[14] SOA 2003, Sch 2, para 8.
[15] SOA 2003, s 80(1) (not listed in Sch 3); see Chapter 14 Tables 14.2–14.5.
[16] Part 2 of the Safeguarding Vulnerable Groups Act 2006 (Prescribed Criteria and Miscellaneous Provisions) Regulations 2009 (SI 2009 No 37) paras 2 and 4; see Chapter 12 para 12.217.
[17] SA 2020, s 345 (not listed in Sch 3 or Sch 5 SOA 2003); see Chapter 16 para 16.07.

(iv) Qualifying 'specified sexual offence' in Schedule 18 (Extended Sentences).[18]

The SOA 2003 repealed both ss 2 and 3 of the SOA 1956, without replacing either offence. **11.18**

D. ADMINISTERING DRUGS TO OBTAIN OR FACILITATE INTERCOURSE

Sexual Offences Act 1956, s 4(1)

Definition

… to apply or administer to, or cause to be taken by a woman any drug, matter or thing with intent to stupefy or overpower her so as thereby to enable any man to have unlawful sexual intercourse with her. **11.19**

Proof

(i) 'Apply or administer to' covers any action which leads to the drug being taken and having an effect. **11.20**
(ii) 'Drug' covers anything capable of having the effect of overpowering or stupefying the victim, as per the Definition.
(iii) The accused must have an intention whilst administering the drug, that the female would be overpowered or stupefied and that a man could have sexual intercourse with her.
(iv) The requirement of corroboration was removed as of 3.2.1995.[19]

Notes

(i) The offence is triable on indictment only. **11.21**
(ii) The offence can be committed upon a girl or woman
(iii) The sexual intercourse relates to penetration of the vagina by the penis.
(iv) A male or female may commit this offence. The victim can only be female.

Indictment

ADMINISTERING DRUGS TO OBTAIN OR FACILITATE INTERCOURSE 1.1.1957 to 30.4.2004 **11.22**

---

[18] SA 2020, s 306, Sch 18, para 29(c); see Chapter 12 para 12.51.
[19] Section 4(2) repealed by Criminal Justice and Public Order Act 1994, Sch 11 para 1, SI 1995/127.

348   11. PREPARATORY OFFENCES

> **Statement of Offence**
> ADMINISTRATION OF DRUGS TO OBTAIN OR FACILITATE (UNLAWFUL) SEXUAL INTERCOURSE, contrary to section 4(1) of the Sexual Offences Act 1956.
>
> **Particulars of Offences**
> D on the ... day of ... administered (state the drug/thing) a drug/matter/thing to C (caused a drug/matter/thing to be taken by C), with intent to stupefy or overpower her so as thereby to enable any man to have (unlawful) sexual intercourse with her.

Alternative Offences

11.23 An attempt to commit this offence. When indicting offences of attempt do so under common law until 26.8.1981, thereafter indict under s 1(1) Criminal Attempts Act 1981.[20] Aver the attempt in both the Statement of Offence and Particulars of Offence. In addition, aver the substantive offence under the relevant Act; see paras 1.51 and 12.157 and *Reed & Others* [2021].[21]

Sentence

11.24 On indictment: **2 YEARS**.[22]

Upon Conviction/Sentence

11.25 (i) Notification not applicable.[23]
(ii) Automatic inclusion in the children's and adults' barred lists with the right to make representations.[24]
(iii) SHPO not applicable.[25]
(iv) Qualifying 'specified sexual offence' in Schedule 18 (Extended Sentences).[26]

11.26 *The SOA repealed SOA 1956, s 4 in full. Section 61 of the SOA 2003 covers this offence (see para 11.35).*

E. BURGLARY WITH INTENT TO COMMIT RAPE, 1.1.1969 TO 30.4.2004

1. Burglary with Intent to Commit Rape

Theft Act 1968, s 9(1)

---

[20] Implementation date 27.8.1981.
[21] *Reed & Others* [2021] EWCA Crim 572.
[22] SOA 1956, Sch 2, para 9.
[23] SOA 2003, s 80(1) (not listed in Sch 3); see Chapter 14 Tables 14.2 -14.5.
[24] Part 2 of the Safeguarding Vulnerable Groups Act 2006 (Prescribed Criteria and Miscellaneous Provisions) Regulations 2009 (SI 2009 No 37) paras 2 and 4; see Chapter 12 para 12.217.
[25] SA 2020, s 345 (not listed in Sch 3 or Sch 5 SOA 2003); see Chapter 16 para 16.07.
[26] SA 2020, s 306, Sch 18, para 29(d); see Chapter 12 para 12.51.

E. BURGLARY WITH INTENT TO COMMIT RAPE

Definition

... A person is guilty of burglary if— **11.27**

(a) he enters any building or part of a building as a trespasser and with intent to commit any such offence as is mentioned in subsection (2) below; ... This includes '(2)...raping any woman [from 3.11.1994: changes to person] therein'.

Proof

(i) Entry of a building or part of a building, as a trespasser. Trespass is defined as any intentional, reckless or negligent entry into a building in possession of another without that person's consent, and the defendant must know or be reckless as to the facts which make the entry a trespass.[27] **11.28**
(ii) Intent to commit the offence of rape.

Notes

(i) The offence is triable on indictment only. **11.29**
(ii) From 3.11.1994 the offence can be committed upon a male or female. Before this date the offence could only be committed upon a female.
(iii) The rape covers penetration of the vagina by the penis, up until (and including) 2.11.1994. Thereafter the offence also covers penile penetration of the anus without consent.[28]
(iv) From 3.11.1994 a male or female may commit this offence and the victim may be male or female.

Indictment

BURGLARY WITH INTENT TO COMMIT RAPE 1.1.1969 to 30.4.2004 **11.30**

Statement of Offence
BURGLARY WITH INTENT TO COMMIT RAPE, contrary to section 9(1)(a) of the Theft Act 1968.

Particulars of Offences
D on the ... day of ... entered as a trespasser a building (part of a building) (being a dwelling) known as ... with intent to rape C, a female (male).

Alternative Offences

An attempt to commit this offence. When indicting offences of attempt do so under common law until 26.8.1981, thereafter indict under s 1(1) Criminal Attempts Act 1981.[29] **11.31**

---

[27] *R v Smith and Jones* (1976) 63 Cr App R 47 CA.
[28] SOA 1956, s 1 as amended by CJPOA 1994, s 142.
[29] Implementation date 27.8.1981.

11. PREPARATORY OFFENCES

Aver the attempt in both the Statement of Offence and Particulars of Offence. In addition, aver the substantive offence under the relevant Act; see paras 1.51 and 12.157 and *Reed & Others* [2021].[30]

Sentence

11.32 On indictment:

- if the building was a dwelling: **14 YEARS**;[31]
- otherwise: **10 YEARS**.[32]

Upon Conviction/Sentence

11.33   (i) Notification not applicable.[33]
(ii) Automatic inclusion in the children's and adults' barred lists with the right to make representations.[34]
(iii) SHPO not applicable.[35]
(iv) Qualifying 'specified sexual offence' in Schedule 18 (Extended Sentences).[36]

11.34 The SOA 2003 repealed that part of the Theft Act (TA) 1968, s 9(2) that referred to the intention of 'raping any person therein'. Section 63 of the SOA 2003 (trespass with intent to commit a sexual offence) now covers this offence, and extends the offence to include an intent to commit any sexual offence. See para 11.51. Section 62 covers the commission of an offence with intent to commit any sexual offence (see para 11.43).

F. ADMINISTERING A SUBSTANCE WITH INTENT, 1.5.2004 TO DATE

1. Administering a Substance with Intent

Sexual Offences Act 2003, s 61(1)

Definition

11.35   (1) A person commits an offence if he intentionally administers a substance to, or causes a substance to be taken by another person (B)—
(a) knowing that B does not consent, and

---

[30] *Reed & Others* [2021] EWCA Crim 572.
[31] TA 1968, s 9(3)(a).
[32] TA 1968, s 9(3)(b).
[33] SOA 2003, s 80(1) (not listed in Sch 3); see Chapter 14 Tables 14.2–14.5.
[34] Part 2 of the Safeguarding Vulnerable Groups Act 2006 (Prescribed Criteria and Miscellaneous Provisions) Regulations 2009 (SI 2009 No 37) paras 2 and 4; see Chapter 12 para 12.217.
[35] SA 2020, s 345, (not listed in Sch 3 SOA 2003. The s 9 offence is listed in Sch 5 SOA 2003 but absent intent to commit the offence of rape); see Chapter 16 para 16.07.
[36] SA 2020, s 306, Sch 18, para 33; see Chapter 12 para 12.51.

F. ADMINISTERING A SUBSTANCE WITH INTENT

(b) with the intention of stupefying or overpowering B, so as to enable any person to engage in a sexual activity that involves B.

Proof

As per Definition. In addition: **11.36**

(i) For 'administering or causing to be taken', see para 11.20.
(ii) 'Substance' covers both alcohol and drugs.
(iii) Intention that the substance be administered, knowing that B does not consent, and with intent to stupefy or overpower B so as to enable any person to engage in sexual activity.

Notes

(i) The offence is triable either way.[37] **11.37**
(ii) SOA 2003, s 74 applies in relation to consent, which qualifies as consent if the person had the freedom and capacity to make that choice.
(iii) The extended jurisdiction provisions apply to this section where the victim was under 18.[38] See Chapter 17 para 17.01.
(iv) The s 45 MSA 2015 defence for slavery and trafficking victims who commit an offence does not apply to this offence.[39]

Indictment

ADMINISTERING A SUBSTANCE WITH INTENT 1.5.2004 to date **11.38**

Statement of Offence
ADMINISTERING A SUBSTANCE WITH INTENT, contrary to section 61(1) of the Sexual Offences Act 2003.

Particulars of Offence
D on the ... day of ... intentionally administered a substance to C (caused a substance to be taken by C) knowing that C did not consent and with the intention of stupefying or overpowering C so as to enable D (or X) to engage in sexual activity that involved C.

---

[37] SOA 2003, s 61(2).
[38] SOA 2003, s 72; provides for the prosecution within the jurisdiction of a sexual offence committed outside it.
[39] Modern Slavery Act 2014, s 45 and Sch 4, para 33.

352   11. PREPARATORY OFFENCES

Alternative Offences

11.39 An attempt to commit the offence. This will be appropriate, for example, where 'administration' as defined by case law is in issue. When indicting offences of attempt do so under s 1(1) Criminal Attempts Act 1981.[40] Aver the attempt in both the Statement of Offence and Particulars of Offence. In addition, aver the substantive offence under the relevant Act; see paras 1.51 and 12.157 and *Reed & Others* [2021].[41]

Sentence

11.40 (i) On indictment: **10 YEARS**.[42]
(ii) Summarily: **6 months**[43] or a **fine** not exceeding the statutory maximum or **both**.

Sentencing Guidance

11.41 The Sentencing Council 'Sexual Offences: Definitive Guideline' contains offence-specific guidelines for section 61 offences. The Guideline applies to all offenders aged 18 and over, sentenced on or after 1 April 2014.

Upon Conviction/Sentence

11.42 (i) Notification applicable.[44]
(ii) Automatic inclusion in the children's and adults' barring lists with right to make representations.[45]
(iii) SHPO applicable.[46]
(iv) Qualifying 'specified sexual offence' in Schedule 18 (Extended Sentences).[47]

G. COMMITTING AN OFFENCE WITH INTENT TO COMMIT A SEXUAL OFFENCE, 1.5.2004 TO DATE

Sexual Offences Act 2003, s 62(1)

Definition

11.43 (1) A person commits any offence under this section if he commits an offence with the intention of committing a relevant sexual offence.

---

[40] Implementation date 27.8.1981.
[41] *Reed & Others* [2021] EWCA Crim 572.
[42] SOA 2003, s 61(2)(b).
[43] 12 months if CJA 2003, s 282(4) implemented.
[44] SOA 2003, s 80(1) and Sch 3, para 30; see Chapter 14 paras 14.01–14.05.
[45] Part 2 of the Safeguarding Vulnerable Groups Act 2006 (Prescribed Criteria and Miscellaneous Provisions) Regulations 2009 (SI 2009 No 37) paras 2 and 4; see Chapter 12 para 12.217.
[46] SA 2020, s 345 and Sch 3 SOA 2003, para 30; see Chapter 16 para 16.07.
[47] SA 2020, s 306, Sch 18, para 38(as); see Chapter 12 para 12.51.

G. COMMITTING AN OFFENCE WITH INTENT TO COMMIT A SEXUAL OFFENCE

(2) In this section, 'relevant sexual offence' means any offence under this Part (including an offence of aiding, abetting, counselling, or procuring such an offence).

Proof

As per Definition. In addition: 11.44

(i) Relevant sexual offence relates to any offence within the SOA 2003, ss 1–56 and 61-71.
(ii) Intent to commit a relevant sexual offence covers the situation whereby the defendant hoped that the sexual activity would be consensual, but intended to rape her if there was no consent.
(iii) The extended jurisdiction provisions apply to this section where the intended offence was against a person under 18.[48] See Chapter 17 para 17.01.
(iv) The s 45 MSA 2015 defence for slavery and trafficking victims who commit an offence does not apply to this offence.[49]

Notes

The offence is triable on indictment only if the initial offence is false imprisonment or kidnapping.[50] Otherwise the offence is triable either way.[51] 11.45

Indictment

COMMITTING AN OFFENCE WITH INTENT TO COMMIT A SEXUAL OFFENCE 11.46
1.5.2004 to date

Statement of Offence

COMMITTING AN OFFENCE WITH INTENT TO COMMIT A SEXUAL OFFENCE, contrary to section 62(1) of the Sexual Offences Act 2003.

Particulars of Offence

D on the … day of … committed the offence of [kidnapping] *or* [false imprisonment] particularized in Count 1, and did so with the intention of committing a relevant sexual offence.

The commission of the offence, in the above example: kidnapping or false imprisonment, ought to be drafted as an additional separate count on the indictment.

The particular sexual activity intended does not have to be averred.

Alternative Offences

(i) The initial offence, whatever that may be. 11.47

---

[48] SOA 2003, s 72; provides for the prosecution within the jurisdiction of a sexual offence committed outside it.
[49] Modern Slavery Act 2015, s 45 and Sch 4, para 33.
[50] SOA 2003, s 62(3).
[51] SOA 2003, s 62(4).

11. PREPARATORY OFFENCES

(ii) An attempt to commit the offence. When indicting offences of attempt do so under s 1(1) Criminal Attempts Act 1981.[52] Aver the attempt in both the Statement of Offence and Particulars of Offence. In addition, aver the substantive offence under the relevant Act; see paras 1.51 and 12.157 and *Reed & Others* [2021].[53]

Sentence

11.48 (i) On indictment:
- if the initial offence is kidnapping or false imprisonment: **LIFE**;[54]
- otherwise: **10 YEARS**.[55]

(ii) Summarily: **6 months**[56] or a fine not exceeding the statutory maximum or **both**.

Sentencing Guidance

11.49 The Sentencing Council 'Sexual Offences: Definitive Guideline' contains offence-specific guidance for s 62 offences. The starting point and range should be commensurate with that for the preliminary offence committed, but with an enhancement to reflect the intention to commit a sexual offence. The enhancement will vary depending on the nature and seriousness of the intended sexual offence but 2 years' custody is suggested as a suitable enhancement where the intent was to commit rape or assault by penetration. The Guideline applies to all offenders aged 18 and over, sentenced on or after 1 April 2014.

Upon Conviction/Sentence

11.50
(i) Notification applicable where the (a) offender was aged under 18 and is sentenced to at least 12 months' imprisonment; or (b) in any other case, the offender is sentenced to a term of imprisonment, hospital detention or community order of at least 12 months.[57]
(ii) Automatic inclusion in the children's barring list with the right to make representations where the relevant sexual offence is also specified in the schedule and intended to be committed in relevant circumstances. Automatic inclusion in the adults' barring list with the right to make representations.[58]
(iii) SHPO applicable.[59]
(iv) Qualifying 'specified sexual offence' in Schedule 18 (Extended Sentences).[60]
(v) Qualifying Schedule 19 offence (Life Sentences) where offender liable on conviction on indictment for imprisonment for life.[61]

---

[52] Implementation date 27.8.1981.
[53] *Reed & Others* [2021] EWCA Crim 572.
[54] SOA 2003, s 62(3).
[55] SOA 2003, s 62(4)(b).
[56] 12 months if CJA 2003, s 282(4) implemented.
[57] SOA 2003, s 80(1) and Sch 3, para 31; see Chapter 14 paras 14.01–14.05.
[58] Part 2 of the Safeguarding Vulnerable Groups Act 2006 (Prescribed Criteria and Miscellaneous Provisions) Regulations 2009 (SI 2009 No 37) paras 2 and 4; see Chapter 12 para 12.217.
[59] SA 2020, s 345 and Sch 3, para 31; see Chapter 16 para 16.07.
[60] SA 2020, s 306, Sch 18, para 38(at); see Chapter 12 para 12.51.
[61] SA 2020, s 307, Sch 19, para 20(l); see Chapter 12 para 12.52.

H. TRESPASS WITH INTENT TO COMMIT A SEXUAL OFFENCE, 1.5.2004 TO DATE

Sexual Offences Act 2003, s 63(1)

Definition

(1) A person commits an offence if– **11.51**
   (a) he is a trespasser on any premises,
   (b) he intends to commit a relevant sexual offence on the premises, and
   © he knows that, or is reckless as to whether, he is a trespasser.

Proof

As per Definition. In addition: **11.52**

(i) Trespasser on any premises. Trespass is defined as any intentional, reckless, or negligent entry into a building in possession of another without that person's consent, and the defendant must know or be reckless as to the facts which make the entry a trespass.[64] Adopting the definition in *R v G* [2003][65] reckless entry is where D is aware that there is a risk he is in a building in the possession of another without their consent, and it is unreasonable in the circumstances known to him to take that risk.
(ii) Intent to commit a relevant sexual offence covers the situation whereby the defendant hoped that the sexual activity would be consensual, but intended to rape her if there was no consent.
(iii) Relevant sexual offence relates to any offence within the SOA 2003, ss 1–56 and 61–71.
(iv) 'Premises' includes a structure or part of a structure. 'Structure' includes a tent, vehicle, or vessel or other temporary or movable structure.

Notes

(i) The offence is triable either way.[66] **11.53**
(ii) The particular sexual activity or intended victim does not have to be averred.[67]

---

[62] SA 2020, ss 267 and 280, Sch 14, para 9(x); see Chapter 12 para 12.77.
[63] SA 2020, ss 273 and 283, Sch 15, para 9(x); see Chapter 12 para 12.123.
[64] *R v Smith and Jones* (1976) 63 Cr App R 47 CA.
[65] *R v G* [2003] UKHL 50.
[66] SOA 2003, s 63(3).
[67] *R v Pacurar* [2016[EWCA Crim 569.

(iii) The extended jurisdiction provisions apply to this section where the intended offence was an offence against a person under 18.[68] See Chapter 17 para 17.01.

(iv) The s 45 MSA 2015 defence for slavery and trafficking victims who commit an offence does not apply to this offence.[69]

Indictment

11.54 TRESPASS WITH INTENT TO COMMIT A SEXUAL OFFENCE 1.5.2004 to date

---

Statement of Offence

TRESPASS WITH INTENT TO COMMIT A SEXUAL OFFENCE, contrary to section 63(1) of the Sexual Offences Act 2003.

Particulars of Offence

D on the … day of … whilst trespassing on premises namely …, knowing that he was a trespasser therein, or being reckless as to whether he was a trespasser, intended to commit a relevant sexual offence on those premises.

Alternative Offences

11.55 (i) An attempt to commit the offence. When indicting offences of attempt do so under s 1(1) Criminal Attempts Act 1981.[70] Aver the attempt in both the Statement of Offence and Particulars of Offence. In addition, aver the substantive offence under the relevant Act; see paras 1.51 and 12.157 and *Reed & Others* [2021].[71]

Sentence

11.56 (i) On indictment: **10 YEARS**.[72]

(ii) Summarily: **6 months**[73] or a **fine** not exceeding the statutory maximum or **both**.

Sentencing Guidance

11.57 The Sentencing Council 'Sexual Offences: Definitive Guideline' contains offence-specific guidelines for section 63 offences. The Guideline applies to all offenders aged 18 and over, sentenced on or after 1 April 2014.

---

[68] SOA 2003, s 72; provides for the prosecution within the jurisdiction of a sexual offence committed outside it.
[69] Modern Slavery Act 2015, s 45 and Sch 4, para 33.
[70] Implementation date 27.8.1981.
[71] *Reed & Others* [2021] EWCA Crim 572.
[72] SOA 2003, s 63(3)(b).
[73] SOA 2003, s 63(3)(a). Increased to 12 months if CJA 2003, s 282(4).

Upon Conviction/Sentence

(i) Notification applicable where the (a) offender was aged under 18 and is sentenced to at least 12 months' imprisonment; or (b) in any other case, the offender is sentenced to a term of imprisonment, hospital detention or community order of at least 12 months.[74]

(ii) Automatic inclusion in the children's barring list with the right to make representations where the relevant sexual offence is also specified in the Schedule and intended to be committed in relevant circumstances. Automatic inclusion in the adults' barring list with the right to make representations.[75]

(iii) SHPO applicable.[76]

(iv) Qualifying 'specified sexual offence' in Schedule 18 (Extended Sentences).[77]

11.58

---

[74] SOA 2003, s 80(1) and Sch 3, para 31; see Chapter 14 paras 14.01–14.05.
[75] Part 2 of the Safeguarding Vulnerable Groups Act 2006 (Prescribed Criteria and Miscellaneous Provisions) Regulations 2009 (SI 2009 No 37) paras 2 and 4; see Chapter 12 para 12.217.
[76] SA 2020, s 345 and Sch 3, para 31; see Chapter 16 para 16.07.
[77] SA 2020, s 306, Sch 18, para 38(au); see Chapter 12 para 12.51.

12
SENTENCING

A.	Introduction	12.01	13. Imposing Extended and Determinate Sentences Together	12.87
B.	Indications of Sentence (Goodyear Indications)	12.16	14. Imposing Consecutive Extended and Determinate Sentences	12.88
C.	Sentencing Multiple Offences	12.19	15. Informing the Offender of the Effect of the Sentence	12.90
	1. Associated Offences	12.20	16. Extended Sentences; Release Provisions	12.91
	2. Sample Counts and Multiple Incident Counts	12.22	17. Determinate Sentences for Specified Offences; Release Provisions	12.92
	3. Multiple Extended Sentences	12.24	18. Pre-Sentence Reports and Dangerousness	12.96
D.	Suspended Sentence Orders and Community Orders	12.25	G. Offenders of Particular Concern	12.101
	1. Suspended Sentence Orders	12.26	H. The Calculation	12.108
	2. Sexual Offending Programmes	12.31	1. Release Provisions	12.111
	3. Custodial and Community Sex Offender Programmes; The Difference	12.32	2. Imposing Both Consecutive Determinate and s 265/278 Sentences	12.114
	4. Community Sentences	12.33	3. Sentencing Offences which Straddle the Sexual Offences Act 2003	12.116
	5. Children and Young People (up to 18 years)	12.35	I. Current Dangerousness Provisions: Offences Committed Post the CJA 2003 and LASPO 2012 and Incorporated into the Sentencing Code 2020	12.117
	6. Adult Offenders (18 years and over)	12.37	1. Life Sentence	12.118
E.	Offences which Straddle Different Acts	12.43	2. Discretionary Life Sentence	12.120
	1. Offences Straddling the Implementation of the Sexual Offences Act 2003	12.45	3. Statutory Life Sentences, ss 273, 274, 283, and 285 Sentencing Code 2020 3.12.2012 to present	12.123
	2. Offences Listed in the Violent Crime Reduction Act 2006, s 55(2)	12.49	4. Whole Life Sentence	12.132
	3. Offences Listed in the Violent Crime Reduction Act 2006, s 55(5)	12.50	J. Sentencing Historic Offences	12.135
F.	Sentencing Regimes for Dangerous Offenders	12.51	1. The Fundamental Principles	12.138
	1. Definition	12.51	2. General Principles to be Drawn from Forbes	12.139
	2. Specified Offences	12.52	3. Abuse of Trust	12.143
	3. The Approach to Sentencing a Specified Offence	12.53	4. Sentencing Relatively Young Offenders for Sexual Offences Committed Some Years Before and When They Were under 18	12.156
	4. Dangerous Offenders under 18 at Time of Sentence	12.56	5. Sentencing Geriatric Offenders	12.157
	5. Discretionary Life Sentence: D under 18 (Required Sentence of Custody for Life for Offence Carrying Life Sentence)	12.57	K. Release, Licence, and Supervision Requirements	12.158
	6. Extended Sentence: D under 18	12.60	1. Sentencing for Offences Committed under a Different Licensing Regime	12.159
	7. Dangerous Offenders aged 18–20 at Time of Sentence	12.64	2. Fixed Term Offenders	12.160
	8. Dangerous Offenders aged 21 or over at Time of Sentence	12.68	3. Licence Period for Sentences of Imprisonment of Less than 12 Months: Offender Rehabilitation Act 2014	12.161
	9. Extended Sentences: The Approach for Offenders of Any Age	12.72		
	10. Calculating the Custodial Term: The Approach when Sentencing More than One Offence	12.78		
	11. Calculating the Extension Period	12.83		
	12. Imposing Consecutive Extended Sentences	12.85	4. Extended Sentence: Release on Licence	12.164

5. The Release of Prisoners (Alteration of Relevant Proportion of Sentence) Order 2020	12.165
L. Application of the Sentencing Guideline and Recent Changes	12.169
1. Recent Changes to the Definitive Guidelines	12.175
2. Harm and Culpability	12.180
3. Determining Culpability when No Sexual Activity Has Taken Place	12.182
4. Psychological Harm	12.185
M. General Principles	12.186
1. Good Character and/or Exemplary Conduct	12.189
2. Good Character Since the Offences	12.190
3. Ostensible or Apparent Consent	12.191
4. The Need to Consider the Overall Picture	12.193
5. Indecent Images	12.194
6. Sentencing Adult Offenders with Mental or Developmental Disorders or Neurological Impairments	12.201
7. Sentencing Children and Young people with Mental Health Disorders	12.203
N. Sentencing Children and Young People	12.204
1. Factors Not Envisaged by the Sentencing Council Guidelines	12.216
O. Orders and Requirements after Conviction	12.217
1. The Children and Adult Barring Lists	12.217
2. The Lists of Offences Attracting Automatic Inclusion	12.219
3. Restraining Orders	12.224
4. Sexual Harm Prevention Orders	12.230
5. Notification Requirements	12.231
6. Orders under the Modern Slavery Act 2015	12.236
7. Serious Crime Prevention Orders, s 19 Serious Crime Act 2007	12.240
8. Recommendation for Deportation	12.242
P. Prosecution Reviews of Sentence (Attorney General's References)	12.247
1. Offences Referable to the Court of Appeal by the Attorney General	12.248
2. Checklist of Matters to be Included in Attorney General's References	12.250

A. INTRODUCTION

12.01 Offenders must be sentenced according to the sentencing regime in place at the time the offence was committed. The maximum sentences available are set out within the chapters of this Referencer at the sentencing paragraph for each offence.

12.02 Following its review of sentencing legislation, the overall recommendation of the Law Commission was for the implementation of a new Sentencing Code to substantially simplify the law of sentencing by removing the need to make reference to historic versions of sentencing legislation when dealing with older offences. It will instead apply the current law to all offenders whose convictions occur after the Sentencing Code has come into force (subject to limited exceptions necessary to respect the fundamental rights of offenders).

12.03 The Sentencing Act (SA) was implemented on 1.12.2020. It applies to those convicted on or after 1.12.2020. Anyone convicted before that date will be sentenced according to the pre-existing law.[1]

12.04 The Act introduces the 'Sentencing Code' in Parts 2–13; a framework which consolidates and streamlines a substantial body of complex and voluminous sentencing laws currently spread across multiple statutes. It is intended to ensure greater transparency and clarity is achieved by Courts when passing sentences. Part 1 of the Act contains an overview (s 1) and deals with the application of the Code (s 2). Consequently, when

---

[1] Schedule 27 to the Act (transitional provisions and savings) provides for continuity of the law if a Court faces pre-Code and Sentencing Code matters.

A. INTRODUCTION 361

referring to Parts 2–13 inclusive, the terms 'Sentencing Act' and 'Sentencing Code' are interchangeable.

For cases where the conviction pre-dates 1.12.2020, the now 'old' law, principally contained in the CJA 2003, PCC(S)A 2000 and CJIA 2008 will apply. The SA is now the principal source of sentencing procedure legislation, with cross-references to other pieces of relevant legislation such as the Road Traffic Offenders Act 1988 and the Proceeds of Crime Act 2002. **12.05**

The SA does not remove any sentencing disposals or introduce new ones. It does not subject the offender to a harsher penalty than was available at the time of the offence and it does not replace Sentencing Guidelines or the work of the Sentencing Council. Pre-existing case law in these areas will, therefore, continue to be germane to the Sentencing Code.[2] **12.06**

The 'Sentencing Code' is a consolidation of existing sentencing procedure law. It brings together over 50 pieces of primary legislation relating to sentencing procedure into one single Act. That exercise provided an opportunity to remove ambiguities in drafting, produce a more coherent structure to the order in which provisions appear, and introduce greater consistency of language. It has been drafted with the needs of judges in mind and seeks to make the law more readily accessible. It will mean that any sentencing exercise should be capable of being resolved by reference to the Code, Sentencing Council Guideline(s) and the CrimPR/CrimPD.[3] **12.07**

The Code applies only to convictions on or after commencement date (1.12.2020). But the 'Clean Sweep' approach in the Code means that it applies to all convictions on or after that date irrespective of the date of the commission of the offence. There will be transitional cases where some offences before the court for sentencing will be governed by the Code and others by the pre-Code law but this will diminish quickly with time. What matters is the date of conviction. Judges will need to be vigilant as to the date of conviction if, for example, an offender absconds and is apprehended, was convicted in absence or, for example, the conviction was before 1.12.2020 but sentencing is after that date because reports were sought. Schedule 27 (transitional provisions) provides for continuity of the law if a court faces pre-Code and Code matters. The Code applies to England and Wales. It extends to Scotland and Northern Ireland only where it is necessary, for example to facilitate the transfer of orders (eg a community order) and the offender proposes to move from order) and the offender proposes to move from one jurisdiction to another.[4] **12.08**

The most innovative aspect of the Code is that it will apply to every person convicted on or after the date of the commencement of the Code (1.12.2020). This is subject to the important safeguard that, because of the way the Code has been drafted, no-one will be at risk of being sentenced to a heavier penalty than could have been imposed at the date of the commission of his or her offence. The way that has been achieved is by a technical drafting device in the Sentencing (Pre-consolidation Amendment) Act 2020. All that any judge or advocate applying the Code needs to know is that where someone is being sentenced under the Code, the provisions already guard against any unfair retrospectivity. Where there was **12.09**

---

[2] Section 17(2) Interpretation Act 1978.
[3] From 'Sentencing Code—10 things you need to know' written by Professor David Ormerod QC CBE, then Law Commissioner for Criminal Law who led the work of the Law Commission to produce the Sentencing Code.
[4] From 'Sentencing Code—10 things you need to know' written by Professor David Ormerod QC CBE.

any risk that retrospectively applying the most modern form of the law (as consolidated in the Code) might expose someone to a harsher penalty than was available at the date of their offence, the 'old' (less harsh) provision has also been included in the Code. It is clear on the face of any such provision to which date range of offending it applies. (See eg the drafting of Cll 273 and 283 of the Bill and Schedule 15). The practical benefit is that courts will no longer have to make reference to historic versions of legislation, and decipher opaque transitional provisions The Code is retrospective but does not contravene art 7 nor any common law principle against retrospectivity because it is drafted in such a way that no one can be sentenced to a harsher penalty than could have been imposed at the date of the commission of their offence. There should be no basis on which an art 7 or retrospectivity argument arises before the court.[5]

12.10 The overall purposes of sentencing those aged 18 and over at the date of conviction are set out in s 57 SA 2020. Section 58 refers to the principle, unaltered aims when sentencing young offenders. The two elements of the assessment of seriousness of an offence remain culpability and harm; s 63 SA 2020.

12.11 The different types of sentence available for dangerous offenders are now contained in the SA 2020. They were previously governed by the Criminal Justice Act (CJA) 2003 and were subject to substantial amendment, in particular by the Legal Aid, Sentencing and Punishment of Offenders Act (LASPO) 2012 (3.12.2013) and the Criminal Justice and Courts Act 2015 (13.4.2015).

12.12 For 'Offenders of Particular Concern' (those convicted of penetrative offences of children under 13 years old) in respect of whom a determinate sentence would otherwise be passed, sentence is governed by ss 265 (offenders aged 18, 19, or 20) and 278 (offenders aged 21 and over) of the SA 2020. See para 12.114.

12.13 Sections 244 and 264 of the CJA 2003 were modified by the Release of Prisoners (Alteration of Relevant Proportion of Sentence) Order 2019 significantly increasing the proportion of the sentence to be served before release on licence from one-half to two-thirds for offenders convicted of relevant sexual or violent offences. See para 12.165.

12.14 There are a number of ancillary orders which need to be considered when sentencing as well as the automatic notification requirement and the likelihood of automatic inclusion in the lists barring offenders from working with children and/or vulnerable adults ('regulated activities'). Neither the notification requirements nor inclusion in the barred lists form part of the sentence; consequently, neither is included in the SA.[6] The notification requirements impose significant limitations and obligations on an offender convicted of qualifying sexual offences and are set out in detail in Chapter 14. The children's and adults' barred lists are set out in paras 12.220–12.223. Offences are either an automatic barring offence or an automatic inclusion offence. If an offence falls into the latter category, the offender will be able to make representations to the Disclosure and Barring Service (DBS) against being placed on a barring list. Unless an offender who is subject to an automatic inclusion offence, either at the time of conviction or caution or after that, seeks to work in a regulated activity with

---

[5] From 'Sentencing Code—10 things you need to know'.
[6] Save for a reference in s 379(2) to the notification requirements, referring the reader back to the SOA 2003 provisions.

either children or vulnerable adults, the position of the DBS is that it will have no reason to consider barring the offender. Sexual Harm Prevention Orders are another important ancillary order and are set out in detail in Chapter 16.

The 'Sexual Offences' Definitive Guideline, issued by the Sentencing Council (SC) in December 2013 and in force from 1.4.2014, and the 'Sexual Offences—Sentencing Children and Young Persons' Definitive Guideline in force from 1.6.2017 are applicable to most sexual offences. The Guidelines are not reproduced in this work; they are subject to change and it is essential to consult the current Guideline online for any offence. **12.15**

B. INDICATIONS OF SENTENCE (*GOODYEAR* INDICATIONS)

Where a defendant is charged with a specified offence[7] to which the dangerousness provisions apply (most sexual offences), a judge should be cautious about giving an indication as to the likely sentence because the question of dangerousness remains undetermined. The issue did not arise in the Guideline case of *Goodyear*[8] but in *R v Kulah*[9] the Court of Appeal judged the assessment of dangerousness in most such cases not to be clear cut. A judge who had not been provided with reports might well feel disinclined to give an indication. A renewed request of a second judge uninformed by defence counsel of the refusal (regarded as proper) from the first was deprecated by the court. Similarly, a judge should be slow to give an indication of sentence in the absence of a victim personal statement. **12.16**

The procedure for the making of an application for an indication of sentence is set out in rule 3.31 CPR 2020. Rule 3.31(4)(a) requires the prosecutor to provide information relevant to sentencing, this includes impact statements from the complainant, the complainant's family or others. Recent case law reminds practitioners that the Goodyear procedure is the indication of the maximum sentence and is not a bargaining process with the Court[10] and that an indication must be accepted in a reasonable time to be binding.[11] **12.17**

See Criminal Practice Directions V11 C (*Goodyear* Indications) and F (Victim Personal Statements). **12.18**

C. SENTENCING MULTIPLE OFFENCES

The Sexual Offences Guidelines are based on a sentence for a single offence. The Sentencing Council Guidelines on Totality[12] provide comprehensive and clear guidance for sentencing more than one offence. **12.19**

---

[7] Listed within Sch 18 or Sch 19 Sentencing Act 2020.
[8] *R v Goodyear* [2005] 3 All ER 117.
[9] *R v Kulah* [2008] 1 All ER 16.
[10] *R v Almilhim* [2019] EWCA Crim 220.
[11] See *R v Utton* [2019] Crim 1341 at para [10] citing *R v Goodyear* [2005] EWCA Crim 888 at para [61].
[12] Offences Taken Into Consideration and Totality: Definitive Guideline.

1. Associated Offences

12.20 In deciding what the appropriate sentence to be passed is, the court may take account of all the offences for which an offender is to be sentenced on the same occasion, as long as they are 'associated offences'. An offence is 'associated' with another offence if the offender is convicted of it in the same proceedings as the other offence or is sentenced for it at the same time as the other offence. The definition includes offences admitted and asked to be taken into consideration by the offender; s 400 SA 2020.

12.21 Associated offences are therefore limited to offences of which a defendant has been convicted, or which he has asked the court to take into consideration. It follows that they must be both individually identified and admitted. Sample counts are not 'associated offences' for the purpose of determining sentence.

2. Sample Counts and Multiple Incident Counts

12.22 Indictments reflecting a course of conduct may contain either sample counts or multiple incident counts;[13] see paras 1.08–1.17/1222-12.23. In sentencing upon conviction of sample counts, the judge will be restricted to what is contained within the indictment unless more than that is both identified and admitted.

12.23 Whilst, therefore, sample counts do not, without more, allow the sentencing judge to pass a longer sentence to reflect that course of conduct, multiple incident counts do and the Court of Appeal has reiterated that they are to be preferred in appropriate cases.[14]

3. Multiple Extended Sentences

12.24 An extended sentence is one entity comprising the custodial term and the extension period. Therefore, when it is necessary to pass multiple extended sentences, if the custodial term is consecutive the extension period must also be consecutive and if the custodial term is concurrent the extension period must also be concurrent. See *Pinnell and Joyce* [2010],[15] *Francis & Lawrence* [2014],[16] and *DJ* [2015].[17] For extended sentences generally see paras 12.51 and 12.72.

D. SUSPENDED SENTENCE ORDERS AND COMMUNITY ORDERS

12.25 All offenders convicted on or after 1.12.2020 will be sentenced in accordance with the provisions of the SA 2020.[18] The transitional provisions of the SA 2020 mean that offenders

---

[13] See para 1.03 *et seq*, including the new rules allowing one count to reflect a continuing course of conduct.
[14] For example *R v Forbes and Others* [2016] EWCA Crim 1388.
[15] *Pinnell and Joyce* [2010] EWCA Crim 2848.
[16] *Francis & Lawrence* [2014] EWCA Crim 631.
[17] *DJ* [2015] EWCA Crim 563.
[18] SA 2020, s 1(1)

D. SUSPENDED SENTENCE ORDERS AND COMMUNITY ORDERS   365

convicted before the Sentencing Code came into force will be sentenced under the pre-existing law.

1. Suspended Sentence Orders

12.26 Suspended Sentence Orders (SSOs) are only available in respect of adult offenders. The provisions in relation to SSOs are contained in ss 264 (offenders aged 18–21) and 277 (offender aged 21+) and Chapter 5 of the SA 2020. An SSO is an order providing that a sentence of imprisonment or detention in a young offender institution in respect of an offence is not to take effect unless (a) an activation event occurs, and (b) a court having power to do so subsequently orders[19] that the sentence is to take effect.[20]

12.27 For suspended sentences of detention in a young offender institution (offenders aged between 18 and 21) the minimum period of detention in a YOI is 21 days[21] the maximum period of detention which may be suspended is not more than 2 years.[22] For suspended sentences for offenders aged 21 or over, the period of imprisonment which may be suspended must be at least 14 days but not more than 2 years.[23] The operational period of an SSO must be a period of at least 6 months and not more than 2 years.[24] The supervision period of an SSO must be specified where requirements are imposed[25] and must be a period of at least 6 months and not more than 2 years or, if less, the operational period.[26] Where consecutive suspended sentences are passed the aggregate sentence must not exceed the 2-year maximum.[27]

12.28 As part of an SSO the court may specify that the offender complies with one or more community order requirements during the supervision period.[28] The requirements which may be attached to an SSO are set out in the community requirements table at s 287 SA and will apply provided it is an available requirement[29] and subject to any entry requirements in column 3 of the table.[30] Where multiple requirements are imposed they must be compatible with one another[31] and the court must ensure, insofar as is practicable, to avoid conflict with the offender's religious beliefs, the requirements of any other court order(s) or the offender's employment or education.[32]

12.29 Note that an offender subject to an SSO which does not include a residence requirement may not change residence without the permission of their responsible officer or the court.[33]

---

[19] Under paragraph 13 of Sch 16 SA 2020.
[20] SA 2020, s 286(1).
[21] SA 2020, s 263(2).
[22] SA 2020, s 264(2).
[23] SA 2020, s 277(2).
[24] SA 2020, s 288(2).
[25] SA 2020, 288(3).
[26] SA 2020, s 288(4). Note that where an SSO includes an unpaid work requirement, the supervision continues until the offender has completed the number of hours specified but does not continue beyond the operational period (s 288(5)).
[27] SA 2020, ss 264(3) (18–21) and 277(3) (21+).
[28] SA 2020, s 286(2).
[29] See SA 2020, s 291.
[30] SA 2020, s 290.
[31] SA 2020, s 292(3).
[32] SA 2020, s 293(4).
[33] SA 2020, s 302.

12.30 See also, the 'Sentencing Council: Imposition of Community and Custodial Sentences' Definitive Guideline which applies to offenders aged 18 or over sentenced on or after 1.2.2017 and *R v Hussain* [2019];[34] credit for guilty plea should not be reflected in the imposition of a suspended sentence. *R v Dawes* [2019];[35] it was wrong, in principle, to impose a suspended period of imprisonment where time spent on remand meant the custodial term would be extinguished if the order was breached.

2. Sexual Offending Programmes

12.31 Sexual offending programmes are programme requirements for the purposes of SSOs, COs, and YROs. A programme requirement (or 'systematic set of activities')[36] for an adult offender is defined as a requirement that the offender must:

> In accordance with instructions given by the responsible officer participate in an accredited[37] programme at a particular place, and
>
> While at that place, comply with the instructions given by or under the authority of the person in charge of the programme.[38]
>
> The order must specify the number of days on which the offender is required to participate in the accredited programme under the requirement.[39]

3. Custodial and Community Sex Offender Programmes; The Difference

12.32 Sexual offending programmes have changed considerably, particularly in relation to their focus. As at date of publication, strengths-based or desistance approaches are considered to be a more effective way of promoting change. The emphasis has moved from identifying the risk factors which led to a sexual offence being committed to determining what strengths a person has or needs to develop in order to promote a positive, offence-free life. The suite of programmes that have been developed for this purpose are not identical in name or detail but all come from the same theoretical perspective and are broadly similar in content. They do however vary in length, dependent upon in which environment the programme is undertaken. Programmes delivered in a custodial environment require the offender to attend a greater number of sessions; however, programmes delivered in a custodial setting can be delivered at a more intense rate. Courts including such a programme to be undertaken within a community environment should ensure that at least 2 years are available within the term of the order to complete it.[40]

---

[34] *Hussain (Tayyab)* [2019] EWCA Crim 1542.
[35] *Dawes (Robert Houghton)* [2019] EWCA Crim 848.
[36] SA 2020, Sch 9, Part 3, para 6(4).
[37] See SA 2020, Sch 9, Part 3, paras 6(2) and (3) re: accredited programmes.
[38] SA 2020, Sch 9, Part 3, para 6(1).
[39] SA 2020, Sch 9, Part 3, para 6(1).
[40] With thanks to Sean Brosnan, Senior Probation Officer.

4. Community Sentences

Where there is a sufficient prospect of rehabilitation, a community order with a sex offender treatment programme requirement under part 3 of Schedule 9 of the Sentencing Code can be a proper alternative to a short or moderate length custodial sentence.[41]   **12.33**

The provisions in relation to community sentences are contained in Part 9 of the SA 2020.   **12.34**

5. Children and Young People (up to 18 years)

Chapter 1 of Part 9 SA 2020 deals with Youth Rehabilitation Orders) (YROs) including YROs with Intensive Supervision and Surveillance[42] (ISS) or Fostering,[43] and Chapter 2, Part 9 with Community Orders (COs).   **12.35**

YROs are available in respect of offenders aged under 18 at the time of conviction[44] but may not be made in combination with hospital or guardianship order for the same offence,[45] or where mandatory sentence requirements apply.[46] A YRO may be made in respect of an offender who is subject to a Detention and Training Order (DTO);[47] the Conditional Release Order (CRO) may be ordered to take effect when the period of supervision begins or at the expiry of the DTO.[48] If the Offender is already subject to a YRO or Reparation Order the court cannot make YRO without revoking the existing order(s).[49] If the court is dealing with offences including one of which the offender was convicted when aged 18 it may not make a YRO if it also makes an SSO.[50]

A YRO is defined as an order imposing one or more of the youth rehabilitation requirements[51] set out in the requirements table at s 174 provided it is an available requirement and subject to any entry requirements in column 3 of the table.[52] Where multiple requirements are imposed they must be compatible with one another[53] and the court must ensure, in so far as is practicable, to avoid conflict with the offender's religious beliefs, the requirements of any other court order(s) or the offender's employment or education.[54] The table of requirements includes programme requirements,[55] namely a 'requirement for the offender to participate in a particular systemic set of activities, which may have a residential component.[56] A programme requirement may only be imposed if recommended by the   **12.36**

---

[41] Sentencing Guidelines; Definitive Guideline Sexual Offences at Step 2.
[42] SA 2020, s 180(1)(a).
[43] SA 2020, s 180(1)(b).
[44] SA 2020, s 177(1).
[45] SA 2020, s 177(2).
[46] SA 2020, s 177(3) subject to reduction in sentence for assistance to the prosecution (s 74 SA 2020).
[47] SA 2020, s 181.
[48] SA 2020, ss 181(a) and (b).
[49] SA 2020, ss 181(4).
[50] SA 2020, ss 181(6).
[51] SA 2020, s 173(1).
[52] SA 2020, s 184.
[53] SA 2020, s 186(10).
[54] SA 2020, s 186(11).
[55] SA 2020, s 174 and Sch6, Part 4.
[56] SA 2020, Sch 6, Part 4, para 12(1).

368   12. SENTENCING

Youth offending Team or a Probation Officer.[57] A YRO must specify an end date not more than 3 years after the date on which the order takes effect.[58] The end date for a YRO with Intensive Supervision and Surveillance Programme (ISSP) must be not less than 3 months after the effective date.[59]

6. Adult Offenders (18 years and over)

12.37 COs are available in respect of imprisonable offences for offenders aged 18 or over at the time of the conviction but may not be made in combination with either an SSO,[60] or a hospital or guardianship order for the same offence.[61] A CO is not available in respect of an offence in relation to which a mandatory sentence requirement applies[62] (s 202(3) SA 2020), subject to s 74 and Chapter 4 of Part 12 (reduction of sentence for assistance to prosecution).

12.38 The maximum length of a CO is 3 years.[63]

12.39 A CO is defined as an order imposing one or more of the community order requirements in the table at s201 SA 2020,[64] provided it is an available requirement and subject to any entry requirements in column 3 of the table.[65] Section 201 includes identical requirements to those available for SSOs, including the programme requirement.[66] The order must include at least one CO requirement for the purpose of punishment[67] unless the court imposes a fine or there are exceptional circumstances which would make it unjust to impose either.[68] Where multiple requirements are imposed they must be compatible with one another[69] and the court must ensure, insofar as is practicable, to avoid conflict with the offender's religious beliefs, the requirements of any other court order(s) or the offender's employment or education.[70]

12.40 Note that, as with SSOs, an offender subject to a CO which does not include a residence requirement may not change residence without the permission of the responsible officer or the court.[71]

12.41 In cases where the custodial sentence would be measured in months it is arguable that a CO may be more appropriate.[72] Careful regard should also now be had to the amendments to licence and supervision requirements which impose, in certain cases, an extended period of supervision (see para 12.37). The maximum period of supervision is usually preferred by the Probation Service when a requirement to address sexual offending is imposed as part of an SSO or CO, in order to allow for ongoing risk management and to monitor change.[73]

---

[57] SA 2020, Sch 6, Part 4, para 13(1).
[58] SA 2020, s 187(2).
[59] SA 2020, s 187(3).
[60] SA 2020, ss 202(2)(a) and s 203.
[61] SA 2020, s 202(2)(c).
[62] SA 2020, (s399 SA 2020)—mandatory sentences, including minimum mandatory sentences.
[63] SA 2020, s 209(2).
[64] SA 2020, s 200.
[65] SA 2020, s 206.
[66] SA 2020, s 201 and Sch 9, Part 3.
[67] SA 2020, s 208(10).
[68] SA 2020, s 208(11).
[69] SA 2020, s 208(12).
[70] SA 2020, s 208(13).
[71] SA 2020, s 216.
[72] See for example *R v Jones* [2014] EWCA Crim 1859; [2015] 1 Cr App R (S) 9 where a community order with a Sex Offender Treatment Programme (SOTP) requirement was considered a proper alternative to a moderate custodial sentence in accordance with the guideline.
[73] With thanks to Sean Brosnan, Senior Probation Officer.

See also, the 'Sentencing Council: Imposition of Community and Custodial Sentences' Definitive Guideline which applies to offenders aged 18 or over sentenced on or after 1.2.2017. **12.42**

E. OFFENCES WHICH STRADDLE DIFFERENT ACTS

Following the implementation of the SA 2020 all offences fall to be sentenced under the Code if the conviction occurred on or after 1.12.2020. If the conviction is on or after 1.12.20 the Code applies irrespective of the date on which the offence was committed. If the conviction occurred before 1.12.20 the previous law will apply (ie that in force and applicable at the date of conviction having regard to the date of the offence. **12.43**

So if a defendant had offended in 2002 and 2005 but was convicted in 2021, the Code would apply to all the offences committed. Care would need to be taken to ensure that the correct criminal offence was charged because of the transition between the respective Acts; using the example just given, from the Sexual Offences Act (SOA) 1956 to the SOA 2003.

When the allegations made straddle the implementation dates of Acts which create two different sentencing regimes, the indictment should be drafted in such a way as to reflect the differing sentencing powers which attach to each time frame; see paras 1.26–1.34. **12.44**

Section 55 of the Violent Crime Reduction Act (VCRA) 2006 provides the mechanism for this when indicting offences which span the SOA 2003 and earlier, repealed legislation.[74] If this has not been done and an indictment spans two sentencing regimes without reflecting the differing powers, then unless it is clear from the evidence under which regime the offence was committed,[75] the court should sentence as if the offence was committed under the preceding legislation assuming that this will be more favourable to the defendant.[76]

1. Offences Straddling the Implementation of the Sexual Offences Act 2003

Following the repeal of the SOA 1956 on 1.5.2004, any sexual offence occurring from this date onwards must be prosecuted under the SOA 2003. The lacuna which existed because no transitional provision had been implemented[77] to deal with the situation where the prosecution could not prove whether the offence occurred before, on or after 1 May, leading to the decisions in *R v Newbon*[78] and *R v C*,[79] has now been filled by s 55 of the VCRA 2006. This section came into force on 12.2.2007.[80] **12.45**

---

[74] See also from 12.38 and para 1.25.
[75] *R v R (Paul Brian)* [1993] Crim LR 541.
[76] CJA 2003 (Commencement No 8 and Transitional and Saving Provisions) Order 2005 (SI No 950); in particular, 'where an offence is found to have been committed over a period of two or more days, or at some time during a period of two or more days, it shall be taken ... to have been committed on the last of those days'.
[77] Despite provision being made by SOA 2003, s 141.
[78] *R v Newbon* [2005] Crim LR 738.
[79] *R v C* [2005] EWCA Crim 3533.
[80] By virtue of the VCRA 2006 (Commencement No 1) Order 2007 (SI 2007 No 74 art 2(c)). See para 12.42 for list of offences it applies to.

12.46 Section 55 provides for the situation where a defendant is charged in respect of the same conduct with both an offence under the SOA 2003 and an offence under the old law, and the only thing preventing him being found guilty of the 2003 Act offence or the offence under the old law is the fact that it has not been proved beyond a reasonable doubt that the time when the conduct took place was either after the coming into force of the enactment providing for the offence or before the repeal of the old law.

> In such circumstances, for the purpose of determining guilt, it will be conclusively presumed that the time when the conduct took place was when the old law applied if the offence attracted a lesser maximum penalty; otherwise it will be presumed the conduct took place after the implementation of the new law.[81]

12.47 For s 55 to have effect, both the SOA 2003 and the earlier legislation must be pleaded in the alternative[82] in the indictment. See also para 1.26.

12.48 To apply s 55 of the VCRA 2006,[83] consider:

- Is the offence charged an offence under the SOA 2003?
- Does the conduct alleged also amount to an offence under one of the repealed offences listed in subsection (2) see para 12.42 or the inchoate offences specified in subsection (5) (see para 12.43)?
- Is the *only thing* preventing D being found guilty that it cannot be proved beyond reasonable doubt whether the conduct took place before or after the commencement of the SOA 2003?

If so:

- Consider whether the maximum penalty of imprisonment available was lower under the old law or the new law.
- Whichever version carries the lower penalty will be conclusively presumed to apply.
- If the penalties are the same, then it shall be conclusively presumed that the conduct took place after the commencement of the SOA 2003.

12.49   2. Offences Listed in the Violent Crime Reduction Act 2006, s 55(2)

(a) Any offence under the SOA 1956 (c 69)
(b) an offence under the VA 1824, s 4 (c 83) (obscene exposure)
(c) an offence under the Town Police Clauses Act 1847, s 28 (c 89) (indecent exposure)
(d) an offence under the OPA 1861, s 61 or 62 (c 100) (buggery etc)
(e) an offence under the MHA 1959, s 128 (c 72) (sexual intercourse with patients)
(f) an offence under the IwCA 1960, s 1 (c 33) (indecency with children)

---

[81] VCRA 2006, s 55(1).
[82] *R v Chaney* [2009] EWCA Crim 52, per Sir Geoffrey Grigson at para 9.
[83] With thanks to Professor David Ormerod QC CBE.

(g) an offence under the SOA 1967, s 4 or 5 (procuring a man to commit buggery and living on the earnings of male prostitution)
(h) an offence under the TA 1968, s 9 (c 60) (burglary, including entering premises with intent to commit rape)
(i) an offence under the CLA 1977, s 54 (c 45) (incitement of girl under 16 to commit incest)
(j) an offence under the PCA 1978, s 1 (c 37) (indecent photographs of children)
(k) an offence under the SO(A)A 2000, s 3 (c 44) (abuse of position of trust)
(l) an offence under the Nationality, Immigration and Asylum Act 2002, s 145 (c 41) (traffic in prostitution).

3. Offences Listed in the Violent Crime Reduction Act 2006, s 55(5)

A reference in s 55 to an offence under the SOA 2003 or to an offence specified in subsection (2) includes a reference to— **12.50**

(a) inciting the commission of that offence;
(b) conspiracy to commit that offence;
(c) attempting to commit that offence.

F. SENTENCING REGIMES FOR DANGEROUS OFFENDERS

1. Definition

A 'dangerous offender' is one who fulfils the following criteria: **12.51**

convicted of an offence specified in Schedule 18 or Schedule 19 of the SA 2020 and assessed by the court as posing a significant risk to members of the public of serious harm by the commission of further specified offences.

2. Specified Offences

The commission of a specified offence requires consideration of dangerousness before sentence. Almost all serious sexual offences are specified offences. Specified sexual offences are listed in Schedule 18 (Part 2) or Schedule 19 SA (2020). Schedule 18 includes those offences for which an extended sentence is available (all specified offences) and Schedule 19 includes those offences for which a life sentence is available (serious specified offences, that is, those carrying a maximum determinate sentence of 10 years or a life sentence.) It follows that some offences will appear in both Schedules. **12.52**

3. The Approach to Sentencing a Specified Offence

12.53 The correct approach when sentencing an offender for a specified offence is:

> Determine whether the offender is dangerous;[84] that is—
> is there a significant risk that
> (a) D will commit further specified offences and
> (b) by doing so, D will cause serious physical or psychological harm to one or more people?
>> If the offender is not found to be dangerous either a determinate sentence or a sentence not involving immediate custody will usually follow.
>> If the Court finds the offender to be dangerous, it must next decide the appropriate sentence:
> Determine the correct type of sentence

12.54 Absent other complicating factors which might lead to a different type of life sentence, there are 3 possible sentences following a finding of dangerousness, following the order of consideration provided in *Burinskas*:

(a) a discretionary[85] life sentence (the 'required sentence of custody for life for offence carrying life sentence')
(b) a determinate sentence (coupled with appropriate protective order/s)
(c) an extended sentence, if a determinate sentence is insufficient to address the risk posed.

12.55 The following remain good law in determining dangerousness:

Lang and Others [2005] EWCA Crim 2864
Johnson and Others [2006] EWCA Crim 2486
Wilkinson and Others [2009] EWCA Crim 1925

4. Dangerous Offenders under 18 at Time of Sentence

12.56 In sentencing young people under the age of 18 the court cannot presume dangerousness, even if the offender has committed previous specified offences. A new assessment of dangerousness must be made each time a young person is convicted of a specified offence on the available evidence. See s 30(3) SA 2020 at para 12.96 in relation to pre-sentence reports.

5. Discretionary Life Sentence: D under 18 (Required Sentence of Custody for Life for Offence Carrying Life Sentence)

12.57 Sections 250 and 258 Sentencing Act 2020 apply; see 12.59.

The court must impose a life sentence where:

(1) the offender is convicted of a Schedule 19 offence

---

[84] Section 308 (1) SA 2020 deals with the assessment of dangerousness.
[85] Discretionary in the sense that it is not automatic.

(2) the court considers that the criteria for a finding of dangerousness are met and
(3) the court considers that the seriousness of the offence, or of the offence and one or more offences associated with it, is such as to justify the imposition of a sentence of detention for life.

12.58 For an offender under 18, a sentence of detention for life should be used as a last resort when an extended sentence is not able to provide the level of public protection that is necessary. In order to determine this, the court should consider the following factors in the order given:

the seriousness of the offence;
the child or young person's previous findings of guilt;
the level of danger posed to the public and whether there is a reliable estimate of the length of time the child or young person will remain a danger; and
the alternative sentences available.[86]

12.59 Section 258 Sentencing Act 2020

(1) This section applies where—
    (a) a person aged under 18 is convicted of a Schedule 19 offence (see section 307),
    (b) the court considers that the seriousness of—
        (i) the offence, or
        (ii) the offence and one or more offences associated with it,
        is such as to justify the imposition of a sentence of detention for life, and
    (c) the court is of the opinion that there is a significant risk to members of the public of serious harm occasioned by the commission by the offender of further specified offences (see sections 306(1) and 308).
(2) The court must impose a sentence of detention for life under section 250.
(3) The pre-sentence report requirements (see section 30) apply to the court in relation to forming the opinion mentioned in subsection (1)(c).
(4) An offence the sentence for which is imposed under this section is not to be regarded as an offence the sentence for which is fixed by law.

6. Extended Sentence: D under 18

12.60 An extended sentence is available for an offender under 18

Sections 254 and 255 Sentencing Act 2020 apply; see para 12.62.

12.61 In deciding whether to exercise its discretion to impose an extended sentence on a young offender, a court should consider the potential impact of both rehabilitation and increasing maturity on the level of risk a young person may pose at the time of sentence.[87]

---

[86] SGC Guidelines: Sentencing Children and Young People at 6.59.
[87] *Lang* [2005] EWCA Crim 2864; *Chowdhury* [2016] EWCA Crim 1341; *Miller* [2018] EWCA Crim 500.

12.62 Section 255 Sentencing Act 2020

> (1) An extended sentence of detention under section 254 is available where a court is dealing with an offender for an offence if—
>> (a) the offence—
>>> (i) is a specified offence (see section 306(1)), and
>>> (ii) is listed in the table in section 249(1) (sentence of detention under section 250: availability),
>>
>> (b) the offender is aged under 18 when convicted,
>> (c) the court is of the opinion that there is a significant risk to members of the public of serious harm occasioned by the commission by the offender of further specified offences (see section 308),
>> (d) the court is not required by section 258(2) to impose a sentence of detention for life under section 250, and
>> (e) if the court were to impose an extended sentence, the term that it would specify as the appropriate custodial term (see section 256) would be at least 4 years.
>
> (2) The pre-sentence report requirements (see section 30) apply to the court in relation to forming the opinion referred to in subsection (1)(c).

12.63 See also **Extended Sentences; the approach for offenders of any age** from para 12.72.

7. Dangerous Offenders aged 18–20 at Time of Sentence

Discretionary life sentence: D aged 18–20 (required sentence of custody for life for offence carrying life sentence)

12.64 Sections 250 and 274 Sentencing Act 2020 apply; see para 12.65.

The court must impose a life sentence where:

(1) the offender is convicted of a Schedule 19 offence
(2) the court considers that the criteria for a finding of dangerousness are met and
(3) the court considers that the seriousness of the offence, or of the offence and one or more offences associated with it, is such as to justify the imposition of a sentence of detention for life.

12.65 Section 274 Sentencing Act 2020

> (1) This section applies where a court is dealing with an offender for an offence where—
>> (a) the offender is aged 18 or over but under 21 when convicted of the offence,
>> (b) the offence is a Schedule 19 offence (see section 307), and
>> (c) the court is of the opinion that there is a significant risk to members of the public of serious harm occasioned by the commission by the offender of further specified offences (see sections 306(1) and 308).
>
> (2) The pre-sentence report requirements (see section 30) apply to the court in relation to forming the opinion mentioned in subsection (1)(c).
> (3) If the court considers that the seriousness of—
>> (a) the offence, or

(b) the offence and one or more offences associated with it,
   is such as to justify the imposition of a sentence of custody for life, the court must impose a sentence of custody for life under section 272.
(4) An offence the sentence for which is imposed under this section is not to be regarded as an offence the sentence for which is fixed by law.

Extended sentence; D aged 18–20
An extended sentence is available for an offender aged 18–20 **12.66**

Sections 266 and 267 Sentencing Act 2020 apply.

Section 267 Sentencing Act 2020

(1) An extended sentence of detention in a young offender institution is available in respect of an offence where—
   (a) the offence is a specified offence (see section 306(1)),
   (b) the offender is aged at least 18 but under 21 when convicted of the offence,
   (c) the court is of the opinion that there is a significant risk to members of the public of serious harm occasioned by the commission by the offender of further specified offences (see section 308),
   (d) the court is not required by section 273 or 274 to impose a sentence of custody for life, and
   (e) the earlier offence condition or the 4 year term condition is met.
(2) The pre-sentence report requirements (see section 30) apply to the court in relation to forming the opinion mentioned in subsection (1)(c).
(3) The earlier offence condition is that, when the offence was committed, the offender had been convicted of an offence listed in Schedule 14.
(4) The 4 year term condition is that, if the court were to impose an extended sentence, the term that it would specify as the appropriate custodial term (see section 268) would be at least 4 years.

See also Extended Sentences; **the approach for offenders of any age** from para 12.72. **12.67**

8. Dangerous Offenders aged 21 or over at Time of Sentence

Discretionary life sentence; D aged 21 or over (required sentence of custody for life for offence carrying life sentence)
Sections 250 and 285 Sentencing Act 2020 apply; see para 12.69. **12.68**

The court must impose a life sentence where:

(1) the offender is convicted of a Schedule 19 offence;
(2) the court considers that the criteria for a finding of dangerousness are met; and
(3) the court considers that the seriousness of the offence, or of the offence and one or more offences associated with it, is such as to justify the imposition of a sentence of detention for life.

12.69 Section 285 Sentencing Act 2020

(1) This section applies where a court is dealing with an offender for an offence where—
   (a) the offender is aged 21 or over at the time of conviction,
   (b) the offence is a Schedule 19 offence (see section 307),
   (c) the offence was committed on or after 4 April 2005, and
   (d) the court is of the opinion that there is a significant risk to members of the public of serious harm occasioned by the commission by the offender of further specified offences (see sections 306(1) and 308).
(2) The pre-sentence report requirements (see section 30) apply to the court in relation to forming the opinion mentioned in subsection (1)(d).
(3) If the court considers that the seriousness of—
   (a) the offence, or
   (b) the offence and one or more offences associated with it,
   is such as to justify the imposition of a sentence of imprisonment for life, the court must impose a sentence of imprisonment for life.
(4) An offence the sentence for which is imposed under this section is not to be regarded as an offence the sentence for which is fixed by law.

Extended sentence: D aged 21 or over

12.70 An extended sentence is available for an offender aged 21 and over

Sections 279 and 280 Sentencing Act 2020 apply.

Section 280 Sentencing Act 2020

(1) An extended sentence of imprisonment is available in respect of an offence where—
   (a) the offence is a specified offence (see section 306(1)),
   (b) the offender is aged 21 or over when convicted of the offence,
   (c) the court is of the opinion that there is a significant risk to members of the public of serious harm occasioned by the commission by the offender of further specified offences (see section 308),
   (d) the court is not required by section 283 or 285 to impose a sentence of imprisonment for life, and
   (e) the earlier offence condition or the 4 year term condition is met.
(2) The pre-sentence report requirements (see section 30) apply to the court in relation to forming the opinion mentioned in subsection (1)(c).
(3) The earlier offence condition is that, when the offence was committed, the offender had been convicted of an offence listed in Schedule 14.
(4) The 4-year term condition is that, if the court were to impose an extended sentence of imprisonment, the term that it would specify as the appropriate custodial term (see section 281) would be at least 4 years.

12.71 See also **Extended Sentences; the approach for offenders of any age** from para 12.72.

9. Extended Sentences: The Approach for Offenders of Any Age

12.72 An extended sentence can be passed for a qualifying offence whenever it was committed; s 279 SA 2020.

F. SENTENCING REGIMES FOR DANGEROUS OFFENDERS

The approach in *Burinskas*[88] is to be followed; if a life sentence is not necessary a court should first consider whether a determinate sentence would meet the risk posed, potentially supported by available ancillary order/s including an Sexual Harm Prevention Order (SHPO). If it would not, the court may then impose an extended sentence. **12.73**

Guidance was also provided by the Court of Appeal in *Pinnell and Joyce* [2010].[89] **12.74**

When a court passes an extended sentence, it should explain its reasons for concluding that a determinate sentence was not appropriate.[90] **12.75**

The extension period is a further period of licence to protect members of the public from the significant risk of serious harm caused by the offender's commission of further specified offences.[91] **12.76**

An extended sentence is only available to a court, subject to an assessment as to future risk, if the offender has previously committed an offence listed in Sch 14 SA 2020 or the instant offence (with associated offences) merits a sentence of at least 4 years; ss 231 and 400 SA 2020. See for example para 12.70 for availability criteria under s 280. See also para 12.72. **12.77**

10. Calculating the Custodial Term: The Approach when Sentencing More than One Offence

The custodial term and the extension period

The court must fix the custodial term and the extension period. These must not, in total, exceed the maximum sentence permitted for the offence; *Pinnell and Joyce* [2010].[92] **12.78**

An extended sentence is one entity comprising the custodial term and the extension period. Therefore, when it is necessary to pass multiple extended sentences, if the custodial term is consecutive the extension period must also be consecutive and if the custodial term is concurrent the extension period must also be concurrent. See *Pinnell and Joyce* [2010],[93] *Francis & Lawrence* [2014],[94] and *DJ* [2015].[95] **12.79**

The CACD has considered the question as to whether it is permissible to impose consecutive extension periods which exceed the 8 year maximum extension period for sexual offences (or 5 for violent offences); *Thompson and others* [2018].[96] The 5-judge court held: **12.80**

> [I]t is open to the court, in an appropriate (albeit exceptional) case to impose consecutive extended sentences where the total extended licence was in excess of the maximum licence

---

[88] Burinskas [2014] EWCA Crim 334.
[89] Pinnell and Joyce [2010] EWCA Crim 2848.
[90] R v Bourke [2017] EWCA Crim 2150.
[91] Ibid.
[92] Pinnell and Joyce [2010] EWCA Crim 2848.
[93] Pinnell and Joyce [2010] EWCA Crim 2848.
[94] Francis & Lawrence [2014] EWCA Crim 631.
[95] DJ [2015] EWCA Crim 563.
[96] Thompson and others [2018] EWCA Crim 639.

period for a single offence. That option should not, of course, be deployed to create what could be considered as the equivalent of life licence or one that is otherwise oppressive in nature [29].

12.81 Absent a previous Schedule 14 offence, the custodial term of at least 4 years must relate to a single offence; the usual criteria apply when determining the correct length.

12.82 It is not permissible for a court to imposes consecutive terms in order to reach a term of 4 years when passing an extended sentence. It is, however, permissible to aggregate associated offences in order to pass a sentence which takes all of the offending into account in order to reach the 4-year term. See ss 231 and 400 SA 2020 and *Pinnell*.[97] This means that where none of the offences individually merits 4 years, a court may impose for one offence the appropriate sentence for both that offence and for any offence for which the defendant is being sentenced at the same time. That sentence must be expressed as the extended sentence with the appropriate extension period calculated and concurrent determinate sentences should then be imposed in respect of the other offences. The court must make clear the custodial term for the offence attracting the extended sentence is a term taking all offences into account.

11. Calculating the Extension Period

12.83 The minimum extension period is 1 year. The maximum period for a sexual offence is 8 years (SA 2020 s 256).

12.84 The length of the extension period should be linked to the level of risk posed; its purpose is protective, not punitive.[98]

12. Imposing Consecutive Extended Sentences

12.85 It is lawful to impose consecutive extended sentences. When doing so, each element (custodial term and extension period) must be made consecutive.[99]

12.86 The Court of Appeal has expressed the view that in many circumstances the use of concurrent extended sentences of a length reflecting the gravity of the offending is preferable to consecutive extended sentences; *R v Falder* [2019].[100]

13. Imposing Extended and Determinate Sentences Together

12.87 An extended sentence may only be passed in relation to an individual offence or individual offences for which the criteria ('offence conditions') are satisfied. If it is to be imposed at the

---

[97] [2010] EWCA Crim 2848.
[98] *R v Phillips* [2018] EWCA Crim 2008.
[99] *R v Francis* [2014] EWCA Crim 631; *R v DJ* [2015] EWCA Crim 563, making reference to *Pinnell*; ibid.
[100] [2019] 1 Cr App R (S) 46.

same time as an offence which does not satisfy the criteria then the non-qualifying offence must be expressed as a determinate sentence.

14. Imposing Consecutive Extended and Determinate Sentences

When passing consecutive sentences which are extended and determinate, the determinate sentence/s should be passed first with the extended sentence made consecutive; *R v Ulhaqdad*,[101] *R v IS*.[102] The reason for this is the effect on the offender's release date. Although in *Ulhaqdad* the Court was informed that the Prison Service had indicated that the calculation it makes does not take account of the order in which sentence is passed, any type of sentence which involves an application to the Parole Board before release depends on a decision by an external body which cannot be known at the time of sentence. **12.88**

It is, however, permissible to impose a determinate sentence consecutive to an extended sentence where necessary. An example would be where the offender is already serving an extended sentence.[103] **12.89**

15. Informing the Offender of the Effect of the Sentence

The court passing sentence should explain to the offender what the effect is. The effect (regardless of the order of the sentences) is that the offender only becomes eligible for release after serving half the determinate and two-thirds of the extended custodial term. He will only become entitled to release after serving half the determinate and the full extended custodial term and will still then remain on licence for the extended licence period. **12.90**

16. Extended Sentences; Release Provisions

Offenders sentenced after 13.4.2015[104] to an extended sentence will serve two-thirds of the custodial term before being referred to the Parole Board for consideration for release. The offender must be released at the expiry of the custodial term (subject to terrorism offences exceptions). **12.91**

---

[101] *R v Ulhaqdad* [2017] EWCA Crim 1216; *R v Lang*; ibid.
[102] *R v IS* [2016] EWCA Crim 1443.
[103] For example *R v Hibbert* [2015] EWCA Crim 507; *R v Gwilym* [2018] EWCA 377.
[104] Criminal Justice and Courts Act 2015 commencement date.

380 12. SENTENCING

17. Determinate Sentences for Specified Offences; Release Provisions

12.92 The law in relation to determinate custodial sentences has been changed by the Release of Prisoners (Alteration of Relevant Proportion of Sentence) Order 2020[105] in relation to offenders convicted of a specified violent or specified sexual offence which carries a life sentence as its maximum penalty, and where the offender has been sentenced to 7 years or more. Those offenders are still released automatically, but now at the two-thirds point of the sentence rather than the half-way point.

12.93 This means that an offender aged 18 or over at sentence who is sentenced (on or after 1.4.2020) for a specified violent or specified sexual offence which carries a life sentence as its maximum penalty to a determinate terms of 7 years or more will not be entitled to release until he has served two-thirds of that sentence. See para 12.111 in relation to release provisions.

It is proposed by the Police, Crime, Sentencing and Courts Bill 2021 that the current release provisions will be amended to include qualifying offenders sentenced to a determinate term of 4 years or more. This will include all the sexual offences already specified. Assuming enactment, the timing seems likely to be not before the latter part of 2022.

12.94 An error by the sentencing judge in announcing the timing of release as half and not two-thirds does not create a 'legitimate expectation' which should affect the correct term to be imposed when the error is realized; *A-G's Ref R v Darren Rose* [2021].[106]

12.95 The calculation which applies to determinate terms of 7 years or more will not apply to a sentence passed under s 278 SA (2020); offenders of particular concern continue to be eligible for, but not entitled to, release after serving up to half of the sentence imposed whatever its length. See from para 12.101 for Offenders of Particular Concern generally and para 12.111 for release provisions in relation to them. Note that a proposal exists in the Police, Crime, Sentencing and Courts Bill to increase the point at which application for release can be made from the half-way point to two-thirds in respect of Offenders of Particular Concern. See para 12.115.

18. Pre-Sentence Reports and Dangerousness

12.96 Sentencing Act 2020 s 30(1)

This section applies where, by virtue of any provision of this Code, the pre-sentence report requirements apply to a court in relation to forming an opinion.

(2) If the offender is aged 18 or over, the court must obtain and consider a pre-sentence report before forming the opinion unless, in the circumstances of the case, it considers that it is unnecessary to obtain a pre-sentence report.

---

[105] This Order modifies the application of ss 244 and 264 of the Criminal Justice Act 2003 (release provisions are not included in the SA 2020).
[106] *A-G's Ref R v Darren Rose* [2021] EWCA Crim 155.

(3) If the offender is aged under 18, the court must obtain and consider a pre-sentence report before forming the opinion unless—
   (a) there exists a previous pre-sentence report obtained in respect of the offender, and
   (b) the court considers—
       (i) in the circumstances of the case, and
       (ii) having had regard to the information contained in that report or, if there is more than one, the most recent report,
       that it is unnecessary to obtain a pre-sentence report.
(4) Where a court does not obtain and consider a pre-sentence report before forming an opinion in relation to which the pre-sentence report requirements apply, no custodial sentence or community sentence is invalidated by the fact that it did not do so.

12.97 The question of dangerousness should usually be addressed by a pre-sentence report.[107] In a case of a serious sexual offence or offences, particularly where the offence is rape, it is almost always advisable to obtain such a report, unless the case is so grave that an indeterminate sentence is inevitable.[108] A judge is not bound by the assessment as to dangerousness in a pre-sentence report; *R v KC*,[109] which also makes reference to the intermediate position when an SHPO can properly address the risk posed by a dangerous offender as set out in *Burinskas* at [25].

12.98 The absence of such a report is not necessarily fatal to a finding of dangerousness; Where there is a sound evidential basis for such a finding and the question of obtaining reports has been carefully considered, the failure to obtain a pre-sentence report will not invalidate an extended sentence; *Allen* [2019].[110]

See also for a serious sexual offender: *R v PH* [2006][111] where the judge at first instance had been correct to impose life sentences for 2 rapes where he found there was a continuing significant risk to the public; no reports were before the court, but the defendant had a previous conviction for firearms offences. The offences revealed the defendant's dominant and aggressive attitude towards women:

> The sentencer will be guided, but not bound by, the assessment of risk in such reports. A sentencer who contemplates differing from the assessment in such a report should give both counsel the opportunity of addressing the point.[112]

12.99 Only in exceptional circumstances would a judge permit cross-examination of the author of the pre-sentence report. The circumstances in which a psychiatric report would be necessary were few.[113] However, where such a report was necessary, it was essential that for

---

[107] Per Rose LJ; *Lang* [2005] EWCA Crim 2864 at para 17(iii) and ss 156(3) and (4) CJA 2003; A-G Ref *Olawale Hassan* [2021] EWCA Crim 412; *A-G's Ref* (No 145 of 2006); *R v Dogra* [2019] EWCA Crim 145, [2019] 2 Cr App R (S)9.
[108] *A-G Ref Olawale Hassan* [2021] EWCA Crim 412 [20].
[109] *R v KC* [2019] EWCA Crim 2311.
[110] *Allen* [2019] EWCA Crim 1772.
[111] [2006] EWCA Crim 2394.
[112] Per Rose LJ; *Lang* at para [17]. See also *R v KC* [2019] EWCA Crim 2311.
[113] *R v S and Others* [2005] EWCA Crim 3616 at para 100.

the guidance of the sentencing judge it addressed the risk of serious harm posed by the offender.[114]

12.100 Section 30(4) SA 2020: where a court does not obtain and consider a pre-sentence report before forming an opinion in relation to which the pre-sentence report requirements apply, no custodial sentence or community sentence is invalidated by the fact that it did not do so.

G. OFFENDERS OF PARTICULAR CONCERN

Sections 265, 278, and Schedule 13 Sentencing Act 2020

12.101 A court must impose a special sentence

> on an offender aged 18 or over when the offence was committed who is convicted of a qualifying offence
> when a determinate immediate custodial sentence is imposed.

12.102 SA 2020 s 265 -Defendant aged 18 or over when offence committed and under 21 when sentenced

Section 265 Required special custodial sentence for certain offenders of particular concern

> (1) This section applies where a court imposes a sentence of detention in a young offender institution for an offence where—
>   (a) the offence is listed in Schedule 13,
>   (b) the offender—
>   (i) was aged 18 or over when the offence was committed, and
>   (ii) is aged under 21 when convicted of the offence, and
>   (c) the court does not impose either of the following for the offence (or for an offence associated with it)—
>   (i) an extended sentence under section 266, or
>   (ii) a sentence of custody for life under section 272.
> (2) The term of the sentence must be equal to the aggregate of—
>   (a) the appropriate custodial term, and
>   (b) a further period of 1 year for which the offender is to be subject to a licence,
>   and must not exceed the maximum term of imprisonment with which the offence is punishable in the case of a person aged 21 or over.
> (3) For the purposes of subsection (2), the 'appropriate custodial term' is the term that, in the opinion of the court, ensures that the sentence is appropriate.

12.103 SA 2020 s 278 —Defendant aged 18 or over when offence committed and over 21 when sentenced

Section 278 Required special custodial sentence for certain offenders of particular concern

> (1) This section applies where the court imposes a sentence of imprisonment for an offence where—

---

[114] *R v Lang* (ibid) and *R v S and Others* [2005] EWCA Crim 3616 at para 101.

(a) the offence is listed in Schedule 13,
(b) the person—
  (i) was aged 18 or over when the offence was committed, and
  (ii) is aged 21 or over when convicted of the offence, and
(c) the court does not impose either of the following for the offence (or for an offence associated with it)—
  (i) an extended sentence under section 279, or
  (ii) a sentence of imprisonment for life.
(2) The term of the sentence must be equal to the aggregate of—
(a) the appropriate custodial term, and
(b) a further period of 1 year for which the offender is to be subject to a licence, and must not exceed the maximum term of imprisonment with which the offence is punishable.
(3) For the purposes of subsection (2), the 'appropriate custodial term' is the term that, in the opinion of the court, ensures that the sentence is appropriate.

12.104 Sentences for offences of particular concern are frequently overlooked, giving rise to difficulty on both appeal and in respect of retrials. Further, if the section is not applied it creates significant difficulties on appeal (see *R v Thompson*) and if there should be retrial (see *R v KPR*).[115] The sentences have been introduced by s 6 of the Criminal Justice and Courts Act (CJCA) 2015 and have been in force since April 2015.

12.105 The full list of offences is set out in SA 2020 Schedule 13. It includes inchoate offences. In relation to sexual offences, it includes penetrative sexual offences against children under 13, both current and historic. Current sexual offences to which it applies are ss 5 and 6 SOA 2003; rape of a child under 13 and sexual assault by penetration of a child under 13 respectively.

12.106 Historic offences[116] will include those offences which were abolished before 13.4.2015[117] which are the equivalent of a current offence which is included in Schedule 13. These are rape and buggery of a child who was under 13 years, sexual intercourse with a girl under 13 and those penetrative indecent assaults which amount to offences under s 5 or s 6 SOA 2003; for example, penile penetration of the mouth or digital penetration of the vagina or anus. For an historic offence, it is important the indictment particularizes the fact of penetration if it is not clear from the charge. In the event of dispute or a lack of clarity, the judge may need to hear evidence to determine the issue.

12.107 The relevant section does not apply when either a life sentence or an extended sentence is imposed. If a life or extended sentence is imposed at the same time for another offence, then the court should impose concurrent determinate sentences for any s 265/s 278 offences.

---

[115] [2018] EWCA Crim 2537.
[116] An equivalent but abolished offence is included by virtue of para 9, Sch 13 SA 2020.
[117] The implementation date of s 236A CJA 2003 under which sentences for offenders of particular concern were first introduced.

384 12. SENTENCING

H. THE CALCULATION

12.108 When a determinate sentence is imposed for a qualifying offence, the court must add to it an extended licence period of 12 months.

12.109 The total sentence imposed, that is, the custodial element plus the mandatory 12 months' licence period, must not exceed the maximum sentence available for the offence.

12.110 It is permissible for a court to impose consecutive sentences for more than one qualifying offence under the section. If this course is adopted, consecutive extended periods of 12 months must be imposed for each such offence.[118]

1. Release Provisions

12.111 A sentence imposed for an offence of particular concern may significantly affect the custodial proportion of the sentence to be served.

12.112 The offender only becomes eligible for release after serving half the sentence and is not entitled to release until he has served the full term. The extra 12 months' licence applies whenever he is released; its purpose is to ensure that such an offender is subject to at least 12 months' licence even if he is not released until the end of the custodial term.

12.113 It is not necessary for the court to find such an offender dangerous. The Parole Board will not permit release until satisfied the offender is not a danger. *Fruen and DS*:[119]

> Treacy LJ: It is clear to us that the purpose of the new legislation was to ensure that such persons were subject to licence for a period after release even though, by definition, they had not been found to be dangerous by the sentencing judge. The effect, therefore, is not dissimilar to a modified form of extended sentence imposed under section 226A, although one important point of difference is that the case must be considered by the Parole Board once the offender under section 236A has served half rather than two thirds of the custodial term.

2. Imposing Both Consecutive Determinate and s 265/278 Sentences

12.114 If the court imposes both determinate sentences and s 265/278 sentences at the same time, the court should impose the determinate sentence first and order the s 265/278 sentence to run consecutively *Clarke*.[120] The reason lies in the release provisions; the offender is only eligible for release after serving half the determinate and half the s 265/278 sentence but will not be entitled to release until he has served half the determinate and the full custodial element of the s 278 sentence. Upon release such an offender, upon whom both determinate

---

[118] *R v Fruen and DS* [2006] EWCA 561.
[119] *Fruen* [2016] EWCA Crim 561.
[120] *R v Clarke* [2017] EWCA Crim 393.

and s 265/278 sentences were imposed, will be subject to both any outstanding licence as well as the extra 12 months.

12.115 For those offenders of particular concern sentenced to a determinate term, it is proposed by the Police, Crime, Sentencing and Courts Bill 2021 that the current release provisions will be amended to increase the point at which application for release can be made from the half-way point to two-thirds. Assuming enactment, the timing seems likely to be not before the latter part of 2022.

3. Sentencing Offences which Straddle the Sexual Offences Act 2003

12.116 When dealing with dangerous offenders whose offences either do or may straddle 4.4.2005, see paras 12.43–12.48 (and paras 1.26–1.34).

I. CURRENT DANGEROUSNESS PROVISIONS: OFFENCES COMMITTED POST THE CJA 2003 AND LASPO 2012 AND INCORPORATED INTO THE SENTENCING CODE 2020

12.117 The CJA 2003 (as amended by LASPO) life sentence powers under ss 224A, 225, and 226 (thereafter contained in the Sentencing Code from 1.12.2020 and applicable to convictions after that date), only apply to offences committed after 4.4.2005 (CJA 2003 implementation date). This needs to be borne in mind when dealing with offences committed between 1.5.2004 (SOA 2003) and 3.4.2005; they must be sentenced under the regime in place for the Act against which they were committed. Whereas a CJA 2003 LASPO extended sentence provisions (as incorporated into the Sentencing Code) can be passed for any offence whether it is committed before or after 4.4.2005. See para 12.66.

1. Life Sentence

12.118 The four situations in which a life sentence may currently arise for consideration were identified by Lord Judge, then Lord Chief Justice, in *Saunders*.[121] The court made clear that a discretionary life sentence may be appropriate in cases which previously would properly have attracted an IPP; see para 12.59, bearing in mind that such a sentence is one of last resort. All but a mandatory life sentence may apply to rape and other serious sexual offences with a maximum term of life imprisonment.

(1) **Mandatory life** sentence; following conviction for murder.[122]
(2) **Statutory life** sentence; following conviction for a second listed offence under s 224A and Schedule 15B of the 2003 Act (inserted by s 122 of LASPO 2012) or ss 273 (adult under 21), 283 (adult over 21) and Schedule 15 of the Sentencing Code, a sentence of imprisonment for life 'must' be imposed, unless the particular circumstances would

---
[121] *R v Saunders and Others* [2013] EWCA Crim 1027.
[122] SA 2020, s 275.

make it unjust.[123]The Sentencing Code specifies that the particular circumstances must relate to the index offence, the previous offence or the offender.

(3) **Discretionary life** sentence; available following conviction for a 'specified offence' under s 225 of the CJA 2003 and Schedule 15 or a Schedule 19 offence under ss 274 and 285 of the Sentencing Code.

(4) **Discretionary life** sentence; available following conviction for both a 'specified' and a 'non-specified offence'. This may be appropriate in a case where an IPP would have been imposed. The question will be whether or not the current, more onerous, form of extended sentence will provide adequate protection for the public.

12.119 Per Lord Judge CJ in *Saunders*:

[11.] This leaves open the further question (addressed in the Criminal Law Review at (2013) Crim LR 508 in commentary on *R v Cardwell* [2012] EWCA Crim 3030) whether a sentence of life imprisonment may be imposed when the case does not fall within either the statutory life sentence or the discretionary life sentence analysed in the previous paragraphs. The jurisdiction to impose a life sentence in an appropriate case has survived the enactment of the 2003 Act and the changes to the sentencing regime affected by LASPO. If it had been intended to abolish it, the appropriate legislative change could readily have been made by provisions restricting the life sentence (other than the mandatory sentence) to the statutory sentence or the discretionary sentence under s 225(1) and (2). As it is, neither the 2003 Act, nor LASPO, imposed any limit on the power of the court to impose a sentence of life imprisonment in such cases. Some of these offences may involve a significant risk of serious harm to the public, but are not included within the list of 'specified' offences in the dangerousness provisions in the 2003 Act. One obvious example is the offender who commits repeated offences of very serious drug supplying which justifies the imposition of the life sentence. In circumstances like these the court is not obliged to impose the sentence in accordance with s 225(2), but its discretion to do so is unaffected.

[12.] In reality, the occasions when this second form of discretionary life sentence is likely to be imposed will be rare, and no inconvenience has yet resulted from applying the description 'discretionary' to both forms of sentence. We have reflected whether any advantages might accrue to sentencing courts if we were able to offer alternative descriptions which would identify the distinction between these two forms of discretionary life sentence. In reality, none is needed.

[13.] For those convicted after 3 December 2012, as a result of s 123 of LASPO the sentence of imprisonment for public protection (IPP) created for serious offences by s 225(1) and (3) of the 2003 Act will no longer be available. As we have explained, for dangerous offenders the statutory life sentence under s 224A of the 2003 Act has been abated and the discretionary life sentence remains. In relation to convictions returned before 3 December 2012 the protection of the public from dangerous offenders was achieved either by the discretionary life sentence or IPP. There are relatively minor distinctions between the two sentences which have no direct bearing on the issue of

---

[123] See s 224A(2). In short, there is a discretionary power in the court to disapply what would otherwise be a provision requiring an obligatory sentence, this is replicated in ss 273(3) and 283(3) of the Sentencing Code. See also *A-G's Ref (No 55 of 2008)* [2008] EWCA Crim 2790.

public protection. In relation to the discretionary life sentence, the court was theoretically able to make a whole life order, but, as far as we are aware, no such orders have been made or, if made, upheld. In relation to the IPP there was a supplementary jurisdiction in the Parole Board to give a direction that supervision under licence should come to an end 10 years after release.

[14.] In the overwhelming majority of cases these distinctions were irrelevant, and so the IPP was normally sufficient to address the protection of the public from a dangerous offender who would, if made subject to the order, continue to be detained until the Parole Board was satisfied that he no longer represented a risk to the public. (See *R v Kehoe* [2009] 1 Cr App R(S) 9.) As the court observed in *R v Wilkinson* [2010] 1 Cr App R(S) 100:

> '... as a matter of principle a discretionary life sentence under s 225 should continue to be reserved for offences of the utmost gravity. Without being prescriptive, we suggest that the sentence should come into contemplation when the judgment of the court is that the seriousness is such that the life sentence would have ... a "denunciatory" value, reflective of public abhorrence of the offence, and where, because of its seriousness, the notional determinate sentence would be very long, measured in very many years.'

[15.] The new statutory life sentence has not replaced the IPP. Many offenders who represent a danger to the public may not 'qualify' for the statutory life sentence. Yet, for some offenders, the imperative of public protection continues undiminished, and is not wholly met by the 'new' extended sentence. Very long term public protection must therefore be provided by the imposition of a discretionary life sentence. That is consequent on s 225(1) and (2) which, in the context of the discretionary life sentence for serious offences continue, as we have explained, in full force.

For Schedule 15 and Schedule 15B CJA 2003 see Appendix 3, for Schedule 15 and Schedule 19 Sentencing Code see Appendix 4.

2. Discretionary Life Sentence

In *R v Saunders* [2013] EWCA Crim 1027 Lord Judge CJ expressed the view that discretionary life sentences could still be passed in addition to life sentences then passed under ss 224A and 225 of the CJA 2003 (for convictions on or after 1.12.2020 ss 273 SA 2020 (adult under 21, second listed offence) , s 274 SA 2020 (adult under 21, required life sentence), s 283 SA 2020 (adult over 21, second listed offence) and s 285 SA 2020 (adult over 21, required life sentence) of the Sentencing Code). **12.120**

The Court of Appeal in *Attorney General's Reference (No 27 of 2013) (R v Burinskas)* rejected criticism of the court in *Saunders* on this point, observing that in its view the approach of the court was correct and pointed to then current SGC Guidelines[124](para 1, p. 24) in support of that view: **12.121**

---

[124] 2007 version. Current version effective from 1 April 2014 and now contains the following guidance on sentencing rape offences: 'Offences may be of such severity, for example involving a campaign of rape, that sentences of 20 years and above may be appropriate.'

Life imprisonment is the maximum for the offence [of rape]. Such a sentence may be imposed either as a result of the offence itself where a number of aggravating factors are present, or because the offender meets the dangerousness criterion.

12.122 See for an example *R v P* [2013][125] in which a discretionary life sentence for assault on a child under 13 by penetration (committed before 4.4.2005) was not excessive. The offender was a predatory paedophile with previous convictions for sexual offences against children and the offence was of sufficient seriousness to warrant life imprisonment.

3. Statutory Life Sentences, ss 273, 274, 283, and 285 Sentencing Code 2020

3.12.2012 to present

12.123 Section 224A of the CJA 2003 (inserted by s 122 of the LASPO 2012) created the new sentence of 'life sentence for second listed offence'. It applied to a defendant convicted on or after 3.12.2012.[126] From 1.12.2020 adult offenders convicted on or after 1.12.2020 will instead be subject to the corresponding provisions of the Sentencing Code, namely ss 273 (adult under 21), 283 (adult over 21) and Schedule 15 SA 2020. These provisions apply to offences committed on or after dates specified in in Schedule 15.[127] Under both the SA and the CJA 2003, where an offence is found to have been committed over a period of 2 or more days, or at some time during a period of 2 or more days, it must be taken to have been committed on the last of those days.[128]

12.124 As per Lord Judge in *Saunders* at para 12.75, this form of sentence does not replace Imprisonment for the Protection of the Public (IPP) but has its own qualifying criteria:

(i) a person aged 18 or over is convicted of an offence [known as the 'index offence' in the Sentencing Code] listed in Part 1 of Schedule 15B to the CJA 2003 [now Part 1 of Schedule 15 of the Sentencing Code];
(ii) the offence is such that the court would have imposed a determinate sentence of 10 years or more (including an extended sentence where the custodial term would have been 10 years or more) [and disregarding any extension period under s 266 of the Sentencing Code]; and
(iii) the offender has a previous conviction for an offence listed in Schedule 15B (not just in Part 1) [now Schedule 15 of the Sentencing Code] for which he received a life sentence (with a minimum term of at least 5 years) or a determinate sentence of 10 years or more (including an extended sentence where the custodial term was 10 years or more);
(iv) the court must impose a life sentence if all the conditions in s 224A apply, unless there are particular circumstances relating to either the current offence or the previous

---

[125] *R v P* [2013] EWCA Crim 1143, also known as *R v DP*.
[126] Section 224A(1)(b) CJA 2003.
[127] The dates relevant to each offence are specified in the Schedule, the earliest date is 3.12.2012.
[128] Section 224A(12) CJA 2003 (added by Criminal Justice and Courts Act 2015 c 2 Pt 1 s 5(1) (13.4.2015), and SA 2020, ss 273(14) and 283(14).

relevant offence, or to the offender which 'would make it unjust to do so in all the circumstances': s 224A(2). [now ss 273(3) and s 283(3) of the SA 2020]

12.125 Part 2 of both Schedules includes any offence that was abolished before 3 December 2012 which would have constituted an offence specified in Part 1. Part 3 of both Schedules includes corresponding offences under service law.

12.126 For the purposes of these provisions, whilst the index offence must be listed in Part 1 of either Schedule 15B CJA 2003 or Schedule 15 Sentencing Code, the previous offence can be listed anywhere in the schedule. This is intended to allow, within the qualifying previous conviction, for offences which have been repealed (such as those under the SOA 1956) but replaced with broadly equivalent offences.

12.127 It is suggested that an offender who qualifies under the criteria would most likely be subject to a discretionary life sentence for the new offence in any event. However, it should be remembered that, whilst in order to pass a discretionary life sentence a judge would have to find an offender to be dangerous within the statutory test, it is not necessary to apply that test in passing a statutory life sentence.

(i) Sections 273 and 283 Sentencing Act 2020 (previously s 224A CJA 2003) apply where an offender is convicted of a second listed offence; the judge must pass a life sentence unless the particular circumstances make it unjust.

(ii) Sections 274 and 285 Sentencing Code (previously s 225 CJA 2003) apply where a person is convicted of a serious offence after 3.12.2012, is dangerous and the seriousness of the offence justifies the imposition of a life sentence. Where the offender is judged to be dangerous and the conditions under the relevant section are met, there is no judicial discretion; a life sentence must be passed.

12.128 *Attorney General's Reference (No 27 of 2013)* [2014] EWCA Crim 334 (*R v Burinskas*) deals with life sentences and extended sentences under the CJA 2003 as amended by LASPO 2012 and will continue to apply to corresponding extended sentences under the Sentencing Code.

12.129 The judgment in *Burinskas* followed consideration of 8 conjoined appeals (only one a prosecution reference) involving dangerous sexual offenders. In 6, life sentences had been imposed under the LASPO provisions (s 224A or s 225 CJA 2003 following the abolition of IPPs); in 2, extended sentences were imposed under LASPO 2012.

12.130 The Court considered the effect of the then new provisions under LASPO on sentencing dangerous offenders, that is, the new route to a life sentence under the CJA 2003; s 224A and the correct interpretation of s 225 after the abolition of IPPs.

12.131 Delivering his judgment, Lord Thomas CJ said:

[8] i) For a life sentence to be imposed under s 224A there is no requirement of a finding that the offender is dangerous within the meaning of the CJA 2003, although it is likely that in most cases he will be. It follows that the fact that an offender is not dangerous is not something that of itself would make it unjust to pass a life sentence under this section.

ii) s 225(2)(b) does not apply to the relevant offence in s 224A. There is no requirement to consider whether the 'seriousness' threshold has been passed.

iii) s 224A could lead in cases that may be rare to the imposition of a life sentence in respect of an offence which does not carry life as a maximum.

...

[12] The critical issue is the interpretation of the condition in s 225(2)(b).

...

[15] ...decisions about the circumstances in which a life sentence was appropriate handed down during the currency of the version of the CJA which was in force between 3 April 2005 and 3 December 2012 are now of limited assistance.[129]

[16] Although the provisions of s 225 ... remain the same, the statutory context in which they are to be interpreted is fundamentally changed ... IPP no longer exists.

[17] We interpret [s 225] in the light of the new regime which includes s 224A and the new extended sentences.

...

[18] Save where imposed under s 224A a life sentence remains a sentence of last resort ... [Given the abolition of IPPs] it is inevitable that sentences of life imprisonment will be imposed more frequently than before [LASPO].

[19] We agree with the view of Lord Judge in *Saunders* that the new extended sentence cannot be treated as a direct replacement for the old IPP ... where the court is faced with facts which ... [pre-LASPO] would have led the court to pass an IPP, it may well be necessary to pass a life sentence....

[22] ...taking into account the law prior to the coming into force of the CJA 2003 and the whole of the new statutory provisions, the question in s 225(2)(b) as to whether the seriousness of the offence (or the offence and one or more offences associated with it) is such as to justify a life sentence requires consideration of—

i) The seriousness of the offence itself, on its own or with other offences associated with it (s 143(1)) ... This is always a matter for the judgment of the court.

ii) The defendant's previous convictions (s 142(2)).

iii) The level of danger posed to the public by the defendant and whether there is a reliable time estimate of the length of time he will remain a danger.

iv) The available alternative sentences.

See para 12.67 for the court's judgment in relation to extended sentences. See also *R v Arifin* [2018][130] in which the offender had been sentenced to a discretionary life sentence under s 225 CJA 2003. Adopting and applying *Burkinsas* the court upheld the sentence and stated (at para 29):

> We draw attention to three particular features of that judgment: (1) a life sentence remains a sentence of last resort; (2) nonetheless, life sentences will be more prevalent in the light of the abolition of sentences of imprisonment for public protection than before that abolition; (3) the protection of the public furnished by an extended sentence is very different from that furnished by an indeterminate sentence, given the fact that the offender must be

---

[129] With the introduction of the SA 2020, it is suggested now of even less assistance.
[130] *R v Arifin* [2018] EWCA Crim 145.

released at a fixed point (the end of the appropriate custodial term) under an extended sentence (now, in accordance with the provisions of s.246A of the Criminal Justice Act 2003), regardless of any continuing danger then posed to the public.

4. Whole Life Sentence

12.132 Whilst whole life sentences have in principle been upheld by the Supreme Court,[131] whole life sentences have been judged rarely appropriate for sexual offences without more.

12.133 *Oakes* [2012]:[132] absent accompanying murder, it is unlikely to include sexual cases. *Oakes* was applied in *R v Reynolds: R v Rosser* [2014][133] in which the court rejected separate appeals against the imposition of whole life orders in respect of two murders of children involving sadistic and sexual conduct. More recently in *R v McCann, Sinaga & Shah* [2020][134] the court declined to impose whole life terms in respect of 2 multiple rape cases of the most extreme gravity. Whilst there was no bar to attaching a whole life term to a discretionary life sentence, 'there is a principled reason for reserving the most serious sentences to cases of murder, save in the most exceptional circumstances'.[135]

12.134 *Hogg* [2007]:[136] the Court of Appeal set a minimum term for the life sentences properly passed, rather than the whole life term imposed by the trial judge. The criteria for deciding whether whole life is necessary relate to the offences themselves, not the question of future risk. It is for the Parole Board to determine the latter.

J. SENTENCING HISTORIC OFFENCES

12.135 Offenders must be sentenced according to the sentencing regime in place at the time the offence was committed. The maximum sentences available at the relevant time for offences appear at each sentencing paragraph within Chapters 2–11 inclusive. The SC Guidelines provide assistance in sentencing historic offences at its Annexes B and C; the latter is based on the table which appears in Chapter 1 of the three editions of this work.

12.136 In an important judgment arising out of a series of conjoined appeals in 2016, Lord Thomas, then Lord Chief Justice, presiding over a 5-judge court provided guidance as to the correct principles and approach when sentencing historic cases involving sexual offences: *R v Forbes and Others*.[137]

---

[131] *McLoughlin & Newell* [2014] EWCA Crim 188. The question was whether a whole life term is lawful, bearing in mind the domestic statutory regime in place governing the hope or possibility of release. The Court of Appeal found that the provision for release by the Secretary of State in exceptional circumstances (C(S)A 1997, s 30) means that the power to impose a whole life sentence is not incompatible Article 3 ECHR.
[132] *Oakes* [2012] EWCA Crim 2435. Suggestion that the whole life order will only be for the most exceptional cases. Absent accompanying murder, it is unlikely to include sexual cases.
[133] *R v Reynolds; R v Rosser* [2014] EWCA Crim 22015.
[134] *R v McCann, Sinaga & Shah* [2020] EWCA Crim 1676.
[135] Per Lord Burnett of Maldon CJ at para [88].
[136] *Hogg* [2007] EWCA Crim 1357.
[137] *R v Forbes and Others* [2016] EWCA Crim 1388.

12.137 *R v H*[138] [2011] was codified by the Sentencing Council in Annex B to the Definitive Guideline on Sexual Offences published in 2013.[139] Annex B is a convenient statement of the applicable principles which, subject to one exception in relation to para 9 set out at (h) below, should apply without the need to refer to *H* or other cases [paras 2 and 3].

1. The Fundamental Principles

12.138 The court in *R v H* restated the two fundamental principles of sentencing offences committed some considerable time in the past.

> The offender must be sentenced in accordance with the regime applicable at the date of sentence. The court must therefore have regard to the statutory purposes of sentencing and to current sentencing practice. The fact that attitudes have changed is of no moment.
>
> The sentence that can be passed is the limited to the maximum sentence available at the time of the commission of the offence, unless the maximum has been reduced, when the lower maximum is applicable.

2. General Principles to be Drawn from Forbes

Have regard to the guidelines for the equivalent offence

12.139 The judge should have regard to any applicable sentencing guidelines for equivalent offences under the SOA 2003. The judge should not simply apply the relevant guideline applicable at the date of sentence, subject to any lower statutory maximum sentence applicable at the date the offence was committed but use the guideline in a measured and reflective manner to arrive at the appropriate sentence (paras [6,7, 9, and 10]).

12.140 It is important for the judge to guard against too mechanistic an approach, either in terms of equivalent offence or in adopting the figures in the guideline without having regard to the fact that generally higher maxima are provided for some of the modern-day offences (para [10]).

The type of sentence: (ref article 7 European Convention on Human Rights, which prohibits retroactive penalties)

12.141 The court is not concerned to ascertain what sentence would have been passed if the case had been tried shortly after the offence had been committed; it is only concerned to ascertain the statutory maximum. There may, however, be rare cases where a broader inquiry is necessary. For example, as in the case of one of the Appellants BD, who was under 14 at the time of the offence and so could not have been sentenced at the relevant time to a custodial sentence on account of his age. The rare circumstances of the appeal of BD should not operate as encouragement or licence to courts to consider a similar exercise in any other situation (paras [13] and [111–121]).

---

[138] Ibid.
[139] Effective from 1.4.2014.

12.142 When an historic case attracts a low maximum sentence it is permissible for the sentencing judge to pass consecutive sentences in order to have regard to current sentencing practice: *Woods* [2012],[140] decided pre *Forbes* but the principle is still applicable, for example *Max Clifford* [2014][141] when art 7 was rejected when sought to be relied on by the appellant.

3. Abuse of Trust

12.143 It was evident from the appeals that the concept of 'abuse of trust' as an express aggravating factor had caused difficulty. The phrase 'abuse of trust' as used in the guideline connotes rather more than the colloquial understanding of trust, such as a parent's trust in a cousin, relation or neighbour to behave properly towards their children. The mere fact of association or the fact that one sibling is older than another does not necessarily amount to breach of trust in this context. The phrase plainly includes a relationship such as between the teacher and pupil (as in the appellant Clark's case); a priest and the pupils in a school for those from a disturbed background (as in the appellant McCallen's case) or a scoutmaster and boys in his charge (as in the appellant Warren's case). It may also include parental or quasi-parental relationships or arise from an ad hoc situation, for example, where a late-night taxi driver takes a lone female fare. What is necessary is a close examination of the facts and clear justification given if abuse of trust is to be found (paras [17] and [18]). For abuse of trust generally, see also para 12.188.

Immaturity and its relevant to the assessment of culpability

12.144 The court was of the view that the approach taken in *H* at [47(c)], namely that immaturity goes to culpability is a better one than the SGC Guidance[142] that it may be regarded as personal mitigation, depending on the circumstances of the offence. In assessing such culpability, it is necessary to look at all of the facts and reach an overall assessment.

12.145 For example, in relation to the appellant Forbes, although he was only 16 when he embarked on the course of offending, he knew it was wrong and continued offending as an adult. Immaturity was therefore a factor of little weight in that appeal (para [48]), but in relation to the appellant Tarrant, it was a factor of greater weight for the offence which had occurred when he was 15 (para [175]).

12.146 The maturity of a youth should be assessed by reference to the maturity of a youth of the offender's age at the material time, absent reliable evidence of the maturity of the particular offender when he committed the offences (para [21]). Since *Forbes*, the CACD has addressed this further in a number of judgments including *Clarke and Others*;[143] an offender aged 18 is not to be regarded as fully mature and aged 21 may not be either. A court must have regard to both chronological age and actual maturity. A helpful article can be found on this topic in the Criminal Law Review: 'The Sentencing of Young Adults; a Distinct Group Requiring a Distinct Approach'.[144]

---

[140] *R v Woods* [2012] EWCA Crim 2753, followed in *R v DCA* [2013] EWCA Crim 1017.
[141] *R v Clifford* [2014] EWCA Crim 2245.
[142] Referring to para 9 to Annex B of the SGC Definitive Guideline; Sexual Offences 2013, effective from 1.4.2014.
[143] [2018] EWCA Crim 18.
[144] Crim LR 2021, 3, 203–17.

12.147 The correct approach when sentencing an immature offender aged 19 for offences committed when he was 15 was to apply the guideline on sentencing children and young people and for the sentence to be that which would have been imposed if he had been convicted at 15 (the age at which he committed the offences), rather than to apply the 'approach to sentencing historic sexual offences' detailed in Annex B of the Definitive Guideline on Sexual Offences; *R v O (Orritt)* [2018]:[145] 'This at all events is not a historical sexual offending case of a kind where the offending occurred at a time when a different statutory regime prevailed. This offending had occurred just 3 or 4 years earlier when the Sexual Offences Act 2003 already applied. It was entirely legitimate, in our view, for the judge to consider the position on the footing that the offender had been sentenced at the time of the offending itself rather than several years afterwards.'

12.148 In relation to the 'maximum sentence' and 'immaturity', see *R v Goldfinch* [2019][146] applying *R v Forbes*, in which a sentence of six and a half years' imprisonment imposed on an offender following his conviction for historical child sex offences was reduced to 3 years' imprisonment. In that case the Recorder had failed to attach sufficient weight to the maximum sentence available at the time of the offences and to the fact that the relevant culpability was that of a 16-year-old boy, not a mature adult offender.

Assessment of harm

12.149 The judge must have regard to the fact that the guidelines provide for the inevitable effect of serious crime on the victim and avoid double counting. 'There has to be significantly more before harm is taken into account as a distinct and further aggravating factor and/or before a judge makes a finding of extremely severe psychological or physical harm so as to justify placing the offence in the top category' [para 26].

Further guidance has more recently been provided in *Chall and Others*.[147]

12.150 The prosecution and police must keep the relevant guidelines on victim personal statements in mind when preparing such statements. They should only contain material which should be in them (para [27]).

See *Perkins* [2013][148] for further guidance as to Victim Personal Statements and *Chall* on assessment of severe psychological harm. See also para 12.185 in relation to the assessment of severe psychological harm.

Good character since the offences

12.151 Paragraph 8 of Annex B makes clear that what is of material significance is proper evidence of positive good character, as distinct from simply having no previous convictions. In each case it will be necessary to examine carefully all of the circumstances. For example, evidence that the appellant Clark had good qualities as a teacher and a constructive life as an organ

---

[145] *R v Orritt* [2018] EWCA Crim 2286.
[146] *R v Goldfinch* [2019] EWCA Crim 878.
[147] [2019] EWCA Crim 865, 73.
[148] *R v Perkins* [2013] EWCA Crim 323. See also Criminal Practice Direction VII Sentencing F: Victim Personal Statements.

J. SENTENCING HISTORIC OFFENCES 395

builder and volunteer organist did not amount to exemplary conduct. Evidence that the appellant T had established a positive lifestyle had to be tempered by the fact that he had lent himself to a cover up (para [24]).

Relevance of the passage of time
This is provided for by para 7 of Annex B. Passage of time in cases where there are threats or other conduct designed to discourage the complainant from reporting the offence is not a mitigating factor of any material weight (para [29]). **12.152**

The Court in *Forbes* also made observations in relation to the framing of the indictment at paras [20–24] (see also Chapter 1) and the application of s 236A of the CJA 2003 at paras [35–36]; (for convictions after 1.12.2020 the corresponding section 265 and 278 of the Sentencing Code apply). **12.153**

As to the position regarding art 7 (the exception to the general principle that the relevant maximum penalty is the maximum penalty available for the offence at the date of the commission of the offence, where the offender could not have received any form of custodial sentence) the limited extent of the exception was confirmed in *R v L* [2017].[149] See also *R v AM* [2018][150] which suggests that the court in *Forbes* erred in its approach to art 7 and the appeal of *LDG* [2018].[151] **12.154**

In relation to the 'maximum sentence' and 'immaturity', see *R v Goldfinch* [2019][152] applying *R v Forbes*, in which a sentence of 6 and a half years' imprisonment imposed on an offender following his conviction for historical child sex offences was reduced to 3 years' imprisonment. In that case the Recorder had failed to attach sufficient weight to the maximum sentence available at the time of the offences and to the fact that the relevant culpability was that of a 16-year-old boy, not a mature adult offender. **12.155**

4. Sentencing Relatively Young Offenders for Sexual Offences Committed Some Years Before and When They Were under 18

The position appears to be somewhat different when sentencing, for example, a 19 year old for offences committed when he was 15. This arose recently in *Att Gen's Ref (O)* [2018][153] EWCA Crim 2286; [2019] 1 Cr App R (S) 28, Davis LJ pointed out that this was not a case where the offending occurred at a time when a different statutory scheme applied and had occurred only 2 or 3 years earlier. It was therefore entirely legitimate for the judge to consider the position on the footing that the offender had been sentenced at the time of offending rather than several years later. Such an approach was consistent with *R v Bowker* [2008] 1 Cr App R (S) 72 and more recently *R v L* [2017] 1 Cr App R (S) 51 which **12.156**

---

[149] *R v L* [2017] EWCA Crim 43.
[150] *R v AM* [2018] EWCA Crim 279 at paras 19–23.
[151] *R v LDG* [2018] EWCA Crim 2264 at para 19.
[152] *R v Goldfinch* [2019] EWCA Crim 878.
[153] EWCA Crim 2286; [2019] 1 Cr App R (S) 28.

restated the importance of age of the offender at the time of the offending going to the issue of culpability.

For a recent example (D 16 when committed serious offence but convicted when he was in his late 30s) see *R v Goldfinch* [2019] EWCA Crim 878.

5. Sentencing Geriatric Offenders

12.157 The issue of sentencing aged offenders in historic offences was considered, to a limited extent, in the case of *R v Forbes* by Lord Thomas CJ at paras [80] and [81]. It was subsequently followed in a conjoined appeal against sentence for historic sexual offences by *Clarke* and *Cooper*[154] aged 101 and 96 respectively, the Court of Appeal considered the issue of the appropriate allowance to be made for extreme old age in the sentencing process and issued the following guidance:

> Sentencing guidelines frequently refer to age as a mitigating factor. In the Sentencing Council's Guideline for Sexual Offences the factor is shown as 'Age and/or lack of maturity where it affects the responsibility of the offender'. That, of course, will cover the case of young offenders, but the reference to age in the case of an older person is a reference to chronological age as a mitigating factor, irrespective of whether it affects the responsibility of the offender [para 19].
>
> Sentencing in cases of historical sexual abuse could not wholly be viewed from the standpoint of the offender, who had either by his inaction or by positive steps avoided justice and been able to enjoy life into old age (para 20).
>
> When sentencing old-aged offenders, especially in historic cases, since rehabilitation and dangerousness were unlikely to be significant questions; the court should focus on finding an appropriate sentence where harm and culpability are the primary considerations [para 21].
>
> Old age was a material mitigating consideration and would frequently be accompanied by considerations of ill health (para 21). However, sentencing should be done on a case-by-case basis, taking into account the individual circumstances of the offender. Old age should not be treated as a special category and there should be no general discount based on assumptions about extreme old age [para 22].
>
> The offender's diminished life expectancy, age, health, and prospect of dying in prison should be balanced against the gravity of the offending (including harm to the victims) and public interest in passing an appropriate punishment for very serious crimes. Consequently, whilst anxious scrutiny should be given to factors of extreme old age and health, allowance for extreme old age would be limited [para 25]. The fact that this may give rise to the possibility of the offender dying in prison is something which is taken into account by the Secretary of State in considering whether a prisoner should be released on compassionate grounds where exceptional circumstances justify release [para 26].

---

[154] *R v Clarke and R v Cooper* [2017] EWCA Crim 393.

K. RELEASE, LICENCE, AND SUPERVISION REQUIREMENTS

12.158 The particular release, licence or supervision requirements applicable to a sentence remain unchanged by the SA 2020. The Sentencing Code, s 328 does, however, enable the Court, when sentencing offenders convicted after 1.12.2020, to recommend licence conditions for adult offenders sentenced to 12 months' imprisonment or more.

1. Sentencing for Offences Committed under a different Licensing Regime

12.159 A reduction should not be made at sentence on the basis that since the time of the offence the early release provisions have been changed and/or the licensing system made more severe *R v Burinskas* [2014].[155] Further, the judge should not consider a 'legitimate expectation' had arisen even where a mistake had been made in initial sentencing remarks; *A-G's Reference (Darren Rose)* [2021].[156]

2. Fixed Term Offenders

12.160 Offenders sentenced to a standard determinate sentence are automatically released halfway though their sentence to serve the remainder of their sentence on licence[157] unless convicted of a specified offence and sentenced to 7 years or more; in which case the 'Release of Prisoners (Alteration of Relevant Proportion of Sentence) Order 2020' applies or a sentence for offenders of particular concern. See paras 12.165 and 12.101.

3. Licence Period for Sentences of Imprisonment of Less than 12 Months: Offender Rehabilitation Act 2014

12.161 On 1.2.2015 the Offender Rehabilitation Act 2014 (ORA) came into force. Sections 1–7 altered the release and supervision requirements under the CJA 2003[158] for offenders serving custodial sentences of less than 2 years. Previously offenders serving less than 12 months would be released unconditionally halfway through their sentence. As amended, ss 243A and 256AA require that all those released from short prison sentences will first be subject to a standard licence period for the remainder of their prison sentence to be served in the community, and then be subject to an additional supervision period. The provisions apply, subject to the exceptions set out in the section,[159] to offenders:

> Whose offence was committed on or after the 1.2.2015.
> Who were sentenced to a prison term of more than 1 day but less than 2 years.
> Who will be 18 years or over when released.

---

[155] *R v Burinskas* [2014] EWCA Crim 334.
[156] *A-G's Reference (Darren Rose)* [2021] EWCA Crim 155.
[157] CJA 2003, ss 244 and 249(1).
[158] Section 243A CJA 2003 youth offenders) and s 256AA for adult offenders.
[159] Sentences to which restricted release applies under the SA 2020, ss 254, 265, 266, 278, 279, or 247A CJA 2003.

398 12. SENTENCING

12.162 Section 2 ORA 2014 inserts a new s 256AA into the CJA 2003 under which Offenders sentenced to less than 2 years and released on licence (as outlined above), will then be subject to an additional period of supervision (for the purposes of rehabilitation), once their licence period comes to an end. The licence and supervision period will together add up to 12 months. Depending on the length of the prison sentence, the length of the supervision period can vary significantly.

12.163 Section 4 ORA 2014 amends s 256B of the 2003 Act, which relates to the supervision of young offenders after release from a s 91 or a s 96 sentence of less than 12 months. Those offenders would previously have been subject to a 3-month period of supervision. The amendments mean that offenders serving s 91 or s 96 sentences in relation to post-commencement offences, who are 18 or over on the last day of the custodial period, will no longer be subject to supervision under section 256B, but will be subject instead to the same arrangements as apply to an adult sentenced to a custodial sentence of less than 12 months. The amendments also have the effect that s 256B continues to apply in any case where the offence for which the sentence was imposed was committed before 1.2.2015. Section 6 ORA 2014 introduces modified supervision requirements for qualifying offenders who are subject to detention and training orders by inserting a new s 106B into the Powers of Criminal Courts (Sentencing) Act 2000.

4. Extended Sentence: Release on Licence

12.164 Offenders sentenced after 13.4.2015[160] to an extended sentence will serve two-thirds of the custodial term before being referred to the Parole Board for consideration for release. The offender must be released at the expiry of the custodial term (subject to terrorism offences exceptions).

5. The Release of Prisoners (Alteration of Relevant Proportion of Sentence) Order 2020

12.165 The 'Release of Prisoners (Alteration of Relevant Proportion of Sentence) Order 2020' came into force on 1.4.2020. The Order makes fundamental changes to the release provisions applicable to qualifying offenders convicted of relevant violent or sexual offences. Sections 244 and 264[161] of the Criminal Justice Act 2003, under which the Secretary of State is required to release on licence prisoners serving fixed-term sentences (subject to certain exceptions) once they have served the requisite custodial period under s 244(3) of the 2003 Act are modified by art 3 of the Order. So that prisoners sentenced to a fixed-term sentence of 7 years or more for a relevant violent or sexual

---

[160] Criminal Justice and Courts Act 2015 commencement date.
[161] As amended by the SA 2020.

offence, who would ordinarily have been automatically released at the halfway point, cannot now be released on licence until they have served two-thirds of their sentence (s 244(3)(a)). Similar modifications are made to those serving consecutive sentences (s 264(6)(d)). Any sentence served consecutively which is not imposed for a term of 7 years or more and for a relevant violent or sexual offence will remain subject to the halfway release provisions.

12.166 The Order applies to relevant specified violent or sexual offences, namely offences listed in Part 1 or 2 of Schedule 15 to the CJA 2003 for which a sentence of life imprisonment may be imposed. The following offences are specified sexual offences in Part 2 of Schedule 15:[162]

- Sexual Offences Act 1956, ss 1–7, 9–11, 14–17, 19–29, 32, and 33A.
- Mental Health Act 1959, s 128.
- Indecency with Children Act 1960, s 1.
- Sexual Offences Act 1967, ss 4, 5.
- Theft Act 1968, s 9 (where burglary with intent to rape).
- Criminal Law Act 1977, s 54.
- Protection of Children Act 1978, s 1.
- Customs and Excise Management Act 1979, s 170 (when related to prohibited goods under s 42 Customs Consolidation Act 1876 (indecent or obscene articles).
- Criminal Justice Act 1988, s 160.
- Sexual Offences Act 2003, ss 1–19 (including 15A) 25, 26, 30–41, 47–50, 52, 53, 57, 58, 59A, 61–70.
- Modern Slavery Act 2015, s 2 (where exploitation consist of or includes behaviour within s 3(3) (sexual exploitation)).
- Offences of aiding, abetting, counselling, procuring or inciting the commission of a sexual offence or an offence conspiring or attempting to commit such an offence.
- Part 2 Serious Crime Act 2007, in relation to which a specified sexual offence is the offence (or one of the offences) which the person intended or believed would have been committed.

12.167 The amended provisions only apply to offenders sentenced after the order came into force and do not apply to those aged under 18 at the time of sentence or those who receive a special custodial sentence (for offenders of particular concern).[163]

12.168 Practitioners and judges alike should be mindful of this Order. The mechanism of the amendment, whilst permissible, is rarely used. It amounts to a non-textual modification of primary legislation. Consequently, great care should be taken if relying upon the original statutory provision.

---

[162] The corresponding Schedule under the Sentencing Code is Sch 18, pt 2.
[163] Article 5, The Release of Prisoners (Alteration of Relevant Proportion of Sentence) Order 2020.

L. APPLICATION OF THE SENTENCING GUIDELINE AND RECENT CHANGES

12.169 The 'Sexual Offences' Definitive Guideline applies to all offenders aged 18 and older, who are sentenced on or after 1 April 2014. The guidelines are not reproduced in this Referencer; it is essential to access them online to ensure use of the most recent version.

12.170 The guideline applies only to offenders aged 18 and older. For offenders aged under 18, courts should follow the Guideline for Sentencing Children and Young People.[164] Annexes B and C deal with historic offences which may include offenders who were then under 18. Annex C is a reproduction of the information in the table created for and first published in this Referencer.[165]

12.171 The Sentencing Council Guidelines remain guidelines which should usually, but not exclusively, be followed.[166] To depart from the 'offence range' requires a finding that to do otherwise 'would be contrary to the interests of justice'; CAJA 2009. S125(1). Such a finding is not necessary in order to move outside the 'category range'.[167]

Section 59 Sentencing Act 2020

Sentencing guidelines: general duty of court

(1) Every court—
   (a) must, in sentencing an offender, follow any sentencing guidelines which are relevant to the offender's case, and
   (b) must, in exercising any other function relating to the sentencing of offenders, follow any sentencing guidelines which are relevant to the exercise of the function, unless the court is satisfied that it would be contrary to the interests of justice to do so.

12.172 The Definitive Guideline for Sexual Offences adopts the now familiar structure of the overarching principles of sentencing. It sets out 9 steps to be followed for each offence. In applying the guideline, it is important to bear in mind that it is concerned with sentence levels for a single offence. It follows that in respect of cases involving more than one offence, sentencers should ensure this is adequately reflected by the overall sentence subject to the principle of totality.

12.173 Part 1 of the guideline contains the Overarching Principles, which should not be overlooked when sentencing non-consensual offences. Many factors may be relevant to the level of culpability and the degree of harm suffered, including sexual offences committed by gangs or groups which is relevant to and increases both.

12.174 The Sentencing Council has issued a series of expanded explanations,[168] which supplement the General Guideline. These add extra information to aggravating and mitigating factors to make it easier for courts to maintain consistency and transparency in sentencing. They

---

[164] Effective from 1.6.2017.
[165] *Sexual Offences Referencer* 1st edn 2007, table created by Lucy Luttman, barrister.
[166] *A-G's Ref (No 21 of 2007) (R v Oakes)* [2007] All ER (D) 281 May 9.
[167] Martin Wasik, Sentencing: Recent Developments (2014).
[168] Implemented on 1.10.2019.

L. APPLICATION OF THE SENTENCING GUIDELINE AND RECENT CHANGES

1. Recent Changes to the Definitive Guidelines

Culpability when no sexual activity; *Reed & Others, Privett*

Equal culpability for remote offending when victim is overseas

New guideline for the offence of sexual communication with a child—s15A SOA 2003

12.175 The Definitive Guideline for Sexual Offences (published in 2013 and implemented on 1.4.2014).[169] They represented a significant change of approach from the 2007 Guideline; the guidelines are now tailored to deal with the specific offending behaviour. This is intended to be achieved by the structure for determining the level of harm caused and the level of culpability varying according to the offence(s) being considered.

12.176 In keeping with this approach, the Sentencing Council has revised the Definitive Guideline in accordance with the judgment in *Reed and Others*,[170] following *Privett*.[171]

The revisions to the guidelines stipulate that where no sexual activity takes place, the court should identify the category of harm on the basis of the sexual activity the offender intended and then adjust the starting point downwards to reflect what actually happened. The final sentence will be influenced by other aspects of the offender's culpability, as well as aggravating and mitigating factors specific to the offence and the offender.

12.177 Current sexual offences guidelines, published in 2013, had been interpreted in some cases to mean that harm should be considered low in these cases, or had placed the absence of actual harm to a child as a mitigating factor in cases where sexual activity was incited but did not actually occur.

See also from para 12.182 **Determining culpability when no sexual activity has taken place.**

12.178 Amongst other changes made by the Sentencing Council after consultation, child sexual offence guidelines now make clear the position that remote offending committed against victims overseas is to be treated as seriously as similar offending against victims in England and Wales.

12.179 As of 2021, a new guideline for the offence of sexual communication with a child (s 15A of the SOA) has been published. Offenders face a maximum penalty of 2 years in prison for sharing images, causing psychological harm, abuse of trust or the use of threats.

---

[169] Subject to updates in 2015, 2016, and 2017.
[170] *Reed and Others* [2021] EWCA Crim 572.
[171] *Privett* [2020] EWCA Crim 557.

2. Harm and Culpability

12.180 For most offences (including rape and sexual assault), harm and culpability[172] are assumed, from which lowest level one or more factors can move it to a higher category of harm or culpability with a higher staring point.

12.181 A different approach is adopted for offences such as meeting a child following sexual grooming (s 15); administering a substance with intent (s 61); trespass with intent to commit a sexual offence (s 63); sex with an adult relative (ss 64 and 65); exposure (s 66); and voyeurism (s 67); here, factors are identified which indicate a level of raised harm and/or culpability. Where both exist, they attract the highest starting points. A conflict arose in the approach to be adopted when determining culpability in a case where no sexual activity, for a variety of possible reasons, has taken place.

3. Determining Culpability When No Sexual Activity has Taken Place

12.182 There are a number of possible factual scenarios which can result in the commission of an offence where no sexual activity takes place and consequently no harm caused. Such cases include police operations involving online communications and self-styled 'paedophile hunters' where no victim ever existed, as well as cases where an attempt to engage with a real child sexually has either failed or been prevented. A number of factors complicate the approach to sentencing such offences, including that they are variously charged under different sections of the SOA 2003 which have different maximum sentences and different sentencing guidelines (or, in the case of s 14 no separate guideline, simply a reference to the applicable guideline for the substantive offence under ss 9–12).

12.183 The conflict (which arose from two contrasting lines of authority following *Privett*[173] and then *Manning* which itself followed the line of reasoning in *Baker*) as to the approach to be adopted when determining culpability in such a case where no harm has been caused, and so the correct starting point within the SGC Guideline, has now been addressed by the CACD in *Reed and others*,[174] following the judgment in *Privett*,[175] both courts led by Fulford LJ, Vice-President CACD. As a consequence, the SGC guideline has been revised in keeping with *Reed* and *Privett*.

12.184 Fulford LJ:

> [5] These six cases have been listed together to consider whether the reasoning in Privett should apply more widely to other offences under the SOA when the defendant has committed a sexual offence with, or in respect of, a person who is, or who the defendant believes to be, a child and no sexual activity occurs. Under consideration in this context are certain offences or attempted offences relating to:

---

[172] See also *R v Forbes*; ibid re: harm at [14]–[15] and culpability at [25] –[26].
[173] *Privett* [2020] EWCA Crim 557.
[174] *Reed and Others* [2021] EWCA Crim 572.
[175] Ibid.

L. APPLICATION OF THE SENTENCING GUIDELINE AND RECENT CHANGES 403

children under the age of 13, namely those of rape (section 5), assault by penetration (section 6), sexual assault (section 7) and causing or inciting a child under the age of 13 to engage in sexual activity (section 8);

children under the age of 16, namely those of sexual activity with a child (section 9), causing or inciting a child to engage in sexual activity (section 10), engaging in sexual activity in the presence of a child (section 11), causing a child to watch a sexual act (section 12), child sex offences committed by children or young persons (section 13), meeting a child following sexual grooming (section 15) and sexual communication with a child (section 15A); and

the sexual exploitation of children, namely paying for the sexual services of a child (section 47), causing or inciting the sexual exploitation of a child (section 48), controlling a child in relation to sexual exploitation (section 49) and arranging or facilitating the sexual exploitation of a child (section 50).

[23] The difference in approach as between *Privett* and *Baker*, which depends simply on the particular offence with which the accused has been charged, is unsustainable; it would mean that the assessment of harm would be markedly different in cases of grave sexual offending involving young people simply because of the particular section under which the perpetrator is charged. As already cited, the court in *Privett* observed '*(w)e recognise that aspects of the decision in Baker may well need to be revisited in light of this judgment*' (at [66]). This is an area in which injustice would undoubtedly result if the law is not able to develop. This decision will end the rigid distinction between those cases where particular sexual activity takes place and those cases where the defendant, for instance, does everything he is able to bring that sexual activity about but for reasons beyond his control it does not materialise. The sentencing judge should make an appropriate downward adjustment to recognise the fact that no sexual activity occurred, as demonstrated by the court in *Privett* (at [67]). Furthermore, we consider this approach should apply to all of the offences set out in [5] above when the defendant attempts to commit these offences or incites a child to engage in certain activity, but the activity does not take place. The harm should always be assessed in the first instance by reference to his or her intentions, followed by a downward movement from the starting point to reflect the fact that the sexual act did not occur, either because there was no real child or for any other reason.

[24] The extent of downward adjustment will depend on the facts of the case. Where an offender is only prevented from carrying out the offence at a late stage, or when the child victim did not exist and otherwise the offender would have carried out the offence, a small reduction within the category range will usually be appropriate. Where relevant, no additional reduction should be made for the fact that the offending is an attempt.

[25] But when an offender voluntarily desisted at an early stage, and particularly if the offending has been short-lived, a larger reduction is likely to be appropriate, potentially going outside the category range.

[26] As indicated in *Privett* at [72], it may eventuate that a more severe sentence is imposed in a case where very serious sexual activity was intended but did not take place than in a case where relatively less serious sexual activity did take place.

See para 1.51 for the postscript to the judgement (at [85]) in relation to ensuring greater clarity in drafting counts or charges of attempted offences. It encourages the inclusion of the

404   12. SENTENCING

substantive offence lying behind the attempt, not least to direct the sentencing judge's mind to the correct guideline.

4. Psychological harm

12.185 The court, in the case of *Chall and Others*[176] gave guidance on the approach to be taken by a sentencing judge when assessing whether a victim of crime has suffered severe psychological harm and the proper working of the Victim Personal Statement (VPS) scheme:

> Expert evidence is not an essential precondition of a finding that a victim has suffered severe psychological harm
>
> A judge may assess that such harm has been suffered on the basis of evidence from the victim, including evidence contained in a VPS and may rely on his or her observation of the victim whilst giving evidence.
>
> Whether a VPS provides evidence which is sufficient for a finding of severe psychological harm depends on the circumstances of the particular case and the contents of the VPS.
>
> A VPS must comply with the requirements of the Criminal Practice Direction and be served on the defence in sufficient time to enable them to consider its contents and decide how to address them. If late service gives rise to genuine problems for the defence, an application for an adjournment can be made.

Note also the case of *R v JM*[177] where it was held that 'severe psychological harm' need not be permanent and could be demonstrated by a serious suicide attempt.

M. GENERAL PRINCIPLES

12.186 *R v Forbes*[178] (also from para 12.136) which, whilst primarily concerned with sentencing historic sexual offences, also provides relevant guidance when sentencing for sexual offences generally.

12.187 **In relation to young offenders:** para 9 of Annex B of the Definitive Guidelines states: 'If the offender was very young and immature at the time of the offence, depending on the circumstances of the offence, this may be regarded as personal mitigation.' The court in *Forbes* preferred the dicta in *R v H* at [47(c)], expressing the view that immaturity goes to culpability stating, 'we consider that to be the approach that better accords with principle than the guidance given at paragraph 9 of Annex B' (see also para 12.137).

12.188 **Abuse of trust:** In *R v DO* [2014][179] the court stated:

> In our view the Sentencing Council did not intend that every case of rape within an established relationship should be treated as a breach of trust. Rather, the change was designed

---
[176] *R v Chall and Others* [2019] EWCA Crim 865 per Holroyde LJ. See also *Forbes* at paras 25–26.
[177] *R v J.M.* [2015] EWCA Crim 1638; [2016] 1 Cr App R (S) 21.
[178] *R v Forbes and Others* [2016] EWCA Crim 1388.
[179] *R v DO* [2014] EWCA Crim 2202 per HHJ Rooke QC at para 31.

so as to include circumstances where the offender may not hold a formal position in relation to the victim, but they have abused the trust engendered by their status and/or standing.

In *R v W* [2018][180] the judge had erred in interpreting *Forbes* (at [16]–[18]). *Forbes* said that an 'abuse of trust' might also include parental or quasi-parental relationships, or could arise from an ad hoc situation, for example a late-night taxi driver and a lone passenger. What was necessary was a close examination of the facts and a clear justification where an abuse of trust was found. Whilst the mere fact of a familiar relationship would not necessarily give rise to a position of trust, on the facts of the present case there had undoubtedly been a quasi-parental relationship between the victim and W. See also *R v Brant* [2018].[181]

1. Good Character and/or Exemplary Conduct

The Sentencing Guidelines provide: **12.189**

(i) Previous good character/exemplary conduct is different from having no previous convictions. The more serious the offence, the less the weight which should normally be attributed to this factor. Where previous good character/exemplary conduct has been used to facilitate the offence, this mitigation should not normally be allowed and such conduct may constitute an aggravating factor.

(ii) For offences attracting a maximum sentence of 14 years or over the Guideline additionally states:

In the context of this offence previous good character/exemplary conduct should not normally be given any significant weight and will not normally justify a reduction in what would otherwise be the appropriate sentence.

2. Good Character Since the Offences

Per Thomas LCJ in *R v Forbes & Others* dealing with historic offences: **12.190**

It is sometimes the case that offences have been committed whilst the offender was considerably younger and it is said that the offender has since that time been a man of good character. Paragraph 8 of Annex B provides:

[8.] Where there is an absence of further offending over a long period of time, especially combined with evidence of good character, this may be treated by the court as a mitigating factor. However, as with offences dealt with under the Sexual Offences Act 2003, previous good character/exemplary conduct is different from having no previous convictions. The more serious the offence, the less the weight which should normally be attributed to this factor. Where previous good character/exemplary conduct has been used to facilitate the offence, this mitigation should not normally be allowed and such conduct may constitute an aggravating factor.

---

[180] *R v W* [2018] EWCA Crim 265; [2018] 1 Cr App R (S) 55.
[181] *R v Brant (David Charles)* [2018] EWCA Crim 2800 at paras [14]–[15], where the defendant, a friend of the complainant's father and a frequent visitor to the home, was in an express position of trust.

As this paragraph makes clear, what is of material significance is proper evidence of positive good character. It is therefore necessary to examine carefully all the circumstances. For example, in the appeal of Clark, he committed the offences whilst teaching at a boys' boarding school; thereafter there was evidence that he had had very good qualities as a teacher and what was said to be a constructive life as an organ builder and volunteer organist. However we were not persuaded that this sufficed to amount to exemplary conduct (see paragraphs [77–79]). In the appeal of Tarrant, the evidence was that he established a positive life style (see paragraph [161]), but that was tempered by the fact that he had lent himself to a cover up (see paragraph [175]).

3. Ostensible or Apparent Consent

12.191 The Sentencing Council agreed with the statement of Pitchford LJ in *Attorney General's References (Nos 11 and 12 of 2012) (Channer and Monteiro)*,[182] that '"ostensible consent" and "willingness" are terms which, in the context of offences against the young in particular, are susceptible to misunderstanding and, even if accurately used, are liable to obscure the true nature of the encounter between the offender and the victim'. The new guideline moves away from the language of 'ostensible consent' so that the focus in relation to children aged between 13 and 15 is placed not on the behaviour of the victim but on the behaviour and culpability of the offender. Accordingly, harm is determined by the nature of the sexual activity involved, so avoiding the need to consider the child's behaviour or their understanding of their 'relationship' with the offender. The guideline places more emphasis on how the offender has persuaded the child to engage in the activity and obtained their apparent consent. Following on from the consideration given to 'remote offending' in *Prince*,[183] the guideline confirms that the approach to sentencing and the starting points and ranges apply equally where the offender commits the offence remotely over the internet.

12.192 In *Attorney General's Reference (No 53 of 2013)*,[184] a case which related to an offence of sexual activity with a child and the making of indecent images and possession of extreme images, the court made it clear that the purpose of the legislation making it a crime punishable with imprisonment to have sexual relations with those under 16 years was to protect those under 16. A reduction of punishment on the basis that the person who needed protection encouraged the commission of an offence is therefore simply wrong. An underage person who encourages sexual relations with her needs more protection, not less (at [20]). The victim's vulnerability was an aggravating rather than a mitigating feature.

4. The Need to Consider the Overall Picture

12.193 Whilst it should be appreciated that under the current guidelines a higher starting point would have been likely, an example of the need to look at the overall picture can be

---

[182] [2012] EWCA Crim 1119, at 34.
[183] [2013] EWCA Crim 1768.
[184] *R v Wilson* [2013] EWCA Crim 2544.

found in *Attorney General's Reference (No 107 of 2007)*.[185] The unpleasant threats and violence, accompanied by multiple acts of penetration, distinguished the case from a single offence of rape for which a 5-year sentence remained the appropriate starting point after a trial. The court sympathized with the trial judge in his conscientious attempt to make the case fit into one or more of the boxes provided by the guidelines. The court considered that the sentencing judge might not have stood back and looked at the overall picture. Whatever was the appropriate pigeonhole starting point, the court was satisfied that the appropriate sentence following a trial would have been in the region of 9 years.

5. Indecent Images

12.194 For offences involving indecent images of children, harm is assessed on the basis of the level of images involved. The Sentencing Council reduced the levels provided in *Oliver* from 5 to 3. Culpability is assessed on the basis of what the offender was doing with the images and is split into three categories: possession, distribution and production. The categories are:

Category A: this broadly coincides with *Oliver* levels 4 and 5 (images involving penetrative sexual activity, sexual activity with an animal and sadism).
Category B: this broadly coincides with *Oliver* level 3 (images involving non-penetrative activity).
Category C: this covers other indecent images not falling within either A or B.

12.195 The guideline states that

[i]n most cases the intrinsic character of the most serious of the offending images will initially determine the appropriate category. If, however, the most serious images are unrepresentative of the offender's conduct a lower category may be appropriate. A lower category will not, however, be appropriate if the offender has produced or taken (for example photographed) images of higher category.

In determining the 'appropriate category' the guideline does not require a mathematical or ratio apportioning exercise. It requires an exercise of judgment by the court in following the approach set out in the guideline.[186] See also *R v Bateman* [2020][187] for the correct approach to categorization of 'hybrid' images which could be categorized fall into either the production or possession category.

12.196 For offences of possession of extreme images (s 83 CJIA 2008) see *R v Oliver* [2011][188] in which it was stated that offences of possession of extreme pornographic images, whilst serious, were not to be equated with the seriousness of images of children.

---

[185] [2008] EWCA Crim 198.
[186] *R v Pinkerton* [2017] EWCA Crim 38, per Treacy LJ at para 17.
[187] *R v Bateman (Paul Michael)* EWCA Crim 1333.
[188] *R v Oliver* [2011] EWCA Crim 3114.

Greater focus on harm to the victim whether physical and/or psychological

12.197 Vulnerability of the victim is treated as a major indicator of harm. Whilst every child is vulnerable, the personal circumstances of some will render them acutely so. This would place them in the highest category for a s 5 rape of a child under 13 offence. For assessment of psychological harm see *R v Chall* (para 12.185).

Grooming

12.198 An appreciation of the greater culpability of an offender who grooms his victim(s) and/or uses the internet to facilitate sex offending is reflected by the guideline. See also the relatively new offence of 'sexual communication with a child' (Chapter 4).

Cultural differences

12.199 Cultural differences provide no mitigation of rape; *MA* [2012] EWCA Crim 1646. The fact that the offender had been brought up in Pakistan to believe that he had a right to rape his wife was no basis for leniency.

Increase in sentencing levels for some offences of rape and assault by penetration

12.200 Where an offender is convicted of a campaign of rape, against single or multiple victims, a sentence of 20 years or more should now be passed. Sentences of such length are not confined only to 'campaign' cases, see *R v JH* [2015][189] and *R v Forbes*[190] for examples of appropriate offending falling into this category. In addition, the starting point for a single offence will be 15 years if its nature reflects Category 1 harm together with higher culpability. The most serious cases of s 2 assault by penetration may attract similar levels of sentence as rape because of the physical harm that will be caused when large or dangerous objects have been used by the offender. Sexual offences involving penetration of a child under 13 are Offences of Particular Concern. See paras 12.101 *et seq*.

6. Sentencing Adult Offenders with Mental or Developmental Disorders or Neurological Impairments

12.201 On 22.07.2020 the Sentencing Council published a new guideline, 'Overarching Principles: Sentencing Offenders with Mental Disorders, Developmental Disorders, or Neurological Impairments'. The guideline applies only to offenders aged 18 and over, who are sentenced on or after 1.10.2020, regardless of the date of the offence. This guideline does not apply to offenders under the age of 18, as mental health and related issues can be substantially different in both diagnosis and impact for children and young people. Courts should instead refer to the Sentencing Children and Young People Guideline,

12.202 For recent guidance discussing the advantages and disadvantages of hybrid orders under s 45A MHA 1983 see *R v Nelson* [2020][191] and *R v Reynolds* [2021][192] for an example of s 45A MHA order properly imposed on an offender convicted of sexual offences.

---

[189] *R v JH* [2015] EWCA Crim 54; [2015] 1 Cr App R (S) 59 at p. 409.
[190] Ibid, at *Forbes* para 197.
[191] *R v Nelson* (Keith) [2020] EWCA Crim 1615.
[192] *R v Reynolds* [2021] EWCA Crim 10.

7. Sentencing Children and Young People with Mental Health Disorders

12.203 The 'Sentencing Offenders with Mental Health Disorders, Developmental Disorders or Neurological Impairments' Definitive Guideline, effective from 1.10.2020 only applies to offenders aged 18 or over. Regard should be had to *R v PS, CF, Abdi Hadir* [2019][193] which clarifies the situation when children (in the cases of PS and CF) who are affected by autism or other mental health conditions or disorders fall to be sentenced.

N. SENTENCING CHILDREN AND YOUNG PEOPLE

12.204 In cases involving those aged under 18 the court must have regard to the following two principles:

> The welfare of the child or young person and shall in a proper case take steps for removing him from undesirable surroundings, and for securing that proper provision is made for his education and training (Children and Young Persons Act 1933 s 44). It shall be the principal aim of the youth justice system to prevent offending by children and young persons (Crime and Disorder Act 1998, s 37(1)).

These considerations remain unaffected by the Sentencing Code.[194]

12.205 The 'Sexual Offences' Definitive Guideline applies only to offenders aged 18 and over.

On 7.03.2017 the Sentencing Council published a new guideline for sentencing children and young people,[195] the 'Sentencing Children and Young People: Overarching Principles' Definitive Guideline. The guideline replaces the Sentencing Guidelines Council's 'Overarching Principles—Sentencing Youths' published in November 2009. The guideline incorporates offence-specific guidelines for sexual offences and offences of robbery. The new Sexual Offences Guideline replaced the 2007 'Sexual Offences Definitive Guideline in Relation to Youths

12.206 The Definitive Guideline (and offence-specific guidelines) apply to all under young persons (under 18 years) sentenced on or after 1.06.2017, regardless of the date of the offence. It applies equally in the Youth Court, the Magistrates' Court and the Crown Court. In accordance with s 125(1) of the CAJA 2009 or s 59(1) of the Sentencing Code when sentencing offenders convicted after 1.12.2020, the court must follow any sentencing guidelines which are relevant to the offenders case unless satisfied that it would be contrary to the interests of justice to do so.

12.207 The overarching guideline is split into six sections: (1) General approach; (2) Allocation; (3) Parental responsibilities; (4) Determining the sentence; (5) Guilty plea and (6) Available sentences. There is an appendix which deals with the breach of orders. The first section sets out the principles to be applied generally when sentencing children and young people. At

---

[193] *R v PS, CF, Abdi Hadir* [2019] EWCA Crim 2286.
[194] SA 2020, s 58.
[195] The terminology of 'youth' and 'young offender' in the former guidelines have been replaced with 'children and young people'.

the forefront of the principles are the statutory requirements of prevention and the welfare of the child or young person (para 12.128). The seriousness of the offence continues to be the starting point but the Guideline states that the approach to sentencing should not be offence-focused; it should be individualistic and focused on the child or young person (para 1.2). There is now a much wider emphasis on consideration of the background of the child or young person, their circumstances and vulnerabilities; the transient nature of offending in some children and young people; the very real impact of sentences on children and young people as compared to adult offenders including to their education (paras 1.16–1.18). Consideration must also be given to the factors and issues relevant to children from deprived or abusive and/or neglectful backgrounds (para 1.13), and black and ethnic minority and looked-after children and young adults, who are over resented in the youth justice system; and the impact of particular sentences upon them (paras 1.16–1.18). Sentencers are reminded that a custodial sentence should always be a measure of last resort for children and young people (para 1.3) and of the importance of avoiding criminalizing children and young people unnecessarily. 'The primary purpose of the youth justice system is to encourage children and young people to take responsibility for their own actions and promote re-integration into society rather than to punish.'

12.208 The Definitive Guideline specific to sexual offences should be read alongside the 'Sentencing Children and Young People—Overarching Principles' Definitive Guideline.

12.209 The Definitive Sexual Offence Guideline sets out that

> sentencing a child or young person for sexual offences involves a number of different considerations from adults. The primary difference is the age and level of maturity. Children and young people are less emotionally developed than adults; offending can arise through inappropriate sexual experimentation; gang or peer group pressure to engage in sexual activity; or a lack of understanding regarding consent, exploitation, coercion and appropriate sexual behaviour.

12.210 The guideline emphasizes that sentencing a child or young person for sexual offences involves a number of different considerations from adults. The primary difference is the age and level of maturity. Children and young people are less emotionally developed than adults; offending can arise through inappropriate sexual experimentation; gang or peer group pressure to engage in sexual activity; or a lack of understanding regarding consent, exploitation, coercion and appropriate sexual behaviour. It goes on to identify a number of non-exhaustive background factors which may have given rise to the offending including neglect or abuse; exposure to pornography; involvement in gangs; association with child exploitation; unstable living or educational arrangements; communication: learning or mental health difficulties or concerns; part of a group where harmful sexual norms and attitudes prevail, or a trigger event.

12.211 The 'Sexual Offences—Sentencing Children and Young People' Definitive Guideline introduces a 5-step sentencing process. The first two steps determine the seriousness of the offence. **The fact that a sentence threshold is crossed does not necessarily mean that that sentence should be imposed.**

(1) Step 1: Sentencers must first assess seriousness based on the nature of the offence, by applying a short (but not exhaustive) list of the type of culpability and harm factors

N. SENTENCING CHILDREN AND YOUNG PEOPLE

to determine whether a particular sentence threshold has been crossed. The offence will then fall within a custodial (custodial/YO with ISS or with fostering) or non-custodial bracket which *may* be appropriate.

(2) Step 2: The second step in determining the overall seriousness of the offence is to consider the aggravating and mitigating factors relevant to the offence in the usual way. The guideline makes explicit that the fact that a sentence threshold is crossed does not necessarily mean that that sentence should be imposed.

(3) Step 3: Having completed the overall assessment of seriousness the sentence moves on to consider the personal mitigation of the child or young person to determine whether a custodial sentence or a community sentence is necessary. It is recognized that personal mitigation may reduce what would otherwise be a custodial sentence to a non-custodial one, or a community sentence to a different means of disposal.

(4) Step 4: The court should take account of any potential reduction for a guilty plea in accordance with s 144 of the Criminal Justice Act 2003 and part one, s 5 of the 'Sentencing Children and Young People' Definitive Guideline. Unlike with adult offenders, the reduction in sentence for a guilty plea can be taken into account by imposing one type of sentence rather than another for example could mean the difference between a custodial and community sentence.

(5) Step 5: The final step requires that the court must review the sentence to ensure it is the most appropriate one for the child or young person. This will include an assessment of the likelihood of reoffending and the risk of causing serious harm. A report from the Youth Offending Team may assist.

The guideline goes on to suggest a length range for referral orders, when appropriate, and the intensity and content of YROs and YROs with ISS or fostering, based on the determination of seriousness. Where a custodial sentence is unavoidable: **12.212**

> the court must state its reasons for being satisfied that the offence is so serious that no other sanction would be appropriate and, in particular, why a YRO with ISS or fostering could not be justified.
>
> the length of custody imposed must be the shortest commensurate with the seriousness of the offence. The court may want to consider the equivalent adult guideline in order to determine the appropriate length of the sentence.

The guideline provides that when considering the adult guideline, the court may feel it appropriate to apply a sentence broadly within the region of half to two thirds of the appropriate adult sentence for those aged 15–17 and allow a greater reduction for those aged under 15. However, it makes clear that this is only a rough guide and must not be applied mechanistically. The individual factors relating to the offence and the child or young person are of the greatest importance and may present good reason to impose a sentence outside of this range. In most cases when considering the appropriate reduction from the adult sentence the emotional and developmental age and maturity of the child or young person is of at least equal importance as their chronological age.[196] **12.213**

---

[196] Final sentence added from para 6.46 Sentencing Children and Young People: Overarching Principles.

12.214 The latest guidelines afford the sentencer substantially more discretion than for adult.

12.215 In *PS; Abdi Dahir; CF* [2019][197] in relation to *CF* it was held that it is inappropriate to sentence an offender under 18 for an offence of causing a child under 13 to engage in sexual activity largely by reference to the adult offence-specific guideline for that offence as, first the sentencing levels in that guideline take into account the inevitable difference in age between an adult offender and the child victim [73]; and secondly, s 13 of the 2003 Act has the effect that for offences contrary to ss 9–12 of the 2003 Act, the maximum sentence for a young offender is limited to 5 years' custody, rather than the 14- and 10-year maxima applicable to adult offenders. That provision does not apply to offences contrary to s 8 but the court took the view it was another statutory recognition that when dealing with sexual offending, the court must be careful not to treat the young offender as if he or she were simply a reduced-size version of an adult offender committing similar offences [74].

1. Factors Not Envisaged by the Sentencing Council Guidelines

12.216 When an SC Guideline presumes, for example, consensual sexual activity but the facts demonstrate otherwise, the guideline will not apply. Although the question of consent is not expressly dealt with in the guideline (presumably because it is not an ingredient of the offence), Category 1 provides a higher starting point and range. An example of this is to be found (using the pre-2013 guideline) in *R v Jones* [2009].[198] The defendant was convicted of sexual activity with a person with a mental disorder by a care worker (s 38 of the SOA 2003). He was a 22-year-old male care worker working in a care home, the victim was a woman aged 76 with severe dementia. The offender had taken the victim to her bedroom for the purposes of putting her to bed and shortly afterwards activated an emergency alarm. The victim was removed to hospital where it was found that she had severe tears to the perineum. The medical evidence was that the injuries had most likely been caused by the insertion into her vagina of a penis or similar object. D denied that he was responsible. He was a man of previous good character with significant learning difficulties. Sentenced to 9 years' imprisonment. Held:

The sentencing judge had considered the (then) Sentencing Guidelines Council Guidelines in relation to sexual offences. The guidelines proceeded on the basis that the sexual activity was essentially consensual, while in the present case it plainly was not; the guidelines were therefore of no particular assistance. The maximum penalty for the offence was 14 years' imprisonment. The sentencing judge made it clear that the guidelines were not applicable to the offence with which he was dealing. In the court's judgment, the sentencing judge was correct to conclude that the guidelines did not apply. The question for the court was whether in all the circumstances the sentence of 9 years was manifestly excessive. In the court's view, the proper sentence, reflecting to the gravity of the offending balanced against the factors in favour of the appellant, would have been 7 years' imprisonment and a sentence of 7 years' imprisonment would be substituted.

---

[197] Ibid.
[198] [2009] EWCA Crim 237.

O. ORDERS AND REQUIREMENTS AFTER CONVICTION

1. The Children and Adult Barring Lists

Barring from working with children and vulnerable adults
Sections 26–34 of the CJCSA have been fully repealed and replaced with effect from 17.06.2013 (Safeguarding Vulnerable Groups Act 2006 (Commencement No 8 and Saving) Order 2012 No 2231). The role of disqualifying an offender from working with children or vulnerable adults now lies with the Disclosure and Barring Service (the replacement to the Independent Safeguarding Authority) (s 87(1) of the Protection of Freedoms Act 2012).[199]

12.217

The role of the judge[200] is now to inform the offender that the Disclosure and Barring Service (DBS) either *will* or *may* be barred, depending on where the offence is found within Part 2 of the Safeguarding Vulnerable Groups Act 2006 (Prescribed Criteria and Miscellaneous Provisions) Regulations 2009 (SI 2009 No 37). For some offences (known as automatic inclusion offences, as opposed to automatic barring offences) the offender is able to make representations to the DBS after conviction/caution, but before he or she is placed on the list; hence, *may* be barred. See para 12.137 for offences which attract automatic barring without the right to make representations (*will* be barred) and for offences in respect of which an offender can make representations (*may* be barred). The court should inform the defendant which list he or she will be included on and under what legislation. In addition, a defendant should be told whether or not they can make representations to be removed from the list.

12.218

Suggested form of words: 'You (may/)will be made subject to the barring regulations under the Safeguarding Vulnerable Groups Act 2006 and (may/)will be placed on the adult/children's list (subject to your right to make representations to be removed from that list).'

2. The Lists of Offences Attracting Automatic Inclusion

There are four lists: two in relation to working with children and two in relation to working with adults. All offences listed are 'automatically included' but not all attract automatic barring. Each pair is divided between those offences in respect of which the offender can make representations as to why he or she should not be placed on the list and those in respect of which they cannot and so barring is automatic.

12.219

Note: these lists are subject to change as the legislation is amended and updated.

Automatically included in the children's barred list with no right to make representations to be removed (Will be Barred)

---

[199] (Commencement No 4) Order 2012 (SI 2012 No 2521).
[200] CPR 2020, r 28(3).

12.220 An offender will be barred automatically from working with children in a regulated activity with no right to make representations to the DBS if convicted of an offence falling within Schedule 1, para 1 of the Regulation, namely:[201]

> s 4 CLA 1885 Carnal knowledge of a girl under 13
>
> s 1 SOA 1956 Rape (where the victim was a child)
>
> s 5 SOA 1956 Sexual intercourse with a girl under 13
>
> s 128 MHA 1959 Sexual intercourse with a mentally disordered patient (where the victim was a child)
>
> s 1 SOA 2003 Rape (where the victim was a child)
>
> s 2 SOA 2003 Assault by penetration (where the victim was a child)
>
> s 5 SOA 2003 Rape of a child under 13
>
> s 6 SOA 2003 Assault of a child under 13 by penetration
>
> s 7 SOA 2003 Sexual assault of a child under 13
>
> s 8 SOA 2003 Causing or inciting a child under 13 to engage in sexual activity
>
> s 30 SOA 2003 Sexual activity with a person with a mental disorder impeding choice (where the victim was a child)
>
> s 31 SOA 2003 Causing or inciting a person with a mental disorder impeding choice, to engage in sexual activity (where the victim was a child)
>
> s 32 SOA 2003 Engaging in sexual activity in the presence of a person with a mental disorder impeding choice (where the victim was a child)
>
> s 33 SOA 2003 Causing a person, with a mental disorder impeding choice, to watch a sexual act (where the victim was a child)
>
> s 34 SOA 2003 Inducement, threat or deception to procure sexual activity with a person with a mental disorder (where the victim was a child)
>
> s 35 SOA 2003 Causing a person with a mental disorder to engage in or agree to engage in sexual activity by inducement, threat or deception (where the victim was a child)
>
> s 36 SOA 2003 Engaging in sexual activity in the presence, procured by inducement, threat or deception, of a person with a mental disorder (where the victim was a child)
>
> s 37 SOA 2003 Causing a person with a mental disorder to watch a sexual act by inducement, threat or deception (where the victim was a child)
>
> s 38 SOA 2003 Care workers: sexual activity with a person with a mental disorder (where the victim was a child)
>
> s 39 SOA 2003 Care workers: causing or inciting sexual activity (where the victim was a child)
>
> s 40 SOA 2003 Care workers: sexual activity in the presence of a person with a mental disorder (where the victim was a child)
>
> s 41 SOA 2003 Care workers: causing a person with a mental disorder to watch a sexual act (where the victim was a child)
>
> Any offence contrary to s 70 Army Act 1955; s 70 Air Force Act 1955; s 42 Naval Discipline Act 1957 or s 42 Armed Forces Act 1957 which corresponds to an offence under the provisions of Part 1 or 2 (all of the above offences)

---

[201] Safeguarding Vulnerable Groups Act 2006 (Prescribed Criteria and Miscellaneous Provisions) Regulations 2009/37, reg 3 and Sch 1, para 1.

Automatically included in the children's barred list with right to make representations to be removed (May be Barred)

An offender will be barred automatically from working with children in a regulated activity, but with a right to make representations to the DBS if convicted of an offence falling within Schedule 1, para 2 of the Regulation, namely:[202]

12.221

Common Law Offences:
Murder
Kidnapping
Infanticide
s 21 OAPA 1861 Attempt to choke, suffocate/strangle in order to commit or assist in the commission of any indictable offence
s 52 OAPA 1861 Indecent assault upon a female
s 53 OAPA 1861 Fraudulent abduction of a girl under age against the will of her father
s 54 OAPA 1861 Forcible abduction of any woman with intent to marry or carnally know her
s 55 OAPA 1861 Abduction of a girl under 16 years of age
s 61 OAPA 1861 Buggery (where the victim was under 16 or did not consent)
s 62 OAPA 1861 Indecent assault upon a male, attempt to commit buggery, assault with intent to commit buggery (where the victim was under 16 or did not consent)
s 2 CLAA 1885 Procuration
s 3 CLAA 1885 Procuring defilement of a woman by threats or fraud or administering drugs
s 5 CLAA 1885 Defilement of a girl under 17 years of age
s 6 CLAA 1885 Householder permitting defilement of young girl on his premises
s 7 CLAA 1885 Abduction of a girl under 18 with intent to have carnal knowledge
s 8 CLAA 1885 Unlawful detention with intent to have carnal knowledge
s 11 CLAA 1885 Outrages on decency (where the victim was under 16 or did not consent, and the conviction has not been disregarded under Chapter 4 of Part 5 of the Protection of Freedoms Act 2012)
s 1 Vagrancy Act 1898 Trading in prostitution
s 1 Punishment of Incest Act 1908 Incest by males (where the victim was a child)
s 2 Punishment of Incest Act 1908 Incest by females aged 16 or over (where the victim was a child)
s 1 C&YPA 1933 Cruelty to children
s 1 Infanticide Act 1938 Infanticide
s 1 SOA 1956 Rape (where the victim was an adult)
s 2 SOA 1956 Procurement of a woman by threats
s 3 SOA 1956 Procurement of a woman by false pretences
s 4 SOA 1956 Administering drugs to obtain or facilitate intercourse
s 6 SOA 1956 Sexual intercourse with a girl under 16
s 7 SOA 1956 Intercourse with a defective

---

[202] Safeguarding Vulnerable Groups Act 2006 (Prescribed Criteria and Miscellaneous Provisions) Regulations 2009 (SI 2009 No 37), Reg 4 and Sch 1, para 2.

- s 9 SOA 1956 Procurement of a defective
- s 10 SOA 1956 Incest by a man (where the victim was a child)
- s 11 SOA 1956 Incest by a woman (where the victim was a child)
- s 12 SOA 1956 Buggery (where the victim was under 16 or did not consent, and the conviction has not been disregarded under Chapter 4 of Part 5 of the Protection of Freedoms Act 2012)
- s 13 SOA 1956 Indecency between men (where the victim was under 16 or did not consent, and the conviction has not been disregarded under Chapter 4 of Part 5 of the Protection of Freedoms Act 2012)
- s 14 SOA 1956 Indecent assault on a woman
- s 15 SOA 1956 Indecent assault on a man
- s 16 SOA 1956 Assault with intent to commit buggery
- s 17 SOA 1956 Abduction of a woman by force or for the sake of her property
- s 19 SOA 1956 Abduction of unmarried girl under 18
- s 20 SOA 1956 Abduction of unmarried girl under 16
- s 21 SOA 1956 Abduction of defective from parent or guardian
- s 22 SOA 1956 Causing prostitution of women
- s 23 SOA 1956 Procurement of girl under 21
- s 24 SOA 1956 Detention of a woman in a brothel or other premises
- ss 25 and 26 SOA 1956 Permitting girl, under 13, or between 13 and 16, to use premises for intercourse
- s 27 SOA 1956 Permitting defective to use premises for intercourse
- s 28 SOA 1956 Causing or encouraging prostitution of, intercourse with or indecent assault on girl under 16
- s 29 SOA 1956 Causing or encouraging prostitution of defective
- s 30 SOA 1956 Man living on earnings of prostitution
- s 31 SOA 1956 Woman exercising control over prostitute
- s 128 MHA 1959 Sexual intercourse with a mentally disordered patient
- s 1 IwCA 1960 Indecency with children under 16
- s 4 SOA 1967 Procuring others to commit homosexual acts
- s 5 SOA 1967 Living on the earnings of male prostitution
- s 9(1)(a) Theft Act 1968 Burglary (with intent to commit rape)
- s 4(3) Misuse of Drugs Act 1971 Supply or offer to supply of controlled drugs (where the supply or offer was to a child)
- s 54 CLA 1977 Inciting girl under 16 to have incestuous sexual intercourse
- s 1 Protection of Children Act 1978 Taking, possessing, distributing, publishing etc indecent photographs of children
- s 170 Customs and Excise Management Act 1979 Fraudulent evasion of duty re importation of obscene material
- s 127 MHA 1983 Ill-treatment or wilful neglect of a patient with a mental disorder
- s 1 Child Abduction Act 1984 Abduction of a child by parent
- s 2 Child Abduction Act 1984 Abduction of child by other persons
- s 160 CJA 1988 Possession of indecent photographs of children
- s 3 SO(A)A 2000 Sexual activity with person under 18 in abuse of trust
- s 145 Nationality, Immigration and Asylum Act 2002 Traffic in prostitution

O. ORDERS AND REQUIREMENTS AFTER CONVICTION

s 1 Female Genital Mutilation Act 2003 Carrying out female genital mutilation (where the victim was a child)

s 2 Female Genital Mutilation Act 2003 Aiding, abetting, counselling or procuring a girl to mutilate her own genitals (where the victim was a child)

s 3 Female Genital Mutilation Act 2003 Aiding, abetting, counselling or procuring a non-UK person to mutilate overseas a girl's genitals (where the victim was a child)

s 1 SOA 2003 Rape (where the victim was an adult)

s 2 SOA 2003 Assault by penetration (where the victim was an adult)

s 3 SOA 2003 Sexual assault

s 4 SOA 2003 Causing a person to engage in sexual activity without consent

s 4(1A) SOA 2003 Trafficking people for labour and other exploitation

s 9 SOA 2003 Sexual activity with a child

s 10 SOA 2003 Causing or inciting a child to engage in sexual activity

s 11 SOA 2003 Engaging in sexual activity in the presence of a child

s 12 SOA 2003 Causing a child to watch a sexual act

s 14 SOA 2003 Arranging or facilitating commission of a child sex offence

s 15 SOA 2003 Meeting a child following sexual grooming

s 16 SOA 2003 Abuse of a position of trust: sexual activity with a child

s 17 SOA 2003 Abuse of a position of trust: causing or inciting a child to engage in sexual activity

s 18 SOA 2003 Abuse of position of trust: sexual activity in the presence of a child

s 19 SOA 2003 Abuse of position of trust: causing a child to watch a sexual act

s 25 SOA 2003 Sexual activity with a child family member

s 26 SOA 2003 Inciting a child family member to engage in sexual activity

s 30 SOA 2003 Sexual activity with a person with a mental disorder impeding choice (where the victim was an adult)

s 31 SOA 2003 Causing or inciting a person, with a mental disorder impeding choice, to engage in sexual activity (where the victim was an adult)

s 32 SOA 2003 Engaging in sexual activity in the presence of a person with a mental disorder impeding choice (where the victim was an adult)

s 33 SOA 2003 Causing a person, with a mental disorder impeding choice, to watch a sexual act (where the victim was an adult)

s 34 SOA 2003 Inducement, threat or deception to procure sexual activity with a person with a mental disorder (where the victim was an adult)

s 35 SOA 2003 Causing a person with a mental disorder to engage in/agree to engage in sexual activity by inducement, threat or deception (where the victim was an adult)

s 36 SOA 2003 Engaging in sexual activity in the presence, procured by inducement, threat or deception, of a person with a mental disorder (where the victim was an adult)

s 37 SOA 2003 Causing a person with a mental disorder to watch a sexual act by inducement, threat or deception (where the victim was an adult)

s 38 SOA 2003 Care workers: sexual activity with a person with a mental disorder (where the victim was an adult)

s 39 SOA 2003 Care workers: causing or inciting sexual activity (where the victim was an adult)

s 40 SOA 2003 Care workers: sexual activity in the presence of a person with a mental disorder (where the victim was an adult) s 41 SOA 2003 Care workers: causing a person with a mental disorder to watch a sexual act (where the victim was an adult)

s 47 SOA 2003 Paying for sexual services of a child

s 48 SOA 2003 Causing or inciting child prostitution or pornography

s 49 SOA 2003 Controlling a child prostitute or a child involved in pornography

s 50 SOA 2003 Arranging or facilitating child prostitution or pornography

s 52 SOA 2003 Causing or inciting prostitution for gain

s 53 SOA 2003 Controlling prostitution for gain

s 57 SOA 2003 Trafficking into the UK for sexual exploitation

s 58 SOA 2003 Trafficking within the UK for sexual exploitation

s 59 SOA 2003 Trafficking out of the UK for sexual exploitation

s 59A SOA 2003 Trafficking people for sexual exploitation

s 61 SOA 2003 Administering a substance with intent

ss 62 and 63 SOA 2003 Committing an offence or trespassing with intent to commit a sexual offence (where that offence leads to automatic barring)

s 66 SOA 2003 Exposure (where the victim was under 16)

s 67 SOA 2003 Voyeurism (where the victim was under 16)

s 72 SOA 2003 Sexual offences committed outside the UK (corresponding to an offence which leads to automatic barring from work with children with the right to make representations)

s 4 Asylum and Immigration (Treatment of Claimants) Act 2004 Trafficking people for exploitation

s 5 Domestic Violence, Crime and Victims Act 2004 Causing or allowing a child or vulnerable adult to die, or suffer serious physical harm

s 44 Mental Capacity Act 2005 Ill-treatment or wilful neglect

s 63 Criminal Justice and Immigration Act 2008 Possession of extreme pornographic images

s 62 CAJA 2009 Possession of prohibited images of children

s 2 Modern Slavery Act 2015 Human trafficking

Any offence contrary to s 70 Army Act 1955; s 70 Air Force Act 1955; s 42 Naval Discipline Act 1957 or s 42 Armed Forces Act 1957 which corresponds to an offence under the provisions in Part 1 or 2 (all of the above offences)

Automatic inclusion in the adults' barred list with no right to make representations to be removed (Will be Barred)

12.222 An offender will be barred automatically from working in a regulated activity related to vulnerable adults with no right to make representations to the DBS if convicted of an offence falling within Schedule 1, para 3 of the Regulation, namely:[203]

s 30 SOA 2003 Sexual activity with a person with a mental disorder impeding choice

s 31 SOA 2003 Causing or inciting a person, with a mental disorder impeding choice, to engage in sexual activity

---

[203] Safeguarding Vulnerable Groups Act 2006 (Prescribed Criteria and Miscellaneous Provisions) Regulations 2009 (SI 2009 No 37), reg 5 and Sch 1, para 3.

s 32 SOA 2003 Engaging in sexual activity in the presence of a person with a mental disorder impeding choice

s 33 SOA 2003 Causing a person, with a mental disorder impeding choice, to watch a sexual act

s 34 SOA 2003 Inducement, threat or deception to procure sexual activity with a person with a mental disorder

s 35 SOA 2003 Causing a person with a mental disorder to engage in or agree to engage in sexual activity by inducement, threat or deception

s 36 SOA 2003 Engaging in sexual activity in the presence, procured by inducement, threat or deception, of a person with a mental disorder

s 37 SOA 2003 Causing a person with a mental disorder to watch a sexual act by inducement, threat or deception

s 38 SOA 2003 Care workers: sexual activity with a person with a mental disorder

s 39 SOA 2003 Care workers: causing or inciting sexual activity

s 40 SOA 2003 Care workers: sexual activity in the presence of a person with a mental disorder

s 41 SOA 2003 Care workers: causing a person with a mental disorder to watch a sexual act

Any offence contrary to s 70 Army Act 1955; s 70 Air Force Act 1955; s 42 Naval Discipline Act 1957 or s 42 Armed Forces Act 1957 which corresponds to an offence under the provisions of Part 1 or 2 (all of the above offences)

Automatic inclusion in the adults' barred list with the right to make representations to be removed (May be Barred)

12.223 An offender will be barred automatically from working with vulnerable adults, but with a right to make representations to the DBS if convicted of an offence falling within Schedule 1, para 4 of the Regulation, namely:[204]

As per the children's list with the right to make representations at para 12.139 with the following additions (which offences appear in the children's list of offences in respect of which no representations can be made):

s 4 CLAA 1885 Defilement of a girl under 14 years of age
s 6 SOA 1956 Sexual intercourse with a girl under 16
s 5 SOA 2003 Rape of a child under 13
s 6 SOA 2003 Assault of a child under 13 by penetration
s 7 SOA 2003 Sexual assault of a child under 13
s 8 SOA 2003 Causing a inciting a child under 13 to engage in sexual activity

but not including the following offences (which offences do appear at para 12.139):

s 30 SOA 2003 Sexual activity with a person with a mental disorder impeding choice (where the victim was an adult)

---

[204] Safeguarding Vulnerable Groups Act 2006 (Prescribed Criteria and Miscellaneous Provisions) Regulations 2009 (SI 2009 No 37), Regulation 6, Schedule 1, para 4.

s 31 SOA 2003 Causing or inciting a person, with a mental disorder impeding choice, to engage in sexual activity (where the victim was an adult)

s 32 SOA 2003 Engaging in sexual activity in the presence of a person with a mental disorder impeding choice (where the victim was an adult)

s 33 SOA 2003 Causing a person, with a mental disorder impeding choice, to watch a sexual act (where the victim was a adult)

s 34 SOA 2003 Inducement, threat or deception to procure sexual activity with a person with a mental disorder (where the victim was an adult)

s 35 SOA 2003 Causing a person with a mental disorder to engage in/agree to engage in sexual activity by inducement, threat or deception (where the victim was an adult)

s 36 SOA 2003 Engaging in sexual activity in the presence, procured by inducement, threat or deception, of a person with a mental disorder (where the victim was an adult)

s 37 SOA 2003 Causing a person with a mental disorder to watch a sexual act by inducement, threat or deception (where the victim was an adult)

s 38 SOA 2003 Care workers: sexual activity with a person with a mental disorder (where the victim was an adult)

s 39 SOA 2003 Care workers: causing or inciting sexual activity (where the victim was an adult)

s 40 SOA 2003 Care workers: sexual activity in the presence of a person with a mental disorder (where the victim was an adult)

s 41 SOA 2003 Care workers: causing a person with a mental disorder to watch a sexual act (where the victim was an adult)

3. Restraining Orders

Sentencing Act 2020, s 359 and Protection from Harassment Act 1997, s 5A.

12.224 Restraining Orders under s 5A of the Sexual Offenders Act 1997 were repealed by the SOA 2003 and replaced by Sexual Offences Prevention Orders (SOPOs). On 8.03.015 SOPOs were replaced with Sexual Harm Prevention Orders (SHPOs).[205] See Chapter 16.

However, a restraining order can be made under s 360 SA 2020 on conviction for any offence. The order must protect 'the victim or victims of the offence, or any other person mentioned in the order, from conduct which—

(a) amounts to harassment, or
(b) will cause a fear of violence.'[206]

12.225 In most sexual cases a SHPO would seem to continue to be the most appropriate way of restraining the defendant from further prohibited activity. However, there will be cases where a Restraining Order, made on conviction, is the more appropriate order due to

---

[205] Anti-Social Behaviour, Crime and Policing Act 2014 c 12 Sch 5 para 2 (8.03.2015: insertion has effect as SI 2015/373 subject to savings and transitional provisions as specified in 2014 c 12 s 114). From 1.12.2020 SHPOs on conviction, are made under the provisions of Part 2, Chapter 2 of the SA 2020.
[206] SA 2020, s 360(2).

the particular circumstances of the case or, for example, where the SHPO provisions do not apply.[207]

12.226 The terms of a Restraining Order should be drafted in clear and precise terms so there is no doubt as to what the defendant is prohibited from doing and should be framed in practical terms that can be readily understood, for example by the use of road name areas identified by a map.[208]

12.227 In *R v Khellaf* [2016][209] the court distilled, from existing authorities, the following applicable principles:

(1) Ordinarily the views of the victim should be sought: either there should be direct evidence of them or the court may be able to draw a proper inference as to those views. If the victim does not want an order to made, only exceptionally should the court make one, but it would have to be borne in mind that if the victim wants contact the order may be impracticable.
(2) An order should not be made unless the judge concludes that it is necessary to make an order to protect the victim.
(3) The terms of the order should be proportionate to the harm that is sought to prevent.
(4) Particular care should be taken when children are involved to ensure that the order does not make it impossible for contract to take place between a parent and child if that is otherwise inappropriate.[210]

12.228 The order is a civil order and the civil standard of proof applies. Further evidence can be called (*Major* [2010] EWCA Crim 3016) and s 362 SA 2020.

12.229 Section 5A of the Protection from Harassment Act 1997[211] permits the court to make a restraining order against a defendant who has been acquitted in order to protect a person from harassment by the defendant.

4. Sexual Harm Prevention Orders

12.230 See Chapter 16.

5. Notification Requirements

12.231 See Chapter 14. Notification is not an order of the court;[212] the notification requirements are automatic, but the judge should deal with the requirement expressly.[213]

---

[207] Where the offence is not listed in Sch 3 or Sch 5 of the SOA 2003.
[208] *R v Debnath (Anita)* [2005] EWCA Crim 3472 at para [20].
[209] *R v Khellaf* [2016] EWCA Crim 1297, followed in *R v Wright* [2020] EWCA Crim 1696.
[210] *R v Khellaf* [2016] EWCA Crim 1297 at para [14].
[211] Inserted by s 12 Domestic Violence, Crime and Victims Act 2004 on 30.9.2009.
[212] *Longworth* [2006] UKHL. 1 and *R v Rawlinson* [2018] EWCA Crim 2825.
[213] Rule 28(3) CPR 2020. See now reference in s 379(2) SA 2020.

12.232 Notification remains a requirement of any offender subject to an SHPO; it is important for every court imposing an SHPO to be mindful of this when fixing the term of such an order.

12.233 It is wrong in principle to pass a lower sentence in order to avoid the operation of the notification requirements: *R v F* [2009].[214]

12.234 A right of review for those subject to indefinite requirements was upheld by the Supreme Court, having been found to breach Article 8: *R (F and T) v Secretary of State for Justice*.[215] Consequently, 'indefinite' rather than 'for life' is appropriate when notification has no fixed term.

Forfeiture under the Sexual Offences Act 2003, s 60A and Modern Slavery Act 2015, s 11

12.235 The power to order forfeiture of land vehicles, ships, aircrafts etc under 60A SOA 2003 was repealed from 31.7.2015[216] by the Modern Slavery Act (MSA) 2015 and replaced by s 11 MSA 2015. The power under 11 MSA 2015 is preserved by s 160(2) of the SA 2020.

6. Orders under the Modern Slavery Act 2015

Slavery and Trafficking Prevention Orders

12.236 The MSA 2015[217] introduced two new protective orders; the Slavery and Trafficking Prevention Order (STPO) under s 14 and the Slavery and Trafficking Risk Order (STRO) under s 23. The power to make a STPO under the MSA 2015 remains available to the court following the implementation SA 2020.[218] The orders are similar in operation to the Sexual Harm Prevention Order and Risk of Sexual Harm Order regime. The STRO is a stand-alone order made on application to a Magistrates' Court absent a conviction. The STPO applies to an offender convicted[219] of a slavery or human trafficking offence, if the court is satisfied that:

> there is a risk the offender may commit a slavery or human trafficking offence; and
> it is necessary to make the order for the purpose of protecting persons generally, or particular persons, from the physical or psychological harm which would be likely to occur if the offender committed such an offence.

12.237 The prohibitions imposed must be necessary for the purpose of the protecting persons generally, or particular persons, from the physical or psychological harm which would be likely to occur if the offender committed a slavery or human trafficking offence. The order may prohibit the offender from doing things in any part of the United Kingdom, and anywhere, outside of the United Kingdom. Under s 18 the order can specifically include a complete

---

[214] [2009] CLR 462.
[215] [2010] UKSC 17.
[216] Subject to transitional provisions and savings specified in SI 2015/1476 art 3.
[217] In force on 31 July 2015, SI 2015/1471 reg 2(b).
[218] SA 2020, s 379(1).
[219] Or (a) found not guilty by reason of insanity or found; or (b) to be under a disability and to have done the act charged (s 14(1)).

prohibition or restriction on foreign travel outside of the UK, for a period of no longer than 5 years, and requires surrender of the offender's passport to a specified police station (s 18(5). As well as imposing prohibitions the order may also require the offender to provide name and address details and change of name and address details under s 19, in a similar way to the notification requirements under the SOA 2003.

The STPO imposes prohibitions on the offender for a minimum period of 5 years or until further order (s 17(4)). **12.238**

Slavery and Trafficking Reparation Orders

Section 8 of the MSA 2015 introduced STROs for defendants convicted of an offence under ss 1, 2, or 4 of the MSA 2015 and against whom a confiscation order has been made. A STRO requires the defendant to pay compensation to the victim for any harm resulting from the offence, but must not be made if a compensation order has been made. In every eligible case the court must consider whether to make an STRO and if one is not made the Judge must give reasons.[220] **12.239**

7. Serious Crime Prevention Orders, s 19 Serious Crime Act 2007

The Crown Court may make a Serious Crime Prevention Order (SCPO) for an offender convicted, on or after 6.4.2008, of a 'serious offence' by virtue of section 19 of the Serious Crime Act (SCA) 2007. A serious offence is any offence listed in Part 1 of Schedule 1 of the SCA 2007. The definition of 'serious offence' is also extended to include the corresponding inchoate offences, the offence under Part 2 of the Act of encouraging and assisting, and offences which fall within the descriptions in Schedule 1 but were offences under preceding legislation at the time of the conduct concerned.[221] The test is whether there are reasonable grounds to believe that the order would prevent, restrict or disrupt the offender's involvement in serious crime in England and Wales.[222] An order under this section may contain such prohibitions, restrictions or requirements and such other terms as the court considers appropriate for the purpose of protecting the public by preventing, restricting or disrupting involvement by the person concerned in serious crime in England and Wales.[223] If the court makes a SCPO in respect of an offender already subject to a SCPO it must discharge the existing order.[224] Sections 20 and 21 cover the powers of the Court to vary or replace the order in the event of a breach. Breach of a SCPO without reasonable excuse constitutes an offence punishable summarily with a maximum of 6 months' imprisonment,[225] a fine not exceeding the statutory maximum or both. On conviction on indictment breach is punishable with maximum 5 years' imprisonment or a fine, or both.[226] **12.240**

---

[220] SCA 2007, s 8(7).
[221] SCA 2007, Sch 1, paras 14 and 15.
[222] SCA 2007, s 19(2).
[223] SCA 2007, s 19(5).
[224] SCA 2007, s 19(2A).
[225] Maximum 6 months increased to 12 months when s 154 CJA 2003 in force.
[226] SCA 2007, s 25.

12.241 The following people trafficking, prostitution and child sex offences are listed in Part 1 of Schedule 1:[227]

> An offence under any of ss 57 to 59A of the Sexual Offences Act 2003 (trafficking for sexual exploitation).
> An offence under s 2 of the Modern Slavery Act 2015.
> An offence under s 33A of the Sexual Offences Act 1956 (keeping a brothel used for prostitution).
> An offence under any of the following provisions of the Sexual Offences Act 2003
>   (a) s 14 (arranging or facilitating commission of a child sex offence);
>   (b) s 48 (causing or inciting sexual exploitation of a child);
>   (c) s 49 (controlling a child in relation to sexual exploitation);
>   (d) s 50 (arranging or facilitating sexual exploitation of a child);
>   (e) s 52 (causing or inciting prostitution for gain);
>   (f) s 53 (controlling prostitution for gain).

8. Recommendation for Deportation

12.242 The Secretary of State is under a duty to make a deportation order in respect of a person who is not a British citizen and who has been sentenced to imprisonment for a period of at least 12 months.[228] This includes indeterminate sentences and detention in a Young Offenders Institution (ss 23–39 UK Borders Act 2007) but does not apply where a sentence of 12 months has been reached by aggregating short consecutive sentences (s 38(1)(b)). Judges should not seek to avoid this provision by reducing what would have otherwise been an appropriate sentence of 12 months or more; *Gebru* [2011].[229] The circumstances in which a judge will now have to make a recommendation for deportation are limited. The approach to be followed was set out in *Kluxen* [2010]:[230]

> i) In cases to which the 2007 Act applies, it is no longer necessary or appropriate to recommend the deportation of the offender concerned.
> ii) In cases to which the 2007 Act does not apply, it will rarely be appropriate to recommend the deportation of the offender concerned, whether or not the offender is a citizen of the EU.
> iii) If in a case to which the 2007 Act does not apply a Court is, exceptionally, considering recommending the deportation of the offender concerned, it should apply the *Nazari* test in tandem with the *Bouchereau* test, there being no practical difference between the two. This is so whether the offender is or is not a citizen of the EU. The test:
>> [25] Is there a genuine and sufficiently serious threat to the requirements of public policy affecting one of the fundamental interests of society? In other words, would the appellant's continued presence in the United Kingdom be to its detriment?

---

[227] SCA 2007, Sch 1, paras 2 and 4.
[228] Section 32, UK Borders Act 2007.
[229] [2011] EWCA Crim 3321, at para 13.
[230] [2010] EWCA Crim 1081.

iv) However, the Court should not take into account the Convention Rights of the offender; the political situation in the country to which the offender may be deported; the effect that a recommendation might have on innocent persons not before the Court; the provisions of Article 28 of Directive 2004/38; or the 2006 Regulations.

Immigration Act 1971, ss 3(6) and 6.

12.243 For offenders convicted after 1.12.2020, s 386 of the Sentencing Code refers the reader back to the 1971 Act, s 6. The law, therefore remains the same.

12.244 *Nazari 1980*: the starting point when deciding whether to recommend deportation under s 3(6) Immigration Act 1971 is for the court to consider whether the offender's continued presence in the United Kingdom is to its detriment, particularly if they have committed serious crimes or have long criminal records. The more serious the offences and extensive the record of offending, the more obvious it may be that there should be a recommendation for deportation.[231] The basic test set out in *Nazari* was reconsidered and left unaltered by *R v Carmona* [2006],[232] however the court clarified that when making a recommendation for deportation, it was no longer necessary or desirable for the sentencing court to consider the likely effect of the recommendation on either the offender's or his family's rights under the Human Rights Act 1998 Schedule 1 Part I art 8, such matters are for the Secretary of State when deciding whether to act on the recommendation.

12.245 A recommendation for deportation cannot be made unless the offender is given at least 7 days written notice,[233] is aged 17 or over and has been convicted of an offence punishable with imprisonment.

12.246 Where there is power to deport a person under either the Immigration Act 1971 or the UK Borders Act 2007, the European Citizens Directive (2004/38/EC) makes further requirements before that power may be exercised in the cases of European Economic Area nationals or their family members.

P. PROSECUTION REVIEWS OF SENTENCE (ATTORNEY GENERAL'S REFERENCES)

12.247 In *Johnson and Others*[234] Judge LJ dealt with references from cases where the rebuttable presumption of an indeterminate sentence applies:

> In cases to which section 229(3) applies, where the sentencer has applied the statutory assumption, to succeed the appellant should demonstrate that it was unreasonable not to disapply it. Equally, where the Attorney General has referred such a case because the sentencer has decided to disapply the assumption, the Reference will not succeed unless it is shown that the decision was one which the sentencer could not properly have reached.

---

[231] *R v Nazari* [1980] 71 Cr App R (S) 87A.
[232] *R v Carmona* [2006] EWCA Crim 508.
[233] Section 6(2) IA 1971.
[234] *R v Johnson and Others* [2006] EWCA Crim 2486 [2007] 1 Cr App R (S) 112.

1. Offences Referable to the Court of Appeal by the Attorney General

12.248 Listed below are all those offences in respect of which it is currently possible for the Attorney General to refer the sentence to the Court of Appeal for its consideration. The list has been subject to a series of amendments, most recently on the 19.11.2019[235] when nine further sexual offences under SOA 2003, two offences concerning indecent photographs of children and offences under the MSA 2015 were added.

SI 2006/116 (as amended)
1. All offences triable only on indictment.
2. Any case tried on indictment following a notice of transfer under the CJA 1987, s 4.
3. Any case where one or more of the counts in respect of which sentence was passed relates to a charge which was dismissed at committal (under CJA 1987, s 6(1)) and further proceedings then brought by means of preferment of a voluntary bill.
4. Any case tried on indictment following a notice given under s 51B of the CDA 1998 (notices in serious and complex fraud cases) or following such notice, in which one or more of the counts in respect of which sentence is passed relates to a charge-
   (i) which was dismissed under para 2 of Schedule 3 to the CDA 1998 (applications for dismissal); and
   (ii) on which further proceedings were brought by means of the preferment of a voluntary bill of indictment.
4. Any sentence passed for any of the following offences under the SOA 1956:

Legislative Provision	Offence
SOA 1956, s 6	Unlawful sexual intercourse with girl under 13
SOA 1956, s 14	Indecent assault on a female
SOA 1956, s 15	Indecent assault on a male

5. Any sentence passed for one of the following either way offences under the SOA 2003:

Legislative Provision	Offence
SOA 2003, s 3	Sexual assault
SOA 2003, s 4	Causing a person to engage in sexual activity without consent
SOA 2003, s 7	Sexual assault of a child under 13
SOA 2003, s 8	Causing or inciting a child under 13 to engage in sexual activity
SOA 2003, s 9	Sexual activity with a child
SOA 2003, s 10	Causing or inciting a child to engage in sexual activity
SOA 2003, s 11	Engaging in sexual activity in the presence of a child
SOA 2003, s 12	Causing a child to watch a sexual act
SOA 2003, s 14	Arranging/facilitating commission of a child sex offence
SOA 2003, s 15	Meeting a child following sexual grooming
SOA 2003, s 16	Abuse of position of trust: sexual activity with a child

---

[235] Criminal Justice Act 1988 (Reviews of Sentencing) Order 2019.

P. PROSECUTION REVIEWS OF SENTENCE (ATTORNEY GENERAL'S REFERENCES) 427

Legislative Provision	Offence
SOA 2003, s 17	Abuse of position of trust: causing or inciting a child to engage in sexual activity
SOA 2003, s 18	Abuse of position of trust: sexual activity in the presence of a child
SOA 2003, s 19	Abuse of position of trust: causing a child to watch a sexual act
SOA 2003, s 25	Sexual activity with a child family member
SOA 2003, s 26	Inciting a child family member to engage in sexual activity
SOA 2003, s 30	Sexual activity with a person with a mental disorder impeding choice
SOA 2003, s 31	Causing or inciting a person with a mental disorder impeding choice to engage in sexual activity
SOA 2003, s 32	Engaging in sexual activity in the presence of a person with a mental disorder impeding choice
SOA 2003, s 33	Causing a person with a mental disorder impeding choice to watch a sexual act
SOA 2003, ss 47–50 incl	Child prostitution offences
SOA 2003, s 52	Causing or inciting prostitution for gain
SOA 2003, ss 57–59A SOA 2003	Trafficking offences
SOA 2003, s 61	Administering a substance with intent

6. Any sentence passed for any of the following offences:

Legislative Provision	Offence
IwCA 1960, s 1	Gross indecency with/towards a child
CLA 1977, s 54	Incitement by man of daughter, granddaughter, daughter or sister to commit incest with him
CLAA 1885, s 5(1)	Defilement of a girl aged between 14 and 17
OAPA 1861, s 52	Indecent assault upon a female
s 16	Threats to kill
CYPA 1933, s 1	Cruelty to persons under 16
PCA 1978, s 1	Taking, possessing, distributing, publishing indecent photographs of children
CJA 1988, s 160	Possession of indecent photographs of children
MSA 2015, s 1, 2, 4	Slavery and human trafficking offences

7. Any offence for either attempting to commit or inciting the commission of any of the above offences (conspiracy to commit any offence is triable only on indictment and so automatically referable).

Note: referable offences under the Misuse of Drugs Act 1971, Customs and Excise Management Act 1979, Protection from Harassment Act 1997, Crime and Disorder Act 1998, Asylum and Immigration (Treatment of Claimants, etc.) Act 2004, Serious Crime Act 2007, Coroners and Justice Act 2009, Serious Crime Act 2015 and anti-terrorism legislation are not set out above.

12.249

2. Checklist of Matters to be Included in Attorney General's References

12.250 The Attorney General's References are dealt with in the Court of Appeal by treasury counsel. Prior to that it is necessary for trial counsel to prepare an advice making reference to relevant SC guidelines and decided cases for consideration by the CPS Unduly Lenient Sentence (ULS) Department and the Attorney General's Office (AGO). This should be done as soon as possible but within 10 days of the sentence as a notice of an application for leave to refer a case to the Court of Appeal must be submitted within 28 days[236] of sentence and is the initial step in the process. The 28-day time limit is absolute. There is no power to extend the time limit or to apply for leave to refer out of time. Part 41 of the Criminal Procedure Rules 2020 sets out the procedure to be followed.

12.251 The following is a list of those matters with which trial counsel should deal in submitting advice for consideration by treasury counsel.

12.252 Checklist[237]

(1) Name and age of defendant.
(2) Name of sentencing judge and court.
(3) The offences and any offences taken into consideration.
(4) Chronology of proceedings.
(5) Details of any basis of plea/concessions by the prosecution.
(6) Full details of the sentence and any orders including reporting restrictions. There is a table (reproduced on the CPS website <https://www.cps.gov.uk/legal-guidance/unduly-lenient-sentences>) in the format recommended by the Court of Appeal, which ought to be used.
(7) Outline of facts (include case summary or opening if available).
(8) Any issues relevant to sentencing such as delay.
(9) Any other unusual features of the case such as whether the judge was explicitly exercising his prerogative of mercy.
(10) Details of previous convictions/breach of bail/licence, etc
(11) A note of sentencing remarks.
(12) Pre-sentence and other reports.
(13) Address the question whether the offender is subject to the 'dangerousness' provisions of the Sentencing Act 2020 and what the prosecution's submissions were on the subject.
(14) List the applicable Harm and Culpability categories in any offence-specific Sentencing Guideline.
(15) List the aggravating features.
(16) List the mitigating features.
(17) Refer to any guideline authority and any authority which the judge was referred to. Resist the temptation to quote reams of old authorities which are not similar on the facts.

---

[236] Criminal Justice Act 1988, Sch 3.
[237] With thanks to Jocelyn Ledward, junior treasury counsel, for compiling this list.

P. PROSECUTION REVIEWS OF SENTENCE (ATTORNEY GENERAL'S REFERENCES)

(18) Explain in a final paragraph why the sentence is unduly lenient. For example, it may be because the judge has not made sufficient allowance for the number of offences, has not applied the principles of totality correctly, has misdirected himself as to his sentencing powers, or that he has not followed the guideline authority or has given too great a reduction for a guilty plea. However, be cautious about relying upon this last ground alone.

Defence advocates should note CrimPR 41.4(1)(a) in particular; a Respondent's Notice must be served if it is intended to make representations (oral or otherwise) to the CACD. **12.253**

13

SPECIAL MEASURES INCLUDING SECTION 28 PRE-TRIAL RECORDED CROSS-EXAMINATION

A. Who is Eligible for Special Measures?	13.01	2. Live Link for Defendants over 18	13.31
1. Witnesses Eligible for Assistance on the Grounds of Age or Incapacity	13.02	3. Intermediaries	13.32
2. Witnesses Eligible for Assistance on the Ground of Fear or Distress about Testifying	13.12	4. Applying for a Defendant's Evidence Direction: Livelink/Intermediary	13.33
B. Applying for Special Measures	13.17	F. Section 28 Youth Justice and Criminal Evidence Act (1999)	13.38
1. Video Recorded Cross-examination or Re-examination, ss 28-30 YJCEA 1999	13.25	G. Section 28 Hearings—Recent Changes	13.51
C. What are the Special Measures Provisions in Force?	13.27	1. Timetable for Hearings	13.55
D. Ground Rules Hearings; Vulnerable Witnesses and Defendants	13.28	2. Matters in Advance of the Plea and Trial Preparation Hearing	13.57
E. What Special Measures Apply to Defendants?	13.29	3. Timetabling; Potential Causes for Delay	13.59
1. Live Link for Defendants under 18	13.30	4. The Plea and Trial Preparation Hearing	13.61
		5. Pre-Trial Court Visit and Memory Refreshing; The Day before S 28	13.64
		6. Section 28 Hearing; the Recording of the Pre-Trial Cross-Examination— 7 days after GRH	13.67

A. WHO IS ELIGIBLE FOR SPECIAL MEASURES?

There are two categories of witness eligible for special measures:[1] **13.01**

(1) Witnesses who are eligible for assistance on grounds of age or incapacity.[2]
(2) Witnesses eligible for assistance on the ground of fear or distress about testifying.[3]

1. Witnesses Eligible for Assistance on the Grounds of Age or Incapacity

These witnesses fall into three subcategories: **13.02**

(a) Witnesses under 18 *at the time of the hearing.*[4]

---

[1] This chapter is limited to special measures issues relevant to sexual offences.
[2] Youth Justice and Criminal Evidence Act (YJCEA) 1999 (as amended by Coroners and Justice Act (CAJA) 2009), s 16.
[3] YJCEA 1999, s 17.
[4] YJCEA 1999, s 16(1)(a).

(b) Witnesses under 18 *at the time of the making of their video-recorded interview*.[5]
(c) Witnesses whose evidence the court considers is likely to be *diminished in quality*[6] by reason of the witness suffering from a mental disorder,[7] significant impairment of intelligence and social functioning;[8] or where the witness has a physical disability or disorder.[9]

Quality of evidence

13.03 References to the quality of a witness's evidence are to its quality in terms of completeness, coherence, and accuracy; and for this purpose 'coherence' refers to a witness's ability in giving evidence to give answers which address the questions put to the witness and can be understood both individually and collectively.[10]

Witnesses aged under 18 and 'qualifying' witnesses

13.04 Witnesses under 18 at the time of the court's determination of eligibility for special measures,[11] or witnesses who were under 18 at the time of the making of their video-recorded interview (known as 'qualifying witnesses')[12] are automatically eligible for special measures.[13]

13.05 The 'Primary Rule'[14] in the case of a child or qualifying witness is that the court must give a special measures direction which:

(a) provides for any video-recorded interview to be admitted (YJCEA 1999, s 27);[15]
(b) for any other evidence to be given by means of a live link (YJCEA 1999, s 24).[16]

13.06 These special measures are presumed to be likely to maximize, so far as practicable, the quality of the witness's evidence.[17]

13.07 The primary rule can be displaced if the special measures are unavailable at the court in question,[18] it is not in the interests of justice to admit the recording,[19] or the court is satisfied that these measures would not maximize the quality of the witness's evidence, for example because another type of special measure would also have that effect.[20] The courts should be slow to disapply the primary rule for a reason other than those contemplated by the statute.[21]

---

[5] YJCEA 1999, s 22(1)(a).
[6] YJCEA 1999, s 16(1)(b).
[7] Within the meaning of the MHA 1983 (YJCEA 1999, s 16(2)(a)(i)).
[8] YJCEA 1999, s 16(2)(a)(ii).
[9] YJCEA 1999, s 16(2)(b).
[10] YJCEA 1999, s 16(5).
[11] YJCEA 1999, ss 16(3); 19(2).
[12] YJCEA 1999, s 22(1)(a).
[13] YJCEA 1999, ss 21, 22.
[14] YJCEA 1999, s 21(3).
[15] YJCEA 1999, s 21(3)(a).
[16] YJCEA 1999, s 21(3)(b).
[17] YJCEA 1999, s 21(2).
[18] YJCEA 1999, s 21(4)(a).
[19] YJCEA 1999, ss 21(4)(b); 27(2).
[20] YJCEA 1999, s 21(4)(c).
[21] *R (D). v Camberwell Green Youth Court* [2005] UKHL 4.

A. WHO IS ELIGIBLE FOR SPECIAL MEASURES?

The child or qualifying witness may also ask the court to disapply the primary rule.[22] In acceding to the request the court must be satisfied that the quality of the witness's evidence would not be diminished, taking into account (a) the age and maturity of the witness; (b) the ability of the witness to understand the consequences of giving evidence using other (or no) special measures; (c) the relationship between the witness and the accused; (d) the witness's social and cultural background and ethnic origins; and (e) the nature and alleged circumstances of the offence to which the proceedings relate.[23]   **13.08**

If the court disapplies the primary rule it must make an order for the use of screens, pursuant to the YJCEA 1999, s 23.[24] However, this provision may also be displaced if, again, the witness informs the court that they do not wish to give evidence using a screen and the court is satisfied that the quality of evidence would not be diminished if a screen is not used.[25]   **13.09**

The court may also refuse to order screens to be used on the basis that it would not be likely to maximize the quality of the evidence, for example because another type of special measure would also have that effect.[26]   **13.10**

There are therefore three stages to the court's consideration of appropriate special measures in the case of a witness who is under 18 or a qualifying witness: **13.11**

(1) Consideration of the use of video recording and live link. In the absence of a request from the witness, the court should compare other available special measures with the efficacy of using video recording and live link in maximizing the quality of the witness's evidence.
(2) If the court disapplies the primary rule, it should conduct a similar comparison exercise using screens as the benchmark.
(3) If, having conducted the comparison, the court decides that a particular special measure (or combination, or none) will be more effective than screens at maximizing the quality of evidence, the court should order that those special measures (or none) to be used.

2. Witnesses Eligible for Assistance on the Ground of Fear or Distress about Testifying

The court must be satisfied that (a) the complainant is in fear or distress, and (b) that this fear or distress would diminish the quality of evidence.   **13.12**

Quality of evidence

Quality of evidence refers to its quality in terms of completeness, coherence, and accuracy.[27]   **13.13**

---

[22] YJCEA 1999, s 21(4)(ba).
[23] YJCEA 1999, s 21(4C).
[24] YJCEA 1999, s 21(4A).
[25] YJCEA 1999, s 21(4B)(a).
[26] YJCEA 1999, s 21(4B)(b).
[27] YJCEA 1999, s 16(5).

Fear or distress

13.14 In assessing whether the court is satisfied that the quality of evidence given by the witness is likely to be diminished by reason of fear or distress on the part of the witness in connection with testifying in the proceedings,[28] the court must take into account: (a) the nature and alleged circumstances of the offence; (b) the age of the witness; (c) the social, cultural and ethnic origins of the witness (where relevant); (d) the domestic and employment circumstances of the witness (where relevant); (e) any religious or political beliefs of the witness; (f) any behaviour of the accused (or their family or associates), co-accused (actual or potential) or other witnesses (actual or potential) in the proceedings towards the witness.[29]

Further, the court must take into account any views expressed by the witness.[30]

Fear or Distress in Cases of Sexual Offences

13.15 In cases of sexual offences or an offence under ss 1 or 2 Modern Slavery Act 2015 where the complainant is to be a witness, that complainant is automatically eligible for special measures under the YJCEA, s 17(4) unless that witness informs the court that they do not wish to avail themselves of such measures.

13.16 In Crown Court[31] trials of sexual offences, where the complainant is over 18 at the time of the hearing,[32] the complainant may request video-recorded evidence-in-chief as the relevant special measure.[33] A direction that video-recorded evidence-in-chief pursuant to the YJCEA, s 27 must then be made,[34] unless it would not be likely to maximize the quality of the complainant's evidence or it would not be in the interests of justice to admit it.[35]

13.17

B. APPLYING FOR SPECIAL MEASURES

Applications for special measures may be made by any party to the proceedings or may be raised by the court of its own motion.[36] The procedure for special measures direction applications is set out in Part 18 of the Criminal Procedure Rules (CPR) 2020. Ordinarily special measures directions are made following an application (but see para 13.23); the content of the application is prescribed by Rule 10.18 of the CPR 2020.[37] An applicant for a special measures direction must:

> explain how the witness is eligible for assistance;
> explain why special measures would be likely to improve the quality of the witness' evidence;

---

[28] YJCEA 1999, s 17(1).
[29] YJCEA 1999, s 17(2).
[30] YJCEA 1999, s 17(3).
[31] YJCEA 1999, s 22A(2).
[32] YJCEA 1999, s 22A(3).
[33] YJCEA 1999, s 22A(4).
[34] YJCEA 1999, s 22A(7).
[35] YJCEA 1999, ss 22A(8); 27(2) as inserted and amended by the Coroner and Justice Act 2009 (27.6.2011).
[36] YJCEA 1999, s 19(1).
[37] CPR 2020, r 18.10.

propose the measure or measures that in the applicant's opinion would be likely to maximize, so far as practicable, the quality of that evidence;

report any views that the witness has expressed about:

his or her eligibility for assistance,

the likelihood that special measures would improve the quality of his or her evidence, and the measure or measures proposed by the applicant;

in a case in which a child witness or a qualifying witness does not want the primary rule to apply, provide any information that the court may need to assess the witness' views;

in a case in which the applicant proposes that the witness should give evidence by live link:

identify someone to accompany the witness while the witness gives evidence,

name that person, if possible, and

explain why that person would be an appropriate companion for the witness, including the witness' own views;

in a case in which the applicant proposes the admission of video recorded evidence, identify:

the date and duration of the recording, and

which part the applicant wants the court to admit as evidence, if the applicant does not want the court to admit all of it;

attach any other material on which the applicant relies; and

if the applicant wants a hearing, ask for one, and explain why it is needed.

13.18 Special measures pro-forma application forms are available on the Ministry of Justice website (<http://www.justice.gov.uk/courts/procedure-rules/criminal/forms#Anchor2>).

13.19 The application must be filed with the court and served on every other party to the proceedings. The application must made as soon as reasonably practicable, and in any event no later than 20 days after the defendant pleads not guilty in a magistrates' court or 10 days after of a not guilty plea in the Crown Court.[38]

13.20 Objections must be made within 10 days of the application in writing, if a hearing is requested the reasons why one is needed must be included. The objection must set out why (a) the witness is not eligible for assistance or (b) if the witness is eligible for assistance, why (i) no special measure would be likely to improve the quality of the witness' evidence, (ii) the proposed measure or measures would not be likely to maximize, so far as practicable, the quality of the witness' evidence, or (iii) the proposed measure or measures might tend to inhibit the effective testing of that evidence; or (c) in a case in which the admission of video recorded evidence is proposed, why it would not be in the interests of justice for the recording, or part of it, to be admitted as evidence.[39]

13.21 Where no objection is received, the application may be dealt with administratively.[40] However, the court must announce, at a hearing in public before the witness gives evidence, the reasons for a decision to either make, vary, discharge or refuse to make an order.[41]

---

[38] CPR 2020, r 18.3.
[39] CPR 2020, r 18.13.
[40] CPR 2020, r 18.8.
[41] CPR 2020, r 18.4.

13.22 The court may shorten or extend the applicable time limits (even if they have expired) on application or of its own motion.[42] An application for an extension of the time limits may be made in writing, orally, or in any form allowed by the court.[43] In each case the applicant must explain the reasons for the delay.[44]

13.23 Special measures directions can be made by the court without the necessity of an application when the making of the direction is unopposed, provided the circumstances prescribed by Rule 18.9 are met namely; the party seeking to introduce the evidence of such a witness must, as soon as reasonably practicable, (a) notify the court that the witness is eligible for assistance; (b) provide the court with any information that the court may need to assess the measure or measures likely to maximize so far as practicable the quality of the witness' evidence, and the witness's own views; and (c) where applicable, file with the court and serve on any other party the video-recorded evidence.[45]

13.24 For further guidance, see also the 2015 Criminal Practice Directions at 3D, 3E, and 3F, the Advocates Toolkits (<https://www.theadvocatesgateway.org/toolkits>), the Ministry of Justice: Achieving Best Evidence in Criminal Proceedings Guidance on interviewing victims and witnesses, and guidance on using special measures (March 2004) (<https://www.cps.gov.uk/sites/default/files/documents/legal_guidance/best_evidence_in_criminal_proceedings.pdf>).[46]

1. Video Recorded Cross-examination or Re-examination, ss 28-30 YJCEA 1999

13.25 The implementation of s 28 has taken place over a number of years and has been piecemeal.

13.26 Section 28 is now in force in all Crown Courts where the witness is eligible for assistance by virtue of s 16 of the Act. In increasing numbers of Crown Courts s 28 is also in force where the witness is eligible for assistance by virtue of s 17(4) of the Act (complainants in respect of a sexual offence or modern slavery offence who are witnesses in proceedings relating to that offence, or that offence and any other offences, who are eligible on grounds of fear or distress about testifying).

C. WHAT ARE THE SPECIAL MEASURES PROVISIONS IN FORCE?

13.27 Table 13.1 sets out the special measures provisions directions available as at date of publication.

---

[42] CPR 2020, r 18.5(1)(a).
[43] CPR 2020, r 18.5(1)(b).
[44] CPR 2020, r 18.5(2).
[45] CPR 2020, r 18.9.
[46] With the caveat that, whilst the 2004 guidance remains of assistance, it is now significantly out of date and does not include, for example, interviewing MSA 2015 complainants or s 28. There are also a number of local police service protocol and guidance documents and NPCA documents available online.

Table 13.1 Special Measures Provisions

Special Measure (YJCEA 1999)	Section 16 Witnesses (children and Vulnerable adults)	Section 17 Witnesses (intimidated/ fear or distress)	Qualification to Applicability
s 23 Screening the witness from the accused	Yes	Yes	The screen must prevent the witness from seeing the defendant but must not prevent the witness from being able to see, and to be seen by, (a) the judge or justices and the jury; (b) at least one of the legal representatives acting for each party in the proceedings. (c) any interpreter or other person appointed to assist the witness.
s 24 Giving evidence via live link	Yes	Yes	The witness may be supported in the live-link room, and the judge must have the regard to the wishes of the witness as to who the supporter is.
s 25 Giving evidence in private	Yes	Yes	This provision only applies to: (a) proceedings for sexual offences under SOA 2003, Part 1 or the MSA 2015, ss1 and 2; or (b) where there are reasonable grounds for believing that there has been or will be witness intimidation by someone other than the accused. The persons to be excluded must be specified. This may not include: (a) the accused; (b) legal representatives acting in the proceedings; (c) any interpreter or other person appointed to assist the witness.
s 26 Removing wigs and gowns s 27	Yes	Yes	This provision has no applicability to the magistrates' court because wigs and gowns are not worn.
Video recorded evidence-in-chief	Yes	Yes	The presumption that this is the most appropriate measure for both adult complainants and child witnesses can be displaced by the court on the basis that it is in the interests of justice not to admit it (taking into consideration any prejudice caused to the defendant balanced against the desirability of showing the recording) or by either: (a) acceding to the witness's request to use a different measure; or (b) determining that playing the video recording would not maximize the quality of the evidence.

(continued)

Table 13.1 Continued

Special Measure (YJCEA 1999)	Section 16 Witnesses (children and Vulnerable adults)	Section 17 Witnesses (intimidated/ fear or distress)	Qualification to Applicability
s 28 Video-recorded cross-examination re-examination	Yes	In the early adopter courts only (see para 13.26).	Section 28 applies where a special measures direction has been made under s 27. The recording must be made in the presence of persons 'specified' in the CPR and s 27 direction not including the defendant, but in circumstances in which (a) the judge or justices (or both) and at least one of the legal representatives acting for each party are able to see and hear the examination of the witness and communicate with the 'specified persons' and the defendant is able to see and hear the examination and communicate with their legal representative(s).
s 29 Examination through an intermediary	Yes	No	Section 29 applies when: A special measures direction has been made; The intermediary has made the intermediary declaration; and (a) The judge or justices, at least one of the legal representatives for each party and the jury should be able to see and hear the examination of the witness. (b) The judge or justices and legal representatives should be able to communicate with the intermediary.
s 30 Aids to communication	Yes	No	

D. GROUND RULES HEARINGS; VULNERABLE WITNESSES AND DEFENDANTS

13.28 A Ground Rules Hearing (GRH) will be appropriate in any case involving a young or otherwise vulnerable witness or a vulnerable defendant to ensure fair questioning and treatment. See also CPD 3E and CPR 2020 r 3.9.

E. WHAT SPECIAL MEASURES APPLY TO DEFENDANTS?

13.29 Defendants have only limited access to two special measures,[47] namely live link[48] and the use of an intermediary.[49]

---

[47] YJCEA 1999, ss 16(1), 17(1), 19(1) apply to defence witnesses but expressly exclude the defendant.
[48] YJCEA 1999, s 33A; added by Police and Justice Act 2006, s 47 (15.1.2007).
[49] Under the courts' inherent power to ensure a fair trial. See para 13.27.

1. Live Link for Defendants under 18

13.30 Defendants who are under 18 when the special measures application is made are eligible to give evidence over a live link if the court is satisfied that (a) their ability to participate in the proceedings as a witness is compromised by their level of intellectual ability or social functioning; and (b) that the use of a live link would enable them to participate more effectively as a witness, whether by improving the quality of their evidence or otherwise.[50]

2. Live Link for Defendants over 18

13.31 Defendants who are over 18 at the time of application are eligible to give evidence over a live link if (a) suffer from a mental disorder[51] or otherwise have a significant impairment of intelligence or social function;[52] (b) they therefore are unable to participate effectively in the proceedings as a witness giving oral evidence in court; and (c) the live link would enable the defendant to participate more effectively in the proceedings as a witness, whether by improving the quality of his evidence or otherwise.[53]

3. Intermediaries

13.32 The CAJA 2009 inserted new ss 33BA–BB into the YJCEA 1999.[54] The effect of s 33BA is that a defendant will be eligible to give evidence with the assistance of an intermediary if the court is satisfied that the same conditions set out earlier for live links are met,[55] and that such a direction is necessary to ensure that the accused has a fair trial.[56] However, these provisions will only come into force on a date yet to be appointed. A defendant must therefore rely upon the court exercising its inherent power to take such steps as are necessary to enable a defendant to participate effectively in a trial by directing the use of an intermediary.[57] An intermediary is likely to perform one of two roles identified by Lady Justice Rafferty in *R. (OP) v Secretary of State for Justice* [2014]:[58] the first is founded in general support, reassurance, and calm interpretation of unfolding events. The second requires skilled support and interpretation with the potential for intervention and on occasion suggestion to the Bench associated with the giving of the defendant's evidence. The Court went on to state that it is not essential for all defendants to have an intermediary for the duration of a trial, the 'pinch point' is likely to be at the time of giving evidence. For further detailed guidance see the 2015 consolidated Criminal Practice Directions from 3F.11 re: intermediaries for defendants.

---

[50] YCJEA 1999, s 33A(4).
[51] Within the meaning of the MHA 1983, YJCEA 1999.
[52] YJCEA 1999, s 33A(5)(a).
[53] YJCEA 1999, s 33A(5).
[54] CAJA 2009, s 104.
[55] YJCEA 1999, s 33BA(5), (6).
[56] YJCEA 1999, s 33BA(2).
[57] *C v Sevenoaks Youth Court* [2009] EWHC 3088 (Admin).
[58] *R. (OP) v Secretary of State for Justice* [2014] EWHC 1944 (Admin) at paras [34] and [41].

4. Applying for a Defendant's Evidence Direction: Livelink/Intermediary

13.33 The application for a defendant's evidence direction must: (a) explain how the proposed direction meets the conditions prescribed by the YJCEA 1999; and (b) in a case in which the applicant proposes that the defendant give evidence by live link (i) identify a person to accompany the defendant while the defendant gives evidence, and (ii) explain why that person is appropriate.[59]

13.34 The application must be filed with the court and served on every other party to the proceedings. The application must made as soon as reasonably practicable, and in any event no later than 20 days after the defendant pleads not guilty in a magistrates' court or 10 days after a not guilty plea in the Crown Court.[60]

13.35 Objections must be made within 10 days of the service of the application.[61]

13.36 Where no objection is received, the application may be dealt with administratively.[62] However, the court must announce, at a hearing in public before the defendant gives evidence, the reasons for a decision to either make, vary, discharge or refuse to make an order.[63]

13.37 For vulnerable defendants, see also the consolidated Criminal Practice Directions 2015 at 3G.

F. SECTION 28 YOUTH JUSTICE AND CRIMINAL EVIDENCE ACT (1999)

13.38 Section 28 provides for the pre-trial cross-examination of a vulnerable witness. The purpose is to ensure that such a witness is able to complete his/her evidence well before the full trial begins. There can, however, be value in a s 28 recording even when it is close to the trial date (arising for example in a case not spotted earlier or for a newly added young/vulnerable witness) because it means that if the trial is ineffective or requires a retrial the evidence is recorded.

13.39 Section 28 cases are expedited and the timescales to be applied, from the grant of s 28 special measures, are those within the Criminal Practice Directions, which supersede the timescales set in the joint protocol for witnesses under 10 years.[64]

13.40 Criminal Practice Directions 18E and the annexe thereto apply to s 28 cases. There is no universal Protocol for the courts at which s 28 is available but local guidance/protocols are available.

---

[59] CPR 2020, r 18.1.
[60] CPR 2013, r 18.3.
[61] CPR 2013, r 18.17.
[62] CPR 2013, r 18.14.
[63] CPR 2013, r 18.4(3).
[64] CrimPD 18E.13.

F. SECTION 28 YOUTH JUSTICE AND CRIMINAL EVIDENCE ACT (1999)

13.41 Section 28 is, at time of publication, in force at all Crown Courts for those witnesses who qualify under s 16 YJCEA, providing pre-recording of evidence for a witness who is either:

Section 16.(1)(a) under 18 years at the time of the hearing[65]

or

(b) if the court considers that the quality of evidence given by the witness is likely to be diminished by any of the following circumstances (as set out in subs (2)):

that the witness—

(i) suffers from mental disorder within the meaning of the Mental Health Act 1983, or
(ii) otherwise has a significant impairment of intelligence and social functioning, or
(b) that the witness has a physical disability or is suffering from a physical disorder.

Note:

Section 16(4) provides: In determining whether a witness falls within subsection (1)(b) the court must consider any views expressed by the witness.

Section 16 (5): references to the quality of a witness's evidence are to its quality in terms of completeness, coherence, and accuracy; and for this purpose 'coherence' refers to a witness's ability in giving evidence to give answers which address the questions put to the witness and can be understood both individually and collectively.

13.42 Following implementation at the three original s 28 pilot Crown Courts (sitting at Liverpool, Leeds, and Kingston-upon-Thames), s 28 is being rolled out across the jurisdiction for those witnesses who qualify for s 28 under s 17(4) YJCEA 1999, providing pre-recording of evidence for:

(i) complainants in respect of a sexual offence; or where the witness is a complainant in proceedings relating to that offence (or to that offence and any other offences), unless the witness has informed the court of the witness' wish not to be so eligible.
(ii) complainants in respect of an offence under ss 1 or 2 of the Modern Slavery Act 2015, where the witness is a complainant in proceedings relating to that offence (or to that offence and any other offences), unless the witness has informed the court of the witness' wish not to be so eligible.

13.43 It is intended that the provisions under s 17(4) will be extended to all other Crown Courts within the jurisdiction.

13.44 Section 28 is also intended to be extended for use by Youth Courts.

13.45 For timetabling of the case, it is imperative that the investigators and prosecutor commence the disclosure process at the start of the investigation.[66] See also paras 13.55 and 13.56.

13.46 All cases need careful consideration by police and the prosecution as a whole to ensure potential s 28 witnesses are not missed. Typically, someone not spotted as eligible will be a witness who is not a complainant in a sex case; anyone who qualifies under the legislation in force is eligible.

---

[65] In subs (1)(a) 'the time of the hearing', in relation to a witness, means the time when it falls to the court to make a determination for the purposes of s 19(2) in relation to the witness.
[66] CrimPD 18E.7.

13.47 A s 28 recording can only occur when a video-recorded interview (ABE) is in place.[67] The fact that a s 9 witness statement has been taken first does not preclude making a video-recorded interview with a witness.

13.48 Every s 28 case requires a GRH to ensure the questions to be asked are fair. All the questions to be asked by either advocate should be agreed in advance by the judge.

13.49 A s 28 from a remote location is, at time of publication, only possible from another court; that can be from a court outside the jurisdiction—the restriction arises from the technology available. The court familiarization visit will take place at the remote location. This restriction may mean that for a witness whose movement is restricted or confined to the home, a live-link may be a better option.

13.50 Consideration should be given to whether a person intended to accompany the s 28 witness to court for the s 28 hearing is also a witness in the case. If such a person is to accompany the witness obviously s/he must remain in a separate room throughout and the usher accompanying the witness must be made aware by the judge of the need to ensure there is no contact. If such a witness must accompany the witness (as the parent of a young child or a carer) it is essential that witness is told formally not to speak to the accompanying witness about his/her evidence and vice versa. The judge and counsel will meet the witness at the s 28 hearing, which is the perfect opportunity to deal with this.

G. SECTION 28 HEARINGS—RECENT CHANGES

13.51 The Criminal Practice Directions were amended as of 24 March 2022; see also CPD 18E.

The judge should pay careful regard to whether a s 28 special measures direction will in fact materially advance the date for the cross-examination and re-examination, so as to maximize, along with any other measures, the quality of the witness's evidence. This will involve detailed consideration of when the s 28 recording and the trial are likely to occur. This in turn will depend, amongst other things, on any waiting list to use the recording equipment, the likely length of the s 28 hearing, and the availability of the judge, the advocates, the witness, and a suitable courtroom.[68]

13.52 Depending on the circumstances of the case, the judge may order that the defence advocate who appeared at the ground rules hearing must conduct the recorded cross-examination.[69]

13.53 When such an order is made, the judge and list office will make whatever reasonable arrangements are feasible to achieve this, assisted by the Resident Judge when necessary. Although continuity of representation is to be encouraged, it is not mandatory for the advocate who conducted the s 28 cross-examination to represent the defendant at trial.[70]

13.54 Depending on the circumstances of the case, the GRH and the s 28 hearing may be ordered to be listed before the same judge. Once the s 28 hearing has taken place, any judge, including recorders, can deal with the trial.[71]

---

[67] Crim PD 18E.6.
[68] CrimPD 18E.19.
[69] CrimPD 18E.61.
[70] CrimPD 18E.61.
[71] CrimPD 18E.63.

G. SECTION 28 HEARINGS—RECENT CHANGES 443

Listing: Section 28 hearings should be listed at a time determined by the list officer, or as directed by the judge or Resident Judge, bearing in mind the circumstances of the witness as well the availability of the judge, the advocates, and a courtroom with the relevant equipment, including the ability to record the evidence. Ground rules hearings, if they are listed in advance of the day when the recorded cross-examination and re-examination is to occur, may be held at any time, including towards the end of the court day, to accommodate the advocates and the intermediary (if there is one) and to minimize disruption to other trials.[72]

1. Timetable for Hearings

The following is envisaged to be best practice.[73] It requires active consideration of disclosure by the prosecution team prior to sending to the Crown Court. 13.55

- Plea and Trial Preparation Hearing (PTPH); within 28 days of date of sending where possible whether for bail or custody cases.[74]
- GRH; 7 days after service of defence statement.
- Section 28 Hearing; 7 days after GRH with pre-trial visit and ABE watched the working day before the s 28. For a young child the s 28 hearing should be in the morning and concluded by lunchtime.[75]
- Mention; for advocates to report back to judge after checking recording.
- Unlikely, but if a problem requiring submissions over editing of the recording arises, a hearing to resolve that.
- Trial

There are 2 forms to be completed: 13.56

The drop-down s 28 part of the PTPH form on the Digital Case System (DCS).
The Defence GRH form:–

<https://www.gov.uk/government/publications/form-ground-rules-hearing-form-defence-ground-rules-hearing-form-section-28>

(link available for e-book). The form needs to be completed by defence counsel and uploaded onto DCS before the GRH; it must include the draft questions. The final version of the questions is to be uploaded after the GRH.

2. Matters in Advance of the Plea and Trial Preparation Hearing

An application for a witness summons to obtain material held by a third party should be served in advance of the PTPH and determined at that hearing, or as soon as reasonably practicable thereafter. The timetable should accommodate any consequent hearings or applications, but it is imperative parties are prompt to obtain third party disclosure material. The prosecution must make the court and the defence aware of any difficulty as soon as it 13.57

---

[72] CrimPD 18E.64.
[73] CrimPD 18E.21.
[74] CrimPD 18 E.12.
[75] CrimPD 18E.24.

13.58 A transcript of the ABE interview and the application for special measures, including under s 28 YJCEA 1999, must be served on the court and defence at least 7 days prior to the PTPH. The report of any registered intermediary must be served with the application for special measures.[77]

3. Timetabling; Potential Causes for Delay

13.59 The timetable should ensure the prosecution evidence and initial disclosure are served swiftly. The GRH will usually be soon after the deadline for service of the defence statement, the recorded cross-examination and re-examination hearing about 1 week later. However, there must be time afforded for any further disclosure of unused material following service of the defence statement and for determination of any application under s 8 of the Criminal Procedure and Investigations Act (CPIA) 1996. Subject to judicial discretion, applications for extensions of time for service of disclosure by either party should generally be refused.[78]

13.60 Where the defendant may be unfit to plead, a timetable for s 28 should usually still be set, taking into account extra time needed for the obtaining of medical reports, save in cases where it is indicated that it is unlikely that there would be a trial if the defendant is found fit.[79]

4. The Plea and Trial Preparation Hearing

13.61 The usual form is completed and the s 28 drop-down form will be used during hearing. This includes a record of any (and a reminder to impose) s 4 Contempt of Court Act postponing publication of the GRH and/or s 28 hearing prior to trial.

> Defence to state trial issue/s.
> Stage dates set but note that Stage 1 is 50 days from sending, whether the defendant is in custody or on bail. Defence Statement must be served on time at Stage 2 given the very tight timing thereafter.
> GRH will usually be fixed 7 days after Stage 2.
> Directions will be made as to who will be required for the GRH; that will include: the defendant,[80] any intermediary for the witness must attend if involved. It is helpful if a police officer Officer in the Case/Sexual Offences Investigation Trained Officer/Family Liaison Officer (OIC/SOIT/FLO) also attends to ensure instructions can be given to prosecution counsel and judicial directions are understood and followed.

---

[76] CrimPD 18E.25.
[77] CrimPD 18E.15.
[78] CrimPD 18E.22.
[79] CrimPD 18E.23.
[80] The Annex (sic) to CrimPD 18E provides: 7. In preparation for trial, courts must take every reasonable step to facilitate the participation of witnesses and defendants (CPR 3.8(4)(d)). The court should order that the defendant attends the GRH.

G. SECTION 28 HEARINGS—RECENT CHANGES

The date for the pre-trial visit and memory-refreshing (watching ABE) will be fixed; this should be the working day before the s 28 hearing.

A date (suggested 14–21 days) thereafter will be fixed as a mention hearing for both parties to notify the judge by email and on the DCS widely shared comments that the sound and visual quality is either good or not, so that if there is a problem which requires the judge to consider submissions as to editing the judge will fix an agreed date for the same advocates to return.

Date set for mention to confirm the recording is ready for use at trial.

This hearing could be either by telephone or remote link and the defendant's attendance excused.

After the s 28 hearing, the recording will be stored in the cloud. A link to the recording will be emailed to the advocates by the court clerk on their Criminal Justice System eMail (CJSM) accounts for them to check it for quality of sound and visibility as well as any other problem envisaged in playing it to a jury.

R v PMH[81] (*Hampson*); Hallett LJ sets out it is the responsibility of counsel to do so. Editing is very rare and the s 28 hearing is to be treated as any other court hearing, not as an opportunity for a 'test run'.

Ensure an email chain is set up between judge and trial advocates; time is tight and you will need a means of speedy communication.

Ensure that both advocates have the correct email address of the intermediary if there is one for the next stage:

Directions will be given re the questions to be included in the GRH form which the defence advocate must complete.

In appropriate cases and in particular where the witness is of very young years or suffers from a disability or disorder, it is expected that the advocate will have prepared his or her cross-examination in writing for consideration by the court.[82] See also *Dinc*.[83]

When the court requires written questions that direction must be complied with:[84]

Rule 3.11(d) of the Crim PR gives the power to the Court to 'limit (i) the examination, cross-examination or re-examination of a witness'. The Court of Appeal Criminal Division will support the proper case management of the cross-examination of a witness, see *E (Edwards)*[85] and *Lubemba*.[86]

Written questions from the advocate who will cross-examine are required in every s 28 case. These must be in full, not just headings, and have headlines so each topic is set out with relevant questions underneath. The cross-examination must follow the document and the witness told what the next topic is and when that topic is finished.

Unnecessary questions will include any preamble and also anything which is not in dispute and therefore can be dealt with by admissions/schedule/family tree.

---

[81] [2018] EWCA Crim 2452.
[82] Annex (sic) to CrimPD 18E at 4.
[83] *Dinc* 2017 EWCA Crim 1206.
[84] *RT & Stuchfield* [2020] EWCA Crim 155.
[85] *E (Edwards)* [2011] EWCA Crim 3028; [2012] Crim LR 563.
[86] *Lubemba and Pooley* [2014] EWCA Crim 2064.

If a witness is capable of understanding and answering questions, it is the duty of an advocate to put the defendant's case—even where limitation on cross-examination was appropriate because of the youth and/or vulnerability of the witness *R v RK (Knight)*.[87]

Ensure the planned questions have options to cover the position if unexpected answers are given: 'if no, then ...'/ 'if yes, then ...'

This will obviate the need for a break to draft more questions during the s 28 hearing. The questions must be provided to the intermediary in advance of their submission to the judge in order to check the witness will understand them (no double-negatives, rolled-up or tagged questions) and at the same time to the prosecution advocate. This is essential to ensure that these hearings are meaningful and that the questions are neither unnecessary or improper in content or structure; the judge will need to hear submissions if there is disagreement.

The questions should not be provided to anyone beyond the trial advocates and intermediary in order to allay any concern about their inadvertent supply to the witness in advance of the s 28 hearing.

After that process between advocates (and intermediary) is complete, the questions must be included in the completed GRH form and that uploaded onto DCS and/or sent by email (as directed) and in an editable Word format to the judge and prosecution advocate at the date and time set by the judge (suggested: at the latest 9 a.m. the day before the GRH).

Judge will fix dates re questions—suggested timetable:

Defence advocate sends draft questions to intermediary (if instructed) and prosecution advocate 28 days after PTPH.

Intermediary to respond within 14 days (copying in both advocates).

Prosecution to send final response to defence 14 days thereafter.

Counsel to then liaise over any matters not agreed and highlight those for Judge in the final document.

Defence to send final version to Judge by 9 a.m. the working day before the GRH.

Any other Special Measures sought to be raised; prosecution to take instructions re wigs and gowns, anything which will assist the witness to relax and give better evidence etc. Intermediary may know if eg intermediary was already in place for ABE. A 'combined special measures' application may arise; some witnesses may want a screen to shield him/her from the defendant's view as s/he gives evidence via the camera.

Applications and rulings on matters which will affect cross-examination:

Any applications under s 100 of the CJA 2003 or under s 41 of the YJCEA 1999 or any other application which may affect the cross-examination must be made promptly, and responses submitted in time for the judge to rule on the application at the GRH.[88] Rulings will be made on any application under s 100 of the CJA 2003 or s 41 of the YJCEA 1999, and on any other application that may affect the conduct of the cross-examination. Any ruling will be included in the trial practice note.[89]

---

[87] *RK (Knight)* [2018] EWCA Crim 603.
[88] CrimPD 18E.28.
[89] Para 20, Annex to CrimPD 18E.

G. SECTION 28 HEARINGS—RECENT CHANGES

Judge and advocates must have watched the ABE/VRI before the GRH.[90] **13.62**

This is important for both drafting questions and considering them; it will crystallize those matters genuinely in issue and those which can be dealt with by agreed facts.

The Ground Rules Hearing **13.63**

Note: A GRH in similar terms will be equally appropriate in any case involving a young or otherwise vulnerable witness or a vulnerable defendant, to address questioning and other matters such as breaks and timing. See also CrimPD 3E and CrimPR 2020 r 3.9

- The judge will state what ground rules will apply. The advocates must comply with them.[91]
- The intermediary must attend if one is instructed.[92] An intermediary should not be instructed unless s/he will be available to attend the GRH and the s 28 hearings ordered by the court.[93]
- The defendant should attend the GRH;[94] that implies a degree of latitude so in appropriate circumstances he may be excused.
- The Ground Rules will be set including:
- where the intermediary will sit (in the sight of the witness and both of them in sight of the usher/member of court staff).
- how the intermediary will signal a concern to the judge.
- what, if any, items the intermediary and/or usher will have in the room.
- how the witness/es will give evidence: who will be in the room with the witness; for a young child it may be better for advocates, and possibly judge, to be with the witness.
- the aids to communication, if any, to be used.
- no witness should be asked to touch or point to any part of his/her own body so if there is any dispute over such an aspect of the evidence a diagram or a doll must be used.[95] The intermediary should have input as to which is best but ultimately the Judge has responsibility for this task and all decisions.
- how the advocates and judge, and any intermediary, are going to interact with the witness, and with each other, including how each will be addressed.
- the length of time after which a break/breaks must be taken.
- any other 'ground rules' for asking questions of the witness.
- how the witness will be shown exhibits or documents.
- any additional questions to be asked by the prosecution in examination in chief.
- the overall length of cross-examination.
- in a multi-handed case, which advocate/s will conduct the cross-examination.
- what the jury are to be told about the limitations imposed and when such an explanation will be given.

---

[90] Para 11 Annex (sic) to CrimPD 18E.
[91] Para 12, Annex to CrimPD 18E.
[92] CrimPD 18E.33.
[93] Para 15, Annex to CrimPD 18E].
[94] The Annex (sic) to CrimPD 18E provides: 'In preparation for trial, courts must take every reasonable step to facilitate the participation of witnesses and defendants' (CPR 3.8(4)(d)). The court should order that the defendant attends the GRH.
[95] CrimPD 3E.6.

(iv) Matters which may affect cross-examination will be argued and ruled on:
S 100 of the CJA 2003
S 41 of the YJCEA 1999 or
other applications that may affect the cross-examination.
Finalize the Questions
The judge should discuss with the advocates the submitted questions and they will be finalized for use at the s 28 hearing following any submissions.

Advocates should follow the 20 Principles of Questioning,[96] Advocates Gateways,[97] and relevant authorities including:

YGM [2018] EWCA Crim 2458
RK (Knight) [2018] EWCA Crim 603
PMH (Hampson) [2018] EWCA Crim 2452
Mark Le Brocq v Liverpool CC [2019] EWCA Crim 1398
Dinc [2017] EWCA Crim 1206 (judge requiring written questions)
RT & Stuchfield [2020] EWCA Crim 155 (continuing trial when cross-examination incomplete because witness no longer willing/available to attend)
Jonas [2015] EWCA Crim 562
RL [2015] EWCA Crim 1215
R v Grant Murray [2017] EWCA Crim 1228 (role of intermediary)
Lubemba and Pooley [2014] EWCA Crim 2064
R v Wills [2011] EWCA Crim 1938 guidance including counsel failing to comply with judge's limitation on cross-examination).

5. Pre-Trial Court Visit and Memory Refreshing; The Day before S 28

13.64 Day 1 of the trial is the s 28 recording.

13.65 The working day before the s 28 the police bring the witness to court to familiarize him/herself with the remote room. This is not cast in stone; if an earlier date may be preferred but the memory refreshing should be on the *working day before the evidence is given.*

13.66 A court usher or member of witness support will meet the witness for the s 28 hearing. Others arriving may include family, a member of the external victim support team and well as a police officer (SOIT/ OIC).

This is also the day on which the memory refreshing by watching the ABE/VRI occurs.

---

[96] *20 Principles of Questioning—a guide to the cross-examination of vulnerable witnesses* —<https://static-documents.easygenerator.com/c9ac3583-bba3-456c-9b46-9b3f17fbee73.pdf>.
[97] https://www.theadvocatesgateway.org/toolkits>.

G. SECTION 28 HEARINGS—RECENT CHANGES   449

6. Section 28 Hearing; the Recording of the Pre-Trial Cross-Examination—7 days after GRH

13.67

- Defendant remains in the dock in the court room throughout the hearing.
- Witness and intermediary remain in link room.
- For a very young witness, advocates may be in link room (subject to available space) and sometimes the judge may be in link room too.
- The CRIM PD provides that both advocates must have watched the ABE before the s 28 hearing.
- Judge meets the witness with the advocates in the dedicated link room. Discuss special measures if not already all agreed: eg wigs and gowns, anything which might assist the witness to feel more relaxed, where advocates will sit to ask questions (once social distancing is lifted/altered to permit), where intermediary will sit, whether any aids to explanation and/or exhibits need to be in the room.
- If, despite the discussion and planning, an unexpected answer is given so that the cross-examiner needs to divert from the agreed questions, then this needs to be raised in the absence of the witness (recording can be switched off or if that is not done edited out later). The judge will then require the advocate to write out the extra questions and go through them just as at the GRH, using the intermediary if there is one and giving opposing counsel an opportunity to make submissions. Advocates must abide by the ruling in relation to the question in *Wills*.[98]
- Prosecution re-examine and then the judge will conclude the hearing. The same rules apply for formulating questions whoever asks them.
- The direction at PTPH for the questions to be provided to all in an editable format (Word document) means that an accurate note of the evidence can be inserted into that document.
- A note of that evidence for the trial judge, in the event that is not the s 28 judge, can be uploaded into the private section of the DCS. Different courts will have different practices in relation to this informal record; it should be remembered that it is not a transcript.

Mention for advocates to check recording and report back to judge, 14–21 days after s 28 (Remote/telephone hearing).

Advocates will receive the recording via secure email from the court clerk once it is accessible; usually a few days after the s 28 hearing. The judge should have made a direction at PTPH to notify him/her within 21 days of the s 28 hearing of any difficulties with it or that there are none.

13.68

Without exception, editing of the ABE interview/examination-in-chief or recorded cross-examination is precluded without an order of the court (CrimPD 18E.43).

13.69

Under s 28(4) YJCEA 1999, the judge, on application of any parties or on the court's own motion, may direct that the recorded examination is not admitted into evidence, despite

13.70

---

[98] *R v Wills* 2011 EWCA Crim 1938 [36] and [37].

any previous direction. Such direction must be given promptly, preferably immediately after the conclusion of the examination (CrimPD 18E.42).

13.71 **Video on Demand** link to training video.

<https://www.youtube.com/watch?v=iFcpJq-JaFQ&feature=youtu.be>.

13.72 If a problem requiring submissions over editing of the recording arises, a hearing to resolve that.

Advocates will need to liaise with the judge over a date so that both can attend this; it can be dealt with remotely and the defendant's attendance excused. Note that editing is rare and the s 28 hearing cannot be regarded by anyone as including an opportunity for a test run.

The Trial

13.73 It is essential to ensure the playback of the s 28 recording is booked accurately in advance of the trial with input from the prosecution trial advocate. The slots come in half days; failure to book for the correct time and correct length of time will lead to a delay whilst another booking is made, probably not until the next day.

13.74 The judge should explain to the jury that the evidence was recorded on an earlier date and give specific directions about the limitations placed on defence counsel both before the recorded evidence is played and a reminder in summing up.

14
NOTIFICATION REQUIREMENTS

A. Applicability	14.02	G. Method of Notification	14.16
B. Role of the Court	14.04	H. Failure to Notify	14.17
C. Children and Young Persons	14.07	I. Conditional Discharges	14.19
D. Initial Notification	14.10	J. Removal of Details	14.22
E. Updating Details	14.12	K. Notification Period	14.27
F. Travel Notification Requirements	14.14	L. Sexual Offences Act 2003, Schedule 3	14.28

Notification requirements have applied since 1.9.1997, falling within the ambit of Part 1 of the SOA 1997.[1] Notification is now governed by Part 2 of the SOA 2003,[2] which came into force on 1.5.2004.[3] The provisions have retrospective application[4] to those who were previously subject to a notification requirement under the 1997 Act. It is important to note therefore that these requirements are now the same for any offence committed after 1.9.1997. Notification requirements do not apply to those individuals who were convicted of Schedule 3 offences before 1.9.1997. **14.01**

A. APPLICABILITY

Notification requirements apply to those who are either convicted of an offence specified in Schedule 3 to the 2003 Act;[5] found not guilty of such an offence by reason of insanity;[6] are found to be under a disability and to have done the act charged against them in respect of such an offence;[7] or are cautioned in respect of such an offence.[8] The offences listed in Schedule 3 also include any attempt, conspiracy, or incitement to commit that offence,[9] and aiding, abetting, counselling, or procuring the commission of that offence.[10] Also included are inchoate offences under Part 2 of the Serious Crime Act 2007 (encouraging or assisting crime offences) where the listed offence is the offence (or one of the offences) which the person intended or believed would be committed.[11] Equivalent service offences are included by virtue of paras 93–93A of Schedule 3. It is important to note that notification does **14.02**

---

[1] Hereafter 'the 1997 Act'.
[2] Hereafter 'the 2003 Act'.
[3] The provisions are unaffected by the SA 2020, see s 379(1).
[4] SOA 2003, s 81.
[5] SOA 2003, s 80(1)(a); see Tables 14.1–14.5. This is unchanged by the Sentencing Act 2020 (see s 379(2)).
[6] SOA 2003, s 80(1)(b).
[7] SOA 2003, s 80(1)(c).
[8] SOA 2003, s 80(1)(d) in England, Wales, or Northern Ireland.
[9] SOA 2003, Sch 3, para 94A(a).
[10] SOA 2003, Sch 3, para 94A(b).
[11] SOA 2003, Sch 3, para 94AA.

not apply to any sexual offences prior to the implementation of the 1956 Sexual Offences Act and not all sexual offences in subsequent sexual offences legislation are included in Schedule 3. Notification periods also attach to Sexual Offence Prevention Orders (SHPOs) (see para 14.23).

14.03 The notification requirements also apply where any of the above conditions are found to be met in a foreign jurisdiction and the chief police officer for the area in which the offender lives or is intending to live applies to the magistrates' court for a notification order.[12]

B. ROLE OF THE COURT

14.04 A notification requirement is not a 'penalty'.[13] It is therefore unnecessary, except in the case of a notification order following conviction abroad, for the court to order notification. Instead, the requirement is automatic. The role of the court is only to state in open court that one of the eligibility criteria in s 80(1) has been satisfied[14] and to certify that fact.[15]

14.05 When a defendant is required to notify upon conviction, the judge should state at the sentencing hearing how long the defendant will be subject to the requirements for. If notification is indefinite, that is the term which should be used, not 'for life'; it is possible for an offender to apply to be removed from the Sex Offender Register.[16] See para 14.20.

14.06 Where the period will be indeterminate, the fact of the defendant's youth may found a reason for cessation of the notification requirement if full rehabilitation can be argued.

C. CHILDREN AND YOUNG PERSONS

14.07 The Court has a further discretionary role with regard to offenders under 18 at the date of conviction or finding; namely, that it may direct that the notification obligation transfers to an individual with parental responsibility for the offender.[17]

14.08 Where a Detention and Training Order has been imposed, the period of 'detention and training' (as opposed to the overall sentence which also includes a period of supervision)[18] is equivalent to a 'sentence of imprisonment' for the purposes of calculating the length of a notification requirement.[19]

14.09 The length of any notification requirement for a young person is half of that imposed on an adult.[20]

---

[12] SOA 2003, s 97.
[13] *Ibbotson v UK* [1999] Crim LR 153.
[14] SOA 2003, s 92(2)(a); Rule 28(3) CPR 2020. *R v Rawlinson* [2018] EWCA Crim 2825.
[15] SOA 2003, s 92(2)(b).
[16] *R (on the application of F (by his litigation friend F) and Thompson (FC) (Respondents)) v Secretary of State for the Home Department (Appellant)* [2010] UKSC 17 E. The Supreme Court ruled that indefinite notification without possibility of review was incompatible with the European Convention on Human Rights. Section 91A SOA 2003 introduces a new provision to remedy this incompatibility. See para 14.10.
[17] SOA 2003, s 89.
[18] *R v Slocombe* [2005] EWCA Crim 2297.
[19] SOA 2003, s 131(1)(a).
[20] SOA 2003, s 82(1), (2).

D. INITIAL NOTIFICATION

14.10 Unless an offender is already subject to a notification requirement,[21] within 3 days of conviction (or the finding), the offender must notify the police of the following information: (a) the relevant offender's date of birth; (b) his national insurance number; (c) his name on the relevant date and, where he used one or more other names on that date, each of those names; (d) his home address on the relevant date; (e) his name on the date on which notification is given and, where he uses one or more other names on that date, each of those names; (f) his home address on the date on which notification is given; (g) the address of any other premises in the United Kingdom at which, at the time the notification is given, he regularly resides or stays.[22]

14.11 The offender must also notify the police of any information prescribed by regulations made by the Secretary of State.[23] This includes the offender's passport and identity document details.[24] It also includes details of the offender's bank accounts, credit and debit cards, whether solely or jointly held.[25] Where an offender resides or stays for at least 12 hours at a household at which a child resides or stays, the offender must provide: (a) the date on which the residence or stay begins; (b) the address of the relevant household; and (c) the period(s) for which he intends to reside or stay at the address.[26]

E. UPDATING DETAILS

14.12 Any changes in name, address, passport, and identity document details,[27] debit, credit card, or bank account details (including the opening and closing of accounts)[28] must be notified to the police within 3 days.[29] The offender must also notify the police when residing or staying (or ceasing to reside or stay) for at least 12 hours at a household at which a child resides or stays. The offender must provide: (a) the date on which the residence or stay begins; (b) the address of the relevant household; and (c) the date from which he resides or stays or ceases to reside or stay at the address.[30]

14.13 In any event, at least once every 12 months the offender must update the information provided to the police.[31] If the offender does not have a sole or main residence they must give notification of a place in the UK that they can regularly be found to the police every 7 days.[32]

---

[21] SOA 2003, s 83(2).
[22] SOA 2003, s 83(5). Under s 83(5)(h)(the Secretary of State may also prescribe by regulations prescribe other information be provided under this section.
[23] SOA 2003, s 83(5)(h), s 83(5A).
[24] Sexual Offences Act 2003 (Notification Requirements) (England and Wales) Regulations 2012 (hereafter 'SI 2012/1876'), r 14.
[25] SI 2012/1876, r 12. In *R (on the Application of Christopher Prothero) v Secretary of State for the Home Department* [2013] EWCA 2830 (Admin) the requirement to provide financial information under the regulations was held to be compatible with Article 8 ECHR.
[26] SI 2012/1876, r 10.
[27] SI 2012/1876, r 14.
[28] SI 2012/1876, r 13.
[29] SOA 2003, s 84.
[30] SI 2012/1876, r 11.
[31] SOA 2003, s 85(5)(b).
[32] SOA 2003, s 85(5)(a); SI 2012/1876, r 9.

F. TRAVEL NOTIFICATION REQUIREMENTS

14.14 Offenders are required to notify of any travel outside of the UK.[33] The notification must disclose (a) the date on which the offender will leave the UK; (b) the country (or, if there is more than one, the first country) to which he will travel and his point of arrival (determined in accordance with the regulations) in that country; and (c) any other information prescribed by the regulations which the offender holds about his departure from or return to the UK or his movements while outside the UK.

14.15 In addition to the statutory information (para 14.14) the offender must comply with regulations prescribed by the Secretary of State under SI 2004/1220 (as amended in 2012).[34] The regulations specify that notification should be given not less than 7 days before departure, if the information is not known then it must be given as soon as reasonably practicable but not less than 24 hours before departure but only if the offender has a reasonable excuse for not providing the information not less than 7 days before.[35] The further required information includes: (a) the destination country (or, if there is more than one, the first) and the point of arrival in that country; the point(s) of arrival in any countries that will be visited in addition to the initial destination country; the carrier(s) the offender intends to use to leave and return to the UK or to any other point(s) of arrival while they are outside the UK (but not internal flights; details of accommodation arrangements for the first night outside the UK); the date of re-entry to the UK and point of arrival.[36] Any changes to the previously notified information must be notified at least 24 hours before departure from the UK.[37] If the offender's date of re-entry into the UK and point of arrival are not notified prior to departure notification must be made within 3 days of the offender's return to the UK.[38]

G. METHOD OF NOTIFICATION

14.16 An offender fulfils his notification obligation by attending his prescribed police station and giving an oral notification to any authorized officer at the station.[39] A person who is changing address may give notification at the police station that would be the prescribed police station had the change of address already occurred.[40]

---

[33] SOA 2003, ss 86(2)(a), (b), and 82(3).
[34] The Sexual Offences Act 2003 (Travel Notification Requirements) Regulations 2004 (hereafter 'SI 2004/1220') in force from 1 May 2004, as amended by SI 2012/1876.
[35] SI 2004/1220, r 5(2) (as amended).
[36] SI 2004/1220 (as amended) r 6.
[37] SI 2004/1220 (as amended) r 7.
[38] SI 2004/1220 (as amended) r 8.
[39] SOA 2003 s 87(1).
[40] SOA 2003, s 87(2).

H. FAILURE TO NOTIFY

A failure to notify without reasonable excuse is an offence triable either way. It is punishable summarily with a maximum of 6 months' imprisonment or a fine not exceeding the statutory maximum. The maximum sentence on indictment is imprisonment for a term not exceeding 5 years.[41] **14.17**

For sentencing see the Sentencing Council 'Breach Offences Definitive Guideline' which applies to any offender aged 18 or over, sentenced on or after 1 October 2018. **14.18**

I. CONDITIONAL DISCHARGES

Anyone conditionally discharged for an offence to which the 2003 Act applies is, by virtue of the express provision of that Act, liable to the notification requirements of that Act for the period of the conditional discharge. **14.19**

A person conditionally discharged before 1.5.2004 (implementation date for the SOA 2003), for an offence to which the 1997 Act applies, is not liable for notification.[42] **14.20**

A conviction resulting in an absolute discharge[43] or a conditional discharge[44] deemed not to be a conviction does not trigger the requirement to notify.[45] **14.21**

J. REMOVAL OF DETAILS

Offences since Decriminalized

Anyone convicted of an offence which has since been decriminalized has the right to have his name and details removed from the list of those required to notify.[46] This will include those convicted of some homosexual offences which are no longer offences by virtue of the lowering of the age of consent, first from 21 to 18[47] and then from 18 to 16.[48] **14.22**

Offenders Subject to Indefinite Notification Requirement

An offender who is subject to an indefinite notification period may apply in writing for a determination by the relevant chief officer of police that the notification requirements **14.23**

---

[41] SOA 2003, s 91.
[42] *R v Longworth* [2006] UKHL 1.
[43] SA 2020, s 79.
[44] SA 2020, s 80.
[45] SOA 2003, s 134(1)(a) and SA 2020, s 82(2).
[46] See Sch 4 SOA 2003 for the applicable procedure.
[47] CJPOA 1994, s 145 commencement date 3.11.1994.
[48] SO(A)A 2000, s 1(1) commencement date 8.1.2001.

should cease to apply in their case.[49] The offender must not be subject to a Sexual Harm Prevention Order (SHPO), interim SHPO, Sexual Offences Prevention Order (SOPO), or interim SOPO.[50] Notification requirements attach to sexual offences preventative orders. An offender whose notification period has technically expired in relation to the offence will still be subject to notification requirements until the expiration date of their SHPO/interim SHPO (or SOPO/interim SOPO), if that term is longer than the notification term.

14.24 The offender may only apply after the qualifying date. The qualifying date is 15 years after initial notification for an offender who was over 18 and 8 years for an offender under 18 at the time of the date of conviction, finding or caution.[51]

14.25 The chief officer of police must determine the application within 6 weeks of acknowledging receipt,[52] taking into account the test under s 91C and applying the factors set out in s 91D of the 2003 Act. Any appeal against a determination must be made to the magistrates' court within 21 days of receipt.[53]

14.26 If an offender's application is unsuccessful the notification requirements will continue without eligibility for further review for a further period of 8 years, rising to a maximum of 15 years dependent upon the chief officer of police's assessment of the risk of sexual harm posed.[54]

K. NOTIFICATION PERIOD

Table 14.1 Notification Periods

Description of relevant offender	Notification period[a]
A person who, in respect of the offence, is or has been sentenced to imprisonment for life, to imprisonment for public protection under s 225 of the Criminal Justice Act 2003 or to imprisonment for a term of 30 months or more	An indefinite period beginning with the date of conviction or finding
A person who, in respect of the offence or finding, is or has been admitted to a hospital subject to a restriction order	An indefinite period beginning with the date of the finding
A person who, in respect of the offence, is or has been sentenced to imprisonment for a term of more than 6 months but less than 30 months	10 years beginning with that date
A person who, in respect of the offence, is or has been sentenced to imprisonment for a term of 6 months or less	7 years beginning with that date
A person who, in respect of the offence or finding, is or has been admitted to a hospital without being subject to a restriction order	7 years beginning with that date

---

[49] SOA 2003, s 91A. On 30 July 2012 the SOA 2003 was amended by the SOA 2003 (Remedial) Order 2012 No 1883 so as to introduce a mechanism for individuals to seek a review of their indefinite notification requirements.
[50] SOA 2003, s 91A(2b).
[51] SOA 2003, s 91B(2).
[52] SOA 2003, s 91C(1).
[53] SOA 2003, s 91E(2).
[54] SOA 2003, s 91B(3)–(5).

Description of relevant offender	Notification period[a]
A person within s 80(1)(d) (cautioned in respect of the offence)	2 years beginning with that date
A person in whose case an order for conditional discharge is made in respect of the offence	The period of conditional discharge
A person of any other description	5 years beginning with the date of conviction or finding

Note:

When an offender is aged under 18 on the relevant date, the notification periods above (which are applicable to adult offenders) are halved. See para 14.09.

When a sentence of custody is suspended, the length of sentence for notification purposes is determined by the length of the term of custody.[b]

When an extended sentence is imposed, the length of the sentence for notification purposes is the full length of the sentence and not only the custodial term.[c]

When a Detention and Training Order (DTO) has been imposed, the length of the sentence for notification purposes is equal to the period of actual imprisonment (as opposed to the overall sentence which also includes a period of supervision). See para 14.08.

A SHPO or SOPO attracts its own notification period which last for the duration of the order. See para 14.23.

Where an offender is sentenced to terms which are wholly or partly consecutive, the length of the sentence will be the aggregate length of the terms.[d]

[a] SOA 2003, s 82.
[b] SA 2020, s 289.
[c] R v Wiles [2004] Cr App R (S) 88.
[d] SOA 2003 s 82(3) and (4).

L. SEXUAL OFFENCES ACT 2003, SCHEDULE 3

14.27

Tables 14.2 to 14.5 are extracted from Schedule 3. They comprise the offence condition and in some cases, an additional sentence condition. Age and sentence thresholds have been applied to some of the offences to ensure that only the more serious offending will trigger the requirements. For example, in the case of the offence of child sex offences committed by children or young persons (s 13 SOA 2003) an offender will only be required to register if they are sentenced to a term of imprisonment of 12 months or more. Where a person is convicted, cautioned etc in relation to an offence, any applicable thresholds have to be met for the notification requirements to be triggered.

14.28

Note that the Schedule 3 offences listed in the tables also include any attempt, conspiracy, or incitement to commit that offence,[55] and aiding, abetting, counselling, or procuring the commission of that offence.[56] Also included are inchoate offences under Part 2 of the Serious Crime Act 2007 (encouraging or assisting crime offences) where the listed offence is the offence (or one of the offences) which the person intended or believed would be committed.[57] Equivalent service offences are included by virtue of paras 93–93A of Schedule 3. It is important to note that notification does not apply to any sexual offences prior to the implementation of the 1956 Sexual Offences Act and not all sexual offences in subsequent sexual offences legislation are included in Schedule 3.

14.29

[55] SOA 2003, Sch 3, para 94A(a).
[56] SOA 2003, Sch 3, para 94A(b).
[57] SOA 2003, Sch 3, para 94AA.

1. Offences Subject to Notification Requirements under the Sexual Offences Act 1956

Table 14.2 Offences Subject to Notification Requirements under the Sexual Offences Act 1956

	Offence	Qualification to applicability of notification requirement *Notification requirements only apply ...*
s 1	Rape	
s 5	Intercourse with a girl under 13	
s 6	Intercourse with a girl under 16	If the offender was 20 or over
s 10	Incest by a man	If the victim or other party was under 18
s 12	Buggery	(a) If the offender was 20 or over, *and* (b) the victim or other party was under 18
s 13	Indecency between men	(a) If the offender was 20 or over, *and* (b) the victim or other party was under 18

s 14	Indecent assault on a woman	(a) The victim or other party was under 18, *or*
		(b) the offender, in respect of the offence or finding, is or has been—
		  (i) sentenced to imprisonment for a term of at least 30 months; *or*
		  (ii) admitted to a hospital subject to a restriction order.

s 15	Indecent assault on a man	(a) The victim or other party was under 18, *or*
		(b) the offender, in respect of the offence or finding, is or has been—
		  (i) sentenced to imprisonment for a term of at least 30 months; *or*
		  (ii) admitted to a hospital subject to a restriction order

s 16	Assault with intent to commit buggery	If the victim or other party was under 18
s 28	Causing or encouraging the prostitution of, intercourse with, or indecent assault on girl under 16	

Note that the Schedule 3 offences listed below also include any attempt, conspiracy, or incitement to commit that offence,[a] and aiding, abetting, counselling, or procuring the commission of that offence.[b] Also included are inchoate offences under Part 2 of the Serious Crime Act 2007 (encouraging or assisting crime offences) where the listed offence is the offence (or one of the offences) which the person intended or believed would be committed.[c] Equivalent service offences are included by virtue of paras 93–93A of Schedule 3. It is important to note that notification does not apply to any sexual offences prior to the implementation of the 1956 Sexual Offences Act and not all sexual offences in subsequent sexual offences legislation are included in Schedule 3.

[a] SOA 2003, Sch 3, para 94A(a).

[b] SOA 2003, Sch 3, para 94A(b).

[c] SOA 2003, Sch 3, para 94AA.

2. Offences Subject to Notification Requirements under Miscellaneous Acts 1960–2002

Table 14.3 Offences Subject to Notification Requirements under Miscellaneous Acts 1960–2002

	Offence	Qualification to applicability of notification requirement *Notification requirements only apply…*
IwCA 1960, s 1	Indecent conduct towards young child	
CLA 1977, s 54	Inciting girl under 16 to have incestuous sexual intercourse	
PCA 1978, s 1	Indecent photographs of children	If the indecent photographs or pseudo-photographs showed persons under 16, *and* (a) the conviction, finding or caution was before 1 May 2004 (the commencement of this Part) *or* (b) the offender— (i) was 18 or over, *or* (ii) is sentenced in respect of the offence to imprisonment for a term of at least 12 months
Customs and Excise Management Act 1979, s 170	Penalty for fraudulent evasion of duty etc. in relation to goods prohibited to be imported under of the Customs Consolidation Act 1876, s 42 (indecent or obscene articles)	If the prohibited goods included indecent photographs of persons under 16, *and* (a) the conviction, finding or caution was before 1 May 2004 (the commencement of this Part) *or* (b) the offender— (i) was 18 or over, *or* (ii) is sentenced in respect of the offence to imprisonment for a term of at least 12 months
CJA 1988, s 160	Possession of indecent photograph of a child	If the indecent photographs or pseudo-photographs showed persons under 16, *and* (a) the conviction, finding, or caution was before 1 May 2004 (the commencement of this Part) *or* (b) the offender— (i) was 18 or over, *or* (ii) is sentenced in respect of the offence to imprisonment for a term of at least 12 months
SO(A)A 2000, s 3	Abuse of position of trust	If the offender was 20 or over

Note that the Schedule 3 offences listed below also include any attempt, conspiracy, or incitement to commit that offence,[a] and aiding, abetting, counselling, or procuring the commission of that offence.[b] Also included are inchoate offences under Part 2 of the Serious Crime Act 2007 (encouraging or assisting crime offences) where the listed offence is the offence (or one of the offences) which the person intended or believed would be committed.[c] Equivalent service offences are included by virtue of paras 93–93A of Schedule 3. It is important to note that notification does not apply to any sexual offences prior to the implementation of the 1956 Sexual Offences Act and not all sexual offences in subsequent sexual offences legislation are included in Schedule 3.

[a] SOA 2003, Sch 3, para 94A(a).
[b] SOA 2003, Sch 3, para 94A(b).
[c] SOA 2003, Sch 3, para 94AA.

3. Offences Subject to Notification Requirements under the Sexual Offences Act 2003

Table 14.4 Offences Subject to Notification Requirements under the Sexual Offences Act 2003

	Offence	Qualification to applicability of notification requirement *Notification requirements only apply…*
s 1	Rape	
s 2	Assault by penetration	

s 3	Sexual assault	If:
		(a) *where the offender was under 18,* he is or has been sentenced, in respect of the offence, to imprisonment for a term of at least 12 months;
		(b) *in any other case*
		   (i) the victim was under 18, *or*
		   (ii) the offender, in respect of the offence or finding, is or has been
		(a) sentenced to a term of imprisonment,
		(b) detained in a hospital, *or*
		(c) made the subject of a community sentence of at least 12 months

s 4	Causing sexual activity without consent	
s 5	Rape of a child under 13	
s 6	Assault of a child under 13 by penetration	
s 7	Sexual assault of a child under 13	If the offender (a) was 18 or over, *or* (b) is or has been sentenced in respect of the offence to imprisonment for a term of at least 12 months
s 8	Causing or inciting a child under 13 to engage in sexual activity	
s 9	Sexual activity with a child	
s 10	Causing or inciting a child to engage in sexual activity	
s 11	Engaging in sexual activity in the presence of a child	
s 12	Causing a child to watch a sexual act	
s 13	Child sex offences committed by children or young persons	If the offender is or has been sentenced, in respect of the offence, to imprisonment for a term of at least 12 months
s 14	Arranging or facilitating the commission of a child sex offence	If the offender (a) was 18 or over, *or* (b) is or has been sentenced, in respect of the offence, to imprisonment for a term of at least 12 months
s 15	Meeting a child following sexual grooming etc.	

Table 14.4 Continued

	Offence	Qualification to applicability of notification requirement *Notification requirements only apply ...*
s 15A	Sexual communication with a child	
s 16	Abuse of position of trust: sexual activity with a child	If the offender, in respect of the offence, is or has been (a) sentenced to a term of imprisonment, *or* (b) detained in a hospital, *or* (c) made the subject of a community sentence of at least 12 months
s 17	Abuse of position of trust: causing or inciting a child to engage in sexual activity	If the offender, in respect of the offence, is or has been (a) sentenced to a term of imprisonment, *or* (b) detained in a hospital, *or* (c) made the subject of a community sentence of at least 12 months
s 18	Abuse of position of trust: sexual activity in the presence of a child	If the offender, in respect of the offence, is or has been (a) sentenced to a term of imprisonment, *or* (b) detained in a hospital, *or* (c) made the subject of a community sentence of at least 12 months
s 19	Abuse of position of trust: causing a child to watch a sexual act	If the offender, in respect of the offence, is or has been (a) sentenced to a term of imprisonment, *or* (b) detained in a hospital, *or* (c) made the subject of a community sentence of at least 12 months
s 25	Sexual activity with a child family member	If the offender (a) was 18 or over, *or* (b) is or has been sentenced in respect of the offence to imprisonment for a term of at least 12 months
s 26	Inciting a child family member to engage in sexual activity	If the offender (a) was 18 or over, *or* (b) is or has been sentenced in respect of the offence to imprisonment for a term of at least 12 months
s 30	Sexual activity with a person with a mental disorder impeding choice	
s 31	Causing or inciting a person, with a mental disorder impeding choice, to engage in sexual activity	
s 32	Engaging in sexual activity in the presence of a person with a mental disorder impeding choice	
s 33	Causing a person, with a mental disorder impeding choice, to watch a sexual act	
s 34	Inducement, threat, or deception to procure sexual activity with a person with a mental disorder	

(continued)

Table 14.4 Continued

	Offence	Qualification to applicability of notification requirement *Notification requirements only apply ...*
s 35	Causing a person with a mental disorder to engage in or agree to engage in sexual activity by inducement, threat or deception	
s 36	Engaging in sexual activity in the presence, procured by inducement, threat, or deception, of a person with a mental disorder	
s 37	Causing a person with a mental disorder to watch a sexual act by inducement, threat, or deception	
s 38	Care workers: sexual activity with a person with a mental disorder	If: (a) *where the offender was under 18*, he is or has been sentenced, in respect of the offence, to imprisonment for a term of at least 12 months; (b) *in any other case*, the offender, in respect of the offence or finding, is or has been (i) sentenced to a term of imprisonment (ii) detained in a hospital, *or* (iii) made the subject of a community sentence of at least 12 months
s 39	Care workers: causing or inciting sexual activity	If: (a) *where the offender was under 18*, he is or has been sentenced, in respect of the offence, to imprisonment for a term of at least 12 months; (b) *in any other case*, the offender, in respect of the offence or finding, is or has been (i) sentenced to a term of imprisonment, (ii) detained in a hospital, *or* (iii) made the subject of a community sentence of at least 12 months
s 40	Care workers: sexual activity in the presence of a person with a mental disorder	If: (a) *where the offender was under 18*, he is or has been sentenced, in respect of the offence, to imprisonment for a term of at least 12 months; (b) *in any other case*, the offender, in respect of the offence or finding, is or has been (i) sentenced to a term of imprisonment (ii) detained in a hospital, *or* (iii) made the subject of a community sentence of at least 12 months
s 41	Care workers: causing a person with a mental disorder to watch a sexual act	If: (a) *where the offender was under 18*, he is or has been sentenced, in respect of the offence, to imprisonment for a term of at least 12 months; (b) *in any other case*, the offender, in respect of the offence or finding, is or has been (i) sentenced to a term of imprisonment (ii) detained in a hospital, *or* (iii) made the subject of a community sentence of at least 12 months

Table 14.4 Continued

	Offence	Qualification to applicability of notification requirement *Notification requirements only apply...*
s 47	Paying for sexual services of a child	If the victim or other party was under 16, *and* the offender (a) was 18 or over, *or* (b) is or has been sentenced in respect of the offence to imprisonment for a term of at least 12 months
s 48	Causing or inciting child prostitution or pornography	If the offender (a) was 18 or over, *or* (b) is or has been sentenced in respect of the offence to imprisonment for a term of at least 12 months
s 49	Controlling a child prostitute or a child involved in pornography	If the offender (a) was 18 or over, *or* (b) is or has been sentenced in respect of the offence to imprisonment for a term of at least 12 months
s 50	Arranging or facilitating child prostitution or pornography	If the offender (a) was 18 or over, *or* (b) is or has been sentenced in respect of the offence to imprisonment for a term of at least 12 months
s 61	Administering a substance with intent	

s 62	Committing an offence with intent to commit a sexual offence	If:
		(a) *where the offender was under 18*, he is or has been sentenced, in respect of the offence, to imprisonment for a term of at least 12 months;
		(b) *in any other case*
		  (i) the intended victim was under 18, *or*
		  (ii) the offender, in respect of the offence or finding, is or has been
		(a) sentenced to a term of imprisonment,
		(b) detained in a hospital, *or*
		(c) made the subject of a community sentence of at least 12 months

s 63	Trespass with intent to commit a sexual offence	If:
		(a) *where the offender was under 18*, he is or has been sentenced, in respect of the offence, to imprisonment for a term of at least 12 months;
		(b) *in any other case*
		  (i) the intended victim was under 18, *or*
		  (ii) the offender, in respect of the offence or finding, is or has been
		(a) sentenced to a term of imprisonment,
		(b) detained in a hospital, *or*
		(c) made the subject of a community sentence of at least 12 months

s 64	Sex with an adult relative: penetration	If:
		(a) *where the offender was under 18*, he is or has been sentenced, in respect of the offence, to imprisonment for a term of at least 12 months;
		(b) *in any other case*, the offender, in respect of the offence or finding, is or has been
		  (i) sentenced to a term of imprisonment
		  (ii) detained in a hospital

(continued)

Table 14.4 Continued

	Offence	Qualification to applicability of notification requirement *Notification requirements only apply ...*
s 65	Sex with an adult relative: consenting to penetration	If: (a) *where the offender was under 18*, he is or has been sentenced, in respect of the offence, to imprisonment for a term of at least 12 months; (b) *in any other case*, the offender, in respect of the offence or finding, is or has been 　(i) sentenced to a term of imprisonment, 　(ii) detained in a hospital
s 66	Exposure	If: (a) *where the offender was under 18*, he is or has been sentenced, in respect of the offence, to imprisonment for a term of at least 12 months; (b) *in any other case* 　(i) the victim was under 18, *or* 　(ii) the offender, in respect of the offence or finding, is or has been (a) sentenced to a term of imprisonment, (b) detained in a hospital, or (c) made the subject of a community sentence of at least 12 months
s 67	Voyeurism	If: (a) *where the offender was under 18*, he is or has been sentenced, in respect of the offence, to imprisonment for a term of at least 12 months; (b) *in any other case* 　(i) the victim was under 18, *or* 　(ii) the offender, in respect of the offence or finding, is or has been (a) sentenced to a term of imprisonment, (b) detained in a hospital, or (c) made the subject of a community sentence of at least 12 months
s 67A	Voyeurism: additional offences	If— (a) the offence was committed for the purpose mentioned in s 67A(3)(a) (sexual gratification), and (b) the relevant condition is met. (2) Where the offender was under 18, the relevant condition is that the offender is or has been sentenced in respect of the offence to imprisonment for a term of at least 12 months. (3) In any other case, the relevant condition is that— 　(a) the victim was under 18, *or* 　(b) the offender, in respect of the offence or finding, is or has been— 　　(i) sentenced to a term of imprisonment, 　　(ii) detained in a hospital, *or* 　　(iii) made the subject of a community sentence of at least 12 months
s 69	Intercourse with an animal	If: (a) *where the offender was under 18*, he is or has been sentenced, in respect of the offence, to imprisonment for a term of at least 12 months;

Table 14.4 Continued

Offence		Qualification to applicability of notification requirement *Notification requirements only apply...*
		(b) *in any other case,* the offender, in respect of the offence or finding, is or has been (i) sentenced to a term of imprisonment, (ii) detained in a hospital
s 70	Sexual penetration of a corpse	If: (a) *where the offender was under 18,* he is or has been sentenced, in respect of the offence, to imprisonment for a term of at least 12 months; (b) *in any other case,* the offender, in respect of the offence or finding, is or has been (i) sentenced to a term of imprisonment, (ii) detained in a hospital

Note that the Schedule 3 offences listed below also include any attempt, conspiracy, or incitement to commit that offence,[a] and aiding, abetting, counselling, or procuring the commission of that offence.[b] Also included are inchoate offences under Part 2 of the Serious Crime Act 2007 (encouraging or assisting crime offences) where the listed offence is the offence (or one of the offences) which the person intended or believed would be committed.[c] Equivalent service offences are included by virtue of paras 93–93A of Schedule 3. It is important to note that notification does not apply to any sexual offences prior to the implementation of the 1956 Sexual Offences Act and not all sexual offences in subsequent sexual offences legislation are included in Schedule 3.

[a] SOA 2003, Sch 3, para 94A(a).
[b] SOA 2003, Sch 3, para 94A(b).
[c] SOA 2003, Sch 3, para 94AA.

4. Offences Subject to Notification Requirements under Miscellaneous Acts 2008–2015

Table 14.5 Offences Subject to Notification Requirements under Miscellaneous Acts 2008–2015

	Offence	Qualification to applicability of notification requirement *Notification requirements only apply...*
CJIA 2008, s 63	Possession of extreme pornographic images	If the offender- (a) was 18 or over, *and* (b) is sentenced to imprisonment for a term of at least 2 years.
CJA 2009, s 62(1)	Possession of prohibited images of children	If the offender- (a) was 18 or over, *and* (b) is sentenced to imprisonment for a term of at least 2 years.
SCA 2015, s 69	Possession of a paedophile manual	If the offender- (a) was 18 or over, *or* (b) is sentenced to imprisonment for a term of at least 12 months.

Note that the Schedule 3 offences listed below also include any attempt, conspiracy, or incitement to commit that offence,[a] and aiding, abetting, counselling, or procuring the commission of that offence.[b] Also included are inchoate offences under Part 2 of the Serious Crime Act 2007 (encouraging or assisting crime offences) where the listed offence is the offence (or one of the offences) which the person intended or believed would be committed.[c] Equivalent service offences are included by virtue of paras 93–93A of Schedule 3. It is important to note that notification does not apply to any sexual offences prior to the implementation of the 1956 Sexual Offences Act and not all sexual offences in subsequent sexual offences legislation are included in Schedule 3.

[a] SOA 2003, Sch 3, para 94A(a).
[b] SOA 2003, Sch 3, para 94A(b).
[c] SOA 2003, Sch 3, para 94AA.

15
PUBLICITY

A. Anonymity of Complainants	15.01	2. Eligibility of Adult Witnesses for Reporting Restrictions	15.09
1. Offences to which the Anonymity Requirement Applies	15.04	3. Applying for Reporting Restrictions	15.11
2. Offences *Not* Subject to Reporting under the Sexual Offences Act 2003	15.05	5. Dispensing with Reporting Restrictions	15.16
B. Anonymity of Witnesses	15.07	6. Young Persons Aged Under 18	15.19
1. Adult Witnesses Aged 18 or Over	15.08	7. Provisions under the Youth Justice and Criminal Evidence Act 1999	15.20

A. ANONYMITY OF COMPLAINANTS

15.01 Where a complainant makes an allegation of any offence specified under s 2 of the Sexual Offences (Amendment) Act (SO(A)A) 1992, *no matter* relating to the complainant *during the complainant's lifetime* should be published if it is likely to lead members of the public to identify the complainant.[1] This is qualified by s 1(4) of the Act and does not extend, for example, to a rape complainant who is accused of perjury.[2]

15.02 This includes, specifically, the complainant's name, address, identity of any school or education establishment attended by the complainant, the identity of any place of work, and any still or moving picture of the person.[3]

15.03 In relation to a complainant who is deceased, there is no protection provided by statute. In a case where the evidence of that complainant is not challenged, with the agreement of defence counsel, the deceased witness could be referred to as Witness A in order to protect his/her identity. (Such a measure was adopted in *R v Delroy Grant* (March 2011)—The 'Night Stalker' trial—where the defence was identification.)

1. Offences to which the Anonymity Requirement Applies

15.04 1. Rape (under any legislative provision).

2. Burglary with intent to commit rape (under any legislative provision).
3. Any attempt, conspiracy, incitement, aiding, abetting, counselling, or procuring of either of the above or any of the offences specified below.
4. Any of the offences below.

---

[1] SO(A)A 1992, s 1(1).
[2] *R v Beale* [2019] EWCA Crim 665 at paras [49–50].
[3] SO(A)A 1992, s 1(3A).

Table 15.1 Offences to which the Anonymity Requirement Applies

Legislative Provision	Offence
SOA 1956, s 2	Procurement of woman by threats
SOA 1956, s 3	Procurement of woman by false pretences
SOA 1956, s 4	Administering drugs to obtain or facilitate intercourse with a woman
SOA 1956, s 5	Intercourse with a girl under 13
SOA 1956, s 6	Intercourse with a girl under 16
SOA 1956, s 7	Intercourse with a defective
SOA 1956, s 9	Procurement of a defective
SOA 1956, s 10	Incest by a man. Except where the complainant is alleged to have committed incest under s 11 against the defendant at the time of the s 10 offence[a]
SOA 1956, s 11	Incest by a woman. Except where the complainant is alleged to have committed incest under s 10 against the defendant at the time of the s 11 offence[b]
SOA 1956, s 12	Buggery. Except where the complainant is alleged to have committed buggery under s 12 against the defendant at the time of the s 12 offence[c]
SOA 1956, s 14	Indecent assault on a woman
SOA 1956, s 15	Indecent assault on a man
SOA 1956, s 16	Assault with intent to commit buggery
SOA 1956, s 17	Abduction of woman by force or for the sake of her property
MHA 1959, s 128	Sexual intercourse with patients
IwCA 1960, s 1	Indecent conduct towards young child
CLA 1977, s 54	Inciting girl under 16 to have incestuous sexual intercourse
MSA 2015, s 2	Human trafficking

[a] SO(A)A 1992, s 4(2), (5).
[b] SO(A)A 1992, s 4(3), (6).
[c] SO(A)A 1992, s 4(4), (7).

2. Offences *Not* Subject to Reporting under the Sexual Offences Act 2003

15.05 *All offences* under the SOA 2003 are subject to the anonymity provisions of the SO(A)A 1992, except for the following.[4]

3. When Can Anonymity be Waived?

15.06 (i) *Before trial*: if the defendant, or another person against whom the complainant may be expected to give evidence, applies to the judge for a direction and satisfies the judge: (a) that such direction is required for the purpose of inducing persons who are likely to be needed

[4] SO(A)A 1992, s 2(1)(da).

Table 15.2 Offences *not* Subject to Reporting under the Sexual Offences Act 2003

SOA 2003, s 64	Sex with an adult relative: penetration
SOA 2003, s 65	Sex with an adult relative: consenting to penetration
SOA 2003, s 69	Intercourse with an animal
SOA 2003, s 71	Sexual activity in a public lavatory

as witnesses at the trial to come forward; and (b) that the conduct of the defendant's defence at the trial is likely to be substantially prejudiced if the direction is not given.[5]

(ii) *At trial*: if: (a) the effect of a reporting restriction is to impose a substantial and unreasonable restriction on the reporting of proceedings at the trial; and (b) it is in the public interest to remove or relax the restriction.[6]

(iii) *After trial*: the outcome of the trial is not reason enough to remove or relax the restriction.[7] If a defendant is convicted and applies to appeal that conviction, the defendant may apply to the appellate court for a direction under the SOA(A) 1992, s 3(4) to displace reporting restrictions. The restrictions shall be displaced if the court is satisfied: (a) that the direction is required for the purpose of obtaining evidence in support of the appeal; and (b) that the applicant is likely to suffer substantial injustice if the direction is not given.[8]

B. ANONYMITY OF WITNESSES

15.07 The provisions regarding the anonymity of both adult and child/young witnesses within the Youth Justice and Criminal Evidence Act (YJCEA) 1999 are all in force.

1. Adult Witnesses Aged 18 or Over

15.08 Section 46 of the YJCEA 1999 gives the court the power to make a 'reporting direction' where an application is made in relation to a witness, other than the accused, who is 18 or over.[9] This provision came into force on 7.10.2004.[10] Breach of such a reporting direction is a summary offence, the maximum penalty for which is a fine not exceeding level 5 on the standard scale.[11]

---

[5] SO(A)A 1992, s 3(1).
[6] SO(A)A 1992, s 3(2).
[7] SO(A)A 1992, s 3(3).
[8] SO(A)A 1992, s 3(4). It is a defence to an offence under s 1 of the Act (inclusion of any matter in a publication) to prove that the complainant gave written consent to that party (s 5(2) SO(A)A 1992)). Unless it is proved that any person interfered unreasonably with the peace or comfort of the person giving the consent, with intent to obtain it or that person was under the age of 16 at the time when it was given (s 5(3)).
[9] YJCEA 1999, s 46(1).
[10] YJCEA 1999 (Commencement Order No 10) (England and Wales) Order 2004 (SI 2004 No 2428) art 2(a).
[11] YJCEA 1999, s 49. Provisions in LASPO 2012 increased the power of Magistrates' Courts so they are able to impose unlimited fines for the most serious offences committed on or after 12.3.2015.

2. Eligibility of Adult Witnesses for Reporting Restrictions

15.09 The court may make such an order if it considers (a) that the witness is eligible for protection and (b) that giving a reporting direction is likely to improve the quality of evidence given by the witness or the level of co-operation given by the witness to any party in connection with the case.[12]

15.10 When determining eligibility, the court must take into account the nature and alleged circumstances of the offence; the age of the witness; the social, cultural, and ethnic origins of the witness (where relevant); the domestic and employment circumstances of the witness (where relevant); and the religious or political beliefs of the witness (where relevant). Further, the court may take into account any behaviour towards the witness by either the accused, members or associates of the accused's family or any other person who is likely to be an accused or witness to the proceedings.[13] The court must also consider any views expressed by the witness.[14]

3. Applying for Reporting Restrictions

15.11 The procedure for application and objection is set out in rule 6.4 of the CPR 2020. The CPR does not specify whether the application must be oral or in writing, leaving the form of the application to the court.[15] However, the content of the application is specified: the application must: (a) specify the proposed terms of the order and for how long they should last; (b) explain the court's power to make the order; (c) explain why the order is necessary; (d) explain, in the case of adult witnesses, how s 46 of the YJCEA 1999 is satisfied both in terms of the witness's eligibility for assistance and why a reporting direction would be likely to improve the witness's quality of evidence or their cooperation in preparing the case.[16]

15.12 The application should be made as soon as reasonably practicable.[17] Any other party to the proceedings and such other persons as the court directs should be notified of it.[18]

15.13 Any representations in response must be filed and served as soon as reasonably practicable after the notice of application. The reasons for any objection must be explained and any alternative terms proposed must be specified. If a hearing is required, it must be requested, and an explanation given as to why it is needed.[19]

15.14 The application can either be dealt with administratively or at a hearing.[20] It may only be dealt with after all parties to the proceedings and any other person directly affected

---

[12] YJCEA 1999, s 46(2).
[13] YJCEA 1999, s 46(4).
[14] YJCEA 1999, s 46(5)
[15] CPR 2020, r 6.4(2).
[16] CPR 2020, r 6.4(c), (d), and (f).
[17] CPR 2020, r 6.4(3).
[18] CPR 2020, r 6.4(3).
[19] CPR 2020, r 6.7.
[20] CPR 2020, r 6.2(2).

have been afforded the opportunity to either attend a hearing or make representations.[21] When dealing with the application the court must have regard to the importance of open justice.[22]

4. Nature and Duration of Reporting Restrictions

15.15 Reporting restrictions last for the lifetime of the witness and apply to any matter that is likely to lead members of the public to identify the witness as being such in the proceedings.[23] This includes, in particular, their name, address, the identity of any educational establishment or place of work attended by the witness, and any still or moving picture of the witness.[24]

5. Dispensing with Reporting Restrictions

15.16 The court or an appellate court may make an 'excepting direction' to dispense with the restrictions, provided: (a) it is satisfied that it is necessary in the interest of justice to do so; or (b) it is satisfied the effect of the restrictions is to impose a substantial and unreasonable restriction on the reporting of proceedings, and that it is in the public interest to remove or relax that restriction.[25] The relaxation can be to any extent specified by the court.[26]

15.17 The abandonment or determination of the criminal proceedings is not a good ground for the making of an excepting direction.[27]

15.18 An excepting direction may be given at the time the reporting direction is given and may be varied or revoked by the court or an appellate court.[28]

6. Young Persons Aged Under 18

15.19 On the 13.4.2015 s 45[29] of the YJCEA 1999 was implemented and a new s 45A.[30] was inserted into the Act (see para 15.31). Section 45 replaced section 39 of the Children and Young Persons Act (CYPA) 1933. Section 39 remains in force but was amended and no longer applies in relation to criminal proceedings.

---

[21] CPR 2020, r 6.2(3).
[22] CPR 2020, r 6.2(1).
[23] YJCEA 1999, s 46(6).
[24] YJCEA 1999, s 46(7).
[25] YJCEA 1999, s 46(9).
[26] YJCEA 1999, s 46(9).
[27] YJCEA 1999, s 46(9).
[28] YJCEA 1999, s 46(11).
[29] Youth Justice and Criminal Evidence Act 1999 (Commencement No 14) (England and Wales) order 2015/818 art 2(a).
[30] Section 45A was inserted by Criminal Justice and Courts Act 2015 c 2, Pt 3 s 78(2).

7. Provisions under the Youth Justice and Criminal Evidence Act 1999

Section 44 YJCE 1999

15.20 Section 44, restrictions on reporting alleged offences involving persons aged under 18 years, came into force on 27.7.1999. Section 44(2) requires that: no matter relating to any person involved in the offence while he is under the age of 18 is to be included in any publication if it is likely to lead members of the public to identify him as a person involved in the offence as a defendant, complainant or *witness*.[31] This includes, in particular, their name, address, the identity of any educational establishment or place of work attended by the witness, and any still or moving picture of the witness.[32]

15.21 These provisions only apply until the institution of criminal proceedings or until the restriction is dispensed with by court order in the interests of justice.[33] A decision to dispense with the order must have regard to the welfare of that person.[34] The power to dispense with the order may be exercised by a single magistrate.[35] Where the decision is made by the Magistrates' Court a right of appeal against the making of an order to/or refusal to dispense with the restrictions lies to the Crown Court.[36] On appeal the Crown Court may (a) make such order as is necessary to give effect to the determination of the appeal: and (b) make also make such incidental or consequential orders as appear to be just.

15.22 Breach of such a reporting direction is a summary offence,[37] the maximum penalty for which is a fine not exceeding level 5 on the standard scale.[38]

15.23 Note: This section does not apply to persons in respect of whom section 1 SO(A)A 1992 applies. See para 15.01.

Witnesses under 18 once proceedings have been instituted: the court may direct that no matter relating to any person concerned in the proceedings while he is under 18 be included in any publication if it is likely to lead members of the public to identify him as a person concerned as a defendant, complainant, or witness in the court proceedings.

Section 45 YJCE 1999

15.24 Section 45 of the YJCEA 1999 gives the court the discretion to restrict reporting of criminal proceedings involving any persons aged under 18 years. This provision was implemented on 13.4.2015. Breach of such a reporting direction is a summary offence,[39] the maximum penalty for which is a fine not exceeding level 5 on the standard scale.[40]

---

[31] YJCEA 1999, s 44(2) and (4).
[32] YJCEA 1999, s 44 (6).
[33] YJCEA s 44 (7).
[34] YJCEA s44 (8).
[35] YJCEA s 44 (10).
[36] YJCEA s 44(11).
[37] YJCEA 1999, s 49(1)(a).
[38] YJCEA 1999, s 49(5).
[39] YJCEA 1999, s 49(1)(a).
[40] YJCEA 1999, s 49(5). Provisions in LASPO 2012 increased the power of magistrates' courts so they are able to impose unlimited fines for the most serious offences committed on or after 12.3.2015.

Note: s 45 does not apply in relation to any proceedings to which s 49 CYPA 1933 applies (automatic reporting restrictions in the Youth Court). **15.25**

Applying for reporting restrictions under s 45

The procedure for application and objection is set out in rule 6.4 of the CPR 2020. See para 15.11. **15.26**

Nature and duration of s 45 reporting restrictions

Reporting restrictions last until the person is 18 and apply to any matter that is likely to lead members of the public to identify them as being concerned in the proceedings.[41] This includes, in particular, their name, address, the identity of any educational establishment or place of work attended by the witness, and any still or moving picture of the witness.[42] When deciding whether to make a s 45 direction the court shall have regard to the welfare of that person.[43] **15.27**

Dispensing with reporting restrictions under s 45

The court or an appellate court may make an 'excepting direction' to dispense with the restrictions, provided: (a) it is satisfied that it is necessary in the interest of justice to do so; or (b) it is satisfied the effect of the restrictions is to impose a substantial and unreasonable restriction on the reporting of proceedings, and that it is in the public interest to remove or relax that restriction.[44] The relaxation can be to any extent specified by the court.[45] The abandonment or determination of the criminal proceedings is not a good ground for the making of an excepting direction.[46] **15.28**

In deciding whether to make an excepting direction the court must have regard to the welfare of that person.[47] **15.29**

An excepting direction may be given at the time the reporting direction is given and may be varied or revoked by the court or an appellate court.[48] **15.30**

Section 45A YJCEA 1999

Section 45A of the YJCEA 1999 gives the court the discretion to make a 'reporting direction' where an application is made in relation to a witness, other than the accused, or a complainant who is aged under 18 when the proceedings commence.[49] This provision came into force on 13.4.2015. Breach of such a reporting direction is a summary offence,[50] the maximum penalty for which is a fine not exceeding level 5 on the standard scale.[51] **15.31**

---

[41] YJCEA 1999, s 45(3).
[42] YJCEA 1999, s 45(8).
[43] YJCEA 1999, s 45(6).
[44] YJCEA 1999, s 45(4) and (5).
[45] YJCEA 1999, s 45(4).
[46] YJCEA 1999, s 45(5).
[47] YJCEA 1999, s 45(6).
[48] YJCEA 1999, s 45(10).
[49] YJCEA 1999, s 45A(2).
[50] YJCEA 1999, s 49(1A).
[51] YJCEA 1999, s 49. Provisions in LASPO 2012 increased the power of magistrates' courts so they are able to impose unlimited fines for the most serious offences committed on or after 12.3.2015.

Eligibility of young persons for reporting restrictions under s 45A

15.32 The Court may make a direction under s 45 if it considers (a) that the person is eligible for protection and (b) that giving a reporting direction is likely to improve the quality of evidence given by the witness or the level of cooperation given by the witness to any party in connection with the case.[52]

15.33 When determining eligibility, the Court must take into account the nature and alleged circumstances of the offence; the age of the witness; the social, cultural, and ethnic origins of the witness (where relevant); the domestic and employment circumstances of the witness (where relevant); and the religious or political beliefs of the witness (where relevant). Further, the court may take into account any behaviour towards the witness by either the accused, members, or associates of the accused's family or any other person who is likely to be an accused or witness to the proceedings.[53] The Court must also consider any views expressed by the person in respect of whom the reporting may be made.[54] If that person is under the age of 16 the views of an appropriate person (other than the accused) must be considered. The Court must also have regard to the welfare of that person, whether it would be in the interests of justice to make the direction, and the public interest in avoiding the imposition of a substantial and unreasonable restriction on the reporting of the proceedings.[55]

Applying for reporting restrictions under s 45A

15.34 The procedure for application and objection is set out in rule 6.4 of the CPR 2020. See para 15.11.

Nature and duration of s 45A reporting restrictions

15.35 Reporting restrictions last for the lifetime of the person in respect of whom they are made and apply to any matter that is likely to lead members of the public to identify the witness as being such in the proceedings.[56] This includes, in particular, their name, address, the identity of any educational establishment or place of work attended by the witness, and any still or moving picture of the witness.[57]

Dispensing with reporting restrictions under s 45A

15.36 The Court or an appellate court may make an 'excepting direction' to dispense with the restrictions, provided: (a) it is satisfied that it is necessary in the interest of justice to do

---

[52] YJCEA 1999, s 45A(5).
[53] YJCEA 1999, s 45A(6).
[54] YJCEA 1999, s 45A(7).
[55] YJCEA 1999, s 45A(8).
[56] YJCEA 1999, s 45A(2).
[57] YJCEA 1999, s 45A(4).

so; or (b) it is satisfied the effect of the restrictions is to impose a substantial and unreasonable restriction on the reporting of proceedings, and that it is in the public interest to remove or relax that restriction.[58] The relaxation can be to any extent specified by the court.[59]

15.37 The abandonment or determination of the criminal proceedings is not a good ground for the making of an excepting direction.[60]

15.38 In deciding whether to make an excepting direction, the court must have regard to the welfare of that person.[61]

15.39 An excepting direction may be given at the time the reporting direction is given and may be varied or revoked by the court or an appellate court.[62]

---

[58] YJCEA 1999, s 45A(11).
[59] YJCEA 1999, s 45A(10).
[60] YJCEA 1999, s 45A(12).
[61] YJCEA 1999, s 45A(13).
[62] YJCEA 1999, s 45A(14).

16

SEXUAL HARM PREVENTION ORDERS

General	16.01
A. Applicability	16.07
1. Within Criminal Court Proceedings	16.07
2. Procedure	16.08
3. Non-conviction SHPOs	16.12
4. Civil Orders	16.13
B. Sexual Harm	16.18
C. Interim SHPOs	16.19
D. Ambit and Content of an SHPO	16.21
1. Clarity of the SHPO	16.25
2. SHPOs and Other Regimes	16.28
3. Computer Access	16.30
4. Personal Contact with Children	16.33
E. Variations, Renewals, and Discharges	16.37
F. Appeals Against the Making of SHPOs and Interim SHPOs	16.45
G. Relationship with Notification Requirements	16.48
H. Relationship with Barring from Working with Children and Vulnerable Adults	16.51
1. The Original Regime under the Safeguarding and Vulnerable Groups Act 2006	16.52
2. The Regime under the Safeguarding and Vulnerable Groups Act 2006 (as amended)	16.53
I. Offences: Breach of SHPO, Interim SHPO and Existing Protective Orders	16.65
J. Sexual Offences Act 2003, Schedule 3	16.70
1. Offences which may be Subject to an SHPO under the Sexual Offences Act 1956	16.71
2. Offences which may be Subject to an SHPO under Miscellaneous Acts 1960–2002	16.72
3. Offences which may be Subject to an SHPO under the Sexual Offences Act 2003	16.73
4. Offences which may be Subject to an SHPO under Miscellaneous Acts after 2003	16.75
K. Sexual Offences Act 2003, Schedule 5	16.76
1. Common Law Offences which may be Subject to an SHPO	16.77
2. Offences which may be Subject to an SHPO under the Offences Against the Person Act 1861	16.78
3. Offences which may be Subject to an SHPO under Miscellaneous Acts 1883 to 1938	16.79
4. Offences which may be Subject to an SHPO under the Firearms Act 1968	16.80
5. Offences which may be Subject to an SHPO under the Theft Act 1968	16.81
6. Offences which may be Subject to an SHPO under Miscellaneous Acts 1971 to 1982	16.82
7. Offences which may be Subject to an SHPO under the Aviation Security Act 1982	16.83
8. Offences which may be Subject to an SHPO under Miscellaneous Acts 1983 to 1985	16.84
9. Offences which may be Subject to an SHPO under the Public Order Act 1986	16.85
10. Offences which may be Subject to an SHPO under Miscellaneous Acts 1988 (including death by dangerous driving)	16.86
11. Offences which may be Subject to an SHPO under the Aviation and Maritime Security Act 1990	16.87
12. Offences which may be Subject to an SHPO under the Protection from Harassment Act 1997	16.88
13. Offences which may be Subject to an SHPO under Miscellaneous Acts/Orders 1994 to 2004	16.89
14. Offences which may be Subject to an SHPO under the Sexual Offences Act 2003	16.90
15. Offence which may be Subject to an SHPO under the Modern Slavery Act 2015	16.91
L. Suggested Forms of Words for SHPOs	16.92
M. SHPO Example	16.97

GENERAL

16.01 The court's power to impose a s 5A restraining order[1] was repealed by the SOA 2003[2] and replaced by the power to impose a Sexual Offences Prevention Order (SOPO). The 2003 Act also introduced the Foreign Travel Order (FTO)[3] and Risk of Sexual Harm Order (RSHO) made by a magistrate on the application of the chief officer of police for an area in which the defendant lives, or to which he may travel, to prohibit the offender from travelling outside the UK for a period of up to 6 months.

16.02 The SOPO, RSHO, and FTO were repealed by the Anti-Social Behaviour Crime Policing Act 2014[4] and replaced with the s 103A Sexual Harm Prevention Order (SHPO) an amalgamation of the SOPO and FTO, and the s 122A Sexual Risk Order; see also para 12.142. Like the SOPO, the SHPO has a wide ambit and is prohibitive in nature. An SHPO may be imposed if the offence[5] was sexual and falls within Schedule 3 to the 2003 Act.[6] The qualifying age and/or sentence requirements previously applicable to SOPOs under Schedule 3 were disapplied in relation to the SHPO regime.[7] Further, an SHPO may be imposed for a number of non-sexual offences falling within Schedule 5 to the 2003 Act.[8]

16.03 On 1.12.2020 the Sentencing Act 2020 (known as the 'Sentencing Code') was enacted. The Act consolidates existing sentencing legislation and applies to offenders convicted on or after that date. The Sentencing Code repealed the SOA 2003 provisions relating to the imposition of SHPOs on conviction, however the transitory provisions of the Sentencing Code mean that SHPO's will continue to be available under pre-Code law for qualifying offenders convicted before 1.12.2020. SHPOs on conviction after 1.12.2020 will be made under the corresponding provisions of Part 11, Chapter 2 of the Sentencing Code. SHPOs in relation to offenders found guilty by reason of insanity, or found to be under a disability but have done the act charged, civil SHPOs, interim SHPOs, and SROs will continue to be governed by the provisions of the Sexual Offences Act 2003.

16.04 The court must, before granting an SHPO following conviction for an offence under either Schedule 3 or Schedule 5, be satisfied that such an order is necessary for the purpose of protecting the public or any particular members of the public from sexual harm from the offender,[9] or protecting children or vulnerable adults generally, or any particular children or vulnerable adults, from sexual harm from the defendant outside the United Kingdom.[10] Note: the test of necessity brings with it the subtest of proportionality.[11] See para 16.25.

---

[1] SOA 1997, s 5A.
[2] Repealed by Sexual Offences Act 2003 c 42 Sch 7 para 1 (1 May 2004).
[3] S 114 SOA 2003.
[4] Repealed by Anti-social Behaviour, Crime and Policing Act 2014 c 12 Sch 5 para 3(1) (8 March 2015: repeal has effect as SI 2015/373 subject to savings and transitional provisions specified in 2014 c 12 s 114.
[5] Whether convicted of, or found guilty by reason of insanity, or found to be under a disability but has done the act charged, in relation to a Sch 3 or 5 offence.
[6] SOA 2003, s 103A(2).
[7] SOA 2003, s 103B(9) provided that any conditions in Sch 3 relating to the age of the offender or the victim, or to the relevant finding or the sentence imposed on the offender may be disregarded in making an SHPO.
[8] SOA 2003, s 103A(2).
[9] SA 2020, s 346(a).
[10] SA 2020, s 346(b).
[11] *R v Smith* [2011] EWCA Crim 1772, per Hughes LJ at paras [4] and [8].

In a slight but significant change, the SHPO legislation replaced the SOPO terminology of 'serious sexual harm' with 'serious harm', thereby creating a lower test for imposing SHPOs. This change is replicated in the 2020 Sentencing Code.

16.05

In dealing with an SHPO in respect of a sibling who is not the victim, it may be wise to involve the family court.[12]

16.06

A. APPLICABILITY

1. Within Criminal Court Proceedings

An SHPO is defined by the Sentencing Code as an order under Part 11, Chapter 2 which prohibits the offender from doing anything described in the order.[13] Such an order may be made in relation to those who are convicted of an offence specified in Schedule 3 or 5 to the 2003 Act.[14] The age and sentence conditions listed in Schedule 3 are specifically disregarded in relation to SHPOs.[15] The offences listed in Schedules 3 and Schedule 5 also include any attempt, conspiracy, or incitement to commit that offence,[16] and aiding, abetting, counselling, or procuring the commission of that offence.[17] Also included are inchoate offences under part 2 of the Serious Crime Act 2007 (encouraging or assisting crime offences) where the listed offence is the offence (or one of the offences) which the person intended or believed would be committed.[18] Equivalent service offences are included by virtue of paras 93–93A of Schedule 3 and paras 172 and 172A of Schedule 5. It is important to note that not all sexual offences are included in Schedule 3 or Schedule 5.

16.07

2. Procedure

Rule 31(3)(5) of the 2020 CrimPR now governs the application for an SHPO, requiring the prosecutor to serve a draft order specifying the prohibitions considered to be necessary for the statutory purposes, on both the defendant and the court, not less than 2 business days before the hearing at which the order may be made. It reflects the Court of Appeal's emphasis in *Smith* 'that it is essential that there is a written draft, properly considered in advance of the sentencing hearing. The prosecutor must serve a draft order on the court officer and on the defendant not less than 2 business days before the hearing at which the order may be made.[19] If the draft is served in paper form.'[20] In *R v McLellan*[21] [2018] the court stated *per curiam*, that a draft SHPO should also indicate a proposed duration or at least flag

16.08

---

[12] *R v D (Sexual offences prevention order)* [2005] EWCA Crim 3360.
[13] SA, s 343(1).
[14] SA 2020, s 345(1). For the Schedules, see tables at the end of this chapter.
[15] SA 2020, s 345(2).
[16] SOA 2003, Sch 3, para 94A(a) and Sch 5, para 173(a).
[17] SOA 2003, Sch 3, para 94A(b) and Sch 5, para 173(b).
[18] SOA 2003, Sch 3, para 94AA and Sch 5, para 173A.
[19] CPR 2020 Rule 31.3 (5)(a).
[20] *R v Smith and Others* [2011] EWCA Crim 1772, at [26].
[21] *R v McLellan* [2018] 1 Cr App R (S) 18.

the question of duration for consideration. The important duty of all parties in relation to SHPOs was expressed in the following terms by Court of Appeal in *Sokolowski*:[22]

> There is a real need for parties to be sensitive to their obligations in relation to this form of order, and properly to advise the court of the relevant statutory provisions and the court's role in such orders, to avoid the court making SHPOs in terms inconsistent with the statutory scheme, necessitating multiple appeals to correct errors in SHPOs.

16.09 The court may grant an SHPO following conviction if it is satisfied that such an order is necessary[23] for the purpose of protecting the public or any particular members of the public from sexual harm from the offender or protecting children or vulnerable adults generally, or any particular children or vulnerable adults, from sexual harm from the defendant outside the United Kingdom.[24] 'Sexual harm' is defined in s 344 of the Sentencing Code as physical or psychological harm caused (a) by the person committing one or more offences listed in Schedule 3 to the Sexual Offences Act 2003; or (b) (in the context of harm outside the United Kingdom), anything which would constitute an offence listed in Schedule 3[25] if done in any part of the United Kingdom.[26] 'The public' means the public in the United Kingdom.[27] For the purposes of this chapter, 'child'[28] means a person under the age of 18 years and 'vulnerable adult' means a 'person aged 18 or over whose ability to protect themself from physical or psychological harm is significantly impaired through physical or mental disability or illness, through old age or otherwise'.[29]

16.10 If further time is needed for proper consideration of the proposed SHPO, it is permissible for the sentencing court to make the order on a date subsequent to sentence, but not outside the 56-day slip rule.[30]

16.11 In *R v Connor* [2019][31] the court commented that all orders sent out from the Crown Court must be in proper form and reflect the order made by the judge.[32] Where there was a discrepancy between the form of the order issued by the Crown Court office and the order announced by the judge, the offender is subject to the latter, not the former.[33] Orders should not be made in haste. Resident judges and listing officers should ensure that in every case which may require an ancillary order the list reflects the time needed to deal effectively with all the issues.[34]

---

[22] *R v Sokolowski* [2017] EWCA Crim 1903. Lord Justice Hickinbottom at para [5(vi)].
[23] For the necessity test see *R v Parsons: R v Morgan* below at para 16.18 at (i). See also *Smith* (as updated by *R v NC*) citations below.
[24] SA 2020, s 346.
[25] The age and sentence conditions set out in Sch 3 are to be disregarded, SA 2020, s 344(2).
[26] SA 2020, s 344.
[27] SA 2020, s 358.
[28] SA 2020, s 358.
[29] SA 2020, s 358.
[30] SA 2020, s 385.
[31] *R v Connor* [2019] EWCA Crim 234.
[32] At para 31.
[33] *R v Pelletier* [2012] EWCA Crim 1060.
[34] *R v Connor* [2019] EWCA Crim 234, at para 32.

3. Non-conviction SHPOs

16.12 SHPO's in relation to offenders found guilty by reason of insanity, or found to be under a disability but have done the act charged[35] will continue to be made under s 103A(2)(a) SOA 2003 where the court is satisfied that it is necessary to make a sexual harm prevention order, for the purpose of: (i) protecting the public or any particular members of the public from sexual harm from the defendant, or (ii) protecting children or vulnerable adults generally, or any particular children or vulnerable adults, from sexual harm from the defendant outside the United Kingdom.[36]

4. Civil Orders

16.13 SHPOs may also be imposed as civil orders at another date upon complaint to a magistrates' court.[37] The effect of imposing a subsequent SHPO is that an existing sexual offences order ceases to have effect;[38] care therefore needs to be taken to ensure that terms from an original order are included if still appropriate.

16.14 The ambit of such an application is wider, extending to all 'qualifying offenders'.[39]

16.15 A 'qualifying offender' means a person who has been either: (a) convicted of an offence specified in Schedule 3 (other than at para 60)[40] or Schedule 5 of the 2003 Act[41] in the UK or an equivalent offence abroad;[42] (b) found not guilty of such an offence by reason of insanity;[43] (c) found to be under a disability and to have done the act charged against them in respect of such an offence;[44] or (d) cautioned for such an offence.[45]

16.16 Such later application must be made by the Director General of the National Crime Agency (NCA)[46] or a chief police officer in respect of a person who resides in his police area or who that officer believes intends to come to his police area.[47] It must appear to them: (a) that the offender is a 'qualifying offender' and; (b) that since being dealt with for the original offence the offender has acted in such a way as to give reasonable cause to believe that it is necessary for an order to be made.[48] Where an order under s 103A(4) is applied for by the Director General, notice of the application must be given as soon as is reasonably practicable to the chief officer of police for the relevant area.[49]

---

[35] In relation to offences specified in Sch 3 or Sch 5, disapplying the age and/or sentence conditions.
[36] SOA 2003, s 103A(2)(b).
[37] SOA 2003, s 103A(4).
[38] SOA 2003, s 103C(6). This also applies to SHPOs made on conviction under SA 2020, s 349.
[39] SOA 2003, s 103A(4)(a).
[40] An offence in Scotland other than is mentioned in [paras 36–59ZL]1 if the court, in imposing sentence or otherwise disposing of the case, determines for the purposes of this paragraph that there was a significant sexual aspect to the offender's behaviour in committing the offence.
[41] SOA 2003, s 103B(2)(a).
[42] SOA 2003, ss 103B(3)(a).
[43] SOA 2003, ss 103B(2)(b) and (3)(b).
[44] SOA 2003, s 103B(2)(c) and (3)(c).
[45] SOA 2003, s 103B(2)(d) and (3)(d).
[46] SOA 2003, s 103A(4).
[47] SOA 2003, s 103A(5).
[48] SOA 2003, s 103A(4).
[49] SOA 2003, s 103A(7).

16.17 The court may grant an SHPO if it is satisfied that the defendant's behaviour since the date of dealing makes such an order necessary for the purpose of protecting the public or any particular members of the public from sexual harm from the defendant or protecting children[50] or vulnerable adults[51] generally, or any particular children or vulnerable adults, from sexual harm from the defendant outside the United Kingdom.[52]

B. SEXUAL HARM

16.18 'Sexual harm' is defined in s 103A of the SOA 2003 and s 344(1) of the Sentencing Code as physical or psychological harm caused by the offender committing one or more offences listed in Schedule 3 or, in the context of harm outside the United Kingdom, by the offender doing, outside the United Kingdom, anything which would constitute an offence listed in Schedule 3 if done in any part of the United Kingdom. The type of sexual harm to which the section refers includes the harm caused to children who are the subject of pornographic photographs or videos: see *R v Beaney* [2004],[53] *R v Collard* [2005],[54] and *R v Terrell* [2008],[55] all of which are cases on the predecessors to s 103A. See also *R v Choung* [2020][56] for the necessity of SHPO in a case involving possession of an extreme pornographic image and multiple Hentai computer-generated images of children.

C. INTERIM SHPOs

16.19 Interim SHPOs may be ordered to cover the period leading up to determination of the main application.[57] Such application may be granted if the court considers it just to do so.[58] The order has effect only for a fixed period that must be specified.[59] It will cease to have effect, at the latest, on determination of the main application.[60]

16.20 On an application for an interim sexual harm prevention order made by a chief officer of police, the court may, if it considers it just to do so, make an interim notification order.[61]

---

[50] Defined as aged under 18, SOA 2003, s 103B(1).
[51] Defined as a person aged 18 or over whose ability to protect himself or herself from physical or psychological harm is significantly impaired through physical or mental disability or illness, through old age or otherwise. SOA 2003, s 103B(1).
[52] SOA 2003, s 103A(3)(b).
[53] *R v Beaney* [2004] 2 Cr App R (S) 441.
[54] *R v Collard* [2005] 1 Cr App R (S) 34.
[55] *R v Terrell* [2008] 2 Cr App R (S) 49.
[56] *R v Choung* [2020] 1 Cr App R (S) 13.
[57] SOA 2003, s 103F(1).
[58] SOA 2003, s 103F(3).
[59] SOA 2003, s 103F(4)(a).
[60] SOA 2003, s 103F(4)(b).
[61] SOA 2003, s 103G(7).

D. AMBIT AND CONTENT OF AN SHPO

16.21 The Sentencing Code requires that an SHPO must specify the prohibitions included in the order[62] and the period for which each prohibition is said to have effect (the 'prohibition period').[63] This will also apply to SHPOs made under the SOA 2003. The prohibition period must be a fixed period (not less than 5 years)[64] or indefinitely, until a further order is made.[65] It is permissible for different prohibitions to have effect for different periods or until further order.[66]

16.22 A prohibition on foreign travel must be for a fixed period or not more than 5 years[67] but can be extended (on application) for a further period[68] of not more than 5 years at a time.[69] Where such a prohibition is imposed, the SHPO must contain a requirement that the offender surrender all of their passports on or before the date the prohibit takes effect or within a specified period.[70] A 'prohibition on foreign travel' means: (a) a prohibition on travelling to any country outside the United Kingdom named or described in the order; (b) a prohibition on travelling to any country outside the United Kingdom other than a country named or described in the order; or (c) a prohibition on travelling to any country outside the United Kingdom.[71] Where a prohibition is made preventing travelling outside of the United Kingdom, the SHPO must also require the offender to surrender their passport(s)[72] to a specified police station and state the period within which they must be surrendered.[73]

16.23 An SHPO should not be made for an indefinite period unless the court is satisfied of the need to do so. Careful consideration should be given, and it should not be made as a mere default. Where an indefinite order is made, unless it is obvious, reason should be given (even if brief) as to why it is necessary.[74]

16.24 The SHPO prohibits the offender from doing anything described in the order.[75] The only prohibitions that may be included in the order are those necessary for the purpose of protecting the public or any particular members of the public from sexual harm from the defendant *or* protecting children or vulnerable adults generally, or any particular children or vulnerable adults, from sexual harm from the defendant outside the United Kingdom.[76]

---

[62] SA 2020, s 347(1)(a) or SA 2020, s 347(1)(a).
[63] SA 2020, s 347(1)(b).
[64] SA 2020, s 347(2)(a) or SOA 2003, s 103C(2)(a).
[65] SA 2020, s 347(2)(b) or SOA 2003, s 103C(2)(b).
[66] SA 2020, s 347(3) or SOA 2003, s 103C(3)(a) and (b).
[67] SA 2020, s 348(1) or SOA 2003, s 103D(1).
[68] SA 2020, s 350 or SOA 2003, s 103D(3).
[69] SA 2020, s 348(2) or SOA 2003, s 103D(3).
[70] SOA 2003, s 103D(3).
[71] SA 2020, s 348(3) or SOA 2003 s 103D(2). See *R v Cheyne (Marco)* [2019] EWCA Crim 182 for an example of an FTO preventing travel outside of the UK.
[72] As defined in section 348(7) SOA 2003.
[73] SA 2020, s 348(4) or SOA 2003, s 103D(4). There is no corresponding requirement under s 103D(4) to specify the police station.
[74] See *R v McLellan and Bingley* [2017] EWCA Crim 1464 at [25]. See also *R v Sokolowski* [2017] EWCA Crim 1903 at paras [15–24] and [25–36] in which indefinite SHPOs were reduced in length to align with the notification periods. See *R v Howarth* [2021] for an example of indefinite SHPO replaced with SHPO of longer duration than the notification period.
[75] SA 2020, 343(1) or SOA 2003, s 103C(1).
[76] SA 2020, s 343(2) or SOA 2003, s 103C(4).

1. Clarity of the SHPO

16.25 The case law relating to SOPOs remains of general application to SHPOs under the SOA 2003 and the Sentencing Code, though it should be amended to reflect the lowered test.[77] The SOPO guideline case of *R v Smith* confirms that the order 'must be sufficiently clear on its face for the defendant, those who have to deal with him in ordinary daily life and those who have to consider enforcement, to understand without real difficulty or the need for expert legal advice exactly what he can and cannot do. Real risk of unintentional breach must be avoided.[78] Such orders need to be carefully drafted and 'bearing in mind that ... they are often made against those of limited education, simplicity is a virtue.'[79]

16.26 In *R v Parsons; R v Morgan* [2017],[80] a case relating to SHPO appeals, the court issued the following overarching guidance:

(i) First, as with SOPOs, no order should be made by way of SHPO unless necessary to protect the public from sexual harm as set out in the statutory language. If an order is necessary, then the prohibitions imposed must be effective; if not, the statutory purpose will not be achieved.

(ii) Secondly and equally, any SHPO prohibitions imposed must be clear and realistic. They must be readily capable of simple compliance and enforcement. It is to be remembered that breach of a prohibition constitutes a criminal offence punishable by imprisonment.

(iii) Thirdly, as restated by *R v NC* [2016] EWCA Crim 1448, none of the SHPO terms must be oppressive and, overall, the terms must be proportionate.

(iv) Fourthly, any SHPO must be tailored to the facts. There is no one size that fits all factual circumstances.

16.27 Note in *R v Sokolowski* [2017][81] at para [5] the important principles applicable to SHPOs were once more restated by the Court of Appeal.

2. SHPOs and Other Regimes

16.28 No SHPO is needed if it merely duplicates or interferes with another regime, such as the notification requirements[82] and a bar from working with children or vulnerable adults.[83]

16.29 An indeterminate sentence needs no SHPO, at least unless there is some very unusual feature which means that such an order could add something useful and does not run the risk of undesirably tying the hands of the offender managers later.[84] Licence conditions should suffice.

---

[77] An exercise undertaken in *R v NC* [2016] EWCA Crim 1448 in relation to the guidance in *Smith*.
[78] *R v Smith and Others* [2011] EWCA Crim 1772, per Hughes LJ at [4].
[79] *Hemsley* [2010] EWCA Crim 225, per HHJ Cooke QC at [4].
[80] *R v Parsons; R v Morgan* [2017] EWCA Crim 2163.
[81] *R v Sokolowski* [2017] EWCA Crim 1903 per Lord Justice Hickinbottom.
[82] *R v Smith and Others* [2011] EWCA Crim 1772, at [9] and [17].
[83] *R v Smith and Others* [2011] EWCA Crim 1772, at [9] followed in *R v NC* [2016] EWCA Crim 1448 at [18].
[84] *R v Smith and Others* [2011] EWCA Crim 1772, at [13]. This approach was endorsed, in relation to SHPOs in the cases of *R v McLellan and Bingley* [2017] EWCA Crim 14 and *R v GD* [2021] EWCA Crim 465.

D. AMBIT AND CONTENT OF AN SHPO   485

3. Computer Access

The case of *Smith* laid down a number of propositions about terms limiting computer use.[85]   **16.30**

(a) A blanket prohibition on computer use or internet access is impermissible.
(b) Restricting internet access to 'job search, study, work, lawful recreation and purchases' prevents a defendant from legitimate use of the internet.
(c) A requirement to notify the police of the possession of any device giving access to the internet is also onerous and of little value, given the proliferation of internet-ready devices such as mobile phones.
(d) A prohibition on internet access without filtering software risks uncertainty about precisely what is required.
(e) The most effective formulation is likely to be the preservation of readable internet history coupled with a submission to inspection on request.

(f) Where the risk includes the use of chat rooms or similar networks for grooming, suitable terms include a prohibition on communicating via the internet with any young person known or believed to be under the age of 16, coupled with an internet history provision.

The issue of restrictions on internet access was revisited by the court in *R v Parsons; R v Morgan* [2017] in which the court considered the previous guidance in Smith. It was held that the guidance in *Smith* remained generally sound and should continue to be followed. However, developments in technology and changes in everyday living called for an adapted and targeted approach in certain specific areas. That was especially so in relation to risk management monitoring software, cloud storage, and encryption software [para 30]. The Court was unwilling to conclude that a blanket ban on internet access could never be justified, but such a prohibition would be appropriate only in the most exceptional cases. In all other cases, a blanket ban would be unrealistic, oppressive and disproportionate—cutting off the offender from too much of everyday, legitimate living (para [10]).   **16.31**

The courts recognition of the importance of the internet to modern day life prevails. See *R v Hewitt* [2018][86] in which the court commented that '[t]here may be a case where a blanket ban ... is proportionate even though oppressive, but we do not consider that the appellants offending repugnant as it is, would justify such a ban. The use of the internet is an essential and integral part of everyone's life and its use essential to transactions between individuals, statutory bodies and other entities.'   **16.32**

4. Personal Contact with Children

It is important to note that SHPO legislation defines 'child' as a person under 18 rather than under 16.[87] Offences under ss 16–19, 21, 25, and 26 of the SOA 2003 are defined with reference to a child under 18 and any prohibition following the commission of such offences should relate to children under 18.[88] However, there is no objection in principle to   **16.33**

---

[85] *R v Smith and Others* [2011] EWCA Crim 1772, at [20].
[86] *R v Hewitt* [2018] EWCA Crim 2309.
[87] SA 2020, s 358 or SOA 2003, s 103B(1).
[88] *R v Smith and Others* [2011] EWCA Crim 1772, at [21].

confining the prohibition to children under 16 in appropriate cases, for the reasons given in *Smith* (at para [21]).[89]

16.34 The court should consider carefully whether it is appropriate to restrict contact with children generally. There should be an identifiable risk of 'contact offences'. In *R v Sokolowski* [2017][90] the court emphasized the importance of the guidance given in previous cases. The guidance in relation to contact with children was summarized as follows:

> Particular care must be taken when considering whether prohibitions on contact with children are really necessary; although such orders may be necessary to prevent the defendant from seeking out children for sexual purposes. Where a defendant is convicted of viewing child pornography, then an SHPO should only contain provisions preventing contact, or permitting only supervised contact, with children where there is a real risk that the offending will progress to contact offences. It is not enough for the prosecution to assert, or for the court to assume, that such provisions are necessary on the safety first principle, irrespective of how remote or fanciful the risk of such progression might be. Even when provisions are necessary, they must still be proportionate in their scope (see *Smith* at [22]–[24] and *Lewis* at [10]).

16.35 If such a condition is imposed it should include a saving for incidental contact inherent in everyday life.[91]

16.36 Where a non-contact prohibition can be justified as necessary it must still be tailored to the specific facts of the case. See *R v Franklin* [2018][92] in which the court said that where there was no evidence that the defendant posed a risk to boys, as opposed to girls, a restriction in the SHPO in respect of 'any child under 16' could not be justified and should be limited to girls.

E. VARIATIONS, RENEWALS, AND DISCHARGES

16.37 The offender,[93] a chief police officer for the area in which the defendant resides[94] (or believes the offender resides)[95] or intends to reside,[96] (or the chief police officer that made the original application)[97] may apply to the court for an order varying, renewing or discharging an SHPO.[98]

16.38 The court may make any order varying, renewing, or discharging the SHPO that the court considers appropriate.[99] Any varied or renewed conditions, including any additional

---

[89] *R v Parsons: R v Morgan* [2017] (n 80), at para [13].
[90] *R v Sokolowski* [2017] EWCA Crim 1903. Lord Justice Hickinbottom at para [5(iii)]. See *R v Alison* [2021] EWCA Crim 324 for more recent application of the principle.
[91] *R v Smith and Others* [2011] EWCA Crim 1772, at [24].
[92] *R v Franklin* [2018] EWCA Crim 1080 at paras 28–29.
[93] SA 2020, s 350(2)(a) SOA 2003, s103E(1) and 2(a).
[94] SA 2020, s 350(2)(b) or SOA 2003, ss 103E(1) and 2(b).
[95] SA 2020, s 350(2)(c) only.
[96] SA 2020, s 350(2)(c) or SOA 2003, ss 103E(1) and 2(c).
[97] SOA 2003, ss 103E(1) and 2(d) only.
[98] SA 2020, s 350(1) or SOA 2003, s 103E(1).
[99] SA 2020, s 350(5) or SOA 2003, s 103E(4).

conditions, must be necessary for the purpose of protecting the public or any particular members of the public from sexual harm from the defendant, or protecting children or vulnerable adults generally, or any particular children or vulnerable adults, from sexual harm from the defendant outside the United Kingdom.[100]

16.39 Care must be taken in the event of a further SHPO once an order is in place. A new SHPO has the effect of revoking the original order,[101] therefore it may, depending on the circumstances and reasons for the new order, be necessary to include the original terms.

16.40 The application to vary should be to the Crown Court where the original application was granted in a Crown Court or in the Court of Appeal.[102] The application, if made in a youth or magistrates' court, should be to a youth or magistrates' court for the area where the defendant lives or, if made by a chief police officer, to a youth or magistrates' court whose commission area includes any part of the chief police officer's area.[103] In the case of an order made under the SOA 2003, where the order was made in a youth court but the offender is now aged 18 or over the application should be made to a magistrates' court for the area where the defendant lives or, if made by a chief police officer, to a magistrates' court whose commission area includes any part of the chief police officer's area.[104]

16.41 The court must not discharge an order before the end of 5 years, beginning with the day on which the order was made, without the consent of the offender and:

(a) where the application is made by a chief officer of police, that chief officer; or
(b) in any other case, the chief officer of police for the area in which the defendant resides.[105]

This does not apply to an order containing a foreign travel prohibition and no other prohibitions.[106]

16.42 In the case of *R v Hoath; R v Standage* [2011][107] relating to variation of SOPOs the court held:

(a) Objections in principle to the terms of a SOPO imposed by the Crown Court should be raised by an appeal to the Court of Appeal and not by subsequent applications to vary to the Crown Court. [9]
(b) Where the defendant relied on particular and unanticipated difficulties arising from the form and/or wording of the order, those difficulties should be identified promptly (in writing and with particularity) and sent to the prosecuting authority to see whether the matter could be put before the Crown Court on an agreed basis and in any event to narrow the area of dispute. [9]
(c) Although minor but necessary adjustments to the order might be required, in which case application should be made to the Crown Court to vary the order, in circumstances where a defendant had not appealed to the Court of Appeal the Crown Court

---

[100] SA 2020, s 350(6) or SOA 2003, s 103E(5).
[101] SA 2020, s 349(1) or SOA 2003, s 103C(6)6.
[102] SA 2020, 350(9)(a) or SOA 2003, s 103E(9)(a).
[103] SA 2020, s 350(9)(b) and (c) or SOA 2003, s 103E(9)(b) and (c).
[104] SOA 2003, s 103E(9)(d).
[105] SA 2020 s 350(7) or SOA 2003, s 103E(7).
[106] SA 2020, s 350(8) or SOA 2003, s 103E(8).
[107] *R v Hoath; R v Standage* [2011] EWCA Crim 274.

would not be expected to make other than minor adjustments to the terms of the order, at least in the short term. [10]

(d) Usually the defendant would need to rely on a change of circumstances. In such a case, the Crown Court would need to be satisfied that the order in its original form was no longer necessary for the statutory purpose of protecting the public (or particular members of the public) from serious sexual harm from the defendant, or that that objective could properly and sufficiently be secured by the proposed variation. [11]

16.43 See also *R v Cheyne*,[108] in which the Court held that knowledge in relation to an offender gained since the imposition of an SHPO could justify the variation of an existing SHPO.

16.44 Appeal against variation or a refusal to vary lies to the Court of Appeal. Whether it is a civil or criminal appeal is unclear. The Lord Chief Justice recognized this as a 'clear legislative oversight' but repeated that it would be 'a matter of complete indifference' to the defendant which division of the Court of Appeal heard the appeal.[109]

F. APPEALS AGAINST THE MAKING OF SHPOs AND INTERIM SHPOs

16.45 A defendant may appeal against the making of an SHPO.[110] This effectively takes the form of an appeal against sentence, even where the defendant was found not guilty by reason of insanity or suffering from a disability.[111] Where the SHPO was granted in the Crown Court, appeal is to the Court of Appeal.[112] In any other case, appeal is to the Crown Court.[113]

16.46 Where the SHPO was made on application to a magistrates' court by a chief police officer or Director General of the NCA, the appeal is to the Crown Court.[114]

16.47 Appeal against the making of an interim SHPO is to the Crown Court.[115]

G. RELATIONSHIP WITH NOTIFICATION REQUIREMENTS

16.48 Where a defendant was subject to notification requirements immediately before the making of the SHPO and would ordinarily cease to be subject to the notification requirements, the defendant remains subject to the notification requirements throughout the period of the SHPO.[116] This also applies when an interim SHPO is made.[117]

---

[108] *R v Cheyne (Marco)* EWCA Crim 18, in which the authorities became aware that the offender, having absconded for 5 years, had been residing in Thailand and the surrounding countries for that period. On appeal the variation to his SHPO adding an FTO preventing any travel outside the UK was held to be perfectly properly made.
[109] *R v Aldridge and R v Eaton* [2012] ECWA Crim 1456.
[110] SA 2020, s 353 or SOA 2003, s 103H(1).
[111] SOA 2003, s 103H(1)(b).
[112] SA 2020, s 353(a) or SOA 2003, s 103H(3)(a).
[113] SA 2020, s 353(b) or SOA 2003, s 103H(3)(b).
[114] SOA 2003, s 103H(1)(c).
[115] SOA 2003, s 103H(2).
[116] SA 2020, s 352(1) or SOA 2003, s 103G(1).
[117] SOA 2003, s 103G(4).

16.49 Where a defendant was not subject to notification requirements but is made subject to an SHPO (this would arise essentially when a defendant is convicted of an offence under the SOA 2003, Schedule 5), the making of an SHPO triggers the notification requirements throughout the period of the SHPO.[118]

16.50 The terms of an SHPO should not duplicate the notification requirements and must operate in tandem with the statutory notification scheme. The SHPO must not therefore conflict with the notification requirements, and it is not normally a legitimate use of an SHPO to use it simply to extend the notification requirements prescribed by law. However, it does not automatically follow that the duration of an SHPO must always be the same as or no longer than the period of the notification requirements.[119]

H. RELATIONSHIP WITH BARRING FROM WORKING WITH CHILDREN AND VULNERABLE ADULTS

16.51 Amendments to the Safeguarding and Vulnerable Groups Act (SVGA) 2006 have resulted in an amended test for inclusion onto the Barred List(s) applicable to some offenders. The consequence of the new test is that a number of sexual offenders who would previously have been included on the List(s) no longer meet the criteria for inclusion. In those cases, it will be necessary to consider applying for an additional prohibition as part of an SHPO. There will also be a number of offenders previously on the List(s) who are entitled to make representations as to their removal from the List(s) and offenders who have already been removed from the List(s). These offenders will need to be identified by the police or prosecution if consideration is to be given as to whether applications for SHPOs or variations to existing SHPOs are required.

1. The Original Regime under the Safeguarding and Vulnerable Groups Act 2006

16.52 The SVGA 2006 introduced the Independent Barring Board which was subsequently renamed the Independent Safeguarding Authority (ISA). The role of the ISA was to prevent unsuitable people from working with children and vulnerable adults by establishing and maintaining the 'children's barred list' and the 'adult's barred list'.[120]

2. The Regime under the Safeguarding and Vulnerable Groups Act 2006 (as amended)

16.53 On 1 December 2012 sections of the Protection of Freedoms Act (PFA) 2012 came into force to form the Disclosure and Barring Service (DBS). The PFA also made amendments to the SVGA. Section 67 of the PFA made specific amendments to Schedule 3 to the SVGA

---
[118] SA 2020, s 352(2) or SOA 2003, s 103G(2).
[119] *R v Parsons: R v Morgan* [2017] (n 80) and *R v Smith* at para [17].
[120] SGVA 2006, s 2 and Sch 3.

2006 which altered the test for barring decisions. Following the amendments, the DBS can now only bar a person from working within a regulated activity with children or adults if they have reason to believe that the person is or has been, or might in the future be, engaged in regulated activity. The only exception to this is where a person is cautioned or convicted for a relevant (automatic barring) offence (under para 1 or 7) and is not eligible to submit representations against their inclusion in a Barred List(s).

16.54 Additionally, where a person is cautioned for or convicted of a relevant offence with the right to make representations (para 2 or 8), the DBS will ask the person to submit their representations and consider them *before* making a final barring decision.

16.55 The consequences of these changes are that only those convicted of the most serious offences (paras 1 and 7) will be certain to be placed on the List(s). Those convicted of less serious offences (para 2 or 8) who do not meet the new test because they have not, do not or will not carry out regulated activities will no longer qualify to be considered for inclusion on the List(s). Those who do qualify under the new test and have been convicted of less serious offences may be placed on the List(s) subject to the consideration of representations *before* they are entered onto the List(s).

16.56 A further relevant change is that, whereas previously the ISA's decision would not be subject to review for a period of 10 years, the position has now been altered so that a review may take place at any time if new information emerges, or there has been a change of circumstances, or it becomes apparent that the DBS has made an error.[121]

16.57 There will be a number of offenders who would previously have been placed on the List(s) who do not fulfil the new criteria and will not now be included on the List(s), as a result of the amendments to the Act.

16.58 See Chapter 12 for the list of barred offences.

16.59 However, this lacuna can be addressed by applying, in appropriate cases, for an SHPO prohibition at the time of sentence prohibiting them from working with children. This is particularly pertinent given that Disqualification Orders under the CJCSA 2000 were abolished as of 17.6.2013.[122]

16.60 The prohibition could be along the lines of:

> Not to seek or undertake any employment (including voluntary work), paid or otherwise, which will or is likely to bring him/her into unsupervised contact with children [specify target gender where appropriate, although arguably a sex offender who targets very young children does so regardless of gender] under the age of 16 years.

16.61 Such a prohibition should be tailored to the individual facts of the offence and may not be suitable in all cases.

16.62 It is important that those who draft, apply for, and make SHPOs are aware of the important changes to the SVGA 2006 and that there are cases which would previously have been

---

[121] SVGA 2006, s 18A, as inserted by the PFA 2012.
[122] SI 2009 No 2611; SI 2012 No 2231.

'caught' by the SVGA which no longer are and therefore careful consideration needs to be given, in appropriate cases, as to whether a further prohibition in an SHPO is required.

16.63 There may well be cases where even though the offender is placed on the Barring List(s), there are risks envisaged which fall outside the remit of the List(s). In those circumstances it is not only permissible (see *R v Smith & Others* [2011] EWCA Crim 1772 per Hughes LJ at para 25) but necessary to consider imposing SHPO prohibitions to address those risks provided there is justification for doing so.

16.64 In the same way that a judge must inform a defendant being sentenced that he will be subject to the Notification Requirements, the judge must inform a defendant of future restrictions imposed upon him by the DBS.[123] The court should inform the defendant which list he or she will be included on and under what legislation. In addition, a defendant should be told whether or not they can make representations to be removed from the list. See paras 16.51–16.56.

I. OFFENCES: BREACH OF SHPO, INTERIM SHPO AND EXISTING PROTECTIVE ORDERS

16.65 A person subject to an SHPO or interim SHPO commits an offence if, without reasonable excuse, he does anything that he is prohibited from doing by that SHPO or interim SHPO.[124] Breach of an existing SOPO, interim SOPO, or FTO remains an offence by virtue of ss 103I(1)(c),(d) and (e) SOA 2003.

16.66 Breach of an SHPO or interim SHPO renders the offender liable: (a) on summary conviction, to imprisonment for a term not exceeding 6 months, or a fine not exceeding the statutory maximum, or both;[125] (b) on conviction on indictment, to imprisonment for a term not exceeding 5 years.[126] A court cannot conditionally discharge a person convicted of breaching an SHPO.[127]

16.67 Where an SHPO is made in respect of an offender under the age of 18, the Court can also consider making a parenting order in respect of the offender's parents.[128]

16.68 For sentencing see the Sentencing Council 'Breach Offences Definitive Guideline' which applies to any offender aged 18 or over sentenced on or after 1 October 2018.

16.69 Note: the Court has no power to impose an SHPO for breach of a SOPO or an SHPO for breach of an SHPO as breach of either is not a 'qualifying offence'. See also *R v Hamer* [2017].[129]

---

[123] CrimPR 2020, r 28(3).
[124] SA 2020, s 254(1) or SOA 2003, ss 103I(1)(a) and (b).
[125] SA 2020, s 54(4)(a) or SOA 2003, s 103I(3)(a).
[126] SA 2020, s 54(4)(b) or SOA 2003, s 103I(3)(b).
[127] SA 2020, s 54(5) or SOA 2003, s 103I(4).
[128] SA 2020, s 355 and CDA 1998, s 8(1)(b).
[129] *R v Hamer* [2017] EWCA Crim 192.

J. SEXUAL OFFENCES ACT 2003, SCHEDULE 3

16.70 The conditions in Schedule 3 relating to the age of the offender or the victim, or to the relevant finding[130] or the sentence imposed on the offender may be disregarded in making an SHPO. The Schedule 3 conditions have not therefore been included in the tables below.

1. Offences which may be Subject to an SHPO under the Sexual Offences Act 1956

16.71 The offences listed in Schedule 3 also include any attempt, conspiracy, or incitement to commit that offence,[131] and aiding, abetting, counselling, or procuring the commission of that offence.[132] Also included are inchoate offences under part 2 of the Serious Crime Act 2007 (encouraging or assisting crime offences) where the listed offence is the offence (or one of the offences) which the person intended or believed would be committed.[133] Equivalent service offences are included by virtue of paras 93–93A of Schedule 3.

	Offence
s 1	Rape
s 5	Intercourse with a girl under 13
s 6	Intercourse with a girl under 16
s 10	Incest by a man
s 12	Buggery
s 13	Indecency between men
s 14	Indecent assault on a woman
s 15	Indecent assault on a man
s 16	Assault with intent to commit buggery
s 28	Causing or encouraging the prostitution of, intercourse with, or indecent assault on girl under 16

2. Offences which may be Subject to an SHPO under Miscellaneous Acts 1960–2002

16.72 The offences listed in Schedule 3 also include any attempt, conspiracy, or incitement to commit that offence,[134] and aiding, abetting, counselling, or procuring the commission of that offence.[135] Also included are inchoate offences under part 2 of the Serious Crime Act 2007 (encouraging or assisting crime offences) where the listed offence is the offence (or one

---

[130] Defined as '(a) a finding that a person is not guilty of the offence by reason of insanity, or (b) a finding that a person is under a disability and did the act charged against him in respect of the offence'.
[131] SOA 2003, Sch 3, para 94A(a).
[132] SOA 2003, Sch 3, para 94A(b).
[133] SOA 2003, Sch 3, para 94AA.
[134] SOA 2003, Sch 3, para 94A(a).
[135] SOA 2003, Sch 3, para 94A(b).

of the offences) which the person intended or believed would be committed.[136] Equivalent service offences are included by virtue of paras 93–93A of Schedule 3.

	Offence
s 1 Indecency with Children Act 1960	Indecent conduct towards young child
s 54 Criminal Law Act 1977	Inciting girl under 16 to have incestuous sexual intercourse
s 1 Protection of Children Act 1978	Indecent photographs of children
s 170 Customs and Excise Management Act 1979	Penalty for fraudulent evasion of duty etc in relation to goods prohibited to be imported under s 42 of the Customs Consolidation Act 1876 (indecent or obscene articles)
s 160 Criminal Justice Act 1988	Possession of indecent photograph of a child
s 3 Sexual Offences (Amendment) Act 2000	Abuse of position of trust

3. Offences which may be Subject to an SHPO under the Sexual Offences Act 2003

16.73 The offences listed in Schedule 3 also include any attempt, conspiracy, or incitement to commit that offence,[137] and aiding, abetting, counselling, or procuring the commission of that offence.[138] Also included are inchoate offences under part 2 of the Serious Crime Act 2007 (encouraging or assisting crime offences) where the listed offence is the offence (or one of the offences) which the person intended or believed would be committed.[139] Equivalent service offences are included by virtue of paras 93–93A of Schedule 3.

	Offence
s 1	Rape
s 2	Assault by penetration
s 3	Sexual assault
s 4	Causing sexual activity without consent
s 5	Rape of a child under 13
s 6	Assault of a child under 13 by penetration
s 7	Sexual assault of a child under 13
s 8	Causing or inciting a child under 13 to engage in sexual activity
s 9	Sexual activity of a child
s 10	Causing or inciting a child to engage in sexual activity
s 11	Engaging in sexual activity in the presence of a child
s 12	Causing a child to watch a sexual act
s 13	Child sex offences committed by children or young persons
s 14	Arranging or facilitating the commission of a child sex offence
s 15	Meeting a child following sexual grooming etc

---

[136] SOA 2003, Sch 3, para 94AA.
[137] SOA 2003, Sch 3, para 94A(a).
[138] SOA 2003, Sch 3, para 94A(b).
[139] SOA 2003, Sch 3, para 94AA.

	Offence
s 15A	Sexual communication with a child
s 16	Abuse of position of trust: sexual activity with a child
s 17	Abuse of position of trust: causing or inciting a child to engage in sexual activity
s 18	Abuse of position of trust: sexual activity in the presence of a child
s 19	Abuse of position of trust: causing a child to watch a sexual act
s 25	Sexual activity with a child family member
s 26	Inciting a child family member to engage in sexual activity
s 30	Sexual activity with a person with a mental disorder impeding choice
s 31	Causing or inciting a person, with a mental disorder impeding choice, to engage in sexual activity
s 32	Engaging in sexual activity in the presence of a person with a mental disorder impeding choice
s 33	Causing a person, with a mental disorder impeding choice, to watch a sexual act
s 34	Inducement, threat, or deception to procure sexual activity with a person with a mental disorder
s 35	Causing a person with a mental disorder to engage in or agree to engage in sexual activity by inducement, threat, or deception
s 36	Engaging in sexual activity in the presence, procured by inducement, threat, or deception, of a person with a mental disorder
s 37	Causing a person with a mental disorder to watch a sexual act by inducement, threat, or deception
s 38	Care workers: sexual activity with a person with a mental disorder
s 39	Care workers: causing or inciting sexual activity
s 40	Care workers: sexual activity in the presence of a person with a mental disorder
s 41	Care workers: causing a person with a mental disorder to watch a sexual act
s 47	Paying for sexual services of a child
s 48	Causing or inciting child prostitution or pornography
s 49	Controlling a child prostitute or a child involved in pornography
s 50	Arranging or facilitating child prostitution or pornography
s 61	Administering a substance with intent
s 62	Committing an offence with intent to commit a sexual offence
s 63	Trespass with intent to commit a sexual offence
s 64	Sex with an adult relative: penetration
s 65	Sex with an adult relative: consenting to penetration
s 66	Exposure
s 67	Voyeurism
s 67A	Voyeurism: additional offences
s 69	Intercourse with an animal
s 70	Sexual penetration of a corpse

16.74 Note that ss 47, 51–53, and 57–59A of the SOA 2003 are found under Schedule 5; see from para 16.54.

4. Offences which may be Subject to an SHPO under Miscellaneous Acts after 2003

The offences listed in Schedule 3 also include any attempt, conspiracy, or incitement to commit that offence,[140] and aiding, abetting, counselling, or procuring the commission of that offence.[141] Also included are inchoate offences under part 2 of the Serious Crime Act 2007 (encouraging or assisting crime offences) where the listed offence is the offence (or one of the offences) which the person intended or believed would be committed.[142] Equivalent service offences are included by virtue of paras 93–93A of Schedule 3.

16.75

	Offence
s 63 Criminal Justice and Immigration Act 2008	Possession of extreme pornographic images
s 62(1) Coroners and Justice Act 2009	Possession of prohibited images of children
s 69 Serious Crime Act 2015	Possession of paedophile manual

K. SEXUAL OFFENCES ACT 2003, SCHEDULE 5

The offences listed in Schedule 5 also include any attempt, conspiracy, or incitement to commit that offence,[143] and aiding, abetting, counselling, or procuring the commission of that offence.[144] Also included are inchoate offences under part 2 of the Serious Crime Act 2007 (encouraging or assisting crime offences) where the listed offence is the offence (or one of the offences) which the person intended or believed would be committed.[145] Equivalent service offences are included by virtue of paras 172 and 172A of Schedule 5.

16.76

1. Common Law Offences which may be Subject to an SHPO

These comprise murder; manslaughter; kidnapping; false imprisonment; and outraging public decency.

16.77

2. Offences which may be Subject to an SHPO under the Offences Against the Person Act 1861

The offences listed in Schedule 5 also include any attempt, conspiracy, or incitement to commit that offence,[146] and aiding, abetting, counselling, or procuring the commission

16.78

---

[140] SOA 2003, Sch 3, para 94A(a).
[141] SOA 2003, Sch 3, para 94A(b).
[142] SOA 2003, Sch 3, para 94AA.
[143] SOA 2003, Sch 5, para 173(a).
[144] SOA 2003, Sch 5, para 173(b).
[145] SOA 2003, Sch 5, para 173A.
[146] SOA 2003, Sch 5, para 173(a).

of that offence.[147] Also included are inchoate offences under part 2 of the Serious Crime Act 2007 (encouraging or assisting crime offences) where the listed offence is the offence (or one of the offences) which the person intended or believed would be committed.[148] Equivalent service offences are included by virtue of paras 172 and 172A of Schedule 5.

Provision	Offence
s 4	Soliciting murder
s 16	Threats to kill
s 18	Wounding with intent to cause grievous bodily harm
s 20	Malicious wounding
s 21	Attempting to choke, suffocate, or strangle in order to commit or assist in committing an indictable offence
s 22	Using chloroform etc. to commit or assist in the committing of any indictable offence
s 23	Maliciously administering poison etc so as to endanger life or inflict grievous bodily harm
s 27	Abandoning children
s 28	Causing bodily injury by explosives
s 29	Using explosives etc with intent to do grievous bodily harm
s 30	Placing explosives with intent to do bodily injury
s 31	Setting spring guns etc. with intent to do grievous bodily harm
s 32	Endangering the safety of railway passengers
s 35	Injuring persons by furious driving
s 37	Assaulting officer preserving wreck
s 38	Assault with intent to resist arrest
s 47	Assault occasioning actual bodily harm

3. Offences which may be Subject to an SHPO under Miscellaneous Acts 1883 to 1938

16.79 The offences listed in Schedule 5 also include any attempt, conspiracy, or incitement to commit that offence,[149] and aiding, abetting, counselling, or procuring the commission of that offence.[150] Also included are inchoate offences under part 2 of the Serious Crime Act 2007 (encouraging or assisting crime offences) where the listed offence is the offence (or one of the offences) which the person intended or believed would be committed.[151] Equivalent service offences are included by virtue of paras 172 and 172A of Schedule 5.

---

[147] SOA 2003, Sch 5, para 173(b).
[148] SOA 2003, Sch 5, para 173A.
[149] SOA 2003, Sch 5, para 173(a).
[150] SOA 2003, Sch 5, para 173(b).
[151] SOA 2003, Sch 5, para 173A.

Provision	Offence
Explosive Substances Act 1883, s 2	Causing explosion likely to endanger life or property
Explosive Substances Act 1883, s 3	Attempt to cause explosion, or making or keeping explosive with intent to endanger life or property
Infant Life (Preservation) Act 1929, s 1	Child destruction
Children and Young Persons Act 1933, s 1	Cruelty to children
Infanticide Act 1938, s 1	Infanticide

4. Offences which may be Subject to an SHPO under the Firearms Act 1968

16.80 The offences listed in Schedule 5 also include any attempt, conspiracy, or incitement to commit that offence,[152] and aiding, abetting, counselling, or procuring the commission of that offence.[153] Also included are inchoate offences under part 2 of the Serious Crime Act 2007 (encouraging or assisting crime offences) where the listed offence is the offence (or one of the offences) which the person intended or believed would be committed.[154] Equivalent service offences are included by virtue of paras 172 and 172A of Schedule 5.

Provision	Offence
s 16	Possession of firearm with intent to endanger life
s 16A	Possession of firearm with intent to cause fear of violence
s 17(1)	Use of firearm to resist arrest
s 17(2)	Possession of firearm at time of committing or being arrested for offence specified in Schedule 1 to that Act
s 18	Carrying a firearm with criminal intent

5. Offences which may be Subject to an SHPO under the Theft Act 1968

16.81 The offences listed in Schedule 5 also include any attempt, conspiracy, or incitement to commit that offence,[155] and aiding, abetting, counselling, or procuring the commission of that offence.[156] Also included are inchoate offences under part 2 of the Serious Crime Act 2007 (encouraging or assisting crime offences) where the listed offence is the offence (or one of the offences) which the person intended or believed would be committed.[157] Equivalent service offences are included by virtue of paras 172 and 172A of Schedule 5.

---

[152] SOA 2003, Sch 5, para 173(a).
[153] SOA 2003, Sch 5, para 173(b).
[154] SOA 2003, Sch 5, para 173A.
[155] SOA 2003, Sch 5, para 173(a).
[156] SOA 2003, Sch 5, para 173(b).
[157] SOA 2003, Sch 5, para 173A.

Provision	Offence
s 1	Theft
s 8	Robbery or assault with intent to rob
s 9(1)(a)	Burglary with intent to— (a) steal; (b) inflict grievous bodily harm on a person; or (c) do unlawful damage to a building or anything in it
s 10	Aggravated burglary
s 12A	Aggravated vehicle-taking involving an accident which caused the death of any person

6. Offences which may be Subject to an SHPO under Miscellaneous Acts 1971 to 1982

16.82 The offences listed in Schedule 5 also include any attempt, conspiracy, or incitement to commit that offence,[158] and aiding, abetting, counselling, or procuring the commission of that offence.[159] Also included are inchoate offences under part 2 of the Serious Crime Act 2007 (encouraging or assisting crime offences) where the listed offence is the offence (or one of the offences) which the person intended or believed would be committed.[160] Equivalent service offences are included by virtue of paras 172 and 172A of Schedule 5.

Criminal Damage Act 1971, s 1	Arson
Criminal Damage Act 1971, s 1(2)	Destroying or damaging property other than an offence of arson
Taking of Hostages Act 1982, s 1	Hostage-taking

7. Offences which may be Subject to an SHPO under the Aviation Security Act 1982

16.83 The offences listed in Schedule 5 also include any attempt, conspiracy, or incitement to commit that offence,[161] and aiding, abetting, counselling, or procuring the commission of that offence.[162] Also included are inchoate offences under part 2 of the Serious Crime Act 2007 (encouraging or assisting crime offences) where the listed offence is the offence (or one of the offences) which the person intended or believed would be committed.[163] Equivalent service offences are included by virtue of paras 172 and 172A of Schedule 5.

---

[158] SOA 2003, Sch 5, para 173(a).
[159] SOA 2003, Sch 5, para 173(b).
[160] SOA 2003, Sch 5, para 173A.
[161] SOA 2003, Sch 5, para 173(a).
[162] SOA 2003, Sch 5, para 173(b).
[163] SOA 2003, Sch 5, para 173A.

s 1	Hijacking
s 2	Destroying, damaging, or endangering safety of aircraft
s 3	Other acts endangering or likely to endanger safety of aircraft
s 4	Offences in relation to certain dangerous articles

8. Offences which may be Subject to an SHPO under Miscellaneous Acts 1983 to 1985

16.84 The offences listed in Schedule 5 also include any attempt, conspiracy, or incitement to commit that offence,[164] and aiding, abetting, counselling, or procuring the commission of that offence.[165] Also included are inchoate offences under part 2 of the Serious Crime Act 2007 (encouraging or assisting crime offences) where the listed offence is the offence (or one of the offences) which the person intended or believed would be committed.[166] Equivalent service offences are included by virtue of paras 172 and 172A of Schedule 5.

Mental Health Act 1983, s 127	Ill-treatment of patients
Child Abduction Act 1984, s1	Abduction of child by parent, etc
Child Abduction Act 1984, s 2	Abduction of child by other persons
Prohibition of Female Circumcision Act 1985, s 1	Prohibition of female circumcision

9. Offences which may be Subject to an SHPO under the Public Order Act 1986

16.85 The offences listed in Schedule 5 also include any attempt, conspiracy, or incitement to commit that offence,[167] and aiding, abetting, counselling, or procuring the commission of that offence.[168] Also included are inchoate offences under part 2 of the Serious Crime Act 2007 (encouraging or assisting crime offences) where the listed offence is the offence (or one of the offences) which the person intended or believed would be committed.[169] Equivalent service offences are included by virtue of paras 172 and 172A of Schedule 5.

s 1	Riot
s 2	Violent disorder
s 3	Affray

---

[164] SOA 2003, Sch 5, para 173(a).
[165] SOA 2003, Sch 5, para 173(b).
[166] SOA 2003, Sch 5, para 173A.
[167] SOA 2003, Sch 5, para 173(a).
[168] SOA 2003, Sch 5, para 173(b).
[169] SOA 2003, Sch 5, para 173A.

10. Offences which may be Subject to an SHPO under Miscellaneous Acts 1988 (including death by dangerous driving)

16.86 The offences listed in Schedule 5 also include any attempt, conspiracy, or incitement to commit that offence,[170] and aiding, abetting, counselling, or procuring the commission of that offence.[171] Also included are inchoate offences under part 2 of the Serious Crime Act 2007 (encouraging or assisting crime offences) where the listed offence is the offence (or one of the offences) which the person intended or believed would be committed.[172] Equivalent service offences are included by virtue of paras 172 and 172A of Schedule 5.

Criminal Justice Act 1988, s 134	Torture
Road Traffic Act 1988, s 1	Causing death by dangerous driving
Road Traffic Act 1988, s 3A	Causing death by careless driving (when under influence of drink or drugs)

11. Offences which may be Subject to an SHPO under the Aviation and Maritime Security Act 1990

16.87 The offences listed in Schedule 5 also include any attempt, conspiracy, or incitement to commit that offence,[173] and aiding, abetting, counselling, or procuring the commission of that offence.[174] Also included are inchoate offences under part 2 of the Serious Crime Act 2007 (encouraging or assisting crime offences) where the listed offence is the offence (or one of the offences) which the person intended or believed would be committed.[175] Equivalent service offences are included by virtue of paras 172 and 172A of Schedule 5.

s 1	Endangering safety at aerodromes
s 9	Hijacking of ships
s 10	Seizing or exercising control of fixed platforms
s 11	Destroying fixed platforms or endangering their safety
s 12	Other acts endangering or likely to endanger safe navigation
s 13	Offences involving threats

12. Offences which may be Subject to an SHPO under the Protection from Harassment Act 1997

16.88 The offences listed in Schedule 5 also include any attempt, conspiracy, or incitement to commit that offence,[176] and aiding, abetting, counselling, or procuring the commission of

---

[170] SOA 2003, Sch 5, para 173(a).
[171] SOA 2003, Sch 5, para 173(b).
[172] SOA 2003, Sch 5, para 173A.
[173] SOA 2003, Sch 5, para 173(a).
[174] SOA 2003, Sch 5, para 173(b).
[175] SOA 2003, Sch 5, para 173A.
[176] SOA 2003, Sch 5, para 173(a).

that offence.[177] Also included are inchoate offences under part 2 of the Serious Crime Act 2007 (encouraging or assisting crime offences) where the listed offence is the offence (or one of the offences) which the person intended or believed would be committed.[178] Equivalent service offences are included by virtue of paras 172 and 172A of Schedule 5.

s 2	Harassment
s 2A	Stalking
s 4	Putting people in fear of violence
S 4A	Stalking involving fear of violence or serious alarm or distress

13. Offences which may be Subject to an SHPO under Miscellaneous Acts/Orders 1994 to 2004

The offences listed in Schedule 5 also include any attempt, conspiracy, or incitement to commit that offence,[179] and aiding, abetting, counselling, or procuring the commission of that offence.[180] Also included are inchoate offences under part 2 of the Serious Crime Act 2007 (encouraging or assisting crime offences) where the listed offence is the offence (or one of the offences) which the person intended or believed would be committed.[181] Equivalent service offences are included by virtue of paras 172 and 172A of Schedule 5.

16.89

Part II Channel Tunnel (Security) Order 1994 (SI 1994 No 570)	Offences relating to Channel Tunnel trains and the tunnel system
Crime and Disorder Act 1998, s 29	Racially or religiously aggravated assaults
Crime and Disorder Act 1998, s 31(1)(a) or (b)	Racially or religiously aggravated offences under the Public Order Act 1986, s 4 or 4A
Regulation of Investigatory Powers Act 2000, s 53	Failure to comply with a notice relating to encrypted information
Regulation of Investigatory Powers Act 2000, s 54	Tipping off in connection with such a notice
Postal Services Act 2000, s 85(3)	Sending a postal package with obscene contents
Postal Services Act 2000, s 85(4)	Sending a postal package with obscene words, marks or designs
International Criminal Court Act 2001, s 51	Genocide, crimes against humanity or war crimes other than one involving murder
International Criminal Court Act 2001, s 52	Conduct ancillary to genocide etc committed outside the jurisdiction other than one involving murder
Communications Act 2003, s 127(1)	Sending or causing to be sent a message or other matter that is grossly offensive or of an indecent, obscene, or menacing character
Domestic Violence, Crime and Victims Act 2004, s 5	Causing or allowing the death of a child or vulnerable adult

---

[177] SOA 2003, Sch 5, para 173(b).
[178] SOA 2003, Sch 5, para 173A.
[179] SOA 2003, Sch 5, para 173(a).
[180] SOA 2003, Sch 5, para 173(b).
[181] SOA 2003, Sch 5, para 173A.

14. Offences which may be Subject to an SHPO under the Sexual Offences Act 2003

16.90 The offences listed in Schedule 5 also include any attempt, conspiracy, or incitement to commit that offence,[182] and aiding, abetting, counselling, or procuring the commission of that offence.[183] Also included are inchoate offences under part 2 of the Serious Crime Act 2007 (encouraging or assisting crime offences) where the listed offence is the offence (or one of the offences) which the person intended or believed would be committed.[184] Equivalent service offences are included by virtue of paras 172 and 172A of Schedule 5.

s 47	Paying for sexual services of a child, where the victim or (as the case may be) other party was 16 or over. See Schedule 3 for victims under 16
s 52	Causing or inciting prostitution for gain
s 53	Controlling prostitution for gain
s 57	Trafficking into the UK for sexual exploitation
s 58	Trafficking within the UK for sexual exploitation
s 59	Trafficking out of the UK for sexual exploitation
s 59A	Trafficking people for sexual exploitation

15. Offence which may be Subject to an SHPO under the Modern Slavery Act 2015

16.91 The offences listed in Schedule 5 also include any attempt, conspiracy, or incitement to commit that offence,[185] and aiding, abetting, counselling, or procuring the commission of that offence.[186] Also included are inchoate offences under part 2 of the Serious Crime Act 2007 (encouraging or assisting crime offences) where the listed offence is the offence (or one of the offences) which the person intended or believed would be committed.[187] Equivalent service offences are included by virtue of paras 172 and 172A of Schedule 5.

s 2	Human trafficking

L. SUGGESTED FORMS OF WORDS FOR SHPOS

16.92 The following are examples SHPO prohibitions, drafted in accordance with current case law, and will be appropriate in many cases. However, it is crucial to tailor the prohibitions of every order to the specific facts of each case and the particular risks posed by the offender.

---

[182] SOA 2003, Sch 5, para 173(a).
[183] SOA 2003, Sch 5, para 173(b).
[184] SOA 2003, Sch 5, para 173A.
[185] SOA 2003, Sch 5, para 173(a).
[186] SOA 2003, Sch 5, para 173(b).
[187] SOA 2003, Sch 5, para 173A.

In particular, consider whether the facts of the offence(s) give rise to a risk of harm to children aged between 16 to 18 (see para 16.32) and whether the prohibitions should extend to all children or be limited to children of a specific gender (see para 16.35). Consider also whether the facts of the offence give rise to an identifiable risk of future contact offences (see paras 16.17 and 16.33).

Internet use (see *R v Parsons and Morgan* at para [58])

The offender is prohibited from: 16.93

> Using any computer or device capable of accessing the internet, unless: (a) He/she has notified the relevant Police Public Protection Unit within 3 days of the acquisition of any such device.
> (b) It has the capacity to retain and display the history of internet use, and he does not delete such history.
> (c) He/she makes the device immediately available on request for inspection by a Police officer, or police staff employee, and he allows such person to install risk management monitoring software if they so choose.

This prohibition shall not apply to a computer at his place of work, Job Centre Plus, Public Library, educational establishment, or other such place, provided that in relation to his place of work, within 3 days of him commencing use of such a computer, he notifies the relevant Police Public Protection Unit of this use.

> Interfering with or bypassing the normal running of any such computer monitoring software.
> Using or activating any function of any software which prevents a computer or device from retaining and/or displaying the history of internet use, for example using 'incognito' mode or private browsing.
> Using any 'cloud' or similar remote storage media capable of storing digital images (other than that which is intrinsic to the operation of the device) unless, within 3 days of the creation of an account for such storage, he notifies the police of that activity, and provides access to such storage on request for inspection by a police officer or police staff employee.
> Possessing any device capable of storing digital images (moving or still) unless he provides access to such storage on request for inspection by a police officer or police staff employee.
> Installing any encryption or wiping software on any device other than that which is intrinsic to the operation of the device.

In appropriate cases:

> Installing and/or using on any internet enabled device, any Peer-to-Peer file sharing software, examples being 'eMule', 'Shareza', 'Limewire'.
> Using the internet to contact or attempt to contact any child known or believed to be under the age of 16/18 years.

Non-contact (see *R v Parsons and Morgan* at para [76] and *R v Smith*)

16.94 The offender is prohibited from:

> Having any unsupervised contact or communication of any kind with any [male/female] child under the age of 16/18 other than:
> Such as is inadvertent and not reasonably avoidable in the course of daily life, or
> With the consent of the child's parent or guardian (who has knowledge of his/her conviction(s)) and with the express approval of Social Services and the relevant Police Public Protection Unit for the area.
> Living in the same household as any child [female/male] under the age of 16/18 or entering or remaining in any household where a child under 16/18 is present unless with the express approval of Social Services and the relevant Police Public Protection Unit for the area in which he resides.

Where the Family Court is involved (see *R v D* at para [36])

16.95 The offender is prohibited from:

> Communicating or seeking to communicate, whether directly or indirectly, with (X) whilst he/she remains under the age of 16 years without the order of a Judge exercising jurisdiction under the Children Act 1989.

Where automatic inclusion in the children's barred lists does not apply

16.96 The offender is prohibited from:

> Undertaking or applying for any work or activity whether paid, unpaid, or voluntary, which is likely to bring the defendant into contact with a [male/female] child under the age of 16/18 years without prior written permission from the relevant Police Public Protection Unit.

16.97

M. SHPO Example

Sexual Harm Prevention Order
(Sentencing Act 2020, s 345)

XX Crown Court
Court Location Code: XX

Date:
To the offender: XX
Address: XXXX

On the complaint of- DC XX

Complainant:	On behalf of the Commissioner of Police of the Metropolis/ Chief Constable of …
Address:	eg: Operation Jigsaw, 12–28 Walworth Police Station Manor Place SE17 3BB

It is adjudged that the defendant is a qualifying offender by reason of his conviction of the following offences:

> Possessing indecent images of a child
> Sexual communication with a child

It is ordered that the offender XX is prohibited from:

1. Having unsupervised contact of any kind with any female child under the age of 16, other than such as is inadvertent and not reasonably avoidable in the course of daily life, or with the consent of the child's parent or guardian who have knowledge of his convictions.
2. Residing or spending the night in the same premises as any female child under the age of 16 years other than with the consent of the child's parent or guardian who has knowledge of his convictions and with the approval of the relevant Police Public Protection Unit and Social Services.
3. Undertaking or applying for any work or activity whether paid, unpaid, or voluntary, which is likely to bring the defendant into contact with a female child or female young person under the age of 16 years without prior written permission from the relevant Police Public Protection Unit.
4. Using any computer or device capable of accessing the internet, unless:
    (a) he has notified the relevant Police Public Protection Unit team within 3 days of the acquisition of any such device.
    (b) it has the capacity to retain and display the history of internet use, and he does not delete such history.
    (c) he makes the device immediately available on request for inspection by a Police officer, or police staff employee, and he allows such person to install risk management monitoring software if they so choose. This prohibition shall not apply to a computer at his place of work, Job Centre Plus, Public Library, educational establishment, or other such place, provided that in relation to his place of work, within 3 days of him commencing use of such a computer, he notifies the police VISOR team of this use.
5. Interfering with or bypassing the normal running of any such computer monitoring software.
6. Using or activating any function of any software which prevents a computer or device from retaining and/or displaying the history of internet use, for example using 'incognito' mode or private browsing.
7. Using any 'cloud' or similar remote storage media capable of storing digital images (other than that which is intrinsic to the operation of the device) unless, within 3 days of the creation of an account for such storage, he notifies the police of that activity, and provides access to such storage on request for inspection by a police officer or police staff employee.
8. Possessing any device capable of storing digital images (moving or still) unless he provides access to such storage on request for inspection by a police officer or police staff employee.

9. Installing any encryption or wiping software on any device other than that which is intrinsic to the operation of the device.

until further order (or XX date)

And while this order (as renewed from time to time) has effect, the defendant shall be subject to the notification requirements of Part 2 of the Sexual Offences Act 2003 and the 'relevant date' within the meaning of that Part is the date of service of this order.

OR *where the defendant is already subject to the notification requirements on the making of this order*:

And the defendant, who was a relevant offender within the meaning of Part 2 of the Sexual Offences Act 2003 immediately before the making of this order, but who would otherwise cease to be subject to the notification requirements of the said Part 2 while this order has effect, shall remain subject to the notification requirements for the duration of this order as renewed from time to time.

Her/His Honour Judge XX

Date

NOTE:

The requirement of a Sexual Harm Prevention Order is that you (the offender) will be subject to the notification requirements of Part 2 of the Sexual Offences Act 2003.

The requirements of that Act include an obligation on you to report to a prescribed police station within 3 days of the service of this order and to notify the police of your name(s), home address, date of birth, and national insurance number.

If you have no such residence, any premises in the United Kingdom at which you can be found, if either are different from the name and address at the time of conviction.

Thereafter you are obliged to:

- Notify the police of any changes to the name and address he/she has registered within 3 days of the date of any change, including release from prison for subsequent offences.
- Notify the police of any address where he resides or stays for 7 days or longer. This means either 7 days at a time, or a total of 7 days in any 12-month period.
- Notify the police no less than 7 days in advance of any intended period of foreign travel, with such information as required by the Act.
- Notify the police weekly where registered as 'no fixed abode'.
- Notify the Police if you have resided or stayed for at least 12 hours at a household or other private place where a person aged under 18 years resides or stays.
- Notify police of passport, credit card and bank account details and certain information contained in a passport or other form of identification held by the relevant offender on each notification.
- All offenders must reconfirm their details every year.

Your local Police Service Headquarters will be able to explain these conditions in more detail—in particular the information you must bring with you when you make your initial notification—and tell you at which local police station you should attend.

The restrictions in this order apply throughout the United Kingdom (England and Wales, Scotland and Northern Ireland).

If, without reasonable excuse, you fail to comply with the notification requirements of Part 2 of the Sexual Offences Act 2003 you shall be liable on conviction to imprisonment for a term not exceeding 5 years.

17

SEXUAL OFFENCES COMMITTED OUTSIDE THE JURISDICTION

A. Offences from 1 May 2004 to 13 July 2008	17.03	B. Offences on or after 14 July 2008 to present	17.11
1. Establishing the Offence Committed in the Foreign Jurisdiction	17.05	1. Establishing the Offence Committed in the Foreign Jurisdiction	17.12
2. Relevant Offences	17.08	2. Relevant Offences	17.15

17.01 Generally, an offence will only be triable in the jurisdiction in which the offence takes place, unless there is a specific provision to extend jurisdiction. The following sexual offence provisions enable the UK to exercise extra-territorial jurisdiction in relation to certain sexual offences:

(a) For certain sexual offences committed between 1.9.1997 to 30.4.2004 extra-territorial jurisdiction was governed by s 7, Sex Offenders Act 1997 (SOA 1997). See para 17.03.
(b) For certain sexual offences committed from 30.4.2004 to 13.07.2008 extra-territorial jurisdiction is governed by s 72 (as enacted at that time) Sexual Offences Act 2003 (SOA 2003). See para 17.04.
(c) For certain sexual offences committed on or after 14.7.2008 to date, extra-territorial jurisdiction is governed by s 72 Sexual Offences Act as currently enacted. See para 17.12.

17.02 From 1.9.1997[1] extra-territorial jurisdiction in relation to the commission of certain sexual offences was governed by the Sex Offenders Act, s 7. Section 7 SOA 1997 was repealed by the Sexual Offences Act on 1.5.2004 and replaced with s 72 SOA 2003. The Criminal Justice and Immigration Act 2008 subsequently amended the section 72 provisions from 14.7.2008.[2] Accordingly, it is necessary to know the date of the alleged offending so that charges may be brought under the appropriate statute and, where it applies, version of the SOA 2003, s 72.

A. OFFENCES FROM 1 MAY 2004 TO 13 JULY 2008

17.03 A person who on or after 1.9.1997 is a British citizen or United Kingdom resident[3] is liable to prosecution for a sexual offence committed outside the jurisdiction if the offence is

---

[1] Enacted by SI 1997/1020 art 2.
[2] Criminal Justice and Immigration Act 2008 (Commencement No 2 and Transitional and Savings Provisions) Order 2008 (SI 2008 No 1586).
[3] SOA 2003 prior to amendment, s 72(2).

recognized as a sexual offence both in the country in which it is committed[4] and within the jurisdiction of England, Wales, or Northern Ireland.[5]

17.04 The offence committed is that sexual offence with which the defendant would have been charged had the offence been committed in the jurisdiction.[6]

1. Establishing the Offence Committed in the Foreign Jurisdiction

17.05 The Court should presume that the defendant's alleged actions constitute an offence under the law in force in the foreign country or territory unless the defendant serves a notice upon the prosecution disputing that this condition has been met.[7]

17.06 The notice must: (a) state that, on the facts as alleged, the condition is not in the defendant's opinion met;[8] (b) show the defendant's grounds for that opinion;[9] and (c) require the prosecution to prove that it is met.[10] The Court can, however, waive the condition to serve such a notice.[11]

17.07 The extra-territorial sexual offence need not be described identically to the offence under the law of England, Wales, or Northern Ireland. All that is necessary is that the *actus reus* of an offence under both sets of laws is satisfied.[12] This is a question for the Judge alone.[13]

2. Relevant Offences

17.08 Paragraph 1 of Schedule 2 to the SOA 2003 lists the sexual offences to which s 72 applies.[14]

Offences under the Sexual Offences Act 2003

17.09 (i) an offence under any of ss 5 to 15 (offences against children under 13 or under 16);

(ii) an offence under any of ss 1 to 4, 16 to 41, 47 to 50, and 61 where the victim of the offence was under 16 at the time of the offence;

(iii) an offence under s 62 or s 63 where the intended offence was an offence against a person under 16;

Offences under Miscellaneous Acts

17.10 Offences under:

(i) the Protection of Children Act 1978, s 1 (indecent photographs of children);[15] or

---

[4] SOA 2003, s 72(1)(a).
[5] SOA 2003, s 72(1)(b).
[6] SOA 2003, s 72(1)(b).
[7] SOA 2003, s 72(4).
[8] SOA 2003, s 72(4)(a).
[9] SOA 2003, s 72(4)(b).
[10] SOA 2003, s 72(4)(c).
[11] SOA 2003, s 72(5).
[12] SOA 2003, s 72(3).
[13] SOA 2003, s 72(6).
[14] SOA 2003, s 72(7).
[15] SOA 2003, Sch 2, para 1(d)(i).

(ii) the Criminal Justice Act 1988, s 160 (possession of indecent photograph of a child);[16] where the photograph or pseudo-photograph showing a child under 16 falls within the ambit of s 72.

The offences above include a reference to any attempt, conspiracy, incitement to commit the offence; and aiding, abetting, counselling, or procuring the commission of the offence.[17]

B. OFFENCES ON OR AFTER 14 JULY 2008 TO PRESENT

17.11 A new s 72 was inserted into the SOA 2003 by the Criminal Justice and Immigration Act 2008. It creates an offence that can be committed in three different ways.

(1) If a UK national does an act in a country outside the United Kingdom (even if legal in that country) that, if done in England and Wales, would constitute a sexual offence listed in Schedule 2.[18]
(2) If a UK national does an act in a country outside the United Kingdom that constitutes an offence under the law in force in that country, and the act, if done in England and Wales, would constitute a sexual offence listed in Schedule 2.[19]
(3) If a person commits an offence in another country that, if done in England and Wales, would have constituted a sexual offence listed in Schedule 2, and that person was not a UK national or resident at the time, but met the residence or nationality criteria.[20]

1. Establishing the Offence Committed in the Foreign Jurisdiction

17.12 For the purposes of offences (2) and (3), the court should presume that the defendant's alleged actions constitute an offence under the law in force in the foreign country or territory unless the defendant serves a notice upon the prosecution disputing that this condition has been met.[21]

17.13 The notice must: (a) state that, on the facts as alleged, the condition is not in the defendant's opinion met;[22] (b) show the defendant's grounds for that opinion;[23] and (c) require the prosecution to prove that it is met.[24] The court can, however, waive the condition to serve such a notice.[25]

17.14 For the purposes of offences (2) and (3), the extra-territorial sexual offence need not be described identically to the offence under the law of England and Wales. All that is necessary

---

[16] SOA 2003, Sch 2, para 1(d)(ii).
[17] SOA 2003, Sch 2, para 3.
[18] SOA 2003 following amendment, s 72(1).
[19] SOA 2003, s 72(2).
[20] SOA 2003, s 72(3), s 72(9).
[21] SOA 2003, s 72(6).
[22] SOA 2003, s 72(6)(a).
[23] SOA 2003, s 72(6)(b).
[24] SOA 2003, s 72(6)(c).
[25] SOA 2003, s 72(7).

is that the *actus reus* of an offence under both sets of laws is satisfied.[26] This is a question for the judge alone.[27]

2. Relevant Offences

17.15 The relevant offences are set out in Schedule 2 to the Sexual Offences Act 2003, as amended by the Criminal Justice and Immigration Act 2008.

Offences under the Sexual Offences Act 2003

17.16 (i) An offence under any of ss 5–19, 25, 26, and 47–50.

(ii) An offence under any of ss 1–4, 30–41, and 61 where the victim of the offence was under 18 at the time of the offence.

(iii) An offence under s 62 or s 63 where the intended offence was an offence against a person under 18.

17.17 Offences under miscellaneous acts

(i) Protection of Children Act 1978, s 1 (indecent photographs of children),[28] or
(ii) Criminal Justice Act 1988, s 160 (possession of indecent photograph of child).[29]

The offences above include a reference to any attempt, conspiracy, incitement to commit the offence; and aiding, abetting, counselling, or procuring the commission of the offence.[30]

Note: Section 72, as referred to above, is replicated as it exists from 1.2.2009.[31] As of 1.2.2009 the references to Northern Ireland were repealed from section 72 and the second Schedule.

---

[26] SOA 2003, s 72(5).
[27] SOA 2003, s 72(8).
[28] SOA 2003, Sch 2, para 1(d)(i).
[29] SOA 2003, Sch 2, para 1(d)(ii).
[30] SOA 2003, Sch 2, para 3.
[31] Sexual Offences Act 2003 (Northern Ireland Consequential Amendments) order 2008/1779.

APPENDIX A

Specified Sexual Offences

A. Specified Sexual Offences under the Sexual Offences Act 1956	513	C. Specified Sexual Offences under the Sexual Offences Act 2003	514
B. Specified Sexual Offences under Miscellaneous Acts 1957–2002	514		

Schedule 15 of Part II of the Criminal Justice Act 2003 provides a definitive list of 'specified' sexual offences for the purposes of assessing 'dangerousness' when sentencing. Aiding, abetting, counselling, procuring, inciting, conspiring or attempting to commit any of the specified offences also falls within the ambit of Sch 15.[1]

A. Specified Sexual Offences under the Sexual Offences Act 1956

Legislative Provision	Offence
SOA 1956, s 1	Rape
SOA 1956, s 2	Procurement of woman by threats
SOA 1956, s 3	Procurement of woman by false pretences
SOA 1956, s 4	Administering drugs to obtain or facilitate intercourse
SOA 1956, s 5	Intercourse with a girl under 13
SOA 1956, s 6	Intercourse with a girl under 16
SOA 1956, s 7	Intercourse with a defective
SOA 1956, s 9	Procurement of a defective
SOA 1956, s 10	Incest by a man
SOA 1956, s 11	Incest by a woman
SOA 1956, s 14	Indecent assault on a woman
SOA 1956, s 15	Indecent assault on a man
SOA 1956, s 16	Assault with intent to commit buggery
SOA 1956, s 17	Abduction of woman by force or for the sake of her property
SOA 1956, s 19	Abduction of unmarried girl under 18 from parent or guardian
SOA 1956, s 20	Abduction of unmarried girl under 16 from parent or guardian
SOA 1956, s 21	Abduction of defective from parent or guardian

---

[1] CJA 2003, Sch 15, Part II, para 153.

Legislative Provision	Offence
SOA 1956, s 22	Causing prostitution of women
SOA 1956, s 23	Procuration of girl under 21
SOA 1956, s 24	Detention of woman in brothel
SOA 1956, s 25	Permitting girl under 13 to use premises for intercourse
SOA 1956, s 26	Permitting girl under 16 to use premises for intercourse
SOA 1956, s 27	Permitting defective to use premises for intercourse
SOA 1956, s 28	Causing or encouraging the prostitution of, intercourse with, or indecent assault on girl under 16
SOA 1956, s 29	Causing or encouraging prostitution of defective
SOA 1956, s 32	Soliciting by men
SOA 1956, s 33	Keeping a brothel

B. Specified Sexual Offences under Miscellaneous Acts 1957–2002

Legislative Provision	Offence
MHA 1959, s 128	Sexual intercourse with patients
IwCA 1960, s 1	Indecent conduct towards young child
SOA 1967, s 4	Procuring others to commit homosexual acts
SOA 1967, s 5	Living on earnings of male prostitution
TA 1968, s 9	Burglary with intent to commit rape
CLA 1977, s 54	Inciting girl under 16 to have incestuous sexual intercourse
PCA 1978, s 1	Indecent photographs of children
Customs and Excise Management Act 1979, s 170	Penalty for fraudulent evasion of duty etc in relation to goods prohibited to be imported under the Customs Consolidation Act 1876, s 42 (indecent or obscene articles)
CJA 1988, s 160	Possession of indecent photograph of a child

C. Specified Sexual Offences under the Sexual Offences Act 2003

Legislative Provision	Offence
SOA 2003, s 1	Rape
SOA 2003, s 2	Assault by penetration
SOA 2003, s 3	Sexual assault
SOA 2003, s 4	Causing a person to engage in sexual activity without consent
SOA 2003, s 5	Rape of a child under 13
SOA 2003, s 6	Assault of a child under 13 by penetration

Legislative Provision	Offence
SOA 2003, s 7	Sexual assault of a child under 13
SOA 2003, s 8	Causing or inciting a child under 13 to engage in sexual activity
SOA 2003, s 9	Sexual activity with a child
SOA 2003, s 10	Causing or inciting a child to engage in sexual activity
SOA 2003, s 11	Engaging in sexual activity in the presence of a child
SOA 2003, s 12	Causing a child to watch a sexual act
SOA 2003, s 13	Child sex offences committed by children or young persons
SOA 2003, s 14	Arranging or facilitating commission of a child sex offence
SOA 2003, s 15	Meeting a child following sexual grooming etc
SOA 2003, s 16	Abuse of position of trust: sexual activity with a child
SOA 2003, s 17	Abuse of position of trust: causing or inciting a child to engage in sexual activity
SOA 2003, s 18	Abuse of position of trust: sexual activity in the presence of a child
SOA 2003, s 19	Abuse of position of trust: causing a child to watch a sexual act
SOA 2003, s 25	Sexual activity with a child family member
SOA 2003, s 26	Inciting a child family member to engage in sexual activity
SOA 2003, s 30	Sexual activity with a person with a mental disorder impeding choice
SOA 2003, s 31	Causing or inciting a person, with a mental disorder impeding choice, to engage in sexual activity
SOA 2003, s 32	Engaging in sexual activity in the presence of a person with a mental disorder impeding choice
SOA 2003, s 33	Causing a person, with a mental disorder impeding choice, to watch a sexual act
SOA 2003, s 34	Inducement, threat, or deception to procure sexual activity with a person with a mental disorder
SOA 2003, s 35	Causing a person with a mental disorder to engage in or agree to engage in sexual activity by inducement, threat, or deception
SOA 2003, s 36	Engaging in sexual activity in the presence, procured by inducement, threat or deception, of a person with a mental disorder
SOA 2003, s 37	Causing a person with a mental disorder to watch a sexual act by inducement, threat or deception
SOA 2003, s 38	Care workers: sexual activity with a person with a mental disorder
SOA 2003, s 39	Care workers: causing or inciting sexual activity
SOA 2003, s 40	Care workers: sexual activity in the presence of a person with a mental disorder
SOA 2003, s 41	Care workers: causing a person with a mental disorder to watch a sexual act
SOA 2003, s 47	Paying for sexual services of a child
SOA 2003, s 48	Causing or inciting child prostitution or pornography
SOA 2003, s 49	Controlling a child prostitute or a child involved in pornography

Legislative Provision	Offence
SOA 2003, s 50	Arranging or facilitating child prostitution or pornography
SOA 2003, s 52	Causing or inciting prostitution for gain
SOA 2003, s 53	Controlling prostitution for gain
SOA 2003, s 57	Trafficking into the UK for sexual exploitation
SOA 2003, s 58	Trafficking within the UK for sexual exploitation
SOA 2003, s 59	Trafficking out of the UK for sexual exploitation
SOA 2003, s 59A	Trafficking for sexual exploitation
SOA 2003, s 61	Administering a substance with intent
SOA 2003, s 62	Committing an offence with intent to commit a sexual offence
SOA 2003, s 63	Trespass with intent to commit a sexual offence
SOA 2003, s 64	Sex with an adult relative: penetration
SOA 2003, s 65	Sex with an adult relative: consenting to penetration
SOA 2003, s 66	Exposure
SOA 2003, s 67	Voyeurism
SOA 2003, s 69	Intercourse with an animal
SOA 2003, s 70	Sexual penetration of a corpse

APPENDIX B

Sentencing Guidelines Council—Sexual Offences Act 2003 Definitive Guidelines

Applicability of guideline	519	Causing a child to watch a sexual act	560
Rape and assault offences	519	Sexual Offences Act 2003 (section 12)	560
Rape	519	Arranging or facilitating the commission of a child sex offence	564
Sexual Offences Act 2003 (section 1)	519		
Assault by penetration	523	Sexual Offences Act 2003 (section 14)	564
Sexual Offences Act 2003 (section 2)	523	Meeting a child following sexual grooming	565
Sexual assault	527		
Sexual Offences Act 2003 (section 3)	527	Sexual Offences Act 2003 (section 15)	565
Causing a person to engage in sexual activity without consent	531	Abuse of position of trust: sexual activity with a child	568
Sexual Offences Act 2003 (section 4)	531	Sexual Offences Act 2003 (section 16)	568
Offences where the victim is a child	531	Abuse of position of trust: causing or inciting a child to engage in sexual activity	568
Rape of a child under 13	536		
Sexual Offences Act 2003 (section 5)	536	Sexual Offences Act 2003 (section 17)	568
Assault of a child under 13 by penetration	540	Abuse of position of trust: sexual activity in the presence of a child	572
Sexual Offences Act 2003 (section 6)	540		
Sexual assault of a child under 13	544	Sexual Offences Act 2003 (section 18)	572
Sexual Offences Act 2003 (section 7)	544	Abuse of position of trust: causing a child to watch a sexual act	572
Causing or inciting a child under 13 to engage in sexual activity	548		
		Sexual Offences Act 2003 (section 19)	572
Sexual Offences Act 2003 (section 8)	548	**Indecent images of children**	576
Sexual activity with a child	552	Possession of indecent photograph of child	576
Sexual Offences Act 2003 (section 9)	552		
Causing or inciting a child to engage in sexual activity	552	Criminal Justice Act 1988 (section 160)	576
		Indecent photographs of children	576
Sexual Offences Act 2003 (section 10)	552	Protection of Children Act 1978 (section 1)	576
Sexual activity with a child family member	556		
		Exploitation offences	576
Sexual Offences Act 2003 (section 25)	556	Causing or inciting prostitution for gain	580
Inciting a child family member to engage in sexual activity	557	Sexual Offences Act 2003 (section 52)	580
		Controlling prostitution for gain	580
Sexual Offences Act 2003 (section 26)	557	Sexual Offences Act 2003 (section 53)	580
Engaging in sexual activity in the presence of a child	560	Keeping a brothel used for prostitution	584
		Sexual Offences Act 1956 (section 33A)	584
Sexual Offences Act 2003 (section 11)	560		

Causing or inciting child prostitution or pornography	588
Sexual Offences Act 2003 (section 48)	588
Controlling a child prostitute or child involved in pornography	588
Sexual Offences Act 2003 (section 49)	588
Arranging or facilitating child prostitution or pornography	588
Sexual Offences Act 2003 (section 50)	588
Paying for the sexual services of a child	592
Sexual Offences Act 2003 (section 47)	592
Trafficking people for sexual exploitation	595
Sexual Offences Act 2003 (sections 59A)	595
Offences against those with a mental disorder	595
Sexual activity with a person with a mental disorder impeding choice	599
Sexual Offences Act 2003 (section 30)	599
Causing or inciting a person, with a mental disorder impeding choice, to engage in sexual activity	599
Sexual Offences Act 2003 (section 31)	599
Engaging in sexual activity in the presence of a person with mental disorder impeding choice	603
Sexual Offences Act 2003 (section 32)	603
Causing a person, with mental disorder impeding choice, to watch a sexual act	603
Sexual Offences Act 2003 (section 33)	603
Inducement, threat or deception to procure sexual activity with a person with a mental disorder	607
Sexual Offences Act 2003 (section 34)	607
Causing a person with a mental disorder to engage in or agree to engage in sexual activity by inducement, threat or deception	607
Sexual Offences Act 2003 (section 35)	607
Engaging in sexual activity in the presence, procured by inducement, threat or deception, of a person with a mental disorder	611
Sexual Offences Act 2003 (section 36)	611
Causing a person with a mental disorder to watch a sexual act by inducement, threat or deception	611
Sexual Offences Act 2003 (section 37)	611
Care workers: sexual activity with a person with a mental disorder	614
Sexual Offences Act 2003 (section 38)	614
Care workers: causing or inciting sexual activity	614
Sexual Offences Act 2003 (section 39)	614
Care workers: sexual activity in the presence of a person with a mental disorder	618
Sexual Offences Act 2003 (section 40)	618
Care workers: causing a person with a mental disorder to watch a sexual act	618
Sexual Offences Act 2003 (section 41)	618
Other sexual offences	622
Exposure	622
Sexual Offences Act 2003 (section 66)	622
Voyeurism	625
Sexual Offences Act 2003 (section 67)	625
Sex with an adult relative: penetration	629
Sexual Offences Act 2003 (section 64)	629
Sex with an adult relative: consenting to penetration	629
Sexual Offences Act 2003 (section 65)	629
Administering a substance with intent	632
Sexual Offences Act 2003 (section 61)	632
Committing an offence with intent to commit a sexual offence	636
Sexual Offences Act 2003 (section 62)	636
Trespass with intent to commit a sexual offence	636
Sexual Offences Act 2003 (section 63)	636
Guidance regarding offences committed by offenders under the age of 18 (no definitive guidelines are included)	
Child sex offences committed by children or young persons (offender under 18)	639
Sexual Offences Act 2003 (section 13)	639
Sexual activity with a child family member (offender under 18)	639
Sexual Offences Act 2003 (section 25)	639
Inciting a child family member to engage in sexual activity (offender under 18)	639
Sexual Offences Act 2003 (section 26)	640
Annex A: Ancillary orders	640
Annex B: Approach to sentencing of historic sexual offences	642
Annex C: Historic offences	643
Annex D: Fine bands and community orders	645

Applicability of guideline

In accordance with section 120 of the Coroners and Justice Act 2009, the Sentencing Council issues this definitive guideline. It applies to all offenders aged 18 and older, who are sentenced on or after 1 April 2014.

Section 125(1) of the Coroners and Justice Act 2009 provides that when sentencing offences committed on or after 6 April 2010:

"Every court—

(a) must, in sentencing an offender, follow any sentencing guideline which is relevant to the offender's case, and
(b) must, in exercising any other function relating to the sentencing of offenders, follow any sentencing guidelines which are relevant to the exercise of the function,

unless the court is satisfied that it would be contrary to the interests of justice to do so."

This guideline applies only to offenders aged 18 and older. General principles to be considered in the sentencing of youths are in the Sentencing Guidelines Council's definitive guideline, *Overarching Principles—Sentencing Youths*.

Structure, ranges and starting points

For the purposes of section 125(3)–(4) of the Coroners and Justice Act 2009, the guideline specifies *offence ranges*—the range of sentences appropriate for each type of offence. Within each offence, the Council has specified different *categories* which reflect varying degrees of seriousness. The offence range is split into *category ranges*—sentences appropriate for each level of seriousness. The Council has also identified a starting point within each category.

Starting points define the position within a category range from which to start calculating the provisional sentence. Starting points apply to all offences within the corresponding category and are applicable to all offenders, in all cases. Once the starting point is established, the court should consider further aggravating and mitigating factors and previous convictions so as to adjust the sentence within the range. Starting points and ranges apply to all offenders, whether they have pleaded guilty or been convicted after trial. Credit for a guilty plea is taken into consideration only at step four in the decision making process, after the appropriate sentence has been identified.

Information on ancillary orders is set out at Annex A on page 640. Information on historic offences is set out at annexes B and C on pages 642 and 643.

Information on community orders and fine bands is set out at Annex D on page 645.

Rape

Sexual Offences Act 2003 (section 1)

Triable only on indictment

Maximum: Life imprisonment

Offence range: 4–19 years' custody

This is a serious specified offence for the purposes of sections 224 and 225(2) (life sentence for serious offences) of the Criminal Justice Act 2003.

For offences committed on or after 3 December 2012, this is an offence listed in Part 1 of Schedule 15B for the purposes of sections 224A (life sentence for second listed offence) of the Criminal Justice Act 2003.

For convictions on or after 3 December 2012 (irrespective of the date of commission of the offence), this is a specified offence for the purposes of section 226A (extended sentence for certain violent or sexual offences) of the Criminal Justice Act 2003.

STEP ONE

Determining the offence category

The court should determine which categories of harm and culpability the offence falls into by reference only to the tables below.

Offences may be of such severity, for example involving a campaign of rape, that sentences of 20 years and above may be appropriate.

HARM	
Category 1	• The extreme nature of one or more category 2 factors or the extreme impact caused by a combination of category 2 factors may elevate to category 1
Category 2	• Severe psychological or physical harm • Pregnancy or STI as a consequence of offence • Additional degradation/humiliation • Abduction • Prolonged detention/sustained incident • Violence or threats of violence (beyond that which is inherent in the offence) • Forced/uninvited entry into victim's home • Victim is particularly vulnerable due to personal circumstances* *for children under 13 please refer to the guideline on page 536
Category 3	Factor(s) in categories 1 and 2 not present

CULPABILITY	
A	B
• Significant degree of planning • Offender acts together with others to commit the offence • Use of alcohol/drugs on victim to facilitate the offence • Abuse of trust • Previous violence against victim • Offence committed in course of burglary • Recording of the offence • Commercial exploitation and/or motivation • Offence racially or religiously aggravated • Offence motivated by, or demonstrating, hostility to the victim based on his or her sexual orientation (or presumed sexual orientation) or transgender identity (or presumed transgender identity) • Offence motivated by, or demonstrating, hostility to the victim based on his or her disability (or presumed disability)	Factor(s) in category A not present

STEP TWO

Starting point and category range

Having determined the category, the court should use the corresponding starting points to reach a sentence within the category range below. The starting point applies to all offenders irrespective of plea or previous convictions. Having determined the starting point, step two allows further adjustment for aggravating or mitigating features set out below.

A case of particular gravity, reflected by multiple features of culpability or harm in step one, could merit upward adjustment from the starting point before further adjustment for aggravating or mitigating features, set out below.

	A	B
Category 1	**Starting point** 15 years' custody **Category range** 13–19 years' custody	**Starting point** 12 years' custody **Category range** 10–15 years' custody
Category 2	**Starting point** 10 years' custody **Category range** 9–13 years' custody	**Starting point** 8 years' custody **Category range** 7–9 years' custody
Category 3	**Starting point** 7 years' custody **Category range** 6–9 years' custody	**Starting point** 5 years' custody **Category range** 4–7 years' custody

The table below contains a non-exhaustive list of additional factual elements providing the context of the offence and factors relating to the offender. Identify whether any combination of these, or other relevant factors, should result in an upward or downward adjustment from the starting point. In particular, relevant recent convictions are likely to result in an upward adjustment. In some cases, having considered these factors, it may be appropriate to move outside the identified category range.

Aggravating factors

Statutory aggravating factors

- Previous convictions, having regard to a) the nature of the offence to which the conviction relates and its relevance to the current offence; and b) the time that has elapsed since the conviction
- Offence committed whilst on bail

Other aggravating factors

- Specific targeting of a particularly vulnerable victim
- Ejaculation (where not taken into account at step one)
- Blackmail or other threats made (where not taken into account at step one)
- Location of offence
- Timing of offence
- Use of weapon or other item to frighten or injure
- Victim compelled to leave their home (including victims of domestic violence)
- Failure to comply with current court orders
- Offence committed whilst on licence
- Exploiting contact arrangements with a child to commit an offence
- Presence of others, especially children
- Any steps taken to prevent the victim reporting an incident, obtaining assistance and/or from assisting or supporting the prosecution
- Attempts to dispose of or conceal evidence
- Commission of offence whilst under the influence of alcohol or drugs

Mitigating factors

- No previous convictions or no relevant/recent convictions
- Remorse
- Previous good character and/or exemplary conduct*
- Age and/or lack of maturity where it affects the responsibility of the offender
- Mental disorder or learning disability, particularly where linked to the commission of the offence

* Previous good character/exemplary conduct is different from having no previous convictions. The more serious the offence, the less the weight which should normally be attributed to this factor. Where previous good character/exemplary conduct has been used to facilitate the offence, this mitigation should not normally be allowed and such conduct may constitute an aggravating factor.

In the context of this offence, previous good character/exemplary conduct should not normally be given any significant weight and will not normally justify a reduction in what would otherwise be the appropriate sentence.

STEP THREE

Consider any factors which indicate a reduction, such as assistance to the prosecution

The court should take into account sections 73 and 74 of the Serious Organised Crime and Police Act 2005 (assistance by defendants: reduction or review of sentence) and any other rule of law by virtue of which an offender may receive a discounted sentence in consequence of assistance given (or offered) to the prosecutor or investigator.

STEP FOUR

Reduction for guilty pleas

The court should take account of any potential reduction for a guilty plea in accordance with section 144 of the Criminal Justice Act 2003 and the *Guilty Plea* guideline.

STEP FIVE

Dangerousness

The court should consider whether having regard to the criteria contained in Chapter 5 of Part 12 of the Criminal Justice Act 2003 it would be appropriate to award a life sentence (section 224A or section 225(2)) or an extended sentence (section 226A). When sentencing offenders to a life sentence under these provisions, the notional determinate sentence should be used as the basis for the setting of a minimum term.

STEP SIX

Totality principle

If sentencing an offender for more than one offence, or where the offender is already serving a sentence, consider whether the total sentence is just and proportionate to the offending behaviour.

STEP SEVEN

Ancillary orders

The court must consider whether to make any ancillary orders. The court must also consider what other requirements or provisions may *automatically* apply. Further information is included at Annex A on page 640.

STEP EIGHT

Reasons

Section 174 of the Criminal Justice Act 2003 imposes a duty to give reasons for, and explain the effect of, the sentence.

STEP NINE

Consideration for time spent on bail

The court must consider whether to give credit for time spent on bail in accordance with section 240A of the Criminal Justice Act 2003.

Assault by penetration

Sexual Offences Act 2003 (section 2)

Triable only on indictment

Maximum: Life imprisonment

Offence range: Community order–19 years' custody

This is a serious specified offence for the purposes of sections 224 and 225(2) (life sentence for serious offences) of the Criminal Justice Act 2003.

For offences committed on or after 3 December 2012, this is an offence listed in Part 1 of Schedule 15B for the purposes of sections 224A (life sentence for second listed offence) of the Criminal Justice Act 2003.

For convictions on or after 3 December 2012 (irrespective of the date of commission of the offence), this is a specified offence for the purposes of section 226A (extended sentence for certain violent or sexual offences) of the Criminal Justice Act 2003.

STEP ONE

Determining the offence category

The court should determine which categories of harm and culpability the offence falls into by reference only to the tables below.

HARM		CULPABILITY	
Category 1	• The extreme nature of one or more category 2 factors or the extreme impact caused by a combination of category 2 factors may elevate to category 1	**A**	**B**
		• Significant degree of planning
• Offender acts together with others to commit the offence
• Use of alcohol/drugs on victim to facilitate the offence
• Abuse of trust
• Previous violence against victim
• Offence committed in course of burglary
• Recording of the offence
• Commercial exploitation and/or motivation
• Offence racially or religiously aggravated
• Offence motivated by, or demonstrating, hostility to the victim based on his or her sexual orientation (or presumed sexual orientation) or transgender identity (or presumed transgender identity)
• Offence motivated by, or demonstrating, hostility to the victim based on his or her disability (or presumed disability)	Factor(s) in category A not present
Category 2	• Severe psychological or physical harm
• Penetration using large or dangerous object(s)
• Additional degradation/humiliation
• Abduction
• Prolonged detention/sustained incident
• Violence or threats of violence (beyond that which is inherent in the offence)
• Forced/uninvited entry into victim's home
• Victim is particularly vulnerable due to personal circumstances*
* for children under 13 please refer to the guideline on page 540		
Category 3	Factor(s) in categories 1 and 2 not present		

STEP TWO

Starting point and category range

Having determined the category, the court should use the corresponding starting points to reach a sentence within the category range below. The starting point applies to all offenders irrespective of plea or previous convictions.

Having determined the starting point, step two allows further adjustment for aggravating or mitigating features, set out below.

A case of particular gravity, reflected by multiple features of culpability or harm in step one, could merit upward adjustment from the starting point before further adjustment for aggravating or mitigating features, set out below.

Where there is a sufficient prospect of rehabilitation, a community order with a sex offender treatment programme requirement under section 202 of the Criminal Justice Act 2003 can be a proper alternative to a short or moderate length custodial sentence.

	A	B
Category 1	**Starting point** 15 years' custody **Category range** 13–19 years' custody	**Starting point** 12 years' custody **Category range** 10–15 years' custody
Category 2	**Starting point** 8 years' custody **Category range** 5–13 years' custody	**Starting point** 6 years' custody **Category range** 4–9 years' custody
Category 3	**Starting point** 4 years' custody **Category range** 2–6 years' custody	**Starting point** 2 years' custody **Category range** High level community order–4 years' custody

The table below contains a non-exhaustive list of additional factual elements providing the context of the offence and factors relating to the offender. Identify whether any combination of these, or other relevant factors, should result in an upward or downward adjustment from the starting point. In particular, relevant recent convictions are likely to result in an upward adjustment. In some cases, having considered these factors, it may be appropriate to move outside the identified category range.

When sentencing appropriate category 3 offences, the court should also consider the custody threshold as follows:

- has the custody threshold been passed?
- if so, is it unavoidable that a custodial sentence be imposed?
- if so, can that sentence be suspended?

Aggravating factors

Statutory aggravating factors

- Previous convictions, having regard to a) the nature of the offence to which the conviction relates and its relevance to the current offence; and b) the time that has elapsed since the conviction
- Offence committed whilst on bail

Other aggravating factors

- Specific targeting of a particularly vulnerable victim
- Blackmail or other threats made (where not taken into account at step one)
- Location of offence
- Timing of offence
- Use of weapon or other item to frighten or injure
- Victim compelled to leave their home (including victims of domestic violence)
- Failure to comply with current court orders
- Offence committed whilst on licence
- Exploiting contact arrangements with a child to commit an offence
- Presence of others, especially children
- Any steps taken to prevent the victim reporting an incident, obtaining assistance and/or from assisting or supporting the prosecution
- Attempts to dispose of or conceal evidence
- Commission of offence whilst under the influence of alcohol or drugs

Mitigating factors
- No previous convictions or no relevant/recent convictions
- Remorse
- Previous good character and/or exemplary conduct*
- Age and/or lack of maturity where it affects the responsibility of the offender
- Mental disorder or learning disability, particularly where linked to the commission of the offence

* Previous good character/exemplary conduct is different from having no previous convictions. The more serious the offence, the less the weight which should normally be attributed to this factor. Where previous good character/exemplary conduct has been used to facilitate the offence, this mitigation should not normally be allowed and such conduct may constitute an aggravating factor. In the context of this offence, previous good character/exemplary conduct should not normally be given any significant weight and will not normally justify a reduction in what would otherwise be the appropriate sentence.

STEP THREE

Consider any factors which indicate a reduction, such as assistance to the prosecution

The court should take into account sections 73 and 74 of the Serious Organised Crime and Police Act 2005 (assistance by defendants: reduction or review of sentence) and any other rule of law by virtue of which an offender may receive a discounted sentence in consequence of assistance given (or offered) to the prosecutor or investigator.

STEP FOUR

Reduction for guilty pleas

The court should take account of any potential reduction for a guilty plea in accordance with section 144 of the Criminal Justice Act 2003 and the *Guilty Plea* guideline.

STEP FIVE

Dangerousness

The court should consider whether having regard to the criteria contained in Chapter 5 of Part 12 of the Criminal Justice Act 2003 it would be appropriate to award a life sentence (section 224A or section 225(2)) or an extended sentence (section 226A). When sentencing offenders to a life sentence under these provisions, the notional determinate sentence should be used as the basis for the setting of a minimum term.

STEP SIX

Totality principle

If sentencing an offender for more than one offence, or where the offender is already serving a sentence, consider whether the total sentence is just and proportionate to the offending behaviour.

STEP SEVEN

Ancillary orders

The court must consider whether to make any ancillary orders. The court must also consider what other requirements or provisions may *automatically* apply. Further information is included at Annex A on page 640.

STEP EIGHT

Reasons

Section 174 of the Criminal Justice Act 2003 imposes a duty to give reasons for, and explain the effect of, the sentence.

STEP NINE

Consideration for time spent on bail

The court must consider whether to give credit for time spent on bail in accordance with section 240A of the Criminal Justice Act 2003.

Sexual assault

Sexual Offences Act 2003 (section 3)

Triable either way

Maximum: 10 years' custody

Offence range: Community order–7 years' custody

For convictions on or after 3 December 2012 (irrespective of the date of commission of the offence), this is a specified offence for the purposes of section 226A (extended sentence for certain violent or sexual offences) of the Criminal Justice Act 2003.

STEP ONE

Determining the offence category

The court should determine which categories of harm and culpability the offence falls into by reference only to the tables below.

HARM	
Category 1	• Severe psychological or physical harm • Abduction • Violence or threats of violence • Forced/uninvited entry into victim's home
Category 2	• Touching of naked genitalia or naked breasts • Prolonged detention/sustained incident • Additional degradation/humiliation • Victim is particularly vulnerable due to personal circumstances* *for children under 13 please refer to the guideline on page 544
Category 3	Factor(s) in categories 1 and 2 not present

CULPABILITY	
A	**B**
• Significant degree of planning • Offender acts together with others to commit the offence • Use of alcohol/drugs on victim to facilitate the offence • Abuse of trust • Previous violence against victim • Offence committed in course of burglary • Recording of offence • Commercial exploitation and/or motivation • Offence racially or religiously aggravated • Offence motivated by, or demonstrating, hostility to the victim based on his or her sexual orientation (or presumed sexual orientation) or transgender identity (or presumed transgender identity) • Offence motivated by, or demonstrating, hostility to the victim based on his or her disability (or presumed disability)	Factor(s) in category A not present

STEP TWO

Starting point and category range

Having determined the category, the court should use the corresponding starting points to reach a sentence within the category range below. The starting point applies to all offenders irrespective of plea or previous convictions. Having determined the starting point, step two allows further adjustment for aggravating or mitigating features, set out below.

A case of particular gravity, reflected by multiple features of culpability or harm in step one, could merit upward adjustment from the starting point before further adjustment for aggravating or mitigating features, set out below.

Where there is a sufficient prospect of rehabilitation, a community order with a sex offender treatment programme requirement under section 202 of the Criminal Justice Act 2003 can be a proper alternative to a short or moderate length custodial sentence.

	A	B
Category 1	**Starting point** 4 years' custody **Category range** 3–7 years' custody	**Starting point** 2 years 6 months' custody **Category range** 2–4 years' custody
Category 2	**Starting point** 2 years' custody **Category range** 1–4 years' custody	**Starting point** 1 year's custody **Category range** High level community order–2 years' custody
Category 3	**Starting point** 26 weeks' custody **Category range** High level community order–1 year's custody	**Starting point** High level community order **Category range** Medium level community order–26 weeks' custody

The table below contains a non-exhaustive list of additional factual elements providing the context of the offence and factors relating to the offender. Identify whether any combination of these, or other relevant factors, should result in an upward or downward adjustment from the starting point. In particular, relevant recent convictions are likely to result in an upward adjustment. In some cases, having considered these factors, it may be appropriate to move outside the identified category range.

When sentencing appropriate category 2 or 3 offences, the court should also consider the custody threshold as follows:

- has the custody threshold been passed?
- if so, is it unavoidable that a custodial sentence be imposed?
- if so, can that sentence be suspended?

Aggravating factors

Statutory aggravating factors

- Previous convictions, having regard to a) the nature of the offence to which the conviction relates and its relevance to the current offence; and b) the time that has elapsed since the conviction
- Offence committed whilst on bail

Other aggravating factors

- Specific targeting of a particularly vulnerable victim
- Blackmail or other threats made (where not taken into account at step one)
- Location of offence
- Timing of offence
- Use of weapon or other item to frighten or injure
- Victim compelled to leave their home (including victims of domestic violence)
- Failure to comply with current court orders
- Offence committed whilst on licence

- Exploiting contact arrangements with a child to commit an offence
- Presence of others, especially children
- Any steps taken to prevent the victim reporting an incident, obtaining assistance and/or from assisting or supporting the prosecution
- Attempts to dispose of or conceal evidence
- Commission of offence whilst under the influence of alcohol or drugs

Mitigating factors
- No previous convictions or no relevant/recent convictions
- Remorse
- Previous good character and/or exemplary conduct*
- Age and/or lack of maturity where it affects the responsibility of the offender
- Mental disorder or learning disability, particularly where linked to the commission of the offence
- Demonstration of steps taken to address offending behaviour

* Previous good character/exemplary conduct is different from having no previous convictions. The more serious the offence, the less the weight which should normally be attributed to this factor. Where previous good character/exemplary conduct has been used to facilitate the offence, this mitigation should not normally be allowed and such conduct may constitute an aggravating factor.

STEP THREE

Consider any factors which indicate a reduction, such as assistance to the prosecution

The court should take into account sections 73 and 74 of the Serious Organised Crime and Police Act 2005 (assistance by defendants: reduction or review of sentence) and any other rule of law by virtue of which an offender may receive a discounted sentence in consequence of assistance given (or offered) to the prosecutor or investigator.

STEP FOUR

Reduction for guilty pleas

The court should take account of any potential reduction for a guilty plea in accordance with section 144 of the Criminal Justice Act 2003 and the *Guilty Plea* guideline.

STEP FIVE

Dangerousness

The court should consider whether having regard to the criteria contained in Chapter 5 of Part 12 of the Criminal Justice Act 2003 it would be appropriate to award an extended sentence (section 226A).

STEP SIX

Totality principle

If sentencing an offender for more than one offence, or where the offender is already serving a sentence, consider whether the total sentence is just and proportionate to the offending behaviour.

STEP SEVEN

Ancillary orders

The court must consider whether to make any ancillary orders. The court must also consider what other requirements or provisions may *automatically* apply. Further information is included at Annex A on page 640.

STEP EIGHT

Reasons

Section 174 of the Criminal Justice Act 2003 imposes a duty to give reasons for, and explain the effect of, the sentence.

STEP NINE

Consideration for time spent on bail

The court must consider whether to give credit for time spent on bail in accordance with section 240A of the Criminal Justice Act 2003.

Causing a person to engage in sexual activity without consent

Sexual Offences Act 2003 (section 4)

Triable only on indictment (if penetration involved)—otherwise, triable either way

Maximum: Life imprisonment (if penetration involved)—otherwise, 10 years

Offence range: Community order–7 years' custody (if no penetration involved)/19 years' custody (if penetration involved)

This is a serious specified offence for the purposes of section 224 and, where the offence involved penetration, section 225(2) (life sentence for serious offences) of the Criminal Justice Act 2003.

For offences involving penetration, committed on or after 3 December 2012, this is an offence listed in Part 1 of Schedule 15B for the purposes of sections 224A (life sentence for second listed offence) of the Criminal Justice Act 2003.

For convictions on or after 3 December 2012 (irrespective of the date of commission of the offence), this is a specified offence for the purposes of section 226A (extended sentence for certain violent or sexual offences) of the Criminal Justice Act 2003.

STEP ONE

Determining the offence category

The court should determine which categories of harm and culpability the offence falls into by reference only to the tables below.

HARM		CULPABILITY	
		A	**B**
Category 1	The extreme nature of one or more category 2 factors or the extreme impact caused by a combination of category 2 factors may elevate to category 1	• Significant degree of planning • Offender acts together with others to commit the offence • Use of alcohol/drugs on victim to facilitate the offence • Abuse of trust • Previous violence against victim • Offence committed in course of burglary • Recording of the offence • Commercial exploitation and/or motivation • Offence racially or religiously aggravated • Offence motivated by, or demonstrating, hostility to the victim based on his or her sexual orientation (or presumed sexual orientation) or transgender identity (or presumed transgender identity) • Offence motivated by, or demonstrating, hostility to the victim based on his or her disability (or presumed disability)	Factor(s) in category A not present
Category 2	• Severe psychological or physical harm • Penetration using large or dangerous object(s) • Pregnancy or STI as a consequence of offence • Additional degradation/humiliation • Abduction • Prolonged detention/sustained incident • Violence or threats of violence • Forced/uninvited entry into victim's home • Victim is particularly vulnerable due to personal circumstances* *for children under 13 please refer to the guideline on page 548		
Category 3	Factor(s) in categories 1 and 2 not present		

STEP TWO

Starting point and category range

Having determined the category, the court should use the corresponding starting points to reach a sentence within the category range below. The starting point applies to all offenders irrespective of plea or previous convictions.

Having determined the starting point, step two allows further adjustment for aggravating or mitigating features, set out below.

A case of particular gravity, reflected by multiple features of culpability or harm in step one, could merit upward adjustment from the starting point before further adjustment for aggravating or mitigating features, set out below.

Where there is a sufficient prospect of rehabilitation, a community order with a sex offender treatment programme requirement under section 202 of the Criminal Justice Act 2003 can be a proper alternative to a short or moderate length custodial sentence.

Where offence involved penetration

	A	B
Category 1	**Starting point** 15 years' custody **Category range** 13–19 years' custody	**Starting point** 12 years' custody **Category range** 10–15 years' custody
Category 2	**Starting point** 8 years' custody **Category range** 5–13 years' custody	**Starting point** 6 years' custody **Category range** 4–9 years' custody
Category 3	**Starting point** 4 years' custody **Category range** 2–6 years' custody	**Starting point** 2 years' custody **Category range** High level community order–4 years' custody

Where offence did not involve penetration

	A	B
Category 1	**Starting point** 4 years' custody **Category range** 3–7 years' custody	**Starting point** 2 years 6 months' custody **Category range** 2–4 years' custody
Category 2	**Starting point** 2 years' custody **Category range** 1–4 years' custody	**Starting point** 1 year's custody **Category range** High level community order–2 years' custody
Category 3	**Starting point** 26 weeks' custody **Category range** High level community order–1 year's custody	**Starting point** High level community order **Category range** Medium level community order–26 weeks' custody

The table below contains a non-exhaustive list of additional factual elements providing the context of the offence and factors relating to the offender. Identify whether any combination of these, or other relevant factors, should result in an upward or downward adjustment from the starting point. In particular, relevant recent convictions are likely to result in an upward adjustment. In some cases, having considered these factors, it may be appropriate to move outside the identified category range.

When sentencing appropriate category 2 or 3 offences, the court should also consider the custody threshold as follows:

- has the custody threshold been passed?
- if so, is it unavoidable that a custodial sentence be imposed?
- if so, can that sentence be suspended?

Aggravating factors
Statutory aggravating factors
- Previous convictions, having regard to a) the nature of the offence to which the conviction relates and its relevance to the current offence; and b) the time that has elapsed since the conviction
- Offence committed whilst on bail

Other aggravating factors
- Specific targeting of a particularly vulnerable victim
- Ejaculation (where not taken into account at step one)
- Blackmail or other threats made (where not taken into account at step one)
- Location of offence
- Timing of offence
- Use of weapon or other item to frighten or injure
- Victim compelled to leave their home (including victims of domestic violence)
- Failure to comply with current court orders
- Offence committed whilst on licence
- Exploiting contact arrangements with a child to commit an offence
- Presence of others, especially children
- Any steps taken to prevent the victim reporting an incident, obtaining assistance and/or from assisting or supporting the prosecution
- Attempts to dispose of or conceal evidence
- Commission of offence whilst under the influence of alcohol or drugs

Mitigating factors
- No previous convictions or no relevant/recent convictions
- Remorse
- Previous good character and/or exemplary conduct[*]
- Age and/or lack of maturity where it affects the responsibility of the offender
- Mental disorder or learning disability, particularly where linked to the commission of the offence

[*] Previous good character/exemplary conduct is different from having no previous convictions. The more serious the offence, the less the weight which should normally be attributed to this factor. Where previous good character/exemplary conduct has been used to facilitate the offence, this mitigation should not normally be allowed and such conduct may constitute an aggravating factor. In the context of this offence, previous good character/exemplary conduct should not normally be given any significant weight and will not normally justify a reduction in what would otherwise be the appropriate sentence.

STEP THREE

Consider any factors which indicate a reduction, such as assistance to the prosecution

The court should take into account sections 73 and 74 of the Serious Organised Crime and Police Act 2005 (assistance by defendants: reduction or review of sentence) and any other rule of law by virtue of which an offender may receive a discounted sentence in consequence of assistance given (or offered) to the prosecutor or investigator.

STEP FOUR

Reduction for guilty pleas

The court should take account of any potential reduction for a guilty plea in accordance with section 144 of the Criminal Justice Act 2003 and the *Guilty Plea* guideline.

STEP FIVE

Dangerousness

The court should consider whether having regard to the criteria contained in Chapter 5 of Part 12 of the Criminal Justice Act 2003 it would be appropriate to award a life sentence (section 224A or section 225(2)) or an extended sentence (section 226A). When sentencing offenders to a life sentence under these provisions, the notional determinate sentence should be used as the basis for the setting of a minimum term.

STEP SIX

Totality principle

If sentencing an offender for more than one offence, or where the offender is already serving a sentence, consider whether the total sentence is just and proportionate to the offending behaviour.

STEP SEVEN

Ancillary orders

The court must consider whether to make any ancillary orders. The court must also consider what other requirements or provisions may *automatically* apply. Further information is included at Annex A on page 640.

STEP EIGHT

Reasons

Section 174 of the Criminal Justice Act 2003 imposes a duty to give reasons for, and explain the effect of, the sentence.

STEP NINE

Consideration for time spent on bail

The court must consider whether to give credit for time spent on bail in accordance with section 240A of the Criminal Justice Act 2003.

Rape of a child under 13

Sexual Offences Act 2003 (section 5)

Triable only on indictment

Maximum: Life imprisonment

Offence range: 6–19 years' custody

This is a serious specified offence for the purposes of sections 224 and 225(2) (life sentence for serious offences) of the Criminal Justice Act 2003.

For offences committed on or after 3 December 2012, this is an offence listed in Part 1 of Schedule 15B for the purposes of section 224A (life sentence for second listed offence) of the Criminal Justice Act 2003.

For convictions on or after 3 December 2012 (irrespective of the date of commission of the offence), this is a specified offence for the purposes of section 226A (extended sentence for certain violent or sexual offences) of the Criminal Justice Act 2003.

STEP ONE

Determining the offence category

The court should determine which categories of harm and culpability the offence falls into by reference only to the tables below.

> Offences may be of such severity, for example involving a campaign of rape, that sentences of 20 years and above may be appropriate.
>
> When dealing with the statutory offence of rape of a child under 13, the court may be faced with a wide range of offending behaviour.
>
> Sentencers should have particular regard to the fact that these offences are not only committed through force or fear of force but may include exploitative behaviour towards a child which should be considered to indicate high culpability.
>
> This guideline is designed to deal with the majority of offending behaviour which deserves a significant custodial sentence; the starting points and ranges reflect the fact that such offending merits such an approach. There may also be exceptional cases, where a lengthy community order with a requirement to participate in a sex offender treatment programme may be the best way of changing the offender's behaviour and of protecting the public by preventing any repetition of the offence. This guideline may not be appropriate where the sentencer is satisfied that on the available evidence, and in the absence of exploitation, a young or particularly immature defendant genuinely believed, on reasonable grounds, that the victim was aged 16 or over and that they were engaging in lawful sexual activity.
>
> Sentencers are reminded that if sentencing outside the guideline they must be satisfied that it would be contrary to the interests of justice to follow the guideline.

HARM		CULPABILITY	
		A	**B**
Category 1	• The extreme nature of one or more category 2 factors or the extreme impact caused by a combination of category 2 factors may elevate to category 1	• Significant degree of planning • Offender acts together with others to commit the offence • Use of alcohol/drugs on victim to facilitate the offence • Grooming behaviour used against victim • Abuse of trust • Previous violence against victim • Offence committed in course of burglary • Sexual images of victim recorded, retained, solicited or shared • Deliberate isolation of victim • Commercial exploitation and/or motivation • Offence racially or religiously aggravated • Offence motivated by, or demonstrating, hostility to the victim based on his or her sexual orientation (or presumed sexual orientation) or transgender identity (or presumed transgender identity) • Offence motivated by, or demonstrating, hostility to the victim based on his or her disability (or presumed disability)	Factor(s) in category A not present
Category 2	• Severe psychological or physical harm • Pregnancy or STI as a consequence of offence • Additional degradation/humiliation • Abduction • Prolonged detention/sustained incident • Violence or threats of violence • Forced/uninvited entry into victim's home • Child is particularly vulnerable due to extreme youth and/or personal circumstances		
Category 3	Factor(s) in categories 1 and 2 not present		

STEP TWO

Starting point and category range

Having determined the category, the court should use the corresponding starting points to reach a sentence within the category range below. The starting point applies to all offenders irrespective of plea or previous convictions. Having determined the starting point, step two allows further adjustment for aggravating or mitigating features, set out below.

A case of particular gravity, reflected by multiple features of culpability or harm in step one, could merit upward adjustment from the starting point before further adjustment for aggravating or mitigating features, set out below.

Sentencers should also note the wording set out at step one which may be applicable in exceptional cases.

	A	B
Category 1	**Starting point**	**Starting point**
	16 years' custody	13 years' custody
	Category range	**Category range**
	13–19 years' custody	11–17 years' custody
Category 2	**Starting point**	**Starting point**
	13 years' custody	10 years' custody
	Category range	**Category range**
	11–17 years' custody	8–13 years' custody
Category 3	**Starting point**	**Starting point**
	10 years' custody	8 years' custody
	Category range	**Category range**
	8–13 years' custody	6–11 years' custody

The table below contains a non-exhaustive list of additional factual elements providing the context of the offence and factors relating to the offender. Identify whether any combination of these, or other relevant factors, should result in an upward or downward adjustment from the starting point. In particular, relevant recent convictions are likely to result in an upward adjustment. In some cases, having considered these factors, it may be appropriate to move outside the identified category range.

Aggravating factors

Statutory aggravating factors

- Previous convictions, having regard to a) the nature of the offence to which the conviction relates and its relevance to the current offence; and b) the time that has elapsed since the conviction
- Offence committed whilst on bail

Other aggravating factors

- Specific targeting of a particularly vulnerable child
- Ejaculation (where not taken into account at step one)
- Blackmail or other threats made (where not taken into account at step one)
- Location of offence
- Timing of offence
- Use of weapon or other item to frighten or injure
- Victim compelled to leave their home, school, etc
- Failure to comply with current court orders
- Offence committed whilst on licence
- Exploiting contact arrangements with a child to commit an offence
- Presence of others, especially other children
- Any steps taken to prevent the victim reporting an incident, obtaining assistance and/or from assisting or supporting the prosecution
- Attempts to dispose of or conceal evidence
- Commission of offence whilst offender under the influence of alcohol or drugs
- Victim encouraged to recruit others

Mitigating factors

- No previous convictions or no relevant/recent convictions
- Remorse
- Previous good character and/or exemplary conduct*
- Age and/or lack of maturity where it affects the responsibility of the offender
- Mental disorder or learning disability, particularly where linked to the commission of the offence

* Previous good character/exemplary conduct is different from having no previous convictions. The more serious the offence, the less the weight which should normally be attributed to this factor. Where previous good character/exemplary conduct has been used to facilitate the offence, this mitigation should not normally be allowed and such conduct may constitute an aggravating factor. In the context of this offence, previous good character/exemplary conduct should not normally be given any significant weight and will not normally justify a reduction in what would otherwise be the appropriate sentence.

STEP THREE

Consider any factors which indicate a reduction, such as assistance to the prosecution

The court should take into account sections 73 and 74 of the Serious Organised Crime and Police Act 2005 (assistance by defendants: reduction or review of sentence) and any other rule of law by virtue of which an offender may receive a discounted sentence in consequence of assistance given (or offered) to the prosecutor or investigator.

STEP FOUR

Reduction for guilty pleas

The court should take account of any potential reduction for a guilty plea in accordance with section 144 of the Criminal Justice Act 2003 and the *Guilty Plea* guideline.

STEP FIVE

Dangerousness

The court should consider whether having regard to the criteria contained in Chapter 5 of Part 12 of the Criminal Justice Act 2003 it would be appropriate to award a life sentence (section 224A or section 225(2)) or an extended sentence (section 226A). When sentencing offenders to a life sentence under these provisions, the notional determinate sentence should be used as the basis for the setting of a minimum term.

STEP SIX

Totality principle

If sentencing an offender for more than one offence, or where the offender is already serving a sentence, consider whether the total sentence is just and proportionate to the offending behaviour.

STEP SEVEN

Ancillary orders

The court must consider whether to make any ancillary orders. The court must also consider what other requirements or provisions may *automatically* apply. Further information is included at Annex A on page 640.

STEP EIGHT

Reasons

Section 174 of the Criminal Justice Act 2003 imposes a duty to give reasons for, and explain the effect of, the sentence.

STEP NINE

Consideration for time spent on bail

The court must consider whether to give credit for time spent on bail in accordance with section 240A of the Criminal Justice Act 2003.

Assault of a child under 13 by penetration

Sexual Offences Act 2003 (section 6)

Triable only on indictment

Maximum: Life imprisonment

Offence range: 2–19 years' custody

This is a serious specified offence for the purposes of sections 224 and 225(2) (life sentence for serious offences) of the Criminal Justice Act 2003.

For offences committed on or after 3 December 2012, this is an offence listed in Part 1 of Schedule 15B for the purposes of section 224A (life sentence for second listed offence) of the Criminal Justice Act 2003.

For convictions on or after 3 December 2012 (irrespective of the date of commission of the offence), this is a specified offence for the purposes of section 226A (extended sentence for certain violent or sexual offences) of the Criminal Justice Act 2003.

STEP ONE

Determining the offence category

The court should determine which categories of harm and culpability the offence falls into by reference only to the tables below.

HARM		CULPABILITY	
		A	**B**
Category 1	The extreme nature of one or more category 2 factors or the extreme impact caused by a combination of category 2 factors may elevate to category 1	• Significant degree of planning • Offender acts together with others to commit the offence • Use of alcohol/drugs on victim to facilitate the offence • Grooming behaviour used against victim • Abuse of trust • Previous violence against victim • Offence committed in course of burglary • Sexual images of victim recorded, retained, solicited or shared • Deliberate isolation of victim • Commercial exploitation and/or motivation • Offence racially or religiously aggravated • Offence motivated by, or demonstrating, hostility to the victim based on his or her sexual orientation (or presumed sexual orientation) or transgender identity (or presumed transgender identity) • Offence motivated by, or demonstrating, hostility to the victim based on his or her disability (or presumed disability)	Factor(s) in category A not present
Category 2	• Severe psychological or physical harm • Penetration using large or dangerous object(s) • Additional degradation/humiliation • Abduction • Prolonged detention /sustained incident • Violence or threats of violence • Forced/uninvited entry into victim's home • Child is particularly vulnerable due to extreme youth and/or personal circumstances		
Category 3	Factor(s) in categories 1 and 2 not present		

STEP TWO

Starting point and category range

Having determined the category, the court should use the corresponding starting points to reach a sentence within the category range below. The starting point applies to all offenders irrespective of plea or previous convictions. Having determined the starting point, step two allows further adjustment for aggravating or mitigating features, set out below.

A case of particular gravity, reflected by multiple features of culpability or harm in step one, could merit upward adjustment from the starting point before further adjustment for aggravating or mitigating features, set out below.

	A	B
Category 1	**Starting point** 16 years' custody **Category range** 13–19 years' custody	**Starting point** 13 years' custody **Category range** 11–17 years' custody
Category 2	**Starting point** 11 years' custody **Category range** 7–15 years' custody	**Starting point** 8 years' custody **Category range** 5–13 years' custody
Category 3	**Starting point** 6 years' custody **Category range** 4–9 years' custody	**Starting point** 4 years' custody **Category range** 2–6 years' custody

The table below contains a non-exhaustive list of additional factual elements providing the context of the offence and factors relating to the offender. Identify whether any combination of these, or other relevant factors, should result in an upward or downward adjustment from the starting point. In particular, relevant recent convictions are likely to result in an upward adjustment. In some cases, having considered these factors, it may be appropriate to move outside the identified category range.

Aggravating factors

Statutory aggravating factors

- Previous convictions, having regard to a) the nature of the offence to which the conviction relates and its relevance to the current offence; and b) the time that has elapsed since the conviction
- Offence committed whilst on bail

Other aggravating factors

- Specific targeting of a particularly vulnerable child
- Blackmail or other threats made (where not taken into account at step one)
- Location of offence
- Timing of offence
- Use of weapon or other item to frighten or injure
- Victim compelled to leave their home, school etc
- Failure to comply with current court orders
- Offence committed whilst on licence
- Exploiting contact arrangements with a child to commit an offence
- Presence of others, especially other children
- Any steps taken to prevent the victim reporting an incident, obtaining assistance and/or from assisting or supporting the prosecution
- Attempts to dispose of or conceal evidence
- Commission of offence whilst under the influence of alcohol or drugs
- Victim encouraged to recruit others

Mitigating factors

- No previous convictions or no relevant/recent convictions
- Remorse
- Previous good character and/or exemplary conduct*
- Age and/or lack of maturity where it affects the responsibility of the offender
- Mental disorder or learning disability, particularly where linked to the commission of the offence

* Previous good character/exemplary conduct is different from having no previous convictions. The more serious the offence, the less the weight which should normally be attributed to this factor. Where previous good character/exemplary conduct has been used to facilitate the offence, this mitigation should not normally be allowed and such conduct may constitute an aggravating factor. In the context of this offence, previous good character/exemplary conduct should not normally be given any significant weight and will not normally justify a reduction in what would otherwise be the appropriate sentence.

STEP THREE

Consider any factors which indicate a reduction, such as assistance to the prosecution

The court should take into account sections 73 and 74 of the Serious Organised Crime and Police Act 2005 (assistance by defendants: reduction or review of sentence) and any other rule of law by virtue of which an offender may receive a discounted sentence in consequence of assistance given (or offered) to the prosecutor or investigator.

STEP FOUR

Reduction for guilty pleas

The court should take account of any potential reduction for a guilty plea in accordance with section 144 of the Criminal Justice Act 2003 and the *Guilty Plea* guideline.

STEP FIVE

Dangerousness

The court should consider whether having regard to the criteria contained in Chapter 5 of Part 12 of the Criminal Justice Act 2003 it would be appropriate to award a life sentence (section 224A or section 225(2)) or an extended sentence (section 226A). When sentencing offenders to a life sentence under these provisions, the notional determinate sentence should be used as the basis for the setting of a minimum term.

STEP SIX

Totality principle

If sentencing an offender for more than one offence, or where the offender is already serving a sentence, consider whether the total sentence is just and proportionate to the offending behaviour.

STEP SEVEN

Ancillary orders

The court must consider whether to make any ancillary orders. The court must also consider what other requirements or provisions may *automatically* apply. Further information is included at Annex A on page 640.

STEP EIGHT

Reasons

Section 174 of the Criminal Justice Act 2003 imposes a duty to give reasons for, and explain the effect of, the sentence.

STEP NINE

Consideration for time spent on bail

The court must consider whether to give credit for time spent on bail in accordance with section 240A of the Criminal Justice Act 2003.

Sexual assault of a child under 13

Sexual Offences Act 2003 (section 7)

Triable either way

Maximum: 14 years' custody

Offence range: Community order–9 years' custody

For offences committed on or after 3 December 2012, this is an offence listed in Part 1 of Schedule 15B for the purposes of section 224A (life sentence for second listed offence) of the Criminal Justice Act 2003.

For convictions on or after 3 December 2012 (irrespective of the date of commission of the offence), this is a specified offence for the purposes of section 226A (extended sentence for certain violent or sexual offences) of the Criminal Justice Act 2003.

STEP ONE

Determining the offence category

The court should determine which categories of harm and culpability the offence falls into by reference only to the tables below.

HARM		CULPABILITY	
		A	B
Category 1	• Severe psychological or physical harm • Abduction • Violence or threats of violence • Forced/uninvited entry into victim's home	• Significant degree of planning • Offender acts together with others to commit the offence • Use of alcohol/drugs on victim to facilitate the offence • Grooming behaviour used against victim • Abuse of trust • Previous violence against victim • Offence committed in course of burglary • Sexual images of victim recorded, retained, solicited or shared • Deliberate isolation of victim • Commercial exploitation and/or motivation • Offence racially or religiously aggravated • Offence motivated by, or demonstrating, hostility to the victim based on his or her sexual orientation (or presumed sexual orientation) or transgender identity (or presumed transgender identity) • Offence motivated by, or demonstrating, hostility to the victim based on his or her disability (or presumed disability)	Factor(s) in category A not present
Category 2	• Touching of naked genitalia or naked breast area • Prolonged detention/sustained incident • Additional degradation/humiliation • Child is particularly vulnerable due to extreme youth and/or personal circumstances		
Category 3	Factor(s) in categories 1 and 2 not present		

STEP TWO

Starting point and category range

Having determined the category, the court should use the corresponding starting points to reach a sentence within the category range below. The starting point applies to all offenders irrespective of plea or previous convictions. Having determined the starting point, step two allows further adjustment for aggravating or mitigating features, set out below.

A case of particular gravity, reflected by multiple features of culpability or harm in step one, could merit upward adjustment from the starting point before further adjustment for aggravating or mitigating features, set out below.

Where there is a sufficient prospect of rehabilitation, a community order with a sex offender treatment programme requirement under section 202 of the Criminal Justice Act 2003 can be a proper alternative to a short or moderate length custodial sentence.

	A	B
Category 1	**Starting point** 6 years' custody **Category range** 4–9 years' custody	**Starting point** 4 years' custody **Category range** 3–7 years' custody
Category 2	**Starting point** 4 years' custody **Category range** 3–7 years' custody	**Starting point** 2 years' custody **Category range** 1–4 years' custody
Category 3	**Starting point** 1 year's custody **Category range** 26 weeks'–2 years' custody	**Starting point** 26 weeks' custody **Category range** High level community order–1 year's custody

The table below contains a non-exhaustive list of additional factual elements providing the context of the offence and factors relating to the offender. Identify whether any combination of these, or other relevant factors, should result in an upward or downward adjustment from the starting point. In particular, relevant recent convictions are likely to result in an upward adjustment. In some cases, having considered these factors, it may be appropriate to move outside the identified category range.

Aggravating factors

Statutory aggravating factors

- Previous convictions, having regard to a) the nature of the offence to which the conviction relates and its relevance to the current offence; and b) the time that has elapsed since the conviction
- Offence committed whilst on bail

Other aggravating factors

- Specific targeting of a particularly vulnerable child
- Blackmail or other threats made (where not taken into account at step one)
- Location of offence
- Timing of offence
- Use of weapon or other item to frighten or injure
- Victim compelled to leave their home, school, etc
- Failure to comply with current court orders
- Offence committed whilst on licence
- Exploiting contact arrangements with a child to commit an offence
- Presence of others, especially other children
- Any steps taken to prevent the victim reporting an incident, obtaining assistance and/or from assisting or supporting the prosecution
- Attempts to dispose of or conceal evidence
- Commission of offence whilst under the influence of alcohol or drugs
- Victim encouraged to recruit others

Mitigating factors

- No previous convictions or no relevant/recent convictions
- Remorse
- Previous good character and/or exemplary conduct*
- Age and/or lack of maturity where it affects the responsibility of the offender
- Mental disorder or learning disability, particularly where linked to the commission of the offence

* Previous good character/exemplary conduct is different from having no previous convictions. The more serious the offence, the less the weight which should normally be attributed to this factor. Where previous good character/exemplary conduct has been used to facilitate the offence, this mitigation should not normally be allowed and such conduct may constitute an aggravating factor. In the context of this offence, previous good character/exemplary conduct should not normally be given any significant weight and will not normally justify a reduction in what would otherwise be the appropriate sentence.

STEP THREE

Consider any factors which indicate a reduction, such as assistance to the prosecution

The court should take into account sections 73 and 74 of the Serious Organised Crime and Police Act 2005 (assistance by defendants: reduction or review of sentence) and any other rule of law by virtue of which an offender may receive a discounted sentence in consequence of assistance given (or offered) to the prosecutor or investigator.

STEP FOUR

Reduction for guilty pleas

The court should take account of any potential reduction for a guilty plea in accordance with section 144 of the Criminal Justice Act 2003 and the *Guilty Plea* guideline.

STEP FIVE

Dangerousness

The court should consider whether having regard to the criteria contained in Chapter 5 of Part 12 of the Criminal Justice Act 2003 it would be appropriate to award a life sentence (section 224A) or an extended sentence (section 226A). When sentencing offenders to a life sentence under these provisions, the notional determinate sentence should be used as the basis for the setting of a minimum term.

STEP SIX

Totality principle

If sentencing an offender for more than one offence, or where the offender is already serving a sentence, consider whether the total sentence is just and proportionate to the offending behaviour.

STEP SEVEN

Ancillary orders

The court must consider whether to make any ancillary orders. The court must also consider what other requirements or provisions may *automatically* apply. Further information is included at Annex A on page 640.

STEP EIGHT

Reasons

Section 174 of the Criminal Justice Act 2003 imposes a duty to give reasons for, and explain the effect of, the sentence.

STEP NINE

Consideration for time spent on bail

The court must consider whether to give credit for time spent on bail in accordance with section 240A of the Criminal Justice Act 2003.

Causing or inciting a child under 13 to engage in sexual activity

Sexual Offences Act 2003 (section 8)
Triable only on indictment (if penetration involved)—otherwise, triable either way
Maximum: Life imprisonment (if penetration involved)—otherwise, 14 years' custody
Offence range: 1–17 years' custody

This is a serious specified offence for the purposes of sections 224 and, where the offence involved penetration, 225(2) (life sentence for serious offences) of the Criminal Justice Act 2003.

For offences committed on or after 3 December 2012, this is an offence listed in Part 1 of Schedule 15B for the purposes of section 224A (life sentence for second listed offence) of the Criminal Justice Act 2003.

For convictions on or after 3 December 2012 (irrespective of the date of commission of the offence), this is a specified offence for the purposes of section 226A (extended sentence for certain violent or sexual offences) of the Criminal Justice Act 2003.

STEP ONE

Determining the offence category

The court should determine which categories of harm and culpability the offence falls into by reference only to the tables below.

HARM	
Category 1	The extreme nature of one or more category 2 factors or the extreme impact caused by a combination of category 2 factors may elevate to category 1
Category 2	• Severe psychological or physical harm • Penetration of vagina or anus (using body or object) by, or of, victim • Penile penetration of mouth by, or of, victim • Additional degradation/humiliation • Abduction • Prolonged detention /sustained incident • Violence or threats of violence • Forced/uninvited entry into victim's home • Child is particularly vulnerable due to extreme youth and/or personal circumstances
Category 3	Factor(s) in categories 1 and 2 not present

CULPABILITY	
A	B
• Significant degree of planning • Offender acts together with others to commit the offence • Use of alcohol/drugs on victim to facilitate the offence • Grooming behaviour used against victim • Abuse of trust • Previous violence against victim • Offence committed in course of burglary • Sexual images of victim recorded, retained, solicited or shared • Deliberate isolation of victim • Commercial exploitation and/or motivation • Offence racially or religiously aggravated • Offence motivated by, or demonstrating hostility to the victim based on his or her sexual orientation (or presumed sexual orientation) or transgender identity (or presumed transgender identity) • Offence motivated by, or demonstrating, hostility to the victim based on his or her disability (or presumed disability)	Factor(s) in category A not present

STEP TWO

Starting point and category range

Having determined the category, the court should use the corresponding starting points to reach a sentence within the category range below. The starting point applies to all offenders irrespective of plea or previous convictions. Having determined the starting point, step two allows further adjustment for aggravating or mitigating features, set out below.

A case of particular gravity, reflected by multiple features of culpability or harm in step one, could merit upward adjustment from the starting point before further adjustment for aggravating or mitigating features, set out below.

	A	B
Category 1	Starting point 13 years' custody Category range 11–17 years' custody	Starting point 11 years' custody Category range 10–15 years' custody
Category 2	Starting point 8 years' custody Category range 5–10 years' custody	Starting point 6 years' custody Category range 3–9 years' custody
Category 3	Starting point 5 years' custody Category range 3–8 years' custody	Starting point 2 years' custody Category range 1–4 years' custody

The table below contains a non-exhaustive list of additional factual elements providing the context of the offence and factors relating to the offender. Identify whether any combination of these, or other relevant factors, should result in an upward or downward adjustment from the starting point. In particular, relevant recent convictions are likely to result in an upward adjustment. In some cases, having considered these factors, it may be appropriate to move outside the identified category range.

Aggravating factors

Statutory aggravating factors

- Previous convictions, having regard to a) the nature of the offence to which the conviction relates and its relevance to the current offence; and b) the time that has elapsed since the conviction
- Offence committed whilst on bail

Other aggravating factors

- Specific targeting of a particularly vulnerable child
- Ejaculation (where not taken into account at step one)
- Blackmail or other threats made (where not taken into account at step one)
- Pregnancy or STI as a consequence of offence
- Location of offence
- Timing of offence
- Use of weapon or other item to frighten or injure
- Victim compelled to leave their home, school, etc

- Failure to comply with current court orders
- Offence committed whilst on licence
- Exploiting contact arrangements with a child to commit an offence
- Presence of others, especially other children
- Any steps taken to prevent the victim reporting an incident, obtaining assistance and/or from assisting or supporting the prosecution
- Attempts to dispose of or conceal evidence
- Commission of offence whilst offender under the influence of alcohol or drugs
- Victim encouraged to recruit others

Mitigating factors

- No previous convictions or no relevant/recent convictions
- Remorse
- Previous good character and/or exemplary conduct*
- Age and/or lack of maturity where it affects the responsibility of the offender
- Mental disorder or learning disability, particularly where linked to the commission of the offence
- Sexual activity was incited but no activity took place because the offender voluntarily desisted or intervened to prevent it

* Previous good character/exemplary conduct is different from having no previous convictions. The more serious the offence, the less the weight which should normally be attributed to this factor. Where previous good character/exemplary conduct has been used to facilitate the offence, this mitigation should not normally be allowed and such conduct may constitute an aggravating factor. In the context of this offence, previous good character/exemplary conduct should not normally be given any significant weight and will not normally justify a reduction in what would otherwise be the appropriate sentence.

STEP THREE

Consider any factors which indicate a reduction, such as assistance to the prosecution

The court should take into account sections 73 and 74 of the Serious Organised Crime and Police Act 2005 (assistance by defendants: reduction or review of sentence) and any other rule of law by virtue of which an offender may receive a discounted sentence in consequence of assistance given (or offered) to the prosecutor or investigator.

STEP FOUR

Reduction for guilty pleas

The court should take account of any potential reduction for a guilty plea in accordance with section 144 of the Criminal Justice Act 2003 and the *Guilty Plea* guideline.

STEP FIVE

Dangerousness

The court should consider whether having regard to the criteria contained in Chapter 5 of Part 12 of the Criminal Justice Act 2003 it would be appropriate to award a life sentence (section 224A or section 225(2)) or an extended sentence (section 226A). When sentencing offenders to a life sentence under these provisions, the notional determinate sentence should be used as the basis for the setting of a minimum term.

STEP SIX

Totality principle

If sentencing an offender for more than one offence, or where the offender is already serving a sentence, consider whether the total sentence is just and proportionate to the offending behaviour.

STEP SEVEN

Ancillary orders

The court must consider whether to make any ancillary orders. The court must also consider what other requirements or provisions may *automatically* apply. Further information is included at Annex A on page 640.

STEP EIGHT

Reasons

Section 174 of the Criminal Justice Act 2003 imposes a duty to give reasons for, and explain the effect of, the sentence.

STEP NINE

Consideration for time spent on bail

The court must consider whether to give credit for time spent on bail in accordance with section 240A of the Criminal Justice Act 2003.

Sexual activity with a child

Sexual Offences Act 2003 (section 9)

Causing or inciting a child to engage in sexual activity

Sexual Offences Act 2003 (section 10)

Triable only on indictment (if penetration involved)—otherwise, triable either way

Maximum: 14 years' custody

Offence range: Community order–10 years' custody

For offences committed on or after 3 December 2012, these are offences listed in Part 1 of Schedule 15B for the purposes of section 224A (life sentence for second listed offence) of the Criminal Justice Act 2003.

For convictions on or after 3 December 2012 (irrespective of the date of commission of the offence), these are specified offences for the purposes of section 226A (extended sentence for certain violent or sexual offences) of the Criminal Justice Act 2003.

> Arranging or facilitating the commission of a child offence (section 14 of the Sexual Offences Act 2003—page 564)
> The starting points and ranges in this guideline are also applicable to offences of arranging or facilitating the commission of a child offence. In such cases, the level of harm should be determined by reference to the type of activity arranged or facilitated. Sentences commensurate with the applicable starting point and range will ordinarily be appropriate. For offences involving significant commercial exploitation and/or an international element, it may, in the interests of justice, be appropriate to increase a sentence to a point above the category range. In exceptional cases, such as where a vulnerable offender performed a limited role, having been coerced or exploited by others, sentences below the starting point and range may be appropriate.

STEP ONE

Determining the offence category

The court should determine which categories of harm and culpability the offence falls into by reference only to the tables below.

THIS GUIDLINE [sic] ALSO APPLIES TO OFFENCES COMMITTED REMOTELY/ONLINE

HARM		CULPABILITY	
		A	**B**
Category 1	Penetration of vagina or anus (using body or object) Penile penetration of mouth In either case by, or of, the victim	• Significant degree of planning • Offender acts together with others to commit the offence • Use of alcohol/drugs on victim to facilitate the offence • Grooming behaviour used against victim • Abuse of trust • Use of threats (including blackmail) • Sexual images of victim recorded, retained, solicited or shared • Specific targeting of a particularly vulnerable child • Offender lied about age • Significant disparity in age • Commercial exploitation and/or motivation • Offence racially or religiously aggravated • Offence motivated by, or demonstrating, hostility to the victim based on his or her sexual orientation (or presumed sexual orientation) or transgender identity (or presumed transgender identity) • Offence motivated by, or demonstrating, hostility to the victim based on his or her disability (or presumed disability)	Factor(s) in category A not present
Category 2	Touching, or exposure, of naked genitalia or naked breasts by, or of, the victim		
Category 3	Other sexual activity		

STEP TWO

Starting point and category range

Having determined the category, the court should use the corresponding starting points to reach a sentence within the category range below. The starting point applies to all offenders irrespective of plea or previous convictions. Having determined the starting point, step two allows further adjustment for aggravating or mitigating features, set out below.

A case of particular gravity, reflected by multiple features of culpability or harm in step one, could merit upward adjustment from the starting point before further adjustment for aggravating or mitigating features, set out below.

Where there is a sufficient prospect of rehabilitation, a community order with a sex offender treatment programme requirement under section 202 of the Criminal Justice Act 2003 can be a proper alternative to a short or moderate length custodial sentence.

	A	B
Category 1	Starting point 5 years' custody Category range 4–10 years' custody	Starting point 1 year's custody Category range High level community order–2 years' custody
Category 2	Starting point 3 years' custody Category range 2–6 years' custody	Starting point 26 weeks' custody Category range High level community order–1 year's custody
Category 3	Starting point 26 weeks' custody Category range High level community order–3 years' custody	Starting point Medium level community order Category range Low level community order–High level community order

The table below contains a non-exhaustive list of additional factual elements providing the context of the offence and factors relating to the offender. Identify whether any combination of these, or other relevant factors, should result in an upward or downward adjustment from the starting point. In particular, relevant recent convictions are likely to result in an upward adjustment. In some cases, having considered these factors, it may be appropriate to move outside the identified category range.

When sentencing appropriate category 2 or 3 offences, the court should also consider the custody threshold as follows:

- has the custody threshold been passed?
- if so, is it unavoidable that a custodial sentence be imposed?
- if so, can that sentence be suspended?

Aggravating factors

Statutory aggravating factors

- Previous convictions, having regard to a) the nature of the offence to which the conviction relates and its relevance to the current offence; and b) the time that has elapsed since the conviction
- Offence committed whilst on bail

Other aggravating factors

- Severe psychological or physical harm
- Ejaculation
- Pregnancy or STI as a consequence of offence
- Location of offence
- Timing of offence
- Victim compelled to leave their home, school, etc
- Failure to comply with current court orders
- Offence committed whilst on licence
- Exploiting contact arrangements with a child to commit an offence
- Presence of others, especially other children
- Any steps taken to prevent the victim reporting an incident, obtaining assistance and/or from assisting or supporting the prosecution
- Attempts to dispose of or conceal evidence
- Failure of offender to respond to previous warnings
- Commission of offence whilst under the influence of alcohol or drugs
- Victim encouraged to recruit others
- Period over which offence committed

Mitigating factors

- No previous convictions or no relevant/recent convictions
- Remorse
- Previous good character and/or exemplary conduct*
- Age and/or lack of maturity where it affects the responsibility of the offender
- Mental disorder or learning disability, particularly where linked to the commission of the offence
- Sexual activity was incited but no activity took place because the offender voluntarily desisted or intervened to prevent it

* Previous good character/exemplary conduct is different from having no previous convictions. The more serious the offence, the less the weight which should normally be attributed to this factor. Where previous good character/exemplary conduct has been used to facilitate the offence, this mitigation should not normally be allowed and such conduct may constitute an aggravating factor.

In the context of this offence, previous good character/exemplary conduct should not normally be given any significant weight and will not normally justify a reduction in what would otherwise be the appropriate sentence.

STEP THREE

Consider any factors which indicate a reduction, such as assistance to the prosecution

The court should take into account sections 73 and 74 of the Serious Organised Crime and Police Act 2005 (assistance by defendants: reduction or review of sentence) and any other rule of law by virtue of which an offender may receive a discounted sentence in consequence of assistance given (or offered) to the prosecutor or investigator.

STEP FOUR

Reduction for guilty pleas

The court should take account of any potential reduction for a guilty plea in accordance with section 144 of the Criminal Justice Act 2003 and the *Guilty Plea* guideline.

STEP FIVE

Dangerousness

The court should consider whether having regard to the criteria contained in Chapter 5 of Part 12 of the Criminal Justice Act 2003 it would be appropriate to award a life sentence (section 224A) or an extended sentence (section 226A). When sentencing offenders to a life sentence under these provisions, the notional determinate sentence should be used as the basis for the setting of a minimum term.

STEP SIX

Totality principle

If sentencing an offender for more than one offence, or where the offender is already serving a sentence, consider whether the total sentence is just and proportionate to the offending behaviour.

STEP SEVEN

Ancillary orders

The court must consider whether to make any ancillary orders. The court must also consider what other requirements or provisions may *automatically* apply. Further information is included at Annex A on page 640.

STEP EIGHT

Reasons

Section 174 of the Criminal Justice Act 2003 imposes a duty to give reasons for, and explain the effect of, the sentence.

STEP NINE

Consideration for time spent on bail

The court must consider whether to give credit for time spent on bail in accordance with section 240A of the Criminal Justice Act 2003.

Sexual activity with a child family member

Sexual Offences Act 2003 (section 25)

Inciting a child family member to engage in sexual activity

Sexual Offences Act 2003 (section 26)

Triable only on indictment (if penetration involved)—otherwise, triable either way

Maximum: 14 years' custody

Offence range: Community order–10 years' custody

For offences committed on or after 3 December 2012, these are offences listed in Part 1 of Schedule 15B for the purposes of section 224A (life sentence for second listed offence) of the Criminal Justice Act 2003.

For convictions on or after 3 December 2012 (irrespective of the date of commission of the offence), these are specified offences for the purposes of section 226A (extended sentence for certain violent or sexual offences) of the Criminal Justice Act 2003.

STEP ONE

Determining the offence category

The court should determine which categories of harm and culpability the offence falls into by reference only to the tables below. This offence involves those who have a family relationship with the victim and it should be assumed that the greater the abuse of trust within this relationship the more grave the offence.

HARM	
Category 1	• Penetration of vagina or anus (using body or object) • Penile penetration of mouth In either case by, or of, the victim
Category 2	Touching of naked genitalia or naked breasts by, or of, the victim
Category 3	Other sexual activity

CULPABILITY	
A	**B**
• Significant degree of planning • Offender acts together with others to commit the offence • Use of alcohol/drugs on victim to facilitate the offence • Grooming behaviour used against victim • Use of threats (including blackmail) • Sexual images of victim recorded, retained, solicited or shared • Specific targeting of a particularly vulnerable child • Significant disparity in age • Commercial exploitation and/or motivation • Offence racially or religiously aggravated • Offence motivated by, or demonstrating, hostility to the victim based on his or her sexual orientation (or presumed sexual orientation) or transgender identity (or presumed transgender identity) • Offence motivated by, or demonstrating, hostility to the victim based on his or her disability (or presumed disability)	Factor(s) in category A not present

STEP TWO

Starting point and category range

Having determined the category, the court should use the corresponding starting points to reach a sentence within the category range below. The starting point applies to all offenders irrespective of plea or previous convictions. Having determined the starting point, step two allows further adjustment for aggravating or mitigating features, set out below.

A case of particular gravity, reflected by multiple features of culpability or harm in step one, could merit upward adjustment from the starting point before further adjustment for aggravating or mitigating features, set out below.

Where there is a sufficient prospect of rehabilitation, a community order with a sex offender treatment programme requirement under section 202 of the Criminal Justice Act 2003 can be a proper alternative to a short or moderate length custodial sentence.

	A	B
Category 1	**Starting point** 6 years' custody **Category range** 4–10 years' custody	**Starting point** 3 years 6 months' custody **Category range** 2 years 6 months'–5 years' custody
Category 2	**Starting point** 4 years' custody **Category range** 2–6 years' custody	**Starting point** 18 months' custody **Category range** 26 weeks'–2 years 6 months' custody
Category 3	**Starting point** 1 year's custody **Category range** High level community order–3 years' custody	**Starting point** Medium level community order **Category range** Low level community order–High level community order

The table below contains a non-exhaustive list of additional factual elements providing the context of the offence and factors relating to the offender. Identify whether any combination of these, or other relevant factors, should result in an upward or downward adjustment from the starting point. In particular, relevant recent convictions are likely to result in an upward adjustment. In some cases, having considered these factors, it may be appropriate to move outside the identified category range.

When sentencing appropriate category 3 offences, the court should also consider the custody threshold as follows:

- has the custody threshold been passed?
- if so, is it unavoidable that a custodial sentence be imposed?
- if so, can that sentence be suspended?

Aggravating factors

Statutory aggravating factors

- Previous convictions, having regard to a) the nature of the offence to which the conviction relates and its relevance to the current offence; and b) the time that has elapsed since the conviction
- Offence committed whilst on bail

Other aggravating factors

- Severe psychological or physical harm
- Ejaculation
- Pregnancy or STI as a consequence of offence
- Location of offence
- Timing of offence
- Victim compelled to leave their home, school, etc
- Failure to comply with current court orders
- Offence committed whilst on licence
- Exploiting contact arrangements with a child to commit an offence
- Presence of others, especially other children
- Any steps taken to prevent the victim reporting an incident, obtaining assistance and/or from assisting or supporting the prosecution
- Attempts to dispose of or conceal evidence
- Failure of offender to respond to previous warnings
- Commission of offence whilst under the influence of alcohol or drugs
- Victim encouraged to recruit others
- Period over which offence committed

Mitigating factors

- No previous convictions or no relevant/recent convictions
- Remorse
- Previous good character and/or exemplary conduct*
- Age and/or lack of maturity where it affects the responsibility of the offender
- Mental disorder or learning disability, particularly where linked to the commission of the offence
- Sexual activity was incited but no activity took place because the offender voluntarily desisted or intervened to prevent it

* Previous good character/exemplary conduct is different from having no previous convictions. The more serious the offence, the less the weight which should normally be attributed to this factor. Where previous good character/exemplary conduct has been used to facilitate the offence, this mitigation should not normally be allowed and such conduct may constitute an aggravating factor.

In the context of this offence, previous good character/exemplary conduct should not normally be given any significant weight and will not normally justify a reduction in what would otherwise be the appropriate sentence.

STEP THREE

Consider any factors which indicate a reduction, such as assistance to the prosecution

The court should take into account sections 73 and 74 of the Serious Organised Crime and Police Act 2005 (assistance by defendants: reduction or review of sentence) and any other rule of law by virtue of which an offender may receive a discounted sentence in consequence of assistance given (or offered) to the prosecutor or investigator.

STEP FOUR

Reduction for guilty pleas

The court should take account of any potential reduction for a guilty plea in accordance with section 144 of the Criminal Justice Act 2003 and the *Guilty Plea* guideline.

STEP FIVE

Dangerousness

The court should consider whether having regard to the criteria contained in Chapter 5 of Part 12 of the Criminal Justice Act 2003 it would be appropriate to award a life sentence (section 224A) or an extended sentence (section 226A). When sentencing offenders to a life sentence under these provisions, the notional determinate sentence should be used as the basis for the setting of a minimum term.

STEP SIX

Totality principle

If sentencing an offender for more than one offence, or where the offender is already serving a sentence, consider whether the total sentence is just and proportionate to the offending behaviour.

STEP SEVEN

Ancillary orders

The court must consider whether to make any ancillary orders. The court must also consider what other requirements or provisions may *automatically* apply. Further information is included at Annex A on page 640.

STEP EIGHT

Reasons

Section 174 of the Criminal Justice Act 2003 imposes a duty to give reasons for, and explain the effect of, the sentence.

STEP NINE

Consideration for time spent on bail

The court must consider whether to give credit for time spent on bail in accordance with section 240A of the Criminal Justice Act 2003.

Engaging in sexual activity in the presence of a child

Sexual Offences Act 2003 (section 11)

Causing a child to watch a sexual act

Sexual Offences Act 2003 (section 12)

Triable either way

Maximum: 10 years' custody

Offence range: Community order–6 years' custody

For offences committed on or after 3 December 2012, these are offences listed in Part 1 of Schedule 15B for the purposes of section 224A (life sentence for second listed offence) of the Criminal Justice Act 2003.

For convictions on or after 3 December 2012 (irrespective of the date of commission of the offence), these are specified offences for the purposes of section 226A (extended sentence for certain violent or sexual offences) of the Criminal Justice Act 2003.

> Arranging or facilitating the commission of a child offence (section 14 of the Sexual Offences Act 2003–guidance on page 564)
>
> The starting points and ranges in this guideline are also applicable to offences of arranging or facilitating the commission of a child offence. In such cases, the level of harm should be determined by reference to the type of activity arranged or facilitated. Sentences commensurate with the applicable starting point and range will ordinarily be appropriate. For offences involving significant commercial exploitation and/or an international element, it may, in the interests of justice, be appropriate to increase a sentence to a point above the category range. In exceptional cases, such as where a vulnerable offender performed a limited role, having been coerced or exploited by others, sentences below the starting point and range may be appropriate.

STEP ONE

Determining the offence category

The court should determine which categories of harm and culpability the offence falls into by reference only to the tables below.

HARM	
Category 1	• Causing victim to view extreme pornography • Causing victim to view indecent/prohibited images of children • Engaging in, or causing a victim to view live, sexual activity involving sadism/violence/sexual activity with an animal/a child
Category 2	Engaging in, or causing a victim to view images of or view live, sexual activity involving: • penetration of vagina or anus (using body or object) • penile penetration of the mouth • masturbation
Category 3	Factor(s) in categories 1 and 2 not present

CULPABILITY	
A	**B**
• Significant degree of planning • Offender acts together with others in order to commit the offence • Use of alcohol/drugs on victim to facilitate the offence • Grooming behaviour used against victim • Abuse of trust • Use of threats (including blackmail) • Specific targeting of a particularly vulnerable child • Significant disparity in age • Commercial exploitation and/or motivation • Offence racially or religiously aggravated • Offence motivated by, or demonstrating, hostility to the victim based on his or her sexual orientation (or presumed sexual orientation) or transgender identity (or presumed transgender identity) • Offence motivated by, or demonstrating, hostility to the victim based on his or her disability (or presumed disability)	Factor(s) in category A not present

STEP TWO

Starting point and category range

Having determined the category, the court should use the corresponding starting points to reach a sentence within the category range below. The starting point applies to all offenders irrespective of plea or previous convictions. Having determined the starting point, step two allows further adjustment for aggravating or mitigating features, set out below.

A case of particular gravity, reflected by multiple features of culpability or harm in step one, could merit upward adjustment from the starting point before further adjustment for aggravating or mitigating features, set out below.

Where there is a sufficient prospect of rehabilitation, a community order with a sex offender treatment programme requirement under section 202 of the Criminal Justice Act 2003 can be a proper alternative to a short or moderate length custodial sentence.

	A	B
Category 1	**Starting point** 4 years' custody **Category range** 3–6 years' custody	**Starting point** 2 years' custody **Category range** 1–3 years' custody
Category 2	**Starting point** 2 years' custody **Category range** 1–3 years' custody	**Starting point** 1 year's custody **Category range** High level community order–18 months' custody
Category 3	**Starting point** 26 weeks' custody **Category range** High level community order–1 year's custody	**Starting point** Medium level community order **Category range** Low level community order–Medium level community order

The table below contains a non-exhaustive list of additional factual elements providing the context of the offence and factors relating to the offender. Identify whether any combination of these, or other relevant factors, should result in an upward or downward adjustment from the starting point. In particular, relevant recent convictions are likely to result in an upward adjustment. In some cases, having considered these factors, it may be appropriate to move outside the identified category range.

When sentencing appropriate category 2 or 3 offences, the court should also consider the custody threshold as follows:

- has the custody threshold been passed?
- if so, is it unavoidable that a custodial sentence be imposed?
- if so, can that sentence be suspended?

Aggravating factors

Statutory aggravating factors

- Previous convictions, having regard to a) the nature of the offence to which the conviction relates and its relevance to the current offence; and b) the time that has elapsed since the conviction
- Offence committed whilst on bail

Other aggravating factors

- Location of offence
- Timing of offence
- Victim compelled to leave their home, school, etc
- Failure to comply with current court orders
- Offence committed whilst on licence
- Exploiting contact arrangements with a child to commit an offence
- Presence of others, especially other children
- Any steps taken to prevent the victim reporting an incident, obtaining assistance and/or from assisting or supporting the prosecution
- Attempts to dispose of or conceal evidence
- Failure of offender to respond to previous warnings
- Commission of offence whilst offender under the influence of alcohol or drugs
- Victim encouraged to recruit others

Mitigating factors

- No previous convictions or no relevant/recent convictions
- Remorse
- Previous good character and/or exemplary conduct*
- Age and/or lack of maturity where it affects the responsibility of the offender
- Mental disorder or learning disability, particularly where linked to the commission of the offence
- Demonstration of steps taken to address offending behaviour

* Previous good character/exemplary conduct is different from having no previous convictions. The more serious the offence, the less the weight which should normally be attributed to this factor. Where previous good character/exemplary conduct has been used to facilitate the offence, this mitigation should not normally be allowed and such conduct may constitute an aggravating factor.

STEP THREE

Consider any factors which indicate a reduction, such as assistance to the prosecution

The court should take into account sections 73 and 74 of the Serious Organised Crime and Police Act 2005 (assistance by defendants: reduction or review of sentence) and any other rule of law by virtue of which an offender may receive a discounted sentence in consequence of assistance given (or offered) to the prosecutor or investigator.

STEP FOUR

Reduction for guilty pleas

The court should take account of any potential reduction for a guilty plea in accordance with section 144 of the Criminal Justice Act 2003 and the *Guilty Plea* guideline.

STEP FIVE

Dangerousness

The court should consider whether having regard to the criteria contained in Chapter 5 of Part 12 of the Criminal Justice Act 2003 it would be appropriate to award a life sentence (section 224A) or an extended sentence (section 226A). When sentencing offenders to a life sentence under these provisions, the notional determinate sentence should be used as the basis for the setting of a minimum term.

STEP SIX

Totality principle

If sentencing an offender for more than one offence, or where the offender is already serving a sentence, consider whether the total sentence is just and proportionate to the offending behaviour.

STEP SEVEN

Ancillary orders

The court must consider whether to make any ancillary orders. The court must also consider what other requirements or provisions may *automatically* apply. Further information is included at Annex A on page 640.

STEP EIGHT

Reasons

Section 174 of the Criminal Justice Act 2003 imposes a duty to give reasons for, and explain the effect of, the sentence.

STEP NINE

Consideration for time spent on bail

The court must consider whether to give credit for time spent on bail in accordance with section 240A of the Criminal Justice Act 2003.

Arranging or facilitating the commission of a child sex offence

Sexual Offences Act 2003 (section 14)

Triable either way

Maximum: 14 years' custody

For offences committed on or after 3 December 2012, these are offences listed in Part 1 of Schedule 15B for the purposes of section 224A (life sentence for second listed offence) of the Criminal Justice Act 2003.

For convictions on or after 3 December 2012 (irrespective of the date of commission of the offence), these are specified offences for the purposes of section 226A (extended sentence for certain violent or sexual offences) of the Criminal Justice Act 2003.

> Sentencers should refer to the guideline for the applicable, substantive offence of arranging or facilitating under sections 9 to 10. See pages 552–556. The level of harm should be determined by reference to the type of activity arranged or facilitated. Sentences commensurate with the applicable starting point and range will ordinarily be appropriate. For offences involving significant commercial exploitation and/or an international element, it may, in the interests of justice, be appropriate to increase a sentence to a point above the category range. In exceptional cases, such as where a vulnerable offender performed a limited role, having been coerced or exploited by others, sentences below the starting point and range may be appropriate.

Meeting a child following sexual grooming

Sexual Offences Act 2003 (section 15)

Triable either way

Maximum: 10 years' custody

Offence range: 1–7 years' custody

For offences committed on or after 3 December 2012, this is an offence listed in Part 1 of Schedule 15B for the purposes of section 224A (life sentence for second listed offence) of the Criminal Justice Act 2003.

For convictions on or after 3 December 2012 (irrespective of the date of commission of the offence), this is a specified offence for the purposes of section 226A (extended sentence for certain violent or sexual offences) of the Criminal Justice Act 2003.

STEP ONE

Determining the offence category

The court should determine the offence category using the table below.

Category 1	Raised harm and raised culpability
Category 2	Raised harm or raised culpability
Category 3	Grooming without raised harm or culpability factors present

The court should determine culpability and harm caused or intended, by reference only to the factors below, which comprise the principal factual elements of the offence. Where an offence does not fall squarely into a category, individual factors may require a degree of weighting before making an overall assessment and determining the appropriate offence category.

Factors indicating raised harm

- Continued contact despite victim's attempts to terminate contact
- Sexual images exchanged
- Victim exposed to extreme sexual content for example, extreme pornography
- Child is particularly vulnerable due to personal circumstances

Factors indicating raised culpability

- Offender acts together with others to commit the offence
- Communication indicates penetrative sexual activity is intended
- Offender lied about age/persona
- Use of threats (including blackmail), gifts or bribes
- Abuse of trust
- Specific targeting of a particularly vulnerable child
- Abduction/detention
- Commercial exploitation and/or motivation
- Offence racially or religiously aggravated
- Offence motivated by, or demonstrating, hostility to the victim based on his or her sexual orientation (or presumed sexual orientation) or transgender identity (or presumed transgender identity)
- Offence motivated by, or demonstrating, hostility to the victim based on his or her disability (or presumed disability)

STEP TWO

Starting point and category range

Having determined the category, the court should use the corresponding starting points to reach a sentence within the category range below. The starting point applies to all offenders irrespective of plea or previous convictions. Having determined the starting point, step two allows further adjustment for aggravating or mitigating features, set out below.

A case of particular gravity, reflected by multiple features of culpability or harm in step one, could merit upward adjustment from the starting point before further adjustment for aggravating or mitigating features, set out below.

Category 1	**Starting point** 4 years' custody **Category range** 3–7 years' custody
Category 2	**Starting point** 2 years' custody **Category range** 1–4 years' custody
Category 3	**Starting point** 18 months' custody **Category range** 1 year–2 years 6 months' custody

The table below contains a non-exhaustive list of additional factual elements providing the context of the offence and factors relating to the offender. Identify whether any combination of these, or other relevant factors, should result in an upward or downward adjustment from the starting point. In particular, relevant recent convictions are likely to result in an upward adjustment. In some cases, having considered these factors, it may be appropriate to move outside the identified category range.

Aggravating factors

Statutory aggravating factors

- Previous convictions, having regard to a) the nature of the offence to which the conviction relates and its relevance to the current offence; and b) the time that has elapsed since the conviction
- Offence committed whilst on bail

Other aggravating factors

- Failure to comply with current court orders
- Offence committed whilst on licence
- Any steps taken to prevent the victim reporting an incident, obtaining assistance and/or from assisting or supporting the prosecution
- Attempts to dispose of or conceal evidence
- Victim encouraged to recruit others

Mitigating factors

- No previous convictions or no relevant/recent convictions
- Remorse
- Previous good character and/or exemplary conduct*
- Age and/or lack of maturity where it affects the responsibility of the offender
- Mental disorder or learning disability, particularly where linked to the commission of the offence
- Demonstration of steps taken to address offending behaviour

* Previous good character/exemplary conduct is different from having no previous convictions. The more serious the offence, the less the weight which should normally be attributed to this factor. Where previous good character/exemplary conduct has been used to facilitate the offence, this mitigation should not normally be allowed and such conduct may constitute an aggravating factor.

STEP THREE

Consider any factors which indicate a reduction, such as assistance to the prosecution

The court should take into account sections 73 and 74 of the Serious Organised Crime and Police Act 2005 (assistance by defendants: reduction or review of sentence) and any other rule of law by virtue of which an offender may receive a discounted sentence in consequence of assistance given (or offered) to the prosecutor or investigator.

STEP FOUR

Reduction for guilty pleas

The court should take account of any potential reduction for a guilty plea in accordance with section 144 of the Criminal Justice Act 2003 and the *Guilty Plea* guideline.

STEP FIVE

Dangerousness

The court should consider whether having regard to the criteria contained in Chapter 5 of Part 12 of the Criminal Justice Act 2003 it would be appropriate to award a life sentence (section 224A) or an extended sentence (section 226A). When sentencing offenders to a life sentence under these provisions, the notional determinate sentence should be used as the basis for the setting of a minimum term.

STEP SIX

Totality principle

If sentencing an offender for more than one offence, or where the offender is already serving a sentence, consider whether the total sentence is just and proportionate to the offending behaviour.

STEP SEVEN

Ancillary orders

The court must consider whether to make any ancillary orders. The court must also consider what other requirements or provisions may *automatically* apply. Further information is included at Annex A on page 640.

STEP EIGHT

Reasons

Section 174 of the Criminal Justice Act 2003 imposes a duty to give reasons for, and explain the effect of, the sentence.

STEP NINE

Consideration for time spent on bail

The court must consider whether to give credit for time spent on bail in accordance with section 240A of the Criminal Justice Act 2003.

Abuse of position of trust: sexual activity with a child

Sexual Offences Act 2003 (section 16)

Abuse of position of trust: causing or inciting a child to engage in sexual activity

Sexual Offences Act 2003 (section 17)

Triable either way

Maximum: 5 years' custody

Offence range: Community order–2 years' custody

For convictions on or after 3 December 2012 (irrespective of the date of commission of the offence), these are specified offences for the purposes of section 226A (extended sentence for certain violent or sexual offences) of the Criminal Justice Act 2003.

STEP ONE

Determining the offence category

The court should determine which categories of harm and culpability the offence falls into by reference only to the tables below.

THIS GUIDLINE [sic] ALSO APPLIES TO OFFENCES COMMITTED REMOTELY/ONLINE

HARM		CULPABILITY	
Category 1	• Penetration of vagina or anus (using body or object) • Penile penetration of mouth In either case by, or of, the victim	**A** • Significant degree of planning • Offender acts together with others to commit the offence • Use of alcohol/drugs on victim to facilitate the offence • Grooming behaviour used against victim • Use of threats (including blackmail) • Sexual images of victim recorded, retained, solicited or shared • Specific targeting of a particularly vulnerable child • Commercial exploitation and/or motivation • Offence racially or religiously aggravated • Offence motivated by, or demonstrating, hostility to the victim based on his or her sexual orientation (or presumed sexual orientation) or transgender identity (or presumed transgender identity) • Offence motivated by, or demonstrating, hostility to the victim based on his or her disability (or presumed disability)	**B** Factor(s) in category A not present
Category 2	• Touching, or exposure, of naked genitalia or naked breasts by, or of, the victim		
Category 3	Factor(s) in categories 1 and 2 not present		

STEP TWO

Starting point and category range

Having determined the category, the court should use the corresponding starting points to reach a sentence within the category range below. The starting point applies to all offenders irrespective of plea or previous convictions. Having determined the starting point, step two allows further adjustment for aggravating or mitigating features, set out below.

A case of particular gravity, reflected by multiple features of culpability or harm in step one, could merit upward adjustment from the starting point before further adjustment for aggravating or mitigating features, set out below.

Where there is a sufficient prospect of rehabilitation, a community order with a sex offender treatment programme requirement under section 202 of the Criminal Justice Act 2003 can be a proper alternative to a short or moderate length custodial sentence.

	A	B
Category 1	**Starting point** 18 months' custody **Category range** 1–2 years' custody	**Starting point** 1 year's custody **Category range** 26 weeks'–18 months' custody
Category 2	**Starting point** 1 year's custody **Category range** 26 weeks'–18 months' custody	**Starting point** 26 weeks' custody **Category range** High level community order–1 year's custody
Category 3	**Starting point** 26 weeks' custody **Category range** High level community order–1 year's custody	**Starting point** Medium level community order **Category range** Low level community order–High level community order

The table below contains a non-exhaustive list of additional factual elements providing the context of the offence and factors relating to the offender. Identify whether any combination of these, or other relevant factors, should result in an upward or downward adjustment from the starting point. In particular, relevant recent convictions are likely to result in an upward adjustment. In some cases, having considered these factors, it may be appropriate to move outside the identified category range.

When sentencing appropriate category 2 or 3 offences, the court should also consider the custody threshold as follows:

- has the custody threshold been passed?
- if so, is it unavoidable that a custodial sentence be imposed?
- if so, can that sentence be suspended?

Aggravating factors

Statutory aggravating factors

- Previous convictions, having regard to a) the nature of the offence to which the conviction relates and its relevance to the current offence; and b) the time that has elapsed since the conviction
- Offence committed whilst on bail

Other aggravating factors

- Ejaculation
- Pregnancy or STI as a consequence of offence
- Location of offence
- Timing of offence
- Victim compelled to leave their home, school, etc
- Failure to comply with current court orders
- Offence committed whilst on licence
- Presence of others, especially other children
- Any steps taken to prevent the victim reporting an incident, obtaining assistance and/or from assisting or supporting the prosecution
- Attempts to dispose of or conceal evidence
- Failure of offender to respond to previous warnings
- Commission of offence whilst under the influence of alcohol or drugs
- Victim encouraged to recruit others

Mitigating factors

- No previous convictions or no relevant/recent convictions
- Remorse
- Previous good character and/or exemplary conduct*
- Age and/or lack of maturity where it affects the responsibility of the offender
- Mental disorder or learning disability, particularly where linked to the commission of the offence
- Sexual activity was incited but no activity took place because the offender voluntarily desisted or intervened to prevent it
- Demonstration of steps taken to address offending behaviour

* Previous good character/exemplary conduct is different from having no previous convictions. The more serious the offence, the less the weight which should normally be attributed to this factor. Where previous good character/exemplary conduct has been used to facilitate the offence, this mitigation should not normally be allowed and such conduct may constitute an aggravating factor.

STEP THREE

Consider any factors which indicate a reduction, such as assistance to the prosecution

The court should take into account sections 73 and 74 of the Serious Organised Crime and Police Act 2005 (assistance by defendants: reduction or review of sentence) and any other rule of law by virtue of which an offender may receive a discounted sentence in consequence of assistance given (or offered) to the prosecutor or investigator.

STEP FOUR

Reduction for guilty pleas

The court should take account of any potential reduction for a guilty plea in accordance with section 144 of the Criminal Justice Act 2003 and the *Guilty Plea* guideline.

STEP FIVE

Dangerousness

The court should consider whether having regard to the criteria contained in Chapter 5 of Part 12 of the Criminal Justice Act 2003 it would be appropriate to award an extended sentence (section 226A).

STEP SIX

Totality principle

If sentencing an offender for more than one offence, or where the offender is already serving a sentence, consider whether the total sentence is just and proportionate to the offending behaviour.

STEP SEVEN

Ancillary orders

The court must consider whether to make any ancillary orders. The court must also consider what other requirements or provisions may *automatically* apply. Further information is included at Annex A on page 640.

STEP EIGHT

Reasons

Section 174 of the Criminal Justice Act 2003 imposes a duty to give reasons for, and explain the effect of, the sentence.

STEP NINE

Consideration for time spent on bail

The court must consider whether to give credit for time spent on bail in accordance with section 240A of the Criminal Justice Act 2003.

Abuse of position of trust: sexual activity in the presence of a child

Sexual Offences Act 2003 (section 18)

Abuse of position of trust: causing a child to watch a sexual act

Sexual Offences Act 2003 (section 19)

Triable either way

Maximum: 5 years' custody

Offence range: Community order–2 years' custody

For convictions on or after 3 December 2012 (irrespective of the date of commission of the offence), these are specified offences for the purposes of section 226A (extended sentence for certain violent or sexual offences) of the Criminal Justice Act 2003.

STEP ONE

Determining the offence category

The court should determine which categories of harm and culpability the offence falls into by reference only to the tables below.

HARM		CULPABILITY	
		A	**B**
Category 1	• Causing victim to view extreme pornography • Causing victim to view indecent/prohibited images of children • Engaging in, or causing a victim to view live, sexual activity involving sadism/violence/sexual activity with an animal/a child	• Significant degree of planning • Offender acts together with others to commit the offence • Use of alcohol/drugs on victim to facilitate the offence • Grooming behaviour used against victim • Use of threats (including blackmail) • Specific targeting of a particularly vulnerable child • Commercial exploitation and/or motivation • Offence racially or religiously aggravated • Offence motivated by, or demonstrating, hostility to the victim based on his or her sexual orientation (or presumed sexual orientation) or transgender identity (or presumed transgender identity) • Offence motivated by, or demonstrating, hostility to the victim based on his or her disability (or presumed disability)	Factor(s) in category A not present
Category 2	Engaging in, or causing a victim to view images of or view live, sexual activity involving: • penetration of vagina or anus (using body or object) • penile penetration of mouth • masturbation		
Category 3	Factor(s) in categories 1 and 2 not present		

STEP TWO

Starting point and category range

Having determined the category, the court should use the corresponding starting points to reach a sentence within the category range below. The starting point applies to all offenders irrespective of plea or previous convictions. Having determined the starting point, step two allows further adjustment for aggravating or mitigating features, set out below.

A case of particular gravity, reflected by multiple features of culpability or harm in step one, could merit upward adjustment from the starting point before further adjustment for aggravating or mitigating features, set out below.

Where there is a sufficient prospect of rehabilitation, a community order with a sex offender treatment programme requirement under section 202 of the Criminal Justice Act 2003 can be a proper alternative to a short or moderate length custodial sentence.

	A	**B**
Category 1	**Starting point** 18 months' custody **Category range** 1–2 years' custody	**Starting point** 1 year's custody **Category range** 26 weeks'–18 months' custody

	A	B
Category 2	**Starting point** 1 year's custody **Category range** 26 weeks'–18 months' custody	**Starting point** 26 weeks' custody **Category range** High level community order–1 year's custody
Category 3	**Starting point** 26 weeks' custody **Category range** High level community order–1 year's custody	**Starting point** Medium level community order **Category range** Low level community order–High level community order

The table below contains a non-exhaustive list of additional factual elements providing the context of the offence and factors relating to the offender. Identify whether any combination of these, or other relevant factors, should result in an upward or downward adjustment from the starting point. In particular, relevant recent convictions are likely to result in an upward adjustment. In some cases, having considered these factors, it may be appropriate to move outside the identified category range.

When sentencing appropriate category 2 or 3 offences, the court should also consider the custody threshold as follows:

- has the custody threshold been passed?
- if so, is it unavoidable that a custodial sentence be imposed?
- if so, can that sentence be suspended?

Aggravating factors

Statutory aggravating factors

- Previous convictions, having regard to a) the nature of the offence to which the conviction relates and its relevance to the current offence; and b) the time that has elapsed since the conviction
- Offence committed whilst on bail

Other aggravating factors

- Location of offence
- Timing of offence
- Victim compelled to leave their home, school, etc
- Failure to comply with current court orders
- Offence committed whilst on licence
- Presence of others, especially other children
- Any steps taken to prevent the victim reporting an incident, obtaining assistance and/or from assisting or supporting the prosecution
- Attempts to dispose of or conceal evidence
- Failure of offender to respond to previous warnings
- Commission of offence whilst under the influence of alcohol or drugs
- Victim encouraged to recruit others

Mitigating factors

- No previous convictions or no relevant/recent convictions
- Remorse
- Previous good character and/or exemplary conduct*
- Age and/or lack of maturity where it affects the responsibility of the offender
- Mental disorder or learning disability, particularly where linked to the commission of the offence
- Demonstration of steps taken to address offending behaviour

* Previous good character/exemplary conduct is different from having no previous convictions. The more serious the offence, the less the weight which should normally be attributed to this factor. Where previous good character/exemplary conduct has been used to facilitate the offence, this mitigation should not normally be allowed and such conduct may constitute an aggravating factor.

STEP THREE

Consider any factors which indicate a reduction, such as assistance to the prosecution

The court should take into account sections 73 and 74 of the Serious Organised Crime and Police Act 2005 (assistance by defendants: reduction or review of sentence) and any other rule of law by virtue of which an offender may receive a discounted sentence in consequence of assistance given (or offered) to the prosecutor or investigator.

STEP FOUR

Reduction for guilty pleas

The court should take account of any potential reduction for a guilty plea in accordance with section 144 of the Criminal Justice Act 2003 and the *Guilty Plea* guideline.

STEP FIVE

Dangerousness

The court should consider whether having regard to the criteria contained in Chapter 5 of Part 12 of the Criminal Justice Act 2003 it would be appropriate to award an extended sentence (section 226A).

STEP SIX

Totality principle

If sentencing an offender for more than one offence, or where the offender is already serving a sentence, consider whether the total sentence is just and proportionate to the offending behaviour.

STEP SEVEN

Ancillary orders

The court must consider whether to make any ancillary orders. The court must also consider what other requirements or provisions may *automatically* apply. Further information is included at Annex A on page 640.

STEP EIGHT

Reasons

Section 174 of the Criminal Justice Act 2003 imposes a duty to give reasons for, and explain the effect of, the sentence.

STEP NINE

Consideration for time spent on bail

The court must consider whether to give credit for time spent on bail in accordance with section 240A of the Criminal Justice Act 2003.

Possession of indecent photograph of child

Criminal Justice Act 1988 (section 160)

Triable either way

Maximum: 5 years' custody

Offence range: Community order–3 years' custody

Indecent photographs of children

Protection of Children Act 1978 (section 1)

Triable either way

Maximum: 10 years' custody

Offence range: Community order–9 years' custody

For section 1 offences committed on or after 3 December 2012, this is an offence listed in Part 1 of Schedule 15B for the purposes of section 224A (life sentence for second listed offence) of the Criminal Justice Act 2003.

For convictions on or after 3 December 2012 (irrespective of the date of commission of the offence), these are specified offences for the purposes of section 226A (extended sentence for certain violent or sexual offences) of the Criminal Justice Act 2003.

STEP ONE

Determining the offence category

The court should determine the offence category using the table below.

	Possession	**Distribution***	**Production****
Category A	Possession of images involving penetrative sexual activity Possession of images involving sexual activity with an animal or sadism	Sharing images involving penetrative sexual activity Sharing images involving sexual activity with an animal or sadism	Creating images involving penetrative sexual activity Creating images involving sexual activity with an animal or sadism

	Possession	Distribution*	Production**
Category B	Possession of images involving non-penetrative sexual activity	Sharing of images involving non-penetrative sexual activity	Creating images involving non-penetrative sexual activity
Category C	Possession of other indecent images not falling within categories A or B	Sharing of other indecent images not falling within categories A or B	Creating other indecent images not falling within categories A or B

* Distribution includes possession with a view to distributing or sharing images.

** Production includes the taking or making of any image at source for instance, the original image. Making an image by simple downloading should be treated as possession for the purposes of sentencing. In most cases the intrinsic character of the most serious of the offending images will initially determine the appropriate category. If, however, the most serious images are unrepresentative of the offender's conduct a lower category may be appropriate. A lower category will not, however, be appropriate if the offender has produced or taken (for example photographed) images of a higher category.

STEP TWO

Starting point and category range

Having determined the category, the court should use the corresponding starting points to reach a sentence within the category range below. The starting point applies to all offenders irrespective of plea or previous convictions. Having determined the starting point, step two allows further adjustment for aggravating or mitigating features, set out below.

Where there is a sufficient prospect of rehabilitation, a community order with a sex offender treatment programme requirement under section 202 of the Criminal Justice Act 2003 can be a proper alternative to a short or moderate length custodial sentence.

	Possession	Distribution	Production
Category A	**Starting point** 1 year's custody **Category range** 26 weeks–3 years' custody	**Starting point** 3 years' custody **Category range** 2–5 years' custody	**Starting point** 6 years' custody **Category range** 4–9 years' custody
Category B	**Starting point** 26 weeks' custody **Category range** High level community order–18 months' custody	**Starting point** 1 year's custody **Category range** 26 weeks–2 years' custody	**Starting point** 2 years' custody **Category range** 1–4 years' custody
Category C	**Starting point** High level community order **Category range** Medium level community order–26 weeks' custody	**Starting point** 13 weeks' custody **Category range** High level community order–26 weeks' custody	**Starting point** 18 months' custody **Category range** 1–3 years' custody

The table below contains a non-exhaustive list of additional factual elements providing the context of the offence and factors relating to the offender. Identify whether any combination of these, or other relevant factors, should result in an upward or downward adjustment from the starting point. In particular, relevant recent convictions are likely to result in an upward adjustment. In some cases, having considered these factors, it may be appropriate to move outside the identified category range.

When sentencing appropriate category 2 or 3 offences, the court should also consider the custody threshold as follows:

- has the custody threshold been passed?
- if so, is it unavoidable that a custodial sentence be imposed?
- if so, can that sentence be suspended?

Aggravating factors

Statutory aggravating factors

- Previous convictions, having regard to a) the nature of the offence to which the conviction relates and its relevance to the current offence; and b) the time that has elapsed since the conviction
- Offence committed whilst on bail

Other aggravating factors

- Failure to comply with current court orders
- Offence committed whilst on licence
- Age and/or vulnerability of the child depicted^
- Discernable pain or distress suffered by child depicted
- Period over which images were possessed, distributed or produced
- High volume of images possessed, distributed or produced
- Placing images where there is the potential for a high volume of viewers
- Collection includes moving images
- Attempts to dispose of or conceal evidence
- Abuse of trust
- Child depicted known to the offender
- Active involvement in a network or process that facilitates or commissions the creation or sharing of indecent images of children
- Commercial exploitation and/or motivation
- Deliberate or systematic searching for images portraying young children, category A images or the portrayal of familial sexual abuse
- Large number of different victims
- Child depicted intoxicated or drugged

^Age and/or vulnerability of the child should be given significant weight. In cases where the actual age of the victim is difficult to determine sentencers should consider the development of the child (infant, pre-pubescent, post-pubescent)

Mitigating factors

- No previous convictions or no relevant/recent convictions
- Remorse
- Previous good character and/or exemplary conduct*
- Age and/or lack of maturity where it affects the responsibility of the offender
- Mental disorder or learning disability, particularly where linked to the commission of the offence
- Demonstration of steps taken to address offending behaviour

* Previous good character/exemplary conduct is different from having no previous convictions. The more serious the offence, the less the weight which should normally be attributed to this factor. Where previous good character/exemplary conduct has been used to facilitate the offence, this mitigation should not normally be allowed and such conduct may constitute an aggravating factor.

STEP THREE

Consider any factors which indicate a reduction, such as assistance to the prosecution

The court should take into account sections 73 and 74 of the Serious Organised Crime and Police Act 2005 (assistance by defendants: reduction or review of sentence) and any other rule of law by virtue of which an offender may receive a discounted sentence in consequence of assistance given (or offered) to the prosecutor or investigator.

STEP FOUR

Reduction for guilty pleas

The court should take account of any potential reduction for a guilty plea in accordance with section 144 of the Criminal Justice Act 2003 and the *Guilty Plea* guideline.

STEP FIVE

Dangerousness

The court should consider whether having regard to the criteria contained in Chapter 5 of Part 12 of the Criminal Justice Act 2003 it would be appropriate to award a life sentence (section 224A) or an extended sentence (section 226A). When sentencing offenders to a life sentence under these provisions, the notional determinate sentence should be used as the basis for the setting of a minimum term.

STEP SIX

Totality principle

If sentencing an offender for more than one offence, or where the offender is already serving a sentence, consider whether the total sentence is just and proportionate to the offending behaviour.

STEP SEVEN

Ancillary orders

The court must consider whether to make any ancillary orders. The court must also consider what other requirements or provisions may *automatically* apply. Further information is included at Annex A on page 640.

STEP EIGHT

Reasons

Section 174 of the Criminal Justice Act 2003 imposes a duty to give reasons for, and explain the effect of, the sentence.

STEP NINE

Consideration for time spent on bail

The court must consider whether to give credit for time spent on bail in accordance with section 240A of the Criminal Justice Act 2003.

Causing or inciting prostitution for gain

Sexual Offences Act 2003 (section 52)

Controlling prostitution for gain

Sexual Offences Act 2003 (section 53)

Triable either way

Maximum: 7 years' custody

Offence range: Community order–6 years' custody

For convictions on or after 3 December 2012 (irrespective of the date of commission of the offence), these are specified offences for the purposes of section 226A (extended sentence for certain violent or sexual offences) of the Criminal Justice Act 2003.

The terms "prostitute" and "prostitution" are used in this guideline in accordance with the statutory language contained in the Sexual Offences Act 2003.

STEP ONE

Determining the offence category

The court should determine which categories of harm and culpability the offence falls into by reference only to the tables below.

HARM	
Category 1	• Abduction/detention • Violence or threats of violence • Sustained and systematic psychological abuse • Individual(s) forced or coerced to participate in unsafe/degrading sexual activity • Individual(s) forced or coerced into seeing many "customers" • Individual(s) forced/coerced/deceived into prostitution
Category 2	Factor(s) in category 1 not present

CULPABILITY		
A	**B**	**C**
• Causing, inciting or controlling prostitution on significant commercial basis • Expectation of significant financial or other gain • Abuse of trust • Exploitation of those known to be trafficked • Significant involvement in limiting the freedom of prostitute(s) • Grooming of individual(s) to enter prostitution including through cultivation of a dependency on drugs or alcohol	• Close involvement with prostitute(s) for example control of finances, choice of clients, working conditions, etc (where offender's involvement is not as a result of coercion)	• Performs limited function under direction • Close involvement but engaged by coercion/intimidation/exploitation

STEP TWO

Starting point and category range

Having determined the category, the court should use the corresponding starting points to reach a sentence within the category range below. The starting point applies to all offenders irrespective of plea or previous convictions. Having determined the starting point, step two allows further adjustment for aggravating or mitigating features, set out below.

A case of particular gravity, reflected by multiple features of culpability or harm in step one, could merit upward adjustment from the starting point before further adjustment for aggravating or mitigating features, set out below.

Where there is a sufficient prospect of rehabilitation, a community order with a sex offender treatment programme requirement under section 202 of the Criminal Justice Act 2003 can be a proper alternative to a short or moderate length custodial sentence.

	A	B	C
Category 1	Starting point 4 years' custody Category range 3–6 years' custody	Starting point 2 years 6 months' custody Category range 2–4 years' custody	Starting point 1 year's custody Category range 26 weeks'–2 years' custody
Category 2	Starting point 2 years 6 months' custody Category range 2–5 years' custody	Starting point 1 year's custody Category range High level community order–2 years' custody	Starting point Medium level community Order Category range Low level community order–High level community order

The table below contains a non-exhaustive list of additional factual elements providing the context of the offence and factors relating to the offender. Identify whether any combination of these, or other relevant factors, should result in an upward or downward adjustment from the starting point. In particular, relevant recent convictions are likely to result in an upward adjustment. In some cases, having considered these factors, it may be appropriate to move outside the identified category range.

When sentencing appropriate category 2 offences, the court should also consider the custody threshold as follows:
- has the custody threshold been passed?
- if so, is it unavoidable that a custodial sentence be imposed?
- if so, can that sentence be suspended?

Aggravating factors

Statutory aggravating factors

- Previous convictions, having regard to a) the nature of the offence to which the conviction relates and its relevance to the current offence; and b) the time that has elapsed since the conviction
- Offence committed whilst on bail

Other aggravating factors

- Failure to comply with current court orders
- Offence committed whilst on licence
- Deliberate isolation of prostitute(s)
- Threats made to expose prostitute(s) to the authorities (for example, immigration or police), family/friends or others
- Harm threatened against the family/friends of prostitute(s)
- Passport/identity documents removed
- Prostitute(s) prevented from seeking medical treatment
- Food withheld
- Earnings withheld/kept by offender or evidence of excessive wage reduction or debt bondage, inflated travel or living expenses or unreasonable interest rates
- Any steps taken to prevent the reporting of an incident, obtaining assistance and/or from assisting or supporting the prosecution
- Attempts to dispose of or conceal evidence
- Prostitute(s) forced or coerced into pornography
- Timescale over which operation has been run

Mitigating factors

- No previous convictions or no relevant/recent convictions
- Remorse
- Previous good character and/or exemplary conduct*
- Age and/or lack of maturity where it affects the responsibility of the offender
- Mental disorder or learning disability, particularly where linked to the commission of the offence
- Demonstration of steps taken to address offending behaviour

*Previous good character/exemplary conduct is different from having no previous convictions. The more serious the offence, the less the weight which should normally be attributed to this factor. Where previous good character/exemplary conduct has been used to facilitate the offence, this mitigation should not normally be allowed and such conduct may constitute an aggravating factor.

STEP THREE

Consider any factors which indicate a reduction, such as assistance to the prosecution

The court should take into account sections 73 and 74 of the Serious Organised Crime and Police Act 2005 (assistance by defendants: reduction or review of sentence) and any other rule of law by virtue of which an offender may receive a discounted sentence in consequence of assistance given (or offered) to the prosecutor or investigator.

STEP FOUR

Reduction for guilty pleas

The court should take account of any potential reduction for a guilty plea in accordance with section 144 of the Criminal Justice Act 2003 and the *Guilty Plea* guideline.

STEP FIVE

Dangerousness

The court should consider whether having regard to the criteria contained in Chapter 5 of Part 12 of the Criminal Justice Act 2003 it would be appropriate to award an extended sentence (section 226A).

STEP SIX

Totality principle

If sentencing an offender for more than one offence, or where the offender is already serving a sentence, consider whether the total sentence is just and proportionate to the offending behaviour.

STEP SEVEN

Ancillary orders

The court must consider whether to make any ancillary orders. The court must also consider what other requirements or provisions may *automatically* apply. Further information is included at Annex A on page 640.

STEP EIGHT

Reasons

Section 174 of the Criminal Justice Act 2003 imposes a duty to give reasons for, and explain the effect of, the sentence.

STEP NINE

Consideration for time spent on bail

The court must consider whether to give credit for time spent on bail in accordance with section 240A of the Criminal Justice Act 2003.

Keeping a brothel used for prostitution

Sexual Offences Act 1956 (section 33A)

Triable either way

Maximum: 7 years' custody

Offence range: Community order–6 years' custody

The terms "prostitute" and "prostitution" are used in this guideline in accordance with the statutory language contained in the Sexual Offences Act 2003.

STEP ONE

Determining the offence category

The court should determine which categories of harm and culpability the offence falls into by reference only to the tables below.

HARM	
Category 1	• Under 18 year olds working in brothel • Abduction/detention • Violence or threats of violence • Sustained and systematic psychological abuse • Those working in brothel forced or coerced to participate in unsafe/degrading sexual activity • Those working in brothel forced or coerced into seeing many "customers" • Those working in brothel forced/coerced/deceived into prostitution • Established evidence of community impact
Category 2	Factor(s) in category 1 not present

CULPABILITY

A	B	C
• Keeping brothel on significant commercial basis • Involvement in keeping a number of brothels • Expectation of significant financial or other gain • Abuse of trust • Exploitation of those known to be trafficked • Significant involvement in limiting freedom of those working in brothel • Grooming of a person to work in the brothel including through cultivation of a dependency on drugs or alcohol	• Keeping/managing premises • Close involvement with those working in brothel e.g. control of finances, choice of clients, working conditions, etc. (where offender's involvement is not as a result of coercion)	• Performs limited function under direction • Close involvement but engaged by coercion/intimidation/exploitation

STEP TWO

Starting point and category range

Having determined the category, the court should use the corresponding starting points to reach a sentence within the category range below. The starting point applies to all offenders irrespective of plea or previous convictions. Having determined the starting point, step two allows further adjustment for aggravating or mitigating features, set out below.

A case of particular gravity, reflected by multiple features of culpability or harm in step one, could merit upward adjustment from the starting point before further adjustment for aggravating or mitigating features, set out below.

Where there is a sufficient prospect of rehabilitation, a community order with a sex offender treatment programme requirement under section 202 of the Criminal Justice Act 2003 can be a proper alternative to a short or moderate length custodial sentence.

	A	B	C
Category 1	Starting point 5 years' custody Category range 3–6 years' custody	Starting point 3 years' custody Category range 2–5 years' custody	Starting point 1 year's custody Category range High level community order–18 months' custody
Category 2	Starting point 3 years' custody Category range 2–5 years' custody	Starting point 12 months' custody Category range 26 weeks'–2 years' custody	Starting point Medium level community order Category range Low level community order–High level community order

The table below contains a non-exhaustive list of additional factual elements providing the context of the offence and factors relating to the offender. Identify whether any combination of these, or other relevant factors, should result in an upward or downward adjustment from the starting point. In particular, relevant recent convictions are likely to result in an upward adjustment. In some cases, having considered these factors, it may be appropriate to move outside the identified category range.

When sentencing appropriate category 1 offences, the court should also consider the custody threshold as follows:

- has the custody threshold been passed?
- if so, is it unavoidable that a custodial sentence be imposed?
- if so, can that sentence be suspended?

Aggravating factors

Statutory aggravating factors

- Previous convictions, having regard to a) the nature of the offence to which the conviction relates and its relevance to the current offence; and b) the time that has elapsed since the conviction
- Offence committed whilst on bail

Other aggravating factors

- Failure to comply with current court orders
- Offence committed whilst on licence
- Deliberate isolation of those working in brothel
- Threats made to expose those working in brothel to the authorities (for example, immigration or police), family/friends or others
- Harm threatened against the family/friends of those working in brothel
- Passport/identity documents removed
- Those working in brothel prevented from seeking medical treatment
- Food withheld
- Those working in brothel passed around by offender and moved to other brothels
- Earnings of those working in brothel withheld/kept by offender or evidence of excessive wage reduction or debt bondage, inflated travel or living expenses or unreasonable interest rates
- Any steps taken to prevent those working in brothel reporting an incident, obtaining assistance and/or from assisting or supporting the prosecution
- Attempts to dispose of or conceal evidence
- Those working in brothel forced or coerced into pornography
- Timescale over which operation has been run

Mitigating factors

- No previous convictions or no relevant/recent convictions
- Remorse
- Previous good character and/or exemplary conduct*
- Age and/or lack of maturity where it affects the responsibility of the offender
- Mental disorder or learning disability, particularly where linked to the commission of the offence
- Demonstration of steps taken to address offending behaviour

---

* Previous good character/exemplary conduct is different from having no previous convictions. The more serious the offence, the less the weight which should normally be attributed to this factor. Where previous good character/

exemplary conduct has been used to facilitate the offence, this mitigation should not normally be allowed and such conduct may constitute an aggravating factor.

STEP THREE

Consider any factors which indicate a reduction, such as assistance to the prosecution

The court should take into account sections 73 and 74 of the Serious Organised Crime and Police Act 2005 (assistance by defendants: reduction or review of sentence) and any other rule of law by virtue of which an offender may receive a discounted sentence in consequence of assistance given (or offered) to the prosecutor or investigator.

STEP FOUR

Reduction for guilty pleas

The court should take account of any potential reduction for a guilty plea in accordance with section 144 of the Criminal Justice Act 2003 and the *Guilty Plea* guideline.

STEP FIVE

Totality principle

If sentencing an offender for more than one offence, or where the offender is already serving a sentence, consider whether the total sentence is just and proportionate to the offending behaviour.

STEP SIX

Ancillary orders

The court must consider whether to make any ancillary orders. The court must also consider what other requirements or provisions may *automatically* apply. Further information is included at Annex A on page 640.

STEP SEVEN

Reasons

Section 174 of the Criminal Justice Act 2003 imposes a duty to give reasons for, and explain the effect of, the sentence.

STEP EIGHT

Consideration for time spent on bail

The court must consider whether to give credit for time spent on bail in accordance with section 240A of the Criminal Justice Act 2003.

Causing or inciting child prostitution or pornography

Sexual Offences Act 2003 (section 48)

Controlling a child prostitute or child involved in pornography

Sexual Offences Act 2003 (section 49)

Arranging or facilitating child prostitution or pornography

Sexual Offences Act 2003 (section 50)

Triable either way

Maximum: 14 years' custody

Offence range: Victim aged under 13 1–13 years' custody

Victim aged 13–15 26 weeks'–11 years' custody

Victim aged 16–17 Community order–7 years' custody

For offences committed on or after 3 December 2012, these are offences listed in Part 1 of Schedule 15B for the purposes of sections 224A (life sentence for second listed offence) of the Criminal Justice Act 2003.

For convictions on or after 3 December 2012 (irrespective of the date of commission of the offence), these are specified offences for the purposes of section 226A (extended sentence for certain violent or sexual offences) of the Criminal Justice Act 2003.

The terms "child prostitute", "child prostitution" and "child involved in pornography" are used in this guideline in accordance with the statutory language contained in the Sexual Offences Act 2003.

STEP ONE

Determining the offence category

The court should determine which categories of harm and culpability the offence falls into by reference only to the tables below.

> For offences that involve wide scale commercial and/or international activity sentences above the category range may be appropriate.

HARM

Category 1	• Victims involved in penetrative sexual activity • Abduction/detention • Violence or threats of violence • Sustained and systematic psychological abuse • Victim(s) participated in unsafe/degrading sexual activity beyond that which is inherent in the offence • Victim(s) passed around by the offender to other "customers" and/or moved to other brothels
Category 2	Factor(s) in category 1 not present

CULPABILITY		
A	**B**	**C**
• Directing or organising child prostitution or pornography on significant commercial basis • Expectation of significant financial or other gain • Abuse of trust • Exploitation of victim(s) known to be trafficked • Significant involvement in limiting the freedom of the victim(s) • Grooming of a victim to enter prostitution or pornography including through cultivation of a dependency on drugs or alcohol	• Close involvement with inciting, controlling, arranging or facilitating child prostitution or pornography (where offender's involvement is not as a result of coercion)	• Performs limited function under direction • Close involvement but engaged by coercion/intimidation /exploitation

STEP TWO

Starting point and category range

Having determined the category, the court should use the corresponding starting points to reach a sentence within the category range below. The starting point applies to all offenders irrespective of plea or previous convictions. Having determined the starting point, step two allows further adjustment for aggravating or mitigating features, set out below.

A case of particular gravity, reflected by multiple features of culpability or harm in step one, could merit upward adjustment from the starting point before further adjustment for aggravating or mitigating features, set out below.

Where there is a sufficient prospect of rehabilitation, a community order with a sex offender treatment programme requirement under section 202 of the Criminal Justice Act 2003 can be a proper alternative to a short or moderate length custodial sentence.

		A	B	C
Category 1	U13	**Starting point** 10 years' custody **Category range** 8-13 years' custody	**Starting point** 8 years' custody **Category range** 6-11 years' custody	**Starting point** 5 years' custody **Category range** 2–6 years' custody
	13-15	**Starting point** 8 years' custody **Category range** 6–11 years' custody	**Starting point** 5 years' custody **Category range** 4–8 years' custody	**Starting point** 2 years 6 months' custody **Category range** 1–4 years' custody
	16-17	**Starting point** 4 years' custody **Category range** 3–7 years' custody	**Starting point** 2 years' custody **Category range** 1–4 years' custody	**Starting point** 1 year's custody **Category range** 26 weeks'–2 years' custody

	A	B	C
Category 2 U13	Starting point 8 years' custody Category range 6-11 years' custody	Starting point 6 years' custody Category range 4-9 years' custody	Starting point 2 years' custody Category range 1-4 years' custody
13-15	Starting point 6 years' custody Category range 4-9 years' custody	Starting point 3 years' custody Category range 2-5 years' custody	Starting point 1 year's custody Category range 26 weeks'-2 years' custody
16-17	Starting point 3 years' custody Category range 2-5 years' custody	Starting point 1 year's custody Category range 26 weeks'-2 years' custody	Starting point 26 weeks' custody Category range High level community order-1 year's custody

The table below contains a non-exhaustive list of additional factual elements providing the context of the offence and factors relating to the offender. Identify whether any combination of these, or other relevant factors, should result in an upward or downward adjustment from the starting point. In particular, relevant recent convictions are likely to result in an upward adjustment. In some cases, having considered these factors, it may be appropriate to move outside the identified category range.

When sentencing appropriate category 2 offences, the court should also consider the custody threshold as follows:

- has the custody threshold been passed?
- if so, is it unavoidable that a custodial sentence be imposed?
- if so, can that sentence be suspended?

Aggravating factors

Statutory aggravating factors

- Previous convictions, having regard to a) the nature of the offence to which the conviction relates and its relevance to the current offence; and b) the time that has elapsed since the conviction
- Offence committed whilst on bail

Other aggravating factors

- Failure to comply with current court orders
- Offence committed whilst on licence
- Deliberate isolation of victim(s)
- Vulnerability of victim(s)
- Threats made to expose victim(s) to the authorities (for example immigration or police), family/friends or others
- Harm threatened against the family/friends of victim(s)
- Passport/identity documents removed
- Victim(s) prevented from seeking medical treatment
- Victim(s) prevented from attending school
- Food withheld
- Earnings withheld/kept by offender or evidence of excessive wage reduction or debt bondage, inflated travel or living expenses or unreasonable interest rates
- Any steps taken to prevent the victim reporting an incident, obtaining assistance and/or from assisting or supporting the prosecution
- Attempts to dispose of or conceal evidence
- Timescale over which the operation has been run

Mitigating Factors
- No previous convictions or no relevant/recent convictions
- Remorse
- Previous good character and/or exemplary conduct*
- Age and/or lack of maturity where it affects the responsibility of the offender
- Mental disorder or learning disability, particularly where linked to the commission of the offence

* Previous good character/exemplary conduct is different from having no previous convictions. The more serious the offence, the less the weight which should normally be attributed to this factor. Where previous good character/exemplary conduct has been used to facilitate the offence, this mitigation should not normally be allowed and such conduct may constitute an aggravating factor. In the context of this offence, previous good character/exemplary conduct should not normally be given any significant weight and will not normally justify a reduction in what would otherwise be the appropriate sentence.

STEP THREE

Consider any factors which indicate a reduction, such as assistance to the prosecution

The court should take into account sections 73 and 74 of the Serious Organised Crime and Police Act 2005 (assistance by defendants: reduction or review of sentence) and any other rule of law by virtue of which an offender may receive a discounted sentence in consequence of assistance given (or offered) to the prosecutor or investigator.

STEP FOUR

Reduction for guilty pleas

The court should take account of any potential reduction for a guilty plea in accordance with section 144 of the Criminal Justice Act 2003 and the *Guilty Plea* guideline.

STEP FIVE

Dangerousness

The court should consider whether having regard to the criteria contained in Chapter 5 of Part 12 of the Criminal Justice Act 2003 it would be appropriate to award a life sentence (section 224A) or an extended sentence (section 226A). When sentencing offenders to a life sentence under these provisions, the notional determinate sentence should be used as the basis for the setting of a minimum term.

STEP SIX

Totality principle

If sentencing an offender for more than one offence, or where the offender is already serving a sentence, consider whether the total sentence is just and proportionate to the offending behaviour.

STEP SEVEN

Ancillary orders

The court must consider whether to make any ancillary orders. The court must also consider what other requirements or provisions may *automatically* apply. Further information is included at Annex A on page 640.

STEP EIGHT

Reasons

Section 174 of the Criminal Justice Act 2003 imposes a duty to give reasons for, and explain the effect of, the sentence.

STEP NINE

Consideration for time spent on bail

The court must consider whether to give credit for time spent on bail in accordance with section 240A of the Criminal Justice Act 2003.

Paying for the sexual services of a child

Sexual Offences Act 2003 (section 47)

Triable only on indictment (if involving penetration against victim under 16) - otherwise triable either way

Maximum:	Victim under 13 (penetrative) Life imprisonment
	Victim under 13 (non-penetrative) 14 years' custody
	Victim aged 13-15 14 years' custody
	Victim aged 16-17 7 years' custody
Offence range:	Victim aged 16-17 Community order–5 years' custody

This guideline should only be used where the victim is aged 16 or 17 years old. If the victim is under 13 please refer to the guidelines for rape of a child under 13, assault by penetration of a child under 13, sexual assault of a child under 13 or causing or inciting a child under 13 to engage in sexual activity, depending on the activity involved in the offence.

If the victim is aged 13-15 please refer to the sexual activity with a child guideline.

Where the victim is 16 or 17 years old – for convictions on or after 3 December 2012 (irrespective of the date of commission of the offence), this is a specified offence for the purposes of section 226A (extended sentence for certain violent or sexual offences) of the Criminal Justice Act 2003.

STEP ONE

Determining the offence category

The court should determine which categories of harm and culpability the offence falls into by reference only to the tables below.

This guideline should only be used where the victim was aged 16 or 17 years old.

HARM		CULPABILITY	
		A	**B**
Category 1	• Penetration of vagina or anus (using body or object) by, or of, the victim • Penile penetration of mouth by, or of, the victim • Violence or threats of violence • Victim subjected to unsafe/degrading sexual activity (beyond that which is inherent in the offence)	• Abduction/detention • Sexual images of victim recorded, retained, solicited or shared • Offender acts together with others to commit the offence • Use of alcohol/drugs on victim • Abuse of trust • Previous violence against victim • Sexual images of victim recorded, retained, solicited or shared • Blackmail or other threats made (including to expose victim to the authorities, family/friends or others) • Offender aware that he has a sexually transmitted disease • Offender aware victim has been trafficked	Factor(s) in category A not present
Category 2	• Touching of naked genitalia or naked breasts by, or of, the victim		
Category 3	• Other sexual activity		

STEP TWO

Starting point and category range

Having determined the category, the court should use the corresponding starting points to reach a sentence within the category range below for victims aged 16 or 17. The starting point applies to all offenders irrespective of plea or previous convictions. Having determined the starting point, step two allows further adjustment for aggravating or mitigating features, set out below.

A case of particular gravity, reflected by multiple features of culpability in step one, could merit upward adjustment from the starting point before further adjustment for aggravating or mitigating features, set out below.

Where there is a sufficient prospect of rehabilitation, a community order with a sex offender treatment programme requirement under section 202 of the Criminal Justice Act 2003 can be a proper alternative to a short or moderate length custodial sentence.

	A	B
Category 1	**Starting point** 4 years' custody **Category range** 2–5 years' custody	**Starting point** 2 years' custody **Category range** 1–4 years' custody
Category 2	**Starting point** 3 years' custody **Category range** 1–4 years' custody	**Starting point** 1 year's custody **Category range** 26 weeks'–2 years' custody
Category 3	**Starting point** 1 year's custody **Category range** 26 weeks'–2 years' custody	**Starting point** 26 weeks' custody **Category range** High level community order–1 year's custody

The table below contains a non-exhaustive list of additional factual elements providing the context of the offence and factors relating to the offender. Identify whether any combination of these, or other relevant factors, should result in an upward or downward adjustment from the starting point. In particular, relevant recent convictions are likely to result in an upward adjustment. In some cases, having considered these factors, it may be appropriate to move outside the identified category range.

When sentencing appropriate category 3 offences, the court should also consider the custody threshold as follows:

- has the custody threshold been passed?
- if so, is it unavoidable that a custodial sentence be imposed?
- if so, can that sentence be suspended?

Aggravating factors

Statutory aggravating factors

- Previous convictions, having regard to a) the nature of the offence to which the conviction relates and its relevance to the current offence; and b) the time that has elapsed since the conviction
- Offence committed whilst on bail

Other aggravating factors

- Ejaculation
- Failure to comply with current court orders
- Offence committed whilst on licence
- Any steps taken to prevent the victim reporting an incident, obtaining assistance and/or from assisting or supporting the prosecution
- Attempts to dispose of or conceal evidence

Mitigating factors

- No previous convictions or no relevant/recent convictions
- Remorse
- Previous good character and/or exemplary conduct*
- Age and/or lack of maturity where it affects the responsibility of the offender
- Mental disorder or learning disability, particularly where linked to the commission of the offence
- Demonstration of steps taken to address offending behaviour

---

* Previous good character/exemplary conduct is different from having no previous convictions. The more serious the offence, the less the weight which should normally be attributed to this factor. Where previous good character/exemplary conduct has been used to facilitate the offence, this mitigation should not normally be allowed and such conduct may constitute an aggravating factor.

STEP THREE

Consider any factors which indicate a reduction, such as assistance to the prosecution

The court should take into account sections 73 and 74 of the Serious Organised Crime and Police Act 2005 (assistance by defendants: reduction or review of sentence) and any other rule of law by virtue of which an offender may receive a discounted sentence in consequence of assistance given (or offered) to the prosecutor or investigator.

STEP FOUR

Reduction for guilty pleas

The court should take account of any potential reduction for a guilty plea in accordance with section 144 of the Criminal Justice Act 2003 and the *Guilty Plea* guideline.

STEP FIVE

Dangerousness

The court should consider whether having regard to the criteria contained in Chapter 5 of Part 12 of the Criminal Justice Act 2003 it would be appropriate to award an extended sentence (section 226A).

STEP SIX

Totality principle

If sentencing an offender for more than one offence, or where the offender is already serving a sentence, consider whether the total sentence is just and proportionate to the offending behaviour.

STEP SEVEN

Ancillary orders

The court must consider whether to make any ancillary orders. The court must also consider what other requirements or provisions may *automatically* apply. Further information is included at Annex A on page 640.

STEP EIGHT

Reasons

Section 174 of the Criminal Justice Act 2003 imposes a duty to give reasons for, and explain the effect of, the sentence.

STEP NINE

Consideration for time spent on bail

The court must consider whether to give credit for time spent on bail in accordance with section 240A of the Criminal Justice Act 2003.

Trafficking people for sexual exploitation

Sexual Offences Act 2003 (sections 59A)

(This guideline also applies to offences, committed before 6 April 2013, of trafficking into/within/out of the UK for sexual exploitation contrary to sections 57 to 59 of the Sexual Offences Act 2003)

Triable either way

Maximum: 14 years' custody

Offence range: Community order–12 years' custody

For convictions on or after 3 December 2012 (irrespective of the date of commission of the offence), this is a specified offence for the purposes of section 226A (extended sentence for certain violent or sexual offences) of the Criminal Justice Act 2003.

The term "prostitution" is used in this guideline in accordance with the statutory language contained in the Sexual Offences Act 2003.

STEP ONE

Determining the offence category

The court should determine which categories of harm and culpability the offence falls into by reference only to the tables below.

HARM

Category 1	• Abduction/detention • Violence or threats of violence • Sustained and systematic psychological abuse • Victim(s) under 18 • Victim(s) forced or coerced to participate in unsafe/degrading sexual activity • Victim(s) forced/coerced into prostitution • Victim(s) tricked/deceived as to purpose of visit
Category 2	• Factor(s) in category 1 not present

CULPABILITY

A	B	C
• Directing or organising trafficking on significant commercial basis • Expectation of significant financial or other gain • Significant influence over others in trafficking organisation/hierarchy • Abuse of trust	• Operational or management function within hierarchy • Involves others in operation whether by coercion/ intimidation/ exploitation or reward (and offender's involvement is not as a result of coercion)	• Performs limited function under direction • Close involvement but engaged by coercion/ intimidation/ exploitation

STEP TWO

Starting point and category range

Having determined the category of harm and culpability, the court should use the corresponding starting points to reach a sentence within the category range below. The starting point applies to all offenders irrespective of plea or previous convictions. Having determined the starting point, step two allows further adjustment for aggravating or mitigating features, set out below.

A case of particular gravity, reflected by multiple features of culpability or harm in step one, could merit upward adjustment from the starting point before further adjustment for aggravating or mitigating features, set out below.

Where there is a sufficient prospect of rehabilitation, a community order with a sex offender treatment programme requirement under section 202 of the Criminal Justice Act 2003 can be a proper alternative to a short or moderate length custodial sentence.

	A	B	C
Category 1	**Starting point** 8 years' custody **Category range** 6-12 years' custody	**Starting point** 6 years' custody **Category range** 4–8 years' custody	**Starting point** 18 months' custody **Category range** 26 weeks'–2 years' custody
Category 2	**Starting point** 6 years' custody **Category range** 4–8 years' custody	**Starting point** 4 years' custody **Category range** 2–6 years' custody	**Starting point** 26 weeks' custody **Category range** High level community order–18 months' custody

The table below contains a non-exhaustive list of additional factual elements providing the context of the offence and factors relating to the offender. Identify whether any combination of these, or other relevant factors, should result in an upward or downward adjustment from the starting point. In particular, relevant recent convictions are likely to result in an upward adjustment. In some cases, having considered these factors, it may be appropriate to move outside the identified category range.

When sentencing appropriate category 2 offences, the court should also consider the custody threshold as follows:

- has the custody threshold been passed?
- if so, is it unavoidable that a custodial sentence be imposed?
- if so, can that sentence be suspended?

Aggravating factors

Statutory aggravating factors

- Previous convictions, having regard to a) the nature of the offence to which the conviction relates and its relevance to the current offence; and b) the time that has elapsed since the conviction
- Offence committed whilst on bail

Other aggravating factors

- Failure to comply with current court orders
- Offence committed whilst on licence
- Deliberate isolation of victim(s)
- Children of victim(s) left in home country due to trafficking
- Threats made to expose victim(s) to the authorities (for example immigration or police), family/friends or others
- Harm threatened against the family/friends of victim
- Exploitation of victim(s) from particularly vulnerable backgrounds
- Victim(s) previously trafficked/sold/passed around
- Passport/identity documents removed
- Victim(s) prevented from seeking medical treatment
- Food withheld
- Use of drugs/alcohol or other substance to secure victim's compliance
- Earnings of victim(s) withheld/kept by offender or evidence of excessive wage reduction, debt bondage, inflated travel or living expenses, unreasonable interest rates
- Any steps taken to prevent the victim reporting an incident, obtaining assistance and/or from assisting or supporting the prosecution
- Attempts to dispose of or conceal evidence
- Timescale over which operation has been run

Mitigating factors
- No previous convictions or no relevant/recent convictions
- Remorse
- Previous good character and/or exemplary conduct*
- Age and/or lack of maturity where it affects the responsibility of the offender
- Mental disorder or learning disability, particularly where linked to the commission of the offence

* Previous good character/exemplary conduct is different from having no previous convictions. The more serious the offence, the less the weight which should normally be attributed to this factor. Where previous good character/exemplary conduct has been used to facilitate the offence, this mitigation should not normally be allowed and such conduct may constitute an aggravating factor. In the context of this offence, previous good character/exemplary conduct should not normally be given any significant weight and will not normally justify a reduction in what would otherwise be the appropriate sentence.

STEP THREE

Consider any factors which indicate a reduction, such as assistance to the prosecution

The court should take into account sections 73 and 74 of the Serious Organised Crime and Police Act 2005 (assistance by defendants: reduction or review of sentence) and any other rule of law by virtue of which an offender may receive a discounted sentence in consequence of assistance given (or offered) to the prosecutor or investigator.

STEP FOUR

Reduction for guilty pleas

The court should take account of any potential reduction for a guilty plea in accordance with section 144 of the Criminal Justice Act 2003 and the *Guilty Plea* guideline.

STEP FIVE

Dangerousness

The court should consider whether having regard to the criteria contained in Chapter 5 of Part 12 of the Criminal Justice Act 2003 it would be appropriate to award an extended sentence (section 226A).

STEP SIX

Totality principle

If sentencing an offender for more than one offence, or where the offender is already serving a sentence, consider whether the total sentence is just and proportionate to the offending behaviour.

STEP SEVEN

Ancillary orders

The court must consider whether to make any ancillary orders. The court must also consider what other requirements or provisions may *automatically* apply. Further information is included at Annex A on page 640.

STEP EIGHT

Reasons

Section 174 of the Criminal Justice Act 2003 imposes a duty to give reasons for, and explain the effect of, the sentence.

STEP NINE

Consideration for time spent on bail

The court must consider whether to give credit for time spent on bail in accordance with section 240A of the Criminal Justice Act 2003.

Sexual activity with a person with a mental disorder impeding choice

Sexual Offences Act 2003 (section 30)

Causing or inciting a person, with a mental disorder impeding choice, to engage in sexual activity

Sexual Offences Act 2003 (section 31)

Triable only on indictment (if penetration involved)—otherwise, triable either way

Maximum: Life imprisonment (if penetration involved)—otherwise 14 years' custody

Offence range: Community order–19 years' custody

These are serious specified offences for the purposes of section 224 and, where the offence involved penetration, section 225(2) (life sentence for serious offences) of the Criminal Justice Act 2003.

For offences involving penetration, committed on or after 3 December 2012, these are offences listed in Part 1 of Schedule 15B for the purposes of section 224A (life sentence for second listed offence) of the Criminal Justice Act 2003.

For convictions on or after 3 December 2012 (irrespective of the date of commission of the offence), these are specified offences for the purposes of section 226A (extended sentence for certain violent or sexual offences) of the Criminal Justice Act 2003.

STEP ONE

Determining the offence category

The court should determine which categories of harm and culpability the offence falls into by reference only to the tables below.

HARM		CULPABILITY	
		A	B
Category 1	The extreme nature of one or more category 2 factors or the extreme impact caused by a combination of category 2 factors may elevate to category 1	• Significant degree of planning • Offender acts together with others to commit the offence • Use of alcohol/drugs on victim to facilitate the offence • Grooming behaviour used against victim • Abuse of trust • Previous violence against victim • Offence committed in course of burglary • Sexual images of victim recorded, retained, solicited or shared • Deliberate isolation of victim • Commercial exploitation and/or motivation • Offence racially or religiously aggravated • Offence motivated by, or demonstrating, hostility to the victim based on his or her sexual orientation (or presumed sexual orientation) or transgender identity (or presumed transgender identity) • Offence motivated by, or demonstrating, hostility to the victim based on the victim's disability (or presumed disability)	Factor(s) in category A not present
Category 2	• Severe psychological or physical harm • Pregnancy or STI as a consequence of offence • Additional degradation/humiliation • Abduction • Prolonged detention/sustained incident • Violence or threats of violence • Forced/uninvited entry into victim's home or residence		
Category 3	Factor(s) in categories 1 and 2 not present		

STEP TWO

Starting point and category range

Having determined the category of harm and culpability, the court should use the corresponding starting points to reach a sentence within the category range below. The starting point applies to all offenders irrespective of plea or previous convictions. Having determined the starting point, step two allows further adjustment for aggravating or mitigating features, set out below.

A case of particular gravity, reflected by multiple features of culpability or harm in step one, could merit upward adjustment from the starting point before further adjustment for aggravating or mitigating features, set out below.

Where there is a sufficient prospect of rehabilitation, a community order with a sex offender treatment programme requirement under section 202 of the Criminal Justice Act 2003 can be a proper alternative to a short or moderate length custodial sentence.

Where offence involved penetration

	A	B
Category 1	Starting point 16 years' custody Category range 13–19 years' custody	Starting point 13 years' custody Category range 11–17 years' custody
Category 2	Starting point 13 years' custody Category range 11–17 years' custody	Starting point 10 years' custody Category range 8–13 years' custody
Category 3	Starting point 10 years' custody Category range 8–13 years' custody	Starting point 8 years' custody Category range 6–11 years' custody

Where offence did not involve penetration

	A	B
Category 1	Starting point 6 years' custody Category range 4–9 years' custody	Starting point 4 years' custody Category range 3–7 years' custody
Category 2	Starting point 4 years' custody Category range 3–7 years' custody	Starting point 2 years' custody Category range 1–4 years' custody
Category 3	Starting point 1 year's custody Category range 26 weeks' –2 years' custody	Starting point 26 weeks' custody Category range High level community order – 1 year's custody

The table below contains a non-exhaustive list of additional factual elements providing the context of the offence and factors relating to the offender. Identify whether any combination of these, or other relevant factors, should result in an upward or downward adjustment from the starting point. In particular, relevant recent convictions are likely to result in an upward adjustment. In some cases, having considered these factors, it may be appropriate to move outside the identified category range.

When appropriate, the court should also consider the custody threshold as follows:

- has the custody threshold been passed?
- if so, is it unavoidable that a custodial sentence be imposed?
- if so, can that sentence be suspended?

Aggravating factors

Statutory aggravating factors

- Previous convictions, having regard to a) the nature of the offence to which the conviction relates and its relevance to the current offence; and b) the time that has elapsed since the conviction
- Offence committed whilst on bail

Other aggravating factors

- Ejaculation (where not taken into account at step one)
- Blackmail or other threats made (where not taken into account at step one)
- Location of offence
- Timing of offence
- Use of weapon or other item to frighten or injure
- Victim compelled to leave their home or institution (including victims of domestic violence)
- Failure to comply with current court orders
- Offence committed whilst on licence
- Presence of others, especially children
- Any steps taken to prevent the victim reporting an incident, obtaining assistance and/or from assisting or supporting the prosecution
- Attempts to dispose of or conceal evidence
- Commission of offence whilst under the influence of alcohol or drugs

Mitigating factors

- No previous convictions or no relevant/recent convictions
- Remorse
- Previous good character and/or exemplary conduct*
- Age and/or lack of maturity where it affects the responsibility of the offender
- Mental disorder or learning disability, particularly where linked to the commission of the offence
- Sexual activity was incited but no activity took place because the offender voluntarily desisted or intervened to prevent it

* Previous good character/exemplary conduct is different from having no previous convictions. The more serious the offence, the less the weight which should normally be attributed to this factor. Where previous good character/exemplary conduct has been used to facilitate the offence, this mitigation should not normally be allowed and such conduct may constitute an aggravating factor. In the context of this offence, previous good character/exemplary conduct should not normally be given any significant weight and will not normally justify a reduction in what would otherwise be the appropriate sentence.

STEP THREE

Consider any factors which indicate a reduction, such as assistance to the prosecution

The court should take into account sections 73 and 74 of the Serious Organised Crime and Police Act 2005 (assistance by defendants: reduction or review of sentence) and any other rule of law by virtue of which an offender may receive a discounted sentence in consequence of assistance given (or offered) to the prosecutor or investigator.

STEP FOUR

Reduction for guilty pleas

The court should take account of any potential reduction for a guilty plea in accordance with section 144 of the Criminal Justice Act 2003 and the *Guilty Plea* guideline.

STEP FIVE

Dangerousness

The court should consider whether having regard to the criteria contained in Chapter 5 of Part 12 of the Criminal Justice Act 2003 it would be appropriate to award a life sentence (section 224A or section 225(2)) or an extended sentence (section 226A). When sentencing offenders to a life sentence under these provisions, the notional determinate sentence should be used as the basis for the setting of a minimum term.

STEP SIX

Totality principle

If sentencing an offender for more than one offence, or where the offender is already serving a sentence, consider whether the total sentence is just and proportionate to the offending behaviour.

STEP SEVEN

Ancillary orders

The court must consider whether to make any ancillary orders. The court must also consider what other requirements or provisions may *automatically* apply. Further information is included at Annex A on page 640.

STEP EIGHT

Reasons

Section 174 of the Criminal Justice Act 2003 imposes a duty to give reasons for, and explain the effect of, the sentence.

STEP NINE

Consideration for time spent on bail

The court must consider whether to give credit for time spent on bail in accordance with section 240A of the Criminal Justice Act 2003.

Engaging in sexual activity in the presence of a person with mental disorder impeding choice

Sexual Offences Act 2003 (section 32)

Causing a person, with mental disorder impeding choice, to watch a sexual act

Sexual Offences Act 2003 (section 33)

Triable either way

Maximum: 10 years' custody

Offence range: Community order–6 years' custody

For convictions on or after 3 December 2012 (irrespective of the date of commission of the offence), these are specified offences for the purposes of section 226A (extended sentence for certain violent or sexual offences) of the Criminal Justice Act 2003.

STEP ONE

Determining the offence category

The court should determine which categories of harm and culpability the offence falls into by reference only to the tables below.

HARM	
Category 1	• Causing victim to view extreme pornography • Causing victim to view indecent/prohibited images of children • Engaging in, or causing a victim to view live, sexual activity involving sadism/violence/sexual activity with an animal/a child
Category 2	Engaging in, or causing a victim to view images of or view live, sexual activity involving: • penetration of vagina or anus (using body or object) • penile penetration of mouth • masturbation
Category 3	Factor(s) in categories 1 and 2 not present

CULPABILITY	
A	**B**
• Significant degree of planning • Offender acts together with others in order to commit the offence • Use of alcohol/drugs on victim to facilitate the offence • Grooming behaviour used against victim • Abuse of trust • Use of threats (including blackmail) • Commercial exploitation and/or motivation • Offence racially or religiously aggravated • Offence motivated by, or demonstrating, hostility to the victim based on his or her sexual orientation (or presumed sexual orientation) or transgender identity (or presumed transgender identity) • Offence motivated by, or demonstrating, hostility to the victim based on his or her disability (or presumed disability)	Factor(s) in category A not present

STEP TWO

Starting point and category range

Having determined the category of harm and culpability, the court should use the corresponding starting points to reach a sentence within the category range below. The starting point applies to all offenders irrespective of plea or previous convictions.

Having determined the starting point, step two allows further adjustment for aggravating or mitigating features, set out below.

A case of particular gravity, reflected by multiple features of culpability or harm in step one, could merit upward adjustment from the starting point before further adjustment for aggravating or mitigating features, set out below.

Where there is a sufficient prospect of rehabilitation, a community order with a sex offender treatment programme requirement under section 202 of the Criminal Justice Act 2003 can be a proper alternative to a short or moderate length custodial sentence.

	A	B
Category 1	**Starting point** 4 years' custody **Category range** 3–6 years' custody	**Starting point** 2 years' custody **Category range** 1–3 years' custody
Category 2	**Starting point** 2 years' custody **Category range** 1–3 years' custody	**Starting point** 1 year's custody **Category range** High level community order–18 months' custody
Category 3	**Starting point** 26 weeks' custody **Category range** High level community order–1 year's custody	**Starting point** Medium level community order **Category range** Low level community order–Medium level community order

The table below contains a non-exhaustive list of additional factual elements providing the context of the offence and factors relating to the offender. Identify whether any combination of these, or other relevant factors, should result in an upward or downward adjustment from the starting point. In particular, relevant recent convictions are likely to result in an upward adjustment. In some cases, having considered these factors, it may be appropriate to move outside the identified category range.

When sentencing appropriate category 2 or 3 offences, the court should also consider the custody threshold as follows:

- has the custody threshold been passed?
- if so, is it unavoidable that a custodial sentence be imposed?
- if so, can that sentence be suspended?

Aggravating factors

Statutory aggravating factors

- Previous convictions, having regard to a) the nature of the offence to which the conviction relates and its relevance to the current offence; and b) the time that has elapsed since the conviction
- Offence committed whilst on bail

Other aggravating factors

- Location of offence
- Timing of offence
- Failure to comply with current court orders
- Offence committed whilst on licence
- Any steps taken to prevent the victim reporting an incident, obtaining assistance and/or from assisting or supporting the prosecution
- Attempts to dispose of or conceal evidence
- Commission of offence whilst under the influence of alcohol or drugs

Mitigating factors
- No previous convictions or no relevant/recent convictions
- Remorse
- Previous good character and/or exemplary conduct*
- Age and/or lack of maturity where it affects the responsibility of the offender
- Mental disorder or learning disability, particularly where linked to the commission of the offence
- Demonstration of steps taken to address offending behaviour

* Previous good character/exemplary conduct is different from having no previous convictions. The more serious the offence, the less the weight which should normally be attributed to this factor. Where previous good character/exemplary conduct has been used to facilitate the offence, this mitigation should not normally be allowed and such conduct may constitute an aggravating factor.

STEP THREE

Consider any factors which indicate a reduction, such as assistance to the prosecution

The court should take into account sections 73 and 74 of the Serious Organised Crime and Police Act 2005 (assistance by defendants: reduction or review of sentence) and any other rule of law by virtue of which an offender may receive a discounted sentence in consequence of assistance given (or offered) to the prosecutor or investigator.

STEP FOUR

Reduction for guilty pleas

The court should take account of any potential reduction for a guilty plea in accordance with section 144 of the Criminal Justice Act 2003 and the *Guilty Plea* guideline.

STEP FIVE

Dangerousness

The court should consider whether having regard to the criteria contained in Chapter 5 of Part 12 of the Criminal Justice Act 2003 it would be appropriate to award an extended sentence (section 226A).

STEP SIX

Totality principle

If sentencing an offender for more than one offence, or where the offender is already serving a sentence, consider whether the total sentence is just and proportionate to the offending behaviour.

STEP SEVEN

Ancillary orders

The court must consider whether to make any ancillary orders. The court must also consider what other requirements or provisions may *automatically* apply. Further information is included at Annex A on page 640.

STEP EIGHT

Reasons

Section 174 of the Criminal Justice Act 2003 imposes a duty to give reasons for, and explain the effect of, the sentence.

STEP NINE

Consideration for time spent on bail

The court must consider whether to give credit for time spent on bail in accordance with section 240A of the Criminal Justice Act 2003.

Inducement, threat or deception to procure sexual activity with a person with a mental disorder

Sexual Offences Act 2003 (section 34)

Causing a person with a mental disorder to engage in or agree to engage in sexual activity by inducement, threat or deception

Sexual Offences Act 2003 (section 35)

Triable only on indictment (if penetration involved)—otherwise, triable either way

Maximum: Life imprisonment (if penetration involved)—otherwise, 14 years' custody

Offence range: Community order–10 years' custody

These are serious specified offences for the purposes of section 224 and, where the offence involved penetration, section 225(2) (life sentence for serious offences) of the Criminal Justice Act 2003.

For offences involving penetration, committed on or after 3 December 2012, these are offences listed in Part 1 of Schedule 15B for the purposes of section 224A (life sentence for second listed offence) of the Criminal Justice Act 2003.

For convictions on or after 3 December 2012 (irrespective of the date of commission of the offence), these are specified offences for the purposes of section 226A (extended sentence for certain violent or sexual offences) of the Criminal Justice Act 2003.

STEP ONE

Determining the offence category

The court should determine which categories of harm and culpability the offence falls into by reference only to the tables below.

THIS GUIDLINE [sic] ALSO APPLIES TO OFFENCES COMMITTED REMOTELY/ONLINE

HARM		CULPABILITY	
		A	**B**
Category 1	Penetration of vagina or anus (using body or object) Penile penetration of mouth In either case by, or of, the victim	• Significant degree of planning • Offender acts together with others to commit the offence • Use of alcohol/drugs on victim to facilitate the offence • Abuse of trust • Sexual images of victim recorded, retained, solicited or shared • Commercial exploitation and/or motivation • Offence racially or religiously aggravated • Offence motivated by, or demonstrating, hostility to the victim based on his or her sexual orientation (or presumed sexual orientation) or transgender identity (or presumed transgender identity) • Offence motivated by, or demonstrating, hostility to the victim based on his or her disability (or presumed disability)	Factor(s) in category A not present
Category 2	Touching, or exposure, of naked genitalia or naked breasts by, or of, the victim		
Category 3	Other sexual activity		

STEP TWO

Starting point and category range

Having determined the category of harm and culpability, the court should use the corresponding starting points to reach a sentence within the category range below. The starting point applies to all offenders irrespective of plea or previous convictions. Having determined the starting point, step two allows further adjustment for aggravating or mitigating features, set out below.

A case of particular gravity, reflected by multiple features of culpability or harm in step one, could merit upward adjustment from the starting point before further adjustment for aggravating or mitigating features, set out below.

Where there is a sufficient prospect of rehabilitation, a community order with a sex offender treatment programme requirement under section 202 of the Criminal Justice Act 2003 can be a proper alternative to a short or moderate length custodial sentence.

	A	**B**
Category 1	**Starting point** 5 years' custody **Category range** 4–10 years' custody	**Starting point** 1 year's custody **Category range** High level community order–2 years' custody
Category 2	**Starting point** 3 years' custody **Category range** 2–6 years' custody	**Starting point** 26 weeks' custody **Category range** High level community order–1 year's custody

	A	B
Category 3	**Starting point** 26 weeks' custody **Category range** High level community order–3 years' custody	**Starting point** Medium level community order **Category range** Low level community order–High level community order

The table below contains a non-exhaustive list of additional factual elements providing the context of the offence and factors relating to the offender. Identify whether any combination of these, or other relevant factors, should result in an upward or downward adjustment from the starting point. In particular, relevant recent convictions are likely to result in an upward adjustment. In some cases, having considered these factors, it may be appropriate to move outside the identified category range.

When sentencing appropriate category 2 or 3 offences, the court should also consider the custody threshold as follows:

- has the custody threshold been passed?
- if so, is it unavoidable that a custodial sentence be imposed?
- if so, can that sentence be suspended?

Aggravating factors

Statutory aggravating factors

- Previous convictions, having regard to a) the nature of the offence to which the conviction relates and its relevance to the current offence; and b) the time that has elapsed since the conviction
- Offence committed whilst on bail

Other aggravating factors

- Severe psychological or physical harm
- Ejaculation
- Pregnancy or STI as a consequence of offence
- Location of offence
- Timing of offence
- Victim compelled to leave their home or institution (including victims of domestic violence)
- Failure to comply with current court orders
- Offence committed whilst on licence
- Any steps taken to prevent the victim reporting an incident, obtaining assistance and/or from assisting or supporting the prosecution
- Attempts to dispose of or conceal evidence
- Commission of offence whilst under the influence of alcohol or drugs

Mitigating factors

- No previous convictions or no relevant/recent convictions
- Remorse
- Previous good character and/or exemplary conduct[*]
- Age and/or lack of maturity where it affects the responsibility of the offender
- Mental disorder or learning disability, particularly where linked to the commission of the offence

[*] Previous good character/exemplary conduct is different from having no previous convictions. The more serious the offence, the less the weight which should normally be attributed to this factor. Where previous good character/exemplary conduct has been used to facilitate the offence, this mitigation should not normally be allowed and such conduct may constitute an aggravating factor. In the context of this offence, previous good character/exemplary

conduct should not normally be given any significant weight and will not normally justify a reduction in what would otherwise be the appropriate sentence.

STEP THREE

Consider any factors which indicate a reduction, such as assistance to the prosecution

The court should take into account sections 73 and 74 of the Serious Organised Crime and Police Act 2005 (assistance by defendants: reduction or review of sentence) and any other rule of law by virtue of which an offender may receive a discounted sentence in consequence of assistance given (or offered) to the prosecutor or investigator.

STEP FOUR

Reduction for guilty pleas

The court should take account of any potential reduction for a guilty plea in accordance with section 144 of the Criminal Justice Act 2003 and the *Guilty Plea* guideline.

STEP FIVE

Dangerousness

The court should consider whether having regard to the criteria contained in Chapter 5 of Part 12 of the Criminal Justice Act 2003 it would be appropriate to award a life sentence (section 224A or section 225(2)) or an extended sentence (section 226A). When sentencing offenders to a life sentence under these provisions, the notional determinate sentence should be used as the basis for the setting of a minimum term.

STEP SIX

Totality principle

If sentencing an offender for more than one offence, or where the offender is already serving a sentence, consider whether the total sentence is just and proportionate to the offending behaviour.

STEP SEVEN

Ancillary orders

The court must consider whether to make any ancillary orders. The court must also consider what other requirements or provisions may *automatically* apply. Further information is included at Annex A on page 640.

STEP EIGHT

Reasons

Section 174 of the Criminal Justice Act 2003 imposes a duty to give reasons for, and explain the effect of, the sentence.

STEP NINE

Consideration for time spent on bail

The court must consider whether to give credit for time spent on bail in accordance with section 240A of the Criminal Justice Act 2003.

Engaging in sexual activity in the presence, procured by inducement, threat or deception, of a person with a mental disorder

Sexual Offences Act 2003 (section 36)

Causing a person with a mental disorder to watch a sexual act by inducement, threat or deception

Sexual Offences Act 2003 (section 37)

Triable either way

Maximum: 10 years' custody

Offence range: Community order–6 years' custody

For convictions on or after 3 December 2012 (irrespective of the date of commission of the offence), these are specified offences for the purposes of section 226A (extended sentence for certain violent or sexual offences) of the Criminal Justice Act 2003.

STEP ONE

Determining the offence category

The court should determine which categories of harm and culpability the offence falls into by reference only to the tables below.

HARM		CULPABILITY	
Category 1	• Causing victim to view extreme pornography • Causing victim to view indecent/prohibited images of children • Engaging in, or causing a victim to view live, sexual activity involving sadism/violence/sexual activity with an animal/a child	**A** • Significant degree of planning • Offender acts together with others in order to commit the offence • Use of alcohol/drugs on victim to facilitate the offence • Abuse of trust • Commercial exploitation and/or motivation • Offence racially or religiously aggravated • Offence motivated by, or demonstrating, hostility to the victim based on his or her sexual orientation (or presumed sexual orientation) or transgender identity (or presumed transgender identity) • Offence motivated by, or demonstrating, hostility to the victim based on his or her disability (or presumed disability)	**B** Factor(s) in category A not present
Category 2	Engaging in, or causing a victim to view images of or view live, sexual activity involving: • penetration of vagina or anus (using body or object) • penile penetration of mouth • masturbation		
Category 3	Factor(s) in categories 1 and 2 not present		

STEP TWO

Starting point and category range

Having determined the category of harm and culpability, the court should use the corresponding starting points to reach a sentence within the category range below. The starting point applies to all offenders irrespective of plea or previous convictions. Having determined the starting point, step two allows further adjustment for aggravating or mitigating features, set out below.

A case of particular gravity, reflected by multiple features of culpability or harm in step one, could merit upward adjustment from the starting point before further adjustment for aggravating or mitigating features, set out below.

Where there is a sufficient prospect of rehabilitation, a community order with a sex offender treatment programme requirement under section 202 of the Criminal Justice Act 2003 can be a proper alternative to a short or moderate length custodial sentence.

	A	B
Category 1	**Starting point** 4 years' custody **Category range** 3–6 years' custody	**Starting point** 2 years' custody **Category range** 1–3 years' custody
Category 2	**Starting point** 2 years' custody **Category range** 1–3 years' custody	**Starting point** 1 year's custody **Category range** High level community order–18 months' custody
Category 3	**Starting point** 26 weeks' custody **Category range** High level community order–1 year's custody	**Starting point** Medium level community order **Category range** Low level community order–Medium level community order

The table below contains a non-exhaustive list of additional factual elements providing the context of the offence and factors relating to the offender. Identify whether any combination of these, or other relevant factors, should result in an upward or downward adjustment from the starting point. In particular, relevant recent convictions are likely to result in an upward adjustment. In some cases, having considered these factors, it may be appropriate to move outside the identified category range.

When sentencing appropriate category 2 or 3 offences, the court should also consider the custody threshold as follows:

- has the custody threshold been passed?
- if so, is it unavoidable that a custodial sentence be imposed?
- if so, can that sentence be suspended?

Aggravating factors

Statutory aggravating factors

- Previous convictions, having regard to a) the nature of the offence to which the conviction relates and its relevance to the current offence; and b) the time that has elapsed since the conviction
- Offence committed whilst on bail

Other aggravating factors

- Location of offence
- Timing of offence
- Failure to comply with current court orders
- Offence committed whilst on licence
- Any steps taken to prevent the victim reporting an incident, obtaining assistance and/or from assisting or supporting the prosecution
- Attempts to dispose of or conceal evidence
- Commission of offence whilst under the influence of alcohol or drugs

Mitigating factors

- No previous convictions or no relevant/recent convictions
- Remorse
- Previous good character and/or exemplary conduct*
- Age and/or lack of maturity where it affects the responsibility of the offender
- Mental disorder or learning disability, particularly where linked to the commission of the offence
- Demonstration of steps taken to address offending behaviour

* Previous good character/exemplary conduct is different from having no previous convictions. The more serious the offence, the less the weight which should normally be attributed to this factor. Where previous good character/exemplary conduct has been used to facilitate the offence, this mitigation should not normally be allowed and such conduct may constitute an aggravating factor.

STEP THREE

Consider any factors which indicate a reduction, such as assistance to the prosecution

The court should take into account sections 73 and 74 of the Serious Organised Crime and Police Act 2005 (assistance by defendants: reduction or review of sentence) and any other rule of law by virtue of which an offender may receive a discounted sentence in consequence of assistance given (or offered) to the prosecutor or investigator.

STEP FOUR

Reduction for guilty pleas

The court should take account of any potential reduction for a guilty plea in accordance with section 144 of the Criminal Justice Act 2003 and the *Guilty Plea* guideline.

STEP FIVE

Dangerousness

The court should consider whether having regard to the criteria contained in Chapter 5 of Part 12 of the Criminal Justice Act 2003 it would be appropriate to award an extended sentence (section 226A).

STEP SIX

Totality principle

If sentencing an offender for more than one offence, or where the offender is already serving a sentence, consider whether the total sentence is just and proportionate to the offending behaviour.

STEP SEVEN

Ancillary orders

The court must consider whether to make any ancillary orders. The court must also consider what other requirements or provisions may *automatically* apply. Further information is included at Annex A on page 640.

STEP EIGHT

Reasons

Section 174 of the Criminal Justice Act 2003 imposes a duty to give reasons for, and explain the effect of, the sentence.

STEP NINE

Consideration for time spent on bail

The court must consider whether to give credit for time spent on bail in accordance with section 240A of the Criminal Justice Act 2003.

Care workers: sexual activity with a person with a mental disorder

Sexual Offences Act 2003 (section 38)

Care workers: causing or inciting sexual activity

Sexual Offences Act 2003 (section 39)

Triable only on indictment (if penetration involved)—otherwise triable either way

Maximum: 14 years' custody (if penetration involved)—otherwise 10 years' custody

Offence range: Community order–10 years' custody

For convictions on or after 3 December 2012 (irrespective of the date of commission of the offence), these are specified offences for the purposes of section 226A (extended sentence for certain violent or sexual offences) of the Criminal Justice Act 2003.

STEP ONE

Determining the offence category

The court should determine which categories of harm and culpability the offence falls into by reference only to the tables below.

THIS GUIDLINE [sic] ALSO APPLIES TO OFFENCES COMMITTED REMOTELY/ONLINE

HARM		CULPABILITY	
		A	**B**
Category 1	Penetration of vagina or anus (using body or object) Penile penetration of mouth In either case by, or of, the victim	• Significant degree of planning • Offender acts together with others to commit the offence • Use of alcohol/drugs on victim to facilitate the offence • Grooming behaviour used against victim • Use of threats (including blackmail) • Sexual images of victim recorded, retained, solicited or shared • Commercial exploitation and/or motivation • Offence racially or religiously aggravated • Offence motivated by, or demonstrating, hostility to the victim based on his or her sexual orientation (or presumed sexual orientation) or transgender identity (or presumed transgender identity) • Offence motivated by, or demonstrating, hostility to the victim based on his or her disability (or presumed disability)	Factor(s) in category A not present
Category 2	Touching, or exposure, of naked genitalia or naked breasts by, or of, the victim		
Category 3	Factor(s) in categories 1 and 2 not present		

STEP TWO

Starting point and category range

Having determined the category of harm and culpability, the court should use the corresponding starting points to reach a sentence within the category range below. The starting point applies to all offenders irrespective of plea or previous convictions. Having determined the starting point, step two allows further adjustment for aggravating or mitigating features, set out below.

A case of particular gravity, reflected by multiple features of culpability or harm in step one, could merit upward adjustment from the starting point before further adjustment for aggravating or mitigating features, set out below.

Where there is a sufficient prospect of rehabilitation, a community order with a sex offender treatment programme requirement under section 202 of the Criminal Justice Act 2003 can be a proper alternative to a short or moderate length custodial sentence.

	A	B
Category 1	**Starting point** 5 years' custody **Category range** 4–10 years' custody	**Starting point** 18 months' custody **Category range** 1–2 years' custody

	A	B
Category 2	**Starting point** 3 year's custody **Category range** 2–6 years' custody	**Starting point** 26 weeks' custody **Category range** Medium level community order–1 year's custody
Category 3	**Starting point** 26 weeks' custody **Category range** High level community order–3 years' custody	**Starting point** Medium level community order **Category range** Low level community order–High level community order

The table below contains a non-exhaustive list of additional factual elements providing the context of the offence and factors relating to the offender. Identify whether any combination of these, or other relevant factors, should result in an upward or downward adjustment from the starting point. In particular, relevant recent convictions are likely to result in an upward adjustment. In some cases, having considered these factors, it may be appropriate to move outside the identified category range.

When sentencing appropriate category 2 or 3 offences, the court should also consider the custody threshold as follows:

- has the custody threshold been passed?
- if so, is it unavoidable that a custodial sentence be imposed?
- if so, can that sentence be suspended?

Aggravating factors

Statutory aggravating factors

- Previous convictions, having regard to a) the nature of the offence to which the conviction relates and its relevance to the current offence; and b) the time that has elapsed since the conviction
- Offence committed whilst on bail

Other aggravating factors

- Ejaculation
- Pregnancy or STI as a consequence of offence
- Location of offence
- Timing of offence
- Victim compelled to leave their home or institution (including victims of domestic violence)
- Failure to comply with current court orders
- Offence committed whilst on licence

- Any steps taken to prevent the victim reporting an incident, obtaining assistance and/or from assisting or supporting the prosecution
- Attempts to dispose of or conceal evidence
- Failure of offender to respond to previous warnings
- Commission of offence whilst under the influence of alcohol or drugs

Mitigating factors

- No previous convictions or no relevant/recent convictions
- Remorse
- Previous good character and/or exemplary conduct*
- Age and/or lack of maturity where it affects the responsibility of the offender
- Mental disorder or learning disability, particularly where linked to the commission of the offence
- Sexual activity was incited but no activity took place because the offender voluntarily desisted or intervened to prevent it

* Previous good character/exemplary conduct is different from having no previous convictions. The more serious the offence, the less the weight which should normally be attributed to this factor. Where previous good character/exemplary conduct has been used to facilitate the offence, this mitigation should not normally be allowed and such conduct may constitute an aggravating factor. In the context of this offence, previous good character/exemplary conduct should not normally be given any significant weight and will not normally justify a reduction in what would otherwise be the appropriate sentence.

STEP THREE

Consider any factors which indicate a reduction, such as assistance to the prosecution

The court should take into account sections 73 and 74 of the Serious Organised Crime and Police Act 2005 (assistance by defendants: reduction or review of sentence) and any other rule of law by virtue of which an offender may receive a discounted sentence in consequence of assistance given (or offered) to the prosecutor or investigator.

STEP FOUR

Reduction for guilty pleas

The court should take account of any potential reduction for a guilty plea in accordance with section 144 of the Criminal Justice Act 2003 and the *Guilty Plea* guideline.

STEP FIVE

Dangerousness

The court should consider whether having regard to the criteria contained in Chapter 5 of Part 12 of the Criminal Justice Act 2003 it would be appropriate to award an extended sentence (section 226A).

STEP SIX

Totality principle

If sentencing an offender for more than one offence, or where the offender is already serving a sentence, consider whether the total sentence is just and proportionate to the offending behaviour.

STEP SEVEN

Ancillary orders

The court must consider whether to make any ancillary orders. The court must also consider what other requirements or provisions may *automatically* apply. Further information is included at Annex A on page 640.

STEP EIGHT

Reasons

Section 174 of the Criminal Justice Act 2003 imposes a duty to give reasons for, and explain the effect of, the sentence.

STEP NINE

Consideration for time spent on bail

The court must consider whether to give credit for time spent on bail in accordance with section 240A of the Criminal Justice Act 2003.

Care workers: sexual activity in the presence of a person with a mental disorder
Sexual Offences Act 2003 (section 40)
Care workers: causing a person with a mental disorder to watch a sexual act
Sexual Offences Act 2003 (section 41)
Triable either way
Maximum: 7 years' custody
Offence range: Community order–2 years' custody

For convictions on or after 3 December 2012 (irrespective of the date of commission of the offence), these are specified offences for the purposes of section 226A (extended sentence for certain violent or sexual offences) of the Criminal Justice Act 2003.

STEP ONE

Determining the offence category

The court should determine which categories of harm and culpability the offence falls into by reference only to the tables below.

HARM	CULPABILITY

HARM	
Category 1	• Causing victim to view extreme pornography • Causing victim to view indecent/prohibited images of children • Engaging in, or causing a victim to view live, sexual activity involving sadism/violence/sexual activity with an animal/a child
Category 2	Engaging in, or causing a victim to view images of or view live, sexual activity involving: • penetration of vagina or anus (using body or object) • penile penetration of mouth • masturbation
Category 3	Factor(s) in categories 1 and 2 not present

A	B
• Significant degree of planning • Offender acts together with others to commit the offence • Use of alcohol/drugs on victim to facilitate the offence • Grooming behaviour used against victim • Use of threats (including blackmail) • Commercial exploitation and/or motivation • Offence racially or religiously aggravated • Offence motivated by, or demonstrating, hostility to the victim based on his or her sexual orientation (or presumed sexual orientation) or transgender identity (or presumed transgender identity) • Offence motivated by, or demonstrating, hostility to the victim based on his or her disability (or presumed disability)	Factor(s) in category A not present

STEP TWO

Starting point and category range

Having determined the category of harm and culpability, the court should use the corresponding starting points to reach a sentence within the category range below. The starting point applies to all offenders irrespective of plea or previous convictions. Having determined the starting point, step two allows further adjustment for aggravating or mitigating features, set out below.

A case of particular gravity, reflected by multiple features of culpability or harm in step one, could merit upward adjustment from the starting point before further adjustment for aggravating or mitigating features, set out below.

Where there is a sufficient prospect of rehabilitation, a community order with a sex offender treatment programme requirement under section 202 of the Criminal Justice Act 2003 can be a proper alternative to a short or moderate length custodial sentence.

	A	B
Category 1	**Starting point** 18 months' custody **Category range** 1–2 years' custody	**Starting point** 1 year's custody **Category range** 26 weeks'–18 months' custody

	A	B
Category 2	**Starting point** 1 year's custody **Category range** 26 weeks'–18 months' custody	**Starting point** 26 weeks' custody **Category range** High level community order–1 year's custody
Category 3	**Starting point** 26 weeks' custody **Category range** High level community order–1 year's custody	**Starting point** Medium level community order **Category range** Low level community order–High level community order

The table below contains a non-exhaustive list of additional factual elements providing the context of the offence and factors relating to the offender. Identify whether any combination of these, or other relevant factors, should result in an upward or downward adjustment from the starting point. In particular, relevant recent convictions are likely to result in an upward adjustment. In some cases, having considered these factors, it may be appropriate to move outside the identified category range.

When sentencing appropriate category 2 or 3 offences, the court should also consider the custody threshold as follows:

- has the custody threshold been passed?
- if so, is it unavoidable that a custodial sentence be imposed?
- if so, can that sentence be suspended?

Aggravating factors

Statutory aggravating factors

- Previous convictions, having regard to a) the nature of the offence to which the conviction relates and its relevance to the current offence; and b) the time that has elapsed since the conviction
- Offence committed whilst on bail

Other aggravating factors

- Location of the offence
- Timing of the offence
- Any steps taken to prevent the victim reporting an incident, obtaining assistance and/or from assisting or supporting the prosecution
- Failure to comply with current court orders
- Offence committed whilst on licence
- Commission of offence whilst under the influence of alcohol or drugs
- Presence of others, especially children

Mitigating factors

- No previous convictions or no relevant/recent convictions
- Remorse
- Previous good character and/or exemplary conduct*
- Age and/or lack of maturity where it affects the responsibility of the offender
- Mental disorder or learning disability, particularly where linked to the commission of the offence
- Demonstration of steps taken to address offending behaviour

* Previous good character/exemplary conduct is different from having no previous convictions. The more serious the offence, the less the weight which should normally be attributed to this factor. Where previous good character/exemplary conduct has been used to facilitate the offence, this mitigation should not normally be allowed and such conduct may constitute an aggravating factor.

STEP THREE

Consider any factors which indicate a reduction, such as assistance to the prosecution

The court should take into account sections 73 and 74 of the Serious Organised Crime and Police Act 2005 (assistance by defendants: reduction or review of sentence) and any other rule of law by virtue of which an offender may receive a discounted sentence in consequence of assistance given (or offered) to the prosecutor or investigator.

STEP FOUR

Reduction for guilty pleas

The court should take account of any potential reduction for a guilty plea in accordance with section 144 of the Criminal Justice Act 2003 and the *Guilty Plea* guideline.

STEP FIVE

Dangerousness

The court should consider whether having regard to the criteria contained in Chapter 5 of Part 12 of the Criminal Justice Act 2003 it would be appropriate to award an extended sentence (section 226A).

STEP SIX

Totality principle

If sentencing an offender for more than one offence, or where the offender is already serving a sentence, consider whether the total sentence is just and proportionate to the offending behaviour.

STEP SEVEN

Ancillary orders

The court must consider whether to make any ancillary orders. The court must also consider what other requirements or provisions may *automatically* apply. Further information is included at Annex A on page 640.

STEP EIGHT

Reasons

Section 174 of the Criminal Justice Act 2003 imposes a duty to give reasons for, and explain the effect of, the sentence.

STEP NINE

Consideration for time spent on bail

The court must consider whether to give credit for time spent on bail in accordance with section 240A of the Criminal Justice Act 2003.

Exposure

Sexual Offences Act 2003 (section 66)

Triable either way

Maximum: 2 years' custody

Offence range: Fine–1 year's custody

For convictions on or after 3 December 2012 (irrespective of the date of commission of the offence), this is a specified offence for the purposes of section 226A (extended sentence for certain violent or sexual offences) of the Criminal Justice Act 2003.

STEP ONE

Determining the offence category

The court should determine the offence category using the table below.

The court should determine culpability and harm caused or intended, by reference only to the factors below, which comprise the principal factual elements of the offence. Where an offence does not fall squarely into a category, individual factors may require a degree of weighting before making an overall assessment and determining the appropriate offence category.

Category 1	Raised harm and raised culpability
Category 2	Raised harm or raised culpability
Category 3	Exposure without raised harm or culpability factors present

Factors indicating raised harm
• Victim followed/pursued
• Offender masturbated

Factors indicating raised culpability
- Specific or previous targeting of a particularly vulnerable victim
- Abuse of trust
- Use of threats (including blackmail)
- Offence racially or religiously aggravated
- Offence motivated by, or demonstrating, hostility to the victim based on his or her sexual orientation (or presumed sexual orientation) or transgender identity (or presumed transgender identity)
- Offence motivated by, or demonstrating, hostility to the victim based on his or her disability (or presumed disability)

STEP TWO

Starting point and category range

Having determined the category, the court should use the corresponding starting points to reach a sentence within the category range below. The starting point applies to all offenders irrespective of plea or previous convictions. Having determined the starting point, step two allows further adjustment for aggravating or mitigating features, set out below.

A case of particular gravity, reflected by multiple features of culpability or harm in step one, could merit upward adjustment from the starting point before further adjustment for aggravating or mitigating features, set out below.

Where there is a sufficient prospect of rehabilitation, a community order with a sex offender treatment programme requirement under section 202 of the Criminal Justice Act 2003 can be a proper alternative to a short or moderate length custodial sentence.

Category 1	**Starting point** 26 weeks' custody **Category range** 12 weeks'–1 year's custody
Category 2	**Starting point** High level community order **Category range** Medium level community order–26 weeks' custody
Category 3	**Starting point** Medium level community order **Category range** Band A fine–High level community order

The table below contains a non-exhaustive list of additional factual elements providing the context of the offence and factors relating to the offender. Identify whether any combination of these, or other relevant factors, should result in an upward or downward adjustment from the starting point. In particular, relevant recent convictions are likely to result in an upward adjustment. In some cases, having considered these factors, it may be appropriate to move outside the identified category range.

When sentencing category 2 offences, the court should also consider the custody threshold as follows:

- has the custody threshold been passed?
- if so, is it unavoidable that a custodial sentence be imposed?
- if so, can that sentence be suspended?

When sentencing category 3 offences, the court should also consider the community order threshold as follows:

- has the community order threshold been passed?

Aggravating factors

Statutory aggravating factors

- Previous convictions, having regard to a) the nature of the offence to which the conviction relates and its relevance to the current offence; and b) the time that has elapsed since the conviction
- Offence committed whilst on bail

Other aggravating factors

- Location of offence
- Timing of offence
- Failure to comply with current court orders
- Offence committed whilst on licence
- Any steps taken to prevent the victim reporting an incident, obtaining assistance and/or from assisting or supporting the prosecution
- Attempts to dispose of or conceal evidence
- Failure of offender to respond to previous warnings
- Commission of offence whilst under the influence of alcohol or drugs

---

Mitigating factors

- No previous convictions or no relevant/recent convictions
- Remorse
- Previous good character and/or exemplary conduct*
- Age and/or lack of maturity where it affects the responsibility of the offender
- Mental disorder or learning disability, particularly where linked to the commission of the offence
- Demonstration of steps taken to address offending behaviour

* Previous good character/exemplary conduct is different from having no previous convictions. The more serious the offence, the less the weight which should normally be attributed to this factor. Where previous good character/exemplary conduct has been used to facilitate the offence, this mitigation should not normally be allowed and such conduct may constitute an aggravating factor.

STEP THREE

Consider any factors which indicate a reduction, such as assistance to the prosecution

The court should take into account sections 73 and 74 of the Serious Organised Crime and Police Act 2005 (assistance by defendants: reduction or review of sentence) and any other rule of law by virtue of which an offender may receive a discounted sentence in consequence of assistance given (or offered) to the prosecutor or investigator.

STEP FOUR

Reduction for guilty pleas

The court should take account of any potential reduction for a guilty plea in accordance with section 144 of the Criminal Justice Act 2003 and the *Guilty Plea* guideline.

STEP FIVE

Dangerousness

The court should consider whether having regard to the criteria contained in Chapter 5 of Part 12 of the Criminal Justice Act 2003 it would be appropriate to award an extended sentence (section 226A).

STEP SIX

Totality principle

If sentencing an offender for more than one offence, or where the offender is already serving a sentence, consider whether the total sentence is just and proportionate to the offending behaviour.

STEP SEVEN

Ancillary orders

The court must consider whether to make any ancillary orders. The court must also consider what other requirements or provisions may *automatically* apply. Further information is included at Annex A on page 640.

STEP EIGHT

Reasons

Section 174 of the Criminal Justice Act 2003 imposes a duty to give reasons for, and explain the effect of, the sentence.

STEP NINE

Consideration for time spent on bail

The court must consider whether to give credit for time spent on bail in accordance with section 240A of the Criminal Justice Act 2003.

Voyeurism

Sexual Offences Act 2003 (section 67)

Triable either way

Maximum: 2 years' custody

Offence range: Fine–18 months' custody

For convictions on or after such date (irrespective of the date of commission of the offence), these are specified offences for the purposes of section 226A (extended sentence for certain violent or sexual offences) of the Criminal Justice Act 2003.

STEP ONE

Determining the offence category

The court should determine the offence category using the table below.

Category 1	Raised harm and raised culpability
Category 2	Raised harm or raised culpability
Category 3	Voyeurism without raised harm or culpability factors present

The court should determine culpability and harm caused or intended, by reference only to the factors below, which comprise the principal factual elements of the offence. Where an offence does not fall squarely into a category, individual factors may require a degree of weighting before making an overall assessment and determining the appropriate offence category.

Factors indicating raised harm

- Image(s) available to be viewed by others
- Victim observed or recorded in their own home or residence

Factors indicating raised culpability

- Significant degree of planning
- Image(s) recorded
- Abuse of trust
- Specific or previous targeting of a particularly vulnerable victim
- Commercial exploitation and/or motivation
- Offence racially or religiously aggravated
- Offence motivated by, or demonstrating, hostility to the victim based on his or her sexual orientation (or presumed sexual orientation) or transgender identity (or presumed transgender identity)
- Offence motivated by, or demonstrating, hostility to the victim based on his or her disability (or presumed disability)

STEP TWO

Starting point and category range

Having determined the category, the court should use the corresponding starting points to reach a sentence within the category range below. The starting point applies to all offenders irrespective of plea or previous convictions. Having determined the starting point, step two allows further adjustment for aggravating or mitigating features, set out below.

A case of particular gravity, reflected by multiple features of culpability or harm in step one, could merit upward adjustment from the starting point before further adjustment for aggravating or mitigating features, set out below.

Where there is a sufficient prospect of rehabilitation, a community order with a sex offender treatment programme requirement under section 202 of the Criminal Justice Act 2003 can be a proper alternative to a short or moderate length custodial sentence.

Category 1	**Starting point** 26 weeks' custody **Category range** 12 weeks'–18 months' custody
Category 2	**Starting point** High level community order **Category range** Medium level community order–26 weeks' custody
Category 3	**Starting point** Medium level community order **Category range** Band A fine–High level community order

The table below contains a non-exhaustive list of additional factual elements providing the context of the offence and factors relating to the offender. Identify whether any combination of these, or other relevant factors, should result in an upward or downward adjustment from the starting point. In particular, relevant recent convictions are likely to result in an upward adjustment. In some cases, having considered these factors, it may be appropriate to move outside the identified category range.

When sentencing category 2 offences, the court should also consider the custody threshold as follows:

- has the custody threshold been passed?
- if so, is it unavoidable that a custodial sentence be imposed?
- if so, can that sentence be suspended?

When sentencing category 3 offences, the court should also consider the community order threshold as follows:

- has the community order threshold been passed?

Aggravating factors

Statutory aggravating factors

- Previous convictions, having regard to a) the nature of the offence to which the conviction relates and its relevance to the current offence; and b) the time that has elapsed since the conviction
- Offence committed whilst on bail

Other aggravating factors

- Location of offence
- Timing of offence
- Failure to comply with current court orders
- Offence committed whilst on licence
- Distribution of images, whether or not for gain
- Placing images where there is the potential for a high volume of viewers
- Period over which victim observed
- Period over which images were made or distributed
- Any steps taken to prevent victim reporting an incident, obtaining assistance and/or from assisting or supporting the prosecution
- Attempts to dispose of or conceal evidence

Mitigating factors
- No previous convictions or no relevant/recent convictions
- Remorse
- Previous good character and/or exemplary conduct*
- Age and/or lack of maturity where it affects the responsibility of the offender
- Mental disorder or learning disability, particularly where linked to the commission of the offence
- Demonstration of steps taken to address offending behaviour

* Previous good character/exemplary conduct is different from having no previous convictions. The more serious the offence, the less the weight which should normally be attributed to this factor. Where previous good character/exemplary conduct has been used to facilitate the offence, this mitigation should not normally be allowed and such conduct may constitute an aggravating factor.

STEP THREE

Consider any factors which indicate a reduction, such as assistance to the prosecution

The court should take into account sections 73 and 74 of the Serious Organised Crime and Police Act 2005 (assistance by defendants: reduction or review of sentence) and any other rule of law by virtue of which an offender may receive a discounted sentence in consequence of assistance given (or offered) to the prosecutor or investigator.

STEP FOUR

Reduction for guilty pleas

The court should take account of any potential reduction for a guilty plea in accordance with section 144 of the Criminal Justice Act 2003 and the *Guilty Plea* guideline.

STEP FIVE

Dangerousness

The court should consider whether having regard to the criteria contained in Chapter 5 of Part 12 of the Criminal Justice Act 2003 it would be appropriate to award an extended sentence (section 226A).

STEP SIX

Totality principle

If sentencing an offender for more than one offence, or where the offender is already serving a sentence, consider whether the total sentence is just and proportionate to the offending behaviour.

STEP SEVEN

Ancillary orders

The court must consider whether to make any ancillary orders. The court must also consider what other requirements or provisions may *automatically* apply. Further information is included at Annex A on page 640.

STEP EIGHT

Reasons

Section 174 of the Criminal Justice Act 2003 imposes a duty to give reasons for, and explain the effect of, the sentence.

STEP NINE

Consideration for time spent on bail

The court must consider whether to give credit for time spent on bail in accordance with section 240A of the Criminal Justice Act 2003.

Sex with an adult relative: penetration

Sexual Offences Act 2003 (section 64)

Sex with an adult relative: consenting to penetration

Sexual Offences Act 2003 (section 65)

Triable either way

Maximum: 2 years' custody

Offence range: Fine–2 years' custody

For convictions on or after 3 December 2012 (irrespective of the date of commission of the offence), these are specified offences for the purposes of section 226A (extended sentence for certain violent or sexual offences) of the Criminal Justice Act 2003.

STEP ONE

Determining the offence category

The court should determine the offence category using the table below.

Category 1	Raised harm and raised culpability
Category 2	Raised harm or raised culpability
Category 3	Sex with an adult relative without raised harm or culpability factors present

The court should determine culpability and harm caused or intended, by reference only to the factors below, which comprise the principal factual elements of the offence. Where an offence does not fall squarely into a category, individual factors may require a degree of weighting before making an overall assessment and determining the appropriate offence category.

Factors indicating raised harm

- Victim is particularly vulnerable due to personal circumstances
- Child conceived

Factors indicating raised culpability

- Grooming behaviour used against victim
- Use of threats (including blackmail)

STEP TWO

Starting point and category range

Having determined the category, the court should use the corresponding starting points to reach a sentence within the category range below. The starting point applies to all offenders irrespective of plea or previous convictions. Having determined the starting point, step two allows further adjustment for aggravating or mitigating features, set out below.

A case of particular gravity, reflected by multiple features of culpability or harm in step one, could merit upward adjustment from the starting point before further adjustment for aggravating or mitigating features, set out below.

Where there is a sufficient prospect of rehabilitation, a community order with a sex offender treatment programme requirement under section 202 of the Criminal Justice Act 2003 can be a proper alternative to a short or moderate length custodial sentence.

Category 1	**Starting point** 1 year's custody **Category range** 26 weeks'- 2 years' custody
Category 2	**Starting point** High level community order **Category range** Medium level community order–1 year's custody
Category 3	**Starting point** Medium level community order **Category range** Band A fine–High level community order

The table below contains a non-exhaustive list of additional factual elements providing the context of the offence and factors relating to the offender. Identify whether any combination of these, or other relevant factors, should result in an upward or downward adjustment from the starting point. In particular, relevant recent convictions are likely to result in an upward adjustment. In some cases, having considered these factors, it may be appropriate to move outside the identified category range.

When sentencing category 2 offences, the court should also consider the custody threshold as follows:

- has the custody threshold been passed?
- if so, is it unavoidable that a custodial sentence be imposed?
- if so, can that sentence be suspended?

When sentencing category 3 offences, the court should also consider the community order threshold as follows:

- has the community order threshold been passed?

Aggravating factors

Statutory aggravating factors

- Previous convictions, having regard to a) the nature of the offence to which the conviction relates and its relevance to the current offence; and b) the time that has elapsed since the conviction
- Offence committed whilst on bail

Other aggravating factors

- Failure to comply with current court orders
- Offence committed whilst on licence
- Failure of offender to respond to previous warnings
- Any steps taken to prevent reporting an incident, obtaining assistance and/or from assisting or supporting the prosecution
- Attempts to dispose of or conceal evidence

Mitigating factors

- No previous convictions or no relevant/recent convictions
- Remorse
- Previous good character and/or exemplary conduct*
- Age and/or lack of maturity where it affects the responsibility of the offender
- Mental disorder or learning disability, particularly where linked to the commission of the offence
- Demonstration of steps taken to address offending behaviour

* Previous good character/exemplary conduct is different from having no previous convictions. The more serious the offence, the less the weight which should normally be attributed to this factor. Where previous good character/exemplary conduct has been used to facilitate the offence, this mitigation should not normally be allowed and such conduct may constitute an aggravating factor.

STEP THREE

Consider any factors which indicate a reduction, such as assistance to the prosecution

The court should take into account sections 73 and 74 of the Serious Organised Crime and Police Act 2005 (assistance by defendants: reduction or review of sentence) and any other rule of law by virtue of which an offender may receive a discounted sentence in consequence of assistance given (or offered) to the prosecutor or investigator.

STEP FOUR

Reduction for guilty pleas

The court should take account of any potential reduction for a guilty plea in accordance with section 144 of the Criminal Justice Act 2003 and the *Guilty Plea* guideline.

STEP FIVE

Dangerousness

The court should consider whether having regard to the criteria contained in Chapter 5 of Part 12 of the Criminal Justice Act 2003 it would be appropriate to award an extended sentence (section 226A).

STEP SIX

Totality principle

If sentencing an offender for more than one offence, or where the offender is already serving a sentence, consider whether the total sentence is just and proportionate to the offending behaviour.

STEP SEVEN

Ancillary orders

The court must consider whether to make any ancillary orders. The court must also consider what other requirements or provisions may *automatically* apply. Further information is included at Annex A on page 640.

STEP EIGHT

Reasons

Section 174 of the Criminal Justice Act 2003 imposes a duty to give reasons for, and explain the effect of, the sentence.

STEP NINE

Consideration for time spent on bail

The court must consider whether to give credit for time spent on bail in accordance with section 240A of the Criminal Justice Act 2003.

Administering a substance with intent

Sexual Offences Act 2003 (section 61)

Triable either way

Maximum: 10 years' custody

Offence range: 1–9 years' custody

For convictions on or after 3 December 2012 (irrespective of the date of commission of the offence), this is a specified offence for the purposes of section 226A (extended sentence for certain violent or sexual offences) of the Criminal Justice Act 2003.

STEP ONE

Determining the offence category

The court should determine the offence category using the table below.

Category 1	Raised harm and raised culpability
Category 2	Raised harm or raised culpability
Category 3	Administering a substance with intent without raised harm or culpability factors present

The court should determine culpability and harm caused or intended, by reference only to the factors below, which comprise the principal factual elements of the offence. Where an offence does not fall squarely into a category, individual factors may require a degree of weighting before making an overall assessment and determining the appropriate offence category. Where no substantive sexual offence has been committed the main consideration for the court will be the offender's conduct as a whole including, but not exclusively, the offender's intention.

Factors indicating raised harm

- Severe psychological or physical harm
- Prolonged detention/sustained incident
- Additional degradation/humiliation

Factors indicating raised culpability

- Significant degree of planning
- Specific targeting of a particularly vulnerable victim
- Intended sexual offence carries a statutory maximum of life
- Abuse of trust
- Recording of offence
- Offender acts together with others to commit the offence
- Commercial exploitation and/or motivation
- Offence racially or religiously aggravated
- Offence motivated by, or demonstrating, hostility to the victim based on his or her sexual orientation (or presumed sexual orientation) or transgender identity (or presumed transgender identity)
- Offence motivated by, or demonstrating, hostility to the victim based on his or her disability (or presumed disability)

STEP TWO

Starting point and category range

Having determined the category, the court should use the corresponding starting points to reach a sentence within the category range below. The starting point applies to all offenders irrespective of plea or previous convictions. Having determined the starting point, step two allows further adjustment for aggravating or mitigating features, set out below.

A case of particular gravity, reflected by multiple features of culpability or harm in step one, could merit upward adjustment from the starting point before further adjustment for aggravating or mitigating features, set out below.

Category 1	**Starting point** 6 years' custody **Category range** 4–9 years' custody
Category 2	**Starting point** 4 years' custody **Category range** 3–7 years' custody
Category 3	**Starting point** 2 years' custody **Category range** 1–5 years' custody

The table below contains a non-exhaustive list of additional factual elements providing the context of the offence and factors relating to the offender. Identify whether any combination of these, or other relevant factors, should result in an upward or downward adjustment from the starting point. In particular, relevant recent convictions are likely to result in an upward adjustment. In some cases, having considered these factors, it may be appropriate to move outside the identified category range.

Aggravating factors

Statutory aggravating factors

- Previous convictions, having regard to a) the nature of the offence to which the conviction relates and its relevance to the current offence; and b) the time that has elapsed since the conviction
- Offence committed whilst on bail

Other aggravating factors

- Location of offence
- Timing of offence
- Any steps taken to prevent reporting an incident, obtaining assistance and/or from assisting or supporting the prosecution
- Attempts to dispose of or conceal evidence
- Failure to comply with current court orders
- Offence committed whilst on licence

Mitigating factors

- No previous convictions or no relevant/recent convictions
- Remorse
- Previous good character and/or exemplary conduct*
- Age and/or lack of maturity where it affects the responsibility of the offender
- Mental disorder or learning disability, particularly where linked to the commission of the offence
- Demonstration of steps taken to address offending behaviour

* Previous good character/exemplary conduct is different from having no previous convictions. The more serious the offence, the less the weight which should normally be attributed to this factor. Where previous good character/exemplary conduct has been used to facilitate the offence, this mitigation should not normally be allowed and such conduct may constitute an aggravating factor.

STEP THREE

Consider any factors which indicate a reduction, such as assistance to the prosecution

The court should take into account sections 73 and 74 of the Serious Organised Crime and Police Act 2005 (assistance by defendants: reduction or review of sentence) and any other rule of law by virtue of which an offender may receive a discounted sentence in consequence of assistance given (or offered) to the prosecutor or investigator.

STEP FOUR

Reduction for guilty pleas

The court should take account of any potential reduction for a guilty plea in accordance with section 144 of the Criminal Justice Act 2003 and the *Guilty Plea* guideline.

STEP FIVE

Dangerousness

The court should consider whether having regard to the criteria contained in Chapter 5 of Part 12 of the Criminal Justice Act 2003 it would be appropriate to award an extended sentence (section 226A).

STEP SIX

Totality principle

If sentencing an offender for more than one offence, or where the offender is already serving a sentence, consider whether the total sentence is just and proportionate to the offending behaviour.

STEP SEVEN

Ancillary orders

The court must consider whether to make any ancillary orders. The court must also consider what other requirements or provisions may *automatically* apply. Further information is included at Annex A on page 640.

STEP EIGHT

Reasons

Section 174 of the Criminal Justice Act 2003 imposes a duty to give reasons for, and explain the effect of, the sentence.

STEP NINE

Consideration for time spent on bail

The court must consider whether to give credit for time spent on bail in accordance with section 240A of the Criminal Justice Act 2003.

Committing an offence with intent to commit a sexual offence

Sexual Offences Act 2003 (section 62)

Triable only on indictment (if kidnapping or false imprisonment committed)

—otherwise, triable either way

Maximum: Life imprisonment (if kidnapping or false imprisonment committed)

—otherwise, 10 years

This is a serious specified offence for the purposes of section 224 and, where kidnapping or false imprisonment was committed, section 225(2) (life sentence for serious offences) of the Criminal Justice Act 2003.

For offences committed by kidnapping or false imprisonment, on or after 3 December 2012, this is an offence listed in Part 1 of Schedule 15B for the purposes of sections 224A (life sentence for second listed offence) of the Criminal Justice Act 2003.

For convictions on or after 3 December 2012 (irrespective of the date of commission of the offence), this is a specified offence for the purposes of section 226A (extended sentence for certain violent or sexual offences) of the Criminal Justice Act 2003.

> The starting point and range should be commensurate with that for the preliminary offence actually committed, but with an enhancement to reflect the intention to commit a sexual offence.
>
> The enhancement will vary depending on the nature and seriousness of the intended sexual offence, but 2 years is suggested as a suitable enhancement where the intent was to commit rape or assault by penetration.

Trespass with intent to commit a sexual offence

Sexual Offences Act 2003 (section 63)

Triable either way

Maximum: 10 years' custody

Offence range: 1–9 years' custody

For convictions on or after 3 December 2012 (irrespective of the date of commission of the offence), this is a specified offence for the purposes of section 226A (extended sentence for certain violent or sexual offences) of the Criminal Justice Act 2003.

STEP ONE

Determining the offence category

The court should determine the offence category using the table below.

Category 1	Raised harm and raised culpability
Category 2	Raised harm or raised culpability
Category 3	Trespass with intent to commit a sexual offence without raised harm or culpability factors present

The court should determine culpability and harm caused or intended, by reference only to the factors below, which comprise the principal factual elements of the offence. Where an offence does not fall squarely into a category, individual factors may require a degree of weighting before making an overall assessment and determining the appropriate offence category. Where no substantive sexual offence has been committed the main consideration for the court will be the offender's conduct as a whole including, but not exclusively, the offender's intention.

Factors indicating raised harm

- Prolonged detention/sustained incident
- Additional degradation/humiliation
- Offence committed in victim's home

Factors indicating raised culpability

- Significant degree of planning
- Specific targeting of a particularly vulnerable victim
- Intended sexual offence attracts a statutory maximum of life imprisonment
- Possession of weapon or other item to frighten or injure
- Abuse of trust
- Offender acts together with others to commit the offence
- Commercial exploitation and/or motivation
- Offence racially or religiously aggravated
- Offence motivated by, or demonstrating, hostility to the victim based on his or her sexual orientation (or presumed sexual orientation) or transgender identity (or presumed transgender identity)
- Offence motivated by, or demonstrating, hostility to the victim based on his or her disability (or presumed disability)

STEP TWO

Starting point and category range

Having determined the category, the court should use the corresponding starting points to reach a sentence within the category range below. The starting point applies to all offenders irrespective of plea or previous convictions. Having determined the starting point, step two allows further adjustment for aggravating or mitigating features, set out below.

A case of particular gravity, reflected by multiple features of culpability or harm in step one, could merit upward adjustment from the starting point before further adjustment for aggravating or mitigating features, set out below.

Category 1	**Starting point** 6 years' custody **Category range** 4–9 years' custody
Category 2	**Starting point** 4 years' custody **Category range** 3–7 years' custody
Category 3	**Starting point** 2 years' custody **Category range** 1–5 years' custody

The table below contains a non-exhaustive list of additional factual elements providing the context of the offence and factors relating to the offender. Identify whether any combination of these, or other relevant factors, should result in an upward or downward adjustment from the starting point. In particular, relevant recent convictions are likely to result in an upward adjustment. In some cases, having considered these factors, it may be appropriate to move outside the identified category range.

Aggravating factors

Statutory aggravating factors

- Previous convictions, having regard to a) the nature of the offence to which the conviction relates and its relevance to the current offence; and b) the time that has elapsed since the conviction
- Offence committed whilst on bail

Other aggravating factors

- Location of offence
- Timing of offence
- Any steps taken to prevent reporting an incident, obtaining assistance and/or from assisting or supporting the prosecution
- Attempts to dispose of or conceal evidence
- Failure to comply with current court orders
- Offence committed whilst on licence

Mitigating factors

- No previous convictions or no relevant/recent convictions
- Remorse
- Previous good character and/or exemplary conduct*
- Age and/or lack of maturity where it affects the responsibility of the offender
- Mental disorder or learning disability, particularly where linked to the commission of the offence
- Demonstration of steps taken to address offending behaviour

* Previous good character/exemplary conduct is different from having no previous convictions. The more serious the offence, the less the weight which should normally be attributed to this factor. Where previous good character/exemplary conduct has been used to facilitate the offence, this mitigation should not normally be allowed and such conduct may constitute an aggravating factor.

STEP THREE

Consider any factors which indicate a reduction, such as assistance to the prosecution

The court should take into account sections 73 and 74 of the Serious Organised Crime and Police Act 2005 (assistance by defendants: reduction or review of sentence) and any other rule of law by virtue of which an offender may receive a discounted sentence in consequence of assistance given (or offered) to the prosecutor or investigator.

STEP FOUR

Reduction for guilty pleas

The court should take account of any potential reduction for a guilty plea in accordance with section 144 of the Criminal Justice Act 2003 and the *Guilty Plea* guideline.

STEP FIVE

Dangerousness

The court should consider whether having regard to the criteria contained in Chapter 5 of Part 12 of the Criminal Justice Act 2003 it would be appropriate to award an extended sentence (section 226A).

STEP SIX

Totality principle

If sentencing an offender for more than one offence, or where the offender is already serving a sentence, consider whether the total sentence is just and proportionate to the offending behaviour.

STEP SEVEN

Ancillary orders

The court must consider whether to make any ancillary orders. The court must also consider what other requirements or provisions may *automatically* apply. Further information is included at Annex A on page 640.

STEP EIGHT

Reasons

Section 174 of the Criminal Justice Act 2003 imposes a duty to give reasons for, and explain the effect of, the sentence.

STEP NINE

Consideration for time spent on bail

The court must consider whether to give credit for time spent on bail in accordance with section 240A of the Criminal Justice Act 2003.

Child sex offences committed by children or young persons (sections 9–12) (offender under 18)

Sexual Offences Act 2003 (section 13)

Sexual activity with a child family member (offender under 18)

Sexual Offences Act 2003 (section 25)

Inciting a child family member to engage in sexual activity (offender under 18)

Sexual Offences Act 2003 (section 26)

Triable either way

Maximum: 5 years' custody

These are 'grave crimes' for the purposes of section 91 of the Powers of Criminal Courts (Sentencing) Act 2000.

For convictions on or after 3 December 2012 (irrespective of the date of commission of the offence), these are specified offences for the purposes of section 226B (extended sentence for certain violent or sexual offences: persons under 18) of the Criminal Justice Act 2003.

> Definitive guidelines for the sentencing of offenders under 18 years old are **not** included. When sentencing offenders under 18, a court must in particular:
>
> - follow the definitive guideline **Overarching Principles—Sentencing Youths**;
>
> and have regard to:
> - the principal aim of the youth justice system (to prevent offending by children and young people); and
> - the welfare of the young offender.

Annex A

Ancillary orders

This summary of the key provisions is correct as at the date of publication but will be subject to subsequent changes in law. If necessary, seek legal advice.

Ancillary order	Statutory reference
Compensation The court must consider making a compensation order in any case in which personal injury, loss or damage has resulted from the offence. The court must give reasons if it decides not to make an order in such cases.	Section 130 of the Powers of Criminal Courts (Sentencing) Act 2000
Confiscation A confiscation order may be made by the Crown Court in circumstances in which the offender has obtained a financial benefit as a result of, or in connection with, his criminal conduct.	Section 6 and Schedule 2 of the Proceeds of Crime Act 2002
Deprivation of property The court may order the offender is deprived of property used for the purpose of committing, or facilitating the commission of, any offence, or intended for that purpose.	Section 143 of the Powers of Criminal Courts (Sentencing) Act 2000
Disqualification from working with children From 17 June 2013 courts no longer have the power to disqualify offenders from working with children pursuant to the Criminal Justice and Court Services Act 2000.	Schedule 10 of the Safeguarding Vulnerable Groups Act 2006 Safeguarding Vulnerable Groups Act 2006 (Commencement No 8 and Saving) Order 2012 (SI 2012/2231) Protection of Freedoms Act 2012 (Commencement No 6) Order 2013 (SI 2013/1180)

Ancillary order	Statutory reference
Restraining order Following a conviction *or an acquittal*, a court may make a restraining order for the purpose of protecting the victim or another person from harassment or a fear of violence.	Sections 5 and 5A of the Protection from Harassment Act 1997
Serious crime prevention order (SCPO) An SCPO may be made by the Crown Court in respect of qualifying offenders, if the court is satisfied such an order would protect the public by preventing, restricting or disrupting the involvement of the offender in serious crime.	Section 19 and Schedule 1 of the Serious Crime Act 2007
Sexual offences prevention order (SOPO) A SOPO may be made against qualifying offenders if the court is satisfied such an order is necessary to protect the public or any particular member of the public from serious sexual harm from the offender. The terms of the SOPO must be proportionate to the objective of protecting the public and consistent with the sentence and other ancillary orders, conditions and requirements to which the offender is subject.	Section 104 and Schedules 3 and 5 of the Sexual Offences Act 2003

Automatic orders on conviction

The following requirements or provisions are not part of the sentence imposed by the court but apply automatically by operation of law. The role of the court is to inform the offender of the applicable requirements and/or prohibition.

Requirement or provision	Statutory reference
Notification requirements A relevant offender automatically becomes subject to notification requirements, obliging him to notify the police of specified information for a specified period. The court should inform the offender accordingly. *The operation of the notification requirement is not a relevant consideration in determining the sentence for the offence.*	Sections 80 to 88 and Schedule 3 of the Sexual Offences Act 2003
Protection for children and vulnerable adults A statutory scheme pursuant to which offenders *will* or *may* be barred from regulated activity relating to children or vulnerable adults, with or without the right to make representations, depending on the offence. The court should inform the offender accordingly.	Section 2 and Schedule 3 of the Safeguarding Vulnerable Groups Act 2006 Safeguarding Vulnerable Groups Act 2006 (Prescribed Criteria and Miscellaneous Provisions) Regulations 2009 (SI 2009/37) (as amended)

Annex B

Approach to sentencing of historic sexual offences

Details of the principal offences are set out in the table at Annex C on page 643.

When sentencing sexual offences under the Sexual Offences Act 1956, or other legislation pre-dating the 2003 Act, the court should apply the following principles[1]:

1. The offender must be sentenced in accordance with the sentencing regime applicable at the *date of sentence*. Under the Criminal Justice Act 2003[2] the court must have regard to the statutory purposes of sentencing and must base the sentencing exercise on its assessment of the seriousness of the offence.
2. The sentence is limited to the maximum sentence available at the *date of the commission of the offence*. If the maximum sentence has been reduced, the lower maximum will be applicable.
3. The court should have regard to any applicable sentencing guidelines for equivalent offences under the Sexual Offences Act 2003.
4. The seriousness of the offence, assessed by the culpability of the offender and the harm caused or intended, is the main consideration for the court. The court should not seek to establish the likely sentence had the offender been convicted shortly after the date of the offence.
5. When assessing the culpability of the offender, the court should have regard to relevant culpability factors set out in any applicable guideline.
6. The court must assess carefully the harm done to the victim based on the facts available to it, having regard to relevant harm factors set out in any applicable guideline. Consideration of the circumstances which brought the offence to light will be of importance.
7. The court must consider the relevance of the passage of time carefully as it has the potential to aggravate or mitigate the seriousness of the offence. It will be an aggravating factor where the offender has continued to commit sexual offences against the victim or others or has continued to prevent the victim reporting the offence.
8. Where there is an absence of further offending over a long period of time, especially if combined with evidence of good character, this may be treated by the court as a mitigating factor. However, as with offences dealt with under the Sexual Offences Act 2003, previous good character/exemplary conduct is different from having no previous convictions. The more serious the offence, the less the weight which should normally be attributed to this factor. Where previous good character/exemplary conduct has been used to facilitate the offence, this mitigation should not normally be allowed and such conduct may constitute an aggravating factor.
9. If the offender was very young and immature at the time of the offence, depending on the circumstances of the offence, this may be regarded as personal mitigation.
10. If the offender made admissions at the time of the offence that were not investigated this is likely to be regarded as personal mitigation. Even greater mitigation is available to the offender who reported himself to the police and/or made early admissions.
11. A reduction for an early guilty plea should be made in the usual manner.

---

[1] *R v H and others* [2011] EWCA Crim 2753.
[2] Section 143.

Annex C

Historic offences

Offence (Sexual Offences Act 1956 unless stated otherwise)	Effective dates	Maximum
Rape and assault offences		
Rape (section 1)	1 January 1957–30 April 2004	Life
Buggery with a person or animal (section 12)	1 January 1957–30 April 2004 (from 3 November 1994 non-consensual acts of buggery were defined as rape)	Life
Indecent assault on a woman (section 14)	1 January 1957–30 April 2004	1 January 1957–31 December 1960: 2 years 1 January 1961–15 September 1985: 2 years or 5 years if victim under 13 and age stated on indictment 16 September 1985 onwards: 10 years
Indecent assault upon a man (section 15)	1 January 1957–30 April 2004	10 years
Offences against children		
Sexual intercourse with a girl under 13 (section 5)	1 January 1957–30 April 2004	Life
Incest by a maleperson (section 10)	1 January 1957–30 April 2004	Life if victim under 13; otherwise 7 years
Incest by a femaleperson (section 11)	1 January 1957–30 April 2004	7 years
Gross indecency (section 13)	1 January 1957–30 April 2004	Male offender over 21 with male under age of consent: 5 years Otherwise: 2 years
Indecency with a child (section 1 of the Indecency with Children Act 1960)	1 January 1961–30 April 2004	1 January 1961–30 September 1997: 2 years 1 October 1997 onwards: 10 years *Note: on 11 January 2001 the age definition of a child increased from 14 to 16.*
Incitement of a girl under 16 to commit incest (section 54 of the Criminal Law Act 1977)	8 September 1977–30 April 2004	2 years
Abuse of position of trust (section 3 of the Sexual Offences (Amendment) Act 2000)	8 January 2001–30 April 2004	5 years

Offence (Sexual Offences Act 1956 unless stated otherwise)	Effective dates	Maximum
Indecent images		
Taking indecent photographs of a child (section 1 of the Protection of Children Act 1978)	20 August 1978– present	20 August 1978–10 January 2001: 3 years 11 January 2001 onwards: 10 years
Possession of indecent photographs of a child (section 160 of the Criminal Justice Act 1988)	11 January 1988–present	11 January 1988–10 January 2001: 6 months 11 January 2001 onwards: 5 years
Exploitation offences		
Procurement of woman by threats (section 2)	1 January 1957–30 April 2004	2 years
Procurement by false pretences (section 3)		
Causing prostitution of women (section 22)		
Procuration of girl under 21 for unlawful sexual intercourse in any part of the world (section 23)		
Detention in a brothel (section 24)		
Permitting a defective to use premises for intercourse (section 27)		
Causing or encouraging prostitution (etc) of a girl under 16 (section 28)		
Causing or encouraging prostitution of a defective (section 29)		
Living on earnings of prostitution (section 30)	1 January 1957–30 April 2004	7 years
Controlling a prostitute (section 31)		
Trafficking into/within/out of the UK for sexual exploitation (sections 57–59 of the Sexual Offences Act 2003)	1 May 2005–5 April 2013	14 years
Offences against those with a mental disorder		
Intercourse with a defective (section 7)	1 January 1957–30 April 2004	2 years
Procurement of a defective (section 9)		

Offence (Sexual Offences Act 1956 unless stated otherwise)	Effective dates	Maximum
Sexual intercourse with patients (section 128 of the Mental Health Act 1956)	1 November 1960 –30 April 2004	2 years
Other offences		
Administering drugs to obtain or facilitate intercourse (section 4)	1 January 1957–30 April 2004	2 years
Burglary with intent to commit rape (section 9 of the Theft Act 1968)	1 January 1969–30 April 2004	14 years if dwelling; otherwise 10 years

With thanks to Sweet & Maxwell, HHJ Rook QC and Robert Ward CBE for their kind permission to reproduce parts of *Sexual Offences Law & Practice*.

Annex D

Fine bands and community orders

FINE BANDS

In this guideline, fines are expressed as one of three fine bands (A, B or C).

Fine Band	Starting point (applicable to all offenders)	Category range (applicable to all offenders)
Band A	50% of relevant weekly income	25–75% of relevant weekly income
Band B	100% of relevant weekly income	75–125% of relevant weekly income
Band C	150% of relevant weekly income	125–175% of relevant weekly income

COMMUNITY ORDERS

In this guideline, community orders are expressed as one of three levels (low, medium and high).

An illustrative description of examples of requirements that might be appropriate for each level is provided below. Where two or more requirements are ordered, they must be compatible with each other.

LOW	MEDIUM	HIGH
In general, only one requirement will be appropriate and the length may be curtailed if additional requirements are necessary	More intensive sentences which combine two or more requirements may be appropriate	

LOW	MEDIUM	HIGH
Suitable requirements might include: - 40–80 hours unpaid work; - curfew requirement within the lowest range (for example, up to 12 hours per day for a few weeks); - exclusion requirement, without electronic monitoring, for a few months; - prohibited activity requirement; - attendance centre requirement (where available).	Suitable requirements might include: - appropriate treatment programme; - greater number of hours of unpaid work (for example, 80–150 hours); - an activity requirement in the middle range (20 to 30 days); - curfew requirement within the middle range (for example, up to 12 hours for two to three months); - exclusion requirement, lasting in the region of six months; - prohibited activity requirement.	Suitable requirements might include: - appropriate treatment programme; - 150–300 hours unpaid work; - activity requirement up to the maximum of 60 days; - curfew requirement up to 12 hours per day for four to six months; - exclusion order lasting in the region of 12 months.

The Magistrates' Court Sentencing Guidelines includes further guidance on fines and community orders.

APPENDIX C

PD-5 CPD I to PD-8 CPD I General matters 3: Vulnerable People, Ground Rules, Intermediaries, Vulnerable Defendants

PD-5 CPD I General matters 3: VULNERABLE PEOPLE IN THE COURTS	647	PD-7 CPD I General matters 3: INTERMEDIARIES	649
PD-6 CPD I General matters 3: GROUND RULES HEARINGS TO PLAN THE QUESTIONING OF A VULNERABLE WITNESS OR DEFENDANT	648	PD-8 CPD I General matters 3: VULNERABLE DEFENDANTS	650

PD-5 CPD I General matters 3: VULNERABLE PEOPLE IN THE COURTS

3D.1 In respect of eligibility for special measures, 'vulnerable' and 'intimidated' witnesses are defined in sections 16 and 17 of the Youth Justice and Criminal Evidence Act 1999 (as amended by the Coroners and Justice Act 2009); 'vulnerable' includes those under 18 years of age and people with a mental disorder or learning disability; a physical disorder or disability; or who are likely to suffer fear or distress in giving evidence because of their own circumstances or those relating to the case.

3D.2 However, many other people giving evidence in a criminal case, whether as a witness or defendant, may require assistance: the court is required to take 'every reasonable step' to encourage and facilitate the attendance of witnesses and to facilitate the participation of any person, including the defendant (Rule 8(4)(a) and (b)). This includes enabling a witness or defendant to give their best evidence, and enabling a defendant to comprehend the proceedings and engage fully with his or her defence. The pre-trial and trial process should, so far as necessary, be adapted to meet those ends. Regard should be had to the welfare of a young defendant as required by section 44 of the Children and Young Persons Act 1933, and generally to Parts 1 and 3 of the Criminal Procedure Rules (the overriding objective and the court's powers of case management).

3D.3 Under Part 3 of the Rules, the court must identify the needs of witnesses at an early stage (Rule 3.2(2)(b)) and may require the parties to identify arrangements to facilitate the giving of evidence and participation in the trial (Rule 3.10(c)(iv) and (v)). There are various statutory special measures that the court may utilise to assist a witness in giving evidence. Part 29 of the Rules gives the procedures to be followed. Courts should note the 'primary rule' which requires the court to give a direction for a special measure to assist a child witness or qualifying witness and that in such cases an application to the court is not required (rule 29.9).

3D.4 Court of Appeal decisions on this subject include a judgment from the Lord Chief Justice, Lord Judge in *R v Cox* [2012] EWCA Crim 549, [2012] 2 Cr App R 6; *R v Wills* [2011] EWCA Crim 1938, [2012] 1 Cr App R 2; and *R v E* [2011] EWCA Crim 3028, [2012] Crim LR 563.

3D.5 In *R v Wills*, the Court endorsed the approach taken by the report of the Advocacy Training Council (ATC) 'Raising the Bar: the Handling of Vulnerable Witnesses, Victims and Defendants in Court' (2011). The report includes and recommends the use of 'toolkits' to assist advocates as they prepare to question vulnerable people at court: <http://www.advocacytrainingcouncil.org/vulnerable-witnesses/raising-the-bar>.

3D.6 Further toolkits are available through the Advocate's Gateway which is managed by the ATC's Management Committee: <http://www.theadvocatesgateway.org/>.

3D.7 These toolkits represent best practice. Advocates should consult and follow the relevant guidance whenever they prepare to question a young or otherwise vulnerable witness or defendant. Judges may find it helpful to refer advocates to this material and to use the toolkits in case management.

3D.8 'Achieving Best Evidence in Criminal Proceedings' (Ministry of Justice 2011) describes best practice in preparation for the investigative interview and trial: <http://www.justice.gov.uk/downloads/victims-and-witnesses/vulnerable-witnesses/achieving-best-evidence-criminal-proceedings.pdf>.

PD-6 CPD I General matters 3: GROUND RULES HEARINGS TO PLAN THE QUESTIONING OF A VULNERABLE WITNESS OR DEFENDANT

3E.1 The judiciary is responsible for controlling questioning. Over-rigorous or repetitive cross-examination of a child or vulnerable witness should be stopped. Intervention by the judge, magistrates or intermediary (if any) is minimised if questioning, taking account of the individual's communication needs, is discussed in advance and ground rules are agreed and adhered to.

3E.2 Discussion of ground rules is required in all intermediary trials where they must be discussed between the judge or magistrates, advocates and intermediary before the witness gives evidence. The intermediary must be present but is not required to take the oath (the intermediary's declaration is made just before the witness gives evidence).

3E.3 Discussion of ground rules is good practice, even if no intermediary is used, in all young witness cases and in other cases where a witness or defendant has communication needs. Discussion before the day of trial is preferable to give advocates time to adapt their questions to the witness' needs. It may be helpful for a trial practice note of boundaries to be created at the end of the discussion. The judge may use such a document in ensuring that the agreed ground rules are complied with.

3E.4 All witnesses, including the defendant and defence witnesses, should be enabled to give the best evidence they can. In relation to young and/or vulnerable people, this may mean departing radically from traditional cross-examination. The form and extent of appropriate cross-examination will vary from case to case. For adult non vulnerable witnesses an advocate will usually put his case so that the witness will have the opportunity of commenting upon it and/or answering it. When the witness is young or otherwise vulnerable, the court may dispense with the normal practice and impose restrictions on the advocate 'putting his case' where there is a risk of a young or otherwise vulnerable witness failing to understand, becoming distressed or acquiescing to leading questions. Where limitations on questioning are necessary and appropriate, they must be clearly defined. The judge has a duty to ensure that they are complied with and should explain them to the jury and the reasons for them. If the advocate fails to comply with the limitations, the judge should give relevant directions to the jury when that occurs and prevent further questioning that does not comply with the ground rules settled upon in advance. Instead of commenting on inconsistencies during cross-examination, following discussion between the judge and the advocates, the advocate or judge may point out important inconsistencies after (instead of during) the witness's evidence. The judge should also remind the jury of these during summing up. The judge should be alert to alleged inconsistencies that are not in fact inconsistent, or are trivial.

If there is more than one defendant, the judge should not permit each advocate to repeat the questioning of a vulnerable witness. In advance of the trial, the advocates should divide the topics between them, with the advocate for the first defendant leading the questioning, and the advocate(s) for the other defendant(s) asking only ancillary questions relevant to their client's case, without repeating the questioning that has already taken place on behalf of the other defendant(s).   **3E.5**

In particular in a trial of a sexual offence, 'body maps' should be provided for the witness' use. If the witness needs to indicate a part of the body, the advocate should ask the witness to point to the relevant part on the body map. In sex cases, judges should not permit advocates to ask the witness to point to a part of the witness' own body. Similarly, photographs of the witness' body should not be shown around the court while the witness is giving evidence.   **3E.6**

PD-7 CPD I General matters 3: INTERMEDIARIES

Intermediaries are communication specialists (not supporters or expert witnesses) whose role is to facilitate communication between the witness and the court, including the advocates. Intermediaries are independent of the parties and owe their duty to the court (see Registered Intermediaries Procedural Guidance Manual, Ministry of Justice, 2012): <http://www.cps.gov.uk/publications/docs/RI_ProceduralGuidanceManual_2012.pdf>.   **3F.1**

Intermediaries for witnesses, with the exception of defendants, are one of the special measures available under the Youth Justice and Criminal Evidence Act 1999 and Part 29 of the Criminal Procedure Rules.   **3F.2**

There is currently no statutory provision in force for intermediaries for defendants. Section 104 of the Coroners and Justice Act 2009 (not yet implemented) creates a new section 33BA of the Youth Justice and Criminal Evidence Act 1999. This will provide an intermediary to an eligible defendant only while giving evidence. A court may use its inherent powers to appoint an intermediary to assist the defendant's communication at trial (either solely when giving evidence or throughout the trial) and, where necessary, in preparation for trial: *R (AS) v Great Yarmouth Youth Court* [2011] EWHC 2059 (Admin), [2012] Crim LR 478; *R v H* [2003] EWCA Crim 1208, *The Times*, 15 April 2003; *R (C) v Sevenoaks Youth Court* [2009] EWHC 3088 (Admin), [2010] 1 All ER 735; *R (D) v Camberwell Green Youth Court* [2005] UKHL 4, [2005] 1 WLR 393, [2005] 2 Cr App R 1; *R (TP) v West London Youth Court* [2005] EWHC 2583 (Admin), [2006] 1 WLR 1219, [2006] 1 Cr App R 25.   **3F.3**

Ministry of Justice regulation only applies to Registered Intermediaries appointed for prosecution and defence witnesses through its Witness Intermediary Scheme. All defendant intermediaries—professionally qualified or otherwise—are 'non-registered' in this context, even though they may be a Registered Intermediary in respect of witnesses. Even where a judge concludes he has a common law power to direct the provision of an intermediary, the direction will be ineffective if no intermediary can be identified for whom funding would be available.   **3F.4**

Assessment should be considered if a child or young person under 18 seems unlikely to be able to recognise a problematic question or, even if able to do so, may be reluctant to say so to a questioner in a position of authority. Studies suggest that the majority of young witnesses, across all age groups, fall into one or other of these categories. For children aged 11 years and under in particular, there should be a presumption that an intermediary assessment is appropriate. Once the child's individual requirements are known and discussed at the ground rules hearing, the intermediary may agree that his or her presence is not needed for the trial.   **3F.5**

In the absence of an intermediary for the defendant, trials should not be stayed where an asserted unfairness can be met by the trial judge adapting the trial process with appropriate and necessary caution (*R v Cox* [2012] EWCA Crim 549, [2012] 2 Cr App R 6). This includes setting ground rules   **3F.6** for all witness testimony to help the defendant follow proceedings; for example, directing that all witness evidence be adduced by simple questions, with witnesses asked to answer in short sentences; and short periods of evidence, followed by breaks to enable the defendant to relax and for counsel to summarise the evidence for him and to take further instructions.

Photographs of Court Facilities

3F.7 Resident Judges in the Crown Court or the Chief Clerk or other responsible person in the magistrates' courts should, in consultation with HMCTS managers responsible for court security matters, develop a policy to govern under what circumstances photographs or other visual recordings may be made of court facilities, such as a live link room, to assist vulnerable or child witnesses to familiarise themselves with the setting, so as to be enabled to give their best evidence. For example, a photograph may provide a helpful reminder to a witness whose court visit has taken place sometime earlier. Resident Judges should tend to permit photographs to be taken for this purpose by intermediaries or supporters, subject to whatever restrictions the Resident Judge or responsible person considers to be appropriate, having regard to the security requirements of the court.

PD-8 CPD I General matters 3: VULNERABLE DEFENDANTS

Before the trial, sentencing, or appeal

3G.1 If a vulnerable defendant, especially one who is young, is to be tried jointly with one who is not, the court should consider at the plea and case management hearing, or at a case management hearing in a magistrates' court, whether the vulnerable defendant should be tried on his own, but should only so order if satisfied that a fair trial cannot be achieved by use of appropriate special measures or other support for the defendant. If a vulnerable defendant is tried jointly with one who is not, the court should consider whether any of the modifications set out in this direction should apply in the circumstances of the joint trial and, so far as practicable, make orders to give effect to any such modifications.

3G.2 It may be appropriate to arrange that a vulnerable defendant should visit, out of court hours and before the trial, sentencing or appeal hearing, the courtroom in which that hearing is to take place so that he or she can familiarise himself or herself with it.

3G.3 Where an intermediary is being used to help the defendant to communicate at court, the intermediary should accompany the defendant on his or her pre-trial visit. The visit will enable the defendant to familiarise him or herself with the layout of the court, and may include matters such as: where the defendant will sit, either in the dock or otherwise; court officials (what their roles are and where they sit); who else might be in the court, for example those in the public gallery and press box; the location of the witness box; basic court procedure; and the facilities available in the court.

3G.4 If the defendant's use of the live link is being considered, he or she should have an opportunity to have a practice session.

3G.5 If any case against a vulnerable defendant has attracted or may attract widespread public or media interest, the assistance of the police should be enlisted to try and ensure that the defendant is not, when attending the court, exposed to intimidation, vilification, or abuse. Section 41 of the Criminal Justice Act 1925 prohibits the taking of photographs of defendants and witnesses (among others) in the court building or in its precincts, or when entering or leaving those precincts. A direction reminding media representatives of the prohibition may be appropriate. The court should also be ready at this stage, if it has not already done so, where relevant to make a reporting restriction under section 39 of the Children and Young Persons Act 1933 or, on an appeal to the Crown Court from a youth court, to remind media representatives of the application of section 49 of that Act.

3G.6 The provisions of the Practice Direction accompanying Part 16 should be followed.

The trial, sentencing or appeal hearing

3G.7 Subject to the need for appropriate security arrangements, the proceedings should, if practicable, be held in a courtroom in which all the participants are on the same or almost the same level.

3G.8 Subject again to the need for appropriate security arrangements, a vulnerable defendant, especially if he is young, should normally, if he wishes, be free to sit with members of his family or others in a like relationship, and with some other suitable supporting adult such as a social worker, and in a place which permits easy, informal communication with his legal representatives. The court should ensure that a suitable supporting adult is available throughout the course of the proceedings.

3G.9 It is essential that at the beginning of the proceedings, the court should ensure that what is to take place has been explained to a vulnerable defendant in terms he or she can understand and, at trial in the Crown Court, it should ensure in particular that the role of the jury has been explained. It should remind those representing the vulnerable defendant and the supporting adult of their responsibility to explain each step as it takes place and, at trial, explain the possible consequences of a guilty verdict and credit for a guilty plea. The court should also remind any intermediary of their responsibility to ensure that the vulnerable defendant has understood the explanations given to him/her. Throughout the trial the court should continue to ensure, by any appropriate means, that the defendant understands what is happening and what has been said by those on the bench, the advocates and witnesses.

3G.10 A trial should be conducted according to a timetable which takes full account of a vulnerable defendant's ability to concentrate. Frequent and regular breaks will often be appropriate. The court should ensure, so far as practicable, that the whole trial is conducted in clear language that the defendant can understand and that evidence in chief and cross-examination are conducted using questions that are short and clear. The conclusions of the 'ground rules' hearing should be followed, and advocates should use and follow the 'toolkits' as discussed above.

3G.11 A vulnerable defendant who wishes to give evidence by live link, in accordance with section 33A of the Youth Justice and Criminal Evidence Act 1999, may apply for a direction to that effect; the procedure in Section 4 of Part 29 of the Rules should be followed. Before making such a direction, the court must be satisfied that it is in the interests of justice to do so and that the use of a live link would enable the defendant to participate more effectively as a witness in the proceedings. The direction will need to deal with the practical arrangements to be made, including the identity of the person or persons who will accompany him or her.

3G.12 In the Crown Court, the judge should consider whether robes and wigs should be worn, and should take account of the wishes of both a vulnerable defendant and any vulnerable witness. It is generally desirable that those responsible for the security of a vulnerable defendant who is in custody, especially if he or she is young, should not be in uniform, and that there should be no recognizable police presence in the courtroom save for good reason.

3G.13 The court should be prepared to restrict attendance by members of the public in the court room to a small number, perhaps limited to those with an immediate and direct interest in the outcome. The court should rule on any challenged claim to attend. However, facilities for reporting the proceedings (subject to any restrictions under section 39 or 49 of the Children and Young Persons Act 1933) must be provided. The court may restrict the number of reporters attending in the courtroom to such number as is judged practicable and desirable. In ruling on any challenged claim to attend in the court room for the purpose of reporting, the court should be mindful of the public's general right to be informed about the administration of justice.

3G.14 Where it has been decided to limit access to the courtroom, whether by reporters or generally, arrangements should be made for the proceedings to be relayed, audibly and if possible visually, to another room in the same court complex to which the media and the public have access if it appears that there will be a need for such additional facilities. Those making use of such a facility should be reminded that it is to be treated as an extension of the court room and that they are required to conduct themselves accordingly.

INDEX

alternative verdicts 1.43–1.44
anonymity
   complainants 15.01–15.03
   witnesses 15.07–15.39
attempts
   indictments 1.49–1.53
Attorney-General's references *see* prosecution reviews of sentence

bestiality 5.18
buggery 5.01–5.130
   22.7.1967 to 2.11.1994 5.55–5.59
   3.11.1994 to 7.1.2001 5.60–5.67
   8.1.2001 to 30.4.2004 5.68–5.70
   1.5.2004 to date 5.71–5.74
   categories of offences and related sentences up to 30.4.2004 5.02–5.09
      offences (pre-Sexual Offences Act 2003) which may be charged 5.05, 5.06
      sentences 5.07, 5.08
      sentencing guidance 5.09
   consent 5.04, 5.13, 5.43, 5.62–5.63
   gross indecency between males 5.41–5.47
      alternative offences 5.45
      definition 5.41
      indictment 5.44
      proof 5.42
      sentence 5.46
      upon conviction/sentence 5.47
   gross indecency with another man 5.101–5.114
      alternative offences 5.107
      attempted gross indecency
         1.1.1961 5.112
         1.5.2004 5.113–5.114
      definition 5.102
      indictment 5.105–5.106
      notes 5.95, 5.104
      proof 5.103
      sentence 5.108–5.109
      upon conviction/sentence 5.111
   intercourse with an animal 5.75–5.83
      alternative offences 5.80
      definition 5.76
      indictment 5.79
      notes 5.78
      proof 5.77
      sentence 5.81
      sentencing guidance 5.82
      upon conviction/sentence 5.83
   offences committed between 1.1.1957 and 30.4.2004 5.48–5.74
      alternative offences 5.52
      definition 5.49
      indictment 5.51
      proof 5.50
      sentence 5.53
      upon conviction/sentence 5.54
   offences committed pre-31.12.1956 5.10–5.47
      alternative offences 5.19
      assault with intent to commit buggery 5.25–5.31
      attempted buggery 5.22
      bestiality 5.18
      definition 5.10, 5.11
      gross indecency between males 5.41–5.47
      indecent assault upon a male person 5.32–5.40
      indictment 5.14–5.17
      proof 5.12
      sentence 5.23
      upon conviction/sentence 5.24
   procuring others to commit buggery 5.124–5.130
      definition 5.124
      indictment 5.128
      notes 5.127
      proof 5.125–5.126
      sentence 5.129
      upon conviction/sentence 5.130
   sexual activity in public lavatory 5.115–5.123
      alternative offences 5.120
      definition 5.116
      proof 5.117–5.119
      sentence 5.121–5.122
      upon conviction/sentence 5.123

children, notification requirements 14.07–14.09
children, offences involving 4.01–4.269
   abuse of position of trust: offences committed between 8.1.2001 and 30.4.2004
      alternative offences 4.149
      definitions 4.142–4.145
      indictment 4.148
      notes 4.147
      persons in position of trust, definition 4.154
      proof 4.146
      sentence 4.150
      upon conviction/sentence 4.151
   abuse of position of trust: offences committed from 1.5.2004 to date
      alternative offences 4.160
      definitions 4.154–4.155
      indictment 4.158–4.159
      introduction 4.152–4.154
      notes 4.157

children, offences involving (cont.)
    persons in position of trust, definition 4.154
        proof 4.156
        sentence 4.161
        sentencing guidance 4.163
        upon conviction/sentence 4.151
    abuse of position of trust: causing child to watch sexual act 4.182–4.190
        alternative offences 4.187
        D under 18 4.190
        definition 4.182
        indictment 4.185–4.186
        notes 4.184
        proof 4.183
        sentence 4.188
        sentencing guidance 4.189
    abuse of position of trust: causing/inciting child to engage in sexual activity 4.164–4.172
        alternative offences 4.169
        definition 4.164
        indictment 4.167–4.168
        notes 4.166
        proof 4.165
        sentence 4.170
        sentencing guidance 4.171
        upon conviction/sentence 4.172
    abuse of position of trust: engaging in sexual activity in presence of child 4.173–4.181
        alternative offences 4.178
        definition 4.173
        indictment 4.176–4.177
        proof 4.174
        sentence 4.179
        sentencing guidance 4.180
        upon conviction/sentence 4.181
    abuse of position of trust: sexual activity with a child 4.155–4.163
        alternative offences 4.160
        definition 4.155
        indictment 4.158–4.159
        notes 4.157
        proof 4.156
        sentence 4.161
        sentencing guidance 4.162
        upon conviction/sentence 4.173
    arranging or facilitating commission of child sex offence 4.213–4.223
        alternative offences 4.220
        definition 4.215
        indictment 4.218–4.219
        introduction 4.213–4.214
        notes 4.217
        proof 4.216
        sentence 4.221
        sentencing guidance 4.222
        upon conviction/sentence 4.223
    assault of child under 13 by penetration 4.98–4.106
        alternative offences 4.103
        definition 4.98
        indictment 4.101–4.102
        notes 4.100
        proof 4.99
        sentence 4.104
        sentencing guidance 4.105
        upon conviction/sentence 4.106
    carnal knowledge of girls aged 13 to 16 4.57–4.66
        alternative offences 4.63
        definition 4.57
        indictment 4.62
        notes 4.59–4.61
        proof 4.58
        sentence 4.64
        upon conviction/sentence 4.65
    carnal knowledge of girls under 13 4.49–4.56
        alternative offences 4.53
        definition 4.49
        indictment 4.52
        notes 4.51
        proof 4.50
        sentence 4.54
        upon conviction/sentence 4.55
    causing child to watch sexual act 4.182–4.190
        alternative offences 4.187
        definition 4.182
        indictment 4.138, 4.185–4.186
        notes 4.184
        proof 4.183
        sentence 4.188
        sentencing guidance 4.189
        upon conviction/sentence 4.190
    causing or inciting child under 13 to engage in sexual activity 4.36–4.48
        alternative offences 4.43–4.46
        definition 4.38
        indictment
            non-penetrative 4.41
            penetrative 4.42
        notes 4.40
        proof 4.39
        sentence 4.46
        sentencing guidance 4.47
        two offences 4.37
        upon conviction/sentence 4.48
    causing/inciting a child to engage in sexual activity 4.21–4.35
        alternative offences 4.31–4.32
        definition 4.24
        indictment 4.27–4.30
            non-penetrative activity where D is over 18 4.27
            non-penetrative where D is under 18 4.29
            penetrative activity where D is over 18 4.28
            penetrative where D is under 18 4.30
        notes 4.26
        proof 4.25
        sentence 4.33
        sentencing guidance 4.34
        upon conviction/sentence 4.35
    charging alternative sections 4.04
    correct section to charge 4.04
    determination of age 4.264–4.267

discretion to remit cases from adult magistrates court to youth court 4.269
doli incapax 4.261
engaging in sexual activity in presence of child 4.173–4.181
  alternative offences 4.178
  definition 4.173
  indictment 4.176–4.177
  proof 4.174
  sentence 4.179
  sentencing guidance 4.180
  upon conviction/sentence 4.181
gross indecency with a child 4.07–4.20
  alternative offences 4.17
  definition 4.07–4.08, 4.09–4.10
  indictment
    D committing act with or towards C 4.14
    D inciting C to commit act 4.15–4.16
  notes 4.13
  proof 4.11–4.12
  sentence 4.18
  upon conviction/sentence 4.19–4.20
intercourse with a person under the age of consent 4.49–4.117
  offences committed pre-31.12.1956 4.49–4.66
  offences committed between 1.1.1957 and 30.4.2004 4.67–4.87
  offences committed from 1.5.2004 to date 4.88–4.117
meeting child following sexual grooming 4.224–4.235
  alternative offences 4.232
  definition 4.225
  indictment 4.228–4.231
  notes 4.227
  proof 4.226
  sentence 4.233
  sentencing guidance 4.234
  upon conviction/sentence 4.235
offences committed by children or young persons 4.256–4.260
penetrative sexual activity with child 4.107–4.117
  alternative offences 4.114
  definition 4.108
  indictment
    defendant over 18 4.111
    defendant under 18 4.112–4.113
  notes 4.110
  proof 4.109
  sentence 4.115
  sentencing guidance 4.116
  upon conviction/sentence 4.117
presumption of age 4.261–4.269
presumption that boys under 14 are incapable of intercourse 4.262–4.263
proving age 4.268
rape of child under 13 4.89–4.97
  alternative offences 4.94
  definition 4.90
  indictment 4.93
  introduction 4.89
  notes 4.92
  proof 4.91
  sentence 4.95
  sentencing guidance 4.96
  upon conviction/guidance 4.97
sexual activity with a child 4.155–4.163
  alternative offences 4.160
  definition 4.155
  indictment 4.158–4.159
  proof 4.156
  sentence 4.161
  sentencing guidance 4.162
  upon conviction/sentence 4.173
sexual assault of child under 13 4.120–4.223
  alternative offences 4.125
  definition 4.120
  indictment 4.123–4.124
  notes 4.122
  proof 4.121
  sentence 4.126
  sentencing guidance 4.127
  upon conviction/sentence 4.128
sexual intercourse with girl under 13 4.67–4.76
  alternative offences 4.83
  definition 4.68
  indictment 4.81–4.82
  introduction 4.67
  notes 4.70
  proof 4.69
  sentence 4.84
  sentencing guidance 4.85
  upon conviction/sentence 4.75–4.76
sexual intercourse with girl under 16 4.77–4.87
  alternative offences 4.83
  definition 4.78
  indictment 4.81–4.82
  introduction 4.77
  notes 4.80
  proof 4.79
  sentence 4.84
  sentencing guidance 4.85
  upon conviction/sentence 4.86–4.87
complainants, anonymity of 15.01–15.03
conditional discharges, notification requirements 14.19–14.21
consent, capacity to 3.37

details, update and removal *see* notification requirements
doli incapax 4.261

familial offences 6.01–6.81
  consenting to penetrative sex with adult relative 6.56–6.63, 6.58
    alternative offences 6.60
    definition 6.56
    indictment 6.59

656 INDEX

familial offences (*cont.*)
   proof 6.57
   sentence 6.61
   sentencing guidance 6.62
   upon conviction/sentence 6.63
  drafting indictments 6.06
  incest, offences committed
       pre-1.1.1957 6.02
   females, by 6.15–6.22
    alternative offences 6.19
    definition 6.15
    indictment 6.18
    proof 6.16
    sentence 6.20
    upon conviction/sentence 6.21
   males, by 6.07–6.14
    alternative offences 6.11
    definition 6.07
    indictment 6.10
    proof 6.08
    sentence 6.12
    upon conviction/sentence 6.13
  incest, offences committed between 1.1.1957 and
      30.4.2004
   females, by 6.32–6.40
    alternative offences 6.36
    definition 6.32
    indictment 6.35
    notes 6.34
    proof 6.33
    sentence 6.37
    upon conviction/sentence 6.38–6.40
   males, by 6.23–6.31
    alternative offences 6.27
    definition 6.23
    indictment 6.26
    notes 6.25
    proof 6.24
    sentence 6.28
    sentencing guidance 6.29
    upon conviction/sentence 6.30
  incest, offences committed between 1.2.1991 and
      30.4.2004 6.41–6.47
  incest, offences committed from 1.5.2004 to
      date 6.48–6.55
  incitement of girls under 16 to have incestuous
      intercourse 6.41–6.47
   definition 6.41
   indictment 6.44
   notes 6.43
   proof 6.42
   sentence 6.45
   upon conviction/sentence 6.46–6.47
  inciting child family member to engage in sexual
      activity 6.74–6.81, 6.76
   alternative offences 6.79
   definition 6.74
   indictment 6.77
   proof 6.75
   sentence 6.80
   upon conviction/sentence 6.81
  indictments 1.53
  penetrative sex with adult relative 6.48–6.55
   alternative offences 6.52
   definition 6.48
   indictment 6.51
   notes 6.50
   proof 6.49
   sentence 6.53
   sentencing guidance 6.54
   upon conviction/sentence 6.55
  sexual activity with child family
      member 6.64–6.74
   alternative offences 6.70
   definition 6.64
   indictment 6.68–6.69
   notes 6.67
   proof 6.65–6.66
   sentence 6.71
   sentencing guidance 6.72
   upon conviction/sentence 6.73
  Sexual Offences Act 2003 6.03–6.04

ground rules hearings (GRHs) 13.28

human trafficking 8.181–8.189

indecency 5.01–5.130
indictments 1.01–1.61
  alternative verdicts 1.43–1.44
    Courtie, principle in 1.45–1.48
  attempts 1.49–1.53
  defective counts 1.35–1.40
  delay 1.60
  drafting 1.01–1.05
  duplicity 1.11–1.15
  either way offences 1.55–1.57
  familial offences 1.53
  historic counts to which Sentencing Act 2020,
      Schedule 13 applies 1.41–1.42
  more than one incident of same offence to be
      charged in one count 1.11–1.12
  'multiple incident' count 1.16–1.20
  offences straddling implementation dates of
      different Acts 1.26–1.28
  offences straddling legislation 1.29–1.34
  offences under Sexual Offences Act 2003, s 13
   defendant under 18 1.54
   familial offences 1.53
  offenders of particular concern 1.41–1.42
  particularizing counts 1.06–1.10
  Practice Direction 1.01, 1.19
  proving counts without jury 1.21–1.25
  quashing 1.58–1.61
  Sentencing Act 2020, Schedule 13 1.41–1.42
  separate counts 1.16
  summary only offences 1.55–1.57
  table of changes in legislation 1.61

mentally disordered, offences involving 7.01–7.192
  abuse of mentally disordered as patients or by those with certain responsibility for them 7.61–7.108
    offences committed between 1.11.1913 and 31.12.1956 7.55–7.60
    offences committed between 1.11.1960 and 30.4.2004 7.69–7.75
    offences committed from 1.5.2004 to date 7.76–7.108
  care workers causing or inciting sexual activity with person with mental disorder 7.85–7.92
    alternative offences 7.89
    definition 7.85
    indictment 7.88
    notes 7.87
    proof 7.86
    sentence 7.90–7.91
    upon sentence/conviction 7.92
  care workers: causing person with mental disorder to watch sexual act 7.101–7.108
    alternative offences 7.105
    definition 7.101
    indictment 7.104
    notes 7.102
    proof 7.102
    sentence 7.106–7.107
    upon conviction/sentence 7.108
  care workers: sexual activity in presence of person with mental disorder 7.93–7.100
    alternative offences 7.97
    definition 7.93
    indictment 7.96
    notes 7.95
    proof 7.94
    sentence 7.98–7.99
    upon conviction/sentence 7.100
  carnal knowledge of female under care/treatment 7.55–7.60
    alternative offences 7.58
    definition 7.55
    notes 7.57
    proof 7.56
    sentence 7.59–7.60
  carnal knowledge of mentally disordered female 7.04–7.10
    alternative offences 7.08
    definition 7.04
    indictment 7.07
    proof 7.05
    sentence 7.09
  causing a person with a mental disorder to engage in sexual activity by inducement, threat or deception 7.130–7.137
    alternative offences 7.134
    definition 7.130
    indictment 7.133
    notes 7.132
    proof 7.131
    sentence 7.135–7.136
    upon conviction/sentence 7.137
  causing a person with a mental disorder to watch a sexual act by inducement, threat or deception 7.145–7.151
    alternative offences 7.149
    definition 7.145
    indictment 7.148
    notes 7.147
    proof 7.146
    sentence 7.150
    upon conviction/sentence 7.151
  causing or encouraging prostitution of a defective 7.153–7.156
    definition 7.153
    notes 7.155
    proof 7.154
    sentence 7.156
  causing or encouraging prostitution of any woman or girl who is a defective 7.164–7.169
    definition 7.164
    indictment 7.167
    notes 7.166
    proof 7.165
    sentence 7.168
    upon conviction/sentence 7.169
  causing or inciting a person with a mental disorder impeding choice to engage in sexual activity 7.31–7.38
    alternative offences 7.35
    definition 7.31
    indictment 7.34
    notes 7.33
    proof 7.32
    sentence 7.36–7.37
    upon conviction/sentence 7.38
  causing person with mental disorder impeding choice to watch a sexual act 7.47–7.54
    alternative offences 7.51
    definition 7.47
    indictment 7.50
    notes 7.49
    proof 7.48
    sentence 7.52–7.53
    upon sentence/conviction 7.54
  engaging in sexual activity in presence of person with mental disorder impeding choice 7.39–7.46
    alternative offences 7.43
    definition 7.39
    indictment 7.42
    notes 7.41
    proof 7.40
    sentence 7.44–7.45
    upon sentence/conviction 7.46
  engaging in sexual activity in the presence, procured by inducement, threat or deception, of a person with a mental disorder 7.138–7.144
    alternative offences 7.142

658 INDEX

mentally disordered, offences involving (*cont.*)
    definition 7.138
    indictment 7.141
    notes 7.140
    proof 7.139
    sentence 7.143
    upon conviction/sentence 7.144
  intercourse with a mentally disordered patient 7.69–7.75
    alternative offences 7.73
    definition 7.69
    indictment 7.72
    notes 7.71
    proof 7.70
    sentence 7.74
    upon conviction/sentence 7.75
  intercourse with an idiot/imbecile woman 7.11–7.21
    alternative offences 7.15
    definition 7.11
    indictment 7.14, 7.21
    proof 7.12
    sentence 7.16
    upon conviction/sentence 7.17
  intercourse with defectives receiving treatment 7.61–7.68
    alternative offences 7.65
    definition 7.61
    indictment 7.64
    notes 7.63
    proof 7.62
    sentence 7.66
    upon conviction/sentence 7.67–7.68
  offences committed pre-31.12.1956 7.109–7.116
  offences committed between 1.1.1957 to 30.4.2004 7.114–7.120
  offences committed from 1.5.2004 to date 7.121–7.151
  offences designed to protect mentally disordered from procuration 7.109–7.151
  offences protecting mentally disordered from prostitution or abuse on premises 7.152–7.192
  permitting a defective to use premises for intercourse 7.170–7.175
    definition 7.170
    indictment 7.173
    notes 7.172
    proof 7.171
    sentence 7.174
    upon conviction/sentence 7.175
  permitting premises to be used for sexual intercourse with a female defective 7.157–7.160
    definition 7.157
    proof 7.158
    sentence 7.160
  procurement of a defective 7.114–7.120
    alternative offences 7.118
    definition 7.114
    indictment 7.117
    notes 7.116
    proof 7.115
    sentence 7.119
    upon conviction/sentence 7.120
  procuring by inducement, threat or deception sexual activity with a mentally disordered person 7.122–7.129
    alternative offences 7.126
    definition 7.122
    indictment 7.125
    notes 7.124
    proof 7.123
    sentence 7.127–7.128
    upon conviction/sentence 7.129
  procuring female to have carnal connection 7.109–7.116
    definition 7.109
    proof 7.111
    sentence 7.112–7.113
  sexual activity with a person who has a mental disorder by a care worker
    alternative offences 7.81
    definition 7.77
    indictment 7.80
    notes 7.79
    proof 7.78
    sentence 7.82–7.83
    upon conviction/sentence 7.84
  sexual activity with a person with a mental disorder impeding choice 7.23–7.30
    alternative offences 7.27
    definition 7.23
    indictment 7.26
    notes 7.25
    proof 7.24
    sentence 7.28–7.29
    upon conviction/sentence 7.30
  sexual assaults upon mentally disordered 7.04–7.54
    offences committed pre-31.12.1956 7.04–7.10
    offences committed between 1.1.1957 and 30.4.2004 7.11–7.21
    offences committed from 1.5.2004 to date 7.22–7.54

notification requirements
  applicability 14.02–14.03
  children and young persons 14.07–14.09
  conditional discharges 14.19–14.21
  court's role 14.04–14.07
  failure to notify 14.17–14.18
  initial notification 14.10–14.11
  method of notification 14.16
  notification period 14.27
  removal of details 14.22–14.25
  Sexual Harm Prevention Orders, and 16.48–16.50
  Sexual Offences Act 2003, Schedule 3 14.28–14.29
  statutory basis 14.01
  travel notification requirements 14.14–14.15
  updating details 14.12–14.13

INDEX 659

obscene publications
  child pornography 9.01, 9.02, 9.05–9.37
  disclosing private sexual photographs or
      films 9.67–9.75
    alternative offences 9.72
    definition 9.68
    indictment 9.71
    notes 9.70
    proof 9.69
    sentence 9.73–9.74
    upon conviction/sentence 9.75
  possession of extreme pornographic
      image 9.46–9.54
    definition 9.46
    indictment 9.50–9.51
    notes 9.48–9.49
    participation in consensual acts SOA s 6.6 9.38
    proof 9.47
    sentence 9.52–9.53
    upon conviction/sentence 9.54
  possession of indecent photographs of
      child 9.25–9.37
    alternative offences 9.34
    definition 9.26
    indictment 9.29–9.33
    notes 9.28
    proof 9.27
    sentence 9.35–9.36
    upon conviction/sentence 9.37
  possession of prohibited image of
      child 9.38–9.45
    alternative offences 9.42
    definition 9.38
    indictment 9.41
    notes 9.40
    proof 9.39
    sentence 9.43–9.44
    upon conviction/sentence 9.45
  publishing an obscene article or having an obscene
      article for publication for gain 9.58–9.66
    alternative offences 9.63
    definition 9.58
    indictment 9.61–9.62
    notes 9.60
    proof 9.59
    sentence 9.64–9.65
    upon conviction/sentence 9.66
  taking, making, distributing, publishing etc.
      photographs of children 9.05–9.24
    alternative offences 9.18
    definition 9.05
    indictment 9.08–9.17
    notes 9.07
    proof 9.06
    sentence 9.19
    sentencing guidance 9.20–9.23
    upon conviction/sentence 9.24
offences against public decency
  exposure 10.22–10.28
    definition 10.22
    indictment 10.25
    notes 10.24
    proof 10.23
    sentence 10.26
    sentencing guidance 10.27
    upon conviction/sentence 10.28
  indecent exposure 10.15–10.21
    definition 10.16
    notes 10.18
    proof 10.17
    sentence 10.19
    upon conviction/sentence 10.20
  outraging public decency 10.04–10.14
    definition 10.07
    indictment 10.10
    notes 10.09
    proof 10.08
    sentence 10.11
    sentencing guidance 10.12
    upon conviction/sentence 10.13
  sexual penetration of a corpse 10.48–10.56
    alternative offences 10.53
    definition 10.49
    indictment 10.52
    notes 10.51
    proof 10.50
    sentence 10.54
    sentencing guidance 10.55
    upon conviction/sentence 10.56
  'upskirting' 10.40–10.47
    definition 10.41
    indictment 10.44
    notes 10.43
    proof 10.42
    sentence 10.45
    sentencing guidance 10.46
    upon conviction/sentence 10.47
  voyeurism 10.29–10.39
    definition 10.30
    indictment 10.36
    notes 10.35
    proof 10.31–10.34
    sentence 10.37
    sentencing guidance 10.38
    upon conviction/sentence 10.39

Practice Directions App C
preparatory offences 11.01–11.58
  administering a substance with
      intent 11.35–11.41
    alternative offences 11.39
    definition 11.35
    indictment 11.38
    notes 11.37
    proof 11.36
    sentence 11.40
    sentencing guidance 11.41
    upon sentence/conviction 11.42

preparatory offences (*cont.*)
   administering drugs to obtain or facilitate
      intercourse 11.19–11.26
      alternative offences 11.23
      definition 11.19
      indictment 11.22
      proof 11.20
      sentence 11.24
      upon sentence/conviction 11.25
   burglary with intent to commit rape 11.27–11.34
      alternative offences 11.31
      definition 11.27
      indictment 11.30
      proof 11.28
      sentence 11.32
      upon conviction/sentence 11.33
   committing offence with intent to commit sexual
      offence 11.43–11.50
      alternative offence 11.47
      definition 11.43
      indictment 11.46
      notes 11.45
      proof 11.44
      sentence 11.48
      sentencing guidance 11.49
      upon conviction/sentence 11.50
   procurement of intercourse by false
      pretences 11.11–11.18
      alternative offences 11.15
      definition 11.11
      indictment 11.14
      proof 11.12
      sentence 11.16
      upon conviction/sentence 11.17
   procurement of woman by threats or
      intimidation 11.04–11.10
      alternative offences 11.08
      definition 11.04
      indictment 11.07
      proof 11.05
      sentence 11.09
      upon conviction/sentence 11.10
   trespass with intent to commit a sexual
      offence 11.51–11.58
      alternative offences 11.55
      definition 11.51
      indictment 11.54
      notes 11.53
      proof 11.52
      sentence 11.56
      sentencing guidance 11.57
      upon conviction/sentence 11.58
prostitution and trafficking
   arranging or facilitating child prostitution or
      pornography 8.64–8.69
      alternative offences 8.68–8.69
      definition 8.64
      indictment 8.67
      notes 8.66
      proof 8.65

   arranging or facilitating sexual exploitation
      of a child for prostitution or
      pornography 8.69–8.77
      alternative offences 8.74
      definition 8.70
      indictment 8.73
      notes 8.72
      proof 8.71
      sentence 8.75–8.76
      upon conviction/sentence 8.77
   causing or encouraging prostitution of girl
      under 16 8.14–8.20
      alternative offences 8.18
      definition 8.14
      indictment 8.17
      proof 8.15
      sentence 8.19
      upon conviction/sentence 8.20
   causing or inciting child prostitution or inciting
      child pornography 8.37–8.42
      alternative offences 8.41–8.42
      definition 8.37
      indictment 8.40
      notes 8.39
      proof 8.38
   causing or inciting prostitution for gain 7.177–7.184,
      8.87–8.93
      alternative offences 7.181, 8.91
      definition 7.177, 8.87
      indictment 7.180, 8.90
      notes 8.89
      proof 7.178, 7.179, 8.88
      sentence 7.182–7.183, 8.92
      upon conviction/sentence 7.184, 8.93
   causing or inciting sexual exploitation of a
      child 8.42–8.50
      alternative offences 8.47
      definition 8.43
      indictment 8.46
      notes 8.45
      proof 8.44
      sentence 8.48–8.49
      upon conviction/sentence 8.50
   causing prostitution of women 8.78–8.86
      alternative offences 8.83
      definition 8.79
      indictment 8.82
      notes 8.81
      proof 8.80
      sentence 8.84
      upon conviction/sentence 8.85–8.86
   controlling a child in relation to sexual
      exploitation 8.56–8.63
      alternative offences 8.60
      definition 8.56
      indictment 8.59
      notes 8.58
      proof 8.57
      sentence 8.61–8.62
      upon conviction/sentence 8.63

controlling a child prostitute or a child involved in
    pornography 8.51–8.56
  alternative offences 7.189, 8.55–8.56
  controlling prostitution for gain 7.185–7.192
  definition 7.185, 8.51
  indictment 7.188, 8.54
  notes 8.53
  proof 7.186, 7.187, 8.52
  sentence 7.190–7.191
  upon conviction/sentence 7.192
controlling prostitution for gain 8.138–8.145
  alternative offences 8.142
  definition 8.138
  indictment 8.141
  proof 8.139, 8.140
  sentence 8.143–8.144
  upon conviction/sentence 8.145
detention of a woman in a brothel or other
    premises 8.110–8.116
  alternative offences 8.114
  definition 8.110
  indictment 8.113
  notes 8.112
  proof 8.111
  sentence 8.115
  upon conviction/sentence 8.116
human trafficking 8.181–8.189
  alternative offences 8.186
  definition 8.182
  indictment 8.185
  notes 8.184
  proof 8.183
  sentence 8.187–8.188
  upon conviction/sentence 8.189
keeping a brothel 8.131–8.137
  alternative offences 8.135
  definition 8.131
  indictment 8.134
  notes 8.133
  proof 8.132
  sentence 8.136
  upon conviction/sentence 8.137
living on the earnings of male prostitution 8.124–8.130
  alternative offence 8.128
  definition 8.124
  indictment 8.127
  notes 8.126
  proof 8.125
  sentence 8.129
  upon conviction/sentence 8.130
living on the earnings of prostitution 8.94–8.145
man living on earnings of prostitution 8.96–8.103
  alternative offences 8.100
  definition 8.96
  indictment 8.99
  notes 8.98
  proof 8.97
  sentence 8.101
  sentencing guidance 8.102
  upon conviction/sentence 8.103

paying for sexual services of a child 8.29–8.36
  alternative offences 8.33
  definition 8.29
  indictment 8.32
  notes 8.31
  proof 8.30
  sentence 8.34–8.35
  upon conviction/sentence 8.36
paying for the sexual services of a prostitute
    subjected to force etc 8.190–8.197
  definition 8.191
  notes 8.193–8.194
  proof 8.192
  sentence 8.195–8.196
  upon conviction/sentence 8.197
procuration of women under 21 into
    prostitution 8.07–8.12
  alternative offences 8.11
  definition 8.07
  indictment 8.10
  proof 8.08
  sentence 8.12
procuring girl under 21 to have unlawful sexual
    intercourse 8.21–8.27
  alternative offences 8.25
  definition 8.21
  indictment 8.24
  proof 8.22
  sentence 8.26
  upon conviction/sentence 8.27
soliciting by men for immoral
    purposes 8.117–8.123
  alternative offences 8.121
  definition 8.117
  indictment 8.120
  notes 8.119
  proof 8.118
  sentence 8.122
  upon conviction/sentence 8.123
trafficking for sexual exploitation 8.146–8.171
trafficking into the UK for sexual
    exploitation 8.150–8.156
  alternative offences 8.154
  definition 8.150
  indictment 8.153
  notes 8.152
  proof 8.151
  sentence 8.155
  upon conviction/sentence 8.156
trafficking out of the UK for sexual
    exploitation 8.164–8.171
  alternative offences 8.168
  definition 8.164
  indictment 8.167
  notes 8.166
  proof 8.165
  sentence 8.169
  upon conviction/sentence 8.170–8.171
trafficking people for sexual
    exploitation 8.172–8.180

prostitution and trafficking (cont.)
    definition 8.172–8.173
    indictment 8.177
    notes 8.176
    proof 8.174–8.175
    sentence 8.178–8.179
    upon conviction/sentence 8.180
  trafficking within the UK for sexual
        exploitation 8.157–8.163
    alternative offences 8.161
    definition 8.157
    indictment 8.160
    notes 8.159
    proof 8.158
    sentence 8.162
    upon conviction/sentence 8.163
  women exercising control over
        prostitute 8.104–8.109
    definition 8.104
    indictment 8.107
    notes 8.106
    proof 8.105
    sentence 8.108
    upon conviction/sentence 8.109
public decency, offences against 10.01–10.56
publicity
  anonymity of complainants 15.01–15.03
  anonymity of witnesses 15.07–15.39

rape 2.01–2.55
  offences committed pre-31.12.1956 2.02–2.13
    alternative offences 2.07
    definition 2.03
    indictment 2.06
    proof 2.04
    sentence 2.11
    upon conviction/sentence 2.13
  offences committed between 1.1.1957 and
        21.12.1976 2.14–2.25
    alternative offences 2.20, 2.21
    definition 2.15–2.16
    indictment 2.19, 2.22
    proof 2.17
    sentence 2.23
    sentencing guidance 2.24
    upon conviction/sentence 2.25
  offences committed between 22.12.1976 and
        2.11.1993 2.26–2.35
    20.9.1993 (as of) 2.36
    alternative offences 2.31
    attempted rape: indictment 2.32–2.34
    definition 2.28
    indictment 2.30
    proof 2.29
    sentence 2.35
  offences committed between 3.11.1994 and
        30.4.2004 2.37–2.45
    alternative offences 2.43

    definition 2.38
    indictment 2.40–2.42
    notes 2.38
    proof 2.39
    sentencing guidance 2.45
  offences committed from 1.5.2004 to
        date 2.46–2.55
    alternative offences 2.52
    definition 2.48
    indictment 2.51
    sentence 2.53
    Sexual Offences Act 2003 2.46–2.47
    upon conviction/sentence 2.55

sentencing 12.01–12.253
  application of Sentencing
        Guidelines 12.169–12.185
  associated offences 12.20–12.21
  Attorney General's References 12.247–12.253
  Attorney-General's references see prosecution
        reviews of sentence
  calculation 12.108–12.116
  children 12.204–12.216
  community orders 12.35
  community sentences 12.33–12.34
  consecutive extended sentences 12.84–12.89
  current dangerousness provisions 12.117–12.134
  custodial and community sex offender programmes,
        difference between 12.32
  dangerous offenders 12.51–12.100 see also
        sentencing regimes for dangerous offenders
  determinate sentences 12.87–12.95
  discretionary life sentences 12.57–12.59,
        12.120–12.122
  extended sentences 12.60–12.91
  general principles 12.186–12.203
  historic offences 12.135–12.157
  indications of sentence (Goodyear
        Indications) 12.16–12.18
  licence requirements 12.158–12.168
  life sentences 12.118–12.119
  multiple extended sentences 12.24
  multiple incident counts 12.22–12.23
  multiple offences 12.19–12.24
  offences straddling implementation of different
        Acts 12.43–12.50
  offenders of particular concern 12.101–12.107
  post-conviction orders and
        requirements 12.217–12.246
  pre-sentence reports 12.96–12.100
  prosecution reviews see prosecution reviews of
        sentence
  prosecution reviews of sentence 12.247–12.253
  release requirements 12.158–12.168
  sample counts 12.22–12.23
  sexual offending programmes 12.31
  statutory life sentences 12.123–12.131
  supervision requirements 12.158–12.168

Suspended Sentence Orders (SSOs) 12.26–12.30
  whole life sentences 12.132–12.134
  young people 12.204–12.216
Sentencing Guidelines Council, Sexual Offences Act
    2003, definitive guidelines App B
sexual, meaning of, SOA 2003 3.37
sexual assaults 3.01–3.66, 3.47
  alternative offences 3.51
  assault by penetration 3.37–3.46
    alternative offences 3.43
    consent 3.39
    definition 3.37
    indictment 3.42
    proof 3.38
    sentence 3.44
    sentencing guidance 3.45
    'sexual' 3.39, 3.42
    specific intention 3.37–3.41
    upon conviction/sentence 3.46
    voluntary intoxication 3.39
  assault with intent to commit buggery 3.33, 5.25–5.31,
      5.84–5.100
    3.11.1994 to 30.4.2004 5.90–5.91
    definition 5.25, 5.84
    indictment 5.28, 5.87
    notes 5.86
    proof 5.26, 5.85
    sentence 5.29, 5.88
    upon conviction/sentence 5.30, 5.89
  causing person to engage in sexual activity without
      consent 3.55–3.66
    alternative offences 3.62
    child complainants 3.66
    definition 3.56
    indictment 3.60, 3.61
      non-penetrative activity 3.60
      penetrative activity 3.61
    penetration 3.58
    proof 3.57, 3.58
    sentence 3.63
    sentencing guidance 3.64
    upon conviction/sentence 3.65
  definition 3.47
  indecent assault 3.03–3.09
    alternative offences 3.07
    definition 3.03
    indictment 3.06
    proof 3.04
    sentence 3.08
    upon conviction/sentence 3.09
  indecent assault on a man 3.25–3.30, 5.92–5.100
    alternative offences 3.30, 5.97
    definition 3.26, 5.93
    indictment 3.29, 5.96
    notes 5.95
    proof 3.27, 5.94
    sentence 3.31, 5.98
    upon conviction/sentence 3.32, 5.99–5.100

  indecent assault on a woman 3.12–3.24
    alternative offences 3.20
    definition 3.12
    indictment 3.19
    proof 3.13
    sentence 3.21
    sentencing guidance 3.22
    upon conviction/sentence 3.23–3.24
  indecent assault upon a male person 5.32–5.40
    alternative offences 5.37
    attempted 5.38
    definition 5.32, 5.33
    indictment 5.36
    proof 5.34
    sentence 5.39
    upon conviction/sentence 5.40
  indictment 3.50
  notes 3.16–3.18
  offences committed pre-31.12.1956 3.03–3.09
  offences committed between 1.1.1957 and
      30.4.2004 3.10–3.31
  offences committed from 1.5.2004 to date
      3.34–3.60
  proof 3.48
  sentence 3.52
  sentencing guidance 3.53
  'touching' 3.49
  upon conviction/sentence 3.54
sexual behaviour with or towards a child 4.07–4.48
  offences committed between 1.1.1961 and
      30.4.2004 4.07–4.20
  offences committed from 30.4.2004 to
      date 4.21–4.48
Sexual Harm Prevention Orders (SHPOs)
  ambit and content of 16.21–16.24
  appeals against 16.45–16.47
  applicability
    Civil Orders 16.13–16.17
    non- conviction SHPOs 16.12
    procedure 16.08–16.11
    within criminal court proceedings 16.07
  barring from working with children and vulnerable
      adults, and 16.51–16.64
  breach 16.65–16.69
  clarity of 16.25–16.27
  computer access 16.30–16.32
  discharges 16.37–16.44
  form of 16.69
  generally 16.01–16.06
  interim SHPOs 16.19–16.20
  notification requirements, and 16.48–16.50
  other regimes, and 16.28–16.29
  personal contact with children 16.33–16.36
  renewals 16.37–16.44
  sexual harm, definition of 16.18
  Sexual Offences Act 2003 Schedule 3 16.70–16.75
  Sexual Offences Act 2003, Schedule 5 16.76–16.97
  variations 16.37–16.44

sexual offences committed outside the jurisdiction
　offences before 14.07.2008 17.03–17.10
　offences on or after 14.07.2008 17.11–17.17
　statutory basis 17.01–17.02
special measures
　application for 13.17–13.26
　current provisions 13.27
　defendants 13.29–13.37
　eligible persons 13.01–13.16
　ground rules hearings for vulnerable witnesses and defendants 13.28
　Section 28 Youth Justice and Criminal Evidence Act (1999) 13.38–13.74
specified sexual offences App A

trafficking *see* prostitution and trafficking
travel notification requirements 14.14–14.15

vulnerable witnesses and defendants, ground rules hearings for 13.28

witnesses, anonymity of 15.07–15.39

young persons, notification requirements 14.07–14.09